1/22

THE BLACK PRESIDENT

THE BLACK PRESIDENT

HOPE AND FURY IN THE AGE OF OBAMA

CLAUDE A. CLEGG III

JOHNS HOPKINS UNIVERSITY PRESS

Baltimore

Johns Hopkins University Press
2715 North Charles Street
Baltimore, Maryland 21218-4363
www.press.jhu.edu

Names: Clegg, Claude Andrew, author.
Title: The Black president : hope and fury in the age of
Obama / Claude A. Clegg III.
Description: Baltimore : Johns Hopkins University Press, 2021.
| Includes bibliographical references and index.
Identifiers: LCCN 2020051674 | ISBN 9781421441887
(hardcover) | ISBN 9781421441894 (ebook)
Subjects: LCSH: Obama, Barack. | Obama, Barack—Public
opinion. | Obama, Barack—Relations with African Americans.
| African Americans—Politics and government. | African
Americans—Attitudes. | United States—Race relations—Political
aspects. | United States—Politics and government—2009-2017.
| United States—Public opinion.
Classification: LCC E907 .C537 2021 | DDC 973.932092—dc23
LC record available at https://lccn.loc.gov/2020051674

Frontispiece: Barack Obama in Selma, Alabama, 2015

Cover and interior design by Amanda Weiss

A catalog record for this book is available from the British Library.

*Special discounts are available for bulk purchases of this book. For more
information, please contact Special Sales at specialsales@jh.edu.*

Johns Hopkins University Press uses environmentally friendly book
materials, including recycled text paper that is composed of at least
30 percent post-consumer waste, whenever possible.

To the ending of
man's inhumanity to man

CONTENTS

PREFACE

ON THE NIGHT OF NOVEMBER 4, 2008, I WATCHED THE US ELEC-
tion returns on CNN while chatting on the phone with a relative
in his seventies. We were both engrossed by the prospect of a Black
person being voted into the country's highest office, a feat no one
had ever seen. As we talked, suddenly on the TV screen appeared
the words "BARACK OBAMA ELECTED PRESIDENT." In that
surreal moment, we both agreed to get off the phone in order to fully
appreciate this unprecedented event.

I would learn later that my older relative's vote for Obama was
the first ballot that he had cast in his life. The next time I saw him I
asked how he had felt when Obama was elected. I suspected that he
was being characteristically guarded in his response when he answered
that he did not think that he would see such a day during his lifetime.
Curious, I asked, "Why not?" He mused, "I thought that the presidency was a white man's job." I probed further, "Why?" He retorted
with a question: "What number president is Obama?" I said, "He's
number forty-four." "How many before him were white men?" my
relative asked. I conceded, "Forty-three." "Yep," he answered smugly
as he checkmated me, "you see, a white man's job. Blacks were not
allowed to serve in the White House."

I still reflect on that conversation in thinking about the historic nature of Obama's two-term presidency and how history will eventually measure it. Soon after the 2008 election, I decided to write a book on the Obama White House years, specifically how they were witnessed, experienced, and interpreted by African Americans, his most supportive constituency. As an observer, I knew that this presidency was uniquely historic as it began and unfolded, but as a historian I wondered how to think about it historically just a few years after the Obamas left the White House. Unlike my previous books, the contemporary nature of this project seemed to demand a more flexible and real-time approach to the research and to the question of how the subject matter could eventually be historically construed. To put it a different way, witnessing the Obama presidency while trying to think about it in contextual terms placed me in the position of constructing a historical archive and a historically informed narrative without the benefit of historical hindsight. The real ability to view the Obama administration—in its entirety—in historical terms did not emerge until January 20, 2017, when his successor was sworn in. Consequently, what historians and the general public ultimately judge to be the significant historical outcomes of the Obama presidency will not come into clearest focus for many years hence.

Despite the immediate-term limitations of historical vision, it is imperative that historians bring their contextual tools and scholarly perspectives to bear on the recent past, lest their hesitance allow the interpretive void to be filled by simplistic narratives and disinformation that mislead the public and even corrupt its capacity for understanding events, contemporary and remote. All historical writings and interpretations are subject to later revision and refinement, which ideally benefit the human record; however, popular myths are hard to dislodge once they have gone unchallenged for too long by factual sources and informed reasoning. In this digital age when conspiracy theories, viral propaganda, and accusations of "fake news" so easily and quickly circulate globally, the grounded work of historians and other serious students of the past becomes all the more relevant and required. These observations thus suggest both the challenges and rewards of this book, which is among the first fully formed historical accounts of Obama's eight years in the White House.

As an interpretative history of the Obama presidency in its entirety, this volume situates the former president in his dynamic, inspirational, yet contentious political context. It captures the America that made Obama's White House years possible, while also rendering the America that resolutely resisted the idea of a Black chief executive, thus making possible the ascent of the most unlikely of his successors. In elucidating the Obama moment in US politics and culture, this book is also, at its core, a sweeping exploration of the Obama presidency's historical environment, impact, and meaning for African Americans—the tens of millions of people from every walk of life who collectively comprised his staunchest supporters and who most starkly experienced both the euphoric triumphs and dispiriting shortcomings of his years in office. In Obama's own words, his White House years were the "best of times and worst of times" for Black America. This book is vitally concerned with the veracity of this claim, along with how Obama engaged the aspirations, struggles, and disappointments of his most loyal constituency and how representative segments of Black America engaged, experienced, and interpreted his historic presidency.

The history presented here is rooted in three guiding themes. First, in this study I contend that the prolific diversity of Black America resulted in complex, layered, and fractured views and experiences of the Obama presidency and its meaning, ranging from the conflicted ruminations of politicians, academicians, clergy, and cultural figures to the realities of the everyday people who attempted to reconcile the historic election of a Black president with their own desperate struggles to survive the dire economic crises that marked his time in office. Second, I argue that the tension between the universalist, seemingly race-neutral policy prescriptions of the Obama administration and the adamant demands by some Black people for more targeted relief for African Americans suffering disproportionately from the effects of the Great Recession, institutional racism, and general marginalization was a persistent feature of the Obama years, and that this tension shaped how many view his White House tenure and eventual legacy. Third, I assert that Obama did, in fact, deploy the substance and symbolism of his office to forthrightly address the challenges and longings of African Americans in significant ways, though he typically couched such attention in official packaging and language meant to avoid conveying a racial favoritism that might offend white supporters and onlookers. As some of his critics regularly pointed out, Obama did occasionally use public platitudes and cultural signification to soothe Black pain and placate dissenters. However, even these gestures were fraught with their own share of potential dangers in the midst of the racial antagonisms and economic angst that characterized his time in the Oval Office.

This book is informed by an expansive and eclectic archive of materials collected and analyzed over the course of more than a decade of research. These sources include government records and reports, interviews, speeches, memoirs and insider accounts, quantitative data, video and audio archives, the journalism of the 24/7 news cycle, existing scholarship, and other literature. Since the book is a history of the Obama presidency within its political and social context and in particular its intricate engagement with African Americans—as opposed to being strictly a biography of Obama—I am less concerned with his day-to-day activities or the detailed maneuverings of his inner circle, which will likely be at least somewhat clarified by the release of his presidential records several years hence. Instead, I range more broadly and deeply to examine Obama's complicated upbringing and early political ambitions, his delicate and often tricky navigation of matters of race, the nature and impacts of his administration's policies and politics, the inspired but carefully choreographed symbolism of his presidency (and Michelle Obama's role), and the spectrum of allies and enemies that he made along the way, all of which constitute an Age of Obama in US political history and cultural discourse. As one of the first studies of his life and presidency that examines his two-decade presence on the (inter)national scene, the volume endeavors to establish an evidence-driven narrative arc and fact pattern of the entire Obama presidency, a timely task in our current historical moment and political climate.

In this vein, part I presents the historical Barack Obama, born in Hawaii, nurtured in Ivy League schools and Chicago activism and politics, and eventually propelled by boundless ambition and the political moment into the White House. Running alongside and through his story are those of Black America, Africa, and the larger diaspora, each constituting an essential component of Obama's identity but also, in their own right, serving as subjects and agents in the larger panorama of his life and presidency. The fascinating history of the 2008 campaign is central to this part of the book, as are Obama's electoral machinery and strategy. In these chapters I also delve into how Black voters responded to his improbable bid for high office during the Democratic primaries while the nation careened into the maw of the Great Recession, which would devastate African American wealth, homeownership, and employment prospects. Part I also examines candidate Obama's efforts to grapple with matters of race in the wake of various controversies and his navigation of the white racial resentment stoked by the campaigns of his primary and general election opponents. It concludes with his election to the presidency and responses of African Americans to this historic occasion.

Part II explores Barack Obama's first term in office. It begins with the staffing of his administration, the president's continuing outreach to and courtship of the diverse communities that formed his electoral coalition, and the interfacing of African Americans with White House policy initiatives. In these chapters I evaluate Obama's ties with Black political actors, including those in his administration, in Congress, and across the nation. His cordial though largely aloof relationship with the Congressional Black Caucus is detailed, as well as how some members of the Black commentariat—composed mostly of academicians, media personalities, and cultural figures—debated and construed Obama's presidency, policy agenda, and symbolism. This part also scrutinizes the American political discourse, often racially tinged, that marked much of Obama's time in the White House. Of interest here is the implacable and unrelenting nature of Republican and conservative opposition to both the agenda and the idea of Barack Obama. In this particular discussion I am less concerned with the minutiae of policy differences between Democrats and Republicans than with the blatant and surreptitious deployment of race to serve political ends, whether as seen in the advent of the Tea Party (which many Black people believed to be racially inflammatory), the tenor of the campaigns, or the incessant efforts of various right-wing personalities and organizations to delegitimize the Obama presidency, which eventually culminated in the presidential campaign of Donald J. Trump. In a related fashion, this part engages Black conservatism and its standard-bearers, illustrating their distinct brands of oppositional politics and anti-Obama idioms. Additionally, I delineate at length the darker world of racial animus directed toward the president, a necessary foray given Obama's reality of being one of the most threatened presidents in US history and the implications of this poisonous political environment for African Americans.

Furthermore, part II depicts how Obama and his presidency have been reflected in, incorporated into, and challenged by various aspects of Black life, including religious realms, educational endeavors, sports, and entertainment. I discuss the ambivalence of some Black clergy and congregations about the president's stance on same-sex marriage and other social issues, along with his reception among Black elites of various ideological stripes. Obama's facility with cultural lexicons and gestures is assayed, too, including his (class-conscious) balancing of golf and basketball, his (and Michelle Obama's) public interactions with Black celebrities, and the president's acknowledgments of Black achievements and civil rights–era commemorations. This part of the book also places Obama and his presidency within the larger African and diasporic world, delineating the high expectations across sub-Saharan Africa and the Caribbean that marked his inauguration and the dampened enthusiasm that followed the realization that stated principles often took a back seat to pragmatic realism during the administration's pursuit of its foreign policy goals. Of course, no history of the Obama presidency would be complete without an examination of Michelle Obama's vital influence on Barack Obama's early life and White House years.

Part III considers the second term of the Obama administration. Similarly to part II, I examine the place of African Americans in the staffing of executive agencies, in the formulation and implementation of policies, and within the broader experiences of the country during those four years. In these chapters I deeply probe the crises and controversies that distinguished his second term, including widespread protests over police violence and the right-wing backlash against Obama's presidency, which was most starkly expressed in the outcome of the 2016 election. In this part I also discuss the emergence of militant, digital-age Black activism and the generational shift that it signified, dynamics that inspired Obama, a former community organizer himself, yet contrasted sharply with his own measured temperament and often cautious governing style.

Undoubtedly for some Black people, the mere fact of the election of Barack Obama to the White House was the fulfillment of the change that he had promised. That is, the event itself was historic—period, end of story. Whatever happened next might have been interesting and newsworthy, but the simple fact of the elevation of a smart, qualified, serious Black man to the highest office in the land was the story to these observers. To other African Americans, the eight years were a protracted and tragically ironic struggle as they endured the greatest economic disaster in generations under the leadership of a Black president whose ability to redress their plight was more circumscribed than many had previously understood.

Black America, and indeed the entire country and the world, had quite the story to tell by the twilight of the Obama presidency. It was an extraordinary eight years, with more than its fair share of peaks and valleys from beginning to end. History's judgment of this era will be long in the making, shaped, expanded, and revised by new information and chroniclers and by future events and temporal distance, which will help further contextualize the Obama years and enrich subsequent analyses of them. At this moment, more than four years after Barack Obama left the Oval Office, his two-term presidency, along with his life before the White House, has acquired enough archival and digital dust and the beginnings of illuminating rays of hindsight to allow for some substantive historicizing of its trajectory and meaning. My fundamental task in this book, then, is to offer an interpretative history of the Obama presidential years in their entirety, with particular focus on the myriad ways in which African Americans encountered that era and its developments. If this work serves as a well-lit guide that assists future researchers, writers, and readers in discovering even more pathways for studying and understanding this important period in US and world history, then I will have accomplished my first, best purpose.

PART I.

A CHRONIC RESTLESSNESS

CHAPTER 1

Wanderers and Dreamers

THE YEAR 1960 WAS RIVETING. THE UNITED NATIONS PRO-
claimed it "The Year of Africa" in light of the seventeen African
countries that gained formal independence by November. From
Senegal and Mali in the west to Somalia and Madagascar in the east,
the ceremonial unfurling of vivid national flags across the continent
symbolized the emergence of indigenous sovereignty in places that
had been ruled by European imperial powers since the nineteenth
century. Those heady days of possibility, laden with liberation's hopes
and challenges, remade maps and birthed new peoples. However,
difficult realities on the ground along with machinations in foreign
capitals tempered many of the nationalist dreams that circulated in
teeming cities and restless countrysides. In most of the new states,
independence came with burdensome amounts of political confusion,
economic distress, ethnic tensions, and outright armed conflict. In the
Republic of the Congo, for example, generations of Belgian dominion
and brutality gave way to Cold War proxy fights and neocolonial
subterfuges that both claimed the life of the new prime minister,
Patrice Lumumba, and tipped a fractured society into civil war. In
populous Nigeria to the northwest, regional strife and military coups
were the unlucky trajectory of nationhood, as the country became

emblematic of the costs of the nonsensical borders that European cartographers had previously graphed onto the continent to facilitate Africa's conquest and division. As one Tanzanian statesman later claimed about this historical moment, African nations that managed to shake themselves loose from foreign domination staggered out of colonialism and into varying states of emergency.[1]

Kenya, a British-ruled colony in East Africa, was the epitome of this fraught phenomenon. Racked by an uprising led by the Kikuyu people and the cruel suppression that followed, the territory's troubles— colloquially known as the Mau Mau Rebellion—were a cautionary tale for both Africans and Europeans who pondered what might lie ahead in the netherworld between colonial rule and national independence. Like other imperial powers, Britain saw fit to hastily cultivate a native elite to assume the official duties of government, while making arrangements to protect the property and privileges that its white settlers and corporate interests fully expected to enjoy well past independence in 1963. For Africans, it was a dirty bargain, but there were enough takers with sufficient motivation to actually make it work.

Of the rising generation of (mostly) young men who were socially positioned just well enough to simultaneously discern and seize a fleeting opportunity with both hands, Barack Hussein Obama Sr. was a representative figure. A Luo born in the remote locale of Nyang'oma Kogelo in western Kenya, Obama was a curious—and, at times, unstable—mosaic of ambition, wanderlust, irreverence, and appetites. He revealed himself as a quick study at an early age, earning good grades in school despite a penchant for foolishness and disruption. His father, Onyango Obama (the future president's grandfather), pushed him hard toward the potential that he saw in the boy, landing him a clerk job in Mombasa on the coast. Barack Obama Sr. reportedly flirted with the budding nationalist movement in the 1950s but was more drawn toward urban nightlife and its pleasures. During this period, he managed to settle down long enough to marry Grace Kezia Nyandega, a Luo woman with whom he had two children. In between jobs and other pursuits, he also met Tom Mboya, a trade unionist and surging presence in Kenyan politics who would be instrumental to setting Barack Sr.'s future course.[2]

While his early experiences were largely confined to colonial Kenya, Barack Obama Sr. was an astute enough observer of international developments to know that by the late 1950s he was standing at the edge of one world and in desperate need of means to cross the chasm that separated him from the next. Even as the rebellion and reprisals dragged on, it was clear that things could never go back to how they were before the British declared an emergency in 1952. The future Kenya would be different, and it would need different kinds of people to manage and give it shape. Mboya could imagine some of the contours and textures of this new country, as could other Africans and a few whites, including the ones who encouraged Barack Sr. to continue with his education through correspondence courses. The bridge that he searched for materialized in the form of an initiative sponsored by William X. Scheinman, an American industrialist who had established the African American Students Foundation (AASF). Reminiscent of colonial missionary projects of an earlier age, this venture was designed to facilitate the training of East Africans in Western colleges so that they could eventually return home to lead postcolonial societies. Between 1959 and 1963, the AASF and an assortment of other sponsors arranged for almost 800 students from Kenya, Tanganyika, Uganda, and Northern and Southern Rhodesia to attend colleges and secondary schools in Europe and the United States. Mboya's support was crucial to the fortunes of the earliest wave as he was able to raise enough money to fund scholarships for 81 Kenyans. Barack Sr., who had cast his net of applications broadly and was eventually admitted into the University of Hawaii, was among the first group of young sojourners.[3]

It is difficult to know what ultimately attracted Barack Obama Sr. to Hawaii to continue his education, though several factors could have been at play that both lured and encouraged him to stay long enough to earn a degree in economics. The mystical island paradise, where an endless sapphire ocean teased glittering beige beaches crowned in lush, tropical greenery, probably reminded Barack Sr. of parts of Kenya since the weather and scenery were similar. Hawaii was a new state, having only been admitted into the United States in August 1959. With its mix of Americans, Asians, Native Hawaiians, and everything in between, it exuded the exotic and the cosmopolitan, characteristics to which the 23-year-old Obama Sr.—who had flown from Nairobi to Rome, to Paris, and then to New York before taking a bus to Los Angeles and finally arriving by plane in Honolulu—could increasingly relate. The young Kenyan, tall, lean, and dark, would have been quite a novelty on and off campus. He was one of the first Africans to attend the University of Hawaii, and in a statewide population—according to the 1960 Census—of 632,772, he would have been counted either as one of the 4,943 "Negroes" in the archipelago or as one of the 5,545 non-European, non-Asian foreigners.[4]

The small Black community of Hawaii had roots that went back to merchant and whaling voyages of the nineteenth century, when some sailors settled in the islands. The native-led Kingdom of Hawaii was overthrown by white landowners and claimed as a US territory in 1898, and most African Americans residing there in the twentieth century were associated with the US military. Distance and the minority status of whites on the island may have initially spared Blacks some of the indignities of the racial discrimination endemic to the US mainland. By 1960, tourism had become the chief industry of the state, which further complicated the cultural and racial dynamics of a population that was already the most diverse in the Union. Still, by the mid-twentieth century, enough of the ways of the States, including segregation and other forms of marginalization, would have been evident to even a roving African visitor like Obama Sr., who had by then become known for both his academic prowess and his love of socializing.[5]

In the fall of 1960, Obama Sr.'s interest in international affairs prompted him to enroll in a Russian language class, a not-so-far-fetched course of study given the ominous Cold War clouds that hung over the Kenyan's host country. In that year, tensions between the United States and the USSR threatened to escalate into direct conflict, fueled by controversial American spy-plane flights over Soviet territory, a new US embargo against revolutionary Cuba, and a commitment of US troops to South Vietnam to fight a communist insurgency. On an island that could be reached as quickly by a Soviet ICBM as any of the lower forty-eight states could, the Russian course seemed timely and drew a mixed crowd of students. One of Obama Sr.'s more thoughtful classmates was Ann Dunham, a young white woman whose family had just recently moved to Hawaii. Born in Wichita, Kansas, Ann and her family had moved several times before settling in Honolulu, with much of the serial relocating a result of the job-hopping of her father, Stanley, a furniture salesman. From Kansas to California, then Oklahoma, Texas, and Washington state, the small Dunham family—Stanley, wife and mother Madelyn, and only-child Ann—never quite seemed to establish roots in any single place before Stanley heard about a better job elsewhere and decided to move the family once more. When Ann graduated from Mercer Island High School in Seattle in June 1960, the family promptly embarked for the country's newest state. Once in Honolulu, Madelyn found suitable work as an officer in a local bank, and her 17-year-old daughter enrolled at the university.[6]

Barack Sr. and Ann seem to have first connected intellectually and as kindred wanderers. As an anthropology major, her personal and professional lives would eventually take her across the Pacific world in search of experiences that fulfilled a restlessness perhaps inherited from her father. The young Kenyan, six years her senior, exuded erudition and confidence, which could have been stoked by him being tapped to lead the International Students Association, as well as his class-topping grades. As a couple, the fall of 1960 was theirs to share at evening parties, along sun-soaked beaches, and in secret intimacies that were a diversion from the rigors of their studies. Sometime around her eighteenth birthday on November 29, Ann became pregnant, which necessitated some life-transforming decisions.

The lovers wanted to marry, but this was not a simple proposition. Perhaps through Mboya, Barack Sr.'s father, Onyango Obama, learned about the situation and wrote Stanley Dunham a "long, nasty letter" expressing disapproval of both the planned nuptials and how the family's blood had been "sullied by a white woman." Moreover, Onyango Obama wrote to his son, threatening to have his visa revoked if he dared marry his pregnant paramour. The correspondence also raised the sensitive matter of Barack Sr.'s first wife, Kezia, in Kenya. He had told Ann that they had divorced, though he could produce no document confirming the separation. The Dunhams counseled caution; Madelyn, in particular, had been put off by reports of the Mau Mau Revolt, which would likely prevent the couple from traveling to Kenya, lest Ann risk falling into the hands of rebels and having her "head chopped off." Notwithstanding their parents' ire and apprehension, the couple chose to act decisively and eloped. They exchanged vows in a private ceremony in Wailuku, Maui, on February 2, 1961, a few days before spring registration at the university.[7]

At 7:24 p.m. on August 4, Barack Hussein Obama II was born in Kapiolani Maternity and Gynecological Hospital in Honolulu. Many years later, Ann reflected on both the life that she and Barack Sr. conceived and the one that they could have had together. "We were so young, you know," she acknowledged, as if things could have been—should have been—different. It was all a torrent of events and emotions. In early 1962, Ann decided to return to Seattle with her newborn, securing an apartment and enrolling for the spring term at the University of Washington. As she struggled with classes and single motherhood back in the States, Barack Sr. applied to graduate school and in 1963 was admitted to Harvard for doctoral work in economics. He went alone to Cambridge; the scholarship that he received would not cover the cost of providing for a family. The following year, Ann moved back to Hawaii and filed for divorce.[8]

By 1966, Ann had married again and begun another life in Jakarta, Indonesia, with her second husband, Lolo Soetoro, and her son. The Soetoros' daughter, Maya, was born in 1970. Barack Jr. spent his formative years between the worlds of American expatriates and Indonesians, as much a racial oddity in the Southeast Asian country as his mother was. Ann tried to smooth the hard edges of exclusion that occasionally broke through the surface of the country's layered religious and ethnic identities, which stymied Barack and reminded him that he did not truly belong. In one instance when Indonesian boys flung rocks and racial epithets at him, Ann did not flinch but instead told an expatriate companion that Barack, who evaded the volley of words and stones "as though playing dodge ball," was "used to it" and would be "O.K." Barack later characterized his mother as an "unreconstructed liberal" who was deeply impressed with the high principles powering the US civil rights struggle and intent upon imparting to her son an abiding respect for Black history and culture. She radiated empathy for the less fortunate and respect for those who challenged injustice. She collected speeches by Martin Luther King Jr. and the songs of Mahalia Jackson to share with her boy, as if to compensate for depriving him of the opportunity to learn firsthand the meaning of being Black in America or in his father's Kenya. "Every black man was Thurgood Marshall or Sidney Poitier, every black woman Fannie Lou Hamer or Lena Horne," Barack recalled of his mother's romanticizations. Perhaps these fictions were comforting for an African American boy who lived through the 1960s largely "filtered through my mother."[9]

In the early 1970s, Barack was sent back to Hawaii to finish grade school. Ann, who had completed her bachelor's degree in anthropology in 1967, decided to pursue graduate study; fieldwork would have her crisscrossing the Pacific for years to come. Barack's grandparents, Stanley and Madelyn Dunham, became his primary source of familial stability as he spent his adolescent years in their home. In a stroke of good fortune, Punahou Academy in Honolulu, a prestigious private school founded by white Protestant missionaries in the 1840s, admitted him on a scholarship. It was not unlike the lucky break that his father had received from the University of Hawaii and then Harvard years earlier, but neither was the experience entirely positive. The

7,517 Black people residing in Hawaii in 1970 represented only 1 percent of the state's population. Their percentage was almost certainly lower at Punahou in any given year. Barack would later recall there being only one other Black student at the school when he arrived, a girl named Joella Edwards. He described the racial isolation that they experienced as a "different kind of pain," though the two never became close. In going to some lengths to avoid being mocked by classmates as Joella's boyfriend, he learned to dissemble more and to "speak less often in class." Edwards, exhausted from enduring "the n-word" and "Aunt Jemima" jeers from classmates, left the school five years after Barack's arrival. Decades later, he still felt that he had betrayed her through his cold treatment and that even "a part of me felt trampled on, crushed."[10]

Barack saw his father only once more: during a month-long visit to Honolulu around Christmas 1971. While their time together would leave an indelible impression on the boy, there was undoubtedly a masquerading quality to the encounter, with the father pretending to be the parent that he had never been. Imperious and temperamental, Barack Sr. chided his son for watching too much television and for not starting on his homework days in advance of the due date. When he on one occasion ordered the boy out of his sight "before I get angry with you," he was reminded by Stanley Dunham that he had limited authority in his former father-in-law's home. As usual, Ann tried to ease tensions by discouraging her son from being upset with his father, assuring him, "He loves you very much." And Barack Sr., in his own way, did make an effort to connect with the boy. He shared dance moves, swaying and gyrating to African records that he had brought with him. A visit to Punahou, in which Barack Jr.'s father mesmerized his classmates with an oration about wild animals, Luo customs, and British colonialism, went better than expected. Even Joella Edwards seemed to appreciate having yet another Black person at the school, no matter how temporary the spectacle. Still, as abruptly as he had appeared, Barack Sr. was gone, back to Kenya to face separation proceedings related to yet another estranged wife,

Ruth Baker, a white American woman whom he had married only months after he and Ann Dunham divorced in 1964. When he recounted in his 1995 memoir, *Dreams from My Father*, his reaction to learning of his father's death in a 1981 car accident, Barack Jr. was not grief-stricken or especially fazed. "I felt no pain, only the vague sense of an opportunity lost," he mused, "and I saw no reason to pretend otherwise."[11]

If there was no immediate pain, there was certainly residual injury, or deprivation, or something akin to these. The 1971 visit had been a blur of Christmas lights, rousing African music on 45 rpm records, a gift of a basketball, and plenty of posturing, bickering, and awkwardness. The most-circulated surviving picture of the two together was taken in a busy airport, with the younger Obama clutching the draped arm of his father, whose eyes are distracted by something off camera. Barack Jr. would spend much of his life trying to process his father's world and meaning, along with whatever utility the Kenyan's legacy might have for his own personal and professional trajectory. His recollections evolved and changed over time, sometimes conditioned by circumstance and at other times appearing to be as unstable and inconsistent as the randomness of his father's rare appearances and sudden departures.

Some of Barack Jr.'s characterizations have been kind, as when he acknowledged in his memoir that following his father's visit, "I realized, perhaps for the first time, how even in his absence his strong image had given me some bulwark on which to grow up, an image to live up to, or disappoint." In a subsequent reflection, he attributed his "fierce ambitions" to his father, along with a "desire to somehow earn his love" and to live up to his expectations or compensate for his mistakes. Family members and acquaintances sometimes discussed Obama Sr. with Barack, and on occasion he learned something revealing. When his half sister Auma Obama visited him in Chicago in 1984, Barack reportedly demurred when she asked, "Do you know that our father always really loved all of us?" Perhaps he was reminded of when his mother had made a similar remark during the Christmas visit in 1971, but this time he expressed his doubts. "No, I don't know that, Auma," he countered. "I didn't actually know him. I only saw him once in my conscious memory, as a ten-year-old. That was too short to learn anything about him." Auma, unprepared for such a reaction, eventually opened up to her brother, conceding that their father "just wasn't capable of showing [love]" and revealing how his treatment had left her with "nothing but anger toward him for many years."[12]

By the time Obama campaigned for the US presidency in 2008, his portrayal of the patriarch could be decidedly candid and even negative, no doubt at least partially influenced by a perceived need to minimize any potential damage that his father's image could do to his candidacy. "My father was a deeply troubled person," he told journalist Jon Meacham in an interview. "My father was an alcoholic. He was a womanizer. He did not treat his children well." Throughout Obama's presidency, glimpses of Obama Sr. could sometimes be distinguished in the son's many pronouncements about fatherhood and personal responsibility—to a degree that irked some of his critics as unnecessary public scolding of Black men. Obama Jr. never backed away from offering such counsel, apparently convinced that he had every right to proclaim, publicly or privately, the detriment that he had suffered through his father's abandonment and that such a broken model of parenting was avoidable and worthy of the censure of a sitting American president. "I spent a lot of time trying to figure out, in the absence of an immediate role model, what it meant to be a man—or in my case, a black man or a man of mixed race in this society," he told a *New York Times* reporter in 2016. "There was a powerful sense that I wanted to get this [being a father] right," he continued, mulling over the life that he had tried to provide for his own children. "Not that I was going to be perfect, but that I was going to be there, and engage, and try to figure this out." For a son caught between alienation, disappointment, and unrequited longing, Obama Sr., perhaps like all fathers, was a foil, a proof of concept—a retrospective model of what to do and what not to do in the realm of parenting.[13]

The concept of race has no evidentiary basis in science or the serious study of the natural world, but as a social construction, it has had a powerful impact on the shaping of the modern era. Race has structured hierarchies and relationships within vast empires and between powerful nation-states and subjugated colonies for centuries. Further, the idea of race diminishes the significance of the individual and the many environmental variables that shape people and societies in favor of exaggerating the assumed existence of collective tendencies and differences between groups. Easily lending itself to racism and other extreme forms of racialized thinking, race is often employed to do its most vigorous labor in the service of justifying existing inequalities and can, in turn, set the stage for rationalizing future privilege and exploitation. As an ideological and a historical phenomenon that has shaped policy, practice, and tradition, race, as experienced in any given setting, also has borders and protocols, which may exhibit varying degrees of porousness depending on conditions. For the individual not easily characterized visually or culturally within conventional racial categories, the navigating of race can be deployed for advantage, allowing for inconspicuous movement across boundaries and even long-term, if precarious, residence in the gray areas between socially acknowledged racial identities.

In this vein, Barack Obama is an intriguing and instructive case study—both in his observed, lived experiences and as a practitioner of narrative self-making—of the nexus of several racial, ethnic, and cultural identities, each of which shaped and helped project his sense of self and being. Many of his early—and more frank and less politically filtered—ruminations on race are presented in his first book, *Dreams from My Father*. At once a memoir, travelogue, and deeply introspective meditation, the volume is a poignant, probing chronicle of his efforts to reconcile himself with his eclectic lineage—embodied in his mixed racial heritage, his geographically dispersed kin and homelands, and his contentious paternal issues—and to discover his place and purpose in the world. In vivid, lively prose, he escorts readers through his childhood in Hawaii and Jakarta, between his undergraduate years at

Occidental College and Columbia University, deep into a transformative stint as a community organizer on the South Side of Chicago, and alongside his Kenyan search for familial origins and affirmation. At its thematic core, the book is as much about coming of age as a Black youth in late twentieth-century America as it is about how Obama grappled with the more exotic circumstances of his birth and far-reaching family ties, though these elements get their fair share of pages. That is, he seeks first and foremost to understand his American experiences—via Hawaii, Los Angeles, New York, and Chicago—through race and his evolving Black identity, even as he invites readers to witness these developments and dynamics from foreign—namely, Indonesian and Kenyan—vantage points.

The alchemy of race and racial identity that Obama spends chapter and verse discussing is fluid and volatile, though its protean nature and contradictions at times seem to escape his notice, or at least do not warrant further efforts at investigation. Obama the chameleon is on full display throughout the book. As he confides early on, "I learned to slip back and forth between my Black and White worlds, understanding that each possesses its own language and customs and structures of meaning, convinced that with a bit of translation on my part the two worlds would eventually cohere."[14] While trial-and-error experiences often tested his racial footing, he was exposed to enough laboratories of race, whether Hawaii, New York, or Chicago, to gain a sense of their parameters and each place's unique balance of possibilities and limitations.

In his book, Obama is generally realistic about the potentialities of race relations, and his reading of African American history, Malcolm X, and his own experiences is typically informed and clear-eyed. Nonetheless, the book strikes some discordant notes, with Obama sporadically lapsing into a pessimism that obscures his ability to see across divides or to cross borders. "The emotions between the races could never be pure," he writes about a particularly depressing incident. "Even love was tarnished by the desire to find in the other some element that was missing in ourselves. Whether we sought out our demons or salvation, the other race would always remain just that: menacing, alien, and apart." Such statements are in line with the stylistic sweep of the book, adding shades of complexity that both illuminate and darken the content and tone.

During the 1980s, Obama deliberately embraced an African American or Black identity. His college experiences on the mainland were an important part of this development, but his stint as a community organizer among economically distressed Black residents on Chicago's South Side was particularly critical. He noticeably matured in his relationships and as a person, symbolized by his preference to be called "Barack" instead of his childhood nickname, "Barry." His writings convey a genuine longing for community of the sort that had not been available to him in Hawaii or Jakarta, where a minuscule or "lonely only" representation (as Joella Edwards termed her tokenism at Punahou) could never approximate the substance or value of true belonging. Immersing himself in the South Side and its many crises involving unemployment, health-care access, affordable housing, drug-related violence, and failing schools moored him in a people and their communal concerns. However, being present was not enough to establish binding ties.

Obama came to believe that membership and belonging could be— had to be—earned. "In the sit-ins, the marches, the jailhouse songs, I saw the African-American community becoming more than just the place where you'd been born or the house where you'd been raised," he opines in consideration of his experiences in Chicago. "Through organizing, through shared sacrifice, membership had been earned. And because membership was earned—because this community I imagined was still in the making . . . , I believe[d] that it might, over time, admit the uniqueness of my own life." To be sure, phenotype and ancestry did matter and could produce meaningful kinship, or at least durable connections and inclusion. In his 2006 book, *The Audacity of Hope*, Obama describes explicitly seeking to merge his own American perspective and experiences as "a black man of mixed heritage" with "generations of people who looked like me" and who "were subjugated and stigmatized, and [experienced] the subtle and not so subtle ways that race and class continue to shape our lives." Still, individual agency, choices, and psychological investment in belonging did count; these factors were the very sinew of community, its reason for being.[15]

In later musings, Obama recognized that facets of his experience, whether the missing father or his "teenage rebellion," were mirrored in the lives of the Black people that he worked with and for in Chicago. He also recognized that he was arriving at an African American identity in a "pretty round-about" fashion and that he had even been compelled "to shape my identity, in some ways, on my own." Such community imagining and self-crafting are, of course, circuits that lead back to his absent Kenyan father, his white mother, Indonesia, Punahou, and all of the features of his biography that convinced him that it was imperative to think of American Blackness (and communal membership) in capacious enough ways to hold his sprawling familial narratives and their far-flung points of origin. If moving to Chicago had not created an entirely new man, the journey had provided the tools and rationale for such a project of self-(re)invention.[16]

In contrast to the nomadic, aspiring Barack Obama, Michelle LaVaughn Robinson was native to the South Side of Chicago, a product of its Black working class forged in the smelter of housing segregation, machine politics, and the lasting reverberations of the Great Migration. Her family had long roots in American soil going back to the time when her great-great-great-grandmother Melvinia Shields left the site of her bondage in Jonesboro, Georgia, to begin a life elsewhere in the 1870s. Generations later, Michelle and her older brother, Craig, were fortunate enough to live relatively stable lives in the care of Fraser and Marian Robinson, their blue-collar parents who tried to prepare them for horizons beyond the one-bedroom apartment they all shared. Following in the footsteps of her athletically inclined sibling, Michelle attended Princeton University, where she earned a bachelor's degree in sociology in 1985.

Michelle's Ivy League years were both advantageous and exacting. While enrollment in the university was the start of her path toward acquiring what one observer would call "ruling-class education credentials," she found it challenging to adjust to being one of the small number of African American students, who accounted for less than 10 percent of the campus population. "My experiences at Princeton have made me far more aware of my 'Blackness' than ever before," she wrote in her senior thesis. "I have found that at Princeton, no matter how liberal and open-minded some of my white professors and classmates try to be toward me, I sometimes feel like a visitor on campus, as if I really don't belong." Michelle was not alone in this sentiment, which was shared by many Black people who gained admission into predominantly white institutions during the generation following the civil rights movement. A network of sympathetic Black students at Princeton did help her to acclimate, and the same happened at Harvard University, where she went to law school in the late 1980s and took part in activism aimed at increasing the number of minority professors on campus.[17]

Shortly after earning a JD degree, Michelle was hired as an associate partner at the Sidley & Austin law firm back in Chicago, where she specialized in marketing and intellectual property. Her parents were justifiably proud of her achievements and her white-collar return to the Windy City. Unfortunately, her father, Fraser, perished in 1991 from the degenerative effects of multiple sclerosis before witnessing much of her adult journey.[18]

Over time, Michelle Robinson found the work at Sidley & Austin professionally unsatisfying, and she began looking around for other opportunities. However, before she left the firm, she was assigned to mentor a summer associate, a Harvard law student by the name of Barack Obama, in 1989. By then a six-foot-one, slender, tannish-brown man with close-cropped black hair and a boyish countenance, Obama, too, was groping for direction in the legal field but would soon enough chart a course elsewhere. Robinson found him charming and funny and was not completely put off by his grinning confidence.

His biracial Hawaiian saga struck her as intriguing, and his easy transitions into moments of seriousness and high-intellect-driven conversations were also pluses. But it was his boldness—including his earnest assertion to his mentor, "I think that we should go out on a date"—and an opportunity to witness him speak passionately about social justice to a community group at a local church that piqued her interest. Beyond being just a "black guy who can talk straight," Obama showed promise. "This guy [was] different," Michelle would later recollect to an interviewer. She liked much about him, except his smoking, which reminded her of the incessant cigarette puffing of her parents. "Why would someone as smart as you do something as dumb as that?" she asked him directly on the first day they met. Obama shrugged and conceded the charge of stupidity, but he would struggle with the smoking urge well into the future.[19]

A date did take place, and more followed. Robinson introduced Obama to her parents and brother, and she met Ann Dunham Soetoro, who completed her doctorate in anthropology at the University of Hawaii in 1992 before succumbing to cancer three years later. A trip to see the Obama clan was scheduled as the couple began to contemplate long-term plans. They visited his stepgrandmother Sarah Onyango Obama and other kith and kin in Kogelo and had a "fine time," according to Barack's memoir, with Auma, who was working on a film project. Since the adventure was Barack's second journey to the country, he displayed a level of comfort that Michelle, relatively new to international travel, could not emulate.

Michelle Robinson had expected, as an African American with ancestral ties to the continent, to be at home in Kenya, or presumably anywhere with a Black population. Visiting the "motherland" would bring her story, her family's story, full circle: a daughter of the diaspora finally returning home to her people. But no one knew her in Nairobi, Kogelo, or anywhere else they went, and she came to reckon that "Africa owed us nothing." It was a sobering realization, the "inbetween-ness" she felt in Africa as a Black woman from America. Statelessness, exile, belonging nowhere: she experienced that sinking feeling that afflicts long-displaced people when they discover that the awaiting homeland was a myth after all and that it was only real for as long as one did not attempt a visit. "It gave me a hard-to-explain feeling of sadness, a sense of being unrooted in both lands," Michelle Obama wrote years later. She was the returnee who arrived too late and found that all of the ancestors had returned to dust, replaced by different people and their new gods and strange ways.[20]

Barack and Michelle married in 1992 and settled on the South Side of Chicago. Both continued to look beyond law firms for fulfillment but in decidedly different directions. Michelle accepted a job as founding executive director of the Chicago office of Public Allies, a community-service initiative affiliated with President Bill Clinton's AmeriCorps program. By 1996, she had moved on to become associate dean of student services at the University of Chicago. In 2002, she accepted an appointment as director for community affairs at the University of Chicago Hospitals, and she received another promotion to vice president for community and external affairs three years later. Administrative employment turned out to be a good fit for her, especially when it entailed opportunities to help young people and to have an impact on the larger community. The jobs at the hospital were especially lucrative, and the income was even more useful once the Obamas had their first daughter, Malia, in 1998, who was followed by Natasha (known as Sasha) in 2001. Things had come together for the couple in ways that they could scarcely have imagined years earlier when Michelle and brother Craig rode trains back and forth between Princeton and Chicago, and Barack dabbled in drugs and alcohol to ease his boredom at Punahou. And then Barack threw a curveball.[21]

Barack Obama had developed a more than casual interest in government and politics by the 1990s. His time as a community organizer in the 1980s had whetted his appetite for organizational leadership and political maneuvering, which was further indulged by his tenure as the first African American president of the *Harvard Law Review* in 1991. He was civic-minded, competitive, and restless, three quintessential traits of politicians, and he thought in practical, methodical ways about how to fix things, such as income inequality and the health-care system. During his relatively brief employment at Sidley & Austin, Obama had seemed perpetually distracted; he requested an official leave to organize voters for the 1992 election, which was followed by more time away to finish *Dreams from My Father*. He did enjoy the classroom and the life of the mind and decided in 1992 to work as a lecturer at the University of Chicago Law School, where for twelve years he intermittently offered courses in constitutional law. During this period, he declined several offers of a full-time, tenure-track position, a prospective career path that promised a remunerative salary and job security at a top university.[22]

Politically, Obama was a liberal with pragmatic stripes, best suited and most at home hunting for deals and compromises in the eye of partisan storms. He was ambitious, deliberate, and strategic, quick to make useful connections with the powerful and cautious enough to concede losing battles in order to fight another day. Early in life, he understood the need for quality advisors and experienced mentors, and he sought to surround himself with both whenever possible. Ever the traverser of boundaries, he could swim with the Hyde Park liberals among whom he lived and just as easily wade in the streams of community activists and Black elites in South Side communities. Although he generally enjoyed cordial relations with Mayor Richard M. Daley and his patronage network, the shark-infested waters of city hall never enticed Obama enough to try his luck, likely due to the age-old reality that Chicago machine politics were notoriously nepotistic and rigged against newcomers. As much as any budding Illinois politician, Obama comprehended the power of money in politics and had to learn how to manage the constant need for campaign funding without utterly compromising his reputation and core convictions.[23]

In 1996, Obama decided to run for a state senate seat representing the Thirteenth District, which covered much of the South Side to the South Shore and Chicago Lawn to the west. He handily vanquished his Democratic opponents in the March primary, including Alice

Palmer, who held the seat at the time but whose petition signatures were found to be mostly invalid following an official challenge by Obama, which prevented her from even appearing on the ballot. In a safe Democratic seat, the newcomer demolished the general election field in November, winning 82 percent of the vote. The victory itself was less a classic political upset—Palmer had gravely blundered by committing to run for reelection only after a failed bid for a seat in the US Congress the previous year—than a gander into Obama the tactician.

Characteristically, Obama was genial, respectful, and gracious, even when it came to his opponents, and he preferred not to burn bridges or alienate potential future allies. Still, he had developed a survivalist sensibility during an itinerant youth marked by absentee parents and the need to adapt to different cultures and places where he did not easily fit in racially or otherwise. His competitiveness and ripening ambitions were likely stoked at Ivy League schools and during subsequent work at an elite law firm. Perhaps most relevantly, his reading of Chicago's political landscape during his time as a community organizer on the South Side undoubtedly contributed to his ability to be calculating in his political dealings, especially when it came to engaging and challenging entrenched politicians. In the corrupt, transactional blood sport that was Illinois politics, Obama learned how to kill, and to kill well, but he was quicker to move on to the next hunt than to express delight or regret over spilled blood—his opponent's or his own. In the end, his quest for the Thirteenth District seat conformed to the guiding ethos behind the state's political culture. In an unforgiving arena with few second chances to go around, any single loss was potentially a mortal wound to one's political longevity and thus was to be avoided at whatever costs.[24]

Obama's years in the Illinois Senate were elemental to his professional biography and experiences but rarely absorbing enough on a day-to-day basis to occupy the totality of his political imagination or career ambitions. He reliably voted with the Democratic members of the chamber, leaning liberal on most issues. Over the course of his eight-year tenure, a number of bills were drafted and enacted by means of his arguments, pen, or vote. For instance, he helped to pass campaign finance reform, increase the state's minimum wage, and provide an earned-income tax credit for struggling families. Moreover, he supported bills to end large tax cuts for businesses and opposed tax credits for parents seeking to defray the costs of private school for their children. He fought against limitations on public funding of abortions and cosponsored a failed effort to protect people from discrimination predicated on sexual orientation.

Obama was especially proud of his work on law enforcement and criminal justice matters, including bills passed in 2003 that sought to minimize racial profiling during traffic stops, require videotaping of police interrogations of suspects accused of certain crimes, and revise the state's implementation of capital punishment. As he prepared to depart the state senate in 2004, he was part of a successful attempt to pass the Health Care Justice Act, which authorized formal consideration of a process for moving toward a universal health-care system for the state of Illinois. Overall, it was a respectable record of achievements, which was rewarded with reelection and an evolving list of campaign donors. During his time in Springfield, Obama made valuable allies as well, such as the senate's Democratic leader, Emil Jones, an African American who also hailed from Chicago and whose ascent to president of the body in 2003 resulted in Obama becoming chair of the Health and Human Services Committee.[25]

Not everyone took well to Obama during his Illinois Senate years. Compared to most of his colleagues, his Ivy League pedigree and lectureship at the University of Chicago placed his credentials well beyond the standard résumé. After Obama's arrival in early 1997, Denny Jacobs, a white Democrat from Rock Island County, actually asked the new senator, "What the hell are you doing here?" Given Obama's academic and professional background, the query was not altogether unreasonable.[26]

Most of the grief that Obama suffered during his senate tenure was at the hands of a clique of Black politicians who needled him

on everything from his education and class status to his racial identity and perceived foreignness. Rickey Hendon and Donne Trotter,
Democrats from Chicago, were reportedly the worst of the lot. Their
insults were unvarnished and to Obama's face, taking him to task
for his alleged hubris, for his elitism, and for being fundamentally
disconnected from the life experiences and political interests of Black
constituents back in Chicago. One newspaper article quoted Hendon as condemning Obama's ambition ("he would like to run for
'president of the world'") and attributed a particularly low blow to
Trotter ("he wasn't black enough"). Given his past lives in Indonesia and Hawaii, such ridicule was not without precedent but must
have still carried a sting. According to friends, Obama thought that
he could "bring those guys around" in time, perhaps assuming that
his easygoing manner and conciliatory ways might squeeze him out
of a tough spot as had sometimes happened in the past. Yet to his
critics, Obama was merely an out-of-place, glad-handing imposter
using the Illinois Senate—and his South Side constituents 200 miles
away—as a stepping-stone to the next big score. That was a charge
and a set of suspicions that could not be dismantled with simply an
eloquent presentation on the senate floor or light banter about the
latest Chicago Bulls game.[27]

The tensions boiled over on June 11, 2002. Hendon, rising to take
the senate floor, gave a gripping speech imploring his colleagues to
maintain financing for a child welfare facility. In and of themselves,
such pleas for district resources were not unusual nor was the skewed
partisan outcome. The entire Republican membership voted against
the measure, and all but four Democrats voted for it. Hendon was infuriated that the naysayers included Obama, and he proceeded to cross
the floor to demand an explanation. According to Hendon's account
of the incident, Obama waved him off with "something about fiscal
responsibility" as the proposal crumpled in defeat. Somewhat oddly,
Obama then stood and requested that his vote be changed to the
affirmative, explaining that he had not wholly understood the nature
of the legislation. No such change was allowed, prompting Hendon

to give a standing denunciation of Obama for dealing in what the believed to be a crude political calculus. The Thirteenth District senator was shocked by Hendon's move and subsequently approached his desk. "You embarrassed me on the Senate floor," he said in a low voice, his hand resting on Hendon's shoulder, "and if you ever do it again, I will kick your ass!" The two men then promptly left the chamber to continue the confrontation in a back room.

What transpired next was a shoving match interspersed with vulgarities, which was ended once Trotter and other colleagues arrived to separate the men. One interpretation of the spectacle would be to single out its dismaying racial imagery: two African American politicians, representing the same liberal metropolis, tussling over legislative scraps in the middle of overwhelmingly white Springfield. In hindsight, a more apt assessment might be that the ruckus simply represented politics by other means. Following the incident, Hendon ceased the pestering, and Obama sided with him more consistently in voting. The relationship never became close, but each man understood the other's potential usefulness in an ever-changing political climate. Illustratively, on the eve of the 2008 presidential election, Hendon declared his support for Obama's candidacy, maintaining that he "will not hesitate to fight on behalf of the United States if it comes down to it, just as he tried to fight me because of his personal beliefs." Hendon had, indeed, come around.[28]

One thing that Hendon and company had gotten right about Obama was the ambition. He oozed it. In fact, the senator himself was among the first to note this persistent feature of his personality. He considered it a flaw, a "chronic restlessness" that kept him from focusing on the here and now or things as they are. If he had inherited anything from his parents, this animating tic topped the list. It shaped his political impulses for good and ill.

Barely having warmed the former senate seat of Alice Palmer, Obama saw another opportunity for an electoral power play. Bobby Rush, a former leader of the Illinois Black Panther Party and a long-time resident of the South Side, was the US representative for the

First Congressional District. It subsumed much of Obama's senatorial territory and was one of the Blackest districts in the country. Rush, unlike Obama, had come up through the ranks of Chicago politics, having served as an alderman and ward committeeman before running successfully for Congress in 1992. He had previously served in the army and earned college degrees locally at Roosevelt University and the University of Illinois at Chicago. While born in Albany, Georgia, he was as homegrown a politician as any transplant could be. And he, too, was ambitious. When Mayor Richard Daley ran for a fourth term in 1999, Rush challenged him but was crushed in a nonpartisan election in February. The incumbent carried almost 70 percent of the citywide vote, including Rush's own Second Ward. Such an electoral skewering made Rush vulnerable to a challenge for his congressional seat. With the 2000 primary season approaching, Obama pounced.[29]

As it turned out, the state senator was not as ready for the campaign as he had thought, and the 53-year-old congressman was not as wounded as he first appeared. Nearly everything that could go wrong for Obama did. One poll revealed that Rush began the campaign with 90 percent name recognition compared to 9 percent for Obama. Moreover, the primary field was crowded, with two other Democrats challenging Rush, including Donne Trotter. Similar to Obama's Springfield tormenters, Rush, his allies, and the other candidates turned his assets against him. His Harvard education made him an "educated fool." His fundraising successes made him beholden to white interests in Hyde Park and elsewhere. His cosmopolitan experiences and international travel made him an outsider to the community. And his mixed racial heritage made him all the more suspect—a "white man in blackface," as Trotter put it. Obama himself did not help matters much. His campaign pitch struck some as arrogant and too professorial, which made him seem even more foreign. His classroom demeanor was rumored to have actually put one church congregation to sleep. Obama's record in Springfield was not distinguishable enough from that of Trotter or even Rush to be of much assistance, and missed votes—such as one on a gun-control measure that he had supported—were used to clobber him in the press.

As the March primary rolled around, things were looking grim for the state senator. Although he was the strongest of Rush's challengers, none of the others bowed out, so the opposition to the incumbent could not be consolidated. Mayor Daley, a canny navigator of Democratic politics, owed Obama no favors and predictably sidestepped the stench of defeat that was now wafting from the senator's campaign bid. President Bill Clinton, still a potent political force even in the wake of impeachment over a sex scandal, issued a ringing endorsement of Rush over the radio, all but clearing the way for the incumbent's fifth congressional term. As many had assumed, the election results were anticlimactic. Obama lost to Rush by a two-to-one margin, faring especially poorly in heavily Black areas.[30]

There were, of course, lessons to be learned from this disaster, but none of them were wholly new or surprising. Incumbency mattered, as did roots, networks, money, and, yes, racial heritage. Furthermore, voters tended not to appreciate being lectured, even for educational purposes, by people with hard-to-remember names and inscrutable credentials. Also, previously crafted and widely circulated narratives about a candidate and his motives—for example, Obama's alleged elitism and congenital ambitiousness—were hard to shake, particularly in below-the-belt campaign fights and round-the-clock media cycles. In an unforced error, Obama had allowed his competitive streak to override his usual inclination to be cautious and strategic. He had made the rookie mistake of marching onto the battlefield against a seasoned, well-armed foe before lining up powerful allies, formulating a meaningful rallying cry, or even learning how to speak the language of the common people whom he hoped to lead and represent. Fortunately for the senator, the pummeling by Rush did not result in politically fatal injuries, but it surely made for longer rides between Chicago and Springfield as he nursed a battered ego and questioned his appetite for further pursuit of higher office.

The restlessness was kept in check for the next few years, partly due to the 2001 birth of the Obamas' second child and some strife at home. Michelle loathed politics and had assumed a disproportionate share of the child-rearing and household responsibilities, despite her own flourishing career. Earlier in her life, she had watched as her father was virtually "conscripted" as a precinct captain to serve the Daley machine, his livelihood as a city employee dependent on playing city hall's patronage game. Subsequently, she was greatly dismayed by having to endure her own husband's absenteeism resulting from his various Chicago campaigns and duties in Springfield. In one instance, she charged him with thinking only of himself, leaving her "to raise a family alone." Her expressed outrage and hurt affected Obama, enough for him to write appreciatively about her sacrifices in his 2006 book. The marriage had already lasted a decade, longer than any of the relationships of his parents. Children, jobs, campaigns, and distance all added stress and unique challenges to the union. Yet they were making it work; they needed to make it work. And not just for themselves.[31]

Like clockwork, the tic flared up again in 2003 as a US Senate seat in Illinois was projected to become open the following year. The Republican incumbent, Peter Fitzgerald, had decided not to stand for reelection, which inspired a stampede of candidates to file papers to run. Obama wanted the office, but this time he had the self-restraint not to lunge into the fray as he had in 1999, when he was mauled by an entrenched veteran politician. Instead, he consulted, deferred, cajoled, and, very important, assembled a team of gifted advisors and dedicated donors. Dutifully, he checked in with those in line ahead of him. Former US senator Carol Moseley Braun, an African American politician who had lost the seat to Fitzgerald in 1998, declined to run again. Another prime candidate, US representative Jesse Jackson Jr. of Illinois's Second Congressional District, was not interested in the position; he had entered Congress in 1996 and was now preparing to run again for reelection in relative electoral security. Members of the Jackson and Obama families had been close for years, with Jesse Jr. having attended the couple's wedding in 1992. If Jackson planned to run for the open seat, Obama confided to him that he would step aside.[32]

Next, the state senator talked with influential people whom he respected, including Steven Rogers, a Black business professor at Northwestern University, who was initially skeptical of a US Senate run. "Look, man, you need to go sit your ass down somewhere," he chided when Obama suddenly appeared on the second hole of one of Rogers's golf outings with friends. "You just got your ass beat by Bobby Rush. You can't win. You got two damn African names. You need to be like my children: Akila Rogers. Or, instead of Barack Obama, you need to be Steven Obama or Jones." The would-be candidate insisted upon his seriousness with Rogers, as he did with others. Despite his dismissiveness, the Northwestern professor was a doorway into the world of Chicago's Black business elite, a group whose generosity and blessings would be needed for any successful Democratic campaign.

On the matter of money, millions would be required in order to actually have a chance of winning. Obama had made previous connections with a number of "lakeside liberals": wealthy professionals and business magnates, many of Jewish background, who were known for supporting progressive candidates and causes. Several joined his campaign in various capacities, thus opening up more networks for fundraising. Ultimately, Obama raised nearly $6 million to run in the primary, with financing coming from groups ranging from the banking and insurance industries to political action committees and lobbyists. As with all candidates who have to raise large sums of cash quickly and from an assortment of sources, the frantic money race risked compromising his integrity and bringing him into contact with people and interests that were less honorable than one would have liked. One such individual was Tony Rezko, a local real-estate mogul, who reportedly contributed more than $120,000 to the US Senate campaign of Obama. In 2008, Rezko would be convicted of corrupt solicitation, money laundering, and other crimes and eventually served time in prison, a cause of embarrassment for Obama.[33]

Obama ran a solid primary campaign with broad appeal across Chicago and downstate. By imitating the charismatic diction of Black pastors whose churches he campaigned in, he managed to adjust his style of retail politics to incorporate colloquialisms that people in the pews and on the streets could relate to. But he was careful not to unduly alienate other constituencies, telling one reporter, "I'm rooted in the African-American community, but I'm not limited by it." In taking race head-on but then quickly setting it aside, he was able to travel around the state and foreground issues like health care, jobs, and education without being easily dismissed as too urban, too liberal, or too Black. Serendipitously, a series of scandals and other stumbles among his primary opponents allowed him to surge in the polls right before the vote. On primary day in March 2004, he ended up capturing 53 percent of the ballots despite competing in a field of seven aspirants.[34]

It was a stunning primary victory, and Obama became a household name overnight among Democrats around the country. A few other stars aligned as well. In July, Sen. John Kerry, the party's presidential nominee, arranged for Obama to give the keynote address at the national convention in Boston. It was quite an honor for an up-and-coming politician to be spotlighted in this way—after all, Obama was technically still just an Illinois state senator. Over the weeks between the primary and the convention, Obama rehearsed diligently and proved up to the task of addressing a national audience.

His televised speech, entitled "The Audacity of Hope," was a feel-good oration about American ideals, diversity, and, of course, the rectitude of John Kerry's quest for the presidency. To start, Obama touched on his own mixed-race heritage and his indebtedness to those who had made his remarkable journey possible. He struck neoliberal chords concerning government not being the solution to unemployment or poor schools, and he showcased his opposition to the putative deceit and incompetence of the Bush administration in its handling of the wars in Iraq and elsewhere. In its crescendo, the talk paid homage to the American Dream and called for all true patriots to be hopeful about the future and to hold fast to those bonds of community that tied the country together.

For years to come, the best-remembered lines of the speech were those that sought to submerge group differences and interests into a national identity. "There's not a liberal America and a conservative America; there's the United States of America," Obama exhorted. "There's not a black America and white America and Latino America and Asian America; there's the United States of America." The language was reminiscent of the uplifting, integrationist moralism of Martin Luther King Jr.'s "I Have a Dream" speech, but it was delivered in the spirited cadence and emphatic gesturing of Malcolm X, both of whom Obama had studied and admired. Throughout the presentation, the crowd responded rapturously with outbursts of applause and shouts of approval, and Obama finished his sixteen-minute national debut beaming with confidence and satisfaction.[35]

It was the right speech for the right audience at the right time. In a period of war and national division, Obama's words were cathartic for many, and his self-possessed delivery was reassuring. But there was still the matter of the general election, now only three months away. Obama's opponent on the Republican side had been Jack Ryan, a deep-pocketed former banker who had eked out a plurality of the vote in a crowded March primary. However, in late June, long-churning rumors of a sex scandal involving Ryan and his ex-wife Jeri finally surfaced in court documents, precipitating his hasty exit from the race. Notwithstanding the well-populated primary contest, the Republican bench was shallow, and Ryan's untimely collapse produced a dire crisis for the Illinois GOP.

In a desperate effort to keep the US Senate seat in Republican hands, the party drafted Alan Keyes, a Black Maryland conservative and serial candidate for public office, to run in the general election. Keyes, a Harvard PhD and former diplomat, had hard-core right-wing credentials on issues such as tax cuts, abortion, and homosexuality but was otherwise an odd choice to succeed Ryan. He was a "carpetbagger," just in from the East Coast, with no real funding and an unenviable string of failed campaign bids. Despite his diplomatic background, he was not endearing as a candidate and came across in debates as both preachy and intellectually snobbish. His charge that Obama was "not really African American" since he was not descended from enslaved people did not stick and was wholly predictable at this point in the Democrat's political career. Keyes did strike a nerve with Obama when he publicly questioned his Christian faith. However, whatever irritation that Keyes was capable of inflicting was limited to just a few months of campaigning. If the Illinois GOP thought that it was being particularly clever in fielding a Black Harvard-trained conservative against a Black Harvard-trained liberal, Keyes's flailing proved this to be a calamitous strategy. In the November 2 election, he lost badly to Obama, who garnered 70 percent of the statewide vote.[36]

To fanfare and accolades, US senator Barack Obama was sworn in on January 3, 2005. Since Reconstruction, the number of African Americans elected to the chamber could be counted on one hand, though Illinois had sent two such officeholders to Washington over the past decade. As he had done in Springfield, Obama quickly learned to move between the factions and fiefdoms of the federal legislature, making alliances with key Republicans, such as Sen. Richard Lugar of Indiana, and taking his place as the only Senate member of the Congressional Black Caucus (CBC). President George W. Bush's reelection and the Republicans' fifty-five-seat majority in the Senate portended ill for any meaningful movement on Democratic priorities related to health care, education, foreign policy, or anything else. Thus, during his first few years in office, Obama sponsored only four bills that became laws, including the Democratic Republic of the Congo Relief, Security, and Democracy Promotion Act of 2006 and the Predominantly Black Institution Act of 2007. In accordance with the cues of party leadership, his voting record was reliably liberal, which earned him membership on three Senate committees (Foreign Relations, Veterans Affairs, and Environment and Public Works).

As a freshman member of a minority caucus, there was nothing especially unique or memorable about Obama's early tenure in Washington.

Like other newly elected Democrats, he settled into the routine of visiting his family as often as possible and got used to cosponsoring and voting for a plethora of symbolic bills that stood no chance of surviving floor votes or receiving Bush's signature. In his spare moments, he worked on his policy book, *The Audacity of Hope*, which appeared in print prior to the midterm elections. A sea change did occur in November 2006, when US House Democrats came to power, and the Senate narrowly switched hands with the help of two left-leaning independents. But by then, Obama, who had learned the ways of Capitol Hill and cultivated valuable allies, was staring in a different direction—toward a storied mansion on Pennsylvania Avenue.[37]

The idea of running for president had been percolating in Barack Obama's mind for many months prior to the midterm elections, likely going back to the start of his tenure in the US Senate or even to the 2004 convention speech in Boston. If he had thought about it before then, the notion could only have been a fleeting, fanciful one, so delicate and dependent on a fortuitous series of unforeseeable events that to speak it too loudly or to share it too widely would have revealed the ethereal dream that it was.

In December 2006, Barack and Michelle Obama met with eight advisors and confidants in the Chicago office of David Axelrod, a political strategist whose advice Obama had relied on in the past. The session was meant to hash out the logistics of a possible run for the presidency, with some informal brainstorming about fundraising, organizational infrastructure, and the primary schedule. Michelle, more invested in the discussion than any other attendee was, pressed her husband, stating frankly, "You need to ask yourself *why* you want to do this." The room fell silent in anticipation of an answer that might credibly suffice. "This I know," Obama said. "When I raise my hand and take that oath of office, I think the world will look at us differently. And millions of kids across the country will look at themselves differently." It was not a bad reply, but it was not an especially convincing one either.[38]

Michelle needed more persuading, which came during a family vacation in Hawaii around Christmas. Barack ceded to her the latitude and authority to veto the proposition. He had had his way about a good number of things in their relationship, and a presidential run was an enormous undertaking. Beyond concerns about the impact on the children and the disruption to the family's already overstretched living arrangements, Michelle was anxious about security, especially the death threats and other dangers that a Black candidate for the highest office in the land would surely attract in abundance. What would happen to her if Barack was assassinated? How would their girls bear the loss? In an interview around this time, Michelle tried to imagine the fallout from the worst-case scenario. "There would be great sympathy and outpouring if something were to happen, but I have to maintain some level of professional credibility not only because I enjoy it, but I don't want to be in a position one day where I am vulnerable with my children," she laid bare to the reporter. "I need to be in a position for my kids where, if they lose their father, they don't lose everything." It was heavy stuff to contemplate, even under the fading embers of a postcard-perfect Hawaiian sunset.[39]

The Obamas decided to move forward with the presidential run, but Michelle's trepidation remained. Valerie Jarrett, a close family friend who had early on been professionally helpful to Michelle, later recounted Mrs. Obama's qualms. "I'm already hanging on by my fingertips," she groaned, "and now he wants to do *this*? How's it going to work?" Jarrett warned that the campaign trail would be tough but assured her that together they would cope. Back from vacation, the Obamas gathered again with a circle of advisors to game out the contours of a presidential campaign. Present were Steve Hildebrand, Alyssa Mastromonaco, Robert Gibbs, Pete Rouse, and David Plouffe, all of whom would bring critical skill sets to a national organization. Plouffe, who would become Obama's campaign manager, offered only hard candor when Michelle inquired about her husband's schedule as a candidate. "Can Barack come home on weekends? . . . What about Sunday?" No and no, Plouffe confirmed with cold finality. Sacrifice would be the unyielding cost of a presidential run, and it would be demanded of all—Barack, Michelle, their children, the staff, everyone. And perhaps most especially Michelle.[40]

With the outlines of a plan coming into focus and a new year dawning, the next thing to do was to determine how best to tell the world that Barack Hussein Obama II was running to become the next president of the United States of America.

CHAPTER 2

Joshua Rising

BARACK OBAMA ANNOUNCED HIS CANDIDACY FOR THE US PRES-
idency on February 10, 2007, a sunny but frigid day. Beneath the
limestone columns of the Old State Capitol in Springfield, he introduced himself and painted the broad strokes of his vision for America.
He started by recounting his days as a community organizer and his
eight years of accomplishments in the Illinois Senate. He went on to
concede that there was a "certain presumptuousness—a certain audacity—to this announcement," a tacit acknowledgment of his status
as a junior US senator. Undeterred, he declared, "I've been there long
enough to know that the ways of Washington must change." He challenged the nation to demand universal health care and to reduce its
dependence on foreign oil. To the thousands gathered to hear him,
Obama called for a living wage for workers, revitalized unions, and
a secure retirement for older Americans. Hope and change would
become signature themes of his budding campaign: an undying faith
in "the essential decency of the American people" and in the collective
will to unite, in spite of divisions, to improve society for the common
good.[1]

Notwithstanding his optimistic rhetoric, the candidate named Republican George W. Bush's administration as the real villain of the

day, citing its interminable warmongering, failed educational policies, and unwillingness to lead the country to a post-partisan consensus. In choosing this site for his campaign rollout, Obama intended to invoke the words and life of another Republican president, who had spoken on the Capitol steps generations earlier. In June 1858, Abraham Lincoln, then a candidate for the US Senate, gave his "House Divided" speech warning against the spread of slavery and the creeping threat of secession. Obama was an admirer of the sixteenth president, and the parallels were not lost on him. He promised that if elected, he would end the US misadventure in Iraq, since "no amount of American lives can resolve the political disagreement that lies at the heart of someone else's civil war."[2]

Back in December, when Michelle Obama had told her husband that he needed to determine *why* he was running for the presidency, she also had asked, "What are you hoping to uniquely accomplish, Barack?" The question was an existential one for his candidacy, posed in the lawyerly, no-nonsense way that Michelle sometimes used to prod her husband to concisely address the problem or situation at hand. In this instance, he was prepared—somewhat. Obama had been working on answers to her questions for some time, and with the release of *The Audacity of Hope* he could confidently say that he had given some thought to a number of critical issues facing the country. This second book was a manifesto—the kind of work that politicians put out when their political stock is rising and when publishing houses are willing to offer lucrative contracts. The volume sold well, which suggests that it was widely read, and it offered substantive insight into Obama's ideological commitments and pragmatic conception of governance. For actual enactment, most of his legislative priorities implicitly assumed either Democratic control of the presidency and a filibuster-proof Congress or some bipartisan epiphany that had yet to occur in Obama's lifetime. In any event, beyond its obvious political purpose and blue-sky prescriptions, *The Audacity of Hope* was part history primer and part political autobiography, revealing Obama as a keen student of the past and its lessons.

The tone of the book is hopeful and forward-looking, stressing the commonalities between Americans and their struggles, aspirations, and shared stake in liberal democracy. In it, Obama regularly asserts his belief in the basic decency of the US people and the need for a new politics worthy of that decency, which could transport the country beyond the partisan acrimony and disunity of the day. The book offers many policy discussions and recommendations concerning family life, poverty, immigration, urban renewal, health care, terrorism, and the environment. It discloses a substantial but not unlimited faith in market forces and favors a role for government in guaranteeing the fair and efficient operation of capitalism. Expanding health-care access was one such area in which Obama envisaged a public-private arrangement that could enlarge the pool of insured people while reining in escalating medical costs and allowing private insurers to earn reasonable profits. Government also has a part to play in addressing climate change by promoting renewable sources of energy, in softening income inequality through making the tax code more progressive, and in policing the excesses of Wall Street with more stringent regulation of the financial industry. In Obama's view, the future belonged to the country that could prepare its people for a world increasingly shaped by globalization and technological innovations, and thus he advocated for more investments in research, education, and job-training programs.

Quite noteworthy, Obama's policy recommendations tended not to be race-specific in packaging or explicit purpose. He did not believe such an approach to be either strategic or viable, since "white guilt had largely exhausted itself in America," leaving little residual tolerance for race-coded policies that were obviously meant to benefit Black people or other marginalized groups. "Mainly it's a matter of simple self-interest," he reckoned. Whites, still the preponderance of citizens, officeholders, and voters, would not support a legislative agenda in which the outcomes were aimed at advantaging specific subsets of Americans, regardless of arguments about historical discrimination or even clear proof confirming its present-day manifestations. Thus, at the end of the day, no grand policy initiative could move forward without substantial white support and buy-in, and overtly race-based policies could not pass this threshold. In lieu of targeted remedies for social and economic inequities, Obama maintained that universal policies were more practical and preferred, especially when complemented by a healthy dose of individual and collective responsibility. Therefore, in common with white Americans, Black people and other disadvantaged groups would benefit from health-care expansion, paid family leave, criminal justice reform, and a fairer tax policy. In some cases, the historically marginalized might even benefit disproportionately from some of these measures.[3]

While the universalist, left-of-center pragmatism of Obama's policy plans was clear and largely consistent over time, his stance on affirmative action was subject to evolutionary fluctuations. As a law student at Harvard, he, like Michelle Robinson, had demanded the hiring of more African American faculty. Moreover, he claimed that he had personally benefited from affirmative action, as had the staff of the *Harvard Law Review*, which he led. Although he did understand the feelings of minority classmates who feared that the policy might lead some white colleagues to question their qualifications, Obama insisted in an open letter that he had never "personally felt stigmatized." With the publication of *The Audacity of Hope*, Obama went on record again in support of affirmative action and recognized that some patterns of "prolonged and systematic discrimination" in government, unions, and the corporate world could warrant accountability-driven "goals and timetables for minority hiring." In accordance with the work of interracial coalition-building that the book was intended to address, he advised African American leaders to be mindful of the "legitimate fears" that affirmative action might stir in some whites. Still, in his by then trademark interests-balancing, center-seeking fashion, Obama came to the conclusion that through rational and good-faith compromise, disparate groups with competing claims could be reconciled. "Affirmative action programs, when properly structured, can open up opportunities otherwise closed to qualified minorities," he posited, "without diminishing opportunities for white students."[4]

In May 2007, presidential candidate Obama blinked on the issue of affirmative action, especially in regard to his past support for its use as a tool for advancing racial equity in the face of historical and contemporary exclusion in education and hiring. In an ABC interview, he seemed to downplay racial discrimination, past and present, as the primary animating justification behind the policy, instead highlighting class disparities. When asked whether his daughters should benefit from any college admissions preferences, Obama replied in the negative, calling Malia and Sasha "pretty advantaged." He then appealed for more consideration of "white kids who have been disadvantaged and have grown up in poverty and shown themselves to have what it takes to succeed." To be sure, his comments were not completely out of line with some of the more experimental public policy ruminations of the day regarding how best to diversify campus student bodies using race-neutral methods. But he did appear to question whether race should be the dominant organizing principle behind affirmative action policies, and whether such policies needed to be principally directed toward redressing legacies of slavery and segregation, and ongoing racial discrimination.[5]

Rather predictably, Obama's remarks generated buzz in the blogosphere and elsewhere. In hindsight, the candidate appears to have been acting tactically in this interview, as opposed to overhauling previously articulated principles. With an eye to the long campaign season ahead, he likely wanted to avoid being tagged too early as the "Black candidate" in a contest in which opponents would increasingly look for openings to reduce his bid to such limited confines. Obama's documented views and known actions related to affirmative action in subsequent years would confirm his decades-long belief in the efficacy of a race-conscious policy. Still, his equivocation on the matter in this moment, and especially his televised steering of his interview response toward the plight of needy "white kids," was indicative of a strategy to reduce racialized overexposure. Despite this, race would eventually be employed against Obama—by both Democrats and Republicans—to damaging effect. In terms of political technique, the interview was another example of Obama's inclination to seek the seemingly neutral, safe center, even when it was not necessarily higher ground.[6]

As a presidential contender, Obama prized order, information, and planning, with ideally little occasion for drama and surprises. His campaign style was a more refined but familiar iteration of his Illinois operations. Based in Chicago, the organizational infrastructure was centralized around a small group of advisors and strategists, such as Plouffe and Axelrod, who helped Obama plot the story arc and logistics of the campaign. Financing networks sprawled across the country, and their fundraising power was amplified by savvy use of the internet to encourage small donors to make repeat contributions. A legion of volunteers eventually formed a disciplined ground game, assisted by cutting-edge analytics and targeted advertising on social media, on radio, and in other venues.

Obama's own persona—mature but down-to-earth, cool and smart—informed the look and feel of the enterprise and was just the right mix of competence and exotic novelty to maintain an ongoing critical mass of interest, especially on the part of the press. Clips of him debating opponents, giving speeches, playing basketball, holding hands with Michelle, and casually chatting with TV hosts came together to create an intriguing mosaic of a different kind of American experience, inviting individual observers to project their own ideals and fantasies on Obama. A telegenic baritone, the candidate understood this mystique and cultivated it, once comparing himself to a Rorschach test that people "might gain something" from even if they were not ultimately inspired to support him. There were certainly warts, including some stilted debate performances that felt like law school expositions and an inner circle that was known to be quite white and male. The smoking—which Obama had promised his wife that he would quit if elected—was mindfully kept out of sight. Aside from a few minor tempests, there were no scandals or egregious blunders during the lead-up to the Iowa caucuses in January 2008.[7]

But of course, there was always race. In a crowded Democratic field composed almost entirely of white men, being Black, Barack

Obama stood out. Being smart and eloquent, Barack Obama stood out. Being tall and slender, Barack Obama stood out. Being named "Barack Obama," Barack Obama stood out. Hillary Clinton, a former First Lady and current US senator from New York, added a bit of gender differentiation to the field, and Bill Richardson, the governor of New Mexico, who was of Mexican descent, added more ethnic diversity. Notwithstanding these two candidates, Obama's origin story, pedigree, demeanor, and complexion set him apart.

Commentators Black, white, and other would exhaust their thesauruses searching for words to describe Obama and his improbable bid for the highest US office. Some, like Black columnist Debra J. Dickerson, writing just days before Obama's campaign announcement in Springfield, declined to validate his Blackness but did appreciate that a "non-black" son of a Kenyan father and Kansan mother could open the door for future candidates of color. Others, such as scholars H. Samy Alim and Geneva Smitherman, imagined that Obama's context-flexible voice soothed white angst over a "foreign Muslim" or "socialist African" seizing the White House and relieved the "irrational insecurities" of Black people who feared that one of their own, less articulate than Obama, could make "the whole race [appear] ignorant." More glowing and less generous characterizations than these were in the offing, and some of the countless interpretations of Obama's race and motives must have amused and bemused the candidate. But even with their increased volume and circulation, these perceptions and judgments had long been par for the course for him, the price of such a public life not easily defined by place or heritage.[8]

The Illinois senator actually took the voice issue seriously, even going so far as to meet with a group of supporters, including Black academicians Charles Ogletree and Cornel West, in June 2007 to fine-tune his delivery for Black audiences. As he practiced in awkward fits and starts, the pretending felt and sounded wrong to him. "I can't sound like Martin," Obama admitted. "I can't sound like Jesse." Fortunately for him, he would not have to imitate wholesale any given style in order to connect with a crowd, though he did channel some of the folksy charisma and casual syntax of the Black preacher archetype in some of his speeches. In deciding that he could not replicate the exhortative approaches of Martin Luther King Jr. or Jesse Jackson Sr., Obama did them one better.[9]

Back on March 4 at Brown Chapel in Selma, Alabama, the Illinois senator gave a speech to commemorate the anniversary of the historic 1965 voting rights march there. Aware of the resonance of biblical deliverance stories in the Black church tradition, he invoked Old Testament scripture regarding leadership succession and the search for the promised land. Before a predominantly Black audience, Obama characterized his age cohort as the "Joshua generation," which had stepped forward to complete the honorable but unfinished civil rights work of the "Moses generation." In a gesture of humility, he portrayed the Joshua generation as possibly lacking the courage and merit of their parents, who had realized 90 percent of the struggle's goals. Nevertheless, he argued, there were "still some battles that need to be fought, some rivers that need to be crossed." And the remaining work mattered, he insisted, and could only be carried out by a younger generation of leaders.

The speech turned out to be less a request for the torch than a bold claiming of it, and it was an opportunity for Obama to fold his own unique African American story into the larger one of the Black freedom movement. In one swelling crescendo, he dramatically exclaimed, "Don't tell me I'm not coming home when I come to Selma, Alabama." Emphatically pressing his demand for inclusion further, he sermonized, "I'm here because somebody marched for our freedom. I'm here because y'all sacrificed for me. I stand on the shoulders of giants." The maneuver was both daring and shrewd; it at once conjured a pantheon of venerable ancestors and then cast them in supporting roles in his crusade to finish the last 10 percent of their mission. For the moment, Obama's merging of these life threads worked well, and many would begin to view his campaign as the apotheosis of long-running struggles for African American civil rights and enfranchisement. Nonetheless, race and notions of belonging would play a more vexing role in the primary contests to come, and not all of the ancestors would come to his aid or go quietly to the sidelines.[10]

The 2008 presidential race drew a solid slate of Democratic contenders. Besides Obama, Hillary Clinton, and Richardson, the contest attracted several sitting and former US senators, including Joe Biden, Chris Dodd, John Edwards, and Mike Gravel, and one congressman, Rep. Dennis Kucinich of Ohio. Of the group, Clinton was the most formidable candidate entering the primary season, having witnessed and, at times, participated substantively in the two-term administration of her husband. She was now a second-term US senator from New York and in the eyes of many the presumptive Democratic nominee for president. In terms of policy matters, Clinton was a center-left liberal on most issues, including health-care expansion, strengthening public education, and protecting abortion rights. But she had voted in favor of authorizing the Bush administration's military intervention in Iraq, a decision that would dog her presidential campaign and that contrasted sharply with Obama's early public opposition. Together, the Clintons, who had left the White House in 2001, still retained a lot of star power and were easily the most powerful duo in Democratic politics almost a decade later. Having survived vicious partisan battles and the embarrassment of impeachment, they had fared quite well beyond the White House years, reportedly earning more than $100 million in book royalties and speaking fees, along with Hillary Clinton's senatorial salary.[11]

In *The Audacity of Hope* and in other instances, Obama offered a mixed assessment of the Bill Clinton presidency. He applauded the former president's effort to get beyond the liberal-conservative binary that stifled effective governance and pragmatic problem-solving, even if his attempts to appeal to Reagan Democrats could come across as "clumsy . . . or frighteningly coldhearted." Obama was less enamored of the seeming smallness of Bill Clinton's strategic vision, which he described as a "scaled-back welfare state" predicated on a broad consensus approach with which even "compassionate conservative"

George W. Bush could not find much fault. Following the announcement of his presidential bid in February 2007, Obama was stunned to learn that his Senate colleague from New York was not especially thrilled about him either, and she declined to shake his hand on the chamber's floor in a chilling sign of campaign battles to come. In an October Gallup poll, Obama and Hillary Clinton enjoyed similar favorability ratings among voters (53 percent and 51 percent, respectively), though the latter's unfavorable score was sixteen points higher. If it was any consolation to the New York senator, she still polled far ahead of the field at that time, outpacing Obama by twenty-nine points on a national test ballot. With the coming of the new year, the real test would, of course, come down to what the voters decided at the ballot box, starting with Iowa on January 3.[12]

The caucuses in the Hawkeye State were ultimately a measurement of organizational strength and campaign style. Obama had invested significant time and resources in the state, including multiple visits and a robust paid staff. More than 40 percent of voters would later tell pollsters that they had been contacted by his campaign, a testament to the extensive ground game of canvassers and other volunteers who had been mobilized to get people registered to vote and through the doors of caucus locations. The final tally showed that Obama won 37.6 percent of the vote, compared to the 29.7 percent garnered by Edwards and the 29.5 percent received by Clinton. Entrance polls signaled that he dominated among young, urban, suburban, and more liberal voters, as well as those who told pollsters that they were caucusing to support the candidate that "can bring change." Turnout was critical to Obama's victory, with the 239,000 Democratic caucusgoers representing double the usual participation. Years later, he would characterize the Iowa win as "my favorite night of my entire political career." White talk-show host and comedian Bill Maher captured the significance of Obama's caucus triumph in another way, labeling the mixed-race candidate "the Halle Berry of American politics—an African-American we can kiss." It was by any measure an electoral breakthrough: a Black northern Democrat had bested seasoned opposition in one of the whitest, most rural, and least demographically representative states in the country.[13]

Clinton, who had come in a close third in Iowa, managed a much-needed win in the New Hampshire primary five days later, carrying 39.1 percent of the vote to Obama's 36.5 percent. This development, along with roughly a split vote in the January 19 Nevada caucuses, was enough to even the delegate count between the two frontrunners and to usher several others, including Biden, Dodd, and Richardson, toward the exits. The next major contest was scheduled to take place on January 26 in South Carolina, a Deep South state with a large Black electorate that had historically played an outsized role in the state's Democratic primaries. At this point, the campaign was still a three-person race. Edwards, a South Carolina native and a former US senator from North Carolina, hoped to open up things with an antipoverty platform that could resonate in the country's poorest region. Obama, assisted by campaign appearances by his wife, Michelle, had targeted South Carolina early on and viewed the state as both winnable and essential, especially given what a loss in such a diverse state might indicate about the viability of his presidential bid going forward. Clinton, coming off an important win in New Hampshire, sought to maintain her campaign's momentum ahead of the Super Tuesday contests of early February. To accomplish this, she made the fateful decision to deploy her most potent and volatile surrogate.[14]

Bill Clinton had been campaigning on behalf of his wife for some time. A master politician, he interpreted the Iowa loss and the continuing competitiveness of the race as underscoring the urgency of dispatching the remaining candidates, especially Obama. On January 4, the former president called Sen. Ted Kennedy of Massachusetts, seeking an endorsement for his wife that might help tip the balance. Kennedy, a prominent Democratic statesman from a powerful political clan, rebuffed Clinton's entreaty. Later, the senator would tell a friend that Clinton had spoken disparagingly about Obama during the call, even declaring, "A few years ago, this guy would have been getting us coffee." The phone calls kept coming until Kennedy finally informed Clinton that he planned to support Obama. The former president, livid over the news, reportedly shot back, "The only reason you're endorsing him is because he's black. . . . Let's just be clear."[15]

Bill Clinton also called Donna Brazile, an African American political strategist who had worked on Al Gore's presidential campaign in 2000. The former president's fury was so intense during their talk that Brazile found herself repeatedly asking, "Why are you so angry?" Clinton was desperate by this time, unable to convince Brazile or a majority of South Carolina primary voters that nominating Obama would be the "worst denigration of public service." To his further detriment, the former president's favorability rating, according to one poll, slid seventeen points in the week leading up to the primary vote. His machinations in public and private would prove costly to him and his wife. In the most convincing victory to date, Obama annihilated the field, capturing 55 percent of the ballots compared to Clinton's 27 percent and Edwards's 18 percent. Significantly, Obama carried a quarter of the white vote, demonstrating that he could pull together the sort of interracial coalition that would be required to win contests elsewhere.[16]

Bill Clinton did not suffer the loss graciously or quietly. At 2:15 a.m. following the South Carolina primary, he was back on the phone, this time awakening James Clyburn, a longtime US congressman who represented a predominantly Black district that swept west from Columbia to Marion and along the coast around Charleston. Clinton was still apoplectic over the events of the previous day and was in no mood for pleasantries. A veteran of the civil rights movement, Clyburn served on the Rules Committee of the Democratic National Committee and had previously declared himself neutral regarding primary candidates. Clinton had taken offense at what he believed to be either the congressman's insincerity or his unwillingness to lean more in Hillary Clinton's direction. "If you bastards want a fight," the former president raged, "you damn well will get one." Clyburn tried to reason with Clinton, but the latter would have no part of it. According to the congressman's account, Clinton once again called him a "bastard" before blaming Clyburn for his wife's defeat and for allegedly insinuating the issue of race into the primary. After the call, Clyburn's wife, Emily, who was now also awake, asked him whom he had voted for in the balloting. Still frazzled by Clinton's half-hour harangue, the congressman caught his breath and replied, "How could I ever look in the faces of our children and grandchildren had I not voted for Barack Obama?" To him, the Illinois senator represented the Joshua that his life's work in civil rights had fruitfully helped to produce. If anything, the Clinton call had affirmed to Clyburn the correctness of his choice.[17]

Bill Clinton had more darts to throw in regard to the South Carolina primary, and some were hurled directly at Obama himself. In response to a reporter's question, he compared the Illinois senator's win in South Carolina to the primary victories of two-time presidential candidate Rev. Jesse Jackson Sr., who won the state in 1984 and 1988. Despite his claims to the contrary, many viewed Clinton's comments, offered with a smile and a nod, as one of his clearest efforts yet to name Obama's race for the purpose of electorally isolating him as "the Black candidate." Initially, Obama responded kindly to the controversial remark and gave the former president a pass. He knew as well as anyone that getting into a public argument about race—especially one that cast him as victim—was not an advisable strategy, especially so early in the primary season. Instead, Obama told journalist George Stephanopoulos on his Sunday news show that no one could question that Jackson had "set a precedent for African Americans running for office." He also denied that the Clintons were attempting to vilify him and urged Americans to stay focused on the issues that mattered.[18]

Bill Clinton continued to litigate the matter in the press for several more weeks—at one point even accusing the Illinois senator of playing "the race card on me." In response, Obama became less charitable in his appraisal. He eventually called out the former president for being dismissive of his win in South Carolina and agreed that it was reasonable for Black voters to be offended by such a tactic. Back at the Virginia headquarters of the Clinton campaign, strenuous efforts were made to rein in the former president following the South Carolina battle. Rising panic resulted in a staff member being secretly dispatched to solicit an open letter from Jesse Jackson Sr. that might minimize the racial tensions of the primary. Jackson, who supported Obama, declined the request, though he did encourage the two campaigns to lower the rhetorical temperature.[19]

Many Democratic insiders were appalled by what Bill Clinton had done for the sake of winning South Carolina and damaging Obama. Much of the dismay was expressed in private; the political class, including Clyburn and Jackson, were not quick to publicly censure a power couple that might yet make its way back to the presidency. Others had also decided to give the Clintons the benefit of the doubt for now, perhaps fondly recalling their tenure in the White House (which was the only break in almost thirty years of Republican occupancy), the diversity of the former president's Cabinet, and the relative economic prosperity of the 1990s. Some African Americans still referred to him as the "first Black president," a bow to his folksy southern vernacular, affinity for jazz saxophone, and endurance of the kinds of ferocious attacks that white reactionaries had traditionally reserved for people of color.

Whatever good feelings remained about the Clintons did not, however, fully insulate them from some criticism following the South Carolina primary. Rev. Al Sharpton, a prominent New York–based activist, called upon the former president to "shut up," lest he further poison the political climate. Dr. Johnnetta Cole, president of Bennett College and a longtime friend of the Clintons, was upset by their "campaign driven by a notion of inevitable victory, of entitlement to the post and carelessness around questions of race." White critics, too, castigated the former president for going too far in his strategy. These included Clinton's former secretary of labor, Robert Reich, who called the assault on Obama "ill-tempered and ill-founded," and a past Senate majority leader, Tom Daschle, who viewed Clinton's tactics as "not [in] keeping with the image of a former president." Even forgotten people from his scandal-laden time in office appeared again on the radar to voice disapproval. In an effort perhaps designed *not* to help, Gennifer Flowers, who had claimed years earlier to have had a long-term affair with the former president, took the opportunity to both endorse Hillary Clinton for president and to write off her spousal surrogate as an "idiot husband."[20]

It is hard to know for certain exactly what kind of harm Bill Clinton was doing to his wife's campaign. Staffers feared that the South Carolina skirmishes would have a lasting negative impact on the candidate's appeal among African Americans and subsequently diverted the former president's schedule toward stirring up votes in predominantly white, working-class towns in Pennsylvania, Indiana, and North Carolina. The twenty-three primaries and caucuses that occurred on February 5 (Super Tuesday) decided little, with Obama and Clinton—Edwards had ended his bid a week earlier—acquiring about the same number of proportionally distributed delegates, though the former won more contests. Some concerning signs began to appear for the Clinton camp, including ominous demographic patterns in some of the polling conducted around this time. In one survey of candidate preferences, African Americans in various states continued to skew toward Obama after South Carolina (their support rising from 68 percent to 77 percent), with his campaign making further inroads among Hispanics, women, independents, and middle-aged voters during February.[21]

But with another month came another controversy that threatened to shake up the race. In this instance, a personality close to home injected himself into the conversation. Louis Farrakhan, head of the Chicago-based Nation of Islam, publicly embraced Obama's candidacy before a crowd of almost 20,000 people during the group's annual Saviour's Day gathering on February 25. The leader was generous with his accolades. "If you look at Barack Obama's [diverse] audiences and look at the effect of his words, those people are being transformed from what they were," he declared. "This young man is the hope of the entire world that America will change and be made better." Farrakhan was a well-known figure among African Americans, having flirted with Black politics since the 1980s. His race-conscious brand of Islam, penchant for conspiracy theories and questionable Middle Eastern alliances, and enduring hostility toward Jews limited his general appeal, but he was never without at least a small, dedicated following during his long public life. The Million Man March of October 1995 was the high point of his influence, when a multitude gathered in Washington, DC, to hear his keynote address, which turned out to be esoteric and anticlimactic. In his mid-seventies and having felt some of the harsh winds of the Islamophobia that swept over the United States in the wake of the September 11, 2001, terrorist attacks, Farrakhan's star was definitely fading by the 2008 primaries, though his impact on the race could have potentially been seismic.[22]

Obama well comprehended the danger to his interracial coalition that any affiliation with Farrakhan and his organization posed. A candidate vying for a predominantly Black district in Chicago or elsewhere might welcome the minister's endorsement. Obama himself was a known admirer of Malcolm X, a former Nation of Islam mentor-turned-adversary of Farrakhan. But for a Black candidate running a national campaign dependent on a largely white electorate, there was no upside to any dealings with the Muslim minister. Jesse Jackson had learned this lesson the hard way during his runs for president decades earlier, when his open engagement with the Chicago firebrand had alienated Jews and many others. Moreover, a whisper campaign characterizing Obama erroneously as a Muslim was flaring, and a Farrakhan connection would be an inconvenient accelerant. Aside from these issues, the Chicago leader was known to be unpredictable and given to self-aggrandizing commentaries and off-color remarks. It was hardly the kind of attention that Obama wished to attract, having only been able to fight the Clintons to a draw over the past two months of campaigning.

Obama's repudiation of Farrakhan's support came in two stages. First, he issued a statement through a spokesman following the February 25 endorsement, affirming that he had been "clear in his objections to Minister Farrakhan's past pronouncements and ha[d] not solicited the minister's support." The wording was meant to distance the candidate from the minister's more brash commentaries while hopefully not arousing his ire. For some, the rebuke was not enough. At a February 27 debate, host Tim Russert pressed Obama further on Farrakhan's backing, asking whether he rejected the support. The senator initially responded with semantic quibbles, stating that he had neither sought nor could he nullify the minister's approval of his campaign. Obama eventually offered a fuller condemnation of Farrakhan and his past controversial statements, being careful to mention that he was a true friend of Israel who wanted to revitalize ties between Blacks and Jews. The simmering crisis blew over, and the debate moved to other subjects. Mercifully, Farrakhan did not belabor matters with recriminations loud enough to attract the press, although he had not said his last word on the subject of Barack Obama.[23]

If handling the Nation of Islam leader's endorsement was like juggling grenades, what came next was a bona fide nuclear explosion with all of the attendant fallout. On March 13, ABC began airing what would become a daily, media-wide loop of incendiary video clips of Rev. Jeremiah Wright, the leader of a Chicago church that the Obama family had periodically attended for two decades. The footage captured the pastor at his most animated and boisterous, railing against everything from US foreign policy to the domestic treatment of African Americans. "The government gives them [Black people] drugs, builds bigger prisons, passes the three strikes law and then wants us to sing 'God Bless America,' " he thundered in a 2003 sermon. "No, no, no. Not God Bless America. God Damn America!" Other excerpts showed Wright condemning the country as "the US of KKK A" and as a sponsor of state terrorism. The clergyman roundly denounced the US use of atomic weapons in World War II and portrayed the September 11 attacks as a case of "chickens coming home to roost." In an instant, the videos went viral on the internet, and ABC aired them with spliced clips of Obama denying that the church was problematic. The suddenly ubiquitous coverage of Wright's fiery jeremiads was such a bombshell at the time that it would have been hard to believe that the worst was yet to come. But that was indeed the case.[24]

Obama's affiliation with Wright's Trinity United Church of Christ began in the 1980s when he was a community organizer in Chicago. He had been impressed with the pastor's dedication to social justice, including as it related to the issues of poverty, discrimination, unemployment, poor housing, and LGBTQ rights on the South Side. Further, Wright's sense of Christian duty mandated concern for oppressed people in faraway places like apartheid South Africa. Trinity's growing congregation provided a sense of community for Obama, something that was vitally important to his evolving racial identity and political maturation on the US mainland. Despite the monstrous image that Wright would acquire in the American media in the midst of the primaries, Obama seemed most affected by the optimism of his rendition of the gospel. Obama was inspired enough to adopt Wright's phrase "the audacity of hope" into his own political ethos and later campaign style. While the Obama family had not been especially regular attendees of Trinity, the pastor had officiated at the couple's wedding and baptized their children. Obama came to view him as a trusted mentor and advisor and perhaps even as a spiritual father who provided the paternal direction that his biological father had not.[25]

According to later accounts, Obama knew that some of Wright's words might come back to haunt him. As early as his February 2007 campaign announcement, Obama had known about the circulation of some of the pastor's sermons as well as a *Rolling Stone* interview that included some inflammatory remarks. He decided not to break with Wright and Trinity at that time but did sideline Wright during the presidential bid's launch in Springfield. Michelle reportedly found the *Rolling Stone* piece to be good cause for cutting ties, and she, like her husband, would later claim that they had not been present during Wright's more controversial tirades. In a campaign that valued discipline and planning above all else, the Obama team was unprepared to defuse the Wright time bomb or to evade its sizable blast radius. The candidate had previously instructed his staff to review tapes of the pastor's sermons so that they could get ahead of any damaging narrative that might play out in the media. Yet no one moved on the issue. David Plouffe, the campaign manager, would later accept blame for the dereliction, but the glaring oversight could have been caught earlier and addressed by any number of others, including David Axelrod or Obama himself. In any event, when the video clips started making the media rounds in March 2008, the campaign was inexplicably caught flat-footed. Several staff members, including Plouffe, were seeing the recordings for the first time and were genuinely horrified by the grim implications for the campaign.[26]

Obama, off-balance and on the defensive, issued a repudiation of Wright's more intemperate remarks, including "any statement that disparages our great country or serves to divide us from our allies." He made clear that he and his family would maintain their affiliation with Trinity, given that it was in the process of elevating pastor Otis Moss III to lead. Shortly after this statement, it was announced that Wright would cease advising the campaign. At the time, none of these damage-control tactics seemed to matter. Cable news outlets aired the video clips through the weekend and for days to come, providing little context for the more controversial sound bites, which were played in an endless rotation. Obama's largely white senior campaign staff had not yet come up with language for discussing and interpreting Wright's words and meaning, and thus could hardly offer much direction. Without question, Obama understood that he was witnessing the possible end of his presidential bid. The Wright tapes threatened to define him not only as "the Black candidate" but as "the Black radical candidate" who had tried to dupe an unwitting America into electing an unpatriotic subversive to the White House.[27]

The conflagration precipitated by the Wright videos was certainly about theology, patriotism, foreign policy, and a host of other issues, all knotted together and emblazoned with the pastor's long list of grievances about the country's shortcomings. But at its core, the predicament was about race and how it still continued to shape and destabilize US politics and the presidential campaign cycle. Wright was not just a minister, he was a Black minister who pastored a Black church that he counseled in matters related to Christian charity and salvation but also on the topics of racism, militarism, poverty, and other worldly problems. And Barack Obama was now his best-known parishioner. It did not matter that Wright was a fairly conventional representative of a larger Black theological tradition in which harsh critiques of US hypocrisy and other sins had been common pulpit praxis since the time of slavery. Nor did the Obamas' claim that they had not been present during Wright's more blistering sermons carry much weight with many observers. In the racialized climate of the primaries, the shared Blackness of the senator and his pastor, along with a presumably shared Black / radical / Christian worldview, mattered most to critics, notwithstanding that a few weeks earlier some had used the Farrakhan dustup to portray Obama as a closet Muslim.

None of the options for quelling the rolling crisis were attractive. The campaign could have decided to issue more strident rebuttals of Wright and the videos, hoping that the calamity would fade away as had happened with the Farrakhan situation. The problem with this approach was that there were no foreseeable upcoming events that could decisively change the ugly media narrative. The next primary was not until Pennsylvania on April 22, a full month away, and the Clintons were being careful not to get in the way of the self-immolation that appeared to be happening in the Obama camp. The only other options were to remain silent and risk political death or to do something bold enough to eclipse the Wright mess without creating a new one. Under intense pressure, Obama chose the latter course.

The Illinois senator wanted to give a speech that directly engaged the issue of race. His communication had always been most effective when he had the floor and could control the terms of the discourse, as opposed to other messaging formats, such as debates and interviews, which exposed him to distractions and possible snafus. Plouffe suggested the National Constitution Center (NCC) in Philadelphia as a site for the presentation, a relatively intimate space that would bring Obama into sharp focus for a TV audience. Michelle, who typically did not question campaign strategy, did second-guess the location choice. She imagined her husband in a grander setting. "He needs to see supportive faces and to be boosted," she told Plouffe. The campaign manager thought that a large crowd would make the event raucous and impersonal when it needed to be serious, even moving. Seeing the logic of Plouffe's point, Michelle assented to his decision regarding the NCC, a location that would also signal to the Clintons that the battle was still on for the Pennsylvania delegates in April.[28]

Entitled "A More Perfect Union," Obama's speech at the NCC was eloquent and weighty, cohering around a number of different themes and evocative refrains. Against a decidedly presidential arrangement of American flags, he started with both his own origins and those of the country. He proclaimed the greatness of the US Constitution, though it was unfinished and "stained by this nation's original sin of slavery." He recognized the document's capacity for growth and its living history of expanding rights and citizenship to cover increasing numbers of Americans over time. He also acknowledged his "unyielding faith in the decency and generosity of the American people" as exemplified by the ability of individuals from various backgrounds to come together in common cause. Merging American heterogeneity into his own story, Obama remarked on his mixed-race heritage and described Michelle as a "black American who carries within her the blood of slaves and slaveholders."[29] The motifs of strength through diversity and improvement through persistent struggle punctuated the opening section of the speech and set the terms of what was to come.

Turning to the Rev. Wright controversy, Obama first mentioned the disquieting presence of race in the presidential campaign, whether one considered the tone of the South Carolina primary or the rumors circulating in some quarters that his campaign was "somehow an exercise in affirmative action." He would later talk in a nuanced way about his interactions with and understanding of his former pastor, but upfront he sought to clear the air of some "nagging questions" that had lingered beyond his initial disavowal of the clergyman's diatribes. "Did I ever hear him make remarks that could be considered controversial while I sat in church? Yes. Did I strongly disagree with many of his political views? Absolutely," Obama confirmed. He described himself as drawing a line on Wright's original sin: his apparent inability to grow and evolve on matters of race or to discern a capacity for growth and improvement in others. In Obama's opinion, the pastor had "expressed a profoundly distorted view of this country—a view that sees white racism as endemic, and that elevates what is wrong with America above all that we know is right with America." The pastor's unwitting failure or purposeful unwillingness to recognize progress made him susceptible to a kind of stasis on the question of race, which in turn doomed him to becoming an anachronistic throwback to a historical moment less modern and advanced than the present.

To be sure, Obama offered many sympathetic words about Wright, including references to his military service, his officiating at the Obamas' wedding, and his inspiration as the candidate's spiritual guide. He also discussed the pastor's work for the poor, the incarcerated, and those afflicted with HIV/AIDS. In an effort to contextualize Wright within African American spiritual traditions, Obama depicted him as being shaped by the eclectic richness and glaring contradictions that one could readily find in the pews of many Black churches, including "kindness and cruelty, the fierce intelligence and shocking ignorance, the success, the love and yes, the bitterness and bias that make up the black experience in America." In offering some cover to both Wright and himself, Obama denied ever hearing him denigrate another ethnic group. Still, in the final analysis, he judged the pastor to be "divisive at a time when we need unity," ultimately making it clear that he sought to publicly chasten the clergyman for his rhetoric—as one would an errant family member—rather than break with him completely. "I can no more disown him than I can disown the black community," he declared plainly. "I can no more disown him than I can my white grandmother," who Obama admitted "on more than one occasion has uttered racial or ethnic stereotypes that made me cringe."

Following the Rev. Wright portion of the speech, Obama turned to race relations more broadly. He outlined Black anger over the "brutal legacies of slavery and Jim Crow," pointing to contemporary evidence of racism and discrimination in patterns of property ownership, union membership, economic mobility, and broken families, the latter exacerbated by failed welfare policies. On the other side of the racial divide, he sketched the causes of white resentment, namely, the outsourcing of jobs, static wages, busing, affirmative action, and accusations of racism. He indicted Republicans and other conservatives for exploiting these sentiments for votes and media ratings "while dismissing legitimate discussions of racial injustice and inequality as mere political correctness or reverse racism." He went on to argue that Black rage and white antipathy were misdirected toward racial bogeymen as opposed to class dynamics, to the detriment of all. According to Obama, the true source of middle-class stagnation was a self-interested, corporate culture of cronyism and greed abetted by a corrupt federal government too cozy with special interests and lobbyists, who advocated for "the few over the many."

In the face of these realities, Obama advised Black people "to insist on a full measure of justice in every aspect of American life" while being strategic enough to attach their "particular grievances . . . to the larger aspirations of Americans" and to take "full responsibility for our own lives," particularly in the realm of fathering. To whites, he counseled recognition of the historical and contemporary manifestations of racism and discrimination, and he insisted that these burdens for Black people "are real and must be addressed." As with African Americans, he encouraged his white audience to not think of improving schools, reforming the criminal justice system, enforcing civil rights laws, or erecting new "ladders of opportunity" as a zero-sum game with winners and losers but as being integral to overall US prosperity. Obama concluded his thirty-seven-minute speech on an optimistic note, exhorting Americans to unite to address the many issues facing the nation and to forsake the politics of division and racial scapegoating. After offering uplifting last words about the "band of patriots" who had signed the Constitution in Philadelphia hundreds of years earlier, he thanked and waved at the audience and then departed the stage.

The March 18 "race speech," as it would later be known, was both vintage Obama and his most daring high-wire performance to date. In essence, he had attempted to integrate the metaphorical bus with Black and white passengers sitting together in honest but civil conversation as they moved in the same direction toward a common understanding and collective action on behalf of the greater good. Even the misunderstood but still too divisive Rev. Wright would have a place on the bus of American decency and reconciliation, and it would not be under the vehicle either. Instead, Wright was dusted off, albeit somewhat roughly, and eased into a suitable storage bin to be remembered, even admired, as a curious, lonely artifact of tribal rituals no longer necessary because that racial world no longer existed.

In the new world that Obama rendered, much progress had been made over the generations, to the point that he felt comfortable objecting to the notion that white racism is endemic to the United States. While acknowledging the ongoing ramifications of the country's long history of racial oppression, he posited that an unholy alliance between government and business was the real obstacle to Black and white middle-class prosperity. As had become his custom, he sought to straddle race by narrating the stories of both sides, hoping to generate empathy once everyone could comprehend the other side's motivating premises and frame of reference. This rhetorical and ideological move set up his appeal for racial rapprochement, his call for universalist policies, and his encouragement of self-help and personal responsibility. In sum, most of what was new in the speech was the determined effort to dispense finally with the Wright imbroglio. The rest of the text was straight out of *The Audacity of Hope* and other policy prescriptions that Obama had by then advocated for years.[30]

The speech was the most important of the entire campaign, and it underscored the visibility that the Wright controversy had garnered in the race. At the time of the oration, only 31 percent of Americans had been exposed to Wright's statements to any notable degree. A week later, 51 percent of respondents told pollsters that they had heard "a lot" about the pastor and his rhetoric. To the relief of the Obama camp, his speech seemed to accomplish the immediate task of containing the Wright situation. According to a May poll, 90 percent of Obama supporters believed that he had dealt with the crisis well, and 66 percent of Clinton supporters agreed. Moreover, nine out of ten of his backers told pollsters that the controversy would not impact their voting preference, though 31 percent of Clinton partisans said that they were less likely to support Obama. These figures were palatable overall, especially since they reflected the continuing solidity of his core support. The enhanced public consciousness of the Wright affair would likely have not mattered much had Obama's speech been the last major litigation of the issue. However, to the consternation of his campaign, it was not.[31]

On April 25, Rev. Wright participated in a PBS interview with Bill Moyers. He was soft-spoken in defense of his ministry, a jarring contrast to the looping video clips that had gained him so much notoriety during the primary campaign. When Moyers asked about Obama's race speech, the pastor smiled. "He's a politician, I'm a pastor," Wright mused in an instructive tone, just above a whisper. "I do what I do, he does what politicians do, so that what happened in Philadelphia where he had to respond to the sound bites, he responded as a politician." Gesturing for emphasis, he added, "But he did not disown me, because I'm a pastor." After the March 18 speech and prior to the PBS interview, Obama had tried to smooth things out with Wright. They had met secretly at the clergyman's Chicago home, where the senator assured him that the speech was less a rebuke than a chance to place the pastor in historical perspective. When the Moyers interview aired, Obama took issue with being characterized as a politician responding to a political crisis. "How could he say that about me?"

he reportedly inquired of Valerie Jarrett. "He knows that's not true. He knows I wasn't being a politician."[32]

On April 28, Wright gave Obama more to fume about as he made a series of media appearances. At a National Press Club event, the pastor offered a historical dissertation on the Black church and the prophetic tradition, marked by informed observations and charismatic exhortations. However, during the wide-ranging, sometimes combative Q&A segment, he reiterated his earlier remarks about Obama as having responded to the offending sound bites as a politician would. He continued to refer to himself as the candidate's pastor but insisted that Obama had not read the sermons that he had condemned and was not a faithful attendee of services. Wright also repeated a warning that he had issued to his famous parishioner a year earlier. "If you get elected, November the 5th, I'm coming after you," Wright had promised, "because you'll be representing a government whose policies grind under people." A Chicago friend of the candidate who had seen an early airing of the Wright appearance called Obama to recommend that he view the video himself. "I don't know if I can," the senator confessed ruefully. "I think it's going to be too painful to watch."[33]

The formal break with Wright came the next day. Following a town hall in Winston-Salem, North Carolina, Obama met with reporters offstage. He talked about his lifelong devotion to bringing people together and juxtaposed his vision of America to that of his former pastor. "I am outraged by the comments that were made, and saddened over the spectacle that we saw yesterday," he seethed. He flatly denied that there were political motives behind his race speech and wondered aloud whether he and the pastor, despite a twenty-year affiliation, ever really knew each other. If anyone had any doubts about the current state of their relationship, Obama totally dispelled them. "His comments were not only divisive and destructive," he contended, "but I believe that they end up giving comfort to those who prey on hate, and I believe that they do not portray accurately the perspective of the black church." The questioning of Wright's interpretation of church doctrine was especially damning, since much of the reverend's media tour was self-styled as a defense of the Black Christian tradition. Somewhat predictably, the pastor would later claim that his erstwhile parishioner "threw me under the bus." Yet to many observers, it appeared that Wright had abused his fleeting time in the spotlight with an unforgivable display of grandstanding arrogance that harmed both him and Obama. The weight of the crisis did not abate quickly; one close associate reported Obama as being "at an all-time low" in the week following the break with Wright. In any event, Obama was convinced that the survival of his campaign required that he cut Wright loose, lest the association—and the clergyman's unpredictable screeds—continue to be a costly burden.[34]

By late April, Obama was still ahead slightly in the delegate count, but he had just lost Pennsylvania, and there were enough remaining contests in May and June to give Clinton a valid rationale for not conceding. In a primary matchup that entranced the country and remained tight going into the spring, Hillary Clinton made the decision not to completely abandon racial appeals, this time choosing to employ language as flagrant as any used by her husband earlier in the year. After being dealt a primary loss in North Carolina and barely eking out a win in Indiana on May 6, Clinton told an interviewer that she was still the stronger candidate with the widest appeal, as demonstrated by "how Sen. Obama's support among working, hard-working Americans, white Americans, is weakening again, and how whites in both states who had not completed college were supporting me." An Obama campaign spokesman called the comments out as false and "frankly disappointing," which was followed by a denial from Clinton that her remarks had been racially charged. To be sure, the New York senator did better among white voters than Obama, but that was principally because she fared better among all white women as opposed to notably outpacing Obama among the white working class.[35]

Clinton's comments, like her husband's maneuvering during the South Carolina primary, reeked of desperation and a willingness to

blatantly appeal to white identity politics, while claiming not to do
so. The Jeremiah Wright controversy, an existential threat to Obama's
presidential bid, had underscored the continuing potency of race in
the campaign as well as the likelihood that any racial eruption involving either candidate, but especially Obama, would have a long
afterlife in the media. The Clinton campaign tried to exploit this
pattern as the primary season's clock wound down but ultimately
converted too few voters in its hour of severest need. Ironically, the
Clinton operation was the more diverse of the two, with several more
women and Blacks—including campaign manager Maggie Williams
and chief of staff Cheryl Mills—in positions of high authority than
was the case with the Obama organization. But even this dynamic
did not neutralize race as an issue that could be weaponized for campaign purposes. When a picture of Obama dressed in East African—
derived attire—probably taken during one of his previous trips to
the region—appeared in the conservative media, Stephanie Tubbs
Jones, a Black congresswoman from Ohio and vocal Clinton surrogate, counseled that Obama should not be reluctant to be seen in
"native clothes."[36]

Running alongside the Wright crisis, which claimed so much attention during the spring primary season, various impressions of the
Obama campaign were evolving among an array of African Americans, with a few developments approaching the importance of some
of the better-known media frenzies. By the time of the Iowa victory
in January, Barack Obama had become a familiar (and more often
correctly pronounced) name among Black people from many walks
of life. The unheard-of opportunity, the glimmering possibility of
electing a person of African descent to the nation's highest office
electrified Black communities and the Black realms of politics, activism, academia, entertainment, and spirituality. Representative voices
emerged in each of these areas to signal support for his candidacy,
and everyday, working-class people—anonymous in the historical
record but no less excited and mobilized—registered to vote in droves

and paid rapt attention to the primary season. The tug-of-war with Clinton over every delegate surely had much to do with the general public's fascination, as did the press's obsession with reporting every detail and minute wrinkle, whether on TV, radio, the internet, or social media. Obama was the phenomenon, the underdog challenger who so inspired the interest of many Black people in the presidential race. In his own Rorschach-test way, he became the vessel for countless dreams and fantasies about equality, citizenship, and postracial futures to the point that his impossibility could seem strangely powered by an unseen inevitability.

Rev. Al Sharpton of New York was an early Obama supporter and would be a valued acquaintance long after the election season. Campaign officials were cautious with him at first, given their fear that he might bring unwanted baggage to the presidential bid. Over time, Sharpton proved to be an asset, using his formidable communication skills and activist networks to get across Obama's message as well as anyone did. He was especially useful in tamping down wild expectations of Obama as a prospective president, recognizing the extra burden that his race would entail and understanding that his universalist approach to health care, education, and other issues could actually provide disproportionate benefits for some marginalized communities. In the field of academia, Cornel West, a Princeton philosopher who initially favored John Edwards's antipoverty platform, became an Obama supporter after meeting with him in early 2007. "He has a different style to Reverend Sharpton and Reverend Jackson," the professor gleaned from their encounter, "but he wants to speak about racism in his own way, and it can be effective." West's opinion would change with time, but during the campaign he was inspired enough to serve as an unpaid advisor.[37]

In the entertainment world, Obama had no less a superstar than Oprah Winfrey doing his campaign bidding. A fellow Chicagoan, Winfrey served as an unofficial warm-up act at events leading up to the Iowa caucuses, braving bone-chilling temperatures to stir up crowds that would eventually number in the tens of thousands. Many attendees were probably as anxious to see the famous talk-show host as they were to hear from the candidate at such gatherings. Regardless of why people showed up, the kind of cross-demographic attention that she could bring to a rally was priceless. Similarly to Winfrey, Houston megachurch pastor Kirbyjon Caldwell brought a kind of notoriety to the Obama presidential bid that definitely had its place in a campaign that relied heavily on Black churches as voter-recruitment venues. Caldwell had supported George W. Bush in previous election cycles, apparently drawn to his public embrace of evangelical Christianity and perhaps his funding of faith-based initiatives. By 2008, he was a committed and visible supporter of Obama, donating financially to his campaign, appearing in TV ads, and facilitating connections with other clergy. Caldwell claimed to be impressed by Obama's "heart," finding his race alone "insufficient for my support." Some critics sensed opportunism in the minister's partisan shift, noting that he had downplayed his opposition to homosexuality and same-sex marriage to appeal to the socially liberal Obama. Whatever the case, the candidate countenanced his advice and support, which may have been especially welcome in the throes of the spring primaries.[38]

In addition to a growing number of supporters, Obama's candidacy attracted its share of Black skeptics and detractors. In a 2007 interview, Andrew Young, a former Atlanta mayor and an early Clinton supporter, tweaked the Illinois senator on both his political and racial credentials. "I want Barack Obama to be president," he stated, pausing dramatically and then adding, "in 2016." Young dismissed Obama as too young and immature for the presidency and as lacking the necessary support networks for the job. On the issue of race, Young was plainly salacious: "Bill [Clinton] is every bit as black as Barack. He's probably gone with more black women than Barack." Young shrugged off his lewder comments as jokes but stuck with his general conclusion that the 46-year-old candidate was not ready for high office. Similarly, in the days before the South Carolina primary, Robert Johnson, founder of Black Entertainment Television

(BET), came at Obama from another low angle. Standing beside Hillary Clinton at a campaign event, the businessman proclaimed that she had been "deeply and emotionally involved in black issues when Barack Obama was doing something in the neighborhood," an indirect reference to the candidate's teenage drug use as chronicled in *Dreams from My Father*. Johnson was not the first to bring up the senator's youthful indiscretions in the midst of the campaign, but his jeering of a Black candidate in this fashion—while standing beside his white opponent—seemed to play into pernicious stereotypes regarding race, crime, and addiction.[39]

Beyond the barbs of Young and Johnson, an implacable critic surfaced in the media world around this time. Tavis Smiley, a talk-show host and commentator, invited Obama to attend the annual "State of the Black Union" gathering held in New Orleans in February 2008. The candidate declined but offered to send his wife, Michelle, as a surrogate speaker, an offer that Smiley publicly rejected. From that moment forward, the commentator would be a relentless censurer of nearly every action of the Illinois senator, including his handling of the Wright crisis and his decision not to attend a ceremony marking the fortieth anniversary of the assassination of Martin Luther King Jr. in April. Smiley would face an avalanche of opprobrium for his perpetual faultfinding, which was likely behind his announced plan to resign in June from the Tom Joyner radio show, with its large Black listenership. Still, he would persist as one of the most vitriolic of Obama's critics far beyond the campaign season.[40]

In the arena of politics, Obama's support among Black elites and power brokers played out in complex ways and with long-term implications. For years, the Clintons had been rigorous in their pursuit of endorsements and commitments from Black political figures, including elected officials, former administration staffers, and assorted advisors who had benefited from friendships and favors linked to one or both of them. In the transactional world of politics, these connections were typically freighted with the implicit understanding that the granting of benefits produced obligations. By the 2008 presidential campaign, this quid pro quo system of favor-based loyalties was visibly evident among Black members of Congress, who represented millions of African Americans across dozens of US House districts.

To be sure, there was no standard set of interests or allegiances; different congresspeople from different regions had different kinds of ties to different stakeholders. Moreover, to safeguard their incumbency, politicians had to always be mindful of the unique variables that impacted their individual circumstances, including the demographic and partisan configurations of their district, the demands of fundraising and donors, and the electoral risks of difficult votes. In terms of the Democratic primaries, these interests and concerns tended to produce several categories of Black congressional responses to the Obama campaign, exemplified by those who embraced his candidacy once it proved viable (usually after he had won their district and/or state), those who equivocated longer but eventually committed to Obama (which often entailed defecting from Clinton), and those who refrained from supporting his bid until after the entire nominating process ended. Calculations and miscalculations, of course, influenced their decision-making timelines, but the delegate math between Obama and Clinton at any given moment was a fairly reliable means of predicting the movements and maneuvers of congresspeople.

The easiest, safest path between Clinton and Obama for many Black representatives in Congress was the wait-and-see approach. This hedging normally involved waiting until their state's primary contest took place and then making a judgment based on the outcome. The wider the margin of victory for the winner, the easier the political calculus, unless there were extenuating circumstances. Illustratively, when Obama won Rep. David Scott's district by a fifty-three-point margin in Georgia's primary on February 5, the congressman switched his support from Clinton to the Illinois senator the following day. Others, like Rep. Donald Payne of New Jersey, took a bit longer but also defected to Obama in the wake of the candidate's primary victories in their states.

The case of Congressman John Lewis is noteworthy primarily because of the symbolism of his candidate switch and the generational dynamic involved. Originally a Clinton supporter, the Georgia representative agonized over his commitment to her after Obama won his state's contest. As a veteran of the civil rights movement, he had fought and suffered at Selma and elsewhere for the opportunity to both vote and elect Black people to office. He was sixty-seven at the time of the Georgia primary, which decidedly made him a member of the Moses generation, and he was now facing the first real opportunity to see an African American elevated to the White House. "I want to be on the right side of history," he repeatedly told himself and his colleague James Clyburn of South Carolina, "and I can't let this moment pass me by." Lewis equivocated for weeks but eventually threw his support behind Obama. When he regretfully broke the news to the Clintons, they expressed respect for his decision, perhaps having been prepared for it by his public waffling. "We were friends before this campaign," candidate Clinton told the distressed congressman, "and we'll be friends after this campaign."[41]

Several congresspeople stayed loyal to Clinton longer than some of their constituents preferred, and in a number of cases this triggered protests and even primary challenges. This was the case with New York representatives Edolphus Towns and Gregory W. Meeks, who both drew electoral opponents after deciding to stick with Clinton as the home-state presidential candidate. Other US House members, such as Charles Rangel of New York, Emanuel Cleaver of Missouri, and Maxine Waters of California, refrained from switching their support to Obama until toward the end of the primary season, when the Clinton campaign was all but defeated. Congresswoman Stephanie Tubbs Jones of Ohio, who had been so avid in her support of Clinton, did not give up the fight until the candidate's concession in June, even though Obama won 70 percent of the vote in her district during the Ohio primary on March 4. James Clyburn also declined to endorse Obama until then, in observance of his pledged neutrality as a party leader in the Congress and as a superdelegate. For some, the price of waiting and vacillating had been appreciable, especially once Obama's ultimate victory in the primaries seemed certain. "You don't understand what it's like," Rep. Meeks told a Clinton aide. "We get called 'house Negro' and 'handkerchief head' by our own constituents because we're supporting Hillary." Obama had won Meeks's district by a single point; the backlash against congresspeople in districts that had gone for the Illinois senator by double digits was worse in a number of instances.[42]

Obama's support among Black members of the US House was hard won. He was the underdog going into the campaign against Clinton, a former First Lady and sitting US senator who had many more years of experience with Black politicians than her rival did. If all of the doubts, hesitations, defections, and calculations of Obama's fellow CBC members had significance, they in general meant that he did not owe them anything moving forward. Only if a congressperson had supported him early on—when such an endorsement mattered— would they have been able to advance a claim on his presidential political capital later. Once Obama had won a representative's district and/or state, their endorsement was much less valuable. If anything, such a late-supporting congressperson was now in his debt, for he had likely stirred up their Democratic base and motivated people to vote in unusually high numbers. That is, he was now the one with the electoral coattails going into the general election. But there might have been an ancillary benefit related to the fickle ways of many of the Black representatives: their reluctance to embrace Obama early perhaps kept him from being portrayed in the conservative media as too chummy with the Black establishment in Congress, particularly those with more outspoken views on race and other potentially controversial tendencies. In any event, by the time Clinton was defeated, most of the CBC had migrated to Obama's camp, just in time to line up in a united front at the convention. But by then, the presumptive nominee no longer needed their often last-minute blessings, a realization that would have bearing on his future relations with congressional officials.

Following the spring primaries and into the summer, other conversations swirled around the Obama candidacy, with some careening into sensitive places. The theme of personal responsibility, a perennial favorite of the Illinois senator, bubbled to the surface again on June 15, Father's Day. As the guest speaker at the 20,000-member Apostolic Church of God on the South Side of Chicago, Obama, accompanied by his family, offered a sometimes quite personal talk on the meaning of fatherhood. He related the negative effects of his own father's absence on his life, likening it to a "hole in your heart." He referred to himself as a less-than-perfect parent who was away from home more often than he would like, but he informed his predominantly Black audience that he had promised himself years earlier that he would "break the cycle" and try to be the good father that he never had. "We need fathers to realize that responsibility doesn't just end at conception," he exhorted. "Any fool can have a child." Instead, he continued, "it's the courage to raise a child that makes you a father."[43]

The address received mixed reviews among Black observers. Rep. Clyburn applauded both the message and Obama's willingness to share on the campaign trail his personal story of being raised without a father. Rev. Sharpton thought the speech was bold and significant but could foresee others dismissing it as parading "dirty laundry" in public and unfairly taking to task African American men who faced challenges to effectively leading healthy, economically secure families. Ronald Walters, a professor of politics and government at the University of Maryland, pointed out that Obama was not running to become "preacher in chief," and thus his moralizing about fatherhood at a Black church was less important than his articulation of policies that would benefit Black communities. In a subsequent address on July 5 at an African Methodist Episcopal (AME) Church gathering in St. Louis, Obama reiterated his call for personal responsibility and responded to criticism that he had unnecessarily victim-blamed some Black men as bad fathers. He recognized that "there are out-standing men doing an outstanding job under the most difficult of circumstances" but maintained that the troubling reality of most Black children being reared in single-parent households had social and economic impacts that should not be ignored. Poverty and injustice were not excuses for bad decision-making, he declared, and the "posture of victim" was not an acceptable approach to fixing things "within our control."[44]

Obama's speeches in June and July on Black fatherhood and accountability were nothing new for him on the campaign trail. During a February rally, he had chided a largely African American audience in Texas about the need to limit their children's access to greasy foods, sodas, video games, and television, since these indulgences were all known causes of obesity and educational underperformance. His race speech in Philadelphia the following month was accented with self-help and personal responsibility tropes, with particular encouragement for fellow Black people to exercise more agency "by demanding more from our fathers, and spending more time with our children." Those who had taken the time to read *The Audacity of Hope* would have scarcely been surprised by his Father's Day comments or any of his post-primary recommendations concerning respectability, including his admonishment that "brothers should pull up their pants" and avoid the underwear-exposing style of sagging trousers.

Public critiques of Obama's more recent remarks took aim at his silence on what some would deem the moral failings of the white community, whether those issues involved absent fathers, drug addiction, or racial biases. Further, it seemed to some a bit too politically convenient that Obama would groan again so loudly about the need for Black responsibility just as his campaign was strategizing ways to appeal to white moderates and conservatives. With the general election on the horizon, how better to veer back toward the ideological center than to administer a dose of neoliberal, up-by-the-bootstraps rhetoric to your own African American base? Obama devotees would argue that such a cynical reading of his motives was not shared by—or at least did not noticeably alienate—the vast majority of Black people, whose overwhelming support in polls remained critical to his electoral prospects. Still, the Illinois senator could only have raised eyebrows when he announced after the Father's Day speech that he and Sen. Evan Bayh of Indiana, a traditionally conservative state that Obama narrowly lost to Clinton and that was in play for the November election, would cosponsor a bill to address the "national epidemic of absentee fathers."

In the face of criticism, Obama consistently stressed that there was no incongruity between recognizing the historical injustices and contemporary racism and discrimination that African Americans continued to face while also calling for Black responsibility on both the individual and communal levels. He frequently posited that his own experience with an absentee father gave him insight into how this phenomenon affected Black families, and he was consequently not reluctant to use whatever authority or credibility that his insider experience bestowed upon him to counsel other Black men, in private and in public, on the duties of fatherhood. Several years after the 2008 primaries, he would come back to this issue, disputing once more the charge that he was not focusing adequate attention on institutional racism in his encouragement of Black self-help. "There's no contradiction to say that there are issues of personal responsibility that have to be addressed," he asserted in a 2014 interview, "while still acknowledging that some of the specific pathologies in the African-American community are a direct result of our history." The crisis of Black fatherhood still ranked high on his list of issues that needed to be ameliorated, a contention that he never backed away from.[45]

One person who was not keen on Obama's public appeals to Black people in regard to personal responsibility and community-generated uplift was Rev. Jesse Jackson Sr. Despite having never held a major elected position, Jackson was a legendary figure in African American politics and still retained a degree of gravitas even as his reputation and clout had declined over the course of recent years. In 1984 and 1988, he had boldly run for the US presidency as a Democrat, juxtaposing his unabashedly liberal vision and multiracial Rainbow Coalition against the conservative ethos of Ronald Reagan's America. Jackson, smart and charismatic, pushed against the Republicans' small-government, ultramilitarized, anti–New Deal agenda with proposals for increased public support for education, agriculture, health care, and civil rights. He advocated a rethinking of the War on Drugs, with its emphasis on criminalizing users that had so devastated minority communities, and proposed nuclear détente with the Soviet Union, tougher measures toward the apartheid government of South Africa, and an independent state for Palestinians. While an inexperienced staff, shallow coffers, and a number of impolitic comments and alliances weakened his odds for success, Jackson ran strongly in both election cycles, coming in second in 1988 to the eventual Democratic nominee, Governor Michael Dukakis of Massachusetts.

The minister's bids for the presidency had deeply inspired African Americans and others, providing rays of progressive light and cross-racial possibilities during the conservative ascendancy of the 1980s, which had depended on a broad, disproportionately white backlash to the social advancements of the 1960s and 1970s in order to take root. Jackson remained politically engaged after his historic runs for the White House and occasionally hinted at a lingering interest in public office. Although he never ran for the presidency again, his earlier attempts to become the chief executive of the United States had concretized an enduring political legacy.[46]

Jackson was an early supporter of Obama's candidacy, but he would turn out to be one of the most conflicted, and even tragic, of all. In the midst of nationwide protests after the 2006 arrest of six Black teenagers charged with the alleged beating of a white classmate in Jena, Louisiana, Jackson reportedly had castigated Obama for "acting like he's white" in not issuing a more strident response to the excessiveness of the charges. Later, during the South Carolina primary, the minister credibly played the senior statesman role, counseling in his trademark metaphorical way that after a bruising "playoff season," the two candidates would need to reconcile in time "for the Super

Bowl, and the Super Bowl is November." Jackson would run hot and cold with Obama for years to come, providing robust praise in some instances and prickly rebukes in others. One of his more volcanic moments erupted on July 9, 2008, in the wake of the presidential candidate's speeches on personal responsibility. An open microphone caught Jackson chatting quietly with Dr. Reed V. Tuckson, a United-Health Group executive, following an interview with a Fox News journalist. With both the video and audio feeds still operating, Jackson whispered to a leaning Tuckson, "See, Barack's been talking down to black people. . . . I want to cut his nuts off." The businessman immediately leaned away from Jackson and made no reply, his face betraying neither agreement nor opposition regarding the remark. Tuckson's silence saved him from making news, leaving Jackson to alone endure the media wildfire that he spontaneously ignited.[47]

And a wildfire it was. Jackson spent the next several days apologizing for his "crude and hurtful" insult, confessing that he was unaware that he was being recorded. According to the minister, he contacted the Obama campaign to express remorse as soon as the offending clip began making the media rounds. Bill Burton, a spokesman for the candidate, confirmed Obama's acceptance of the apology but reiterated the themes of the June and July speeches. "As someone who grew up without a father in the home, Sen. Obama has spoken and written for many years about the issue of parental responsibility, including the importance of fathers participating in their children's lives," Burton relayed. "He also discusses our responsibility as a society to provide jobs, justice, and opportunity to all." The campaign's statement, while not backtracking on core tenets, was gracious and painless compared to what was heading Jackson's way.[48]

Rep. Jesse Jackson Jr., who had stepped aside to allow Obama to run for the US Senate in 2004, bluntly excoriated his father for his castration comment. As a cochair of Obama's presidential campaign, he was virtually compelled to respond. However, his statement was more direct and reprimanding than many would have guessed it might be. "I'm deeply outraged and disappointed in Rev. Jackson's reckless statements," the younger Jackson conveyed in a public message. "He should know how hard that I've worked for the last year and a half" for the Obama campaign. While professing love for his father, Jackson Jr. let it be known that he had been disgusted by the video clip, which awkwardly forced him to publicly reaffirm his support for the Illinois senator over the "ugly rhetoric" of his father.[49]

Others were hardly more kind to Jackson Sr. Larry Elder, a Black libertarian and talk-show host, wondered on air whether Obama's comments about fatherhood and personal responsibility "hit a little too close to home for Reverend Jackson," who years earlier had weathered a scandal involving his fathering of a child during an extramarital affair. Making the skewering even worse, the *National Enquirer*, which had first published the story about Jackson Sr.'s infidelity in 2001, located his former mistress, Karin Stanford, who provided her own take on the situation. "Somewhere in the back of his mind, Rev. Jackson has to acknowledge that he has his own responsibility to his daughter," she asserted in an interview, making reference to their nine-year-old offspring. For Jackson, who had never been averse to press attention, a fortnight's worth of such media manhandling must have been both embarrassing and humbling on several levels.[50]

Given his historic runs for US president and some of his subsequent contributions, Jesse Jackson Sr. probably deserved better than he received during the 2008 election cycle, despite the fact that many of his wounds and sorrows had been self-inflicted. To a significant extent, he had made Obama possible, conceivable. Their political fortunes had intertwined long before they actually met, with both of their presidential campaigns having come up through some of the same Illinois activist networks and political associations that had given the country a significant number of Black US senators. When Jackson was running for the presidency in the 1980s, Obama was organizing neighborhoods on the South Side, each laboring under the weighty legacy of Chicago's first African American mayor, Harold Washington, who had mobilized Black voters in ways that would benefit all three men over time.

In the aftermath of his open-mic comments in July 2008, Jackson denied any suggestion that a bruised ego colored his view of Obama and the candidate's ascendancy in US politics. "It is ridiculous to think I have any resentment or jealousy toward Obama or any other younger person coming up," he avowed in a *Newsweek* interview. His denial, indeed, alluded to the Moses-Joshua tension again, now evoked in a context where one could almost hear the telltale rustling of the changing of the guard. A Gallup poll conducted between June 5 and July 6 quantified the generational shift. When asked to name a US leader who could speak for them on issues of race, 29 percent of the Black Americans surveyed chose Obama, with Al Sharpton coming in a distant second (6 percent). Jackson registered as the preference of 4 percent of those polled but was clumped together with Bill and Hillary Clinton (3 percent each) and Oprah Winfrey (2 percent). Having officially endorsed Obama, Jackson told the *Newsweek* reporter that he was "part of the winning team." The difference now, of course, was that he was no longer the star player.[51]

For Barack Obama, the counterweight to the duplicitous political allies, scandalmongering media, and overall griminess of the nomination process was Michelle. Young, statuesque, with a milk-chocolate complexion, she was not the typical candidate's wife, particularly among those seeking high office. She detested politics and despised fundraising even more, but the campaign had no truer supporter than Michelle. She was professionally accomplished and familiar enough with both white and Black worlds to approximate the racially diplomatic ways of her husband. She swam in political waters for years prior to the presidential bid, with Barack's regular trips to Springfield and Washington, DC, requiring her to multitask through neck-deep duties as a working professional, wife, and mother. When she had agreed to the presidential run so many months ago on those balmy Hawaiian shores, she could hardly have guessed the rigors of the trail. In service to the campaign, she gave speeches across the country while her mother, Marian Robinson, watched the girls. She tried not to be away from Malia and Sasha for more than one night at a time but did acclimate to the constant grind of meeting and greeting strangers, piling onto buses and planes, and always living under the watchful eye of Secret Service agents. The spotlight was inescapable, but this was the public stage that she and Barack had chosen to inhabit. It was life altering in all of the ways that one might imagine, and then some.[52]

Michelle Obama had entered the presidential campaign as a good public speaker and became exceptional over time. Of course, she was not perfect, and in the crucible of the 2008 primary season, every blemish and misstep fell under a harsh microscope and was magnified, even distorted, for all to see. One episode in particular became emblematic of this tendency. At a Milwaukee event in February 2008, Michelle made the mistake of inadvertently giving opponents an opening for questioning her patriotism, which was then used to shimmy open a window for exaggerating her racial otherness and challenging her suitability as a prospective First Lady. "For the first time in my adult lifetime, I am really proud of my country," she said of her husband's campaign success, "because it feels like hope is finally making a comeback." The phrasing was clunky, for sure, but no more than that. Yet once the statement splashed into the media cycle, it was immediately weaponized by conservative news outlets. Michelle tried to explain away the brewing controversy by claiming that she was referring to her excitement about the political mobilization that the campaign had inspired among Americans. Predictably, this clarification did not quench the flames.[53]

Other rumors, false impressions, and outright lies about Michelle Obama began to spread across the mediascape during the spring and early summer to create a full-blown caricature. On the right, the *National Review* called her "Mrs. Grievance," playing into a developing narrative of her as an angry, dominating, and emasculating Black woman, while Fox News referred to her as "Obama's baby mama," as if her fifteen-year marriage to Barack readily lent itself to stereotypes about Black family dysfunction. On the left, the July 21 cover of the *New Yorker*, in a questionable attempt at satire, featured a drawing of Michelle with an afro and an assault rifle giving a fist bump to her husband, who was depicted in full jihadist attire in front of a framed picture of Osama bin Laden and a burning US flag. Michelle was horrified and hurt by the portrayals and at first did not know how to respond to a threat that she could not quite comprehend. "It was as if there were some cartoon version of me out there wreaking havoc," she later wrote, "a woman I kept hearing about but didn't know—a too-tall, too-forceful, ready-to-emasculate Godzilla of a political wife named Michelle Obama." By this time, the Obamas had survived the primaries, but the crusade to cast them as racial others ahead of the general election was in full swing. According to an Associated Press poll, Michelle was viewed by Americans more negatively than positively by midsummer (35 percent and 30 percent, respectively), an unenviable position for the campaign to be in, especially if it planned to deploy her to soothe Clinton voters still smarting from the primary battles of the spring.[54]

Both figuratively and literally, Michelle and the campaign decided to undergo a complete makeover. For starters, she more frequently emphasized her experience as an ordinary American who was grateful for the rare opportunities that she had enjoyed in an extraordinary country. In popular forums like the women-hosted talk show *The View*, she presented herself as a supportive wife and conventional mother. For Black outlets such as *Essence* magazine, she rhapsodized about how living on the South Side kept her family grounded, despite the swarm of Secret Service vehicles and personnel. Moreover, to complement her revised public persona, which now stressed the campaign's themes of unity, decency, and common cause across racial lines, Mrs. Obama and her handlers conjured a visual image of the professional political wife: middle class, refined, and appealing to the eye but down-to-earth and sympathetic to the struggles of working-class people.

In dramatizing this persona, she wore J. Crew cardigans and sleeveless summer dresses that took advantage of her hourglass figure and toned, svelte arms. Her Chicago makeup artist was enlisted to lower her eyebrow arches to give her a less "angry" look, and her hair was permed, parted, and delicately styled to wreath her face, falling straight into a partial tuck or curled bob at the base of the neck. By July, Michelle incessantly talked about working-class roots, middle-class motherhood, and patriotic "hope and change," and she now had the look to match. At forty-four, she was being groomed to become the youngest First Lady since Jacqueline Kennedy lived in the White House during the "Camelot" years of the early 1960s; some observers were already fantasizing about a future "Bamelot" in the event of an Obama victory in November. It was an admirable—and, to a degree, self-effacing— act of reinvention that Michelle Obama wore well going into the fall campaign, which promised to be at least as eventful and trying as the spring and summer.[55]

By June 3, Barack Obama had won the 2,118 delegates and superdelegates necessary to become the Democratic Party's presumptive nominee for the US presidency. The primary race had been trending in his direction for months but officially clinching it in such a close matchup with Hillary Clinton required waiting until the last primaries in Montana and South Dakota. The New York senator worked through the difficulty of conceding and eventually issued a full-throated endorsement of Obama's presidential bid on June 7. Meanwhile, Obama swallowed whatever bad taste lingered after the primaries and reached out to his vanquished challenger with kind words and a request for support in the general election. He desired a united front going into the Democratic National Convention in August, including public appearances and speeches by both Clintons. At this junction, no one was surprised by the roles that they would be called on to play in order to elect a Democrat to the White House. Hurt feelings were set aside in favor of political calculus and ambitions, a traditional, intricate dance that takes place between erstwhile primary rivals during every campaign season. In the end, Obama needed Hillary Clinton to keep her formidable base of primary voters energized and loyal to the party, and she needed to endeavor to do so if she hoped to have any political future, including another shot at the presidency someday. That was the new math going into the fall campaign against the Republicans.[56]

In hindsight, there was no single reason behind Clinton's failure to win the nomination but instead a myriad of factors. Many of her campaign's misjudgments stemmed from faulty assumptions and the neglect of a long-game strategy. She ran against Obama with the mentality of an incumbent, convinced that her credentials and experience would expose his relative newness to the political scene and thus his alleged unpreparedness for the presidency. This hubris, which was trumpeted by Bill Clinton and other surrogates, infected her campaign with a lethal myopia.

The Clinton campaign had assumed that the nominating contest would end quickly with a decisive, irreversible triumph by Super Tuesday (February 5). Consequently, it failed to adequately set up the required infrastructure and ground game to compete effectively in several states with later voting dates. Starting with Iowa, Clinton and her strategists fatally underestimated the importance of caucus states, which Obama aggressively cultivated and almost totally swept. She can perhaps be excused for not fully comprehending the exponentially enhanced role of the internet in fundraising during the 2008 election cycle. Even so, the cost of this oversight was that Clinton was heavily dependent on big contributions from traditional sources, leaving her organization in financial straits once donors had reached the statutory spending limits. Obama, with his legions of small donors, never faced this problem, and his team used internet contributions to devastating effect in both the primaries and the general election. At bottom, the Clinton campaign mistakenly ran on a record of incrementalism and past achievements in a year in which voters were demanding change and a clear break with the status quo. Her experiential strengths as a former First Lady, two-term US senator, and longtime Washington power player became weaknesses for a changing Democratic electorate—increasingly populated by minorities and millennials—that had fainter memories of her previous life in the White House.[57]

With the conclusion of the primary season, the Obama campaign made preparations for the fall campaign, when it would face off against Sen. John McCain of Arizona. The 71-year-old Republican presumptive nominee had secured his party's nod in a far less protracted nomination struggle, though doing so had required him to keep his distance from the unpopular GOP incumbent, George W. Bush. In thinking about how best to counter the criticism that Obama did not have the foreign policy background and governmental experience needed to run the country, the campaign settled on Sen. Joe Biden of Delaware as the vice presidential running mate. The gregarious, six-term senator brought a deep store of knowledge about international affairs to the ticket, as well as a folksy narrative about his working-class, Roman Catholic roots in Pennsylvania, an important swing state. On the less positive side, Biden, who had dropped out of the 2008 presidential campaign and subsequently endorsed Obama, was known for occasional misstatements and gaffes. As he announced his bid for the presidency in early 2007, he had referred to Obama as "the first mainstream African-American who is articulate and bright and clean and a nice-looking guy," a dubious compliment that caused a momentary stir and occasioned a private apology. With an eye to the future, Obama took no umbrage at Biden's misstep, but instead made note of how the Delaware senator could potentially anchor a Democratic ticket in a bedrock of seasoned experience like few others could.[58]

To be sure, Obama had seriously entertained the notion of offering Hillary Clinton the VP position, but his staffers were quick to recount all of the reasons not to do so. "You don't just get Hillary, you get Bill," warned one advisor, an apprehension generally shared among the candidate's inner circle. On further reflection, Obama abandoned the idea.[59]

CHAPTER 3

The Pendulum
Swings Forward

NOT SINCE THE GREAT DEPRESSION, WHEN FRANKLIN D. Roosevelt first took office, had a US election taken place amid the kind of economic destruction that the country was experiencing by late 2008. The fiscal catastrophe that unfurled during the waning months of the presidency of George W. Bush resulted from a confluence of events, decisions, and mistakes that would have been detectable if one had looked hard enough at certain data, institutions, and actors. A gargantuan housing bubble, inflated with bad loans to desperate borrowers from shady lenders, burst in 2008 with enough explosive power to gravely damage large banking and investment institutions, such as Lehman Brothers and the American International Group, which undergirded much of the financial industry. Credit markets that had enjoyed a decade's worth of deregulation suddenly froze, sending shock waves through every group, entity, and sector that depended on borrowing money to survive. Companies laid off workers, banks foreclosed on homes, and the stock market began a death spiral that decimated the retirement savings of entire generations of workers. The recession was a mile deep: the economy contracted almost 10 percent and was savaged further by the eventual loss of 8 million jobs and $15 trillion in paper wealth. And it was a mile wide: European countries, drowning in ruinous debt, threatened default, and developing economies staggered and backpedaled under crushing fiscal blows.

When the catastrophic impact of what would become known as the Great Recession came into clearer focus in financial data and real-world experiences, it was apparent that the United States had fallen into a deep economic ditch. Even worse, Black America had not only fallen into the same ditch but had rolled down a mountain and then plummeted off a cliff. Nearly every metric, from statistics on household wealth and homeownership to measurements of employment and poverty, told the same disheartening tale: while the country was experiencing a recession, African Americans were collectively weathering a depression.

During the downturn, Black people were disproportionately affected by both the steep decline in property values and the high-interest subprime loans that predatory lenders had marketed to them. Waves of foreclosures devastated many communities, with the home-ownership rate for Blacks falling to 45 percent by 2011, compared to 74 percent for whites. Between 2004 and 2009, the median net worth of Black households dropped 83 percent (from $13,450 to $2,170), in contrast to a decline of 27 percent among white households (from $134,280 to $97,880). The wealth collapse was tied closely to the widespread loss of homes during the 2007-2009 recession, which was all the worse for Black people for whom homeownership accounted for 60 percent of household assets. Historical patterns of private and governmental discrimination, including redlining, racially biased distribution of Federal Housing Administration (FHA) loans, and early exclusion of Black agricultural and domestic workers from Social Security, were certainly behind the economic inequities that were laid bare in 2008. But even given this history, the calamity was a more hellish nightmare than most people alive had ever witnessed before.

Since African Americans entered the Great Recession with lower amounts of wealth, they could not rely on savings, inheritance, home equity, or relatives to stanch the economic bleeding. For millions of families, these deficiencies were not ameliorated by a tax code that favored middle-class homeowners and businesses and were, of course, exacerbated by a reeling job market that had shed hundreds of thousands of jobs by the end of the 2008 election season. The Black unemployment rate, which had for decades been twice that of whites, spiked during the Great Recession and even afterward, approaching 17 percent by 2011, compared to the overall national rate of 9 percent. In the spring of that year, only 57 percent of African American men over 20 years of age were employed, compared to 68 percent of white men. Black people in public-sector jobs were also grievously impacted by the economic downturn. More than half a million jobs were lost between 2007 and 2011, including in the postal service where a quarter of the workforce was African American. For Black people at the very bottom of the economic disaster, a 27 percent poverty rate afflicted them by 2010; for their children, the rate surged to 39 percent, three times the percentage of white youths living in poverty. As one might expect, African Americans with college degrees fared much better than the non-degreed, enduring only a 7 percent unemployment rate by mid-2011. Still, this was almost twice as high as the rate among white college graduates and did not account for ongoing income disparities based on race.[1]

In the realm of health and wellness, Black America was a mixed picture relative to national trends in the early twenty-first century. Between 1999 and 2014, the life expectancy gap narrowed between Blacks and whites, contracting to 75.6 and 79 years, respectively, the smallest differential on record. Declines in African American infant mortality, homicide rates, and suicides among Black men were partly responsible for this shrinking disparity. A negative factor contributing to this rough equivalency in life expectancy was the explosion in opioid-related deaths among whites, which ravaged communities across both age and gender categories. This epidemic, coupled with an aging baby-boomer generation, suggested there would be future declines in white life expectancy and population growth rates in the new century. During roughly this same period, cancer rates fell for Blacks and whites (29 and 20 percent, respectively), with the widespread availability of Medicare, Medicaid, and better health-care access in general playing a role. However, other health risks accompanied the economic ruin brought on by the Great Recession, confirming the ever-present links between race, class, and morbidity. Between 2007 and 2010, 19.6 percent of African Americans were diagnosed as being afflicted with diabetes, double the white rate of 9.5 percent. HIV / AIDS continued to disproportionately impact Black communities, where the prevalence rate of the virus in 2008 was eight times higher than among whites and three times greater than among Hispanic / Latinx populations.[2]

In many significant ways, there have always been multiple Black Americas, with factors such as region, income, age, complexion, and education sometimes playing determinative roles in individuals' experiences, life chances, and identity formation. Gender has also been a crucial variable. By the time the recession began in 2007, many African American men were already in dire situations. A relatively high percentage were already crippled economically by long-standing patterns of unequal access to employment, education, housing, health care, and civic life in general. The War on Drugs and other hard-on-crime policies of the twentieth century had produced a culture of mass incarceration that ensnared generations of Black men, their sons, and less frequently their daughters. According to one study, an estimated 1.5 million Black men in the 25- to 54-year age bracket were missing from American life by the time the Great Recession started to abate. About 600,000 of these men were incarcerated, and others had suffered early deaths disproportionately caused by heart disease, respiratory ailments, accidents, or homicide, the latter often at the hands of other African American men. Compared to whites in this age subgroup, who were evenly balanced by sex, the ratio of Black men to Black women was 83:100, with obvious implications for marriage opportunities, family stability, and household income. The highest proportion of absent Black men was traceable to the South, but several northern and midwestern cities were also known for their disturbing numbers of such individuals "missing from everyday life," including New York City (120,000), Chicago (45,000), and Philadelphia (30,000+).[3]

Black women and girls were, of course, directly impacted by the circumstances shaping the lives of Black men and boys. In areas that endured the highest incarceration rates, African American women were more likely to be employed and to pursue more educational opportunities. Related to this latter point, Black girls had a slightly better high school graduation rate than their male counterparts as of 2012 (86 percent to 85 percent, respectively), which was substantially superior to the rate among Latinas (66 percent) though below those of white and Asian girls (93 percent and 88 percent, respectively). According to a survey conducted in 2014, Black girls were more likely than girls from other demographic groups, as well as most boys, to be penalized with out-of-school suspension. As adults, Black women were more likely to earn poverty-level wages and to be among the working poor than any other demographic. Further, in the area of health and wellness, they accounted for 64 percent of women infected with HIV, were 40 percent more likely to perish from breast cancer than white women were, and endured an infant mortality rate that was twice as high as that of white women.

By 2010, the life expectancy of Black women was 79, a year longer than white men and 7 years more than Black men. Their relatively high longevity could be a net positive if other things in their lives went well. Unfortunately, Black women who lived long enough to become senior citizens had the lowest household income of any group in the United States. This grim economic reality was aside from the shocking vulnerability of African American women to violence. Of all demographics, they were more likely to be assaulted, raped, or murdered, often at the hands of those they knew, trusted, and loved. Interestingly, Black women, undoubtedly motivated in large part by their individual circumstances and collective condition, would be the demographic most likely to participate in the 2008 presidential election, leading all other groups in voter turnout.[4]

If determining the contours of Black America was complicated by factors such as gender, age, and income, locating it and mapping its geographies were even more challenging by the early twenty-first century. The Great Migration had reconfigured US cities and states between 1910 and 1970, creating populous communities of African Americans in New York, Pennsylvania, Michigan, California, and elsewhere. A subsequent reverse migration of Black people to the South during the last decades of the twentieth century again remade the country's racial landscape. Many of the new migrants were young, well-educated sojourners pursuing careers and adventures in the Sun Belt, a place that they only knew secondhand from the stories of their parents and grandparents. Others were retirees who had moved north during the reign of Jim Crow but found the post–civil rights movement South inviting and affordable. Common destinations included North Carolina, Georgia, Florida, and Texas, where upwardly mobile professionals and comfort-seeking seniors further vitalized cities like Charlotte, Atlanta, Orlando, and Houston. By 2010, more African Americans lived in suburban areas than in larger urban centers, indicative of both the existence of a thriving Black middle class and steady advancements in housing integration. But alongside this phenomenon, residential segregation persisted throughout the country. The traditional pattern of predominantly Black inner cities ringed by mostly white suburbs could easily be found in several metropolitan areas, and Asians and Hispanics tended to be less segregated from whites and each other than was the case for Blacks. Nevertheless, the Great Recession, which destroyed so much home equity, descended upon a Black America that was less racially isolated than in the past.[5]

Along with the continuing mobility of the native-born Black population, a steady stream of Black immigrants arriving in the United States since the late twentieth century has repeatedly and substantively challenged any singular, monolithic notion of what or who constitutes Black America. Starting with the Immigration and Nationality Act of 1965 and continuing with the diversity visa program of 1990, federal policy had gradually made moving to the United

States easier for refugees, those with desired skill sets, and members of underrepresented groups. In 2005, 2.8 million foreign-born Black people lived in America. Ten years later, the number had risen to 3.8 million, representing 8.7 percent of the country's total Black population and a fourfold increase over the 1980 immigrant figure. Half of the newcomers were from the Caribbean region, with large numbers from Jamaica, Haiti, and the Dominican Republic. Africans represented 36 percent of the Black immigrant population by 2015, with Nigerians and Ethiopians comprising the largest subgroups.

Compared to US-born Black people, the foreign-born population tended to be older, better educated, and more prosperous in terms of household income. They were also more likely to be married than were native African Americans, a characteristic that was often associated with age and with immigration policies geared toward family reunification. Foreign-born Black people are projected to account for 16 percent of the US Black population by 2060, and patterns of immigration were already revealing noteworthy ramifications by the 2010 Census, when foreign-born Black people accounted for 28 percent of the Black population of New York, 25 percent in Minnesota, and 19 percent in Florida. Instances of integration, cooperation, and conflict have marked encounters between native-born and foreign-born Black people and, of course, among immigrants themselves. Common racial interests have served as an organizing principle in cases where institutionalized racism and episodic discrimination have affected Black people in a broad, homogenizing way. But more narrow ethnic allegiances and especially class identities have surfaced and been of paramount importance on many occasions, highlighting differences between Black groups as the United States becomes more diverse.[6]

In multilayered, fractured, and ever-evolving ways, Black America emerged as a complex patchwork of identities and experiences in the early twenty-first century. With its plethora of origins, aspirations, and contradictions, its oneness was more imagined and sentimental than solid and tangible, except when the haunting omnipresence of race and the real burdens of racial discrimination compelled a tactical cohesiveness necessary for both group and individual survival. The Black America that Barack Obama sought to win over in the 2008 election was not the same Black America that existed when his father, the gifted and restless Kenyan student, pursued his fortune under a Hawaiian sun so many years earlier. The son's Black America was self-aware and better connected, more varied in texture and tone, and full of high expectations, but it was simultaneously looking up at the horizon and down into darkness.

Early on, Barack Obama had a good sense of the powerful symbolism of a Black man running for the country's highest office. During his trip to Hawaii in December 2006, he had discussed the significance of a presidential run with several people, including Marty Nesbitt, a Chicago acquaintance and businessman who would eventually serve as campaign treasurer. Walking along Waikiki Beach, Obama had mused aloud, "I wonder what impact it would have on African American boys if I were elected president." Nesbitt, not likely caught off guard by the question, had a ready reply. "Wow, that might be the single most influential event since the Emancipation Proclamation," he announced to his friend, "even if you didn't do anything beyond that." Obama pushed further. "But just think if I went to an inner-city school once a month," a proposal that would indeed be a novelty for a US president. "I wonder what impact that would have?" Nesbitt, intrigued, played along with the scenario. "What would it really say about the country?" he queried. "And what would it say about incumbent politicians? What would be the message to them if the American people elected *you*?" Obama, already leaning toward a presidential bid and no doubt encouraged by such banter with a confidant, exclaimed, "Well, they'd be quaking in their boots."[7]

There were other times when the gravity of this proposition seized Obama and others, and as it turned out, the Democratic National Convention (DNC) in Denver was full of such moments. A practice run through the candidate's speech led to a "choked up" Obama, moved by a reference to Martin Luther King Jr. ("a young preacher from Georgia"), having to pause the session long enough to collect himself in a nearby bathroom. His acceptance of the Democratic nomination actually took place on August 28, the anniversary of King's "I Have a Dream" speech at the 1963 March on Washington—and the anniversary of the 1955 lynching of 14-year-old Chicago native Emmett Till in Money, Mississippi. Before a Denver crowd estimated to number 90,000, Obama's oration was the main event, with the candidate juxtaposing his liberal vision for change against what he described as John McCain's continuation of Bush-era policies.

Beyond Obama, an array of other personalities and developments at the convention demonstrated just how much energy could be generated by the possibility of an African American president. Roughly 30 percent of the 4,233 delegates present were African American, an unprecedented number that graphically illustrated the changing face of the Democratic Party. Singer Jennifer Hudson made the national anthem soar with soul, while Stevie Wonder served as the opener for the nominee's speech. To enthusiastic applause, Hillary and Bill Clinton each gave speeches that strongly endorsed Obama's candidacy and confirmed their commitment to help solidify the party ahead of the general election. If there were any hitches or missteps during the gathering, they were well camouflaged from the viewing public and managed quietly behind the scenes.[8]

The historic convention in Colorado, with its ebullient speeches and choreographed performances, was the calm before the storm. With the nomination question finally settled, the general election campaign officially began in earnest. Obama expected a tough fight against the Republicans in the fall that would draw on that party's traditional playbook of attacking Democrats as lacking in patriotism and assailing him in particular, with his "funny name," as too unconventional a nominee to elect to the presidency. Of course, he turned out to be right in this prediction. However, neither he nor many others could have guessed how vicious the GOP onslaught would be, especially the portion of it perpetrated by the top of the ticket itself. Nor would many have assumed that such a negative campaign posture would eventually create a downright dangerous political atmosphere that would aggravate both partisan and racial divisions for years to come.[9]

The Republicans' game plan was not new; in fact, it was in some ways a reversion to previous methods. Since the late nineteenth century, conservatives had employed explicit appeals to white racial bias to win elections, whether this involved dramatic opposition to school desegregation and voting rights or flagrantly racist campaigns by politicians like Strom Thurmond and George Wallace. By the 1970s, more subtle but still easily decipherable means were crafted to attract voters into the Republican fold, including a "southern strategy" that targeted whites in the South who were disaffected by the Democratic Party's support of civil rights. No longer was it necessary or politic to directly use crude racist language to appeal to white social and economic anxieties. Instead, certain ideas and catchphrases that Republican politicians injected into public discourse, such as affirmative action, busing, welfare abuse, voter fraud, and law and order, accomplished the same objective without opening them up to charges of outright bigotry. Lee Atwater, a Republican strategist who created racially incendiary ads to assist the presidential campaign of George H. W. Bush in 1988, perhaps best described the new messaging landscape. In a 1981 interview, he stated:

> You start out in 1954 by saying, "Nigger, nigger, nigger." By 1968 you can't say "nigger," hurts you, backfires. So you say stuff like, uh, forced busing, states' rights, and all that stuff, and you're getting so abstract. Now you're talking about cutting taxes, and all these things you're talking about are totally economic things, and a by-product of them is blacks get hurt worse than whites. "We want to cut this" is much more abstract than even the busing thing, uh, and a hell of a lot more abstract than "nigger, nigger."

Republican local, state, and federal campaigns since then have relied on concepts outlined by Atwater to different degrees and with varying outcomes. The principal distinction between the 2008 presidential election and earlier ones was that elements of the GOP would now pursue an approach that leaned more heavily on the "nigger, nigger" model than any Republican campaign strategy had in quite some time.[10]

John McCain's willingness to countenance such a political methodology and to only rarely and perfunctorily repudiate its excesses allowed it to become a defining part of his bid for the White House. Furthermore, central to the Arizona senator's approval of or at least acquiescence to a racial othering strategy against Obama was his selection of Alaska governor Sarah Palin as his running mate. Entirely new to the national political scene, Palin was a curious vice presidential pick. She had served as mayor of the small city of Wasilla before being elected to the governorship in 2006. At 44, she was the youngest candidate for the VP position since Al Gore in 1992, and she and her husband, Todd, still presided over a household of several minor children. As became clear over time, Palin had limited policy experience and did not clearly make any particular state more competitive for Republicans in the general election.

Palin's selection by the McCain camp for the second slot was primarily based on a perceived need to revitalize his sagging poll numbers and to directly appeal to voters who, with the primary defeat of Hillary Clinton, might consider voting for a Republican ticket that included a woman. Her folksy vernacular and frequent references to outdoor living may have appealed to a certain segment of working-class voters, especially those in rural areas, or the multitasking "hockey mom." In the end though, Palin brought little that was helpful to the McCain presidential bid. Her initial splash into the campaign on August 29, a day after Obama's acceptance speech in Denver, eventually became an uncontrollable vortex that likely damaged the Arizona senator's presidential chances as much as any other single factor.

What Sarah Palin did bring to the presidential race was a rhetorical venom infused with a feverish populism, which would nearly extinguish whatever civility might have otherwise characterized the election process. Her rallies were master classes in incitement and mass hysteria. Obama's passing acquaintance with William Ayers, a professor of education at the University of Illinois at Chicago and a former member of the militant Weather Underground, was characterized by Palin as "palling around with terrorists." At an October 9 campaign event in Clearwater, Florida, she stirred the crowd with warnings about the Democratic nominee's otherness and his questionable patriotism. "I'm afraid that this is someone who sees America as imperfect enough to work with a former domestic terrorist who targeted his own people," she decried, referencing Ayers's involvement in a series of antigovernment bombings during the early 1970s. Stoked by her allusions to Obama as a terrorist sympathizer, members of the crowd at Clearwater and elsewhere participated in the dark spectacle, with some calling out "Kill him!" "Treason!" "Terrorist!" while others exclaimed "Off with his head!" Television reports and YouTube uploads captured several of the threats on video and audio, and many were pronounced audibly enough for Palin to hear. Yet the vice presidential candidate never paused to quiet the crowd or to denounce an off-color remark.[11]

The lynch-mob atmosphere of some of Palin's rallies became so intense that Rep. John Lewis felt compelled to issue a statement on October 11 accusing McCain and his VP pick of "playing with fire" and likening their rhetoric to the racially charged campaigns of segregationist George Wallace. The Arizona senator took exception to Lewis's reproach and called on Obama to denounce it. A spokesman for the Democratic nominee offered McCain the benefit of the doubt by disagreeing with the Wallace comparison but pointedly called out Palin's accusations of terrorist coddling as "baseless and profoundly irresponsible."[12]

If McCain's outrage about Lewis's remarks seemed to some observers both feigned and disingenuous, it was not the case that he was entirely comfortable with the inflammatory climate that his campaign was helping to create. At the start of the general election cycle, he had reportedly told aides that he would not abide attacks on Obama's lack of military service, his wife, or his former pastor, Jeremiah Wright.

At one town-hall-style gathering, McCain even took a microphone from a woman who fumblingly mischaracterized Obama as an Arab and instead described his rival as "a decent family man, a citizen, that I just happen to have disagreements with on fundamental issues." Despite McCain's intervention in this instance, there were other occasions when he declined to correct audience members who shouted insults and falsehoods about Obama, and he appeared unwilling or unable to decisively rein in Palin.[13]

Regardless of the Republican nominee's instructions to his staff to avoid certain kinds of attacks, it was not difficult for many campaign observers to sense that something had, in fact, changed during the fall presidential campaign. Hatemongering demagoguery was more palpable now than anything coming out of the spring primaries or even hard-fought general election battles of the recent past. According to Secret Service reports and other intelligence analyses, white supremacists were attracted to Palin's message in particular, with some preparing to go further than simply spewing harsh language in opposition to Obama's candidacy. After Secret Service officials informed the Obamas in mid-October that they had noticed a spike in the quantity of threats against them, Michelle was taken aback. "Why would they try to make people hate us?" she asked her friend Valerie Jarrett. To Michelle, who had been personally smeared throughout the campaign, the new threat environment fomented by the GOP ticket and some of its allies seemed out of bounds and beyond anything that one might reasonably expect in a US political campaign.[14]

The security issue had been a general concern of the Obama team for more than a year prior to the 2008 general campaign. Given the racial animus that he would face as a Black man running for the presidency, the Illinois senator was assigned a Secret Service contingent in May 2007, earlier than any candidate in US history. His code name was "Renegade," and his wife and two daughters were also given protection and aliases. Security provided by the Secret Service is among the best in the world, and Obama more than once advised voters fearful about his safety to stop worrying. In spite of such counsel, he was daily reminded that the threats to his life and to his family's well-being were real and becoming more numerous as he steadily approached the Democratic nomination.[15]

More than a year prior to her husband's bid for the presidency, Michelle, a realist about most things, had gone as far as to speak privately with Coretta Scott King, the wife of the late Dr. Martin Luther King Jr., about the topic of assassination. This step may have been meant to steel her nerves with comforting guidance from America's most famous living widow, as well as to help her put the fragility of life, even among the most revered, into perspective. She would eventually have to learn how to live with that grim possibility of loss as it hung over the lives of her loved ones, understanding that with each electoral success and political milestone came new dangers. "I don't lose sleep over it," she told an interviewer in 2007, "because the realities are, as a black man, Barack can get shot going to the gas station, you know." Similar to the frequent family division, bad press, and political chicanery, death threats were one of the enduring costs of presidential runs. They could be terrifying and even paralyzing if one allowed them to be, which was often the main objective of the perpetrators.[16]

Threats—minor and serious, online and off—were plentiful by the fall of 2008. In late October, law enforcement officials uncovered a plot by neo-Nazis to first assassinate Obama and then murder an additional eighty-eight African Americans in Jackson, Tennessee. The two would-be assailants had planned to rob a gun store before going on a shooting spree at a local predominantly Black high school. In Kentucky, Oregon, and California, Obama was lynched in effigy, and in North Carolina a coffin with an anti-Obama sticker affixed to it was sent to a Craven County polling site. Hours after the outcome of the November 4 election was announced, Macedonia Church of God, a largely African American meetinghouse in Springfield, Massachusetts, was razed to the ground by arsonists who, at the trial, admitted to having been motivated by hatred of Obama. More threats were discovered by officials prior to and after the election, but they

were discreetly monitored by the Secret Service and other law enforcement agencies and not publicized. In a late October interview,
Obama claimed not to be concerned about such troubling reports,
even asserting that the success of his campaign had resulted in the
marginalization of hate groups. It was the kind of optimism expected
from him in public remarks and very much in keeping with the calm,
self-possessed, and positive persona that he had promised to bring to
the Oval Office. But despite Obama's upbeat outlook, the threats did
continue and in time escalated.[17]

In contrast to the disturbing tone of some of his campaign's rhetoric
during the general election cycle, John McCain's concession speech
was generous and elevated. With Sarah Palin on one side and his wife,
Cindy, on the other, the Arizona senator congratulated Barack Obama
for winning the White House and for running a race that "commands
my respect." He recognized the historic nature of the election and its
particular meaning for African Americans, recalling a less enlightened
time when a visit to the White House by even the famous Black educator Booker T. Washington had caused widespread alarm. "America
today is a world away from the cruel and prideful bigotry of that
time," McCain proclaimed. "There is no better evidence of this than
the election of an African-American to the presidency of the United
States." The senator's demeanor was sober and reassuring. He seemed
comfortable with the outcome of the race, though much of his campaigning had dwelled on his rival's relative inexperience and assumed
unreadiness for the highest office. After kissing his wife and waving at
the cheering crowd, McCain departed the stage, officially ending his
second and final run for the presidency. In January, he would return
to the US Senate in the role of senior statesman, still smarting from
defeat but ready to challenge much of the new president's agenda.[18]

As for Palin, her tenure as Alaska governor was cut short by a bliz-
zard of ethics probes, which compelled her to resign in July 2009.
She would shortly reappear as a conservative media pundit and as a
provocative ideologue behind the Tea Party, an emergent faction of

boisterous insurgents within the Republican Party. But her time as an elected official and as a force in US politics came largely to an end after her turbulent nine weeks as McCain's running mate.[19]

By nearly every measure, Obama had crushed McCain in the presidential contest. The Democrat won 52.7 percent of the popular ballots and 365 electoral votes, the highest counts in each category since 1988 and 1992, respectively. States such as North Carolina, Indiana, and Virginia, which had not been won by a Democratic nominee since the 1970s fell into the blue column, along with the prize swing states of Florida and Ohio. According to exit polls, voters who identified their top concerns as the economy, the war in Iraq, health care, and energy cast their lot with Obama. In terms of demographics, the Illinois senator's appeal crossed lines of race, gender, age, and geography. He won 95 percent of the Black vote, 66 percent of Hispanics, and 43 percent of whites. Fifty-six percent of women voted for Obama, as did 66 percent of voters between 18 and 29 years of age and 52 percent of those in the 30-44 age bracket (the two candidates split the 45-64 age bracket). Furthermore, the Democrat excelled in urban areas, garnering 63 percent of the vote, and managed to beat his challenger among suburban voters, 50 percent to 48 percent.

McCain's strength lay among white voters (especially men and those without college degrees), senior citizens, the rural electorate, and those with annual incomes over $100,000. These constituencies were traditionally Republican leaning, though the Arizona senator underperformed in several instances relative to the records of recent GOP presidential nominees. Conversely, Obama outperformed among a number of demographic groups, especially nonwhite voters. The number of African Americans participating in the 2008 election notably increased over the 2004 figure, with the Black turnout rate reaching 65 percent, a historic high for a national election. Their greater numbers in the electorate provided the margin of victory for Obama in several states, including Florida, North Carolina, Virginia, and Indiana, shattering GOP Electoral College strongholds in the South and Midwest.[20]

Along with his ability to put together a trans-demographic coalition, Obama's election victory was aided by a number of other factors. The long primary fight against Hillary Clinton had forced him to compete in every state, thus requiring the development of campaign infrastructure and an electoral ground game from Guam to Maine to Puerto Rico. The struggle against a determined, competitive opponent had strengthened Obama the candidate, making him calibrate his words, deeds, and resources to appeal to diverse and ever-changing state electorates month after month. By the time of the general campaign, the Obama team was ready to seriously compete in places that Democrats had historically written off as unwinnable. Although more of a tactical bluff than anything else, the campaign brazenly showcased this fifty-state electoral approach by announcing late-cycle plans to run TV ads in McCain's home base of Arizona, a solidly red state that had not gone to a Democrat since 1948.

As in the primaries, the Obama camp reached out to voters across an array of platforms, including TV, internet, radio, and social media, a strategy that both McCain and Clinton struggled to emulate. By Election Day, Obama had almost four times the number of Facebook friends as McCain had, more than twenty times the amount of Twitter followers, and 3 million more unique visitors to his campaign's website. Fundraising told a similar story: Democratic operatives' facility with using the internet as a campaign-financing vehicle outmatched McCain's overreliance on traditional methods of securing donations. One electoral strategy in particular paid handsome rewards for Obama. Early-voting laws in various states allowed the Democrats to lock in millions of votes before the official election date of November 4. In ten such states, a majority of voters cast ballots *before* Election Day, with Democrats overrepresented among this group, thanks in no small measure to the Obama campaign's brisk, multipronged get-out-the-vote regime. If ever there was a starker disconnect between old and new styles of political mobilization, financing, and advertising than was displayed during the 2008 presidential campaign, only a few would have been able to recall such a time. McCain (and

Clinton) had run on the certainties of the past, not counting on the need to innovate for the future.[21]

Post-election polling tried to capture and quantify the tone of the historic moment. According to a Gallup survey, 71 percent of Americans believed that Obama's win was among the top three most important advances for Black people over the previous century. Seventy percent opined that race relations would improve slightly due to the election, with 28 percent of those polled asserting that relations would get much better. Two-thirds of respondents agreed that "a solution to relations between blacks and whites will eventually be worked out," the same as the percentage who felt "optimistic" and "proud" after the November 4 decision. Predictably, McCain voters were less enthused about the outcome of the election and its implications for the future. More than half of them reported being fearful, and a full 60 percent were pessimistic about Obama's win. Only a third described themselves as proud in the wake of the election, despite McCain's encouragement during his concession speech. In contrast, Obama voters were ecstatic about the success of their candidate, with 93 percent saying that they were excited, 85 percent feeling optimistic, and 95 percent experiencing pride.[22]

While the tens of millions of people who voted for the Democratic nominee did so based on their individual beliefs, hopes, and interests, observable patterns could be discerned in the reactions of a cross-section of the African Americans who had just witnessed history in the making. John Lewis, a congressman who had marched with Martin Luther King Jr., viewed Obama's election as a harbinger of a kind of progress that "never in my wildest imagination did I ever believe I would see." Measured in his expectations, he comprehended the moment as a big first step, a "major down payment" on Dr. King's dream and not as the end of the struggle. "The rejected are still among us, heaped with indignity and despair," Lewis noted in the wake of Obama's inauguration. "Maybe, just maybe, our history will help us to see the error in our law, in our policies, customs and traditions, so they will not have to rise up again to prove their worth." Another

Black politician, Van R. Johnson II, a vice chair of the Savannah City Council, expressed similar sentiments in a letter to the new president, requesting that he use his authority responsibly, remember the less fortunate, and be a model public servant. "I ask that you not use your awesome power to put African-Americans in a place of advantage," the Georgia official implored, "but for you to use your power to ensure that 'every mountain and hill shall be made low: and the crooked shall be made straight, and the rough places plain.'" Other politicians would have plenty more to say to and about Obama as he entered the Oval Office, but the initial well wishes from officials such as Lewis and Johnson must have been heartening.[23]

Black academicians assessed the historic development through both personal and intellectual lenses and would continue to interpret the Obama presidency for years to come. Henry Louis Gates Jr., a Harvard professor, "laughed and shouted, whooped and hollered" when the election results were announced. In between smiles and tears, he offered a quiet prayer of thanks that his 95-year-old father had lived long enough to see such a day. Gates was careful to temper his expectations of an Obama presidency, aware that one Black man in the White House could not alone reduce teenage pregnancies, drug abuse, or high school dropout rates in the African American community. Still, he celebrated the crossing of the "Ultimate Color Line . . . by our very first postmodern race man . . . who embraces his African cultural and genetic heritage so securely that he can transcend it." History and law professor Annette Gordon-Reed, known for her award-winning scholarship on Thomas Jefferson, understood the election as an attempt by the country to revise its national identity. In electing Obama, she posited, "Americans were willing to put on a new face for the world." Similarly to Black politicians, Black professors would in time engage in robust debates across books, articles, blogs, and TV screens over what they believed to be the benefits and deficiencies of the Obama presidency vis-à-vis African Americans. For now, the uniqueness and potential global importance of the rise of a Black man so high into the stratosphere of US politics was difficult to question.[24]

In the world of arts and entertainment, Black voices chimed in with poetry and prose, rhapsodizing about the place of Barack Obama in the arc of the African American experience and bringing a cold-eyed realism to bear on the difficulties of the tasks ahead. Pulitzer Prize–winning writer Alice Walker, starting with the salutation "Dear Brother President," wrote adoringly of the new head of state in an open letter. "We knew, through all the generations that you were with us, in us, the best of the spirit of Africa and of the Americas," she unabashedly gushed. "Seeing you take your rightful place, based solely on your wisdom, stamina, and character, is a balm for weary warriors of hope, previously only sung about." Interspersed with her flowery praise, Walker did strike somber notes in her missive, such as her condemnation of Bush-era legalized torture and the "crushing of whole communities." But generally hers was a tender testimony of hope for humanity, which she nudged gently into the illuminating, clarifying light of the "healthy self-worth" that she had detected in Obama's smile.[25]

In a less sentimental fashion, jazzman Wynton Marsalis highlighted the credentials of the new president, praising the country for finally choosing the "most qualified man" for its highest office. Moreover, he pointed out that "Obama didn't run as a black president" or on a "black platform," cautioning African Americans to expect only a competent chief executive who was not specifically committed to the agenda of any particular group. Interestingly, Marsalis alluded to the universalist pragmatism behind Obama's approach to policy matters and seemed to take comfort in the assumption that Black people would benefit from such a governing style. Obama's "top issues *are* our issues," he emphasized. "Joblessness, home foreclosures and lack of health care all resonate within the African American community." In the view of comedian Wanda Sykes, the main message that the new chief executive needed to hear concerned the imperative to stand up for the rights of the LGBTQ community. Feeling personally affronted by a California ban of same-sex marriage that had passed on the same night as Obama's election, she demanded of the president and the country: "The same way he fell in love with a beautiful woman and had the right to marry her, I should be able to do the same."[26]

African Americans from other walks of life expressed a wide variety of thoughts, emotions, and predictions regarding Obama's victory. While the firsthand views and experiences of the working class, the poor, and the otherwise marginalized are rarely captured and preserved for historical reference and interpretation, the occasion of the 2008 election did produce some glimpses into the reactions of members of such groups. Lisha Crenshaw, a 34-year-old Chicago schoolteacher, had never placed much faith in politicians to address acute problems such as the mass incarceration of Black men or the devastating impact of HIV/AIDS on the well-being of Black women. "I'm sure Bush didn't give a hoot about" such problems, she told an interviewer. "Clinton was called the first black president but he put some of those three-strikes rules on the books." Despite her disappointment with past presidents, Obama made her optimistic. Although Crenshaw was firm in her expectation that "Obama needs to care" about Black women suffering from the AIDS epidemic, she thought that he understood, that he "gets it like no one has before," a notion that she found "overwhelming."[27]

Janese Sinclair, a single mother of a 12-year-old son, saw similar promise in the new first family, especially as models of stable, dignified Black relationships. "I want my son to see first-hand what two people can do when they work together and respect each other," the 34-year-old executive assistant confided to a reporter. "The Obamas are going to teach us that love and happiness [are] not just for others but for us too." Elise Ryan of Los Angeles also had new hopes. As a 23-year-old single mother who had not completed high school, she had stopped dreaming about a better future, even for the sake of her two children. She was initially unfazed by Obama and his message, shrugging both off as so much chatter. "But the more I saw him and his family," she reflected, "I was like, OK, maybe he can make things better for me. Maybe he can change the way black people get treated." Powerful in meaning but far too sparse and wispy in their presence in

the historical record, such words and stories display a depth and richness of experience that polls and surveys can hardly probe or render.
Apparent in the common threads winding through these narratives
was one of the prime takeaways of the election: it was a moment in
which Black America came together, if only temporarily, as a coherent
thing, an anchored idea, to marvel and try to collectively appraise
where it was in place and time.[28]

Two days before the inauguration, the president-elect called Martin
Luther King III. The son of the slain civil rights leader had spoken at
the DNC in August, but the two men were not close acquaintances,
so King was surprised by the outreach. To commemorate the MLK
holiday, Obama offered to pick him up the next morning at his DC
hotel. The two ultimately decided to paint the walls of the Sasha
Bruce Youthwork shelter for homeless teens in northeastern Washington to honor the public service of the late clergyman. According to
King, he brought up the issue of poverty with the incoming president
who, like nearly every other candidate, had dwelled on the plight
of the middle class during the election campaign. The 51-year-old
activist was bothered that the poor received so little attention from
the candidates, though it is unclear whether Obama offered any assurances concerning future action. The president-elect did invoke the
elder King in a message celebrating the holiday and anticipating his
own inauguration. "Tomorrow, we will come together as one people
on the same mall where Dr. King's dream echoes still," his statement
read. "And as we go forward in the work of renewing the promise of
this nation, let's remember King's lesson—that our separate dreams
are really one." The younger King was observant enough to notice the
weight on Obama, despite his own concerns about fighting poverty.
"I think the honeymoon was over a while ago," he said of the new
president to a reporter. "He knows everyone wants something at this
point, and someone is going to be disappointed." His words were
more prescient than he could have known at the time.[29]

For now, Black America and much of the nation rejoiced. January 20, 2009, was a luminous day in the capital, and well over a million gathered to witness history. The Obamas attended the swearing-in ceremony at the US Capitol Building, walked and waved from streets cordoned off by the Secret Service, and made cameo appearances at almost a dozen inaugural balls before taking up official residence at the White House. The president's inauguration speech before a packed National Mall touched on his standard themes of enhancing government efficiency, better regulating the private sector, safeguarding the nation against terrorism, and encouraging public service and responsibility. Facing an almost unprecedented economic crisis and entanglement in two foreign wars, Obama called for national action and bipartisan cooperation. Further, he recognized the country's diversity and its travails through "civil war and segregation," expressing his belief that "the old hatreds shall someday pass; that the lines of tribe shall soon dissolve." Overall, the speech was less memorable than the occasion, with his very existence being the real story. There was, of course, much work ahead and more of the Great Recession and international turmoil to be endured. But in this moment, in this instant, nothing else seemed as fascinating to so many as the ambitious young president who had just stepped onto the world's grandest stage.[30]

PART II.

HOPE AND CHANGE

CHAPTER 4

Bamelot

WHEN THE OBAMAS ARRIVED IN JANUARY 2009, THE WHITE
House was more than 200 years old and had been successively occupied by more than forty presidents and first families. The US Constitution and the 1790 Residence Act provided for the founding of a
national capital along the Potomac River, and George Washington
planted the first stakes for an executive mansion in 1792. Among the
motley collection of men who labored to erect what would become
the White House were enslaved African Americans leased from their
enslavers. By that time, neither Black people nor human bondage
were new to the site of the capital. In 1800, one in four inhabitants of
the city were Black, and the District would become a hub of the domestic slave trade during the nineteenth century. Similar to northern
states, Washington gradually leaned toward emancipation, though it
was geographically situated in the South and shared many of its social
mores. In 1860, the Census enumerated 14,316 Black people in the
capital, almost a quarter of whom were enslaved. The slave trade had
been legally banned in the city a decade earlier, and slavery would be
abolished there in April 1862.

For African Americans not in bondage, life in the District was a
case study in second-class citizenship. As early as 1807, their children

had access to schooling, and it was possible to own property. There were even limited opportunities to secure government employment but always of a menial sort. Still, curfews, fugitive slave laws, and a general prohibition against Black people acquiring business licenses dispelled any illusions that observers may have harbored concerning the existence of racial equality in the national capital. After the Civil War and into the next century, Black Washington had a dependent, paradoxical relationship with official Washington, being crucial to the servicing of its needs while at the same time being excluded from sharing in its power and prestige.[1]

The presence of Black people in the White House has mirrored the larger history of race relations in the District. Prior to emancipation, Elizabeth Keckley, who was born enslaved in Virginia, was likely the longest-residing African American in the White House, where she worked as a seamstress for Mary Todd Lincoln and consoled the First Lady in the wake of her husband's assassination in April 1865. The famous abolitionists Frederick Douglass and Sojourner Truth met with President Lincoln during the Civil War, and Douglass, as the DC recorder of deeds, returned to the White House in the 1880s for an inaugural reception for Grover Cleveland. The Black statesman scandalized southern conservatives by showing up with his white wife, Helen Pitts, and Booker T. Washington also provoked opprobrium when he appeared for a scheduled dinner with President Theodore Roosevelt in 1901.

Rigid segregation premiered in the White House during the William H. Taft administration, and this was further fortified by Woodrow Wilson's decision to reorder the DC federal bureaucracy along racial lines. This institutionalized bigotry hung over the residence for decades, including during the infamous 1929 First Lady's tea, when the composure of Jessie De Priest, the wife of Illinois representative Oscar De Priest, the lone African American in Congress, ennobled an otherwise awkward gathering. With burgeoning US engagement with the globe occasioned by World War II, the countenancing of nonwhite guests at the White House became increasingly necessary.

In May 1943, President Edwin Barclay of Liberia spent the night at the executive mansion, followed by Emperor Haile Selassie of Ethiopia in 1954 and Haitian president Paul Magloire a year later. By the 1960s, Black American leaders, such as Martin Luther King Jr., Roy Wilkins, and Whitney Young, were regular visitors who would prod hesitant presidents to support the Black freedom movement.

In general, Black entertainers were more welcome in the White House—and less likely to stir white racial anxieties—than people of African descent arriving there on business, especially anything having to do with the substance or symbols of civil rights. As early as 1878, coloratura soprano Marie Selika (Williams) performed for the family of President Rutherford B. Hayes, and four years later the world-renowned Fisk Jubilee Singers brought spirituals to Chester Arthur's White House. In 1939, contralto Marian Anderson sang Franz Schubert's "Ave Maria" before the Roosevelts and British royalty, the same year that she mesmerized a crowd of more than 75,000 from the steps of the Lincoln Memorial. By the later twentieth century, Republican presidents like Richard Nixon and Ronald Reagan, who fared poorly with African American voters, were comfortable enough with interracial White House gatherings to host celebrities such as Michael Jackson and Sammy Davis Jr., who stayed in the executive residence overnight with his wife, Altovise, in 1973.[2]

As the matron of a new first family, Michelle Obama's early impression of life in the White House was substantially shaped by the preservation work that had taken place there since the 1960s. "I thought initially that it would be like living in a museum," she admitted as her family transitioned to their new home. To a certain extent, she was right. The position of curator of the White House had been created by an executive order in 1964, and significant structural repairs and cosmetic updates, mostly meant to maintain the traditional character of the edifice, had taken place between the Jimmy Carter and Bill Clinton presidencies. However, the new First Lady would soon learn that there are multiple White Houses, each with varying degrees of privacy and customization possibilities.

The public-access areas are the state floor and the ground floor. Two residential levels are reachable by elevator and allow for a range of personal options regarding decor. The Oval Office, situated at the southeast corner of the West Wing, is the president's official domain, symbolizing the power and authority of the chief executive. Aside from the private quarters upstairs, the president's office typically reflects the occupant's individual taste and values more than most other rooms. For example, while a large circular rug with the presidential seal emblazoned on it is standard issue, the border of Obama's custom-made floor covering included a quote from Martin Luther King Jr. The new president also installed a bronze bust of the civil rights leader, replacing one of Winston Churchill. Notwithstanding that certain elements of the Oval Office can be tailored to personal taste, the room does, like a museum, project history and continuity. Portraits of Presidents Washington and Lincoln have remained on the walls through presidential tenures, and the Resolute Desk, a gift from Queen Victoria of England, adds an enduring weightiness to the furnishings.[3]

The presidential mansion comes with accessories befitting high office. For ground transportation, the president's official vehicle is a black limousine with five-inch-thick windows, puncture-proof tires, and enough body armor to resist a bomb attack. Formally designated *Cadillac One* but nicknamed "the Beast," the vehicle is part tank, part land yacht, and part bunker. In the case of a biological or chemical attack, it can be completely sealed, with passengers sustained by an internal ventilation system. If offensive power is needed, teargas cannons can be activated to clear the area of immediate threats. To cope with a more serious crisis, the trunk contains a blood supply matched to the president's type, and a helicopter is routinely close by for evacuation purposes.

When crossing long distances by air, the president relies on two Boeing 747-200B airplanes, both named *Air Force One*. Capable of traveling up to 700 miles per hour, each plane is six stories tall, includes three interior levels, and can be refueled midflight. The aircraft is designed to serve as an autonomous command center with dozens of secure phone lines and other critical amenities. Room is ample, and there are specified areas for staff, reporters, and the president and first family. For shorter trips, *Marine One*, a roomy, white-topped helicopter, can be deployed for pickups from the South Lawn of the White House and then carry the president, his family, and/or advisors to places such as Andrews Air Force Base, where *Air Force One* is kept. While in office, no president drives a car, flies a plane, or in any way exposes himself directly to the hazards of congested streets or unsafe skies. Such are the privileges and constraints of the job.[4]

As was the case with his predecessors, securing the Obama White House was a full-time, round-the-clock job for several teams of security personnel. Back when he first visited the presidential mansion in 1984 with a cohort of student leaders, Obama had noticed how open the property was to visitors and passersby. Such accessibility "said something about our confidence as a democracy," he wrote years later, "the notion that our leaders were not so different from us." By the time he returned to Washington as a newly elected US senator in 2005, things had changed drastically enough to affect him with a "glancing sadness at what had been lost." Now, as the first family moved in, the executive residence was surrounded by guards, vehicles, barricades, and checkpoints, all aimed at discouraging unauthorized entry and terrorist attacks. From the bulletproof presidential limo to the watchful snipers on rooftops, the first family's security, not public access, was the primary, secondary, and tertiary objectives of White House guardians.[5]

In time, President Obama discovered favorite spots around the mansion and grounds for personal moments, such as the Truman Balcony, which allows for an unobstructed view across the verdant South Lawn, over treetops, and to the austere majesty of the Washington Monument. Some evenings he and Michelle enjoyed the vantage together, catching glimpses of ordinary people walking along Constitution Avenue. Integrated layers of ubiquitous security cocooned them from that world across the lawn but did not entirely shield them from gut-level concerns about safety. Illustratively, when Malia and Sasha (ages 10 and 7, respectively, on Inauguration Day) left with Secret Service agents on their first trip to school, Michelle was suddenly struck by the loss of the ordinary, albeit hectic, and full life they had left behind in Chicago. "What on earth am I doing to these babies?" she asked herself, blindsided by yet another hidden cost of the November victory. As they settled into the White House, the Obamas had to search for a new normal.[6]

The West Wing is the administrative nerve center of the White House. In addition to housing the Oval Office, this multistory sector of rooms and corridors features meeting places for the Cabinet and press briefings, as well as offices for the vice president, the Secret Service, and the White House chief of staff. Although hundreds of people circulate through the veins of the West Wing on any given day, President Obama's time was primarily occupied by advisors, Cabinet members, VP Joe Biden, and whatever else Alyssa Mastromonaco, the director of scheduling and advance, placed on his agenda. Of the senior officials who carried out the business of the White House and the Obama executive branch, many were African American, and several had worked on the presidential campaign.[7]

In the immediate orbit of the West Wing were people such as Rob Nabors, Melody Barnes, and Mona Sutphen. Nabors, an alumnus of the Clinton administration, had previously served as staff director of the US House Appropriations Committee before being named deputy director of the Office of Management and Budget in 2009. In this capacity and subsequently as the director of the Office of Legislative Affairs, he proved to be a vital liaison to Congress as the new administration attempted to first pass a stimulus bill for jump-starting the economy and later negotiated with recalcitrant Republican lawmakers to keep the country from sliding off a fiscal cliff. Barnes, the director of the Domestic Policy Council, entered the Obama White House along with a number of other women appointed to important positions, including senior advisors Valerie Jarrett and Stephanie Cutter, communications director Anita Dunn, "energy czar" Carol Browner, and chair of the Council of Economic Advisers Christina Romer. During her three years in the administration, Barnes was instrumental in guiding the work of the White House Task Force on Childhood Obesity, whose final report was championed by First Lady Michelle Obama as "setting really clear goals and benchmarks and measurable outcomes" for countering the escalating epidemic. A graduate of the London School of Economics, Mona Sutphen, similar to Barnes, had worked on the Obama transition team. Her deep knowledge of East Asian affairs—especially her ideas and policy proposals concerning China and Japan—had previously earned her a spot in the campaign's core group of foreign policy advisors. After the inauguration, Sutphen was appointed White House deputy chief of staff for policy, a position that she held for two years.[8]

To represent the country to the world in the areas of international relations and trade, the new president chose two seasoned African American professionals. Susan Rice, a native of Washington, DC, and an Oxford PhD, had served on the staff of the National Security Council before being appointed assistant secretary of state for African affairs during the Clinton administration. She advised candidate Obama prior to the election, after which he nominated her for US ambassador to the United Nations. The president thought the position important enough to elevate it to Cabinet-level status, and much of Rice's attention was occupied with ongoing conflicts in Iraq and Afghanistan, new civil wars in Syria and Libya, and belligerent regimes in Iran and North Korea. She served as ambassador until 2013, at which time she was considered for other governmental appointments.

Complementing Rice's diplomatic portfolio, Ron Kirk was confirmed by the US Senate in March 2009 to serve as the country's trade representative. A former Texas secretary of state and two-term mayor of Dallas, the lawyer-turned-negotiator spent most of his four years in the Obama administration striking free-trade agreements with countries such as South Korea, Colombia, and Panama. During this time, the United States also pursued greater enforcement of trade rules against China and other rival economies, nudged by labor unions dismayed by the perceived laxity of the Bush administration. Kirk's biggest agenda item was the Trans-Pacific Partnership, an ocean-spanning, multinational agreement that would have further engaged the United States economically with several Asian countries. This deal was not completed during Kirk's time as trade representative and faced insurmountable obstacles to its passage years later.[9]

Obama made a consequential selection for the nation's environmental steward. Lisa P. Jackson was nominated to serve as director of the Environmental Protection Agency (EPA). A sixteen-year veteran of the organization and a former commissioner of the New Jersey Department of Environmental Protection, Jackson dedicated her tenure as EPA head to protecting vulnerable communities from ecological and health risks and implementing policies to address climate change. Her concern for the environment was at least partly personal; she had driven her relatives out of New Orleans in the wake of Hurricane Katrina and cared for an infant son suffering with asthma. During her watch at the EPA, mandated reductions in car emissions and cuts in power-plant pollution were enacted, along with stronger prohibitions against the contamination of waterways with mining waste. By the time she resigned from the agency's directorship in February 2013, Jackson had acquired her share of critics among Republican congressmen, who had subjected her to dozens of committee grillings, and among business executives, who claimed that she was waging a "war on coal" and a "regulatory jihad" against the fossil fuel industry. But many environmentalists and others distressed about the future health of the planet considered Jackson a paragon of public service, especially in light of the instances in which she pushed for tougher policies than did the Obama White House, which sought to balance environmental protections and private-sector interests.[10]

In the realm of health and fitness, Obama made a number of choices for the country's well-being and his own. For the position of surgeon general, he chose Dr. Regina M. Benjamin. An Alabama native, she had served as the CEO of a health clinic, as a dean in a medical college, and as a vice admiral in the US Public Health Service Commissioned Corps before being unanimously confirmed as the nation's top doctor by the US Senate in October 2009. During her four years of service, she emphasized disease prevention, tobacco-free lifestyles, and healthier diets. She was especially concerned about obesity and its medical implications and focused many of her efforts on improving health-care access for underserved groups.

While Dr. Benjamin counseled the nation on matters of health and wellness, the president's own exercise and fitness regimen was managed by personal trainer Cornell McClellan, a martial artist who had worked with both Obamas since around 2000. Now dividing his time between Chicago and DC, McClellan guided the president in a variety of exercises, including cardio-intensive activities and plyometrics. According to Obama, he smoked his last cigarette in 2010, around the time that the Affordable Care Act (ACA), his trademark legislative accomplishment, was passed. He had promised Michelle years earlier that he would quit smoking once in the White House; he had struggled with the habit for decades. In the midst of a concerted campaign to sell the health-care bill to the public, he could hardly justify giving his adversaries ammunition with which to attack him in the form of an ongoing tobacco addiction. If he ever regressed, only those closest to him, such as his family, advisors, or personal aide Reggie Love, know. The press, which was ever-present, publicized no images of any backsliding, though Obama was sometimes recorded chewing Nicorette gum.[11]

Not every African American appointed by or in some way affiliated with the early Obama White House worked out. There were a couple of conspicuous, even noisy departures that warrant mention, mostly because of how uncharacteristic they were of a White House that coveted order and calm. Van Jones, an eloquent speaker and progressive thinker, was named special advisor for green jobs, enterprise, and innovation in March 2009. This portfolio interfaced with the White House Council on Environmental Quality, placing him on the frontlines of the administration's efforts to transition the country to sustainable sources of energy. Yet by the time of his appointment, it was clear that Jones had made many enemies on the right and that they would not relent in their pursuit of him, even if it meant slinging mud across 1600 Pennsylvania Avenue.

Only somewhat damaging to Jones's tenure at the White House was a video that emerged showing him referring to Republicans as "assholes," a remark for which he apologized and characterized as not representative of the administration's views. The more nagging issue was a report that he had signed a petition calling for an investigation of whether the Bush administration had allowed the September 11 terrorist attacks to occur as a "pretext to war." It was an ugly accusation that turned out not to be true, but the public litigation of the matter critically wounded Jones's reputation in the administration. In September, he made, in his words, a "rough exit" from the White House but was gracious in future reflections on his short employment there. At 41, Jones was talented enough to land on his feet and secure opportunities elsewhere in politics and media. In 2011, he founded his own activist organization, the American Dream Movement, as a counterweight to what he called the Republicans' "slash-and-burn" vision of governance. Eventually his stints as a progressive commentator on CNN led to the premiere of his own segment, *The Van Jones Show*, in January 2018.[12]

Compared to the Jones case, the circumstances surrounding the departure of the White House social secretary were similarly embarrassing but far more foreboding of a true catastrophe. Desirée Rogers had been a part of the world of Black elites for her entire life. A Harvard MBA, she was a Chicago financial executive who had raised money for the Obama presidential campaign; her ex-husband, John

W. Rogers Jr., had played basketball with Michelle's brother, Craig Robinson, at Princeton decades earlier. When Barack Obama won the presidency, it was hard to imagine an acquaintance better suited for orchestrating the social calendar of the White House. Rogers was comely, chic, and self-assured, a socialite's socialite who exuded glamour in Chanel stilettos and Comme des Garçons gowns. In accordance with the Obamas' wishes, she tried to make the executive mansion the "People's House" during her fourteen-month tenure as social secretary. As the first African American to hold the job, she hosted an array of visitors from an assortment of backgrounds, from local students and disabled veterans to NASCAR drivers and Easter egg hunters. Rogers brought competence, grace, and dignity to the work, along with other qualities and instincts. Drawing on her business training and marketing sensibilities, she sought to brand the White House with an Obama insignia, custom-created by her hand. To some, this promotional turn was inappropriate, especially given that past social secretaries tended not to be as visible as Rogers was. Still, she retained the confidence of the Obamas until a highly publicized oversight put her under the harsh glare of an unforgiving spotlight.

On November 24, 2009, Tareq and Michaele Salahi, a Virginia couple known for their reality TV show aspirations, were able to walk into a state dinner on the White House grounds uninvited and unimpeded. The pair passed through checkpoints, around security personnel, across at least one metal-detecting magnetometer, and into the residence of the president of the United States. After shaking hands with Barack Obama in the Blue Room, the Salahis went downstairs to greet Vice President Biden and Chief of Staff Rahm Emanuel. At 9:00 p.m. (around three hours after their arrival), the interlopers left the dinner crowd of 200 people, posting eight minutes later on their joint Facebook account, "Honored to be at the White House for the state dinner in honor of India with President Obama and our First Lady!" Into the early morning hours, they were still posting pictures of the event under the title "White House State Dinner."

The whole episode was more than a security lapse: it was a complete system failure from top to bottom. The Salahis had used passports, business cards, and smiles to get past concentric rings of security, including Secret Service agents and uniformed police officers, and into the White House itself. No one had flagged any suspicious aspects of the intrusion, such as the absence of the couple's names from the guest list or their initial rejection at the pedestrian gate by a plain-clothes official. It was not until the following afternoon that the breach was even formally acknowledged by White House officials. Ultimately, Mark Sullivan, director of the Secret Service and a hold-over from the Bush administration, accepted responsibility for the Salahi affair. The supreme charge of his office was the protection of the president, and he and his subordinates had been negligent in that duty. Further, Sullivan had ceded too much control over security matters to the Office of the White House Social Secretary, which at the time was led by Rogers, who had been on the job only since January.

As more unflattering details came out and scrutiny increased, De-sirée Rogers announced in February 2010 that she planned to leave the White House. The Obamas, in a joint statement, wished her well as she headed back to Chicago, where she still had personal connections and business ties. Asked by a reporter what she might do next, Rogers offered a response that likely summarized her lasting impression of her short time in Washington. "I am headed back to the private sector," she emailed tersely. "I like meritocracies." Comparable to Van Jones's post–White House success, Rogers landed softly in the Windy City. In August, she was hired as the chief executive officer of the Johnson Publishing Company, a storied Black-owned business that had produced long-running periodicals such as *Ebony* and *Jet*. It seemed a good match for her branding talents, which would be put to good use as the company struggled to remain profitable in a media ecosystem that was very different from the one in which it was founded in 1942.[13]

Of all the presidential appointees, advisors, and allies, Valerie Jarrett was in it for the long haul, with the support and blessings of both Barack and Michelle Obama. She was born in Iran in 1956 to James and Barbara Bowman during her father's employment as a pathologist in a local hospital. The family traveled widely, and Jarrett became fluent in Farsi and French at an early age. Originally from Washington, DC, the Bowmans eventually settled in Chicago. Jarrett's grandfather Robert Taylor was behind the construction of much of the city's public housing. Following undergraduate and law school at Stanford and the University of Michigan, respectively, her career interests led her to public service, working for the administrations of Mayors Harold Washington and Richard M. Daley. It was during this time that she met Michelle Robinson, an applicant for a position with the city. Now deputy chief of staff for Daley, Jarrett was impressed by the new Harvard graduate's credentials, knowledge, and confidence and ended up offering her a job on the spot. She soon met Barack Obama and in time became a close family friend, mentoring Michelle through subsequent professional moves and offering her husband advice regarding his political ambitions.[14]

Jarrett was an inner-circle advisor for the presidential campaign. She was unusual in this group, since she was both a woman and Black. However, her added value was related to her many years in public service and the wisdom that she had acquired along the way. She reliably raised important issues during the presidential run that would have otherwise received short shrift from Obama's other confidants and was not afraid to point out racial dynamics on the campaign trail. Importantly, she encouraged the Obamas to tell their stories to the American people. When Black voters in South Carolina expressed concerns about the candidate's safety, Jarrett convinced Michelle to give a speech there in November 2007 to calm their fears. She was solidly behind Barack Obama's decision to give his race speech in Philadelphia in the midst of the Jeremiah Wright controversy, though she was not quite as pleased to see him denounce

Louis Farrakhan in a debate during the fall of 2007. Jarrett helped to ground the couple when the whirlwind primaries became a hurricane of a general election. Once the election was over, a few people suggested that she place her name in contention for Obama's open US Senate seat. Although backed by senior Illinois senator Richard Durbin, the idea was fleeting and ultimately squashed by none other than her friend Michelle. "We need you in the White House," the new First Lady almost demanded, which was enough to get Jarrett packing for the trip east.[15]

Jarrett's official title in the White House was senior advisor and assistant to the president for intergovernmental affairs and public engagement. Unwieldy and oblique, the designation hardly did justice to either her wide-ranging influence in the West Wing or her ready access to the president. Jarrett weighed in on judicial nominations and Cabinet selections, guest lists for formal dinners and the composition of the First Lady's box at State of the Union addresses. She was the Oval Office's liaison to the business world, civil rights activists, LGBTQ groups, and the Latinx community; in other words, anyone outside of the White House who wanted the president's ear did well to contact her first. It is likely that the Obamas intended for Jarrett to have such gatekeeping responsibilities, even if her distinctive style did not appeal to all.

Similar to her role during the campaign, Jarrett was a pivotal intermediary between the Obama administration and the African American community. She managed to have a functional relationship with the CBC even though it irritated her when vocal members publicly accused the president of not paying enough attention to the economic plight of Black people. Rev. Al Sharpton, whom the White House occasionally relied on to gauge sentiment in the African American community, respected her candor and tended to give her the benefit of the doubt. But Professor Cornel West, a supporter-turned-critic of the president, considered her "ruthless" in her defense of her boss and too dismissive of his own critiques. She could, indeed, be protective of her friend the chief executive, and acquired a reputation for calling people late at night for reprimands that seemed to always begin with the accusatory words "You are hurting the president." It is hard to know whether Obama knew about the frequency or severity of such scoldings, or whether they were helpful or harmful to his administration's goals.[16]

Jarrett received mixed reviews among other staffers in the West Wing. She had a reputation for bringing fresh insights to many different kinds of conversations, but the outsized purview of her job responsibilities—and the way that she interpreted them—led to a blurring of the conventional hierarchy of reporting lines and resulted in tensions. She got along with David Axelrod, the other senior advisor who was closest to the president, but was less chummy with campaign manager David Plouffe, according to one report. Chief of Staff Emanuel and his successor, William Daley (brother of the Chicago mayor), both tussled with Jarrett over matters of authority and access to the president. Emanuel's penchant for profane outbursts and fits of screaming never sat well with Jarrett and created, in her view, an intimidating workplace atmosphere, especially for women staffers.

Despite such pressures, Jarrett's unique relationship with the first family gave her concrete advantages over her rivals, which she used for maximum leverage. In some circles, she became known as the "Night Stalker" since she was the only official who routinely followed the president home to the residential areas of the White House. One aide characterized her influence with the chief executive as "almost like Nancy Reagan was with President Reagan, but more powerful." To her credit, Jarrett, unlike several others who worked in and with the administration, never lost Obama's confidence, even though complaints about her maneuvering and power plays must have occasionally reached him. He trusted her to manage her sprawling portfolio while bringing a sensitive, informed voice to policy matters and keeping him abreast of office politics and morale. "She is family," he told a reporter during a July 2009 interview, affirming a kind of latitude and job security that no one else ever enjoyed during his tenure in office.[17]

If there was a male equivalent of Valerie Jarrett in the Obama administration, the closest contender would be Attorney General Eric H. Holder Jr. While he did not share the same personal history with the first family and his leadership of the Justice Department spared him the day-to-day politicking and turf battles of the West Wing, Holder became a close friend and advisor of the president during his long stint as the nation's chief law enforcement official. Born and raised in New York City, he earned bachelor's and law degrees from Columbia University. During the 1970s, Holder worked for the US Justice Department and was eventually promoted to US attorney for Washington, DC. Under Attorney General Janet Reno, he was elevated in 1997 to deputy attorney general, the department's second-highest office. His accomplishments in the organization were respectable, though President Clinton's last-minute pardon of Marc Rich, a wealthy fugitive charged with tax evasion and other crimes, stained both men's records.

Holder's first encounter with newly elected senator Barack Obama was at a Washington dinner party in late 2004. The two chatted freely about basketball and policy and quickly became friends. They had similar origin stories that placed their Black roots outside of the continental United States, with Obama's Kenya-Kansas-Hawaii history echoing refrains of Holder's tale of how his father, a Barbados-born realtor, met his mother, a New Jersey telephone operator. "We are both basically a little bit outside of the typical black experience," Holder said of himself and Obama during an interview. "But we have wives who remind us of what that was like." As a partner in the Covington & Burling law firm, Holder provided legal advice to Sen. Obama's staff. When Obama decided to run for the presidency, Holder agreed to serve on the vice presidential search team that ultimately selected Joe Biden.[18]

Like Jarrett, Attorney General Holder took on issues of race more frequently than did others in Obama's advisory circle. But unlike her, he did so in public and when the stakes were higher and more fraught, given his office and the Republican opposition that was coalescing against the administration and its policies. During a meeting of Justice Department employees in February 2009, he castigated the United States for priding "itself as an ethnic melting pot, [while] in things racial we have always been and continue to be, in too many ways, essentially a nation of cowards." Predictably, conservatives boisterously accused him of inscribing racial grievances in the new administration's playbook. The speech, which had not been vetted with White House aides, caught the president off guard and seemed inappropriate for the opening days of a presidency predicated on "hope and change" optimism. Top advisors, presumably with Obama's acquiescence, were careful to keep Holder off Sunday news shows for years to come, lest he go off script again and be too indelicate in his commentaries about racial matters.

Aside from such stumbles, there were other instances when the attorney general vocally championed the cause of African Americans in ways that Obama, given his position and temperament, never could, though the president almost certainly nodded in silent approval. When House Republicans took Holder to task for allegedly being too lenient on New Black Panther Party members accused of interfering at a Philadelphia polling station in 2008, Holder read them the riot act. He declared that the incident in question, while inappropriate, hardly measured up to the obstacles that Black people had faced historically in trying to vote and that for a congressman to make such a comparison "does a great disservice to people who put their lives on the line, who risked all, for my people." Over time, Holder endured more hostile attacks from Republican lawmakers and GOP-led congressional committees than any other Cabinet official in the administration. He attributed much of the enmity to ideological and policy differences, but he thought some of it was based on his relationship with Obama. Since Republicans were unable to subject the president to bruising congressional interrogations and other humiliations, Holder believed that they viewed him as a convenient stand-in due to "the fact that we're both African-Americans." It was not an unreasonable conclusion, given some of the rhetoric and conduct directed toward both Holder and Obama by the GOP and its conservative allies in the media and elsewhere. The real news was that the attorney general was willing to make such a claim out loud and before the press.[19]

During his tenure as attorney general, Holder's most explosive run-ins with Congress revolved around investigations into the Fast and Furious gunwalking program. Beginning in late 2009 and lasting until early 2011, the Phoenix field division of the Bureau of Alcohol, Tobacco, Firearms and Explosives (ATF) authorized local gun dealers to sell firearms to illegal "straw buyers." The purchasers would presumably then take (or gunwalk) the weapons into Mexico and sell them to members of drug cartels. Each gun was to be tracked and ideally could lead to the arrest of drug lords and their underlings, who would have illegally acquired the firearms. Due to mismanagement and other factors, the program was handled ineptly, and thousands of firearms were lost and never accounted for. In one instance, rifles associated with the gunwalking program were recovered at the scene of the murder of Brian Terry, a US Border Patrol agent, in December 2010. While the aims of the Fast and Furious program were in line with US drug enforcement policy, its methods and implementation left much to be desired. As its most troubling outcome, there were now better-armed drug gangs and a more violent situation in Mexico and along the southern US border than may have otherwise been the case.[20]

As the Justice Department head and supervisor of the ATF, Holder was roundly condemned by congressional investigative committees for the botched gunwalking, and subpoenas for documents were issued by Republican chairs in the House. Holder provided some materials and claimed that other information was protected by executive privilege and thus was exempt from congressional requests. In June 2012, the Oversight and Government Reform Committee, led by Rep. Darrell Issa of California, voted to hold Holder in criminal contempt of Congress, which was followed days later by an affirming 255-67 vote by the entire House. Members of the CBC and

most other Democrats, led by John Lewis and minority leader Nancy
Pelosi, walked out of the chamber in protest during the vote. To no
one's surprise, the Justice Department announced on June 29 that
Holder would not face criminal prosecution in the wake of the congressional contempt citation. In the middle of the political brawling
over the gunwalking program, the agency's inspector general concurrently conducted an investigation into the handling of Fast and
Furious and its aftermath. Its report, released in September, pointed
out managerial negligence in the operation of the program but found
that Holder had not known of the existence of the ATF initiative
prior to early 2011. No one was recommended for criminal prosecution, though fourteen referrals for disciplinary action were issued.
Acting ATF director B. Todd Jones released a statement accepting
responsibility for the organization's blunders, and two officials, Jason
Weinstein and Ken Melson, immediately resigned from the Justice
Department.[21]

Holder weathered the Fast and Furious storm but was clearly damaged during his battle with GOP enemies, acquiring the unfortunate distinction of being the first attorney general held in contempt
of Congress. Further, since the US House had also voted to hold
Holder in civil contempt for not abiding by its subpoena, which had
demanded a range of documents related to Fast and Furious, he was
still vulnerable to legal action. In August, Rep. Issa filed a lawsuit
against the attorney general, hoping to get via litigation what had
not been obtained through congressional censure. Two years later,
US district judge Amy Berman Jackson ordered that the documents
that Holder had guarded so closely against congressional scrutiny
be turned over to the House Oversight and Government Reform
Committee, but additional legal wrangling stalled the release of the
material for several more years. As it turned out, the skirmishes and
fallout over subpoenas and records represented, at best, a Pyrrhic
victory for the Republicans. None of their investigations of gunwalking had a substantive impact on US drug policy and enforcement
practices, though Holder's Mexican counterpart, Attorney General

Marisela Morales, excoriated the ill-fated ATF program as an "attack on the safety of Mexicans."[22]

If anything, Holder was emboldened by his confrontations with congressional Republicans and continued to be assertive on matters of voting rights, criminal justice, and immigration policy for the rest of his tenure as attorney general—to the dismay of many conservatives. He actually seemed to revel in challenging his opponents in public and in front of cameras, and a number of Black journalists, including Roland Martin, Eugene Robinson, Michele Norris, and Juan Williams, reportedly had sent him texts and emails encouraging him to fight for control of the media narrative that emerged from combative committee hearings. When the CBC honored Holder at an awards ceremony in September 2012, he thanked them for standing with him "during my little dust-up" and received warm applause from a crowd that included dozens of the House Democrats who had walked out of the chamber during the contempt vote in June. His reputation for engaging in aggressive one-upmanship with Republicans raised his profile among Democrats and African Americans in particular, especially as he appeared to shrug off the personal and professional costs of such hyperpartisan warfare.[23]

At the end of the day, Holder was aware that he had to satisfy only one other person, and he managed to meet that standard year after year. Barack Obama continued to both like and respect the attorney general, and the two men shared similar positions on protecting civil rights, punishing Wall Street excesses, and the use of armed drones in fighting foreign adversaries. In addition, the president's relatively scandal-free administration did not trigger harmful Justice Department probes or embarrassing prosecutions that might have otherwise strained the men's relationship. Subsequently, Obama allowed Holder to choose when and how he would exit government service and return to private life, a degree of discretion that resulted in Holder becoming the third-longest-serving attorney general in US history.

CHAPTER 5

President of the
Entire United States

THERE IS NOTHING ESPECIALLY MAGICAL OR SIGNIFICANT ABOUT
the first hundred days of a presidency other than it is a good round
number, and there is usually a tacit expectation that the opposition
party, following a hard-fought campaign, will courteously allow the
new chief executive a brief respite of civility and goodwill. However,
in the face of an existential crisis that could spell doom for many people, the first months of a new government can matter more than the
next several years. Just before leaving office in 2009, President George
W. Bush had moved to break the fall of the financial heavens by
signing a bill that bailed out failing banks and soaked up hundreds of
billions of dollars in toxic mortgages and other bad debts. To address
mounting job losses and their ramifications for every sector of the
economy, the incoming Obama administration pushed an $800 bil-
lion economic stimulus package, the largest ever, through Congress.
The bill, officially titled the American Recovery and Reinvestment Act
and signed into law on February 17, was a collection of funding measures that included everything from big-ticket infrastructure spending
and direct financial assistance to states to enhanced unemployment
insurance and tax abatements. Billions of dollars were also directed

toward scientific research, green energy projects, modernizing the electrical grid, and digitizing health-care records.

As the stimulus package churned through Congress, near-death experiences of automobile manufacturers General Motors and Chrysler, both saddled with massive debts and unloved cars, also commanded the federal government's attention. Initiated under the Bush administration in December 2008, billions of dollars in taxpayer-funded loans were floated to the car giants, which in exchange were required to restructure their businesses and allow for a substantial amount of government oversight of their operations. As with the big-bank bailouts, the rescue of the auto companies turned out to be a good bet in the long run, since the money was recouped once the economy improved. But the whole thing smelled bad to many Americans who disliked the idea of writing eleven-figure checks to lenders who sold people cruel subprime loans or to vehicle manufacturers that had no viable business strategy for the contemporary marketplace. Replete with shocking displays of tone-deaf entitlement—such as General Motors CEO Richard Wagoner's expectation that he would receive a severance package of $20 million after nearly running the company into the ground—the entire economic mess and the assortment of rogues, gamblers, and dimwits behind it were galling in the extreme.[1]

Beyond the urgent task of snatching the country from the economic void of the Great Recession, a number of other measures were passed and decisions made in the early days of the Obama presidency that would have both short-term and lasting consequences. The Lilly Ledbetter Fair Pay Act of 2009 was actually the first bill that the new president signed. The measure overturned a limited US Supreme Court decision regarding income equity in the case of *Ledbetter v. Goodyear Tire & Rubber Co.* and made it easier for individuals to challenge instances of pay discrimination. On February 27, the president outlined plans for ending the US military deployment in Iraq, a campaign pledge that he intended to fulfill through phased withdrawals over the next two years. The war, which began in 2003, cost more than $800 billion by the time of its official conclusion in December

2011. About 4,500 US soldiers had died trying to conquer and sta-bilize the country, and 32,000 others suffered a wide spectrum of injuries. Complementing the huge expenditures on corporate bailouts and the stimulus package, Congress passed the Omnibus Appropri-ations Act, which Obama signed on March 11. Totaling $410 billion, the legislation provided funding for a range of government agencies through the end of the fiscal year on September 30, along with monies earmarked for thousands of pet projects in the districts and states of various lawmakers. Capping his first hundred days in office, President Obama signed the Edward M. Kennedy Serve America Act on April 21, 2009. Among other provisions, the bill established the Summer of Service program for grade-school students, bolstered the membership of the AmeriCorps program, and designated September 11 as National Day of Service and Remembrance.[2]

Along with these policy initiatives, much of the new president's political capital was spent on his early plans for an overhaul of the health insurance system. A reinvention of the US model of medical coverage had been a dream of Democrats for much of the twentieth century. The creation of Medicare and Medicaid during the 1960s presidency of Lyndon B. Johnson marked a milestone in the march toward universal coverage, but tens of millions of Americans still lacked health insurance a half century later. Obama proposed a hy-brid public-private system in which the government would partner with existing health-care insurers to offer a menu of variably priced plans. Federal subsidies would go both to the insurance companies, which would ideally keep premiums affordable, and to means-tested consumers who would have otherwise been unable to afford cover-age. Basic services and features were to be associated with all plans, including certain types of preventive-care coverage, the option to cover offspring through their parent's plan until age 26, and a ban on discriminatory premium pricing related to preexisting medical con-ditions. To bring healthy people into the new system for the purpose of stabilizing costs, a government-enforced mandate would require that everyone obtain health insurance or else pay a fine. Additionally,

Medicaid would be expanded under the Patient Protection and Affordable Care Act (ACA or "Obamacare," as it became colloquially known), and states could opt into the expansion with the federal government covering at least 90 percent of the resulting expense.

The ACA was passed by Congress in March 2010 on a party-line vote. Democrats celebrated it as a breakthrough in slowing runaway medical costs and bringing the country more in line with other nations that provided universal health care to their citizens as a fundamental right. Republicans denounced it as "socialized medicine" or worse, and promised to repeal it at the first opportunity. Largely due to a combination of sometimes lackluster messaging from the administration, incessant attacks by conservatives, and ongoing public confusion about the law's provisions, the ACA was never very popular during Obama's tenure in office. Still, following some initial hiccups with the enrollment website, the law eventually extended insurance coverage to tens of millions of Americans, including large numbers of new Medicaid enrollees. The legislation has remained mostly intact beyond Obama's time in the White House and has gained the approval of more Americans as they came to understand its benefits and to subsequently resent continuing GOP efforts to undermine it.[3]

Alongside major pieces of legislation that he was able to maneuver through Congress in one form or another, Obama issued several executive orders that advanced elements of his policy agenda during his first years in office. Similar to his predecessors, he fully embraced the idea of the administrative presidency. This concept cloaks the chief executive in powers assumed to be inherent in his office and that can thus be used to shape national security, environmental rules, economic policy, or other matters related to the public interest. In some cases, Obama's orders simply reversed Bush-era measures that restricted abortion access or that terminated federal funding for human embryonic stem cell research. Other executive actions strengthened fuel efficiency standards for vehicles and allowed immigrants who had been brought to the country illegally as children to stay and work without fear of deportation. In function and intent, such presidential directives sidestepped legislative gridlock in Congress and bureau-cratic red tape in order to realize more immediate results. To imple-ment several of his orders impacting the environment, private indus-try, and other areas, Obama appointed "czars" who reported to the White House, though their duties frequently interfaced with esta-blished government departments and agencies. Ridiculed by some GOP lawmakers as executive overreach, Obama's orders were occa-sionally blocked by Congress, such as in the case of his unsuccessful attempt to close the US detention center at Guantánamo Bay, Cuba. On big issues, the president usually preferred congressional action, with its legislative legitimacy and bipartisan veneer, to executive or-ders, which were vulnerable to reversal by Congress or a future pres-ident. Nonetheless, he issued 274 such directives during his tenure in office, which was lower than the number issued by his most recent two-term predecessors.[4]

Although the first hundred days of the new administration were bedeviled by a plague of economic woes the likes of which no one had seen in more than six decades, Barack Obama was blessed with the well wishes and forbearance of the American people as he and others tried to find a way out of the recession. A Gallup poll tracked his approval rating at 65 percent during the week of April 20-26, which was twelve points higher than George W. Bush's number at that point in his presidency and twenty points higher than Bill Clinton's figure. Majorities of polled Blacks, whites, and Hispanics endorsed Obama's performance, with the former registering a 96 percent ap-proval rating compared to 85 percent among Hispanics and 57 percent among whites. By the first anniversary of the president's election, a plurality (47 percent) of African Americans told pollsters that they were satisfied with the direction of the country, more than double the percentage of non-Hispanic whites (22 percent) who said so. While Black people generally fared worse than other racial or ethnic groups according to most economic measurements, they were still more likely than any other demographic to concede to Obama the benefit of the doubt in nearly every survey of his presidency.[5]

The Affordable Care Act was emblematic of Barack Obama's view that a universalist, pragmatic, race-neutral approach to progressive policy could, if carefully crafted, pay disproportionately high dividends to individuals and groups, including African Americans, who were the most disadvantaged segments of the society. As he articulated in *The Audacity of Hope* and throughout the presidential campaign, this ideal was at the foundation of his governing philosophy and informed most of his major domestic policies, or at least the stated reasoning behind them. Yet as the recession continued to sink Black wealth, homeownership, employment prospects, and life chances in general, the tension between Obama's universalist methodology and calls for more targeted relief aimed directly at Black communities experiencing depression-like conditions became more noticeable and more visceral. To be sure, the president had a lot on his to-do list, including reversing millions of job losses, saving financial and manufacturing industries from total collapse, decelerating the appalling home foreclosure crisis, and managing treasury-draining wars abroad. And these pressing items were ahead of any positive plans for reform of the health-care, banking, and criminal justice systems. But as the economic pain went from bad to severe among many African Americans, some raised questions about Obama's commitment to his staunchest constituency.

In statements in various venues, the president was consistent in his position, especially early in his administration. In a December 2009 interview with journalist April D. Ryan of the American Urban Radio Networks, he recognized "grumbling" among African Americans hit hard by the economic turmoil. However, he was convinced that as "president of the entire United States" he could not design policies that specifically addressed the concerns of Black people. Instead, he committed to "passing laws that help all people, particularly those who are most vulnerable and most in need." Such an approach would, in his view, "help lift up the African American community." During an Oval Office meeting with selected civil rights leaders in February 2010, the president reiterated both his concern for African American suffering and his reluctance to target the victims of the economic trauma with race-specific remedies. One attendee, Rev. Al Sharpton, later stated that Obama had obviously been affected by the plight of stricken Black communities and had pledged to address "some of the structural inequalities that are currently in place." Benjamin Jealous, president of the National Association for the Advancement of Colored People (NAACP), seemed to agree with Obama that poverty was a more general problem that needed a solution beyond any kind of race-based plan, though he maintained that "all Americans . . . want to see the pace of progress quicken." Rev. Jesse Jackson, who was not invited to the White House meeting, let it be known that more needed to be done about the home foreclosure epidemic, charging that Obama's economic team seemed more concerned about the well-being of big businesses than about individual Americans in distress.[6]

As the midterm elections approached, Obama trained his sights on Republican obstructionism and reminded African American audiences that the November vote would be a referendum on his presidency. "Don't make me look bad, now," he chided a crowd at historically Black Bowie State University, advising those in attendance to turn up at the polls. During a White House interview, he took the Bush administration to task for setting the groundwork for the Great Recession. "We had 10 years of policies that did not help the African-American community," he reminded radio talk-show host Joe Madison of Sirius XM. "Nobody's been more damaged than the African-American community by that. We've got to make sure that we turn out to vote." Obama's election eve outreach to African Americans was both genuine and tactical. He truly believed that his policies had been more helpful to Black communities than anything Republicans would readily offer in terms of reforming health care, saving public-sector jobs, enhancing Pell Grants for college students, or protecting basic support, such as unemployment insurance and food assistance. Nevertheless, when he was interviewed on Tom Joyner's radio show in September, he was compelled to suggest that their chat was more politically pragmatic than casual. "We haven't heard from you in a while," Joyner poked in good humor. "You know, I don't get a chance to do much radio these days," Obama parried, before circling around to acknowledge that "especially in the African-American community, Tom Joyner and black radio [are] what people listen to."[7]

For the president and his party, the pre-midterm rallying cries turned out to be too little, too late. Ill omens were in the air as early as the spring of 2010, when the Black unemployment rate topped out at almost 17 percent and Obama's job approval rating among African Americans slipped below 90 percent for the first time in his presidency. In off-year elections, the party controlling the White House has traditionally had a harder time with voters, but the 2010 elections were uniquely awful for Democrats. The Republican Party, energized and well funded, successfully made the congressional contests about the president. Conservative politicians and media, particularly outlets such as Fox News, condemned Obama and the Democrats for the big government expenditures of bailouts and stimulus measures, often mischaracterizing policies such as the ACA as federal takeovers of the private sector. The Tea Party revolt in the GOP further fueled the ire of voters by releasing a combustible mix of antitax, antiestablishment hysteria into the political atmosphere.

Although the massive federal spending and the ongoing economic pain were behind much of the Republican mobilization for the midterms, many of those who went to the polls were motivated by animus toward Obama himself as the embodiment of all things wrong in the country. He was regularly lambasted at Tea Party rallies, in right-wing cable news commentaries, and in the chambers of Congress as a veritable tyrant. Some critics charged him with bringing socialism, communism, fascism, Islamism, racism, and nearly every other dreadful -ism into the Oval Office. In some ways, the character attack was simply a continuation of the McCain-Palin 2008 crusade to insidiously portray Obama as an anti-American racial other. But in this instance, such dark language and histrionics caused a seismic shift in the electoral landscape, deepening partisan rifts and social cleavages.[8]

The president called the congressional losses endured by his party a "shellacking," and his assessment could not have been more apt. The Republicans took control of the House by winning 63 seats, the most gained in a single election since 1948. The GOP narrowed the Democrats' majority in the Senate with a net gain of 6 seats. Beyond the capital, the electoral carnage in the rest of the country was just as bad for the Democrats. At least 675 legislative seats were lost, which flipped twenty-six state legislatures to Republican control and left only seventeen in Democratic hands, with the rest split between the parties. Factoring in gubernatorial victories, Republicans completely controlled twenty-one state governments after the election (up from twelve previously), and Democrats controlled only eleven (down from sixteen). With congressional redistricting on the horizon, such outcomes were terrible news for Obama and his party. They had lost legislatures and governor's mansions in states that they previously controlled or that candidate Obama had carried just two years earlier.[9]

Adding to the misery, not only had the Democratic Party suffered dismal losses across the board, but key components of its 2008 winning electoral coalition did not show up at the midterm polls. The 44 percent Black turnout rate was five points below that of whites (60 percent of whom voted Republican) and far below the 65 percent figure for African American voters during the 2008 election. Some other Democratic-leaning groups had even lower rates: only one out of three Hispanic and Asian voters showed up at the polls. In the South, where race and party affiliation tend to closely align, Black legislators found themselves carrying the Democratic banner as an isolated minority in several states, with only 5 percent of them being members of the majority party in the region's legislatures. The only good news for Obama and his colleagues in Congress was that the Democrats had managed to hold on to the Senate by one seat, which would protect their legislative achievements over the past two years. Even so, they would face a raucous lot in the new Republican-led House, which was now suffused with Tea Party dogma and hardly under the control of incoming House speaker John Boehner, who was more a flavorless manager than a unifying visionary.[10]

Obama did not wallow in defeat. After a short, perfunctory call to Boehner on the night of the election, he began planning for the future and in particular the 2012 campaign. If nothing else was clear to the Democrats after the November walloping, it was unmistakably obvious that their voters had not shown up in 2010. There were, of course, traceable reasons behind this dip in participation, including the ongoing economic disorder, which had become especially associated with the party in power, and the fact that core Democratic demographics, such as minorities, the young, and less-wealthy voters, are among the least likely to show up for midterm elections. Yet the scale of the defeat strongly suggested that much work needed to be done to shore up those constituencies, which had been so essential to the stunning victories of the president and his party just two years earlier. Much of the heavy lifting would need to take place in the world of messaging, which the Republicans and their media allies dominated going into the election. The other necessary tasks could only be accomplished through concrete actions that convinced voters that they would actually be better off if Democrats were back in control—or at least were not shut completely out of the White House and US Capitol in 2012.[11]

Throughout 2011, the Obama administration, its staff, and its allies tried to tell their story on everything from economic recovery and health-care reform to education policy and civil rights. This time, the president directly and methodically engaged African American communities with a narrative of deep concern for their condition, underscoring ways in which his policies had materially helped and would continue to improve their circumstances. In November, the White House released a forty-four-page report, "The President's Agenda and the African American Community," that outlined Obama's achievements in detail. As one might expect, the economy was front and center. The document touted the stimulus package, claiming that during 2010 alone its various provisions, including expanded unemployment insurance benefits, had kept 1.8 million African Americans from falling below the poverty line. Other government policies, including the earned income tax credit and the child tax credit, were mentioned as having helped "an estimated 2.2 million African American families and almost half of all African American children." Additionally, those facing food insecurity were aided by a 13.6 percent increase in Supplemental Nutrition Assistance Program (SNAP) benefits, which purportedly kept 332,000 individuals from sinking into poverty. The report noted the "unacceptably high rate" of Black unemployment, which stood at 15.1 percent at the time. To address this crisis, it proposed the American Jobs Act that, if approved by Congress, would incentivize businesses to hire the unemployed, invest in schools and infrastructure, and "create new job opportunities in African American communities across the country."

The report also discussed how the lives of African Americans had been improved in the areas of health care, housing, business development, and education. As the crowning policy triumph of the Obama administration thus far, the ACA was cited as having reduced the cost of health insurance through tax credits, as well as having streamlined Medicaid eligibility to the point that almost 4 million African Americans would be extended coverage. Moreover, the act concentrated more attention and resources on reducing racial disparities in the provision of health care. In the area of housing, the report disclosed that approximately 90,000 Black homebuyers avoided foreclosure by receiving permanent mortgage adjustments under the Home Affordable Modification Program. Further, 60 percent of African Americans seeking to buy homes in 2009 were able to do so with FHA insurance. Along with these advances, Black people in the business world were able to obtain almost $7 billion in contracts and assets through the Minority Business Development Agency, a division of the Department of Commerce. According to the report, this office had already "created nearly 11,000 new jobs and saved tens of thousands of existing jobs" during the first two years of the Obama administration. Finally, in the field of education, the president made college more affordable by increasing the maximum Pell Grant by 17.4 percent and devoting more than $40 billion to the program to ensure its future accessibility and inflation-adjusted growth.[12]

The president's report was comprehensive and optimistic, and it did not seem—based on available corroborating information—to unduly stretch the scope or significance of these various policies and programs vis-à-vis African American individuals and communities. Furthermore, in the document and elsewhere Obama justifiably highlighted other ways that Black people had benefited during his tenure in office, including continuing government attention on the HIV/AIDS epidemic, a settlement of decades-old racial discrimination claims filed by African American farmers against the Department of Agriculture, and enhanced funding for teenage pregnancy prevention programs. Obama could even take some credit for continuing the Bush administration's effort to build levees and other infrastructure throughout southern Louisiana in the aftermath of Hurricane Katrina, which had become a potent symbol of death, destruction, and racial inequalities. While the White House Office of Urban Affairs, created by an executive order in February 2009, never completely got off the ground, several federal partnerships, along with the stimulus package and the ACA, did benefit some metro areas with large Black populations.[13]

To fairly balance the ledger concerning Obama's efforts to assist African Americans, one would also have to take into account the areas in which the president and his administration fell short. Despite some mortgage relief to selected homeowners, the federal government did far more to keep afloat the financial institutions that had created and benefited from risky loans and the real-estate bubble than it did to relieve borrowers whose properties were underwater or who faced foreclosure. Furthermore, the administration and Congress accomplished very little in regard to criminal justice reform during President Obama's first years in office, though he was fully aware of the devastating impact that the War on Drugs, harsh sentencing guidelines, and the country's culture of mass incarceration had on communities of color. Put another way, the white-collar fraudsters who capsized the economy were much less likely to be held to account for their actions than the inner-city street hustler who was caught selling a few grams of marijuana or crack cocaine. And the gloomy statistics regarding Black unemployment, wealth loss, home foreclosures, and student loan debt told as powerful a story as anything the president or any other government official could write in a promotional pamphlet. Of course, not all of these issues originated during Obama's watch, nor were many entirely solvable during his first years in office. Still, a disproportionate amount of Black suffering occurred during his early tenure in the White House that should be figured into any evaluation of his record in that time period.

On educational matters, the Obama administration made several efforts to strengthen African American institutions, fortify affirmative action policies, and improve scholastic outcomes for Black students and others. On February 26, 2010, the president hosted a White House ceremony that featured the signing of an executive order before an audience of representatives of historically Black colleges and universities (HBCUs). The directive extended the White House Initiative on HBCUs and continued a related advisory board first established during the Reagan presidency. "I want everyone to understand that you've got a partner in me," Obama announced, further assuring the gathering that his Department of Education was "absolutely committed to making sure that you can succeed in your mission." The words were matched with a funding request in his 2011 budget that called for $98 million in additional monies for HBCUs as part of a ten-year, $850 million outlay for the institutions. The president, in a symbolic flourish, declared the time period of the meeting "National HBCU Week" in honor of "our history and to remember all of the men and women who took risks and made extraordinary sacrifices" to establish these predominantly African American schools.[14]

It was unusual for a US president to officially host HBCU supporters at the White House, and the visibility afforded these institutions during the executive order signing was certainly welcomed by the attendees and others. Aside from this cordial affair, relations between the Obama White House and these schools and their advocates were rocky for much of his first term due in part to the administration's misunderstanding of both the funding models behind the operation of many HBCUs and the financial wherewithal of the typical student who matriculated at them. In the opinion of some stakeholders, the president actually started on the wrong foot by recommending that $80 million be cut from federal funding of HBCUs in his first budget of 2009. Concerned members of the CBC in the US House protested the proposed reduction and, with assistance from Education and Labor Committee chair George Miller, were able to have the money restored to the budget. In the midst of a historic fiscal collapse, the impulse to shift resources to areas of perceived greater need and to find savings seems understandable, though that rationale did not likely satisfy many in this instance.

A more consequential clash over HBCU funding occurred in October 2011 when the Department of Education raised the credit requirements for the Parent PLUS loan program. The move was part of the government's effort to streamline lending systems that had once been under the purview of private entities. As a primary effect of the credit standards revision, many Black parents were no longer able to acquire approval for loans to fund their children's tuition and fees. By 2013, 200,000 fewer loan applications were approved than in 2011, and HBCUs, along with other higher education institutions, were hit hard by the policy change. Outcries reached the White House, along with talk of lawsuits challenging the new lending standards, which, according to one estimate, would cost HBCUs collectively more than $150 million in tuition revenue and disrupt the academic progress of more than 25,000 students.

Stung by the criticism, the administration hastily put in place a process for reconsidering denied applications, and eventually the vast majority of loans were approved. In September 2013, Department of Education secretary Arne Duncan took responsibility for the revised lending rules and issued an apology concerning the "real impact" that his agency's actions were having on students and families. According to some observers, the government's initial attempt to change the eligibility criteria for the Parent PLUS program, apparently without consulting affected institutions or recipients beforehand, was part of a larger preoccupation with quality controls at HBCUs. Rep. Hank Johnson of Georgia, a CBC member and a graduate of historically Black Clark Atlanta University, thought that the focus on such metrics—and in particular what he understood to be Obama's desire to correlate federal funding formulas with a school's graduation rate—displayed a "somewhat callous view of the unique niche HBCUs fill." Julianne Malveaux, a former president of Bennett College, was even more candid in her assessment of the perceived premises behind the administration's policies. "HBCU students aren't taking eight years to finish their degree because they're stupid, but because they started school, and then they stopped because of money," she explained sharply. "And if we had more financial aid available, they wouldn't have to do that." Undoubtedly not alone in his appraisal, Rep. James Clyburn, an alumnus of South Carolina State College, considered the fallout from the changes to Parent PLUS eligibility to be the "lowest point" in the relationship between the Congressional Black Caucus and the Obama administration.[15]

If the Parent PLUS episode revealed some White House insensitivity to or unfamiliarity with the financial realities of HBCUs, such a characterization could not be readily applied to how the president viewed the political and electoral relevance of such institutions. In advance of the 2012 election, his campaign made a concerted effort to get college-age voters to the polls. Stephanie Brown, a Howard University alumna and national African American vote director of the group African Americans for Obama, was featured on the president's reelection website encouraging others affiliated with HBCUs to become involved in the 2012 contest. "Can you commit to registering 20 of our HBCU friends and current students to vote?" she asked of site visitors. "Will you volunteer with the campaign for just a few hours? Are you able to host an Obama tailgate during homecoming?" After the election, Obama continued this outreach by publicly offering warm regards to newly named Morehouse College president John Silvanus Wilson Jr.

"as he continues to inspire more of our nation's youth to pursue higher education." Prior to the Morehouse presidency, Wilson had been the director of the White House Initiative on HBCUs, a position that was filled in September 2013 by George E. Cooper, a former president of South Carolina State University with experience in vetting federal legislation pertinent to Black academic institutions.[16]

Despite some turbulence in his relationship with HBCUs and their advocates, Obama was generally embraced by these institutions, just as he was by a supermajority of Black people, according to every credible poll taken during his time in office. In May 2013, he spoke at the Morehouse commencement ceremony, probably as a professional favor to Wilson, the campus president. Before a hyped crowd, Obama counseled the new graduates to pursue their dreams, be responsible role models, and make no excuses about past hardships. Three years later, he spoke at Howard University's graduation gathering and offered similar advice. By this last year of his presidency, he was much less reluctant to engage race directly, in part due to a number of well-publicized, racially tinged crises that he had to contend with during his second term. To the cheering Howard crowd, he proclaimed:

> First of all—and this should not be a problem for this group—be confident in your heritage. Be confident in your blackness. One of the great changes that's occurred in our country since I was your age is the realization there's no one way to be black. Take it from somebody who's seen both sides of debate about whether I'm black enough. In the past couple [of] months, I've had lunch with the Queen of England and hosted Kendrick Lamar in the Oval Office. There's no straightjacket, there's no constraints, there's no litmus test for authenticity.

By 2016, such open talk of race and Blackness was not uncommon for Obama, though years earlier in his presidency one would have been hard pressed to find such candor in his public remarks on racial identity. While some were piqued by his now time-honored penchant for referencing the theme of personal responsibility before predominantly Black audiences, others found such advice to be wholly reasonable in the larger context of far-ranging addresses to young people.[17]

On balance, Obama's treatment of HBCUs was decent, if a bit uneven in policy application and messaging. Federal funding for these institutions grew during most years of his presidency, though legislative cuts to domestic spending in fiscal years 2011-2013 resulted in sizable budgetary reductions for the Strengthening HBCUs Program. Steady augmentation of Pell Grants during the Obama presidency disproportionately helped students attending HBCUs, since approximately half of them received these federal awards in any given year. As mentioned earlier, the administration could rightly be taken to task for its handling of revisions to the Parent PLUS loan program in addition to some early naïveté or indifference in regard to the funding paradigms that shaped HBCUs and their student bodies. With that said, Obama was both morally committed and politically savvy enough to see the value of cultivating the leadership and constituencies of HBCUs before and after election cycles.[18]

Paralleling his relationship with Black academic institutions, the president was a consistent advocate of utilizing affirmative action to diversify access to educational resources and quality scholastic experiences. In December 2011, the Departments of Justice and Education issued a set of guidelines that superseded Bush-era interpretations of how race could be used in shaping college admissions practices. The previous instructions had prohibited racial quotas and called for the application of race-neutral approaches to improving equity in educational access. In setting aside this 2008 protocol, the Obama administration affirmed that "an institution may permissibly aim to achieve a critical mass of underrepresented students" through the use of race as an admissions criteria, particularly when a race-neutral strategy "would be unworkable." The new guidelines also allowed for race to inform K-12 efforts to diversify student bodies, including decisions concerning the geographical placement of schools and the operation of student transfer policies.[19]

Attorney General Holder's articulated rationale for the new interpretation was consistent with the administration's overarching ethos on affirmative action. "Diverse learning environments promote development of analytical skills, dismantle stereotypes and prepare students to succeed in an increasingly interconnected world," he maintained in a statement, which drew immediate praise from such groups as the NAACP Legal Defense and Educational Fund and the Leadership Conference on Civil Rights. For good measure, the president signed an executive order in July 2012 creating the White House Initiative on Educational Excellence for African Americans. This data-driven program, embedded in the Department of Education, was aimed at improving scholastic outcomes for Black students from preschool to college, as well as addressing the disproportionately high number of African American children who were subjected to punitive "disciplinary tools" at school.[20]

As the US Supreme Court prepared to again consider the legality of affirmative action as it related to college admissions policies in 2012, the Obama administration was one of many groups and entities that filed an amicus brief supporting the use of race as a factor in determining the demographic texture of student bodies. Current court precedent, based on the *Grutter v. Bollinger* (2003) decision, allowed for race to be used as an element of college recruitment and diversification strategies, an ideal that was being challenged by a plaintiff who claimed that she had been denied entrance into the University of Texas at Austin because of an allegedly unconstitutional use of race in application screening. The administration's brief was robust and detailed. It deemed the maintenance of open access to a range of professional careers and occupations as "vital to the national interest" and in particular pertinent "in an era of intense competition in the global economy." In military service and government employment, health-care professions and scientific research, the brief championed the intrinsic value of recruiting "well-qualified graduates who are diverse and prepared to succeed in a diverse society." The educational missions of selective universities, according to the administration, benefited directly from having a rich racial, ethnic, and cultural mix of students on their campuses, aside from the issues of fairness and civic responsibility that were at the heart of the affirmative action debate.[21]

Initially decided in 2013 and upheld in a relitigated second challenge in 2016, the Supreme Court's rulings in *Fisher v. University of Texas* confirmed the legality of the use of race in college admissions to achieve diverse student classes. Writing for the majority in *Fisher II*, Justice Anthony Kennedy largely concurred with those who believed that racial and ethnic diversity on college campuses and in other areas of society was a positive good that enriched the learning and occupational environment. "Considerable deference is owed to a university in defining those intangible characteristics, like student body diversity, that are central to its identity and educational mission," Kennedy wrote, reflecting the majority opinion of his colleagues. This outcome was the one that the Obama administration had hoped for, though this decision did not preclude future challenges to affirmative action.[22]

Three months before the rendering of the 2016 ruling, President Obama had advanced his own view of what was at stake in the *Fisher* cases. "I'm a strong supporter of Affirmative Action as a way of opening more doors," he said in an interview. "And I think that there are ways of structuring Affirmative Action so that everybody's getting more of a chance." As he was increasingly likely to do toward the end of his tenure in office, Obama offered a bit of candor regarding how race and privilege had traditionally functioned in shaping college admissions. "And the truth of the matter is, there's always been Affirmative Action, it just hasn't always been minority focused," he contended. "If you make a big donation to a university, your kid is more likely to get into the university. It's not called Affirmative Action, it's called legacies." In implicating racial privilege as a historical factor in perpetuating white access to elite universities, the president also hinted at how class operated in admissions processes.[23]

Although he probably made the point inadvertently, his remarks illuminated how Harvard's system of legacy admissions benefited Black elites like him personally, replicating prerogatives among them and their descendants. That is, his father's earning of a master's degree in economics there in 1965 perhaps smoothed the way for his own admission into Harvard Law School in 1988, which in turn possibly facilitated the 2016 admission of his daughter Malia into the Ivy League institution. If any of these family ties did indeed pay dividends at the admissions office for the Obamas and other elite Black people, the legacy system was creating new genealogies of privilege and access for only a tiny subset of African Americans. Legacy admissions criteria still function less to the benefit of the small numbers of Black students at highly selective schools than to the advantage of the much larger proportion of white—and increasingly Asian American—alumni and their descendants who attend these universities and colleges.[24]

If ever there was a mismatch between a problem of colossal proportions and government's will to fix it, the crisis of US criminal justice, and especially its mass incarceration component, epitomizes such a disjuncture. Between 1980 and 2013, incarceration rates at the federal, state, and local levels increased dramatically in large part due to harsh drug laws and mandatory minimum sentencing policies. The federal rate alone grew by 518 percent during this period, with a 595 percent increase in annual costs, from $970 million to $6.7 billion. State and local expenditures on corrections rose from $17 billion to $71 billion annually, far outpacing yearly public funding for preschool through twelfth-grade education. To place these figures in global perspective, the United States accounted for 5 percent of the world's population in the early twenty-first century but detained more than a quarter of the planet's prisoners. As the number of US inmates surpassed 2 million in the 2010s, several states found their bloated criminal justice budgets to be unsustainable and searched for means to adjudicate crimes without resorting to imprisonment. In some cases, incarceration rates dropped, though recidivism remained high due to a dearth of public and private investment in the post-release housing, educational, and employment needs of ex-prisoners. Thus, while the country freed roughly 600,000 inmates per year, the vast majority were arrested again for new crimes within three to five years. Such revolving doors maintained the size and operation of the current system of mass incarceration while nurturing a private prison industry that profited from the dysfunction of US criminal justice.

The system is not only a means of punishment but also a method of social ordering, especially around categories of race and class. Although Blacks and Hispanics comprised about 30 percent of the US population by the second decade of the twenty-first century, they made up 50 percent of the country's prison population, with African Americans alone accounting for 38 percent of state and federal inmates. Moreover, while incarceration rates for Blacks declined during the first decade of the twenty-first century, they remained much higher than those for either whites or Hispanics. Along with drug laws that balloon imprisoned populations, racial bias is a significant factor in the arrest rates for Black people, the crimes that they are charged with, and the lengths of their sentences. According to various studies, African Americans are more likely to be stopped, searched, and arrested on suspicion of possessing contraband—though their likelihood of possessing such substances is approximately the same as that of whites—and they are more likely to encounter prosecutors who seek mandatory minimum sentences, thus ensuring long stays behind bars.[25]

Once a person is branded an offender and brought into the parameters of the criminal justice system, they experience a loss of status, rights, and opportunities that is nothing short of social death. Ex-convicts are denied the right to vote, to serve on juries, and to receive public assistance in many jurisdictions, and it is not uncommon for them to be subjected to housing and employment discrimination along with other forms of ostracism. A prison record can be akin to the loss of citizenship, a permanent marker of social and legal disability for Black people because of the reality that they are disproportionately accused of crimes and incarcerated. That is, their color and criminal histories are tied closely together in the American popular mind and media. Thus, mass incarceration is as much a means of stripping people of their future claims to rights and opportunities as it is a method of punishing crimes committed. The system creates a whole racialized caste of individuals who struggle to reclaim legal status and protected personhood long after they have paid the penal costs of their offenses.[26]

Late in 2012, President Obama gestured toward a more focused and systematic approach to criminal justice in the coming years. This signaling was a tacit admission that little had been accomplished in this area during his initial term in office despite the magnitude of the problem. In an interview, he expressed little sympathy for those who committed violent crimes but decried the number of people imprisoned for nonviolent offenses. "It's having a disabling effect on communities," he lamented. "You have entire populations that are rendered incapable of getting a legitimate job because of a prison record. And it gobbles up a huge amount of resources."[27]

There were a few accomplishments during Obama's first four years in office. The most noteworthy was a reduction in the sentencing disparity for those prosecuted for possession of crack cocaine compared to those caught with the powder form of the narcotic. Signed by the president in August 2010, the Fair Sentencing Act significantly reduced the crack–powder sentencing differential from 100:1 to 18:1, which ostensibly would result in shorter sentences for Black people, who were more likely to possess the solid (crack) version of the substance. However, the act was not made retroactive until June 2011, and possessors of crack cocaine remained much more exposed to substantial prison time for possessing fewer grams of the narcotic than someone possessing the powder variety of cocaine. Along with this legislation, the administration's other achievements in the realm of criminal justice consisted mainly of awarding grants to nonprofit organizations through the Reintegration of Ex-Offenders program and the Community-Centered Responsible Fatherhood Ex-Prisoner Reentry pilot project. Cumulatively, the initiatives distributed thirty-eight grants totaling $38.2 million to groups dedicated to helping former inmates acquire job training, employment, and support services after release.[28]

All together, these were small steps toward reform. Monumental systemic changes to the criminal justice system could only be accomplished through federal, state, and local legislation and remedial practices that would challenge and remake policing, the court system, penal institutions, and even notions of racial equity and justice. No president has ever possessed the kind of power to fix something as deeply entrenched in American life and as decidedly broken as the criminal justice system. Further, Obama, facing a gutted economy, multiple wars, and other crises, hardly had the resources or authority, especially after the midterm elections, to alone achieve a grand solution to the country's woes in this area. Such a public policy feat would have to wait until a more willing Congress, along with state and local governments, prioritized the issue.

In common with every other US president, Obama did have the constitutional power to grant clemency to individuals through pardons, reprieves, or commutations of sentences. This Article II power, unlike most other presidential prerogatives, is nearly absolute when it comes to the practice of extending mercy to those charged with federal crimes and is not subject to the review or consent of Congress or the courts. The only real concern affecting the exercise of clemency powers is that they are subject to moral interpretation and can be abused. On their limousine trip to the Capitol on Inauguration Day 2009, George W. Bush had advised the incoming president to "announce a pardon policy early on, and stick to it." The Republican had been lobbied for clemency by countless people during his years in the White House and was "disgusted" by what he believed to be the system's ripeness for favoritism. Late in his presidency, he had even drawn the ire of his vice president, Richard Cheney, for not pardoning a friend whose offenses were steeped in scandal and corruption.[29]

Upon entering office, Obama and his staff had good intentions regarding clemency, with a special focus on reforming the pardoning process. Notwithstanding these plans, the administration's execution was abysmal and ultimately would cost thousands of people cumulatively thousands of more years behind bars than they arguably deserved. The ideas for reform were plentiful. Some officials suggested that independent commissions replace prosecutors as the main evaluators of pardon applications. Others believed that an executive order from the president could change how the pardon process operated. In the end, nothing was done as job turnover among the early advocates of pardon reform deprived the issue of much of its urgency.

Obama, without a clear-cut policy or process and with seemingly little compelling interest in the problem, resorted to simply denying nearly all clemency requests that reached his desk. By the 2010 midterm elections, he had not pardoned a single person or commuted a single sentence. By the end of the following year, he had rejected 1,019 pardon applications, topping the number denied by Bill Clinton during his entire eight years in office. Even as his reelection campaign was in full swing in May 2012, Obama had pardoned just 22 people, with only one commutation, a record that placed him in the running for the most merciless president in more than a century.

Throughout his first term, Obama was moved neither by obscure supplicants seeking relief nor by high-profile pardon requests that would symbolically address historical injustices. Illustratively, repeated bipartisan calls from members of Congress, including Senators John McCain and Harry Reid, for a pardon of the late boxing heavyweight champion Jack Johnson went unheeded, though the pugilist had essentially been prosecuted for the "crime" of consorting with white women. Furthermore, the few that Obama chose to actually pardon were an odd bunch: their average age was 61, and they were granted clemency an average of twenty-four years after the original sentence. When the president participated in the annual ritual of pardoning Thanksgiving turkeys at elaborate White House gatherings, he, of course, exposed himself to ridicule of his clemency record. In a 2012 open letter on her cable TV show, host Melissa Harris-Perry beseeched the president "to show as much mercy to humans in his second term as he has shown to poultry in his first." The snarky request would have been funnier if the costs of executive inaction had not proven to be so high for thousands of individual Americans.[30]

Although Obama did pledge to undertake greater efforts on the criminal justice front in his second term, those languishing behind bars for nonviolent offenses and socially crippled by criminal records would have to wait another day for the possibility of mercy. The president's penchant for caution was in part motivated by political considerations, particularly ahead of the 2012 election. While he did not hold elective office in 1988, he was certainly old enough to recall how the presidential campaign of Democratic nominee Michael Dukakis was pilloried by Republican operatives. Lee Atwater, in particular, had used devastating TV ads to firmly link the candidate to the violent recidivism of Willie Horton, a Black convict who had abused the state's weekend furlough program during Dukakis's governorship. A pardon or commutation for even one felonious backslider—especially a person of color—would almost certainly come back to haunt Obama, and it was not hard to imagine how Fox News and other right-wing outlets might use such a story to inflict maximum carnage on his reelection hopes. As late as 2014, administration officials expressed fear of a Willie Horton–style episode, which may have contributed to the ongoing anemia of Obama's clemency rate. Despite his pronouncements and intentions to the contrary, the president did not positively distinguish himself on the matter of criminal justice in any meaningful way during his first four years in office.[31]

Looking back over several generations, it was hard to recall a time when voting rights were under such a coordinated nationwide attack as was the case during the early twenty-first century. The Fifteenth Amendment (1870), the Voting Rights Act of 1965, and various court decisions had extended the franchise to African Americans, providing protections against measures and machinations enacted by states to limit access to the ballot box. The right to vote had been won across decades of struggle and sacrifice and was duly recognized by Black people from the antebellum period to the digital age as a hallmark of citizenship. With party realignments during the 1960s and 1970s and increasingly close elections by the turn of the twenty-first century, US democracy entered a period of coarseness that often brought out the worst that partisan politics could offer.

Much of this political tribalism was a result of a more racialized party system, with the Republican Party becoming increasingly white and conservative and the Democrats more racially diverse and liberal. Other factors encouraging such division included partisan gerrymandering that elevated and protected extremist candidates, politicized radio and cable stations and social media bubbles that thrived on hyperpartisanship, and the deluge of special-interest money that continued to inundate the political system, ensnaring candidates from both parties. Even in this context, the relentless efforts of the Republican Party and its conservative allies to restrict the franchise during the first decades of the new millennium had no recent precedent, and popular and legal resistance to these disfranchisement schemes was reminiscent of the civil rights activism of earlier eras.

Modern voter suppression policies and practices are in the same lineage as Operation Eagle Eye, an organized attempt by the Republican Party to challenge the eligibility of voters in dozens of urban areas during the 1964 election. They are also derivations of GOP voter intimidation projects of the 1980s that were egregious enough to justify consent decrees that forbade the Republican National Committee from challenging the credentials of African American voters and that required court approval of any future efforts to ostensibly combat electoral chicanery. In the twenty-first century, the Bush administration diverted personnel and funding away from probing charges of voter suppression, instead placing a greater emphasis on searching for fraud. For many Republican strategists, the wave election that gave Democrats control of the Congress and the White House in 2008 increased the urgency for blunting the Democratic Party's electoral potency, much of which was built on a base of urban, young, minority, and college-educated voters. With the countrywide rout of Democrats during the 2010 midterms, the big prize was now the 2012 election cycle, and in particular the White House and the US Senate. Swing states—such as Florida, North Carolina, Ohio, and Pennsylvania—known for hard-fought elections with close margins were considered the frontlines of the fight over voters and voting and consequently featured prominently, though not exclusively, in GOP efforts to diminish access to the ballot for traditionally Democratic-leaning constituencies.[32]

Republican leaders in Florida and Ohio, two of the most populous and consequential swing states, strenuously tried to make voting more inconvenient in 2012. The GOP-controlled legislature of the Sunshine State cut early-voting days from fourteen to eight, aware that pre–Election Day balloting was disproportionately popular among Black voters. The lawmakers even ended voting on the Sunday before Election Day, when African American churches traditionally made "souls to the polls" trips to polling sites. NAACP president Benjamin Jealous reported that voter registration workers were threatened with imprisonment for signing up new voters. Ironically, the biggest voter fraud scheme uncovered during the cycle was led by a Republican-affiliated firm accused of attempting to enfranchise deceased people. In Ohio, the effort to reduce early-voting days was led by Secretary of State Jon Husted, whose directives caused so much confusion among voters that the US Supreme Court ordered the state to keep polls open during the days leading up to the election. In the wake of this decision, billboards turned up in minority neighborhoods in Columbus and Cleveland grimly warning "Voter Fraud Is a Felony."[33]

Although Florida and Ohio were at the center of the 2012 voter suppression campaign, they were by no means solely affected by such efforts. In Texas, officials in Harris County, a reliably Republican area, informed 9,000 people, many residing in traditionally Black neighborhoods, that their voter registrations were subject to cancellation if they could not prove that they were still alive. On the day before the election, NAACP officials reported lynched effigies of Barack Obama and other elected officeholders near a polling place in Goldsboro, North Carolina, not unlike the graphic displays that had appeared during the 2008 campaign. The US Department of Justice agreed to provide Election Day security for that site and others across the state to protect voting rights.[34]

All of these devices and ploys were effective in sending a chilling message to prospective (Democratic) voters, though it is unclear how many people were ultimately discouraged from attempting to cast a ballot. In any event, the linchpin of voter suppression efforts during the 2012 election cycle was voter ID laws, which were enacted in several states. Typically such statutes require voters to show an official identification during the registration and/or voting process, which supporters of such measures do not consider onerous. Yet beneath the requirement are several realities that disproportionately impact African Americans and other marginalized groups. First, Black, Latinx, and young people—demographics that tend to vote Democratic— have access to the requisite IDs, whether driver's license, passport, birth certificate, Social Security card, or college identification, in lower percentages than do whites as a group. Second, acquiring the necessary ID cards might compel a person to incur the additional costs of securing transportation, scheduling childcare, or paying for copies of documentation. Third, considering that the government offices that issue such IDs are usually closed after business hours and over the weekend, a person might actually have to miss a day or more of work in order to acquire the necessary identification. Opponents of such laws consider them both discriminatory and overzealous, since in-person voter fraud is exceedingly rare. Still, more than twenty states passed such measures prior to the 2012 election, though several statutes, such as those crafted in Pennsylvania and South Carolina, were blocked by courts and were not implemented in time to impact the November voting.[35]

The courts were an important, if not wholly predictable, line of defense against the voter suppression crusade that swept across the country between the 2008 and 2012 elections. The Justice Department was also an important bulwark, as were voting rights organizations and civil rights activists that mobilized to inform Americans of their rights and to get them to the ballot box. During a speech before the NAACP in July 2012, Attorney General Holder declared his intention to "not allow political pretexts to disenfranchise American citizens of their most precious right." He labeled voter ID laws "poll taxes," insofar as Blacks in places like Texas were less likely to have the required identification compared to whites, and he promised that his office would be vigilant in protecting voting rights. In September, the CBC launched the For the People initiative aimed at better publicizing voter ID laws and educating voters regarding the eligibility requirements for voting in various states. The Obama campaign, which was deeply invested in ensuring ballot access, enlisted churches, barbershops, and beauty parlors as sites for disseminating campaign literature and registration documents. While combatting voter suppression in the courts and intimidation on the ground consumed much attention, the president's reelection team also was absorbed by voter mobilization and maximizing early-voter numbers. Days before the election, the campaign reported that African American early voting was up at least 17 percent in several states, including Florida, Ohio, Colorado, Nevada, and North Carolina. These preliminary figures boded well but were in no way conclusive regarding what might happen on November 6.[36]

As had become customary for US elections, reports of irregularities of all sorts abounded on the national day of voting. One of the by-products of voter ID laws, especially those that became the subject of litigation, was that they created uncertainty and confusion among voters. Such scenarios played out in Pennsylvania and elsewhere as some poll workers reportedly demanded to see voters' identification documents, even though current state law did not require them as a prerequisite to casting a ballot. Long waits characterized polling stations in New York and New Jersey, which had been recently devastated by a hurricane that made voting for many all the more difficult. In Florida, some voters waited in line for up to three hours on Election Day, which was an improvement over the six- to seven-hour waits that were reported during early voting in Miami on the Saturday before the election. Al Gore, who had lost the 2000 presidential contest in part due to the questionable conduct of the balloting in Florida, pointed out the problematic nature of such delays in voting, relating them to the "racist Jim Crow tactics that were used in the wake of the Civil War to prevent black people from voting." When Barack Obama delivered his victory speech in Chicago later that evening, he thanked those who had waited in line for hours to cast a ballot. "We have to fix that," he pledged, adding yet another item to his long list of things to do in his second term.[37]

Along with expanding health-care access, the issues of educational equity, criminal justice reform, and voting rights protection are arguably the great civil rights causes of the twenty-first century. They are big, far-reaching matters that touch nearly every American in some form or fashion but are especially relevant to Black communities. In an interview with *Black Enterprise* magazine three months before the 2012 election, President Obama again asserted his faith in universalist solutions that would both help large swaths of the population and operate in a manner that brought additional relief to those truly disadvantaged. "I'm not the president of black America. I'm the president of the United States of America," he reiterated, further asserting, "I'll put my track record up against anybody in terms of us putting in place broad-based programs that ultimately had a huge benefit for African American businesses." The claim was not without merit; the administration had assisted Black businesses in obtaining billions of dollars in contracts and other resources. However, in the context of an economic storm that continued to disproportionately flood Black communities with high unemployment, wealth loss, home foreclosures, and other bad news, many were poised to expect much more in terms of accomplishments during Obama's next four years in office.[38]

CHAPTER 6

Dancing with the Caucus

BARACK OBAMA WAS BOTH AN INSIDER AND AN OUTSIDER IN relation to the Congressional Black Caucus. Founded in 1971, the organization began as a small conference of African American representatives in the US House, made possible by the Voting Rights Act of 1965 and the resulting increase in Black participation in elections. When he was elected to the US Senate in 2004, Obama became the only CBC member in that chamber; the other forty-two Black legislators were in the US House. At that time, the group publicly stated its principal mission as being "to close (and, ultimately, to eliminate) disparities that exist between African-Americans and white Americans in every aspect of life." It was a broad enough mandate to encompass the range of policy interests and geographical diversity reflected in the caucus, without alienating the sizable number of members, including Obama, who represented electorates with non-Black majorities.[1]

When he entered the White House, the new president had an ambivalent relationship with the CBC. Back in 2000, he had unsuccessfully tried to unseat Rep. Bobby Rush, a veteran caucus member in good standing, and years later Obama found himself in a grueling war of attrition with Hillary Clinton, who had, along with her husband, meticulously lined up much of the CBC behind her bid for the presidency. Regardless of these rough patches, Obama made durable connections with caucus members such as Jesse Jackson Jr., John Lewis, and James Clyburn, and he continued to seek their advice beyond the 2008 campaign. Most of the CBC was hopeful about his presidency, channeling the post-election euphoria that coursed through Black America. Yet others understood the ebb and flow of US politics well enough to know that overblown expectations of the new chief executive would need to be kept in check. "I think every African American supporter of Obama can safely assume that Obama will do everything within his power to create a level playing field for all Americans by ensuring that they have a government that is just and fair," Rep. Emanuel Cleaver II of Missouri opined in a December 2008 editorial. "But it is important to note that Obama will not be the nation's highest-profile civil rights leader. He will be the leader of the free world." It was a timely call for forbearance that some, including Cleaver himself, would occasionally forget in the future, and it concisely summed up the kinds of tensions that periodically defined the relationship between the caucus and the new administration.[2]

CBC–White House interactions fell into a pattern early on that gave them a certain degree of predictability for years to come. Intimately familiar with the economic pain in their districts still caught in the teeth of the Great Recession, selected members of the caucus would periodically vocalize their disappointment with the pace of improvements along with their dismay over the perceived lack of presidential attention to their constituents' plight. After some delay, Obama would meet with disgruntled members or give a speech in which he would assure them that he recognized the hard circumstances and intended to do all that he could, primarily through a universalist policy approach, to address them. The tide of complaints would then subside until a new wave of grievances swelled, crashing once again into 1600 Pennsylvania Avenue. The pattern operated like clockwork from as early as a month following the inauguration.

With a meeting set with the president for February 26, 2009, CBC chair Barbara Lee of California and others let it be known beforehand that they did not appreciate Obama contemplating the appointment of Republican senator Judd Gregg as secretary of commerce. General concerns regarding the diversity of the new administration were also aired and were perhaps agitated further by Obama's decision not to appoint "just the usual suspects" that the CBC might recommend for positions. Timing was also an issue, as some were put off by being scheduled to meet with the president only after he had held gatherings with conservative Democrats and House and Senate Republicans.[3]

The February 26 meeting was cordial and generative, with Lee referring to it as a "historical moment." The attendees discussed a spectrum of topics with the president, including the economy, health care, civil rights, and education. From a political angle, the meeting was a necessary exercise for all in attendance. The caucus members were granted the time and attention of a popular president whose party exercised unitary control of the capital, though some of them were late in endorsing him during the primaries even after he carried their districts. For the president, the optics of a decision *not* to meet with the CBC would have been atrocious, and besides, he needed them—and every last one of their votes in the House—to push through his policy agenda. The caucus included some of the most senior and powerful politicians in Congress, among them the chairs of four committees and sixteen subcommittees. Thus, the main question about the meeting had always been *when*, not *if*.[4]

Months later, things soured. During a House committee meeting on a regulatory reform bill that the president and others supported, ten CBC members boycotted the scheduled vote. They had several complaints, most focusing on a perceived lack of federal concern for the suffering of Black communities. Led by congresspeople representing a geographical mix of districts, the protest drew the president's attention and shined more light on issues of home foreclosures, tight credit, and unemployment, which for Black people was approaching 16 percent by this time (compared to the national rate of 10.2 percent). Obama, who had initially sent his chief of staff, Rahm Emanuel, to the Capitol to assess the standoff, was compelled to personally intervene in early December. He was sympathetic but obviously annoyed by the committee members' remonstration. "I think it's a mistake to start thinking in terms of particular ethnic segments of the United States," he warned, "rather than to think that we are all in this together and we are all going to get out of this together." The bill was soon voted on and advanced beyond the committee, but criticism from CBC members continued into the new year.[5]

In March, Rep. John Conyers of Michigan rebuked the White House for ignoring Black legislators, and Alcee Hastings of Florida fretted that "there's not enough attention to poor people." A CBC aide told the press that Valerie Jarrett had canceled lunch dates between the president and the caucus eight times by the anniversary of their February 2009 meeting, though Jarrett had visited CBC chair Lee's district in recent weeks for scheduled events. When the president met with Black civil rights leaders in early 2010, some CBC members reportedly griped about not being invited. In an attempt to reset the relationship, Obama gave a speech in September at a CBC awards dinner in which he invoked the activist spirit of the civil rights movement to encourage Black turnout in the upcoming midterm elections. Such late hour outreach did not salvage the strained ties or stave off the Democratic shellacking in November. The president met for a second time with CBC members in May 2011 to hear more complaints about their constituencies and to offer yet more broad-based prescriptions for economic revival. During the meeting, Rep. Emanuel Cleaver, now chair of the caucus, called for a targeted jobs program for African Americans to address their high unemployment but left with little more than an assurance that Obama's attention was focused on the issue. Now a minority caucus in a minority party, the CBC's voice carried less resonance in both the Congress and the White House, a development that few misunderstood in terms of its significance.[6]

A gifted orator, Obama could sometimes get quite a bit done in a single speech. He had propelled himself to political stardom with his rousing presentation at the DNC in 2004 and later saved his presidential bid from looming disaster with his race speech in 2008. Since that time, he had learned to better calibrate his orations to the intended audience, avoiding the default law school lecturer mode that had hampered some of his earliest campaigning. In September 2011, he again brought his talent for elocution to bear at another CBC awards gathering in an effort to elucidate his concerns and plans regarding African Americans and the larger country.

Stressing primarily economic themes, Obama laid out the ways in which he had helped Blacks and other Americans with the earned income credit and child tax credit, the ACA, enhanced Pell Grants, and Strong Cities, Strong Communities partnerships aimed at revitalizing urban areas like Detroit and Cleveland. He then shared his multi-pronged strategy to combat joblessness with the enactment of the American Jobs Act, which would put people to work rebuilding infrastructure; an extension of unemployment insurance, which would serve as a safety net for those who had lost jobs; and the creation of a summer program that would train youth in marketable skills. After roundly castigating Republican obstructionism, which had ramped up significantly since the midterms, the president called for a fairer tax code in which the wealthy would pay a more progressive rate. While he expressed compassion for the tough conditions faced by African Americans and others, he counseled against discouragement and excuses. The speech reached a sermonic climax as Obama pledged to do all that he could to turn the economic tide for drowning families and called upon those in attendance to do the same. "I expect all of you to march with me and press on!" he rallied, conjuring civil rights–era imagery as the crowd roared. "Take off your bedroom slippers, put on your marchin' shoes! Shake it off! Stop complainin', stop grumblin', stop cryin'! We are gonna press on! We've got work to do, CBC!"[7]

As an indication of the stakes attached to the speech, reviews and reactions emanated immediately from various quarters and continued to do so for weeks. To CBC chair Cleaver, the speech had not wholly allayed a number of his concerns about the economic situation nor had the president's stated strategy for dealing with it. "If

Bill Clinton had been in the White House and had failed to address this problem [of Black unemployment and economic despair]," he told one reporter, "we probably would be marching on the White House." Cleaver was particularly irritated by budgetary concessions that Obama had made to Republicans over the summer in order to keep the government from defaulting on its debts. However, Cleaver remained sensitive to the perceived need of Democrats, and especially the CBC, to not "do anything that would empower the people who hate the president." Rep. James Clyburn's response to the speech contextualized dissenting views among African Americans in regard to the president's handling of the economy, noting that Black people are not "monolithic" and that Obama had not received 100 percent of their vote during the 2008 election. Congresswoman Karen Bass of California made a similar observation, arguing that any disagreement with the president over policy did not equate to a general lack of support for his administration.[8]

Appraisals of the speech by other CBC members were less charitable. Rep. Maxine Waters of California was a persistent critic of the president's approach to the economy. Serving a South Los Angeles district with a large population of African Americans and Hispanics, she regularly contended that the federal government had not done enough to help communities disproportionately affected by the recession. Seasoned and plainspoken, she was known for fighting battles big and small, sometimes employing language that drew instant attention. In the span of a week in August, she had roiled the right with her declaration that "the Tea Party can go straight to hell" and discomforted some on the left with her admission that she was "getting tired" of defending President Obama's job performance. Following the September 24 CBC event, Waters expressed continuing support for the president and asserted that her intention had always been to simply heighten Obama's awareness of distressed African American communities. She denied previously complaining about anything—or even owning bedroom slippers. However, she did find some of the president's phraseology to be "curious," pointing out that he was not known for telling Hispanics, LGBTQ activists, or supporters of Israel to "stop complaining" when they pushed their policy agendas.[9]

Prior to the CBC speech, Waters had no relationship with the White House, though there were a few small signs of rapprochement by 2011. Illustratively, Obama invited her to the October 16 dedication ceremony for the new Martin Luther King Jr. monument in Washington, DC, and Waters defended his jobs plan during a cable TV appearance. A savvy politician, she was aware that her criticism of Obama had, in her words, "created a lot of concern" among Black people who thought that her vocal faultfinding might impact his reelection chances. Based on the available contemporary evidence and hindsight, these fears were largely unwarranted. Nonetheless, there were some indications that Waters could possibly do damage to her own electoral viability by attacking the president too stridently. Throughout the remainder of his first term, polls showed the president's job approval rating among African Americans to be well above 80 percent, making Black critics like Waters outliers. Closer to home, Obama had topped her relatively high 69 percent vote in her own congressional district in 2008 and would do even better in 2012. Thus, the possibility of a political backlash was not lost on Waters, nor was it lost on African Americans elsewhere. When asked about the president's speech at the MLK dedication event, one Black woman in attendance instead offered her unsolicited opinion about the California congresswoman. "We as African Americans have to be smarter," Ruby Hicks of Racine, Wisconsin, told the inquiring reporter. "And Maxine Waters needs to shut up." The admonition was a reminder that most of the president's critics were decidedly less popular than he was among African Americans and that there were those who still earnestly defended him as both a leader and a symbol of a certain kind of racial progress, despite the faltering economy.[10]

Aside from animating members of the CBC, the September 24 speech elicited reactions beyond the Capitol Building. L. Douglas Wilder, a former Virginia governor and Democratic presidential candidate, affirmed his support for Obama in a published editorial but thought that his advice to the caucus—and, by extension, its constituents—was harsh and discouraging. Rev. Al Sharpton believed that many of the negative commentaries related to the CBC speech had taken Obama's words out of context and ignored the fact that most of the crowd of 2,000 had cheered the president's call to action. Sharpton went further and wrote off much of the hand-wringing as hypocrisy and sour grapes. "[President Bill Clinton] did things that I felt was detrimental to our community," the clergyman divulged on his cable TV talk show, pointing his finger for emphasis. "Now you go from who some of you call a black president to a real black president and you talk about 'unleash us' and 'let me at 'em' and all that," he continued, referencing comments that Rep. Maxine Waters had made at a Detroit rally in August. "And when he responds, you act like he hurt your feelings or you don't know who he's talking to."[11] Obama responded to the reactions to his speech during an interview with BET a few days later. He underscored his efforts to improve the conditions of the American people broadly and dismissed his detractors as comprising only a "handful of African-American leaders." To his CBC doubters in particular, he retorted, "They were critical when I was running for president," a not so subtle reminder that many caucus members had years earlier supported the Clintons during the 2008 presidential race.[12]

Much of the CBC criticism of Obama for not doing more to directly assist troubled African American communities reflected genuine concern for constituents. Nevertheless, the more vehement assessments of the president's performance did have electoral consequences for selected caucus members. Several representatives, including John Conyers and Laura Richardson of California, drew primary challengers who claimed to be motivated by the incumbents' critiques of the president. In 2011, Conyers, the longest-serving Black member of the US House, had called for a protest march on the White House in response to Obama's budget negotiations with Republicans. He also charged the president with supporting a weakened health-care bill and welcoming advice from "clowns," a remark that reportedly triggered a phone call from the chief executive. Despite these barbs, the two ultimately reconciled, and Obama endorsed a grateful Conyers for a twenty-fifth term.[13]

Unlike Conyers, who went on to win reelection in November 2012, Rep. Richardson was not as fortunate. A three-term incumbent representing a heavily minority district that stretched across southwestern Los Angeles County, the congresswoman was one of the most vociferous critics of the Obama administration. During August 2011, she called the president's broad-based approach to policy a "bunch of bull" at a CBC event in Miami and told a news organization that the president was reluctant to be too closely associated with the African American community. In truth, her rhetoric was no more caustic than things that had been said by Maxine Waters or John Conyers. The big difference was that she did not have the long congressional records of either of them and subsequently ended up attracting competitive opponents. On the eve of an all-party primary, Richardson was further hampered by an ethics investigation that found her guilty of violating federal law and House rules. Her second-place finish in the primary and her general election defeat in November were less of a surprise than the size of her loss. Janice Hahn, a white Democrat who ran well among the Black and Latinx neighborhoods of the district, won the seat by a twenty-point margin.[14]

If the electoral fates of Conyers and Richardson were both lessons in the power of seniority and the fragility of reputations, the odd case of Congressman Charlie Rangel symbolized a confluence of these factors and more. Elected to the US House in 1970, the New York representative had been in the CBC from the beginning, and by 2010 he had served twenty consecutive terms. He had wielded real power in the chamber, including a stint as the chair of the powerful Committee on Ways and Means between 2007 and 2010. Yet by the time of the Republican takeover of the House during the midterms, the 80-year-old congressman faced a dire situation among both his colleagues in Washington and his constituents in Upper Manhattan and the Bronx. An ethics probe found that he had violated eleven

House rules ranging from tax evasion and failing to disclose a half million dollars in assets to inappropriately using his chairmanship to squeeze money out of corporations with business before his committee. In December 2010, he endured the humiliation of being formally censured by his House colleagues in a decisive bipartisan rebuke. Defiant, Rangel decided to run for another term in 2012, though his district was being redrawn in a way that pushed the number of Latinx voters above the number of African American constituents. Once a strong primary challenger appeared in the person of state senator Adriano Espaillat, the longtime congressman's career seemed to be at an ignoble end.[15]

Given that the seat was in a safe Democratic district, President Obama publicly recommended that Rangel "end his career with dignity" by stepping aside. The veteran congressman would have no part of such an exit strategy and instead chastened the president for even making the suggestion. Rangel's survival blueprint was simple and a bit ironic. He would fully embrace Barack Obama and hope that he could ride the president's coattails to victory in 2012. Toward this end, he littered his district with flyers depicting him shaking hands with Obama and emphasizing his role in facilitating the passage of the health-care law. Moreover, his campaign sent out mailings to constituents that proclaimed "Rangel's got Obama's back!" During interviews, the congressman lavished praise on the president, who enjoyed strong support in the New York district. "Quite frankly, in all of my years I've never known a president whose political and legislative agenda is more in line with mine," he told an interviewer days before the June 26 primary. The vote was close. Out of the roughly 38,000 ballots cast, Rangel won by fewer than 1,000, with Espaillat only conceding nearly two weeks later. Rangel went on to win reelection in a landslide and stayed in Congress until 2017, leaving public service less than three weeks ahead of Obama.[16]

While the bumpy finale of Rangel's long tenure in government was a survivalist tale with tragicomic elements, the crumbling of the once-promising career of Jessie Jackson Jr. was a catastrophe of stunning proportions. An erstwhile ally of President Obama, the Illinois congressman became known for occasional critiques of the administration as the recession ravaged his district, but he was never given to some of the more acerbic complaints that other CBC members leveled. Still, his differences with the White House over policy matters attracted a 2012 primary challenge from former representative Debbie Halvorson, who believed that Jackson's constituents "really should have a person who stands with this president, who in this district is loved and revered." As it turned out, neither Obama nor Halvorson were the congressman's main concerns by Election Day. Instead, he was preoccupied with the ramifications of a series of decisions that he had made that threatened his career, family, and even his freedom. At the root of the unfolding calamity were the commonplace afflictions of the ruling class, including hubris, greed, and corruption. But in this particular instance, the spiral of misfortune reverberated across the political landscape with tremors that could only have been produced by the public downfall of one of Black America's most prominent dynastic brands.[17]

Following Barack Obama's election, Jackson had met with Gov. Rod Blagojevich in early December 2008. The next morning, the Illinois chief executive was arrested at his North Side home for what a federal prosecutor called a "political corruption crime spree" that involved, among other things, an effort by Blagojevich to sell the newly vacated US Senate seat of the president-elect. Jackson fell under immediate suspicion as a party to the scheme, and a US House ethics investigation was launched to probe into the matter. After being promptly impeached and removed from office only days following Obama's inauguration, the former governor was charged with seventeen counts of corruption in 2011 and sentenced to fourteen years in federal prison. During the trial, Jackson served as a witness for the defense, which was of little benefit to either man. By the end of the year, the vise was tightening on the Illinois congressman and others. A report issued by the Office of Congressional Ethics in December found that Jackson had inappropriately bartered campaign contributions for an appointment as Obama's senatorial successor. The House document named Raghuveer Nayak as the damning link between Blagojevich and Jackson, stating that the Chicago business-man and campaign fundraiser had been ordered by Jackson to help finance the governor's reelection bid in exchange for the Senate seat. For his part, Jackson denied the accusations, declaring that he had made every effort "to protect the integrity of my office and the people who elected me to serve them."[18]

Things got progressively worse over the course of the election year. In June, Nayak was charged with seventeen counts of fraud. Around that time, Jackson reportedly collapsed at his home and then fell completely out of public view for several weeks, having first been admitted into the Sierra Tucson treatment center in Arizona and then seeking therapy from the Mayo Clinic in Rochester, Minnesota, for bipolar II disorder. By August, he was back at his Washington, DC, residence. Days before the election, Jackson learned that the FBI and federal prosecutors were opening a new investigation into possible financial crimes, including whether he had misused congressional funds. His attorneys were successful in sparing the representative a humiliating public arrest before the November balloting, a decision that may have impacted the outcome. Having defeated Halvorson in the Democratic primary, Jackson won his reelection bid with 63 percent of the vote. The electoral vindication was primarily symbolic and could not protect the triumphant incumbent from what was to come. Almost as quickly as he had savored victory from his room at the Mayo Clinic, he slumped in defeat, tendering his letter of resignation to House speaker Boehner on November 21.

The unraveling continued into the new year. Some of the details of Jackson's federal offenses and ethical lapses leaked into public view, and tales of the extravagant spending of campaign funds on furs, vacation getaways, a Rolex watch, and a Michael Jackson hat made newspaper headlines. These disclosures were aside from reports that some of the largesse had gone to a female acquaintance in the DC area, or the fact that the federal probe had also netted Jackson's wife,

Sandi, a Chicago alderman. The couple's convictions on separately charged financial crimes then began a new chapter of the tragedy. The congressman was allowed to serve his thirty-month sentence while his wife cared for their two children. In turn, she served a one-year sentence. No charges were ever filed against Jackson in the Senate seat scandal, and the House investigation was shelved following his resignation and federal conviction.

The fall was as precipitous and dizzying as it appeared. Jackson, from the safe perch of incumbency in a reliably Democratic district, had risked it all for a Senate seat that would have had to be defended again in just two years. Blagojevich's price was steep, and the scheme could hardly have been kept secret for long, given the governor's auction plan for selecting Obama's Senate successor. Although Jackson was never charged with a crime in this instance, his association with Blagojevich, Nayak, and perhaps other unsavory characters could only have given added incentive for House investigators and federal prosecutors to look deeper into his political and financial affairs.

Beyond the damage to himself and his household, Jesse Jackson Jr. had diminished his namesake and his legacy, though both men were ultimately responsible for their own actions and lives. Unlike Barack Obama Jr., who existed in the eponymous shadow of a father he could not know and from whose intemperate legacy the son had fled once he entered US political life, Jackson Jr. was a political incarnation of his father, fashioned and willed into being through his parent's storied civil rights–era narrative and historic runs for the presidency. At only 47 when he resigned from Congress, he had certainly heard whispers encouraging him to run for the US Senate, or for mayor of Chicago, or even for something higher—after all Obama was exactly 47 when he took up residence in the White House. Alas, there would be no political redemption or a second act for Jackson. Following prison, he went back to private life, moving to a South Shore neighborhood and parting ways with Sandi after twenty-seven years of marriage. His Second District seat was now safely in the hands of another Democratic incumbent.[19]

In collaboration, division, triumph, and despair, President Obama and the CBC coexisted. They danced with and maneuvered around each other, eyeing their true partners, their constituents, all the while. It was indeed true that Obama seemed reluctant to get too close, lest he be accused by opponents of pursuing a Black agenda or risk guilt by association with the more militant or scandal-prone of the caucus's membership. Many of the representatives, too, calibrated their movements for maximum political advantage, lovingly embracing the White House Rangel-style around election time or theatrically brushing it off with Waters-like attitude to appease their base in times of trouble. On the big bills, such as the ACA, the stimulus package, and banking reform, the CBC was a reliable ally of the administration, even if members quibbled over its handling of matters like the Parent PLUS program. Furthermore, there were instances when legislators came to the president's aid in ways that gave their Blackness added authority and power, such as when André Carson of Indiana called out Tea Party bigotry or when Rep. Clyburn challenged racist lies about Obama's place of birth. When he so desired or felt enough pressure, the president could be indulgent of the group and did at time include their ideas—or some version of them—in proposed legislation.

Nonetheless, given the new balance of power after the loss of the House to the Republicans during the 2010 midterms, the caucus did not factor into Obama's political calculus as much as did House speaker Boehner or Senate minority leader Mitch McConnell, who had acquired quite a reputation for abusing the filibuster in order to stymie nearly every bill that the White House supported. The CBC would pick up three new members following the 2012 election, which was a sign of its ongoing political relevance. Still, its effectiveness was confined to one chamber of Congress and further limited by its minority party status.[20]

Beyond the CBC, the Obama era was overall a lively time for African Americans seeking federal and statewide office. Seventy-two Black candidates ran for the US House in 2012, a record that was broken by the no fewer than eighty-three Black people who sought congressional seats two years later. Inspired in part by the high Black turnout during the 2012 presidential cycle, more than two dozen African Americans ran in statewide elections in 2014 for the offices of US senator, governor, and lieutenant governor. As had historically been the case, few Black candidates, whether Democrat or Republican, won these races, which required a broad appeal to a more diverse—and often predominantly white—electorate and exponentially more funding than most municipal and district contests needed. Despite these outcomes, more Black people than ever before were willing to pursue higher office, though opportunities in the private sector diverted many of the most talented individuals away from public service. The electoral successes of Barack Obama and Black representatives in Congress, as well as Black officials in other levels of government, no doubt encouraged such aspirations—even as the president and his CBC supporters and critics regularly danced to political themes that appealed to very different audiences.[21]

CHAPTER 7

Man on a Tightrope

THURSDAY, JULY 16, 2009, WAS A LONG DAY FOR HARVARD PRO-
fessor Henry Louis Gates Jr. An accomplished scholar of African
American studies and a well-known public intellectual, he had arrived
at his home in Cambridge, Massachusetts, around noon and discovered that the front door was jammed. It was a minor and perhaps expected trifle; the residence had been broken into recently, which had
apparently misaligned the doorframe. The driver who had delivered
the professor from the airport—he had just returned from a trip to
China—offered to help. The door eventually opened, and Gates entered. However, within minutes a police cruiser arrived, and a Cambridge officer approached the house. The details of what happened
next vary by account, but Gates and the policeman exchanged words
before the former was arrested for disorderly conduct. The professor's
display of his Harvard identification and his physical disability did
not spare him the indignity of being hauled away in handcuffs. "This
is what happens to black men in America," Gates reportedly declared
to onlookers, as Sergeant James Crowley and other officers led him
toward a waiting car. News of the arrest spread quickly, along with an
image of the 58-year-old academician shackled in front of his home.

On first learning of the event, many were bewildered. There were several questions that seemed to beg for answers. How does a known Harvard professor get arrested in broad daylight after shouldering his way into his own house? Why was the short, bespectacled Gates perceived as enough of a threat to warrant a perp walk? And how much did it matter that the white woman who had initially called the police described Gates and the driver as "two black males with backpacks on the porch . . . trying to force entry" into the home? Over the next several days, some further details became public, though several questions remained unanswered. Early on, Gates, incensed and mortified, had contemplated a lawsuit but dismissed the idea once the disorderly conduct charge against him was dropped. On July 21, the city of Cambridge and the Harvard professor, in an effort to put the whole affair to rest, issued a joint statement calling the circumstances surrounding the arrest "regrettable and unfortunate." Despite this mutual gesture, the denouement of this drama turned out not to be so simple. When President Barack Obama spoke publicly about the affair during a July 22 press event, the story sprouted wings.[1]

The president and the professor were not close acquaintances. They had met when Obama was a candidate for the US Senate, a time when he was crossing paths with many luminaries and people of influence. Like others, the president was confounded and then angered by Gates's treatment by law enforcement officers. In his first public statement about the event, he enumerated his reaction, stating, "not having been there and not seeing all the facts, [including] what role race played in that, . . . I think that it's fair to say, number one, any of us would be pretty angry; number two, that the Cambridge police acted stupidly in arresting somebody when there was already proof that they were in their own home." Making a larger point about racial profiling, he continued, "Number three, what I think we know separate and apart from this incident is that there's a long history in this country of African-Americans and Latinos being stopped by law enforcement disproportionately. This is just a fact." To his surprise, the president's remarks triggered an avalanche of reactions, many of which were much more visceral than his own response to the arrest.[2]

Conservative media and other opponents of the White House portrayed the president's interpretation of the Cambridge affair as motivated by ideological impulses and a lack of regard for the police. Law enforcement groups, including the 15,000-member International Brotherhood of Police Officers, denounced his statement as offensive, and Steve Killion, president of the Cambridge Police Patrol Officers Association, said that he was "disgraced that he [Obama] is our commander-in-chief." The media kept the story boiling for several more days, distracting the administration from its work on the health-care bill and other matters. In an effort to extinguish the all-consuming coverage, Obama invited both Professor Gates and Officer Crowley to the White House. As with many other situations inflamed by racial antagonism, the gesture of conciliation carried costs and further highlighted divisions. Valerie Jarrett reported receiving "immediate blowback" from Black people who related traumatic stories of police harassment and who thought that the president should stick with his original blunt reaction to the Gates arrest. Writer and educator Julianne Malveaux counseled the president to search closer to home for victims of police misconduct to invite to his residence, such as "a brother who lives a stone's throw from the White House and just got pulled over in his new car because race still matters way too much in matters of so-called law enforcement." Tightly managed with limited press access, the White House meeting with Gates and Crowley took place on July 30. As one might expect, it was as cordially awkward as a Black president, a white vice president, a Black professor, and a white policeman drinking alcohol together could be.[3]

Obama made an obligatory statement of optimism following the "beer summit": "I have always believed that what brings us together is stronger than what pulls us apart." In the days to come, polls and other indicators told a different story, one to which he and his staff paid close attention. Some whites had been put off by the president's comments on the Gates arrest, particularly his reference to the police having acted "stupidly." According to a Pew Research Center survey, Obama's job approval rating among white respondents slipped seven points in just the week of the Cambridge incident, falling from 53 percent to 46 percent. Gallup polling showed a similar decline, from 51 percent to 46 percent, and the president's rating among whites never again reached 50 percent for the rest of his time in office.[4]

Obama would later deny that the Gates affair influenced him to stay clear of racial matters, instead characterizing the incident as an unnecessary diversion from more pressing policy issues. However, in a moment of candor, he attributed real weight to the lessons of the experience. "To see the cultural reaction [to my initial remarks], and in retrospect to see how my poll numbers with white voters dropped really significantly off this tempest in a teapot, that was instructive," he acknowledged in a 2016 interview. His close advisor Jarrett was even more to the point. "The seemingly innocuous statement taught us how quickly we could lose the narrative if we said *anything* off message," she later wrote of the president's reaction to the Cambridge incident. "And also it taught us that on the third rail of race, every word mattered." Some later claimed, citing evidence beyond just the president's awareness of poll numbers, that the blowup in the wake of his remarks about the Cambridge police curtailed the administration's willingness to speak frankly about race, racism, or any related matters for fear of offending white sensibilities and harming the president's legislative agenda and reelection chances. Another explosive event would soon test this thesis and lend it greater gravity.[5]

Almost a year to the day that Professor Gates was arrested in front of his home in Massachusetts, Shirley Sherrod, the Georgia director of rural development for the US Department of Agriculture (USDA), was informed by a deputy undersecretary that the White House wanted her to resign. A March 2010 video clip of Sherrod had surfaced in which she was shown allegedly telling an audience at an NAACP event that she had discriminated against a white farmer twenty-four years earlier by not making a good-faith effort to help him retain his land. First posted online by right-wing provocateur Andrew Breitbart, the footage made the rounds on conservative media and created such a stir that even the NAACP applauded Sherrod's firing on July 20. The 62-year-old Georgia director had tried to save her job with an explanation of the video, but the Agriculture Department was not interested. "There is zero tolerance for discrimination at USDA," Secretary Tom Vilsack declared in a statement. "We have a duty to ensure that when we provide services to the American people we do so in an equitable manner."[6]

And then the whole story detonated. Breitbart had edited the video of Sherrod to take her comments out of context. Instead of attempting to harm the white farmer with halfhearted assistance, Sherrod had actually tried her best to aid him and his family, surmounting her own racial assumptions and setting aside bitterness about the murder of her father at the hands of a white planter in 1965. It was the kind of racial redemption story that could have been prominently featured on the president's reelection campaign website but for the deceitful manipulation of Breitbart and others. Benjamin Jealous of the NAACP was among the first to backpedal, claiming that his group had been "snookered" by the doctored video and calling for Sherrod's reinstatement at the USDA. Rep. James Clyburn was livid about the termination, charging that not "a single black person was consulted before Shirley Sherrod was fired." Roger Spooner, the white farmer in question, even came forward to tell how the Black agricultural official had relentlessly tried to save his land from government auction decades earlier. "She [Sherrod] had a right to be mad at every white farmer after her daddy got killed," the 87-year-old Spooner maintained, adding to the sense that the firing had amounted to a grave injustice.[7]

The official story from the administration was that Vilsack had made the decision to request Sherrod's resignation, and thus he was dispatched to apologize to the fired official and offer her a new position with the agency. Sherrod continued to assume that the president had something to do with her release, though Obama denied such a role. After describing Vilsack as having "jumped the gun" in dismissing Sherrod, the president conceded that the course of events had been shaped by "this media culture where something goes up on YouTube or a blog and everybody scrambles." He could have easily added that the scrambling was always made more frantic and error-prone when animated by the sizzling heat of race.[8]

To clear the air, Obama privately phoned Sherrod days later after she was offered the deputy directorship of the Office of Advocacy and Outreach, a position that he and Vilsack had created and that she hesitated to accept, trusting neither the ambiguous job title nor those who were offering it. Sherrod recalled the president as being sympathetic to the grief that she had experienced around the firing, though not expressly apologetic. He directed her to his first book, *Dreams from My Father*, as proof that he understood how race was operating in the Breitbart-USDA controversy. While she had read the president's memoir, Sherrod was not impressed by his line of reasoning. "With all due respect, you don't understand issues the way I do," she retorted plainly. "We haven't lived the same kind of life. I'm not saying you would have had to live as a black person in the rural South to understand it, I'm just saying we are coming from different places." Sherrod went on to invite Obama and his wife, Michelle, to southern Georgia. The president committed to a future visit, and the two concluded their phone discussion.[9]

Years later, Sherrod was still clearly disturbed by the events of July 2010, especially the administration's initial response to the Breitbart smear. In her 2012 book, *The Courage to Hope: How I Stood Up to the Politics of Fear*, she characterized Obama, "our supposedly race-transcendent president," as "*terrified* of race" to the point that he had shrunk from the right-wing attack by Breitbart and others and attempted to hastily short-circuit it by firing her. Going into the 2012 election, Sherrod still intended to vote for Obama, and she did accept a job at the USDA as a contract employee in charge of a southwestern Georgia initiative to improve the agency's relations with Black farmers and ranchers. Still, her book left readers with a lingering question that exuded an aroma of disappointment and even mockery. "Where was my *audacious* president?" she asked, noting that Obama had still not made his way to Georgia.[10]

The Gates and Sherrod incidents were racial tightropes pulled taut and high above the US political landscape, each with its own set of perils swirling underneath. As president, Barack Obama was the premier tightrope walker, the funambulist in chief who, to his consternation more often than his choosing, was tasked with crossing the treacherous heights. If he lost his balance amid countervailing political winds and divergent constituent agendas, ideally the opposing forces eventually steadied him in the middle, allowing for further slow, deliberate steps toward the ledge at the end of the tether. But as with all such plans, missteps were both easy to make and inevitable in the scheme of things, so that the real question was not whether equilibrium would occasionally be lost but whether a safety net existed in the misty depths below to break otherwise fatal falls. Such harrowing concerns are the province of all officials with diverse, conflicted electorates and reelection math to consider. They are doubly the preoccupation of the centrists and the pragmatists, those species of politician who barter policies and promises at the crossroads, hoping never to have to sacrifice too much principle. Beyond his own instincts to lean toward the middle ground (or just left of it), Obama's tightropes were different; the ones that bridged issues connected to race were often greased with slick, flammable oils needing only a spark to ignite or a strong gust to upset his footing. Friend and foe alike understood the dangers below but often squinted to comprehend the view from above, where only the tightrope walker could see the true horizon that merged the heavens with the abyss. Gradual and shaky, crossing one foot in front of the other, the walk proceeded, rarely reaching a fixed destination as opposed to measuring progress by distance traveled or yet to be traversed.

Around the time that the Obama administration was straining to quench the flames of the Shirley Sherrod controversy, other debates about its handling of racial matters flared beyond Washington, DC. Most of the exchanges were not new but instead carry-overs from as far back as the 2008 primaries when various people attempted to take the measure of the junior senator from Illinois. However, the inept handling of the Sherrod episode, along with its embedded commentaries about the racial climate of the Obama years, seemed to provoke more intense public conversations about the president's role in the nation's ongoing struggles with race. A range of advice and assessments came from places high and low, with a small cohort of prominently placed gadflies and pundits wielding influence far out of proportion to their numbers. Many of the voices were academic, clerical, and governmental, with the latter not limited to the CBC. Others represented the tongues of the ancestors, the Moses generation, that had watched with both excitement and dismay as the Joshuas took up the mantle of leadership. At times, the brilliance, ferocity, and pettiness of some commentators were meant for others, though Barack Obama might be invoked as a foil to cover tracks and true intentions. In other instances, the president himself was the object of observers' fascination and censure, especially on occasions when he seemed to be paying them no heed.

Throughout the eight years of Obama's presidency, there were scholars who expressed sympathy for his high-wire performances, even while they almost invariably asked for better, quicker, and more death-defying acts. Around the time USDA secretary Vilsack was trying to rehire Shirley Sherrod in July 2010, Georgetown University professor Michael Eric Dyson lamented that Obama's presence was not more explicitly felt in societal discussions of race. "You've got one of the great intellects on race in the presidency, and yet he is hamstrung, there's a gag order," he told the *New York Times* in an interview. Dyson believed that a fear of alienating white America stayed Obama's hand, and he considered such perceived reticence a "legitimate concern." The compromise bothered him, since he felt that the country could benefit from the president's leadership on matters of race.[11]

Citing somewhat different reasons, Professor Fredrick Harris of Columbia University also expressed disappointment with elements of the Obama presidency. His publications generally argued that the powerful symbolism of a Black chief executive—and the hesitancy of many African Americans to criticize him—reduced any possibility of holding Obama accountable to Black communities suffering disproportionately during the economic crisis. While he did give the president credit for the ACA, the stimulus package, and other achievements, Harris regretted that the putative price of having an African American in the White House was that Black people had to endure a "racially defused electoral and governing strategy" that repudiated policies that specifically targeted the unique plight of Obama's most loyal constituency. In Harris's view, the historic presidency represented less a transformative culmination of African American political power than a tragic diminution of influence. That is, the hazy euphoria that shrouded Obama as a "Black first," along with all of the pride and deference that status conferred, only obscured the high cost of settling for racial symbolism over transactional models of electoral politics, which held politicians responsible for addressing the interests and agendas of their voters.[12]

In contrast to Dyson and Harris, Harvard law professor Randall Kennedy counseled a more "carefully scripted" approach to presidential involvement in racialized situations and discourses. Kennedy had met the president years earlier when Obama was a student at Harvard and could still recall his "very fine reputation" among his peers and law school faculty, though Kennedy never taught, advised, or mentored Obama. Following the 2008 election, the professor did find Obama to be occasionally "hyper-cautious" on matters of race and believed that his administration, and in particular the Justice Department, missed several opportunities to better inform the public of the critical need for criminal justice reform. Aside from these perceived missteps, Kennedy generally saw little to be gained from Obama offering "the country an ongoing and contentious seminar on race," which was "more likely to exacerbate anxiety than to nourish understanding." Further, he singled out those on what he called the "black left" who "seem to want Obama not only to agree with them but to be like them." Kennedy criticized such urges as narcissistic and suggestive of a misunderstanding of how politicians have to negotiate various constituencies and interests in order to win elections. "They are unused to the politics of governance," he wrote in a 2011 book on the Obama presidency, "and appear at times to prefer a merely theoretical progressivism that is marginal and thus insulated from the contamination of strategy and compromise." The professor characterized such thinking as outside the mainstream of African American sentiment about Obama and his presidency. Most Black people, according to his observations, were "remarkably savvy, patient, and loyal" regarding the administration, and they understood the political realities that it faced as it attempted to pursue a progressive agenda.[13]

Of all of Obama's critics in academia—and most everywhere else—Professor Cornel West was easily the most persistent and abrasive. As mentioned earlier, West was initially supportive of Obama during the 2008 primaries but over time came to believe that the president's domestic agenda was not sufficiently aimed at alleviating poverty and that his foreign policies were too imperialist and destructive. His criticisms were sweeping and needling, and little that Obama did went unnoticed or unchallenged, sometimes in off-color language that overshadowed the substance of West's critiques. In July 2010, the professor questioned the president's credentials as a progressive and warned that "Black folk can't be blindsided by Obama's pigmentation and historical symbolism." He expressed disappointment that the commander in chief was not more like Martin Luther King Jr., apparently assuming that civil disobedience and prophetic theology were appropriate models of modern statecraft and national defense. By the following year, West's commentaries had become more acidic, such as when he labeled Obama a "black mascot of Wall Street oligarchs and a black puppet of corporate plutocrats." Even when West was given to cogent analyses of institutional racism, class inequality, or the power of corporations in US politics, rhetorical excess often got the better of him, at least when it came to outlining what he considered to be the president's many flaws and shortcomings.[14]

When disagreement over policy did not seem a large enough battlefield on which to wage a fight, West was not above applying racial litmus tests to opponents, measuring their progressiveness, Blackness, and/or sincerity against his own or some idealized paradigm. "I think my dear brother Barack Obama has a certain fear of free black men," he opined during a 2011 interview. "All he has known culturally is white. . . . When he meets an independent black brother, it is frightening. And that's true for a white brother." If the president was listening, it must have been déjà vu, for West's comments were out of an old "blacker-than-thou" playbook used previously against him by Bobby Rush, Rickey Hendon, Jesse Jackson Sr., Alan Keyes, and so many others. On a few occasions, West did admit that some of his disdain for the president was indeed personal. Years after the fact, he still fumed about Obama not returning his calls during the presidential campaign and not providing tickets for his relatives to attend the inauguration. These alleged offenses were aside from Obama not being sufficiently thankful to the professor for the many—West put the number at sixty-five—events that he had sponsored on behalf of the Illinois senator's bid for the White House. "What it said to me on a personal level," West told an interviewer, "was that brother Barack Obama had no sense of gratitude, no sense of loyalty, no sense of courtesy, sense of decency, just to say thank you." West routinely mixed the political, the intellectual, and the personal when it came to condemning the president and others over some perceived outrage or slight.[15]

Obama was irritated enough by some of West's diatribes to confront him in person. Following a Washington speech on education before a largely Urban League audience in July 2010, the president immediately approached the professor and, according to the latter, upbraided him. "I'll be damned, telling me I'm not progressive enough," Obama jabbed. "Is that the best you can do? Who do you think you are?" Caught off guard by the president's frankness, West smiled and shook his hand, though he later recalled being "cool on the outside but burning inside." Such a direct facing-down of a critic was unusual for Obama, which partly explains West's shock at being, as he put it, "cussed out" by the president. The chief executive usually left such work to supporters and surrogates, a number of whom were quite willing and able to take on detractors such as West, even on their own combative terms.[16]

Influenced by these rhetorical confrontations and the recent Shirley Sherrod incident, Obama invited a number of prominent African Americans to the White House. The group included Al Sharpton, Michael Eric Dyson, radio host Tom Joyner, and other members of the Black commentariat, most of whom supported the president and at least parts of his policy agenda. Obama reportedly told the attendees that while he respected honest disagreements over his approach to policy, he was much less willing to overlook criticism that questioned his Blackness or second-guessed his commitment to Black communities. He reiterated the logic behind his broad-based approach to legislative solutions, arguing that such a methodology actually helped the most vulnerable and needy. "If I go out there saying 'black, black,' do you think that will help black people?" he queried, referencing the resistance that proposals targeted explicitly toward Black people would face in Congress. On the other hand, boosting Pell Grants or pushing for health-care expansion, he argued, would disproportionately help African Americans, though neither initiative was expressly race-specific.[17]

Such periodic palavers with influential African Americans were helpful to Obama in several ways. They kept him abreast of internal developments among certain quarters of Black communities and connected him with other Black professionals who, as a demographic, were not plentiful in the West Wing. The meetings were also good optics, countering claims from disgruntled CBC members and others that the president paid no attention to African American concerns. Moreover, such contacts allowed Obama to cultivate prominent allies who could take on critics in ways that might be unseemly for a sitting president to contemplate. Certain Black leaders, such as Sharpton, Benjamin Jealous, and Marc Morial of the National Urban League, even sought to protect Obama from the scandalmongering of some media outlets by collectively resolving not to openly bicker with the president or each other. In return, their public civility and private counsel earned them regular access to the Oval Office. While the ongoing tussle with Black naysayers was privately considered, according to one Obama confidant, nonsense (or "bull—") and the president still publicly wrote them off as merely a "handful" of discontents, the need to control media narratives was as important in this instance as in any other.[18]

And fight over narrative control they did. When West and his close associate Tavis Smiley embarked on a fifteen-week Poverty Tour in 2011 to ostensibly draw Obama's attention to destitute Americans, several supporters of the president took them to task. "The poor did horribly under every president before Obama, and yet there wasn't this level of outcry toward them by these men," Michael Eric Dyson said. "That makes folks skeptical about the intent." Tom Joyner portrayed the bus tour as more of a stratagem for gaining attention and selling books than a sincere effort to help the less fortunate. Al Sharpton, a reliable but not wholly uncritical supporter of Obama, condemned some of the name-calling that had been directed at the president by critics and advised the chief executive to be tougher on Republican foes. "I am a Christian preacher," he told an interviewer, and then laughed, "and he is more forgiving than I am." Of all of the public rebukes of West and Smiley, the most biting possibly came from West's Princeton colleague-turned-cable-news-host, Professor Melissa Harris-Perry. In a bare-knuckled editorial in the *Nation*, she accused West of being an egotistical Ivy League elitist who trafficked in self-serving "victimology . . . deceptively wrapped in the discourse of prophetic witness." Although West was the focus of her commentary, she hardly spared Smiley, who she claimed steered Black people toward the kinds of predatory mortgages that left many homeless and, somewhat ironically, below the poverty line.[19]

From there, the discourse careened toward the gutter. In May 2012, West announced that Obama was preferable to his 2012 election challenger, former Massachusetts governor Mitt Romney, but his statement turned out to be the faintest of praise. "Mitt Romney is a catastrophic response to a catastrophe," West told an interviewer, "whereas Obama is a disastrous response to a catastrophe." Smiley emailed a similar assessment to the *New York Times* later that year, deploring "this particular president's calibrated, cautious, and sometimes callous treatment of his most loyal constituency." To purportedly again bring attention to the plight of the poor, West and Smiley launched the Poverty Tour 2.0 in September. This time, they planned stops in Florida, Ohio, Pennsylvania, and Virginia, all swing states in which the margins of victory in the November presidential election promised to be close. BET editorialist Cord Jefferson pondered the timing of the tour, given that a President Romney "could be disastrous not just for Black Americans, but also poor Americans." In the end, the tour had no discernible impact on the electoral outcome. However, West still felt compelled to take a new swipe at the victorious Obama, writing him off in November as a "Rockefeller Republican in blackface." Deeper cuts were reserved for others on the professor's list of racial outcasts. "I love Brother Mike Dyson . . . but we're living in a society where everybody is up for sale," West contended in an interview. "And he and Brother Sharpton and Sister Melissa [Harris-Perry] and others, they have sold their souls for a mess of Obama pottage. And we invite them back to the black prophetic tradition after Obama leaves." For those who had followed this epic drama of shrinking proportions up to this point, this newest act could hardly have been surprising or heartening.[20]

Before it had degenerated into political posturing and personal recriminations, the debate over Obama's approach to policy as it pertained to Black communities was useful and even necessary. It brought to bear some of the sharpest minds on issues of economic inequality, social justice, and responsible governance and placed them in often constructive conversation. Collectively, Black intellectuals, politicians, and assorted commentators were attempting to balance—some more consciously than others—their instinctive drive to analyze the Obama presidency and its policy implications for Black people against the coalitional imperatives of electoral politics, the stark human and budgetary realities of the Great Recession, and the president's own tendencies toward political pragmatism and ideological moderation. Most of them understood that Obama was not simply the president of Black America: his election was made possible by a largely white base of voters. However, many of them were dismayed that Obama and the Democratic Party had not paid closer attention to the plight of their most loyal constituency, which suffered disproportionately from the housing crisis, unemployment, wealth loss, mass incarceration, HIV/AIDs, and a host of other social maladies. For a number of these individuals, the symbolism of an African American president—though powerful and important—was not enough, nor were his universalist policies, which purported to lift all boats, even those riddled with holes from bow to stern. In the opinion of several of these observers, the Obama presidency and its policy trajectory were a real dilemma, and any simple interpretations of them were probably wrong or incomplete.

Ultimately, the academicians, CBC members, media types, and others who fervently demanded a more progressive, pro-Black agenda from the White House were mostly relegated to the philosophical fringes of Black America. Throughout the Obama presidency, polls consistently showed African Americans overwhelmingly supportive of the chief executive and not especially eager to blame him for the many problems facing Black communities or the nation as a whole. Still, from their position as outliers, various individuals continued to believe that there should be explicit, racially tailored policy payoffs for Black people as a dedicated subset of the Democratic coalition and that such a case for Black relief should be pressed, just as Latinx organizations, the LGBTQ community, pro-Israel Jews, and others aggressively brought their concerns to the attention of the White House. But race—particularly the exploitation of white racial grievances by the GOP and some of its conservative allies even before 2008—complicated any transactional, quid pro quo politics that might exist between Black voters and the Obama administration.

As early as 2006, Obama had written that white guilt had largely evaporated in the United States and that even well-meaning whites would only go so far in supporting policies blatantly designed to assist distressed Black communities. He was arguably correct in his analysis; one need only view polls showing middling white support for watered-down and perennially besieged policies such as affirmative action to detect the trend. Moreover, in the racial atmosphere of Obama's first term, simply calling out white police officers for acting "stupidly" in arresting a Black professor on his own porch was enough for the president to permanently lose several percentage points of white support for the duration of his presidency. In the midst of an economic cataclysm that helped fuel conservatives' scapegoating of minorities, immigrants, the welfare state, and anything that remotely seemed to assist the downtrodden (especially those of color), the appearance of Obama choosing favorites or being overtly mindful of the circumstances of a subset of Americans—in particular, Black Americans—would have been more than enough to provoke Republican howls of reverse racism. Consequently, such a scenario—following on the heels of the 2010 midterm rout—would have likely been calamitous for the electoral viability of Obama and other Democrats around the country.[21]

The seeming clarity of this logic was not enough to carry the day with some Black participants in the debate, since other interests were often at play. Many CBC members represented predominantly minority districts and believed that an avowedly Black agenda was either sound in principle, or good politics, or both. Furthermore, some academicians researched, wrote, published, and taught about race as a significant element of their intellectual and professional pursuits and were thus most comfortable assessing the Obama presidency and its context in accordance with these interests. In any event, the Black public discourse about Obama's White House tenure was a serious exercise, at least in its more thoughtful incarnations.

Overall, the exchanges revealed the wide diversity of opinion among Black scholars, media personalities, political figures, and others, further debunking the notion of a unitary African American community, shared experiences, or immutable sets of values. At its most productive, the debate even drew in the president, encouraging—and occasionally compelling—him to articulate the rationale behind his legislative agenda and how it could benefit African Americans. At its worst, the decaying civility of the discourse made some of the more argumentative and self-absorbed participants appear small and myopic, unable to see that their Ivy League perches or other privileged vantage points were rarefied spaces for abstract ideas and insider intrigues that few in the outside world either understood or cared about. Such extraneous preoccupations risked transforming vibrant intellectual exchanges that could translate into real policy influence into nonsensical sideshows that were not worth anyone's attention, especially the president of the United States. As the clamor and maneuvering among the Black commentariat grew more trivial, its collective relevance declined to a corresponding degree.

As some of Obama's most vocal supporters and detractors settled in for protracted trench warfare during his first term, the Moses generation occasionally chimed in with words of wisdom and much-needed levity. Andrew Young, who had supported Hillary Clinton during the primaries, cheered the president's legislative achievements and actions on the world stage. While Obama had not reached out to him for advice, the former ambassador and mayor was full of praise for the chief executive on the eve of the dedication of the MLK monument in October 2011. "He is smart and he works hard—he is amazingly humble," Young rhapsodized to a reporter. "I don't think we can do any better." Civil rights icon and former Georgia congressman Julian Bond was not quite as effusive about Obama and had a well-grounded understanding of the limitations of presidential power. Still, he was surprised by the extensive Republican resistance to Obama, considering that the president was "not as liberal as I had hoped he would be." John Lewis, who shared experiences with both Young and Bond in civil rights circles and Georgia politics, was a valued supporter of Obama since the 2008 primaries, when the congressman's endorsement added additional momentum to Obama's appeal to Black voters. In February 2011, the president honored Lewis with the Presidential Medal of Freedom, which, along with the Congressional Gold Medal, is the country's highest civilian award. Months later, the congressman recalled the moment, that feeling of a Black president fastening a medallion around his neck and embracing him at a White House ceremony. "I just kept thinking," he recollected with a hint of sorrow, "I wish Dr. King were here."[22]

Rev. Jesse Jackson Sr., the quintessential Moses-era figure, was sporadically critical of the president's performance but could be insightful, even sagacious, in his unsolicited counsel. In general, he believed that Obama was a bit too moderate and tended to give in too easily to Republican demands for budget cuts to domestic spending, for which the president received precious little in return. Jackson thought that the president could rise to true greatness but had not yet found his voice or learned how to effectively counter GOP opposition. At times, Jackson came to Obama's defense, such as when conservatives questioned the president's citizenship or labeled him a socialist. Nonetheless, the two remained estranged following the 2008 campaign, and Jackson was not invited to the White House as regularly as were Black spokespeople of lesser stature. Apparently, Obama, too, kept a list of personae non gratae, as had many of his Oval Office predecessors. In late October 2012, Jackson endorsed the incumbent president for a second term, lauding his "intelligence, judgment and dignity." At the time, the stamp of approval was probably less valuable than it otherwise could have been, since it came when Jackson's son was dragging the family name through a murky swamp of ethics probes and criminal investigations. The Jackson-Obama standoff remained a glaring, somewhat tragic oddity in US political culture. It was as if the two men, forever linked by their bold, hopeful bids for the nation's highest office, were living in separate historical eras, even though they were both members of the same Democratic Party, Chicago community, and Black political elite.[23]

In May 2012, President Obama announced his support for same-sex marriage. Like many other Americans, his views on the issue had evolved over time. In an interview, he couched his newfound approval in the Golden Rule but acknowledged that his revised stance on the issue would put him "at odds with the views of others," including many Christians like himself. To some extent, his change of heart was not completely out of the blue, since he had signed a 2010 law ending the Don't Ask, Don't Tell policy that kept gays and lesbians from openly serving in the military. Moreover, LGBTQ individuals and organizations had worked and lobbied hard for a more expansive civil rights agenda during the Democratic ascendancy in Washington, efforts that did not go unnoticed by liberal politicians like Obama, who would count them as a core constituency around election time. As with other Americans, Black people's disapproval of same-sex marriage had been dropping over recent years, falling below 50 percent in the month before Obama's statement. Despite these favorable signs, Obama knew that the public response to his announcement would be swift and mixed. In preparation, he tried to blunt some of the intensity of the reactions by conducting a conference call with selected Black ministers two hours after his announcement. The country was still divided over the issue, and the clergy would be important allies, especially in an election year.[24]

Civil rights activists and ministers who were friendly to the administration helped the president to get out in front of the issue before an oppositional narrative could take hold. In a May 11 open letter, Reverends Al Sharpton and Joseph Lowery, Julian Bond, and Melanie Campbell, president and CEO of the National Coalition on Black Civic Participation, characterized same-sex marriage as a civil rights matter. They further asserted that religious organizations would be free to determine for whom they would conduct marriage ceremonies and that conversations about the issue should be managed in a "civil and respectful way." A week later, the board of directors of the NAACP approved a resolution supporting marriage equality, predicating the organization's position on the equal protection clause of the Fourteenth Amendment. "Civil marriage is a civil right and a matter of civil law," the statement emphasized in a secular tone that contrasted with the more religious language found in some other pronouncements.[25]

Sympathetic government officials also weighed in. Rep. Clyburn, whose home state of South Carolina, along with thirty-seven other states, legally prohibited same-sex marriage, publicly expressed his support for Obama's position. He, like Bill Clinton and many other Democrats, had supported the Defense of Marriage Act of 1996, which federally defined marriage as a union between a man and a woman, but now favored an overturning of the law through either a Supreme Court challenge or congressional action. Mayor Cory Booker of Newark, a rising star in the Democratic Party, also approved of Obama's stance and the "very powerful and symbolic effect" it would likely have in expanding civil equality.[26]

The public struggle of Black clergy and congregations over same-sex marriage was contentious, wrenching, and at times indecorous. Some ministers tried to disaggregate their support for the president from their own beliefs on same-sex marriage. Rev. Wallace Charles Smith of the Shiloh Baptist Church in Washington, DC, disagreed with Obama's position but encouraged his parishioners to "keep him lifted up in prayer." Likewise, pastor Wil Nichols of Victorious Praise Fellowship Church in Durham, North Carolina, distinguished his political support for Obama from his own spiritual commitments. "I was always proud of him," the clergyman said of Obama in a 2020 interview, expressing appreciation for the "dignity and class" that he believed Obama brought to the White House. However, "as a spiritual man," Nichols was never able to reconcile himself with the president's approval of same-sex marriage or abortion rights. Rev. Michael Toliver of First Baptist Church South Hill in Chesapeake, Virginia, also continued to support Obama as an elected official but struggled with the paradox that he discerned in "the fact that our president is a devout Christian, yet takes a stance that is not in line with Christianity." To rationalize this perceived disconnect, Rev. S. Benjamin Brown of the Kingdom Life Church of God in Christ in Melbourne, Florida, separated the president's endorsement of same-sex marriage from the life that he personally led. "He and Michelle are raising children, taking them to church, acknowledging God, acknowledging that they are a Christian family," the minister noted, affirming his own heteronormative understanding of matrimony.[27]

Other religious leaders embraced a politically pragmatic approach to Obama's announcement. "He's the president of the United States, not pastor of the United States," Fred Robinson, a Charlotte minister, observed. "I'm not going to vote on one issue." With an eye to the 2012 election, Rev. Joseph E. Lamb Sr. of St. Thomas AME Zion Church in Norfolk, Virginia, adopted a similar view. "We need to make our parishioners aware," he declared to other clergy who had gathered for the president's conference call on the day of his statement, "that not voting is a vote for the other guy." Based on hard-learned lessons, Bishop Carlton Pearson offered advice on other kinds of practical calculations. Having lost his church of 6,000 members as a result of preaching in support of same-sex marriage, he characterized ministerial positions on the matter as primarily career choices and not questions of belief. "A lot of preachers actually don't have a theological issue [with same-sex marriage]," he professed in a CNN interview. "It's a business decision. They can't afford to lose their parishioners and their parsonages and salaries." Pearson's words probably captured more faithfully the dilemma faced by his clerical colleagues than many would publicly acknowledge.[28]

If clergy members who supported the president's position tended to do so quietly or with a number of caveats, those who vehemently opposed his approval of same-sex marriage sometimes vented righteous anger and political heat directly toward the White House. Emmett Burns, the pastor of Rising Sun First Baptist Church in Maryland, had endorsed Obama during his 2008 presidential bid but felt compelled to publicly withdraw his support in the wake of the May 2012 announcement. "I love the president," Burns declared, "but I cannot support what he has done." He predicted that Obama would lose his reelection campaign over the issue. Ministers such as William Owens, the president and founder of the Coalition of African American Pastors, went as far as to organize their coreligionists against same-sex marriage, launching a campaign to "save the family." At a National

Press Club event in July, he told attendees, "I am ashamed that the first black president chose this road, a disgraceful road," and he later claimed that 3,742 Black pastors had joined his crusade against Obama. During a press conference, Owens questioned the president's commitment to African Americans and alluded to his mixed-race background. Two years later, he would call for the impeachment of Attorney General Holder for alleged "lawlessness in attempting to impose same-sex marriage throughout the nation."[29]

While Rev. Patrick L. Wooden of the Upper Room Church of God in Christ in Raleigh, North Carolina, did not publicly challenge Obama's credentials as a Black man, he did criticize him for supporting both same-sex marriage and abortion rights. In radio ads aired in the fall, Wooden encouraged listeners to join him in saying "no more to President Obama." A registered independent, the clergyman admitted in an interview that Mitt Romney would likely get just 0.1 percent of the votes of his 3,000-member congregation, yet he still maintained that it was "time we let both parties know we're relatable."[30]

In terms of clerical predictions about the election, some turned out to be accurate, and others did not. Burns was wrong about the outcome, and Wooden was right that Romney would do poorly among Black Christians. The issue of same-sex marriage was by no means settled by the vote, and many church leaders and congregations remained conflicted for years to come. But despite the continuing sparring in the spiritual realm, the legal tides and societal winds were moving in favor of same-sex marriage by the time Obama began his second term. While the characteristically cautious president did not announce his historic nomination of Judge William Thomas, an openly gay African American man, to a US District Court in Florida until several days following his reelection, his commitment to extending greater rights to LGBTQ people was genuine and repeatedly demonstrated. In June 2015, the US Supreme Court ruling in *Obergefell v. Hodges* legalized same-sex marriage in all fifty states. Three months later, Obama nominated Eric K. Fanning to become the next secretary of the army. A former undersecretary of the air force and chief of staff to defense secretary Ash Carter, Fanning's confirmation the following year not only made him the first openly gay leader of a branch of the US armed services; it also made him the head of an army that had just a decade earlier ordered people like him to "don't ask, don't tell."[31]

CHAPTER 8

Pitchforks, Daggers, and Carnival Barkers

UPON ENTERING THE WHITE HOUSE, BARACK OBAMA ASSUMED
that the Republicans in Congress would work with him to address the
Great Recession and all of the other challenges that the country faced
at the time. He thought that the GOP, suddenly a minority party in
the capital, would undergo a period of uncertainty about its identity
and then fall back on its ideological base for comfort but would
ultimately adjust to the new reality and join him in addressing the
needs of the nation. Some of his hopeful analysis was based in history.
The Democrats had experienced a similar electoral wilderness during
the Reagan presidency but chose to cooperate with the Republican
president on Social Security reform, tax policy, and national security.
During his career in state politics, Obama had reached across the
aisle in Springfield to advance several bipartisan pieces of legislation.
While his relatively short tenure in the US Senate was influenced by
escalating Democratic opposition to an increasingly unpopular Bush
presidency, he and others in his party did collaborate with Republicans to carry out the basic requirements of federal governance.

Such functional bipartisanship, even in minimal doses, was hard to
find during Obama's tenure in the White House. The outnumbered
Republicans in Congress never transitioned into a loyal opposition

party during Obama's first two years in office. Their allegiances remained largely with their campaign donors and base voters, who often resided in gerrymandered districts that amplified the importance of ideological purity over any national unity of purpose. Even for those Republicans who would have otherwise worked with the administration on issues such as health care, tax code revisions, or criminal justice reform, the daily barrage of anti-Obama messaging from conservative cable, internet, and social media outlets scared them into silence, as did the periodic threat of facing a well-funded primary challenger from the right. By the time of the Republican takeover of the US House in the 2010 midterm elections, the will and means to oppose the president and the Democrats on most substantive policy matters were routinely on display. Moreover, the Tea Party insurgency proved that the more vocal and theatrical a candidate's opposition to Obama and his policies, the more likely they were to draw both votes and campaign contributions. This observation became a truism once the US Supreme Court rendered its 2010 decision in the case of *Citizens United v. Federal Election Commission*, a landmark ruling that allowed unlimited amounts of hard-to-trace "dark money" to flood into the bloodstream of US politics.

At the twilight of his presidency, Obama would acknowledge that he was wrong in his assumption that the GOP would eventually decide to work with him on a common policy agenda once it got over the sting of the 2008 election. He would also recognize that there was something unique about some of the conservative attacks against him. "I do think that there has been a degree of venom and viciousness and anger that has been unleashed in our national politics that is qualitatively different in at least our modern history," he opined in a September 2016 interview. An overabundance of evidence supports his thesis, reflecting an unfortunate reality that he and the nation lived through for almost a decade.[1]

The primal scream of Republican enmity toward the president was heard earliest and most audibly during Obama's address to a joint session of Congress in September 2009. Obama, standing before the body with Vice President Biden and Speaker Nancy Pelosi behind him, was abruptly cut short by a lawmaker who yelled "You lie!" as he explained that his proposed health-care bill would not cover illegal immigrants. The words cut sharply through the chamber, prompting immediate groans of disapproval and head-shaking stares at the culprit, Republican representative Joe Wilson of South Carolina, from Pelosi, Obama, and others. The president handled the outburst and awkwardness well, simply answering it with the retort "Not true" and continuing his speech. Years later, he recalled being more stunned than angered by the interruption, but his face in the moment told another tale. Wilson later offered an apology for the unprecedented insult, which Obama accepted. In a largely party-line vote, the congressman was formally rebuked for a "breach of decorum [that] degraded the proceedings of the joint session, to the discredit of the House." Back home in his district, Wilson and his midterm Democratic challenger, Rob Miller, both reaped the rewards of the contrasting partisan reactions to the affair, each reporting that they raised more than $1 million in its aftermath. The incident portended future displays of disrespect toward the president and illuminated widening partisan divisions in Congress and elsewhere.[2]

In its crudeness, Wilson's barb was a rare type of expression of GOP animus toward the president during the public conduct of congressional business. Much more common were other Republican tactics that were aimed at derailing the agenda of Democrats and that transgressed long-observed norms and protocols governing interbranch relations. The routine resorting of minority leader Mitch McConnell to the filibuster procedure in order to require a supermajority vote to move bills or nominations through the Senate was new and inimical to the chamber's operation and comity. According to a report of the nonpartisan Congressional Research Service, Senate confirmation votes for Obama's nominees to district and circuit courts were delayed longer on average than those of the four other most recent presidents. Democrats had previously filibustered selected circuit court nominations of Republican presidents, but unlike McConnell and his GOP colleagues, they had not required *every* nominee for both circuit and district court appointments to receive sixty votes. If the Republican leader's intentions were unclear to anyone, he offered a moment of lucidity on the eve of the midterms. "The single most important thing we want to achieve is for President Obama to be a one-term president," he stated frankly in an interview, though he asserted a willingness to work with Obama if he did a "Clintonian backflip" toward more centrist or center-right positions. It was an unlikely proposition, and McConnell knew it. In any event, such ideological acrobatics would probably not have reined in the Republican's profligate abuse of the filibuster or his single-minded focus on defeating Obama in 2012.[3]

In the House, the post-midterm Republican caucus posed similar problems for Obama's legislative agenda and the operation of government itself. When bipartisan budget negotiations soured in 2011, fiscal ultraconservatives, many of whom were aligned with the newly empowered Tea Party faction, threatened to force the government into default of its debt obligations. Such a course of action would have almost certainly led to an international financial crisis, which the nation's limping economy could scarcely afford. The mere threat of default actually led to an unprecedented downgrade of the country's debt rating by the Standard and Poor's agency, an ominous sign of the potential costs of protracted hyperpartisanship and governmental dysfunction. Emblematic of the president's unpleasant relationship with congressional GOP leadership, Speaker John Boehner ignored multiple phone calls from him at the height of the stalemate, slights that Obama reportedly found offensive.[4]

Instances of disrespect toward the president were ongoing and not limited to Congress. None became quite as engrained in the public consciousness as the Joe Wilson affront. However, enough episodes occurred with enough regularity to produce patterns that were unique to the Obama presidency. During Obama's January 2012 trip to Arizona, Gov. Jan Brewer met the president on the airport tarmac and exchanged heated words with him over immigration policy. A photo of the encounter captured the Republican executive, mouth agape, pointing her finger in Obama's face as he appeared to attentively lean his head forward. It was an unusually belligerent reception of a sitting president by a governor, even considering the difference in party affiliation. In August of the following year, Obama returned to Arizona, and Brewer's tarmac etiquette was more cordial and refined. By then, she had become one of the higher-profile Republican governors to embrace the ACA, particularly its Medicaid expansion component. The conciliatory stance did not last, however. During the 2016 campaign, she was again colorfully criticizing the president, this time on behalf of a Republican presidential candidate who had promised to address the issue of illegal immigration by erecting a wall along the southern US border with Mexico.[5]

Several episodes of public disrespect toward the president were captured on video, and at least a few cases occurred at the White House itself. In June 2012, Obama was interrupted repeatedly by Neil Munro, a reporter for the conservative blog the *Daily Caller*, as he delivered remarks in the Rose Garden. Munro's shouted questions about the president's immigration policy broke the structure of the event and drew a rebuke from Obama. "Excuse me, sir. It's not time for questions, sir," the president admonished. "Not while I'm speaking." Years later, he juxtaposed the Munro interruption with the Wilson outburst and came to different conclusions about the rudeness of each. "I was probably more mad on that one," he recalled about Munro's blurted comments. "Because—whereas Joe Wilson you got a sense of just this weird impulsive action on his part—this felt orchestrated and showed a lack of respect for the office that I think was unprecedented in a Rose Garden statement." Such occasional incidents became par for the course for Obama. Around election time in 2012, more indecencies were hurled his way. In Denver, someone fired a gun into his campaign's reelection headquarters. None of the workers inside were injured, though a window was shattered. Reminiscent of the 2008 campaign, Obama was again lynched in effigy. In one instance in Moreno Valley, California, the imagery was disturbing enough to justify a Secret Service visit and a warning to the perpetrator.[6]

Some of the hostility toward Obama and government in general was generated by the Tea Party. Emerging around the time of the 2009-2010 debates over the health-care bill and lasting well after the midterms, the phenomenon was an explosive mixture of conservative political agendas and both spontaneous and orchestrated protests. To a significant degree the Tea Party was a media creation that fed off right-wing screeds on cable networks such as Fox News and CNBC and found its organizational legs through arranging highly publicized rallies and other events over the internet and social media. Fragmented and diffuse, the Tea Party's community of activists did not produce a recognized leadership cohort or a political infrastructure; its disruptive demonstrations were often stoked by Republican politicians and bankrolled by corporate lobbying groups, such as FreedomWorks and Americans for Prosperity, in pursuit of their own policy interests.

Against the backdrop of the Great Recession, much of the animating dynamism of the Tea Party was derived from a sense that the government had failed to protect the American people from disaster. Other energies behind the movement were libertarian and populist in nature and ignited by the notion that federal authorities had gone too far in using taxpayer dollars to save big banks, big car companies, and other bad actors who did not deserve billions of dollars in bailout funds. Similarly, its supporters also believed that government initiatives such as the ACA and the stimulus package flirted with socialism, though they seemed reluctant to criticize long-established programs such as Social Security or Medicare. Demographically reflective of their allies in politics, the media, and the corporate world, Tea Party members, as far as it could be ascertained, were mostly white, male, married, and more than 45 years of age, with a large segment holding traditional Republican views on issues such as taxes, immigration, abortion, and gay rights.

One of the foundational catalysts behind the rise of the Tea Party was the presidency of Barack Obama. For many drawn to its message, he was the new poster boy for everything that was wrong with the federal government and American culture more broadly. He was too

liberal, too pro-bailouts, too pro-abortion, too pro–socialized medicine, too pro-immigration, and too untraditional a chief executive.
According to a 2009 poll, only 41 percent of self-identified Tea Party
activists believed that Obama was born in the United States, with a
full 30 percent maintaining that he was foreign-born. Thus, when
rallies in the capital featured "Take Our Country Back" signs, the underlying subtext regarding who had "taken" the nation was clear.[7]

The Tea Party was too inchoate and disorderly in its initial incarnation to warrant characterization in any singular, all-encompassing
way. However, white racial grievances were certainly detectable in its
DNA by 2010 and not only as evinced in the loud attacks on the president as a socialist, communist, fascist, Muslim, and/or foreign-born
aspiring dictator. Some Congressional Black Caucus members got
a taste of Tea Party antipathy firsthand when Representatives John
Lewis and André Carson were harassed by a crowd chanting "nigger, nigger" at the Cannon House Office Building in DC in March
2010. In one particularly tense encounter, a protester allegedly spat on
Rep. Emanuel Cleaver, who then had to secure a police escort as he
traveled to the Capitol. Republican lawmakers and candidates were,
on the whole, reticent in the face of such Tea Party excesses. Hoping
to ride the insurgent fervor to victory during the midterm elections,
they often cheered on the activists as fellow conservatives and constitutional originalists, even as they plotted ways to ensure their own
places in the establishment that the rebels so loathed.[8]

Following the 2010 midterms, the Tea Party lost much of its potency. A number of factors were at play, but among the most important was the inability of the insurgency to institutionalize itself after
achieving electoral success. With dozens of new House members,
several US senators, and many more state and local officials winning
office under its banner, the rebellion was successful in pushing the
Republican Party—indeed, US political culture in general—further
to the right on fiscal policy especially and away from any notions
of compromise or collaboration with the likes of Barack Obama or
his party. However, without organizational leadership, infrastructure,

or funding sources that were independent of the Republican Party and its many appendages in the world of lobbying, think tanks, and corporate donors, the Tea Party was simply subsumed into existing structures and recast to align with their interests. Some hoped for a resurgence of the movement in the 2012 election, but by then many of its vital energies were spent or completely absorbed by Republican incumbents who had figured out how to outmaneuver Tea Party–flavored challengers during the primaries. In many cases, the quality and behavior of some Tea Party politicians elected during the Republican wave of 2010 did their ideological kinfolk no favors, as several seemed to showcase their inexperience and extremism at every opportunity. Once the Republican establishment regained its traction in 2012, the only other thing it needed to do to maintain its supremacy in the party was to keep a newly reelected Barack Obama in its sights as a unifying motif for all conservatives and would-be insurgents.[9]

Whether in business or politics, Donald J. Trump had an uncanny knack for instigating controversies about race. The son of a New York developer of German descent and a Scottish mother, he became deeply involved in the city's rental market during the 1970s, working alongside his father and benefiting from his advice and financial support. The real-estate business could be cutthroat, and the Trumps plied the trade with wily and opportunistic deal-making. The business was also known for its patterns of racial discrimination against minorities, and the family participated in that side of it as well. In 1975, Trump Management Inc. settled a federal lawsuit that charged that its employees had systematically steered African Americans and Puerto Ricans away from apartment buildings with a preponderance of white tenants and toward those with higher proportions of minority residents. In addition to ordering the company to desist in its discriminatory practices, the terms of the settlement required the Trumps to "thoroughly acquaint themselves personally on a detailed basis" with the stipulations of the Fair Housing Act. The developers never acknowledged wrongdoing in this case, and the younger Trump quickly turned to other propositions. His pet project involved the construction of the multipurpose Trump Tower on Fifth Avenue, the iconic heart of Manhattan's high-end landholdings. Completed in 1983, the fifty-eight-story skyscraper served as both Donald's primary residence and the headquarters of the Trump Organization.[10]

During the 1980s, Donald Trump, an avid self-promoter and publicity seeker, spent much of his time dabbling in business ventures related to sports teams and the airline industry, in addition to ongoing pursuits in real estate. In the spring of 1989, he veered again into a racial morass when he purchased $85,000 worth of ads in New York newspapers demanding the return of the death penalty in the wake of the arrest of several minority youths charged with brutally assaulting a white woman in Central Park. Even when the accused were exonerated of the crime years later, Trump neither apologized for having previously called for executions nor supported the city's financial settlement for the wrongful convictions. The episode revealed two enduring traits about the developer that would take center stage in American life in the decades to come. First, he was not given to mea culpas or acknowledgment of indisputable facts when doing so would not advance his interests. Second, he was capable of exhibiting derogatory opinions of Blacks and other people of color, at times graphically expressing such sentiments in private conversations and in public forums.[11]

Navigating the world of real-estate acquisition and development brought Trump into regular contact with government agencies and officials ranging from mayors and tax auditors to zoning departments and bankruptcy courts. Whether in local matters or in regard to grander ambitions, he tended to approach politics as he would a business plan, directing attention and resources toward individuals or endeavors that were beneficial to him at the time and switching directions and allegiances when things went south or no longer suited his purposes. Trump was far less concerned about ideology or principle than with loyalty and outcomes, which also would be displayed more fully to the American people in later years. Between 1999 and

2012, he reportedly changed his party affiliation seven times, finally settling for the GOP. To get close to the Clintons, who became more visible in New York's elite circles after Hillary won a US Senate seat in 2000, Trump contributed money to both the Clinton Foundation and the senator's war chest. The businessman's easy migration between political parties, reality TV shows, and branding schemes did not faze anyone who understood his transactional mentality and his personal need to be close to celebrities and the powerful. Although he eventually endorsed John McCain for president in 2008, he had kind words for Barack Obama two years earlier. In the midst of the controversy over the Illinois senator's involvement with Chicago real-estate magnate Tony Rezko, Trump described the dustup as "not a good sign" but extended to Obama the benefit of the doubt. "He's got some wonderful qualities," Trump said of the future president, which he believed warranted a second chance.[12]

Trump had flirted with the possibility of running for public office since the 1980s. During the 2000 election cycle, he launched an "exploratory campaign" to pursue the presidential nomination of the Reform Party but abandoned the idea once he discovered the organization had, in his words, too many "Elvis look-alikes . . . anxious to give me a pamphlet explaining the Swiss-Zionist conspiracy to control America." He publicly teased a run for the White House in 2004 as well but ultimately declined, concluding, "Business is my greatest passion and I am not ready to leave the private sector." After the 2008 election, Trump was again hinting at a bid for the presidency, though by this time his public flirtations with the idea had become a long-running joke in many quarters. Despite the fact that he had never held public office, he seemed to genuinely believe that he could manage the country and its affairs better than people with many years of experience in government service. In the past, his signature policy ideas had focused on trade, with his main argument being that the United States needed to do more to defend its industries and workers from foreign competitors, such as Japan and China. While such protectionist themes might have occasionally resonated among certain segments of the population, they were anathema to both major parties, which had long embraced the putative merits of free trade and the reality of globalization. To jump into the political fray with the glittery splash that he desired, Trump needed an issue, a head-turning topic that would bring instant publicity, whether good or bad.[13]

Trump decided on a direct, low-road battle plan aimed at the highest-value target available: President Barack Obama. His weapon of choice: a fiction that had been lingering since before the 2008 presidential campaign. Innuendo about Obama's place of birth had been in circulation since at least 2004, when Illinois conspiracy theorists tried to portray him as a foreign Muslim during the US Senate campaign. Four years later, some Clinton supporters floated similar rumors, but the campaign itself made no overt or concerted efforts to make Obama's birthplace an issue. For all of its screeching attempts to portray the Democratic presidential nominee as an un-American racial other, the McCain-Palin campaign did not explicitly embrace a strategy of questioning the Illinois senator's nativity. Considering that McCain himself was born to American parents in the Panama Canal Zone, picking a fight over origins probably would not have made much political sense. Nonetheless, in the context of the intense hostility directed toward Obama during and after the campaign, unflattering calumnies about him still held sway in some corners of the country, whether regarding his political ideology, religious affiliation, racial identity, or other attributes. Moreover, Tea Party rallies, Fox News commentaries, right-wing blogs, and easily abused social media platforms provided ample conditions for a whisper campaign about the president's origins to flourish. Subsequently, Trump proffered the brash showmanship and shameless ambition necessary for birtherism—defined as the false belief that Obama was not born in the United States and was thus not eligible to be president—to take firm root among receptive right-wing constituencies.[14]

Paired with more teasing about a presidential bid, Trump went public with questions about the president's birthplace, appearing on several cable news segments and talk shows. In one notably conten- tious March 2011 encounter on *The View*, Trump and cohost Whoopi Goldberg clashed over the motivations behind his skepticism. "I want him to show his birth certificate," Trump repeatedly stated. "There's something on that birth certificate that he doesn't like." Visibly shaken by the birther claims, Goldberg responded, "I think that's the biggest pile of dog mess I've heard in ages." She then asked plainly, "It's not because he's black, is it?" Trump denied that there was any racial angle to his doubts about the president's nativity, a reply that prompted Goldberg to add, "Because I've never heard a white president being asked to show his birth certificate." In other venues, Trump went further, demanding that Obama release his college transcripts. "I heard he was a terrible student. Terrible," he asserted in one interview. "How does a bad student go to Columbia and then to Harvard?" The attacks were full frontal, nothing subtle or hidden. Not only was Trump assailing the president's eligibility and fitness for his office, but he also seemed to suggest that Ivy League schools had a questionable mechanism for admitting "terrible" students who happened to look like Obama.[15]

Into the spring, Trump kept pounding the drum of birtherism, giving it legs across various media outlets and primetime slots. The White House, annoyed by the smear and the reality TV show star's ability to inject it so deeply into US political discourse so quickly, decided to act in order to regain control of the media narrative. On April 22, Obama had his personal attorney, Judy Corley, travel to Hawaii to retrieve certified versions of his original Certificate of Live Birth. Two copies were provided by the state's director of health, who noted that she hoped fulfilling the request would "end the numer- ous inquiries . . . [that] have been disruptive to staff operations and have strained State resources." The president hoped for the same. In a televised statement on April 27, he presented copies of the birth certificate to the press and remarked on how trivial the whole matter was compared to the problems facing the country. "We do not have time for this kind of silliness. . . . We have big problems to solve," he said in a cadence that emphasized seriousness and urgency. "We are not going to be able to solve our problems if we get distracted by sideshows and carnival barkers." As if on cue, Trump made his way to the first available microphone to congratulate himself. "Today, I'm very proud of myself," he told a gaggle of reporters, adding about the birth certificate, "I'd want to look at it, but I hope it's true so that we can get on to much more important matters, so the press can stop asking me questions." The maneuver was classic Trump: (mis)construe reality to fit the immediate situation, even if doing so required listeners to suspend their understanding of the known facts.[16]

Unbeknown to him at the time, Trump called "checkmate" too soon. Obama actually had one more move that would finish the match in a most unexpected way. In his hubris and longing to be recognized by those whom he considered social peers, Trump accepted an invitation to the White House Correspondents' Association dinner at the Washington Hilton on April 30, 2011. This is an annual gathering of the capital's elite, often featuring a lighthearted address by the president as the highlight. In this instance, it was also a trap set so openly that only someone with their head in the clouds could have missed it. Obama's seventeen-minute speech was chockfull of humor, showcasing his aptitude for comedic delivery. It also incorporated what seemed like an eternity of roasting directed specifically toward Trump. The president, with a mock seriousness that was occasionally belied by an inadvertent chuckle, lampooned Trump's credentials, architectural taste, and *Celebrity Apprentice* TV show. Birtherism, which was referenced throughout the presentation, was relentlessly ridiculed at Trump's expense. "No one is happier, no one is prouder, to put this birth certificate matter to rest than 'the Donald,'" Obama announced with feigned solemnity. "Because he can finally get back to focusing on the issues that matter, like did we fake the moon landing, what really happened in Roswell, and where are Biggy and Tupac!" The crowd howled with laughter, with nearby guests looking at Trump for a reaction. Grimacing through squinting

1. Barack Obama Sr. and Jr., 1971.

2. Ann Dunham, 1973.

3. LEFT TO RIGHT, Michelle, Malia, Barack, and Sasha Obama, 2011.

4. Barack and Michelle Obama at a second inaugural ball, 2013.

5. Henry Louis Gates Jr., James Crowley, and Barack Obama at the "beer summit," 2009.

6. President Obama and Ruby Bridges Hall at White House display of Norman Rockwell painting, 2011.

7. President Obama hosts B. B. King and other blues artists at the White
House, 2012.

8. President Obama welcomes the Golden State Warriors to the White House, 2016.

9. Attorney General Eric Holder, 2015.

10. Staff meeting in the Oval Office, 2016. Valerie Jarrett is standing in the center, and newly appointed attorney general Loretta Lynch is to her left.

11. President Obama and staff, including Vice President Joseph Biden and Secretary of State Hillary Clinton, await word of the outcome of the 2011 Navy SEAL raid on Osama bin Laden's compound in Abbottabad, Pakistan.

12. President Obama gives the commencement address at Howard University, 2016.

13. The Obamas at the Martin Luther King Jr. monument, Washington, DC, 2011.

14. President Obama dances with his sister Auma and Kenyan president Uhuru Kenyatta (FAR LEFT), July 2015.

15. The Obamas at the Door of No Return, Gorée Island, Senegal, 2013.

16. Tea Party demonstrators protest the passage of the Affordable Care Act, 2010.

17. Activists protesting police violence, 2015.

18. Tracy Martin and Sybrina Fulton, the parents of Trayvon Martin, 2012.

19. President Obama visits with inmates at El Reno Federal Correctional Institution, Oklahoma, July 2015.

20. President Obama delivers the eulogy at the funeral of pastor Clementa Pinckney, 2015.

21. Reverend Jesse Jackson Sr., 2011.

22. Professor Cornel West, 2018.

23. Reverend Al Sharpton, 2011.

24. Herman Cain, 2011.

25. Dr. Ben Carson, 2015.

26. Senator John McCain (LEFT) and Governor Mitt Romney (RIGHT), 2015.

27. Women's March, Washington, DC, January 21, 2017.

28. Presidents and First Ladies at the funeral of President George H. W. Bush, December 2018. *Left to right*, Donald Trump, Melania Trump, Barack Obama, Michelle Obama, Bill Clinton, Hillary Clinton, Jimmy Carter, and Rosalynn Carter.

eyes and a forced smile, the reality TV host rocked nervously in his chair, scratched his neck, and at one point waved at the president as if to signal that he had had enough. But the brickbats kept coming.[17]

Trump's dash for the limelight and his misunderstanding of Obama's character had gotten the better of him. He had either not comprehended or simply did not care that the birther assault had irritated the president and many others who saw it as a racist attack on Obama and African Americans more generally. Furthermore, he did not appreciate Obama's capacity for retaliating to the point of publicly embarrassing a person who longed for respect and praise, even as that person disrespected and abused others. Only in the very moment of his humiliation did Trump realize that he had stumbled into a buzz saw gleefully operated by none other than the president of the United States himself. Worse still, he could not pull away from the laceration and leave the dinner, lest he appear a spoilsport who loses the game and then takes his ball home in a huff. Instead, he had to sit through it and wait for the derision to end.

In valuing loyalty and deference over other traits, Trump can be a poor judge of character, and in this case he apparently mistook Obama for an unconditionally nice guy: the aboveboard sailor who would never stoop to the ways of the pirate. His estimation of the president was generally accurate regarding most situations. However, when Obama was pushed too far, he could find a foe's jugular with cool deftness and kill as ferociously and quickly as any political animal fending for his life or hungry for the next meal. To dramatically stress this point, at the same time as Trump was being skewered at the White House Correspondents' dinner, US Navy SEALs were invading a compound in Abbottabad, Pakistan, that was believed to be the sanctuary of Osama bin Laden, the architect of the September 11, 2001, terrorist attacks. Nothing in the president's monologue offered the slightest clue that he had just authorized such a risky—and ultimately successful—undertaking. This bold, aggressive move subsequently gave him complete control of the news cycle for the next several days.

The public disparagement at the correspondents' dinner, along with the April 27 birth certificate disclosure and the death of Osama bin Laden, marked the end of Donald Trump's teasing of a 2012 presidential run. Nonetheless, it did not dissuade the reality TV host from espousing the birther canard. In October 2012, he offered to donate $5 million to a charity of the president's choosing if he would release his college and passport records by month's end. Obama brushed aside such lingering particles of birtherism with good humor, going as far as to have his birth certificate inscribed on coffee mugs, which were sold to support his reelection bid. He could now afford to be dismissive of the issue, since polls showed that fewer Americans, including Republicans, believed the president was foreign-born following his open caricaturing of Trump. Despite the dampening public support for birtherism, there were some serious ramifications attached to Trump's trafficking in the conspiracy theory. Republican officials in several states, including Arizona, Kansas, and Iowa, made unsuccessful efforts to keep Obama off the 2012 ballot, citing questions about his citizenship. Closer to home, Michelle Obama viewed the whole affair as an insidious attempt to weaponize racism and xenophobia for crude political purposes. She tried not to worry too much about it, but troubling questions haunted her. "What if someone with an unstable mind loaded a gun and drove to Washington?" she wondered. "What if that person went looking for our girls?" After leaving the White House in 2017, the president's wife still could not get over what she characterized as Trump's "loud and reckless innuendos," which had put "my family's safety at risk." Given Trump's starring role in igniting and spreading the birther firestorm, she vowed never to forgive him.[18]

Immediately after the April 30 correspondents' dinner, the Obamas made an official visit to Ireland that allowed the president to put further distance between himself and questions of birthright and belonging. In Moneygall, he was welcomed like royalty, though his link to the tiny village was through his great-great-great-grandfather Falmouth Kearny, a shoemaker. Unlike his father's Kenyan immigrant tale or his own travels through Hawaii and Indonesia, Obama's conscious insertion of himself into a European immigrant narrative made this part of his origin story, in the minds of some, more recognizably and indisputably American. In extolling his Scotch-Irish heritage, he again moved nimbly between identities as political necessity required and as much as cultural realities would allow, an ability that distinguishes him from most African Americans. Whether one considers his visit to Ireland to emphasize his Irish roots or his biography on the White House website, which referenced his white grandfather's service in George Patton's army in World War II, Obama's discursive unspooling of his racial identity, including his purposeful interweaving of African, European, and American ancestries, relates directly to who he believes he is and who his people are. Thus, this exercise was neither a fleeting whim nor did it always seem calculated. Nevertheless, these shifting identity options were political assets, even though he foregrounded his Blackness—which was inescapable but still debated by some—in most settings. Like all identities, Obama's was always in the making, malleable and still evolving. At least in public, he managed these strands of being as well as could be expected, given the ambiguities and contradictions of race that lay just under his skin and society's scarred surface.[19]

Michelle Obama's concerns about the effects of racial demagoguery and widely circulated conspiracy theories were not unfounded. A report by the Southern Poverty Law Center recorded more than 1,000 hate groups in operation in the United States in 2012, as well as a historically high 1,360 antigovernment "patriot" factions. Moreover, FBI data revealed that fifty out of every million African Americans were victims of hate crimes that year, the highest ratio among any racial group and very likely an undercount. During President Obama's first term, the Department of Defense stepped up efforts to remove known white supremacists and neo-Nazi elements from the military. This new vigilance was partly inspired by a 2009 report by the Department of Homeland Security that chronicled initiatives by right-wing extremists to recruit veterans following their deployments abroad. If anyone had questions about the authenticity of the threats, they need only have followed the case of marine lance corporal Kody Brittingham. While posted at Camp Lejeune in North Carolina in late 2008, he conceived Operation Patriot, a plan to assassinate President Obama. Among other incriminating evidence, his arrest netted a "letter of intent," elaborate maps of the Capitol Building, pictures of the commander in chief, and chilling information about his vital statistics. But for Brittingham's arrest for attempted armed robbery in December 2008, the 20-year-old rogue soldier might have been in a position to encounter the president during the latter's visit to the marine corps base in February 2009.[20]

As Obama made history as the first African American president, he also acquired the unfortunate distinction of being the most threatened chief executive since Abraham Lincoln. The instances of expressed ill intent spiked 400 percent in the initial years of his White House tenure, reaching a high of about thirty threats per day. In later years, the number tapered off to a third of that, roughly the same number faced by George W. Bush while in office. The threats came from everywhere—from white supremacists and the mentally ill to high school students and even junior high school students—and across every medium, with the internet and social media allowing for exponentially more perpetrators and audiences for such communications. Some threats were pranks or were issued with no intention of implementation. Others were more serious and could result in the culprit, if located, being confronted by the Secret Service, which has broad discretion in dealing with those who might pose a credible danger to the president. Since any kind of threat against the chief executive is a federal offense, some perpetrators were surprised to find agents at their doors after posting crude comments on Facebook or Twitter, which were apparently meant more to shock others than to result in concrete action.

Threats against President Obama shared common elements with hostile communications directed at previous chief executives, including stated intentions to do harm to the First Lady or to their children.

But because he was the first Black president, threats against Obama often had a racial component that drew on some of the extremist rhetoric and conspiracy theories that characterized the political climate of his years in office. In an era of budget cuts to many government programs, the funding of the Secret Service was prioritized, enabling the expansion of its Internet Threat Desk and other security protocols. It was the one federal agency that could not be ceded any margin for error, lest it fail its primary mission of presidential and first family protection.[21]

Beyond incendiary placards at Tea Party rallies and effigies hung at election time, serious threats emerged regularly during the president's tenure and were usually addressed in a coordinated way by various local, state, and federal law enforcement units. While the American people would never know the magnitude and details of every threat against Obama and his family, several of the more noteworthy incidents did become public knowledge. In July 2011, James McVay, a 41-year-old South Dakota man, fatally stabbed an elderly woman before stealing her car and heading for Washington, DC. He was apprehended in Madison, Wisconsin, which interrupted his stated plan to assassinate President Obama. In September 2012, Donte Sims of Charlotte, North Carolina, was arrested for making Twitter threats against the chief executive ahead of the DNC in that city. He was eventually sentenced to six months in prison, though he claimed that he had been impaired by marijuana when he issued the hostile tweets. Around this same time, Jarvis Britton of Birmingham, Alabama, made repeated threats against Obama on Twitter, which landed him, too, in federal prison.

Sims and Britton were almost certainly not the typical perpetrators of threats against the president, given that they were both young Black men who claimed to be either drunk or stoned when they issued their tweets. However, even unrepresentative examples of the dangers facing the first family could be disturbing. In July 2012, several members of the DC police department claimed that they had heard a colleague assert that he would kill Michelle Obama with a gun pictured in a cellphone photo that he shared. The unnamed

seventeen-year veteran of the force was a member of the motor escort tasked with protecting the First Lady, an assignment that did
indeed afford opportunities for such a treacherous assault. The threat
was considered credible enough to justify investigations by both the
police department's internal affairs division and the Secret Service.[22]

There were continuities between the first and second Obama terms
in the White House regarding the kinds of threats that the first family
faced. While the years following the president's reelection in 2012 were
marked by a decline and eventual leveling off of communicated and
demonstrated intentions to do harm, such instances remained alarming in variety and seriousness. In April 2013, James Everett Dutschke,
a 41-year-old Mississippi man, was arrested for sending a ricin-laced
letter to President Obama. His guilty plea the following year resulted
in a twenty-five-year prison sentence. In March 2015, Cameron James
Stout was criminally charged with making multiple threats to gun
down the chief executive. The Missouri man's scheme was discovered only after he solicited an informant and an undercover officer,
the latter posing as a member of the Aryan Nation, for assistance in
acquiring a rifle with which to shoot Obama during his next visit to
Kansas City. In a Wisconsin case, Brian Dutcher was convicted in
January 2016 of communicating death threats against the president,
including a Facebook posting. Dutcher's attorney tried to convince
the court that his client had not meant anything sinister when he
posted, "Killing him [Obama] is our CONSTITUTIONAL DUTY!"
However, considering that Dutcher actually traveled to La Crosse a
day before a scheduled visit by the president and told a guard at a
public library of his assassination plans, his trial defense was found
unconvincing, and he was sentenced to prison for his crimes. By this
time, online and digital platforms such as Facebook were the most
common venues for the issuing of threats against the president, accounting for more than 60 percent of all instances. In addition to
Dutcher, at least sixty-five people were indicted for communicating
harmful intentions toward Obama by the last quarter of his presidency, though this figure represented a very small percentage of the

total number of threats that he received during his time in the White House.[23]

Along with domestic hazards, expressions of deadly intent by international actors were commonplace during Obama's presidency, as they had been for his predecessors. To thwart any real or prospective plotting, foreign governments worked closely with the Secret Service and other agencies during state visits and other occasions. The US involvement in Middle Eastern wars, along with the ongoing operations of global terrorist networks, probably heightened both the number of threats during Obama's White House tenure and the sensitivity of law enforcement agencies to their existence. In this fraught context, an early example of foreign perils arose in Turkey in April 2009, when authorities uncovered a plot to assassinate President Obama during his scheduled appearance at the Alliance of Civilizations summit in Istanbul. An apprehended Syrian citizen admitted to being part of a conspiracy to stab the visiting president once he arrived in the country from a North Atlantic Treaty Organization meeting in France. Much attention was given to the fact that the would-be assassin had managed to acquire press credentials, though it was initially unclear whether they were authentic. In a stateside incident two years later, Ulugbek Kodirov, a 22-year-old Uzbek man, was arrested for threatening to murder Obama during his reelection campaign. In court proceedings, the foiled plotter was shown to have tried to coordinate a potential attack with the Islamic Movement of Uzbekistan, using the internet as the medium of communication. Although his defense lawyer claimed that he was not a "big, bad terrorist," Kodirov was sentenced to more than fifteen years in prison for charges that included providing material support to terrorism.[24]

Of all of the publicly known threats to the Obamas, a 2011 incident at the White House was the most harrowing and memorable. On November 11, a man driving a 1988 black Honda Accord parked on Constitution Avenue and fired several semiautomatic rifle rounds from the passenger window into the presidential residence. One bullet shattered a second-floor window near the formal living room.

Another struck a window frame, while others blasted wood and concrete from the roof. A minimum of seven bullets hit the upstairs residential area of the mansion, where the first family spent much of its time. In the wake of the shooting, on-site Secret Service agents had initially responded by scanning the South Lawn with rifle scopes until a misinformed supervisor radioed that the suspicious sounds had come from a backfiring construction vehicle in the vicinity. For the next four days, those in charge of White House security did not figure out what had actually happened until a member of the custodial staff discovered shards of glass and pieces of cement on a floor inside the residence.

During the shooting, the first couple was in San Diego en route to a trade summit in Honolulu. Malia was out with friends but expected back at the White House at any time, and Sasha was inside the residence with her grandmother Marian Robinson. When Michelle arrived back at the executive mansion—the president was still away in Australia—she inadvertently learned of the shooting from an usher who had wrongly assumed that Secret Service director Mark Sullivan had informed her of the incident during their flight back from Hawaii. The First Lady was livid about the oversight, as was President Obama when he arrived home five days later. Michelle reportedly interrogated Sullivan in a tone that could be heard through shut doors, demanding to know why his agents had missed rifle bullets embedded in walls and other fixtures. Reminiscent of the Secret Service missteps that had cost Desirée Rogers her social secretary job almost two years earlier, another system failure had occurred on Sullivan's watch that could have entailed tragic consequences. Notwithstanding the security agency's inept performance, Oscar R. Ortega-Hernandez of Idaho Falls was caught and eventually sentenced to twenty-five years in prison for the attack. His incarceration in 2014 brought some measure of justice, but it hardly made up for the fact that the gunman had robbed the Obamas of yet another dream of creating a secure, semi-normal life in the White House. Years later, Michelle could still freshly recall that one bullet had struck a window in the Yellow Oval Room, where she occasionally sat for tea. Likewise, the Truman Balcony, where the president had sometimes longingly watched crowds shuffle along Constitution Avenue, was never again the same sanctuary for him.[25]

If the November 2011 shooting was the most troubling assault on the White House during the Obama years, a 2014 incident was a close second in terms of intrusiveness and potential lethality. On September 19, Omar J. Gonzalez, a 42-year-old army veteran from Texas, scaled the White House fence, ran across the North Lawn, and entered the front door of the residence. Armed with a serrated knife, he sprinted through the East Room, past the stairway leading to the Obamas' living quarters, and toward the door to the Green Room, which overlooks the South Lawn. An agent finally tackled him before he could penetrate farther into the mansion, and no injuries were suffered by anyone on the premises. Like the November 2011 episode, the Gonzalez intrusion was made possible by a complete failure of White House security personnel to detect and neutralize the threat before the residence was breached. Officers posted outside had not seen the interloper jump the fence, nor had they been able to intercept him as he crossed the lawn. Rather inexplicably, a decision was made not to unleash an available attack dog, and a SWAT team and front-door guard were also not deployed. When Gonzalez entered the residence, an alarm was not triggered due to it having been muted earlier, and he was thus able to brush past the unprepared guard stationed inside the main entrance.

The Obamas were not at home when Gonzalez arrived. They had earlier left for Camp David and would only learn about the incident later. The details of the home invasion were gripping; perhaps even more disquieting were the facts known to authorities prior to the September 19 break-in. In July, Virginia state troopers had stopped Gonzalez for a traffic violation and seized a number of weapons and ammunition, including an illegal sawed-off shotgun. They also found a map of Washington stuffed inside a Bible with the White House and other structures circled. The discoveries were unsettling enough for the Virginia State Police to inform the ATF and the Secret Service, but ultimately Gonzalez was not considered an imminent threat and was not detained. On August 25, he was again stopped by police at the southern fence of the White House. At the time, Gonzalez had a hatchet tucked in his rear waistband. After checking his nearby car and finding no firearms, the authorities allowed him to leave. Although enough information was available at that time to warrant a more thorough investigation into Gonzalez, it was only after his invasion of the White House that authorities connected the dots between his marked DC map, his casing of the executive mansion in August, and his subsequent assault. When his car was searched following his September arrest, officials found more than 800 rounds of ammunition, two hatchets, and a machete.[26]

The president, who had been publicly sympathetic toward the Secret Service during past security breaches, acted decisively in the aftermath of this most recent breakdown in protocol. Having lost confidence in the agency's leadership, he accepted the October 1 resignation of Director Julia Pierson, who had succeeded Mark Sullivan in March 2013. In her place, Homeland Security secretary Jeh Johnson announced the appointment of Joseph Clancy, a former head of the Presidential Protective Division, who came out of retirement to accept the position. Even with these immediate changes in personnel, the Secret Service had suffered enough reputational damage from security lapses to produce an ongoing buzz concerning its competence and mission.

Illustratively, Rep. Emanuel Cleaver told the press that he had heard a number of African Americans complain that the agency was purposefully "trying to expose the president," a charge that raised all sorts of tragic imagery concerning the assassinations of past Black leaders. Donald W. Tucker, a retired Black Secret Service agent, echoed Cleaver's remarks in the wake of the September break-in. "I would say over 75 percent of the African-American community are suspicious," he estimated, "based on all the other things they think has happened to President Obama because he's an African-American." Political analyst Charles D. Ellison boiled down the agency's failures to two theories: "Either agents missed the memo that he's the first black president, or they really are just that overwhelmed." None of these explanations or hypotheses were especially comforting to the Obamas or the staff members around them. Moving forward, the residence that the first couple desired to be known as the "People's House" was further transformed into more of a fortress. In July 2015, a month after Gonzalez was sentenced to seventeen months in prison for his White House invasion, spikes were added to the fencing surrounding the mansion. Undoubtedly, these structural additions sent as ominous a message to those inside the new fortifications as they did to the world beyond.[27]

Despite widely publicized blunders by the Secret Service, the Obamas had a reputation for being friendly and respectful toward the agency's personnel. During the 2008 campaign, candidate Obama had agents over for dinner at the family's Chicago home, having become familiar with a number of them during the protracted primary season. The First Lady was especially known for her pleasantness, insisting that Secret Service agents call her by her first name. "Michelle is friendly," one member of her detail recalled. "She touches you." The gestures were both a reflection of who the Obamas were as people and their awareness that their lives were literally in the hands of well-armed strangers who had access to some of the most intimate aspects of their existence. That is, they needed to trust these watchful men and women, even with the safety of their daughters, and it might be easier to cope with that if they at least made an effort to get to know, or even like, a few of them. With the passage of a law at the beginning of the president's second term that extended lifelong Secret Service protection to First Ladies, the Obamas would eventually be able to leave the White House with a certain amount of continuity in their security arrangements. But, of course, there were tradeoffs. They had to prepare themselves for living post-presidency lives amid the omnipresent vigilance of state guardians, whom they would have to continue to accommodate and, as best they could, endeavor to know and trust.[28]

CHAPTER 9

Guess Who's Coming to Tea

IN COMMON WITH ITS DEMOCRATIC COUNTERPART, THE REPUB-
lican Party has historically had a complicated relationship with African Americans. Emerging from the sectional divisions that racked the
nation during the 1850s, the Republican Party achieved early electoral
success by running on a platform of economic reform and opposition
to the expansion of slavery. The US Civil War explicitly became a
struggle over human bondage after 1862, and the Republicans, led
by progressive factions in Congress, leveraged the eventual Union
victory to pass constitutional amendments and other measures that
extended citizenship and the franchise to freed people. Into the first
decades of the twentieth century, Black voters still heavily favored the
party of Abraham Lincoln, the storied Great Emancipator, though
subsequent GOP leaders had shown declining interest in protecting
African American rights following the Reconstruction era. The four-
term presidency of Democrat Franklin Roosevelt, with its popular
economic and social programs, did much to realign the party system, drawing Black people in greater numbers toward the party that
had once supported their enslavement and ruthlessly crushed their
post-emancipation hopes. By the Second World War, many Republican politicians saw little political value in appealing to Black voters or

becoming involved in burgeoning civil rights activism. For the most part, northern GOP officials were content with allowing southern states to handle their racial problems internally, lest Republicans risk riling their base of white voters, who were not particularly sympathetic to the plight of African Americans in the North or South.[1]

The Democratic Party's gradual embrace of many of the legislative objectives of the civil rights movement during the 1960s completed the pendulum swing of African Americans away from the GOP. The shift was accelerated further by the presidential campaign of Arizona senator Barry Goldwater, who opposed the Civil Rights Act of 1964, and by the Republicans' southern strategy, which sought to attract white Democrats who were put off by the party's evolving liberalism on matters of race. Although they were a shrinking share of the African American electorate, Black Republicans continued to exist, and some found ideological solace in the presidencies of Ronald Reagan and George H. W. Bush. However, they were hardly a uniform or consistent group in terms of their political beliefs and policy prescriptions, despite their relatively small numbers. Some Black GOP supporters were attracted to the party's traditional promotion of private enterprise, limited government, and individual responsibility, even if they could envisage instances when public-private initiatives might be preferable to complete reliance on market-based solutions. Others were enticed by the party's articulation of a Christian social morality that clearly drew lines against abortion, homosexuality, feminism, and drug use, even if they thought the party's "color-blind" approach to addressing lingering racial disparities was not entirely realistic.

As the Republicans increasingly relied on an older, disproportionately white, regionally bounded electorate to win elections, Black people in the GOP became more confined to the margins of the party. Vocal Republican campaigns that centered affirmative action, social welfare programs, and inner-city crime as objects of scorn likely chased some Black voters away from the GOP altogether. Conversely, policies related to tax cuts, national defense, and school choice may have encouraged others not to flee the fold. Much depended on the political climate of the day and the issues at play, along with how individual African American voters calculated their investment in certain electoral outcomes.

Into the twenty-first century, Black Republicans continued to be the outlying exceptions that proved the partisan rule among African Americans, though a few high-profile individuals, such as Supreme Court justice Clarence Thomas and Oklahoma congressman J. C. Watts, confirmed their ongoing relevance in some areas of government. Black Republicans who witnessed the electoral trouncing of 2008 were, like other GOP supporters, forced to come to terms with the defeat and what it meant for the party and their allegiances. There were a few prominent figures, such as Colin Powell, a former army general and secretary of state under George W. Bush, who seemed to have little trouble in endorsing Barack Obama (in both 2008 and 2012) and turning the page on their former political lives. Others, like Condoleezza Rice, who also served a stint as secretary of state under Bush, were more protective of the GOP legacy, which sometimes led them to make strained efforts to see rosy continuities between successful Obama policies—such as the elimination of Osama bin Laden—and Bush-era antecedents. Somewhat ironically, an unusually high number of African American Republicans ran for congressional seats in 2010, largely motivated by the historic election of Barack Obama and serious efforts by the GOP to recruit candidates of any background who could halt his legislative agenda. As with many white candidates, the Tea Party insurgency helped some contenders and hindered others. Nonetheless, the Black Republicans' cumulative efforts to pursue elected office under the GOP banner signaled a continuing diversity of opinions, interests, and goals in Black America as it endured an age of momentous political and economic upheaval.[2]

Among those who rode the conservative wave that swept legions of Republicans into office during the 2010 midterm elections, Allen West became an iconic figure in the Tea Party era. Born in Atlanta, he had made a career in the US Army, rising to the rank of lieutenant colonel before his retirement in 2004. Only 43 at the time of discharge, he pursued additional employment opportunities as a military contractor and advisor to the Afghan army. In 2008, West decided to run for a US House seat. Florida's Twenty-Second Congressional District was roughly split between the parties, and the incumbent Democrat, Ron Klein, had only been in office since 2007, having succeeded Clay Shaw, a seven-term Republican. With his attention still split between the United States and Afghanistan, West lost the race but not by much. Two years later, he sought a rematch against Klein, which he won by a nine-point margin. This victory made him one of only two Black Republicans in the new Congress and the first from Florida since the 1870s, when Civil War veteran Josiah T. Walls, who had previously been enslaved, served three terms. Having benefited from strong Tea Party backing and the anti-incumbent tone of the midterms, West attributed his win to his conservative values, particularly his faith in "limited government, constitutional principles and [the] free market for enterprise solutions."[3]

Like many other newly elected Tea Party Republicans with a presumed mandate to disrupt the status quo, West entered Congress with no officeholding experience and seemingly little interest in governing. He readily picked fights with ideological foes, sometimes offering odd reasons for doing so, and rarely stepped outside of Tea Party dogma to work with representatives of different political stripes. One of his first and more enduring squabbles was with the CBC, which he joined, becoming its only Republican member. In August 2011, he likened the Democratic Party to a "21st century plantation," with "perceived leaders" and "overseers," such as Representatives Maxine Waters and Barbara Lee, Jesse Jackson Sr., and Al Sharpton, being used to keep Black people loyal to the party "regardless of the failures of our social welfare policies." While he acknowledged that the GOP needed to do better in its outreach to African American voters, he portrayed CBC members as puppets of white liberal leaders. The immediate blowback was predictable—Waters called the remarks "ridiculous"—but West was not finished. Days later he attacked a number of Black congresspeople for their criticism of the Tea Party and publicly threatened to leave the CBC. The caucus's chair, Emanuel Cleaver, talked him down from his outrage posture, and Rep. André Carson apologized for "figuratively" likening the Tea Party to a lynch mob.[4]

If West's relationship with his CBC colleagues was at best rocky, his belligerent approach to the White House and to Democrats in the Capitol Building was nothing short of open ideological warfare backed by opportunistic political sniping. In line with his brand of fiscal conservatism, the congressman was especially critical of the US welfare state that had been developed over the previous seventy years by largely Democratic architects. In January 2012, he expressed agreement with the assertion of Republican presidential candidate and former House speaker Newt Gingrich that Obama was the "food stamp president," a characterization that some viewed as a veiled stereotypical reference to Black people who received federal assistance. In July, West went further by claiming that the president wanted the average American to "be his slave and be economically dependent upon him," a racially charged critique of the federal government's stewardship of the economy in general and the Social Security disability insurance program in particular. When four US embassy officials were killed by militants in Libya in September, West accused Obama of being the "weakest and most ineffective person to ever occupy the White House."[5]

As the 2012 election approach, the congressman seemed to become even more free in his histrionics but more narrowly doctrinaire in his thinking. He compared Democrats to Nazis in their alleged "propaganda" efforts and recommended that President Obama and House minority leader Nancy Pelosi "get the hell out of the United States." In a nod to the red-baiting McCarthyism of another era, West claimed at a Jensen Beach town hall meeting that "there's about 78 to 81 members of the democratic party that are members of the communist party." The accusation would have seemed strangely out of place so long after the Cold War period but for all of the other conspiracy theories that had already polluted public discourse.[6]

Having decided to run for reelection in 2012, West faced a couple of obstacles to a second term. First, his district had been redrawn as part of the decennial redistricting process, making it more Democratic. To improve his odds of electoral success, he decided to run instead for the US House seat in the Eighteenth Congressional District, a more Republican-friendly political unit that stretched along the southeastern Florida coast and encompassed St. Lucie, Martin, and Palm Beach Counties. Another complication was that West had drawn a Democratic challenger who, though new to politics, was running competitively in the polls. Patrick Murphy, a 29-year-old businessman and former Republican, had more than enough shocking video footage and sound bites of West to persuasively paint him as an extremist ill prepared to represent a moderate swing district. Nevertheless, the congressman's star power in Republican circles and fundraising prowess kept things close.

As predicted, the election turned out to be tight. When the numbers trended Murphy's way, West charged that "disturbing irregularities" had occurred during the balloting and demanded a recount. Ultimately, the Democrat was declared the victor by a 0.58 percent margin, despite the whopping $18.5 million war chest that West had accrued, the biggest of any US House candidate in the country. "Allen West was quite a character to run against," Murphy declared during his victory speech. "And I'll keep it at that, and hopefully that's the last time I ever need to mention his name, too." Having lost political luster commensurate with the fading influence of the Tea Party, the defeated congressman did indeed retire from electoral politics. His name would come up again in the future connected with the National Rifle Association and Fox News, but his days in the national spotlight were over.[7]

If Allen West was the proverbial light that burns twice as bright for half as long, Tim Scott, the other Black Republican in the US

House, was the steady flame that blazed far into the night. Elected in the same Tea Party wildfire of 2010, the two men, even as Black southerners and ideological siblings, could hardly have been more different in background, temperament, and foresight. Scott was raised in a conservative Christian household by a single mother in a poor, predominantly Black neighborhood in North Charleston, South Carolina. In school, he was a less-than-stellar student but managed to win an athletic scholarship that partially paid for his tuition at a local college. A strong work ethic earned him a job with the Allstate insurance company, and over time he became one of its best agents before launching his own franchise. At age 29, he successfully ran for a seat on the Charleston City Council in 1995, endearing himself to local conservatives by distributing copies of the Ten Commandments. In a controversial move, he agreed to serve as cochair of the 1996 reelection campaign of Sen. Strom Thurmond. Years later, Scott rationalized his decision by contending that the former archsegregationist was having "more of a positive effect in the black community" by the 1990s. Such displays of party loyalty kept him popular among local Republican voters, who reelected him to the city council in 2000 and 2004. Instead of seeking a fourth term in local government, Scott ran for a seat in the South Carolina House of Representatives in 2008. After winning the primary with 53 percent of the vote, he appeared unopposed on the general election ballot, becoming by default the District 117 representative.[8]

With his political ambitions still rising, Scott was not in the state legislature long. In an interesting twist, he decided to run for an open US House seat in 2010, facing off in the Republican primary against Paul Thurmond, son of the late US senator, who had died seven years earlier. In a runoff vote, Scott received two-thirds of the primary ballots cast and went on to beat his general election challenger, Democrat Ben Frasier, by a thirty-six-point margin. In winning the race, the new congressman carried the boot-shaped First Congressional District, which stretched from Myrtle Beach to Charleston and was more than 70 percent white. He also became the first Black

Republican to represent the state in the US House since 1897, when teacher George W. Murray, who had been enslaved, completed his second and final term in the wake of state constitutional amendments that would disfranchise most African Americans for generations.

Although cut from the same deep-red cloth as Allen West, Scott's ideological disposition and interpersonal skills were more refined than those of West and thus not as likely to lead to explosive conflict. The South Carolina congressman was for tax cuts, gun rights, a balanced-budget amendment, and school-choice programs, and he opposed cap-and-trade policies, amnesty for undocumented immigrants, same-sex marriage, and the ACA. He considered affirmative action unnecessary and seemed content to leave some issues of social justice either beyond the reach of limited government or in the purview of the marketplace. His was a coherent vision of the world that mated Republican orthodoxy with Tea Party platitudes. Such a species of conservatism was safe in South Carolina, which made Scott—and arguably his Blackness—safe for the predominantly white electorate that he cultivated.

If there was anything truly novel about Scott in the bitter über-partisanship of the Obama era, it was his reserved demeanor and collegiality. His style belied his home state's reputation for producing fire-breathing secessionists and rabid segregationists, and he appeared to model his own—or his mother's—take on southern gentlemanliness. Even as he critiqued the president's economic policies and campaigned for his defeat in 2012, Scott routinely exhibited decency and could rise to pay a compliment. "We can be proud of what he's accomplished," he said of Obama's historic election, though "the only thing that matters to the American people and to me is what he does . . . not what he looks like." Intriguingly, Scott's ascent from a single-parent household to high posts in state and federal government mirrored Obama's path to power. The South Carolina congressman, too, could sense doorways of opportunity and position himself at exactly the right angle to slip through them. Having won reelection to the House in November 2012, he was appointed by South Carolina governor Nikki Haley to complete the US Senate term of Jim De-Mint, a retiring Tea Party stalwart, making Scott the first Black US senator from the South since Reconstruction. Whether in the House or the Senate, Scott, unlike Obama, declined invitations to join the CBC. In line with his general avoidance of public engagement with matters of race, he believed that such groups amplified the "divisions I've been pushing forward to erase."9

Herman Cain believed in lucky numbers, and his was forty-five. Although not an avid numerologist, he was struck by how often the number appeared in his life experiences in ways that were meaningful and seemingly portentous. In his 2011 book, *This Is Herman Cain! My Journey to the White House*, he described patterns of the number's presence around him and prognosticated about their relevance:

> And given that I was born on December 13, 1945—my con-ception, gestation, and birth all occurred within that year—that number has been with me, literally, for all my life, to date. The number 45 keeps on popping up as I go about the business of being elected—you guessed it—as the forty-fifth president of the United States. . . . That isn't all: next year will be the forty-fifth anniversary of my college graduation. And in 2013, my first year in the White House, Gloria and I will be celebrating our forty-fifth wedding anniversary. . . . Isn't it amazing how often 45 keeps popping up in my life?

While the number was probably not a decisive factor in Cain's de-cision to run for president in 2012, it likely confirmed for him the rectitude of that course of action and helped fortify him for the rigors of a national campaign. Some of the forty-fives, like his birth year, were set and perpetual, while others, such as anniversaries, were time dependent and relative to other happenings. Whatever the ultimate meaning of the number to his journey, Cain assumed that it was mo-mentous enough to notice and remember.10

Herman Cain grew up poor in Georgia, with his father having to work three jobs in order to purchase a family home. As a teenager, he labored to pay for his schooling at Morehouse College before attending Purdue University to study computer science. By his thirties, Cain had demonstrated an interest in and aptitude for managerial assignments and was eventually hired as a vice president at the Pillsbury Company. Hoping to one day run his own corporate enterprise, he entered the training program of Burger King, a Pillsbury subsidiary, and was promoted to administrative head of his region in just a couple of years. His big break came when he was assigned to manage the recovery of the Godfather's Pizza chain, which was languishing in debt and disorder. As the new CEO, Cain prescribed tough medicine, closing more than 200 stores and dismissing thousands of employees. The company returned to profitability by the late 1980s, and Cain and other investors pooled enough resources to buy the pizza chain from Pillsbury.[11]

In the 1990s, Cain began to engage with politics and government agencies in various capacities. From 1992 to 1996, he served as deputy chair and then chair of the Federal Reserve Bank of Kansas City, where he enhanced his knowledge of monetary policy. From 1996 to 1999, he ran the National Restaurant Association, which lobbied lawmakers to oppose minimum-wage increases and restaurant bans on smoking. Having served as an advisor to Robert Dole's presidential campaign in 1996, Cain briefly ran for the Republican presidential nomination four years later but dropped out once his campaign foundered. In that same year, he moved back to Georgia in time to prepare for a 2004 run for the US Senate but lost badly to Rep. Johnny Isakson in the Republican primary. Two years later, Cain had a life-clarifying moment when he was diagnosed with stage 4 cancer and had to undergo a debilitating regimen of chemotherapy. Perhaps it was during that time when the fine details of his life and its meaning came into sharper focus, including the ubiquitous number forty-five. In any event, his desire to run for high office still remained. On May 21, 2011, the 65-year-old businessman announced his candidacy for the Republican presidential nomination before a cheering Atlanta crowd. "I'm running for president of the United States," Cain shouted for all to hear and then assured the audience just as loudly, "and I'm not running for second."[12]

In terms of background and temperament, Cain was somewhat of a mix of Allen West and Tim Scott. A fellow southerner and a generation older than the other men, the businessman-cum-politician could relate to Scott's poverty-afflicted childhood and entrepreneurial skills but shared West's electoral inexperience and flare for melodrama. Cain's more deliberate policy ruminations distinguished him from the congressmen, and he was the only one of the three to author a book that broadcasted his political ambitions. On most issues, he held familiar conservative positions, though some of his views placed him on the far right of the Republican Party. He opposed abortion under all circumstances, derided global warming as a fiction, supported more restrictive immigration policies, and prescribed more warships and missile deployments for containing Iran. Like others who sought to reconfigure or shrink the social safety net, he proposed personal retirement accounts to replace the Social Security system, and enhanced health-care savings accounts to supplant the ACA.

Tax policy was the centerpiece of Cain's economic platform and included his most original idea. Proceeding from the premise that tax cuts would spur economic growth, he advocated a 9-9-9 plan that set corporate, personal income, and federal sales taxes at a flat 9 percent rate. Around the time of his campaign announcement, he proposed reducing the capital gains tax to zero and suspending levies on repatriated foreign profits, measures that would supposedly bring the economy out of the doldrums. Cain was never clear about how the lost federal revenue would be recouped to avoid widening deficits and mounting national debt. Moreover, he could be oblique and even flippant concerning other policy matters as revealed in his admitted lack of a strategy for the Afghanistan conflict and his joking suggestion that an electrified fence be erected along the US border with Mexico. Nevertheless, he was certain about the internal rhyme and reason behind his presidential bid. "I think of this stuff as I go," he told a *Newsweek* interviewer in 2011. "My messages are spontaneous." When asked about the inspiration behind his political beliefs and policies, Cain, who was still an associate minister of the Antioch Baptist Church in Atlanta, readily replied, "The Holy Spirit."[13]

Even more so than Allen West, Cain took on the subject of race head-on and was not shy about inveighing against President Obama. Some of his criticisms were policy related, including his charge that the administration had advanced a "wealth redistribution agenda" that was dependent on increasing the tax burden of "America's job creators." As a Black politician, Cain thought that he could assail the president in ways that most white conservatives would not, lest they be charged with racial animus. In March 2011 as Donald Trump's birther claims were making the news rounds, Cain endorsed calls for Barack Obama to prove his citizenship, while admitting that he had not studied the issue well enough "to have a view one way or the other." By the time he announced his White House bid two months later, the businessman had conjured further racial imagery by claiming that Democrats and liberals were planning to inflict a "high-tech lynching" on him, invoking Clarence Thomas's characterization of his tumultuous Supreme Court confirmation hearings two decades earlier. During an August conference call with the press, Cain supported the impeachment of the president for the passage of the ACA and the Department of Justice's decision not to strictly enforce the Defense of Marriage Act. "It would be a great thing to do," he told reporters, though he was sure that the Democratic-controlled Senate would never vote to remove Obama from office.[14]

Given that his candidacy was supported by Tea Party groups and funding, much of Cain's time was spent defending the right-wing insurgency from charges of bigotry. "You are not racists!" he sometimes proclaimed before predominantly white crowds interspersed with Tea Party supporters. Like West and others, he referred to the Democratic Party as a plantation and vowed that he would never return to it. Despite his efforts to attract Black support, Cain was no more successful in doing so than other GOP candidates. If anything, he may have been more repellent. Michael Eric Dyson portrayed Cain's high standing among some white Republicans as related to his pandering and his skin color. "He makes them feel they aren't racist because they support him," the professor told an interviewer, echoing sentiments expressed by others. Rev. Joseph Lowery was harsher in his assessment, dismissing Cain as an unqualified candidate. "He's done nothing to further black people's lives," the clergyman asserted in October 2011. "All he's doing is saying the racist stuff the mainstream GOP candidates can't say and he's having the time of his life doing it." Singer and actor Harry Belafonte deemed Cain a "bad apple" and questioned his intelligence as well as his sense of history.[15]

The dismissive opinions of prominent African Americans regarding the Cain candidacy were representative of his polling among the broader Black population. A survey taken during the height of his ascent in the Republican nomination race showed Cain receiving only 6 percent of the African American vote in a hypothetical matchup against Obama, who was preferred by 93 percent of respondents. Cain's numbers matched the polling performance of eventual nominee Mitt Romney, which was hardly an achievement since the latter had expended little energy in trying to appeal to Black voters. Ultimately, the polls, in the case of Cain, said less about race than the fact that African Americans largely perceived him as just another Republican candidate whose views and policies were incongruent with their own aspirations and interests.[16]

As it turned out, the most decisive month of Cain's run for the White House was not November 2012 but November 2011, which was undoubtedly the nadir of his campaign. On Sunday evening, October 30, the news broke that two women employed by the National Restaurant Association in the 1990s were publicly accusing Cain of having exhibited "sexually suggestive behavior" toward them during his tenure as head of the organization. Financial settlements with the restaurant group precluded the women from discussing the details of their experiences or the terms of their subsequent departures, but both claimed that Cain's conduct had discomforted and infuriated them. The campaign initially wrote off the story as a character assassination by the "political trade press," though neither the candidate nor his staff denied the core aspects of the accusations. During the early days of November, Cain's poll numbers held firm, and several high-profile conservatives and Tea Party activists came to his defense. "This is about blacks and Hispanics getting uppity," radio talk-show host Rush Limbaugh contended. "[Liberals] cannot have a black Republican running for office, can't have a Hispanic, the Left owns those minorities, those two groups can't be seen rising on their own." The rallying continued for several days, but more damage was done to Cain's campaign when two other women came forward alleging that the businessman had made unwanted sexual advances toward them. By late November, he was slipping in the polls, with one showing that both Romney and Gingrich had passed him. Cain continued to argue that the charges were false, but disaster appeared to be closing in on him.[17]

On November 28, a bombshell exploded on Cain's presidential hopes. Ginger White, an unemployed former businesswoman and mother of two, claimed in a televised interview that she had engaged in an extramarital affair with the candidate for thirteen years, with the relationship ending just before his May 2011 campaign announcement. The Atlanta woman described being lavished with gifts and periodically flown to romantic getaways around the country, attention that "took me away from my humdrum life at the time." White's decision to go public with her story was apparently made only after seeing Cain's other accusers smeared in the press. "They were treated as if they were automatically lying," she told an interviewer, "and the burden of proof was on them." In the face of this new allegation, Cain admitted that he and White were friends and that he had tried to help her financially but denied any affair. But by the end of the week, the weight of the women's charges, along with the interminable grind of the negative news cycle, made his position untenable.[18]

On December 3, Cain, standing beside his wife, Gloria, ended his pursuit of the Republican presidential nomination. He characterized his decision as necessary for halting "the continued distraction, the continued hurt to me and my family" that had ostensibly resulted from the allegations of inappropriate sexual behavior. While there was nothing inevitable about the collapse of Cain's campaign, a number of factors, in addition to the various charges of sexual impropriety, had made his bid for the presidency an unlikely proposition from the beginning. Despite past unsuccessful runs for office and his work for the Federal Reserve, Cain's business background and force of character were no substitutes for actual experience in campaign management and elective officeholding. During his six-month candidacy, he routinely displayed a lack of preparation in debates and in one-on-one interviews, even concerning topics that he had recently written about in his book. Moreover, his campaign operation suffered from chaos and understaffing, problems that Cain never remedied even when he rode high in the polls. It is likely that voters' interest in him was always as fragile and fleeting as the Tea Party's electoral appeal, needing only a mishap, scandal, or short passage of time to allow for the resurgence of more traditional, establishment candidates. Some even speculated that the whole enterprise was less a presidential campaign than an opportunity for Cain to burnish his business brand and sell books, all the while diminishing the seriousness of the nomination process.[19]

Following his aborted presidential bid, Herman Cain never ran for office again. He dabbled a bit more in the 2012 candidate field, suggesting that Republican nominee Mitt Romney consider Rep. Allen West as a running mate, a recommendation also advanced by Sarah Palin. After the election, Cain remained in high enough demand to warrant a stint as a commentator on Fox News, which briefly extended his visibility in the conservative media world. Beyond these diversions, he seemed resigned to moving to the political sidelines. If it was any consolation, he and Gloria did celebrate anniversary number forty-five together, though not while serving as the forty-fifth president and First Lady. That enchanting dream had been shattered by the public allegations of four women and especially those of a fifth, Ginger White, who, in the year of Cain's presidential bid, was 45 years old.[20]

Despite their flashy celebrity, flamboyant personas, and soaring ambitions, none of the Black Republican candidates who ran for office in 2010 or 2012 could claim that they were the most important African American in the party. That distinction went to Michael Steele. A former seminarian and corporate lawyer, the Maryland Republican rose swiftly through the party's ranks by way of both administrative and electoral routes. In 2000, he became chair of the Republican Party State Central Committee and two years later ran successfully to become Maryland's first African American lieutenant governor. In 2004, when Barack Obama's star rose at the DNC in Boston, Steele was tapped to speak at the Republican National Convention in New York. A failed bid for a US Senate seat in 2006 revealed him to be a bit too conservative for Maryland voters despite his known support for affirmative action and efforts to improve public education. Shortly after the 2008 presidential election, Steele won the chair of the Republican National Committee (RNC), becoming again a Black first. His selection for the post signaled a renewed effort by the GOP to reach out to African Americans in the aftermath of a devastating election for the party but a historic one for the nation.[21]

Steele became RNC chair among the flames of the Tea Party revolt. Being from an Upper South state that trended Democratic, he had learned to politically dissemble enough to make himself palatable to a purplish statewide electorate while staying in good stead with the Bush administration and the national GOP apparatus. The Tea Party and other Republican factions, however, persistently forced him rightward into a ruby-red ideology and required him to take on directly their archnemesis, Barack Obama. Steele more than obliged them, at least at first.

In May 2009, Steele vowed to take an "aggressive new approach" in challenging the president, who he claimed had not been evaluated thoroughly enough for the position. Drawing on the McCain-Palin playbook from the fall 2008 campaign and anticipating Trump's birtherism, Steele portrayed Obama as a stranger, an imposter who had stumbled into the White House on the coattails of liberal white guilt. "The problem that we have with this president is we don't know him," Steele contended. "He was not vetted, folks. He came out of nowhere." In the same instant that he rendered Obama as someone who was unfamiliar, despite more than a decade of public life in state and federal politics and two widely available autobiographical books, the RNC chair did not hesitate to disclose who he thought the president was: a disciple of Rev. Jeremiah Wright. It was a name that had been known on the national political scene for only a year, but by the time Steele invoked it, it had become a rather passé slur against Obama, since it had not helped to get either Hillary Clinton or John McCain elected. Still, the RNC chair was just getting started in his crusade against Obama and the Democrats, and Rev. Wright was simply the opener.[22]

Notwithstanding his early gambit for a "new approach," Steele's stated differences with the Obama administration over policy were traditional Republican fare. In his 2009 book, *Right Now: A 12-Step Program for Defeating the Obama Agenda*, he took exception to what he believed to be the president's "old liberal, big-government agenda," which empowered the state more than citizens. He accused the president of being irresponsible and unaccountable in his exercise of power, as well as neglecting any efforts at bipartisanship. When the Department of Homeland Security issued a report in April 2009 warning of attempts by right-wing extremists to recruit military veterans, Steele dutifully chided the president and Secretary Janet Napolitano for going after conservatives and dissenters. As the GOP swung further right over the course of the next several months, the chair tried to ride the wave of Tea Party–fueled anger and vitriol, which was expressed in incendiary rhetoric and racially charged rallies. The political survival skills that he had learned in Maryland somewhat suited him for such a role, and he navigated well enough in various forums. What Steele was not prepared for was the speed at which the ideological ground shifted beneath him, or how his place in the GOP would be jeopardized by forces beyond his control.[23]

By the spring of 2010 when the Tea Party insurgency was in full bloom, Steele was losing faith. At a speech at DePaul University in April, he struggled to answer a question about why African Americans should consider voting for Republican candidates, a query that should not have caught him off guard. "You really don't have a reason, to be honest," he told the audience of approximately 200 students. "We haven't done a very good job of giving you one." Steele's candor was not new. Back in November, he had recalled instances in which he felt that white Republicans were afraid of him. "I've been in the room and they've been scared of me," he stated with amazement during an interview. Such occasions must have been confounding for him, especially given his swift rise in the GOP over the previous decade. In Maryland, he had broken through multiple racial barriers and appeared poised to continue making history. Yet on the national terrain of Republican politics, he was unable to steady himself as the party moved jarringly to the right.[24]

By nearly any standard, Steele was an effective RNC chair. Following the Republican rout in the 2008 election, he had helped to rebuild state parties and encouraged new candidates to run in the midterms. He showed himself to be a gifted fundraiser, generating almost $200 million and wiping out much of the GOP's debt. The dramatic Republican capture of the US House and hundreds of state and local offices in 2010, accentuated by the election of a handful of Black candidates, occurred during his watch. Despite these achievements, it became clear that Steele, while assisting the party in winning important battles, was becoming a casualty of a larger ideological and cultural war. Based on some of his comments, he seemed to understand that the heightening partisan and racial polarization of the Obama era had implications for him as the face of the GOP. He countenanced the tensions for as long as he could and even sought a second term as RNC chair following the historic midterm success. But by then, party leaders and activists, mindful of the ascendant Tea Party elements that had so skillfully used Obama as a bugbear to bolster Republican turnout, had little further use for Steele.

To be sure, Steele's troubles in the party had evolved over a period of years, though they intensified in the wake of the Tea Party eruption. He was occasionally not helpful to his own cause or his political longevity, given that he was prone to contradictory statements of policy and off-message controversies. He was not drummed out of the party leadership as unceremoniously as was Anthony Miller, the Black district chair of the Arizona GOP, who resigned in January 2011 after receiving racist death threats from fellow Republicans. However, Steele was soundly defeated in his quest for another term as RNC chair only two months after having led the party to historic gains in local, state, and federal offices. The former lieutenant governor appeared to be finished with electoral politics; he had left the RNC on unpleasant terms, and no one motioned publicly for his return. As had become the pattern for vanquished political celebrities, Steele found a warm seat as a political commentator on MSNBC, the liberal equivalent of Fox News. In short order, he migrated back to the center-right waters that he had inhabited for most of his political career, a turnabout that was not surprising to anyone who had watched him swim in the purple streams of Maryland politics. It was a more comfortable, natural place for him, especially after having been so severely blistered in trying to manage the boiling-hot Tea Party.[25]

Even in the ebb and flow of the rough political tides of the Obama era, the odd case of Democrat-turned-Republican-turned-Democrat Artur Davis was singularly instructive concerning the perils of mixing repeated self-reinvention with flagrant opportunism. Raised in Alabama poverty by his mother and grandmother, Davis proved studious and resilient enough to excel in public school and gain admission into Harvard University. During his time in Cambridge, his path crossed that of *Harvard Law Review* president Barack Obama, whose "combination of command and comfort" Davis admired. After earning bachelor's and law degrees, Davis returned to his native Montgomery in the 1990s and served as the assistant attorney for the Middle District of Alabama. In 2002, he ran successfully for the congressional seat representing the Seventh District, covering the central-eastern part of the state. When Obama decided to run for president, Davis was the first member of Congress outside of Illinois to endorse his bid. He went on to serve as the campaign chair for Alabama, which Obama decisively carried on Super Tuesday.[26]

Similar to his Harvard Law classmate and CBC colleague, Davis had big political aspirations and strategized to realize them. He wanted to become governor of his home state, which would have been a truly historic achievement, given that Alabama had never voted to elect an African American to a statewide executive office. During his eight years in Congress, Davis moved more toward the political center, positioning himself to appeal to enough conservative white voters to piece together a winning coalition. Toward this end, he racked up votes in favor of "partial-birth" abortion bans, a "traditional marriage" amendment, and other conservative policies, and to the dismay of many became the only CBC member to oppose the passage of the ACA. With centrist record in hand, he risked his congressional seat to run for governor of Alabama just as the Tea Party wave gathered momentum. Davis never made it past the Democratic primary, which he lost to agriculture commissioner Ron Sparks by twenty-four points. Out of public service entirely, the former congressman waded further right, apparently hoping to dock at some destination not reserved for defeated southern Democrats. In August 2011, he expressed support for Alabama's voter ID law, citing the conventional Republican rationale that the measure would make elections less susceptible to fraud. In May of the following year, he left the Democratic Party altogether and announced his defection to the GOP during a Fox News segment.

With only six months before the election, Davis was taking another gamble, tying whatever political future he might have to the fate of

Republican presidential candidate Mitt Romney. His new party used him to its advantage, and Davis employed his momentary notoriety to maximum political effect. In interviews, he expressed disappointment with the Democratic Party, claiming that it was not tolerant of a range of opinions. Barack Obama was especially a letdown, according to Davis, since he had failed to embody "the kind of center-wing of the Democratic Party that Bill Clinton represented." The former congressman predicted that once the president was out of office, Black people would be more open to electing GOP candidates who made efforts to earn their votes. During the Republican National Convention in August, Davis was given a primetime slot to publicly embrace the party and to declare his political apostasy. To some who had followed his career, it was an arresting sight, especially because the nationally televised event featured so few Black delegates and audience members. Fourteen of Davis's former CBC colleagues wrote an open letter to him deploring his decision to leave the Democratic fold and questioning his sincerity. Channeling Herman Cain, Allen West, and others who used demeaning language to describe Black support for the Democratic Party, Davis responded by discounting what he believed to be the CBC's stance that "someone who leaves the reservation [is] . . . something of a traitor."[27]

Davis's political hopes did not end with Romney's defeat in November, but his slippery partisan loyalties earned him no lasting friends of any stature on either side of the aisle. In 2015, he set his sights on the Montgomery mayoral race and ran against Republican incumbent Todd Strange. Davis's pro–job creation, anticrime platform availed him little, and he barely received a quarter of the vote despite his hometown connections. In defeat, he did not give up his pursuit of public office; he simply set his aspirations lower and waded leftward across the political spectrum.

In October, Davis appeared before the executive board of the State Democratic Executive Committee to make a case for being allowed to run as a Democrat for the office of Montgomery County commissioner. His request was rejected outright, with the board members citing a rule barring candidates from running for office after recently changing party affiliation. During the meeting, Davis praised Democratic priorities, such as the expansion of Medicaid, increasing the minimum wage, and the reopening of motor vehicle licensing offices that had been closed in areas with predominantly Black populations following the implementation of the state's voter ID law, which he had previously supported. Despite his pandering, Davis was notified that he would be eligible to run again as a Democrat in 2017 at the earliest, coinciding with the close of the Obama presidency. "I have been with you on the issues that define the Democratic Party," he assured the wary board members, apparently assuming that none of them had even casually followed his zigzagging political journey over the previous decade.[28]

The Black conservatives of the Obama era, including shaky centrists like Davis, were a reflection of the variety of experiences, values, and interests among African Americans, as well as the limitations of the US party system and political culture in general. None of these politicians were particularly popular among Black people at the ballot box, but their assorted backgrounds in poverty, conservative Christian households, and entrepreneurial endeavors were relatable to the lives of many African Americans. Some of their limitations were personal and idiosyncratic; other shortcomings had much to do with their political ideologies and policy prescriptions. Moreover, the two-party system and the hyperpartisanship of the day reduced their attractiveness further by compelling Black voters to accept the entire Republican platform—and the party's racially problematic history, rhetoric, and policies—when they considered voting for a GOP candidate, especially at the national or statewide level. That is, both Black conservatives and Black voters in general were more complicated and diverse in their views than the party system would allow, with some being liberal on matters of economic policy and conservative on social or cultural issues, and vice versa. The same African American voter that might support the ACA, stricter banking regulations, and a more progressive tax code might also be against abortion, same-sex marriage, and gun-control laws. However, in a polarized two-party system, there is little room for such blended, hybridized spaces between liberal and conservative, blue and red, Democrat and Republican.

Consequently, given only the two options, African Americans tended to choose the party that addressed at least some of their concerns and interests without routinely casting them as racial pariahs in order to draw white votes. These systemic limitations of the US partisan arrangement were the great conundrum for Black Republicans who sought to attract a larger African American audience. Aside from the racially coded messaging, special-interest money, and gerrymandered districts that skewed and limited the GOP's appeal to the masses of Black people, the starkness of the choice between Republicans and Democrats—with no viable, party-based middle ground between them—further diminished the electability of Black conservative candidates among African American constituencies.

CHAPTER 10

Signifier in Chief

WORTHINGTON WHITE HAD SEEN A LOT OF THINGS DURING HIS three decades of service as a White House usher. Hired in 1980, he had worked for five first families prior to the arrival of the Obamas in 2009 and had stories to tell about each of them. He could recall the heady, rushing times of presidential transitions and the sad good-byes to departing children whom he had watched grow up during their father's years in office. He knew the pain of the place as well, whether symbolized by Ronald Reagan's near-assassination less than three months into his first term or by Hillary Clinton's personal request that White clear the premises for privacy's sake as her husband publicly confessed his role in a sex scandal. His job at the mansion primarily involved discreetly moving people and managing time without conspicuously appearing to do so. Ushering also required patience, finesse, and the ability to make sure that idle chit-chat never became too political. "I was an independent Republicrat," White said of his party affiliation while on duty in the White House. "I would say I voted for the president, no matter who it was." His long tenure on the staff undoubtedly entailed some occasional fibbing, if only to protect the stately quiet of the residence from the partisan wars that raged just outside its walls. In many ways, the place was home to White as much as it was to any of the first families who passed through, and his investment in its maintenance and well-being was appreciable over the years.[1]

On January 20, 2009, White found himself in the service of yet another first family, whose premier night in the White House would be memorable to him for years to come. The usher was tasked with delivering some papers to the president who, just in from an exhausting round of inaugural balls and other events, had retired to the residential level. As he climbed the stairs to the second floor, White could hear Barack Obama speaking to someone in his confident baritone voice. "I got this, I got this," the new commander in chief reassured. "I got the inside on this now." Suddenly, Mary J. Blige's hit song "Real Love" started pumping through the halls. And around the corner, there they were, the first couple of the United States, dancing as if they were the only two people in the world. The song had been released as a single just weeks before Barack and Michelle Obama had married in 1992, and Blige's stirring vocals and hip-hop beats likely brought back memories of their earlier romance. Noticing the usher, the president hailed him: "I bet you haven't seen anything like this in this house, have you?" An amused White, who had recognized the song despite being some years older than the Obamas, replied, "I can honestly say I've never heard *any* Mary J. Blige being played on this floor." The first couple continued their merriment, he in shirt-sleeves and she in a T-shirt and sweatpants. And Blige sang on with soulful passion, evoking more feelings of nostalgia.[2]

In addition to this first night of dancing, there were a number of moments when the Obamas and guests enjoyed a cultural palette that had never been experienced before in the White House. On the president's fiftieth birthday in August 2011, the first family celebrated with a musical barbeque party that sprawled between the East Room and the Rose Garden. The guest list was impressive, ranging from political types, such as House leader Nancy Pelosi, Sen. Tim Kaine, and Secretary of State Hillary Clinton, to cultural icons like Jay-Z, Oprah Winfrey, Herbie Hancock, and Tom Hanks. The event started with performances of old-school classics: Stevie Wonder sang "Signed, Sealed, Delivered I'm Yours," which had been a theme song of Obama's presidential campaign. Once the White House press corps was dismissed at 4:00 p.m., the summer gathering became more relaxed, with more dancing and casual interactions. According to attendee Chris Rock, the music list trended "blacker and blacker" as afternoon turned into evening and more of the white guests departed. Seeing African American celebrities grooving carefree at a White House birthday celebration for a Black president took the comedian to a euphoric place. "I felt like I died and went to black heaven," he later said of the event, a sentiment likely shared by other revelers.[3]

In several instances during his time in office, President Obama explicitly participated in signifying Black culture, sometimes in ways that both elevated its visibility and lightheartedly spotlighted his own middling talents. During a fundraising event at the legendary Apollo Theater in January 2012, he credibly crooned a line from Al Green's classic "Let's Stay Together," rousing the crowd to shouts and applause. Obama assured the artist, who was in attendance, that he knew that his skills were not in the same league but still "wanted to show my appreciation." It was a win-win performance. Sales of Green's song spiked 500 percent, and the president was invited to join the singer for a duet on the popular TV show *American Idol*. Such gestures were good humor and good politics; they further humanized the White House and played to a popular longing among some Americans to occasionally put aside partisan bickering and the stresses of life. Obama's facility with Black culture also reminded people of the historic nature of his presidency and likely primed many of his supporters for his reelection bid, which was in full swing by the time he sang the Green lyric. Other impromptu performances, such as his joining in to sing a few lines of "Sweet Home Chicago" during a 2012 Black History Month visit of B. B. King and other jazz legends to the White House, added further pop culture elements to the campaign trail and focused attention on Obama as a kind of entertainer in chief. Harking back to Bill Clinton's saxophone playing two decades earlier, the president seemed remarkably comfortable in the role of amateur performer, revealing a willingness both to take risks and to not take himself too seriously.[4]

One especially painful moment in Obama's tenure that required cultural adeptness and presidential empathy was a mass shooting at the historic Mother Emanuel African Methodist Episcopal Church in Charleston, South Carolina. Dylann Roof, a self-avowed white supremacist, entered the meetinghouse on the evening of June 17, 2015, and was welcomed for Bible study. However, his purpose was not to worship but to murder. After lingering among the congregation for several minutes, he pulled out a .45-caliber pistol and killed nine people, including Rev. Clementa Pinckney. The 21-year-old gunman then fled the scene but was captured the following day in Shelby, North Carolina. Obama, who knew Pinckney personally, agreed to eulogize the slain clergyman. During his visit to Charleston on June 26, he offered stirring, uplifting words about grace and the enduring human spirit of the congregation. Toward the end of his speech, the president broke into song, leading the audience in verses of "Amazing Grace." It was a Black signification that evoked his channeling of Al Green at the Apollo Theater years earlier and seemed wholly appropriate to the tragic circumstances at hand. By this point in his presidency, Obama was used to meeting devastated families and friends in the wake of mass shootings, and he did the best he could to console the Charleston survivors. "He hugged each one of us individually—and I mean hug, so that I was able to smell his cologne," one woman grieving the loss of several relatives in the church assault recollected later. "It was not a little pat on the back. The intimacy of the hug is what I'll always remember." According to his rambling manifesto, Roof had hoped to instigate a race war. Instead, the Charleston community and thousands of well-wishers came out in force in the days following the shooting and, like Obama, wrapped Mother Emanuel in a loving embrace.[5]

To a certain extent, incorporating some golden oldies into his cultural and political messaging, whether in jest or in the midst of tragedy, was easy since Obama had grown up with the music, and some of it still had broad cross-demographic appeal. What was trickier and required a more deliberate approach was navigating the taste of younger people, especially those who came of age a generation after the Obamas. This was a necessary endeavor, given that voters under age 30 were at the center of the president's winning electoral coalition. The upshot: Obama needed to learn to speak in a language that attracted members of the hip-hop generation, as well as those older Americans who actually knew who Al Green and B. B. King were.

In other words, it was yet another balancing act. Obama had to engage rap and hip-hop as the ubiquitous national and, indeed, international phenomena that they were without appearing to be either dismissive or pandering. He also needed to recognize the rich diversity of the music, people, and cultures that produced—and were produced by—hip-hop and rap, while at the same time understanding that with such a wide range of artists and genres, there was plenty that a politician with a national constituency needed to avoid. That is, the value of rap and hip-hop music and performances was, as with other cultural expressions and artistic forms, in the eye of the beholder and the ear of the listener. Lyrical screeds that might amuse and inspire one person might confuse and offend the next. Rap is especially known for its colorful commentaries, which offer a cultural lexicon and many different kinds of lenses for examining a plethora of issues, including sexuality, violence, urban life, criminality, poverty, race relations, and, yes, electoral politics. The messages, rhythms, artists, and hybridity are endless, thus necessitating careful assessments of individual performers and their crafts in a fashion that avoids sweeping generalizations about the genres. Consequently, it was not so much that Obama needed to either evade or apologize for rap and hip-hop cultures and their peculiarities and occasional excesses. He could probably do neither to the satisfaction of most people and would have tried to do so at his peril. Instead, he needed to recognize them as global realities and to harness their vital, positive energies and networks to reach people and places that may not have otherwise readily discerned the relevance of his message and policies to their lives.

In 2012, Ice-T, a baby-boom rapper, claimed that rap "put Barack Obama in the presidency," insofar as the music's crossing of cultural and racial boundaries conditioned some white people to accept the possibility of a Black head of state. The contention was impossible to prove and likely overblown but did accurately reflect the growing importance of the genre in the cultural politics of the nation. Obama recognized the utility of having at least an informal rap and hip-hop outreach program during the 2008 campaign, though he proceeded with a caution that was strictly enforced by jittery staff members. Occasionally, the candidate name-dropped artists like Jay-Z, Kanye West, and the Fugees, and some were requested to perform at campaign events. Inspired by the Illinois senator's bid for high office, Busta Rhymes, Young Jeezy, Nas, and others signaled that they would cast the first presidential votes of their lives for Obama. Artists honored the candidate by dropping tracks with titles like "Black President" and "My President Is Black." Jay-Z and Beyoncé performed at inaugural balls on the same day that the Obamas shimmied to Mary J. Blige at the White House.

There were, of course, times when discretion and omission were the better courses, and forgoing a rapper's support was preferable to being associated with a controversial performance. When Ludacris released a July 2008 single titled "Politics as Usual," which lewdly critiqued Hillary Clinton and John McCain, the Obama camp steered clear and tightened its scrutiny of other rappers. At the behest of the campaign, Jay-Z agreed not to make a profane reference to George W. Bush during an October 5 concert in Miami, though members of the crowd did so anyway when an image of the Republican president was displayed. In other cases, the potential benefits of calling on friendly rappers to spread the campaign's message simply outweighed the potential pitfalls, and some concerts resulted in the registration of hundreds of new voters.[6]

Once in the White House, Obama continued to cultivate the rap and hip-hop communities. During an October 2010 interview, he let it be known that his "rap palate" now included Lil Wayne and others and that his daughters were "hipping me to things" to listen to. He invited fellow Chicagoan, rapper, and poet Common to perform at an "evening of poetry" in the East Room the following May, and at the 2012 White House Correspondents' Association dinner the president joked that he would be transitioning to Young Jeezy over Al Green during his second term. Many rappers and hip-hop artists, whether drawn to Obama's style, substance, or both, returned the accolades, sometimes even giving a pitch on behalf of the administration's policies. When the president proposed raising taxes on the wealthy in order to pay for his proposed jobs program and other priorities, actor and former rapper Will Smith publicly supported the idea, as did Jay-Z with the condition that the additional revenue go toward education and antipoverty initiatives. Jay-Z was also one of the first entertainers to openly support the president's endorsement of same-sex marriage, characterizing his position as a stand against discrimination. Even rapper Kanye West, known for his media antics, assisted the president's reelection campaign in an indirect way by releasing a track that alleged that Mitt Romney did not pay taxes, an assertion that amplified widespread suspicion about the Republican nominee's reluctance to publicly disclose his income tax returns. Although his circle of hip-hop and rap supporters was not as lively in 2012 as it had been in 2008, there were still at least a few artists who went all in for Obama's reelection bid. The Game, a rapper from Compton, California, reportedly financed the transporting of voters to the polls, even going as far as to give New Yorkers money to facilitate their access to the franchise.[7]

While it would be reasonable to assume that the rap and hip-hop communities mirrored African American and younger voters in their support for Barack Obama over Republican candidates, it would be inaccurate to characterize this backing as universal or absolute. Chicago-born rapper Lupe Fiasco was harshly critical of the administration's response to the Israeli bombing and invasion of the Gaza Strip in 2009. In later interviews, he labeled the president the "biggest terrorist" and as someone who "kills little children," an apparent reference to civilian casualties that resulted from US antiterrorism activities abroad. Likewise, Atlanta rapper Killer Mike criticized the president's foreign policy, as well as his truthfulness, but supported his reelection. "If you don't vote for Obama this time," he warned Black voters ahead of the 2012 balloting, "you're a fuckin' race traitor."[8]

If explicitly supporting or opposing Obama could be controversial in the world of rap and hip-hop, expressing preference for his Republican rivals was something else entirely. Trinidad and Tobago–born rapper Nicki Minaj learned this lesson the hard way. Two months before the 2012 election, she declared herself a "Republican voting for Mitt Romney" on a track featured on a Lil Wayne mixtape. To her surprise, Twitter exploded with insults and death threats from users who condemned her avowed partisanship. When asked about the row, President Obama generously offered Minaj an out, positing that she might have been misunderstood given her penchant for role playing. The rapper leapt at the lifeline. "Ha!" she retorted in a tweet. "Thank you for understanding my creative humor & sarcasm Mr. President, the smart ones always do . . . *sends love & support* @Barack Obama." But Minaj's original intention—as well as her political allegiance—remained unclear. In any event, her unpleasant experience on Twitter after the release of the pro-Romney track was indicative of the committed support that Obama still had among fans of her genre.[9]

Despite Obama's efforts to understand and appreciate the contemporary iterations of rap and hip-hop cultures, the engagement did not always seem natural for the fiftyish Harvard-trained lawyer-cum-politician, even given his familiarity with Black cultural expressions and his community-minded sensibilities. His willingness to repeatedly try to countenance these cultural phenomena on their own terms appeared to be as much a reflection of his political dexterity and electoral needs as anything else. Undoubtedly, he enjoyed some of the music and respected some of the artists; after all, playing Mary J. Blige in the White House was no small matter. Nonetheless, there was a tellingly precipitous drop in his public outreach to rap and hip-hop figures after his reelection, though his relations with a few artists, such as Jay-Z and Beyoncé, appeared to be meaningful and durable.

Like their musical counterparts, Black people who had established themselves in the realm of television and film, or at least the ones who publicly disclosed their political leanings, tended to be supportive of President Obama. However, their sentiments were sometimes qualified and directly related to their understanding of current happenings in the country. While favoring the president's reelection, singer and actor Harry Belafonte gave his first term a mixed review. In his 2012 memoir, he applauded the stimulus package and the ACA but chastised Obama for moving pragmatically to the political center and not being a stronger advocate for criminal justice reform and antipoverty programs. Some of Belafonte's critique seemed eminently reasonable, including his argument that more should have been done to improve the conditions of Black people in inner cities. Other claims were at odds with known facts, such as his statement that the president had not expressed concern about persistent racial inequities. In a similar vein, actor Samuel L. Jackson sympathized with the criticism that the president had not done enough to address poverty, but he was irked by the reluctance of many Republicans to recognize any of his accomplishments, including the dispatching of Osama bin Laden. In the face of such relentless opposition, film star Morgan Freeman wanted to see Obama "get pissed off, get fighting mad," but he did not believe that the president would consider such advice "politically smart." Like Belafonte and Jackson, Freeman hoped to see an Obama second term, pledging he would "vote for him 1,000 times" if it were possible.[10]

During the 2012 election cycle, endorsements came from all over the Black entertainment world. Some came with words of sympathy and advice, such as actor Tim Meadows's stated wariness concerning the "wishy-washy" support of white liberals and Chris Rock's mantra that "being the first black *anything* sucks." Reflecting the spectrum of music performers, gospel singer Yolanda Adams was featured on the campaign website touting the ACA and educational reform, and Mary J. Blige gave the president an A for his efforts following her performance at the DNC in September. Such displays of support were not always without costs. Actress Kerry Washington reported receiving social media death threats, some serious enough to warrant blocking Twitter, after speaking at the nominating convention. Conversely, expressing a preference for Mitt Romney also entailed risks, as actress Stacey Dash learned. After Dash's fall endorsement of the Republican candidate, TV personality Star Jones disputed that decision on a segment of *The Wendy Williams Show*. "I encourage African-Americans, brown people to be involved in politics, because you know I encourage you to be a part of both national parties," Jones asserted. "But if you have a vagina, brown skin, and a brain, I don't see how you could have endorsed Romney." Jones's rebuke was kind compared to the drubbing that Dash endured on Twitter. In a CNN interview that aired a month before the election, Dash evoked Martin Luther King Jr.'s words in defending her preference for Romney, contending, "I chose him not by the color of his skin, but the content of his character."[11]

In terms of Obama's reelection chances, the individual opinions swirling around Black Hollywood and other celebrity haunts were ultimately less important than the financial resources that these cultural elites could bring to bear to support the president's bid for a second term. In other words, their star power and endorsements only mattered if they could be readily translated into money or votes. Celebrities of any notable stature generally understood this political calculus, and several who supported Obama contributed accordingly. In January 2012, filmmaker Spike Lee and his wife, Tonya, sponsored a $38,500-per-person fundraiser at their Upper East Side residence in New York to help underwrite the cost of the campaign. Debra Lee, the executive head of BET, hosted a forty-person event in her DC home in April; the cost of admittance was $40,000. Two weeks before the election, Hollywood power couple Will and Jada Pinkett Smith opened their Santa Monica Mountains estate for a $2,500-per-person luncheon, where a contribution of $40,000 allowed attendees the chance to meet, dine, and pose for photographs with First Lady Michelle Obama. In their enthusiasm and demonstrated support for the Obama presidency, the Smiths were the approximate equivalent of hip-hop's royal duo Jay-Z and Beyoncé and enjoyed the kind of notoriety that was invaluable to facilitating the campaign's access to multiple donor networks.[12]

To at least nominally circumscribe the dominance of the wealthy, corporations, and other well-heeled interests over the electoral system, campaign finance laws limit the amount of money that can be given directly to candidates. However, contributions to independent expenditure-only political committees, or super PACs, that support particular policy agendas but not individual candidates are not capped, nor is the amount of money that these entities can spend in an election cycle. Consequently, during Obama's reelection campaign celebrities and other rich donors were able to give large sums of money to groups like Priorities USA Action, a super PAC established in 2011 by former Obama White House officials Bill Burton and Sean Sweeney. Morgan Freeman availed himself of this opportunity when he gave a million dollars to the super PAC in the summer of 2012. In praising—and somewhat conflating—the achievements of the Obama administration and the work of Priorities USA Action, he challenged others to join him in his extravagant generosity.[13]

If there was an obvious cost in dealing with Hollywood types, it was the near-certainty that some celebrity supporter would go off script and embarrass or otherwise distract the campaign from the objective at hand. Fortunately for the Obama camp, such occurrences were rare among TV actors and movie stars, unlike the situation with rappers. When awkward moments did arise, they tended to be more exasperating and fleeting than truly controversial. For example, Obama's racial identity, that ever-present curio, was a subject that some celebrities found too tempting to avoid discussing. In a 2012 interview, Chris Rock termed Obama "our zebra president." "Black and white, white and black," he continued. "I love our president, but he's black and white. . . . We ignore the president's whiteness, but it's there." Similarly, around the time that he was writing the big super PAC check, Morgan Freeman opined that people "just conveniently forget that Barack had a mama, and she was white—very white American, Kansas, middle of America." The actor went on to describe the president's heritage in a somewhat arbitrary, pseudoscientific way that assumed that Black identity can be reduced to fractions and percentages. "America's first black president hasn't arisen yet," Freeman declared emphatically. "He's not America's first black president, he's America's first mixed-race president." The 75-year-old actor did not clarify what "racial" admixture or DNA metric would have satisfied his litmus test for bona fide, indisputable Blackness. In a more flippant commentary on Obama's race, comedian Sinbad took for granted Obama's Blackness but still noted his relative uniqueness in US politics. "There are no [more] black men raised in Kansas and Hawaii," he had joked in 2010. "That's the last one. Ya'll better treat this one right. The next one gonna be from Cleveland. He gonna wear a perm. Then you gonna see what it's really like."[14]

While the worlds of Hollywood elites and millionaire rappers were stages that Obama performed on for votes, contributions, and the occasional personal high derived from a well-received impromptu croon, he served as the emcee in chief in his own official domain in Washington. Much of his job as president was ceremonial and social, and he was expected to celebrate the country's achievements both big and small. In one representative example of his commemorative efforts, he invited veteran Tuskegee Airmen to the White House theater to watch a film about their World War II accomplishments. During Black History Month 2012, the president led the groundbreaking for what would become the majestic National Museum of African American History and Culture. Later that year, he signed a bill that brought a statue of abolitionist Frederick Douglass into the Visitor Center of Emancipation Hall in the Capitol. Similarly, in March 2013, he endorsed proclamations, backed by the authority granted to him by the Antiquities Act, that established the Charles Young Buffalo Soldiers National Monument in Ohio and the Harriet Tubman Underground Railroad National Historical Park in Maryland.[15]

A cluster of anniversaries associated with milestones of the civil rights movement made Obama's second term especially active in terms of commemorations. A nine-foot-tall statue of Rosa Parks unveiled in Statuary Hall in the Capitol in February 2013 allowed the president the opportunity to publicly praise her courage and integrity on the hundredth anniversary of her birth. In August, the half-century recognition of the 1963 March on Washington was an occasion for Obama, during a speech before the Lincoln Memorial, to remind listeners: "To secure the gains this country has made requires constant vigilance, not complacency." In February 2015, the president submitted a budget to Congress requesting $50 million for the maintenance of sites and monuments related to the nation's civil rights history. A year later, the US Treasury Department announced that the likeness of Harriet Tubman would be placed on the twenty-dollar bill, moving Andrew Jackson to the back of the currency and making the famous abolitionist the first Black woman to appear on US paper money. As he prepared to leave office in December 2016, Obama signed a law that extended indefinitely the time frame for investigating and prosecuting unsolved, racially motivated killings that took place during the civil rights era. The legislation was named after Emmett Till, whose murder in Mississippi in 1955 helped spark the modern Black freedom movement.[16]

Each December, the Obamas celebrated Kwanzaa, an African American holiday that honors family and community. In 2011, their season's greeting on the White House website assured Americans that "in the spirit of unity, *Umoja*, we can overcome those [ongoing economic] challenges together." As a couple and in their respective official capacities, the president and the First Lady made it a point to highlight Black accomplishments throughout their stay in the White House, often hosting key individuals and groups associated with certain deeds and events. Such tributes were usually marked by a measure of sensitivity and reverence that simultaneously emphasized the uniqueness of the African American experience and inclusively wove it into the larger tapestry of US history. With each event that celebrated or commemorated some aspect of Black life in the United States, the Obamas helped embed these occasions more firmly in the historical calendar and popular consciousness of the nation.[17]

The cultural geography of the White House shifted during the Obama years but not to the extent that a casual observer would have noticed much difference between his presidential decor and that of his predecessors. The aesthetic feel of the place, especially in the public areas, was still museum-like and indicative of a stately stasis, but certain decorative choices did project sentiments and meanings that were a change from the past. On the way to the Oval Office, a visitor might see a pamphlet announcing the 1963 March on Washington, or William H. Johnson's painting of Booker T. Washington. Such artifacts were in addition to a bust of Dr. King and a framed copy of the Emancipation Proclamation hanging on the wall. In 2011, Obama had Norman Rockwell's painting *The Problem We All Live With* displayed in the White House. It was a rather bold move for an otherwise cautious chief executive, given its depiction of young Ruby Bridges stoically walking into a desegregating school accompanied by white guards in front of and behind her and a racial epithet scrawled on an adjacent wall. At least one skeptic read the White House exhibition of the painting as a campaign tactic and noted that many US school systems were as segregated in 2011 as they had been when six-year-old Ruby integrated the all-white William Frantz Elementary School in New Orleans in 1960. Others around the president claimed that he drew inspiration from the young girl's quiet courage and perseverance, which perhaps reminded him of his own experiences as a Black first. When the adult Ruby Bridges Hall visited the White House to see the portrait of herself, she confirmed the weight of such historic feats. "Doing the work we do, it gets really lonely," she said of herself and Obama, with whom she met during her visit. "I felt like we understood each other because we belong to the same club."[18]

If not for his professional turn toward academia and politics, Barack Obama could have easily imagined a life as a big-league athlete. He loved basketball and had played it as an amateur throughout his youth. Early on, he had hoped to play in the National Basketball Association (NBA), but after his last adolescent growth spurt he was stuck with only a six-foot-one frame, instead of that of a six-foot-five power forward. Thus, he had to make do with pursuing other career options. Commensurate with the degree to which he adored the game and admired many of its players, he was highly regarded by athletes across leagues and generations, some of whom he played ball with before and during his White House years. Several former and current NBA stars, such as Magic Johnson, Patrick Ewing, Carmelo Anthony, and Vince Carter, participated in reelection fundraisers. A number of players opened their checkbooks in order to shore up Democrats' chances in November; former Chicago Bull and Obama favorite Michael Jordan gave $40,000 to the Obama campaign and the Democratic National Committee. A few players provided political support of a different kind. Hall of Famer Charles Barkley endorsed Obama's reelection bid early on and was not coy when asked whether he thought the Republicans were too hard on the president. "If you disagree with every single thing a person says, of course you are," he told talk-show host Jay Leno. "I think if the president shot himself, they'd complain that he only shot himself once." In total, NBA players and other affiliates, representing a league whose players were more than 70 percent Black, raised millions of dollars for the reelection effort, with a $20,000-per-person campaign event in New York City alone bringing in $3 million.[19]

As president, Obama hosted and interacted with an array of sports and athletes. He routinely invited championship teams to the White House to congratulate them personally, including the 2009 World Series–winning New York Yankees, the 2010-2011 Stanley Cup–winning Boston Bruins, and the Baylor University Bears, which reigned as the 2012 NCAA women's basketball champions. Venerable sports figures, such as home-run king Henry Aaron, who also knew the loneliness of being a Black first, both empathized with his historic presidency and campaigned on his behalf. Heisman Trophy winner and professional football star Charles Woodson was featured in ads that highlighted the jobs-saving impact of the auto industry bailout on his home turf of Ohio, a perennial swing state. Following the 2012 election, Obama maintained ties with a number of prominent sports figures. On several occasions, iconic athletes publicly supported his policies, which helped the administration to reach audiences that were not in the president's immediate orbit. For example, Magic Johnson appeared on the White House website in January 2014 promoting the virtues of the ACA. Two months later, basketball superstar LeBron James did the same, directing viewers to the health insurance marketplace.

While most Black athletes who spoke publicly about Obama tended to do so in favorable terms, there were a few who had less positive things to say. NBA legend Dennis Rodman, who had cultivated a rather curious relationship with North Korean dictator Kim Jong-un, criticized Obama for not engaging Kim in diplomacy. "Obama can't do shit," the former power forward scoffed in May 2013 as the administration refused to negotiate with the isolated regime on behalf of an American imprisoned there. Rodman's periodic trips to the Asian country certainly made for good theater, but they were not nearly as helpful in tempering Kim's threatening posture toward his neighbors or the United States. If Obama did not see the strategic sense of joining in Rodman's eccentric efforts at diplomacy, he did support the right of San Francisco 49ers quarterback Colin Kaepernick to protest against police brutality during National Football League games. In his characteristically straddling approach to controversies tinged by race, the president acknowledged the offense that some had taken over the NFL player's kneeling during the playing of the national anthem. Nonetheless, in a September 2016 interview he recognized that the 28-year-old passer "cares about some real, legitimate issues that have to be talked about," a statement that was as much a testament to Obama's own evolving willingness to take on criminal justice issues as it was about Kaepernick's demonstrations.[20]

Aside from basketball, Obama had learned how to play golf before becoming president and continued to participate in the sport while in the White House. Beyond it allowing him to establish a balance between the country club (white) imagery of playing eighteen holes and the more common (Black) man's sport of shooting hoops, golf was also politics by other means, and Obama played with partners ranging from House speaker John Boehner to Bill Clinton. Some time on the putting green with Tiger Woods in February 2013 confirmed for the president that the number-one-ranked golfer "plays a different game than I do." Speaking candidly, Obama confessed that Woods's talent was "on another planet" compared to his own. Notwithstanding his dalliances with golf, the president's first love was basketball, which one could easily tell from his following of the NBA on ESPN and his annual NCAA March Madness bracket. On Election Day 2012, he forwent last-minute campaigning in favor of a pickup game with friends and staff members at Chicago's Attack Athletics gym. Apparently, he could think of no better way to relieve the stress of the campaign season.[21]

CHAPTER 11

Renaissance Woman

MICHELLE OBAMA KNEW THAT BEING FIRST LADY WOULD BE hard. And the first African American one? Exponentially harder. The long nominating process and the general campaign of 2008 were a trial by fire. The incessant media exposure, crude personal attacks, unrelenting travel schedule, and days away from family, especially the girls—it was a wonder that she had not cracked under the pressure like many others would have. But actually living in the White House was different, more intense and intrusive than anything that she had previously experienced. Michelle had had the foresight to anticipate some of the changes ahead, even as the Obamas packed up their Chicago house. However, she could not foresee everything. There was no manual or guidebook for how to be a First Lady. Only six people alive in a world of almost 7 billion had firsthand experience in the role, and four of them were in their eighties or nineties. To be sure, several former First Ladies reached out to the newest member of their tiny club, including Rosalynn Carter and Nancy Reagan. Laura Bush was gracious and informative during the transition period, and Hillary Clinton, who would shortly be nominated for the Cabinet position of secretary of state, shared sage advice, including suggestions regarding schools for Malia and Sasha. Still, Michelle Obama knew that she would be a different kind of First Lady, and none of the previous ones, for all of their kindness and sympathy, could fully prepare her for the singular journey ahead.

As Michelle acknowledged in her 2018 memoir, the anxiety and fears were gripping, even as she smiled through them on Inauguration Day and beyond. Despite all of the well wishes and her husband's clear electoral mandate, the honeymoon was short and the scrutiny unending.

> I understood already that I'd be measured by a different yard-stick. As the only African American First Lady to set foot in the White House, I was "other" almost by default. If there was a presumed grace assigned to my white predecessors, I knew it wasn't likely to be the same for me. . . . My grace would need to be earned. . . . I wouldn't have the luxury of settling into my new role slowly before being judged. And when it came to judgment, I was as vulnerable as ever to the unfounded fears and racial stereotypes that lay just beneath the surface of the public consciousness, ready to be stirred up by rumor and innuendo.

As all First Ladies soon learn, the White House can be both a cocoon and an island, protecting its inhabitants from the outside world by the sheer expansiveness of the executive branch and its layers of bureaucracy. It can also be the world's highest pillory, which exposes first families to all manner of attacks, as well as a sandstone mausoleum for hapless presidencies that end long before the next election. The precocious Malia Obama, who was 10 years old when her family moved to Washington, sensed the high bars that were being set. "First African-American president," she remarked to her father just before the inauguration, adding pointedly, "better be good." The advice could have easily been offered to her mother regarding her elevation to First Lady, a White House role that is more vaguely defined than the chief executive's duties.[1]

Michelle Obama, who was initially struck by the museum-like qualities of her new residence, decided early on to have an active agenda as First Lady. Both the caretaker and the organizer in her came to the fore, resulting in the casting of a protective, but not stifling, net over the girls and the mobilization of her staff for a robust, public-facing engagement with community affairs. During the campaign, prior to the Iowa caucuses, she had become interested in the plight of veterans and military families. Her husband had campaigned on an antiwar platform, pledging to reduce troop deployments in Iraq and Afghanistan, and her proposed work with Americans directly affected by these conflicts complemented this campaign promise. As First Lady, she spent the opening months of her time in Washington visiting with veterans and their families and assessing their needs. It was sobering work but less grim than the president's periodic trips to Dover Air Force Base to salute the flag-draped coffins of the fallen. The Obama tenure, in its entirety, was a wartime presidency, laden with the kinds of false hopes, reversals, and weariness that long, costly conflicts abroad usually entail. The uncertain national mood, dampened further by the economic crisis, undoubtedly impacted the First Lady's choice of causes to champion and the urgency with which she pursued them.[2]

Along with interacting with military families, Michelle Obama prioritized education and mentoring as key components of her mission as First Lady. As she had during her professional life in Chicago, she actively engaged young people in the DC metropolitan area and elsewhere. She made trips to schools in Anacostia, a poor, predominantly Black neighborhood southeast of the Capitol, to establish a mentoring program that better connected the White House to high school students. In February 2012, she invited several young musicians to the executive mansion to meet blues artists, including Keb' Mo', Trombone Shorty, and Shemekia Copeland, and to learn more about African American contributions to the nation's cultural heritage. Michelle was consistently in high demand for speaking engagements around the country and often used these occasions to promote educational pursuits, particularly among Black people. Her counsel typically involved references to past civil rights struggles and accomplishments and an exhortation of her audience to take responsibility for their lives and be accountable agents in regard to future endeavors. "And make no mistake about it, change absolutely starts at home," she told an applauding audience at an AME Church conference in June 2012. "We know that we won't close that education gap until we turn off the TV, and supervise homework, attend those parent-teacher conferences, and serve as good role models for our own children. That's on us." Like her husband, the First Lady advanced a mix of individual, communal, and governmental approaches to addressing problems facing Black communities and was not especially tolerant of those who dwelled on past injustices as an excuse for inaction.[3]

While education and veterans' needs were central to her first-term agenda, health and wellness became Michelle Obama's signature issue during her eight years in the White House. Under the general rubric of her Let's Move! initiative, the exercise and fitness side of the project gained needed visibility through appearances of the First Lady on television and in other media. The South Lawn was the preferred staging ground for many of her events, which often involved children who joined her in exercise and other health-related activities. A lighthearted fitness competition with talk-show host Jimmy Fallon in the East Room both generated public awareness of Michelle's health agenda and demonstrated her own physical prowess when it came to push-ups, sack racing, and dodgeball. In 2013, she collaborated with several rap and hip-hop artists to release an album named after her initiative that included songs such as "U R What You Eat" and "Veggie Luv." That same year, the First Lady announced that a partnership between the US Department of Education and private entities like Nike, Kaiser Permanente, and the General Mills Foundation had resulted in a $100 million commitment of resources to assist schools in developing new physical education programs. In hindsight, the First Lady's initiative came together like a multipronged business plan that deliberately leveraged interconnected marketing, modeling, and financing strategies.

As the nutritional complement to Let's Move! Michelle Obama pushed for more informative and transparent food labels that clearly stated the fat, sugar, and salt content of products. Although she generally avoided wading too far into political waters, the First Lady was particularly invested in this issue, given the country's escalating rates of obesity and diabetes. Thus, just as she had called out Republicans in Congress who tried unsuccessfully to overturn the ACA in 2013, she refused to bow to corporate opposition to the proposed label changes. "As consumers and as parents, we have a right to understand what's in the food we're feeding our families," she asserted at a White House event in 2014. It was not until the last year of the Obama presidency, however, that significant progress was made in her battle for updated food labels. In May 2016, the First Lady announced the first successes of her campaign, which included a new labeling policy that required companies to disclose how much sugar was added to a product versus the recommended consumption limit. The mandate, the first of its kind in more than two decades, was scheduled to take effect in 2018 and would have impacted hundreds of thousands of products and brands.[4]

Michelle Obama's active—and infrequently political—agenda as First Lady was appreciated by most Americans. Polls consistently rated her high on the favorability scale. According to a May 2012 Gallup survey, she scored a 66 percent positive rating among respondents for most of her first term in the White House, compared to 73 percent for Laura Bush and 56 percent for Hillary Clinton during the same period of their White House tenures. The First Lady's average rating was the same in February 2014, according to a subsequent Gallup poll. Some of the good feelings toward Michelle were related to her savvy and well-managed use of various media to highlight her projects and causes, such as Let's Move! and her Joining Forces campaign, which supported military families. By the time of the 2012 election, she had become the most televised First Lady, having made forty-four appearances on shows such as *Late Night with David Letterman*, *Jimmy Kimmel Live!*, and Disney's *iCarly*. In its annual ranking of the world's most influential women, *Forbes* magazine placed her fourth in 2013, behind German chancellor Angela Merkel, Brazilian president Dilma Rousseff, and philanthropist Melinda Gates. The following year, a survey by the Siena College Research Institute ranked Michelle Obama fifth among the greatest of First Ladies, coming in behind Eleanor Roosevelt, Abigail Adams, Jacqueline Kennedy, and Dolley Madison. In this particular annual exercise, which was based on the opinions of 242 historians and political scientists, Mrs. Obama scored highest in the categories of "being her own woman" and "value to the president" and lowest in the area of "being the White House steward."[5]

Aside from such popularity metrics and in addition to her role as First Lady, wife, mother, and top White House influencer, Michelle proved an invaluable asset on the campaign trail. With favorability ratings that routinely topped the president's by an average of nine points, she was the administration's best surrogate. During her speech at the DNC in September 2012, public interest in her performance as measured by Twitter crested at 28,003 tweets per minute, doubling the peak rates of both GOP nominee Mitt Romney during his presentation at the Republican National Convention and President Obama's 2012 State of the Union address. Beyond her strength at the podium, the First Lady was a formidable fundraiser as well. Between January and September 2012, she raised at least $17.5 million for the reelection campaign and the Democratic National Committee, having participated in fifty-six different events. Considering her regular appearances on television, on the campaign trail, and in other settings, overexposure and overfamiliarity were, rather remarkably, not an issue for her in terms of public perception. Well before the end of her husband's tenure in the Oval Office, several talk-show hosts and journalists began to inquire whether she had any plans to run for public office, including the presidency. Her answer was always the same, an emphatic no or "absolutely not," but the question kept arising anyway.[6]

Similarly to her husband, Michelle Obama in the role of First Lady embodied a unique significance for many people throughout the country, and especially for African American women. Part of her appeal was related to her public embrace of other Black women during her time in the White House. Beyond friend and fellow Chicagoan Oprah Winfrey, whom she readily invited to the campaign trail, Michelle honored African American women openly and in ways that stressed their shared womanhood and racial heritage. In January 2012, she presented Maya Angelou with a literary arts award at the BET Honors ceremony in DC and referred to the 83-year-old writer-activist as one of her "she-roes." This accolade complemented the Presidential Medal of Freedom that her husband had bestowed on Angelou two years earlier. Perhaps related to the latitude that the public ceded to each of them in their different White House roles, Michelle was at least as good as the president at signifying Black cultural themes, and in certain instances she seemed more comfortable and less scripted in doing so. In March 2015, the First Lady attended an annual BET gathering to celebrate women of color and was met with a roaring ovation when she came on stage chanting the theme of the event, "Black Girls Rock!" "No matter who you are, no matter where you come from, you are beautiful," she proclaimed to the audience. Given both his style and the political tone of the times, it was hard to imagine the president crossing a stage while articulating a similar chant.[7]

The adoring gaze between Michelle Obama and other Black women went both ways, and female observers around the nation routinely voiced their opinions about the First Lady throughout her eight years in the White House. "What a privilege to have such a smart and powerful first lady," Laura Murphy, a lawyer with the American Civil Liberties Union, declared on Mother's Day 2012. "She can do push-ups one day, then regally float into a state dinner in a designer gown." Eleanor Hinton Hoytt, president and CEO of the Black Women's Health Imperative in DC, was even more personal in her appraisal. "Black women look at Michelle Obama and see ourselves," she contended. "We see our potential, and we see our future." Princeton University emerita professor Nell Painter viewed the First

Lady as projecting a special meaning in her highly visible role. "It's a kind of assurance that is also something new for a black woman in public," the historian admiringly noted in a 2016 interview. "She is the symbol of what an American can be."[8]

In a culture preoccupied with defining, assessing, and marketing femininity and women's beauty, few were surprised that Michelle Obama came under the public microscope in ways that were familiar, novel, and disconcerting. As early as the 2008 campaign, much was made of her clothing choices, a scrutiny that continued throughout her White House years and afterward. The digital age has mated omnipresent visual technologies and media with the fickle consumer tastes and corporate deceits of the global marketplace, instantaneously transforming First Ladies into celebrities and brands on Inauguration Day, if not months earlier during the nomination convention. Whether at home or from abroad, the stare and its attendant judgments came from every angle, and the First Lady could only hope to manage or beguile it, never to truly be rid of it. Michelle Obama knew this reality and did not seem too resistant to its rules, and she did not allow herself to be completely captured by one particular designer or fashion trend. In describing the First Lady's DNC appearance in September 2012, the *New York Times* virtually reached out to touch her tailor-made dress, bringing its readers in for an intimate inspection. "From a distance, the dress had a shimmering effect, like wet paint in a blast of unreadable pastels," writer Eric Wilson discerned, "but in close-ups, viewers could practically study the patterns of the gold brocade." Michelle topped the Best Dressed List of the *Times* of London six months later, and the newspaper made no secret of what it thought a First Lady should be. It complimented her "for understanding that, as her primary role as first lady is visual, fashion can be a force for good used to inspire and entertain." The words both celebrated and circumscribed, revealing some lingering allegiance to the royal ornamentalism through which some still judged the worth of women from powerful families.[9]

Of course, to notice the First Lady's sleeveless dresses and her accessories meant that observers took stock of—and often commented on—her other features, including her height, weight, hair, hips, shoulders, and complexion. Matched only by predecessor Eleanor Roosevelt in her five-foot-eleven stature, Michelle Obama is tall by American standards, which campaign critics noted derisively in 2008. Her choice of clothing styles tended to flatter her height and build, and Tracy Reese, a Black designer from Detroit, had a lot to do with this coordination. The First Lady wore a number of Reese's products during her White House years, elevating the designer to international visibility. She, too, offered an impression of Michelle's physique, which, in her words, is "tall and lean and curvy through the hips." Novelist Terry McMillan added even more color in her description of what the First Lady bestowed on the United States. "She brought sexy to the White House," the writer said in 2013, adding, "Even funky and hip." During a visit to India in 2010, the geometry of Mrs. Obama's figure attracted vivid commentary as she interacted with people in New Delhi. She "demonstrated she could swing to desi beats with the best of them," according to the *Times of India*, which made specific reference to the First Lady's "matkas and jhatkas," or hip-gyrating dance moves.[10]

If her clothing choices and hairstyles—a brief flirtation with bangs in 2013 generated much comment—were malleable and evolving, Michelle's natural features did not change but were no less subject to public interpretation. In regard to the First Lady's skin tone, fashion designer Michaela Angela Davis plainly deemed her a "real black girl" who was recognizable as such from a distance. "A lot of people have tried to make diversity into this weird beige thing," Davis posited. Having lobbied for better representation of Black women in media, Davis said, "[Michelle's] presence is just really powerful to interject into the global consciousness." For McMillan (and many others), one feature set the First Lady apart from all others: her arms. "I screamed at the television after seeing their smooth bronze glow," the writer effused. "My cheeks hurt from smiling at her dancing like a black Cinderella at the first Inauguration." Toward the end of his presidency, Barack Obama became more likely to openly comment on his wife's appearance, noting her height and "great legs" during 2016 interviews.[11]

Despite the expressed appreciation for and admiration of Michelle Obama that emanated from many quarters, she was not exempt from crude caricatures of her image and appearance. Such disparagement is a known cost of life in the public eye, made all the more harsh by the hyperpartisanship, racial bias, and female objectification that course through US society and culture. In keeping with the general tenor of his partisan commentaries, Rush Limbaugh repeatedly made reference to the First Lady's posterior on his conservative radio show. In December 2011, Rep. James Sensenbrenner of Wisconsin was overheard making similar remarks as he mocked her campaign for healthier diets. The congressman apologized publicly for the comment once it was widely reported, but his was not the last such affront that Michelle Obama endured. Some questionable musings on her race and gender came from abroad, such as a depiction of her as a bare-breasted enslaved woman on the August 2012 cover of the Spanish periodical *Fuera de Serie*. Karine Percheron-Daniels, the French-English artist who created the image, assumed that she was doing the First Lady a favor by featuring her with an Aunt Jemima–style headscarf and seated on a US flag. "I'm sure Obama would love it," she reportedly told an interviewer, "and I hope that someday she can see it."[12]

Always mature and unflappable in the face of such controversies, Michelle typically did not betray her emotions when journalists asked her for a response to the latest affront. Only after leaving the White House did she publicly share some of her pain. "I've heard about the swampy parts of the internet that question everything about me, right down to whether I'm a woman or a man," she confided in her memoir. "I've been hurt. I've been furious. But mostly, I've tried to laugh this stuff off." As First Lady, she learned to smile when it was the most unnatural response to a situation; perhaps that was the only response that a Black first like herself could get away with conveying.[13]

Michelle Obama had to withstand other things, both big and small, that sometimes had little or nothing to do with race and/or gender and at other times had everything to do with them. When People for the Ethical Treatment of Animals called her out in 2014 for using real eggs in the annual White House Easter egg roll, it was probably more annoying than anything else. A bit more irritating was a heckler who interrupted her speech at a June 2013 fundraiser to demand that her husband sign an executive order banning anti-LGBTQ discrimination. The crowd rallied to the First Lady's defense after she let it be known that she was prepared to leave the event if the discourtesy continued. Race may very well have been a factor in a parent-student protest against Mrs. Obama giving a graduation address at a Topeka high school on the sixtieth anniversary of the *Brown v. Board of Education* Supreme Court decision, which banned public school segregation. In this instance, tensions were abated by the First Lady's agreement to give the speech another day.

Later, looking back on such events, including the mass murder of Black parishioners in a Charleston church in June 2015, Michelle could not help but recognize that the success of Black people like herself, her husband, and others in various professions and walks of life was a provocation, a pretext for some to vent resentment. In her last months in the White House, she publicly pondered the surreal dissonance between being the First Lady of the United States and "[waking] up every morning in a house that was built by slaves." Even at that late date, she was still trying to reconcile the potentially explosive mix of possibility and peril, future and past that Black people living in the White House symbolized in a racially conflicted country. "We lived with it as a family, and we lived with it as a nation," she wrote after returning to private life. "And we carried on, as gracefully as we could."[14]

As complicated and exposed as her public life and image were, Michelle Obama continued to seek people and experiences that would keep her grounded during her time in Washington. She cultivated a close circle of Black women with whom she socialized, and she was sometimes able to surreptitiously enjoy their company in local restaurants before other patrons noticed her. These friends included longtime acquaintances, such as Princeton classmate Angela Acree and fellow Chicagoan Kelly Dibble, as well as newer confidants like Sharon Malone, the wife of Eric Holder. Michelle's exercise routines also allowed her to decompress, and budding interests in yoga and tennis (with Malia) kept her active. Her much-admired biceps required consistent anaerobic attention, a regimen that she balanced with brisk walks through Rock Creek Park.

For her fiftieth birthday in January 2014, the First Lady celebrated the milestone with a White House party that lasted well into the early morning hours. The list of celebrities in attendance was fitting for such a momentous occasion and included Beyoncé, John Legend, Paul McCartney, Ashley Judd, Billie Jean King, and Stevie Wonder. A smattering of Democratic stalwarts and other well-connected notables were sprinkled in the crowd for good measure, including Susan Rice, Nancy Pelosi, and Kathleen Sebelius. But the gathering was hardly about them, given the frequency of their visits to the White House. Instead, old friends from Chicago, such as Marty Nesbitt and Paula and Jim Crown, likely absorbed a disproportionate share of the first couple's time, as they reminisced about the past and looked at the road ahead. Energized by the R&B and club music that turned the East Room into a dance hall, Michelle, in a "flowing red blouse and pants," reveled in the rhythms of her good fortune. These were the kinds of people and events that anchored her, helping to keep the White House bubble in perspective. And these were the times when her smile was most natural.[15]

After moving into the White House, Barack and Michelle Obama lived full time in the same residence for the first time since 1996, when he ran for a seat in the Illinois state senate. The consolidated living arrangements were one of the perks of the presidency and allowed the girls to live with both parents year-round. The First Lady and the president each had their own routines, and much of their typical day was spent in the West Wing, East Wing, or away at some event or function. They regularly saw their daughters off to school in the morning and exercised together, often meeting up again as a family for dinner in the evening. Michelle was usually earliest to bed; the president, after kissing her goodnight, stayed up hours longer, reading briefing books and the day's newspapers. Their house rules made it all function, with the most important being to communicate with each other whether happy, mad, or sad. Early on, Barack Obama lamented that the hermetically sealed presidential cocoon did not allow the couple to enjoy many nights out together, even for special occasions. For Michelle, the hectic life of a First Lady, along with the full schedules of teen and tween children, became quite the grind by the second term. In an April 2013 interview, she referred to herself as a "busy single mother," an accidental slip that she immediately corrected and laughed off but that made the media rounds anyway. The characterization was not wholly off the mark, considering the family-scattering reelection campaign that they had just endured. Even her husband conceded the spirit of her remark weeks later, knowing better than anyone all of the sacrifices that Michelle Obama had made in the interests of their family.[16]

Along with open communication, normalcy was the ever-elusive objective that Michelle Obama pursued most vigorously during her time in Washington, DC. She especially wanted her daughters to grow up to be mature, responsible, and well-adjusted people. By necessity, their lives, too, were cordoned off from much of the outside world. Once when young Sasha tried to open a White House window, a member of the security detail immediately commanded, "Shut the window." Such was life as the first family. Nonetheless, the Obamas did discover ways to soften some of the edges. At least initially, Michelle's mother, Marian Robinson, who also lived in the executive mansion, accompanied the children to their private school so that they would not have to ride alone with Secret Service agents.

When the inevitable efforts to commoditize the girls arose, the First Lady was quick to tell one toymaker that its plan to market Sweet Sasha and Marvelous Malia dolls was an improper infringement on the rights of private citizens. If normalcy was not always within reach, parental engagement was and thus became essential to the Obamas' child-rearing efforts. The couple attended the girls' sporting events and teacher conferences, and the family took the occasional vacation together. Perhaps above all else, the Obamas encouraged their children to project decency and to value moderation in everything from television watching and social media to sweets and dating. Consciously and publicly, the first couple modeled a caring and healthy relationship, and for nearly a decade, they—with help from their daughters—presented the country with an idealized version of what an American nuclear family could be.[17]

One decision that the Obamas were noticeably slow and cautious in making was determining what kind of religious affiliations they would establish after entering the White House. The Rev. Wright controversy was still a fresh memory when the family arrived in Washington in 2009, and the first couple was loath to bring yet another congregation the kind of scrutiny under which Trinity United Church had labored during the campaign. The family did visit a number of African American meetinghouses and made a special effort to participate in services during holidays. However, they never settled on a church home and over time became less eager in their quest for one; according to one count, the Obamas only attended nineteen church services during their first six years in the White House. Despite these infrequent appearances, the first family did engage in religious activities in other ways. For example, the president maintained a circle of spiritual advisors who visited the White House, spoke with him by phone, and sent messages to his BlackBerry. Moreover, during trips to Camp David, the family sometimes attended services at Evergreen Chapel, which was a less disruptive way of worshipping than trying to connect with a congregation in busy, congested Washington, DC. Like many other aspects of their existence, the rather erratic pattern of the Obamas' religious associations in the capital was a result of the intermingling of matters of convenience, time, and, of course, politics. For Michelle, the cost of such a rootless, itinerant journey during her time in the White House was high, and she was unused to the church hopping. Although the campaign drama had forced her family to part ways with Trinity, she sorely missed the "warmth of a spiritual community" that she had once enjoyed there.[18]

CHAPTER 12

The Blood of Africa

NELSON MANDELA WAS AMONG THE MANY FOREIGN LEADERS who congratulated President-elect Barack Obama after his historic election. Having recently turned 90, the South African statesman was the face of the resistance against apartheid and still embodied the spirit of self-determination and social justice that came to define post–World War II human rights campaigns. During his twenty-seven-year imprisonment for attempting to end white minority rule, Mandela became the world's most famous political prisoner, and his election to the presidency in 1994 marked a final end of formal colonialism—as opposed to neocolonialism—on the African continent. His five-year leadership of South Africa as it transitioned to a multi-racial democracy was marked by high hopes. However, his relatively short tenure in office was not nearly enough to rectify deeply engrained societal inequities that had developed over generations.

When Sen. Obama met him briefly at a DC hotel in 2005, Mandela had already had a life-changing impact on the young politician. During Obama's freshman year at Occidental College in 1979-1980, his activism was ignited by the anti-apartheid movement on campus, which inspired the first of his political speeches. The arc of the South African leader's life and politics would in some ways be mirrored by

Obama's own, with their similar preferences for universalist policies, center-left moderation, and racial reconciliation. Thus, when Mandela sent his congratulatory letter in November 2008, the mutual admiration had come full circle. "Your victory has demonstrated that no person anywhere in the world should not dare to dream of wanting to change the world for a better place," the former president wrote. "We trust that you will also make it the mission of your presidency to combat the scourge of poverty and disease everywhere." It was a noble charge from a venerable figure whom the US president-elect had revered for decades. But it was simply a recommended mandate and well wishes. Mandela offered no road map for addressing "poverty and disease everywhere." In truth, Obama could hardly have expected one; Mandela's own efforts to remedy these plagues at home had not produced much of a model. Facing the pit of the Great Recession as a new head of state, Obama would have to lead a battered nation by way of prompt action and hopeful experimentation, just as Mandela had been compelled to do a decade earlier under even more trying circumstances.[1]

In addition to the encouraging words of his South African hero, Obama received a wealth of support from people across the African continent as he entered the White House. Polls showed that he was greatly preferred over John McCain in the 2008 election by people in countries such as Uganda, Tanzania, Ethiopia, and Mali; respondents in Kenya, his father's homeland, supported him by a gaping eighty-four-point margin. Obama's approval ratings, along with those gauging US leadership more generally, continued to crest among selected African countries for the next three years, tapering off at 74 percent across the surveyed populations of thirty-three nations. The president's support was highest in sub-Saharan Africa and weakest in North Africa, with people in Tunisia, a new democracy, offering a split verdict in 2012. A number of factors appeared to influence Obama's ratings in various countries, such as his racial and cultural heritage, local attitudes toward democracy, US antiterrorism efforts in Africa, and lingering distaste toward some Bush-era policies. In

Muslim-majority countries in particular, perceived US bias in dealing with the Israeli-Palestinian conflict played at least a nominal role in depressing Obama's approval numbers.[2]

Just as Africans had opinions about him, Obama had thoughts about the continent and its people, which stretched back to his Hawaiian childhood and found expression in his writings and campaign platforms. In *The Audacity of Hope*, he telegraphed his policy approach toward Africa by revealing democratic governance, human rights safeguards, and ethical economic stewardship as the dominant metrics by which he would measure the continent's nations and their rulers. He also articulated the self-help and personal responsibility imperatives that he so often counseled when addressing African American audiences. "We should not expect to help Africa," he warned, "if Africa ultimately proves unwilling to help itself." These themes remained largely consistent elements of Obama's foreign policy toward much of the continent, though at times principles would give way to more pragmatic handling of certain issues and interests.[3]

In a brief visit to Ghana in July 2009, Obama articulated early in his presidency the terms of his engagement with the nations of the continent, as well as his expectations of the parties involved. Before the country's parliament, he asserted his membership in the African family ("I have the blood of Africa within me") and traced his lineage to oppressed Kenyans who toiled under British imperialism. He acknowledged the colonial past and some of its abuses, as well as the post-independence tendency of Western countries to view the continent as a place to be exploited instead of as a potential partner. However, the thrust of his speech was forward looking, and he implored Africans to be the change agents in the realization of their aspirations. He roundly condemned corruption, warmongering, and human rights abuses, all of which putatively discouraged foreign investment and economic development. "Africa doesn't need strong men," he declared in a denunciation of tyrannical rule. "It needs strong institutions." The president offered a partnership with Africa that entailed mutual responsibilities, and he left the unmistakable impression that US aid and support would be contingent on certain conditions being met. In a show of agreement with at least some of Obama's points, the Ghanaian legislators chanted in unison "Yes we can!" the crowd-rousing slogan of the president's 2008 campaign.[4]

Obama's stay in Ghana lasted less than twenty-four hours, just long enough for him to speak to the parliament, meet with selected politicians and luminaries, and tour the Cape Coast "slave castle," where hapless captives were once imprisoned before being shipped across the ocean during the transatlantic slave trade. Reviews of his trip, and especially his speech, were immediately forthcoming and varied, revealing that he had captured the attention of a wide and eclectic audience. P. L. O. Lumumba, a Kenyan activist, applauded the US president's criticism of corruption and believed that he should continue to use his high office to put unscrupulous governments on notice. Olara A. Otunnu, a former Ugandan foreign minister, also thought that the good governance theme was one that Africans wanted and needed to hear from the White House, though he did not expect Obama to push for action prematurely. "He meets, he consults and then he decides," the former official outlined in a comparison of the president with a traditional African ruler. "The chief doesn't rush." Other observers assumed that Obama's racial identity and ancestral ties boded well for the future of US-Africa relations, potentially allowing him to deal more openly and thus more productively with African leaders than past (white) presidents had felt comfortable doing.[5]

Not every listener was impressed with the speech. Rosa Whitaker, a former assistant US trade representative to Africa, questioned why Western leaders like Obama so readily chastised Africans about corruption when they regularly failed to raise the issue when meeting with Chinese or Russian officials, whose governments were known for their venality. Paul Tiyambe Zeleza, a Malawian historian, also pointed out a perceived overemphasis on Africa's postcolonial shortcomings and claimed that Obama had not adequately acknowledged the well-documented role that the US government had played in supporting dictatorships across Africa. In common with several other observers, Zeleza found the "tough love" tone of the speech "almost hectoring," especially since it seemed to him that the president reserved such a style principally for Black audiences. A number of critics discerned neoliberal assumptions behind Obama's exhortations, which appeared designed to shift responsibility for Africa's ills from the West onto Africans entirely, in effect perpetuating the dominance of the former. A common theme among such critiques related to both the tenor and substance of the president's remarks, which some evaluated as high-handed and ahistorical.[6]

Obama's pronouncements about and policies toward Africa attracted persistent scrutiny across the continent and beyond, and some reactions occasionally induced revisions of his approach—at least at the margins. As was the case among African Americans, particularly harsh assessments of Obama and his actions by some activists, academicians, government officials, and others were often at odds with the generally high regard that he enjoyed among the masses of Africans, as polls and the teeming crowds who rushed to meet his motorcade in Accra and elsewhere confirmed. Perhaps many citizens were of the same mind as Margaret Sigale, a 29-year-old Tanzanian woman, who did not believe that Africa would reap much of a "material gain" from a Black man in the White House. "In my opinion, President Obama has no obligation to return to Africa simply because he is in a way connected," she stated during his trip to her country in 2013. "We should not make him feel he has to give anything, or has any obligation." Ample evidence suggests that Obama was sympathetic to her view. He had said as much during his speech in Ghana.[7]

In June 2012, the White House released a strategic plan regarding US policy toward sub-Saharan Africa. While little in the document was entirely new, it again illuminated the rationale behind the administration's approach to the continent, and it proposed measures aimed at achieving mutually beneficial outcomes. The promotion and defense of democratic governments, institutions, and processes were considered key goals, along with related commitments to upholding "the principles of equality, justice, and the rule of law." Second, and tied to democratization and the cultivation of sound institutions, Obama advocated for trade and investment arrangements that would allow Africans greater access to transregional and global markets, promote economic diversification, and encourage the ethical management and development of resources for the common good. He vowed to urge US companies to pursue opportunities on the continent with an eye toward assisting African nations in gaining the skills, capital, and technology needed for broad-based economic prosperity, which he believed would also help "to create jobs here in America." In addition to an economic partnership, the plan called for a robust US-Africa alliance that would facilitate the deescalation of conflicts, peace initiatives, and coordination of counterterrorism efforts. In terms of concrete policy proposals, the document offered several, including extensions of the African Growth and Opportunity Act and the Generalized System of Preferences, redoubled efforts to defeat al-Qaeda and its African affiliates and surrogates, and the establishment of a framework for actively grooming the next generation of African leaders.[8]

Many of the stated ideals and policies of this strategic plan did inform the Obama administration's engagement with Africa over the coming years, though not as consistently or evenly as some would have perhaps preferred. The president used the authority and symbolism of his office to promote democratic transitions in various African countries, and he rewarded leaders who came to power through constitutional means. After issuing a statement calling for a fair presidential election in Côte d'Ivoire in late 2010, Obama worked with African heads of state to usher the defeated but recalcitrant incumbent, Laurent Gbagbo, out of office. In March 2012, he hosted Ghanaian president John Atta Mills at the White House and lavished praise on him for a number of accomplishments, including the protection of election integrity, bolstering food security and foreign investment, and working with US businesses and government agencies to build infrastructure in the country. Mills returned the accolades, thanking Obama for the "high level of cooperation that exists between our two countries" and lauding the American vision of democracy. A year later, the US president welcomed heads of state from Sierra Leone, Senegal, Malawi, and Cape Verde to the White House and publicly recognized their support for democratic institutions, human rights, and economic development. Besides displaying public solidarity with these African leaders, who acquired and maintained power through electoral means, the Obama administration often provided incentives, typically in the form of financial aid and technical assistance, to these favored governments.[9]

It was considerably easier to host African leaders at the White House who demonstrated a propensity for democratic governance and economic reform than to countenance those rulers who violated daily the high principles set forth in the president's strategic plan for Africa. Nonetheless, the Obama administration did both, and its political calculations were not hard to figure out. US officials, whether in consideration of geostrategic or economic factors, believed that certain countries on the continent had to be engaged, regardless of the nature of their leadership or manner of their rule. It was not a new approach to African realities or those at play elsewhere; many a dictatorship, kleptocracy, and even genocidal regime had been enabled historically by the single-minded pursuit of political and/or economic interests by successive US governments. Thus, the Obama team was not the first to play the game this way, nor was it the only US administration that sometimes failed to elevate the quality of foreign engagements by insisting on rules that were up to its own articulated standards and code of ethics.

Instances of the starkest hypocrisy could sometimes be slightly offset by US interactions and interventions that achieved notable humanitarian or otherwise life-improving results for large numbers of Africans. But the glaring contradictions could not be hidden or easily excused altogether. Even as Obama pushed for democracy or the departure of notorious autocrats in some quarters of the continent, he was less insistent on challenging the misrule of friendly counterparts in places like Ethiopia, Rwanda, and Congo, which had sordid records of corruption and human rights violations. In many cases, economic concerns got in the way of principle, as exemplified in the deepening US dependence on African oil, which lubricated close diplomatic ties with undemocratic, crooked regimes in Nigeria and Equatorial Guinea. Antiterrorism campaigns led to sometimes unpleasant bedfellows in countries like Niger, Djibouti, and Burkina Faso, all in the name of US national security.[10]

Besides its pragmatic methodology toward US-Africa relations, which could occasionally sideline concerns about democracy, transparency, and human rights, the Obama administration also construed the continent's place in the world as embedded in a multifaceted struggle between great powers for global influence. In the twenty-first century, it was not so much the former colonial powers or the more recently consolidated European Union that concerned administration officials as the rising powers in the East, in particular the Chinese. By the first year of Obama's presidency, China surpassed the United States as Africa's biggest trading partner. In 2013, the Asian country drew on the continent for a quarter of its crude oil imports, bringing it in close alignment with nations such as Angola, Equatorial Guinea, Sudan, and Nigeria. As it nourished its industries with African raw materials, China offered low-interest loans and development aid, much of which was directed toward infrastructure investments. When Obama visited Tanzania in June 2013, in many ways he was coming late to the party. The value of trade between the East African nation and China had topped $2.47 billion the prior year, almost seven times the worth of US-Tanzanian economic exchanges.

During a second visit to East Africa in 2015, Obama was in the odd and unenviable position of trying to persuade Africans to do more business with the United States. Although he characterized trade with China as a "good thing," the president warned of a creeping eastern neocolonialism that sought to monopolize and exploit the material wealth of the continent. He explicitly advised Africans to avoid trade relationships in which the rewards went only to "a few elites and the Chinese," leaving the masses no better off. It was the kind of clear-eyed critique of big power politics and global structures of in-equality that some would fault Obama for not applying to the Africa policies of the United States and European countries. In any event, new realities on the ground had changed much over the course of several years. The terms of engagement that Obama had confidently dictated to the Ghanaian parliament in 2009 had given way to earnest supplications for attention on the other side of the continent. Again, the political calculus behind the new stance was not difficult to inter-pret, nor should the pragmatic shifts in tone have been surprising. In 2017, the value of two-way trade between China and African nations would approach $150 billion, dwarfing the continent's $39 billion in similar exchanges with the United States. It was enough of a shift in economic relations and political influence to get anyone's attention.[11]

Born in crisis, the Obama administration had to quickly fend off worst-case scenarios and learn the ways of catastrophe avoidance. Its eight-year engagement with Africa was a long master class in the sci-ence of choosing sides and hoping for the best, as well as the art of selecting middling to poor options from among a bushel of worse ones, while blindfolded and with the clock running down. Under such conditions, mistakes were made, lessons were learned, and then new mistakes were made, which taught new lessons—or simply re-affirmed the old ones. At least in the realm of humanitarian aid and relief work, efforts to extract people from cycles of calamity caused by both man-made and natural factors had their frustrations, but suc-cesses were often measurable in lives saved or improved, a metric that was its own reward.

President Obama could tout a number of achievements in this area, though they were rarely ones that wholly rooted out the more intractable, underlying problems. Started under the Clinton and Bush administrations, US attempts to reduce the worldwide incidence of HIV / AIDS infections and to treat the afflicted continued under the

Obama White House. Special emphasis was placed on targeting anti-retroviral drugs toward pregnant HIV-positive women so that their babies might be born HIV-free. Furthermore, during a G8 meeting of wealthy countries in 2012, the president revealed $3 billion in private-sector commitments to improving food production methods in Africa. These pledges followed $22 billion of government-backed commitments in 2009, $3.5 billion of which was promised by the United States. Additionally, the ambitious Power Africa initiative was launched in 2013. Conceived as a partnership between the US government, private utility companies, and selected African countries to generate up to 30,000 megawatts of new electricity by 2030, the project held out the prospect of lifting millions out of deprivation and isolation. Despite $7 billion in American seed money, the electrification plan was slow to advance and was producing only 374 megawatts by 2016. However, a number of large-scale power sources joined the grid over the next several years, and by July 2019 more than fifty "financially closed projects" were producing 3,486 megawatts of electricity across the continent.[12]

One of the more noteworthy humanitarian challenges that faced the Obama administration occurred in Liberia. The West African country has long-standing ties with the United States dating back to the nineteenth century when Black American migrants ventured there seeking the first-class citizenship and freedom denied them in the land of their birth. As one of the first acts of his presidency, Obama extended the temporary protected status of thousands of Liberians in the United States, allowing them to reside in the country longer while their homeland continued to recuperate from almost two decades of civil war. In 2014, an outbreak of the Ebola virus compelled the Liberian president, Ellen Johnson Sirleaf, to reach out to the world for assistance in containing the plague, which had killed more than 1,000 of her fellow citizens by September. Sirleaf, a Harvard graduate, a Nobel Peace Prize laureate, and the first woman elected as a head of state in Africa, sent an urgent appeal to her US counterpart, requesting that the US military promptly set up hospitals across the country that could accommodate 1,500 patients. "I am being honest with you when I say that at this rate," she wrote to Obama, "we will never break the transmission chain and the virus will overwhelm us."[13]

In response to Sirleaf's plea, Obama deemed the crisis a national security priority, yet his administration's initial actions did not quite match that weighty designation. US officials revealed plans to open a twenty-five-bed facility for the treatment of health-care workers, a move that was criticized by some disease specialists as grossly inadequate. Sirleaf pressed her case harder and let it be known that the situation was dire. Obama met personally with an Ebola survivor in the Oval Office and was briefed in Atlanta by the Centers for Disease Control and Prevention. On September 16, he announced that the United States would send up to 3,000 military personnel to Liberia to help organize the response to the disease. He also called on Congress to allocate $88 million to defray the cost of the effort, which included plans for seventeen hospitals stocked with a hundred beds each. The Liberian president, relieved by the fortified American response, issued additional calls for international assistance the day after Obama announced his commitments. Australia, following the US lead, committed $6.4 million to the emergency effort, complementing a $1 billion Ebola relief plan published by the World Health Organization. Other nations prepared similar blueprints for action.

It is difficult to know the exact impact of the US response to the Ebola crisis in Liberia, given that infection rates tapered off drastically by November and prior to the full deployment of US personnel, financial resources, and technical assistance. What is known is that the response was extensive, with almost a billion dollars spent on moving nearly 3,000 troops into the country and constructing and/or funding eighteen treatment facilities. Also known is the human toll of the spreading plague, which killed more than 3,700 people in Liberia before the last declared case of Ebola was treated in March

2015. The disease continued to ravage neighboring Sierra Leone and Guinea for months longer, driving total deaths for the region toward 10,000. When President Obama announced plans to end the US deployment, Sirleaf requested that he not curb the US presence but instead continue to assist in building infrastructure in the country. She knew that new roads, clean water, and sanitation facilities were the best defense against another disease outbreak and could mean the difference between a containable scourge and an epidemiological disaster. The country's vulnerability to Ebola had made it more susceptible to other endemic diseases, such as malaria, which also spiked in lethality during 2014-2015. The Liberian president was aware of ongoing US efforts to reduce malarial mortality in Africa and elsewhere and thus understood that sufficient institutions and infrastructure were proven weapons in the fight against disease and sickness. Notwithstanding Sirleaf's request, the United States quickly drew down its forces in Liberia, handing off residual elements of its mission, designated Operation United Assistance, to other parties.[14]

The Liberian intervention was an overall success and showed the United States at its best concerning its engagement with Africa. A more complicated affair in East Africa, one involving the heavy lifting of actual nation-building, tested US commitment to the region as well as the viability of its policy tools for effecting change and stability. The Obama administration had inherited from its predecessor a shaky peace in the country of Sudan, which was preparing itself for a rare referendum in 2011 that would allow the southern portion of the nation to secede and become independent. Tensions and outright war between North and South Sudan had taken a heavy toll on the people of Africa's third-largest country, and two decades of oppressive rule by President Omar al-Bashir had completely exhausted any goodwill between the two regions. A further strain was the merciless conflict that had erupted in the western Darfur zone in 2003-2005, when the Sudanese Armed Forces, in league with local Janjaweed irregulars, unleashed an indiscriminate wave of violence against the population in response to military losses at the hands of the insurgent Sudan People's Liberation Army (SPLA). A 2005 peace agreement officially ended the civil war, though sporadic clashes flared in later years.

The Obama administration, like the Bush government before it, tried to hold things together with constant diplomacy and large infusions of aid into the southern region, the latter amounting to $6 billion by the end of 2010. Some progress was achieved, including the building of roads, schools, government ministries, and the rudiments of a South Sudanese army. However, the sprawling, landlocked region had poor infrastructure and facilities in even the best of times and was hardly prepared to put such a flood of money and resources to good use. On the eve of national independence, many southern locales still looked as they had generations earlier. The region's dependence on oil revenues, foreign assistance, and its northern neighbor's port facilities did not bode well for the future.[15]

The referendum was planned for January 9, 2011, and Obama wanted it to happen on time with minimal hitches. Secretary of State Hillary Clinton and Vice President Joe Biden were both in contact with Sudanese leaders, and the president himself worked closely with the African Union in an effort to smooth the way to independence. The plebiscite occurred on schedule. Turnout was high, and secession was endorsed by 99 percent of the electorate. It was a clear mandate for the government of Salva Kiir, an ethnic Dinka and former SPLA commander who had been elected president-in-waiting the previous year. More noteworthy than the near unanimous vote was the process: only one other modern African nation, Eritrea, had attained national sovereignty through seceding from another. That precedent, too, had been produced through war and referendum, and it did not end hostilities between the new nation and its mother country, Ethiopia.

Unfortunately, peace would also be a scarcity in the new South Sudan. While formally recognizing the emerging nation on July 9 and expressing confidence about future relations, Obama could not hold back the forces of disunity that threatened the fragile détente. Faced with political dissent and ethnic strife, the Kiir government, young and unseasoned, assumed its default posture as an armed insurgency and tried to settle matters on the battlefield. Neither money—Washington, DC, sent nearly a half a billion dollars in humanitarian aid by May 2014—nor reason halted the violence, which eventually left 400,000 dead and many more displaced. When he visited Ethiopia the following year, the US president tried to hastily arrange yet another peace initiative, reminding an assembly of African leaders, "We don't have a lot of time to wait." Notwithstanding his desperate efforts at ending the crisis, few were listening to him by the late stages of his presidency. In the end, Obama was stuck with the option of trying to convince the United Nations to support limited sanctions and an arms embargo against the warring South Sudanese. Even this largely symbolic gesture proved futile; the proposed measure never passed the Security Council.[16]

It was too early to tell whether South Sudan would prove to be another failed state when Barack Obama left the White House in 2017. The prognosis was not encouraging, but peace feelers were beginning to test the waters by the following year. Such was the management of international crises thousands of miles away on the world's second-largest continent. Paralleling emergencies in Liberia and Sudan were several other critical developments that seemed to demand the attention of the Obama administration.

When the Arab Spring dawned in North Africa in 2011, its mixed fruits brought democracy to Tunisia but ignited civil war in Libya and raised new autocrats to power in Egypt. Fanned by propaganda and rumor, anti-American sentiment blazed across the Muslim world, leading to the storming of US embassies in Sudan and Libya and heightened terrorism alerts. Stretched thin across the Muslim world from Afghanistan to Libya, US forces and the government in Washington were often on the defensive in terms of messaging and response times. The US Africa Command, founded in 2007 and based in Djibouti, had yet to gain its operational footing on the continent and was frequently reduced to borrowing forces from the European Command in order to address an assortment of dilemmas.

Given the war weariness that had beset the American public over the previous decade, Obama was reluctant to send US troops into harm's way. There were cases in which he authorized the deployment of small numbers of US forces to, for example, chase Joseph Kony and his Lord's Resistance Army across Central Africa or to track down Boko Haram militants in Cameroon. But these assignments were the exception rather than the norm. In lieu of dispatching US military personnel to hotspots, the president preferred to rely on African forces to handle African conflicts. Over time, the US military and other agencies became experienced at airlifting indigenous troops into conflict zones and training drug enforcement personnel in various countries. As an alternative to applying force, the administration sometimes threatened sanctions or cuts to aid in order to encourage a regime to change its behavior, as it did in Rwanda in 2012 to curb its support for rebels in other countries. In other instances, Washington simply supported UN forces in maintaining a shaky status quo, which was the essence of US policy in Congo. Despite appearances, there were guiding principles behind the US approach to Africa, though no standard tools were created and consistently applied to every situation, including those of a similar sort. Consequently, outcomes could be as scattered as the crises themselves, leaving some observers unclear regarding Obama's ultimate motives and goals.[17]

Of all of the tools and methods that the Obama administration employed in Africa, drone aircraft became the most emblematic of its counterinsurgency and antiterrorism activities. Relatively small, lightweight, and fast, these unmanned aerial vehicles allow for intelligence gathering and enemy surveillance from high above as their human handlers remotely maneuver them over difficult-to-access terrain and isolated locations. Costing several million dollars each, these planes are outfitted with a range of technologies, including video cameras, infrared thermometers, and sensors for detecting radio and cellphone signals. Payloads can also include a variety of missiles and other weapons systems, which unlock the offensive potential of drones. First appearing in the Afghan war zone in 2007, hunter-killer craft, such as the MQ-9 Reaper, were increasingly used to pursue and eliminate leaders whom US authorities designated as especially dangerous foes. In Africa, the heavy reliance of US Special Forces on drones for surveillance purposes elevated the military's role in foreign intelligence collection, once the almost exclusive domain of the Central Intelligence Agency. Over time, the deployment of armed variants of the mosquito-shaped craft significantly changed the nature of warfare on the continent in ways that were both novel and highly controversial.

As with all vehicles, drone aircraft require a dedicated infrastructure in order to operate. Across Africa, a hodgepodge of military bases, civilian airports, out-of-the-way airstrips, and makeshift hangars were linked together by US forces to make the refueling and servicing of the unmanned planes possible. Another necessity was the cooperation of African countries whose territories and airspace would host drone flights, which often involved the traversing of national borders. Besides Djibouti, East African countries including Uganda, Kenya, and Ethiopia provided the requisite permission for the establishment of drone installations and flight routes; the Seychelles became a particularly important base of operation in the Indian Ocean region. To the west, Niger, Mauritania, Burkina Faso, and Cameroon allowed US aircraft to crisscross their skies. Complemented by manned aircraft, drones were principally used for surveillance and tracking purposes, whether to locate Boko Haram rebels who had abducted hundreds of girls from northern Nigeria in 2014 or to keep up with the activities of groups such as al-Qaeda in the Islamic Maghreb during the twilight of the Arab Spring. Ultimately, the United States sought to create an overlapping aerial surveillance net that would allow it to literally have eyes watching broad expanses of the African continent. In addition to this usage, offensive employment of unmanned aircraft accelerated during the last years of the Obama presidency, when more intransigent enemies had clearly demonstrated that they could not be bowed by ground forces alone.

One of the more relentless opponents that the United States and its allies faced in Africa was al-Shabaab, which operated out of Somalia and its environs. A creature of Islamic fundamentalism, foreign interventions, and assorted social maladies attributable to poverty and discontent, the group had aligned itself with al-Qaeda by the start of the Obama administration and was in open rebellion against the frail government in Mogadishu. Its methods were brutal and left both combatant and civilian casualties in their wake. By 2012, US Navy SEALs were engaged in ground operations against al-Shabaab operatives, and they were aided by Ethiopian and African Union soldiers who pressed the group from other locations in Somalia. The US State Department, which had designated al-Shabaab a terrorist organization, offered more than $20 million in bounties for information concerning the whereabouts of the group's leadership, a tactic that was not immediately successful. When al-Shabaab took credit for a September 2013 bombing that killed dozens at a Nairobi mall, Navy SEALs raided the home of one of its leaders only to find that the targeted man had departed.

The following year, the US military took its war against the group to the skies. Drones and manned planes bombarded an al-Shabaab camp and an affiliated vehicle, killing Ahmed Abdi Godane, a top leader. The group struck back at the United States and its allies with its characteristic ferocity, which included a lethal truck bombing of a Mogadishu hotel a day after Obama left Kenya for Ethiopia in late July 2015. A year later, US Special Forces, in coordination with troops from Uganda, Kenya, and Somalia, were launching more than six raids per month on al-Shabaab forces and positions, supported by the rocket fire of drone aircraft. In an especially deadly attack in March 2016, 150 suspected al-Shabaab members were killed in a US strike on a camp north of the Somali capital. The escalating violence likely had some degrading impact on the group's offensive capability, but it definitely committed the United States and its allies to a widening war in the Horn of Africa.[18]

In his own opinions about drone combat, President Obama could be both adamant in his support for the devastating new instrument of war and pensive about its meaning and limitations. In interviews, he defended the use of armed unmanned aircraft as a means of protecting the United States from foreign adversaries or even against Americans who might join al-Qaeda or other outlawed groups. He preferred dispatching drones to carry out missions that might otherwise result in higher combatant and civilian casualties if ground troops were sent instead. On several occasions, Obama stated that he struggled with making such decisions and that he never wanted "to be a president who is comfortable and at ease with killing people." As US engagement with al-Shabaab intensified in 2013, he acknowledged that clearer policies were needed for governing drone warfare, as well as more transparency regarding his endorsement of lethal strikes. In the absence of legislative action by Congress, the administration promulgated its own legal framework for the use of armed drones. In late November 2016, the White House released a document that expansively interpreted the 2001 congressional authorization of a war against the perpetrators of the September 11 terrorist attacks, claiming that it covered the escalating war against al-Shabaab. More than anything else, the executive statement offered legal cover for Obama's successor to continue the offensive in Somalia, absent any congressional objections.[19]

Opinion polls revealed that Americans were more tolerant of the use of armed drones in combat zones than were people in other parts of the world. A 2013 survey revealed that 65 percent of US respondents approved of the use of such aircraft against suspected terrorists abroad. When asked whether drone strikes were appropriate against US citizens living in other countries and engaging in terrorist activities, support fell to 41 percent and was even lower for airstrikes against Americans and noncitizens on US soil. Among other countries, disapproval of such methods of warfare was high, especially in Muslim nations. Eighty-nine percent of Jordanian respondents opposed drone strikes, which was similar to the percentage of their disapproving counterparts in Egypt (89 percent), Turkey (81 percent), and Tunisia (72 percent). Outside of the Islamic world, opposition to drone strikes was consistently higher than in the United States, with citizens in Brazil (76 percent), Japan (75 percent), Mexico (73 percent), and China (55 percent) all expressing greater opposition. Even in Western European countries that the United States counted among its closest allies and that sometimes materially assisted the nation in its African affairs, the use of armed drones was generally frowned on by respondents in Spain (76 percent), France (63 percent), and Germany (59 percent).[20]

Although drone strikes were tactically efficient and spared US ground troops potentially fatal combat exposure, they had many associated costs that were reflected in their high disapproval ratings among many countries. The secrecy behind their usage bred suspicion, fear, and hatred, certainly among targeted groups and probably among some of those in whose name the strikes were launched. Moreover, such premeditated killings of political figures—whether on the battlefield, in their homes, or among their family members—were assassinations, regardless of what the Obama administration chose to call them. Further, while the use of armed drones may have reduced the likelihood of combat casualties among US and allied forces, the strategy steadily accrued a global tally of more than a thousand civilian deaths, according to some estimates. It was, again, the Obama balance between principle and practice, the ideal and the pragmatic, but with more deadly and far-reaching consequences. Arguably, Obama had followed Nelson Mandela's advice "to combat the scourge of poverty and disease" by sinking billions into indigent South Sudan and applying a healing balm to Ebola-ridden Liberia. However, he brought the sword to Somalia to a degree that could scarcely have been predicted back in 2008 when the South African statesman sent his post-election greetings to the new US president.[21]

Years after leaving the White House, Obama would characterize his foreign policy as being inspired by the "realist" tradition, which, among other things, sought to pair "a belief in American exceptionalism with a humility about our ability to remake the world in our image." This was, of course, a generous way of describing his approach to Africa and other regions, and he was the first to admit that as a "liberal president [I] couldn't afford to look soft on terrorism." Otherwise, he might have fallen prey to conservative critics at home for not being more proactive against foreign threats. At the same time, Obama understood the price of such an aggressive posture and occasionally reflected on its costs to Africans. In recounting his April 2009 order to have Navy SEALs dispatch three Somali men who had captured an American cargo ship captain off the East African coast, Obama wrote ruefully a decade later: "They were dangerous, these young men, often deliberately and casually cruel. Still, in the aggregate, at least, I wanted somehow to save them—send them to school, give them a trade, drain them of the hate that had been filling their heads. And yet the world they were a part of, and the machinery I commanded, more often had me killing them instead." These words illuminate how Obama understood his role in the international arena during his eight years as president. Further, they are indicative of his penchant for engaging "the world as it is," even when the methods of the realist were not always the most palatable or consistent.[22]

To many Kenyans, Barack Obama was a native son. Regardless of the fact that he was born more than 10,000 miles away in Hawaii to a foreign mother and a father of questionable repute back home, his election to the US presidency was a source of immeasurable pride for many in the East African country. US relations with the former British colony during the Obama administration did not represent a sharp break with the past and continued to be marked by extensions of development aid and maintenance of cordial diplomatic ties. USAID supported livestock-related projects in the northeastern region of the nation, and the US military worked closely with the Kenya Defence Forces to contain al-Shabaab and other regional threats. One wrinkle in the bilateral relationship did emerge during the March 2013 presidential election in Kenya. A contested result in the race between Uhuru Kenyatta and Raila Odinga strained the nation's capacity for a peaceful transfer of power, harking back to the election-related violence that had engulfed the country six years earlier. Kenyatta, a deputy prime minister and son of the nation's first president, was eventually declared the winner of the race, but his victory was severely tainted. The International Criminal Court (ICC) had previously charged him with crimes against humanity stemming from his alleged role in fomenting election-related violence in 2007, and his trial was scheduled to begin in the Netherlands on February 5, 2014. The impending prosecution was not a good beginning for a newly elected president from a prominent political dynasty, but the country was spared the violent spasms that had shaken its democratic institutions years earlier.[23]

In late March 2013, Obama congratulated Kenyatta on his then still-contested victory over Odinga. But even after the dust settled and Kenyatta was confirmed as president, delicate issues remained. Obama had planned a trip to Africa for the summer, which would be his third as president. Many observers believed that such a visit, for both substantive and symbolic reasons, was entirely appropriate, especially with the US reelection campaign and birther innuendos no longer serving as complications. Yet there was a new conundrum. What to do about Kenya? It was reasonable to expect that the president might visit his father's homeland at some point during his term in office. The country was at least moderately democratic, progressing economically, and a proven ally against terrorism and other international hazards. Nonetheless, appearing in a photo op with an ICC-indicted Kenyatta did not appeal to Obama. It would almost certainly give the impression that the US president took the charges against his Kenyan counterpart lightly or even sought to place his thumb on the scales of justice in The Hague.

Making the final decision probably felt as bad as it looked, but Obama, ever averse to needless drama, chose relatively safe democracies to visit at the western, southern, and eastern corners of sub-Saharan Africa: Senegal, South Africa, and Tanzania. Some in the Kenyan leadership took the news hard and let their disappointment be known. "We respect America but Obama's failure to visit the country does not stop us [from] running the government," Deputy President William Ruto told the local press. "We have other friendly nations we will partner with." It was a slight for a slight, perhaps all the more cutting since Obama had explicitly mentioned the outstanding ICC trial as having influenced his itinerary. While he did assure Ruto and others that his connections to the East African country "by definition are going to be strong and will stay strong," he did not alter his travel plans even though the Tanzanian leg of his journey brought him within 150 miles of the Kenyan border.[24]

Obama did ultimately make his way to Kenya later in his second term. In 2015, the East African nation and the United States jointly sponsored the sixth Global Entrepreneurship Summit (GES) in Nairobi. Started in 2009, the annual gathering is dedicated to bringing together businesspeople and investors from around the world to network and share ideas. Given Kenya's expanding economy and innovative leadership in mobile money systems—along with the dropping of ICC charges against President Kenyatta in March—the country was a logical place for such a forward-looking conference. However,. the logistics of the trip proved to be daunting. The US State Department issued a travel warning for citizens traveling to Kenya a week before the summit, an acknowledgment of the ongoing al-Shabaab threat. The tenuous security situation compelled a low-key entry for the US president into the country. *Air Force One* arrived in Nairobi on Friday evening, July 24, and Obama was greeted on the tarmac by the Kenyan president and other officials after nightfall. The main streets had been closed that afternoon, allowing *Cadillac One* a wide berth as it took Obama into the city. It was an unusually quiet ride, punctuated by US flags that lined the road and a billboard that read "Karibu POTUS" (Swahili for "Welcome President of the United States"). The historic nature of the occasion was only made obvious when crowds took to the streets the next day to see and celebrate the first visit of a sitting US head of state in the country's five-decade existence.

At a news conference on Saturday, the two presidents presented an interesting juxtaposition of identities and journeys. Also born in 1961, Kenyatta was a US-trained Kikuyu whose father, Jomo Kenyatta, had been a leading figure in the pro-independence movement. The younger Kenyatta entered local politics in 1997, the same year Obama entered the Illinois state senate, and he ran for president (albeit unsuccessfully) ten years later, just as the junior US senator did a half a world away. Kenyatta had been in business and trade prior to rising through the ranks of the dominant Kenya African National Union, and in some ways his early attraction to the marketplace and finance was similar to the truncated career arc of the economist Barack Obama Sr. Conversely, Barack Obama Jr., the lawyer-writer, would have likely found Jomo Kenyatta a kindred intellectual spirit, especially considering the latter's youthful fascination with anthropology and published musings about identity in his 1938 book, *Facing Mount Kenya*. As fate would have it, the two older men diverged temperamentally and politically to the point of estrangement, and Jomo Kenyatta, during his presidency, made it difficult for Obama Sr. to find a job in the country. When the sons met in 2015 and sat down before the press in Nairobi, much of this awkward history was known to them; Obama had actually written in some detail about his father's run-ins with Kenyatta in his first book, *Dreams from My Father*. Although their roles had not been reversed—they were technically equals as the leaders of sovereign, independent states—power relations undoubtedly tilted in Obama Jr.'s favor. The son of the wandering, intemperate Luo had come home, and his arrival mattered even to a Kikuyu patrician like Kenyatta who had been born into privilege and prestige.

The news conference was scripted and largely uneventful, though disagreements were evident. Obama recognized Kenya's partnership in the struggle against al-Shabaab but counseled that fighting terrorism should not be used as a pretext for squelching dissent. He especially condemned antigay discrimination in the country and likened it to racial segregation in the United States. This was not the first time that Obama had raised this concern on African soil. In 2013, he had mentioned the need to protect gay rights during a meeting with Senegalese president Macky Sall at his palace in Dakar. Like Kenyatta, the West African leader balked, claiming that his people were not ready for such a cultural shift and that more time would be needed to change attitudes. Obama did not press the issue too far with either man but added gay rights to his expanding vision of what human rights should mean in Africa and elsewhere. Additionally, during the 2015 visit the US president brought up the issue of corruption and how it could have a dampening effect on Kenya's economic health. The two leaders had previously discussed this matter and together released a twenty-nine-point proposal for checking venality in the nation's institutions and culture. Also noteworthy, they signed an "action plan" for strengthening the country's defenses against al-Shabaab, which had killed fourteen people in a nighttime assault in northeastern Kenya just two weeks earlier.

In the shadow of terrorism, Chinese overtures, and a steadily unfolding climate crisis, Obama's speech at the GES was a mix of cheerleading and warnings. "Africa is on the move," he announced, acknowledging growing economies across East Africa and other regions of the continent. As had become his tendency, he also informed delegates that African governments needed to abide by the rule of law and to make serious efforts to quell corruption. At least in this context, the themes were not received as merely Western condescension or idle talking points with no real-world relevance. When asked about what they wanted most from the US president's visit, Kenyan citizens on the street highlighted corruption as a problem that they hoped that he would raise with the nation's leaders. Moreover, they cited aspirations that did not find much of an outlet at the GES or the presidents' news conference but were stirred during Obama's time in the country. Joshua Onyango, a florist, wanted the president to implement direct airline flights between Kenya and the United States "to increase trade between the two countries." Janet Wairimu, an employee of the Sankara Hotel in Nairobi, desired an end to travel advisories that warned people away from the region after every terror-ist attack. "Tourists are the backbone of [the] Kenya economy," she told a reporter, "and we expect Obama to address the issue." On July 26, the US president left Kenya in much the same condition that he had found it: struggling but hopeful and at least temporarily inspired by his presence and words. He did not return again before he left the White House but mindfully kept up with the affairs of the country and remained invested in its progress.[25]

During his 2015 visit, Obama was able to reconnect with a number of his Kenyan relatives, including his half sister Auma and stepgrand-mother Sarah Onyango Obama, who both visited him at his Nairobi hotel on the evening of his arrival. Granny Sarah, as he affectionately called her, had come quite a distance to see him, traveling several hours by car through the rustic countryside and over taxing roads. Upon Obama's election in 2008, she had celebrated as much as any-one and four years later waved her cane joyously when she heard that her grandson had been reelected. By the time they met again during the GES trip, she was 93 and had lost a good deal of her former vitality; the trip from Kogelo to Nairobi must have been no small feat for her. The president had tried to care for her from afar, though geography and his duties limited his impact. When al-Qaeda and al-Shabaab threatened to harm her in the wake of Osama bin Laden's demise, extra security was stationed in the village to protect the elderly woman and other relatives. The family tie made her a celebrity in the region, and her humble homestead became almost a site of pilgrimage for tourists and journalists. In the midst of it all, age and experience bestowed on her the wisdom to keep such changes in perspective.

Aside from death threats and the occasional curious stranger, gen-uine benefits came with being related to the most powerful man in the world. In Sarah Obama's case, such perks included paved roads, access to electricity and running water, and even a local thoroughfare named in her honor. Moreover, the Kenyan government prudently assigned a female civil servant to look after her. In 2014, the cheerful nonagenarian told a reporter that the US president was "still very central to my life today," revealing how clearly she understood her good fortune and his. If Barack Obama Jr. had been born in Kogelo, he might never have seen his fifth birthday due to an infant mortality rate that was more than twice the national average. If he had survived, he would have faced a life of hardship and disease and likely would have died in his forties or fifties, given the life expectancy of residents of the region. After he left the White House, Kogelo, no longer such an attraction, lapsed back into the sleepy village it had been before 2008. No stranger to changing circumstances, Granny Sarah endured and remained thankful. Rather remarkably, she lived long enough to see her famous grandson once more.[26]

Barack Obama's family ties to Kenya were almost quaint when it came to his Granny Sarah, who reveled in his success and stayed in his good graces. The situation with other African relatives, especially those who reached the United States, was more complicated, particularly once he entered the White House. The American journey of Onyango Obama, the president's uncle, was one of the less troublesome tales but still included its share of awkward elements and inconveniences. Born in Kenya in 1944 and the half brother of Barack Obama Sr., Onyango migrated to the United States in the 1960s and apparently lived and worked without incident for decades. After he failed to renew an application for continuing residency, an immigration judge ordered his deportation in 1992. For almost two decades, Onyango evaded the government's radar until he was stopped on suspicion of drunk driving in Framingham, Massachusetts, in 2011. His resources were such that he could not immediately afford bail. When asked by law enforcement officials whether he wanted to make other arrangements, he replied, "I think I will call the White House." The maneuver was not completely outlandish; Barack Obama had briefly lived with this Kenyan uncle in Cambridge during his Harvard years, but they had not kept in touch. In any event, no call was made to the Oval Office to bail out Onyango, and his presidential nephew expressly declined to intervene in the normal operation of the legal process. In light of Onyango Obama's otherwise law-abiding history in the United States, a judge granted him permission to stay in the country in December 2013.[27]

In the case of Zeituni Onyango, the puzzle pieces of her Kenyan and American lives came together to render a more unfortunate picture, one that likely affected the president in a personal way. She was Barack's aunt—his father's half sister—whom he had first met during a visit to Kenya in 1988. Their initial encounter was memorable and occurred in Jomo Kenyatta International Airport, where she approached him and declared, "Welcome home," before kissing him on both cheeks. His later recollections of his time with her reveal a true fondness for "Auntie Zeituni," which was returned in the form of rich and emotional family lore that she shared with him about his father and others. In 2000, Zeituni, at age 48, migrated to the United States on a visa and made her way to Chicago to meet her nephew's family.

According to relatives, Zeituni was there when the newborn Sasha needed a sitter and to help an overwhelmed Michelle Obama with household chores. In 2004, her application for political asylum was denied after years of waiting, and she, like her brother Onyango Obama, decided to remain in the shadows. Inconveniently, she did not reemerge until just before the 2008 election. News reports linked Zeituni Onyango to the presidential candidate and described her as being in the country illegally and residing in "run-down public housing" in Boston. Obama, in the heat of the White House race, sought distance from his Kenyan aunt. Publicly, he expressed surprise that she was still in the country and returned a $265 contribution that she had given to his campaign. Privately, he almost certainly struggled with the matter, having been so warmly received in Kenya two decades earlier and having entrusted her with the care of his youngest child in 2001. After an immigration judge granted her asylum in 2010, Zeituni was ecstatic and told the world who she was. "President Obama, I'm his aunt," she explained to an interviewer. "If he does a wrong thing, I'm the only person on earth allowed to pinch his ears and smack him." Her jubilation did not last. In April 2014, she died in Boston after a battle against cancer. Her nephew sent his condolences in a letter and helped cover the costs of the funeral but did not attend.[28]

If Onyango Obama's situation was embarrassing and Zeituni Onyango's tragedy was poignant and conflicting, Malik Obama's appearance on the stage of US history was both ill timed and grating. An older half brother of Barack Jr., Malik was a US citizen and had lived in the DC area since 1985. He, like their father, pursued a career in studying market forces and found work as a financial consultant. Auma Obama, their sister, had not expected much when Barack was elected president and considered the achievement itself worthy of the clan's respect. "As a family . . . we support Barack but have no expectations," she told a reporter after the 2008 election. "Because we are very, very clear that this is something he's doing in America and that he's an American president." Malik, however, had high expectations of his brother once the latter entered the White House and felt that his access to power should benefit Africa, Kenya, and the extended Obama family. He waited eight years for the fruits of Obama's presidency to manifest and publicly expressed disappointment when he did not reap them. In the thick of the 2016 campaign, Malik proclaimed his love for his brother but called him a "hypocrite" who had not done enough for the African continent or his people there. Malik also went into darker territory by endorsing for president Donald Trump, a fellow businessman whom he found to be "down to earth" and a "humble and honest guy." As if enough Obama half siblings and other relatives had not already appeared, Mark Obama Ndesandjo, the son of Barack Obama Sr. and his third wife, told the *New York Times* that he objected to Malik's public support for Trump. "I love my brothers," he said in a conciliatory tone, "but no one member represents the Obamas."[29]

It seemed like an unplanned, unwanted family reunion had convened to hash out long-standing rivalries and jealousies while the whole world watched. For President Obama, the dangers of such a spectacle were real and potentially damaging across oceans and generations, and both the politician and the private man tried to avoid the pitfalls as much as possible. The illegal immigration elements of the stories reminded Americans of his family's foreignness and gave conservative foes and conspiracy theorists ammunition to concoct more rumors and smear campaigns. The Kenyan component raised anew his Black Africanness, which further compounded the perceived foreignness. It was not the tidy tale of the long-dead Scotch-Irish shoemaker whose warts and blemishes had been airbrushed by time and soothing mythologies. Instead, these immigrant Black folks were living, breathing relatives who had broken US laws and then reached out to embrace the sitting president as one of their own. At bottom, it all pointed back to the image of the errant father—the irresponsible African with too many wives and children and too few resources and redeeming qualities. The situation was the antithesis of the respectability rhetoric that the president had been preaching to Black people for years, and it was now squatting at his doorstep.

Barack Obama wanted nothing to do with any of it, at least not publicly. When he first learned of Onyango Obama's legal problems in 2011, he first claimed that he had never met the wayward uncle, but that story began to strain credulity. Similarly, while he did not completely disown Zeituni Onyango, who figured so prominently and favorably in *Dreams from My Father*, the president did decide to play golf on the day of her funeral, which would have almost certainly disappointed her mother, Sarah Onyango Obama, and others back in the old country. Once again, it was principle versus pragmatism, made even murkier by the ever-present politics and the unrelenting need to manage the media narrative. By the last year of his presidency, it was probably easier to ignore Malik Obama, who cast insults of the worst sort, including giving aid and comfort to Trump and his birtherism. Nevertheless, navigating the wanderers, hangers-on, and eccentric personalities of the family was still irritating and tiring.

Illustratively, when a reporter asked the White House in June 2016 why the president had not responded to a 2013 invitation to view his father's personal papers at the Schomburg Center in New York, the president put off a possible visit until after he left office. He was simply unwilling to stir up more unflattering news stories about his African heritage and family prior to again becoming a private citizen.[30]

Obama family drama aside, the president projected optimism about Africa and tried especially in his second term to leave a positive legacy, despite unpleasant loose ends in places like Somalia and South Sudan. His administration had a record of real and substantive achievements, some of which required years of commitment and persistent work on both sides of the Atlantic. Initiatives aimed at combatting disease, food insecurity, and climate change paid varying degrees of dividends in lives saved and improved. The Power Africa project continued to inch along through the end of the Obama presidency and seemed poised to benefit the populations of several of the continent's nations in years to come. Of signal importance, the Young African Leaders Initiative, started in 2010, brought 500 Africans between the ages of 18 and 35 to the United States in 2014 as part of its Washington Fellowship program. Designed to cultivate leadership skills, entrepreneurship, and vital networks between young Africans and Americans, the venture connected participants to university campuses, US leaders, and other resources that could potentially assist them in shaping the Africa of the future. Additionally, the Obama administration provided billions in humanitarian aid and peace-keeping support to African countries and fended off a number of crises in Liberia, Congo, Côte d'Ivoire, and Senegal that likely would have become dire situations without US engagement.[31]

The other side of the ledger, of course, revealed the shortcomings and troubling aspects of US involvement in Africa during the Obama years, which became part of the president's legacy. Antiterrorism and counterinsurgency efforts accelerated the militarization of several nations, escalating conflicts throughout the Horn of Africa and elsewhere. Pragmatic and self-interested relationships with corrupt, autocratic rulers contradicted some of the principled rhetoric coming out of Washington concerning the value that it placed on democracy, human rights, and transparency. Further, cooperating with such regimes in countries like Ethiopia, Rwanda, and Equatorial Guinea extended to them a veneer of legitimacy and likely helped prolong their rule, at the expense of US credibility. In some instances, the administration seemed content with treading water on issues that it had inherited from the Bush government and consequently had to play catch-up when China and al-Shabaab shook up existing paradigms and relationships. At other times, Obama seemed confident that the force of his personality and articulated policies could themselves change behaviors and convert the opposition.

At a historic US-Africa summit with fifty heads of state in Washington, DC, in August 2014, the world got a glimpse of the US vision of the continent, underscoring the administration's values, aspirations, contradictions, and limitations. To applause, the president announced billions of dollars in investments and assistance related to trade, energy, infrastructure, security, and other matters. As he had in his 2009 speech in Ghana, Obama reiterated his personal ties to the continent, proclaiming to the audience, "The blood of Africa runs through our family." If anyone needed to be reminded of his thoughts on combatting corruption in Africa, they needed only to look around to see that longtime autocrats Robert Mugabe of Zimbabwe and Omar al-Bashir of Sudan had not been invited to the gathering, which was a purposeful snub. Yet despite all of the choreographed optics, the inconsistency in standards and the enduring supremacy of pragmatism were on full display. Interspersed with the more democratic and conscientious leaders in attendance was a rogues' gallery of authoritarians, crooks, and cutthroats whose presence was directly related to the costs of doing business in certain parts of Africa. The jarring juxtaposition of such disparate personalities and records was not lost on protesters outside, such as Obang Metho of the Solidarity Movement for a New

Ethiopia. "Now [Obama] is sitting with strongmen," he lamented as he and others demonstrated against the summit. "Where are the strong institutions?" His question was, of course, a fair one, but it was inaudible to those inside the meeting hall.[32]

Michelle Obama was at least several degrees removed from the Africa and Africans, particularly Kenyans, that her husband occasionally encountered during his life and presidency. Her Africa was not the same as Barack's, even though she understood and appreciated his path. She was a member of a different diaspora, one spawned by the transatlantic slave trade centuries earlier, not the one set in motion by the wanderings and ambitions of people like Zeituni Onyango, Onyango Obama, and Barack Obama Sr. When the couple stood together at the "slave castles" in Ghana and Senegal, their emotional registers were different, partially due to the nature and timing of the passage of their ancestors from Africa into diaspora. In recalling the first family's 2013 visit to the Door of No Return on Gorée Island, through which imprisoned Africans were herded into cargo holds and shipped into American slavery, the president initially described his experience in empathetic and instructional terms. As "an African American president," the visit had encouraged him to press harder to protect human rights globally. By the time he met with African leaders at the DC summit the following year, his impression of the Gorée doorway had lapsed into historical time. "We walked the steps of a painful past," he told the gathered heads of state, placing the horrors in a fixed era with chronological bookends. It was not so much that his empathy had diminished; instead, he was simply looking backward at someone else's story, which appeared farther away than his own.[33]

In contrast, Michelle's recollections of the doorway were not quite as abstract and remote as her husband's. In her 2013 travelogue, she noted "the heartbreak and despair I felt standing at the site," particularly as "a descendant of slaves." The experience at Gorée Island had a stifling effect on her as she contemplated the long Middle Passage. "It was hard for me to breathe as I thought about the terror and grief," she wrote hours after the tour as she tried to process "such unthinkable cruelty and suffering." As a diasporan daughter journeying with her own daughters to a site of ancestral trauma, Michelle's thoughts about the doorway reflected a visceral, internal familiarity that was wholly absent from her trips to Kenya to see her husband's people. While her West African story both drew and repelled her, it grounded her heritage in a haunting but seemingly knowable past that was still alive and transcendent.[34]

Beyond the Obamas' travels in Africa and subsequent ruminations on diasporic identities, the president's administration interacted with a number of countries and regions across the Americas with substantial Black populations. The Caribbean nation of Haiti received focused humanitarian assistance from the United States after a 7.0-magnitude earthquake convulsed the island country on January 12, 2010. With an epicenter just twenty miles north of the capital of Port-au-Prince, the seismic event killed as many as 160,000 people within six weeks of the first shock, and many more were internally displaced. President Obama responded quickly to the catastrophe, committing $100 million to relief efforts and dispatching thousands of military personnel to provide security. He also asked former presidents George W. Bush and Bill Clinton to organize the global response to the tragedy, a move that created momentum for international aid efforts. At a press conference, Obama was visibly affected by the calamity, having to stop at one point to gather himself. "You will not be forsaken," he promised the stricken Haitian people. "You will not be forgotten."[35]

The administration took the lead in aid efforts, assisted by the United Nations and other countries. Deportations from the United States of Haitians were curtailed for the rest of the year but resumed in 2011 for those convicted of serious crimes. Despite the ongoing, multifaceted turmoil that plagued Haiti years after the earthquake, the United States continued a policy that reunified Cuban families while denying the same relief to similarly situated Haitian families. In 2014, persistent lobbying by Haitian Americans, supported by a bipartisan group of allies in Congress, encouraged the Obama administration to implement the Haitian Family Reunification Parole program, which allowed family members residing in Haiti to come to the United States up to two years before the processing of their immigrant visas. This loosening of immigration restrictions benefited thousands of Haitians and relieved some of the misery that still gripped the island in the aftermath of the earthquake.[36]

While Haiti received the most US attention due to the 2010 natural disaster, other Caribbean nations were also cultivated by the Obama administration. In April 2015, the president traveled to Jamaica to participate in a meeting of the Caribbean Community (CARICOM). At the gathering, Obama promoted trade and alternative energy projects, committing $20 million to help finance clean energy programs. He also announced the establishment of the Young Leaders of the Americas Initiative, a Caribbean and Latin American version of the Africa-focused youth leadership project. Some observers characterized the US president's visit as designed to counter Venezuela's growing influence in the region, which was facilitated by its export of deeply discounted petroleum across the Caribbean Basin. Whatever the case, Obama did hear some disgruntled voices during his time in Kingston, including that of Bahamian prime minister Perry Christie, who insisted that more be done about illegal gunrunning between the United States and Caribbean gangs. Moreover, Jamaica was enduring a stringent austerity program mandated by the International Monetary Fund that aimed to address its national indebtedness, unemployment, and structural impediments to economic growth. Considering the dependence of their countries on foreign tourism and fair weather, the assembled representatives hoped to discuss several matters with Obama beyond just solar panels and wind turbines.

Notwithstanding the tough realities facing the region, Obama's trip, for the most part, was as mellow as the Bob Marley Museum in Kingston, which he visited on the eve of his meetings with the fifteen-member CARICOM. Jamaicans had lined the roads in anticipation of his motorcade, and Prime Minister Portia Simpson-Miller expressed warm affection for her American counterpart. "So I just wanted to say you're well-loved in Jamaica," she told Obama during one meeting. "Well, first of all I can say to you publicly, 'I love you.'" Along with the prime minister's smiles and hugs, it was almost enough love to make Obama blush. Following the trip, the local media and elites applauded Simpson-Miller on her ability to get a sitting US president to come to Jamaica, the first such visit since 1982. Given the economic straits that the country was currently navigating, it was a politically savvy move on her part. Other observers were, however, quick to remind her that their big neighbor to the north had no permanent friends, just permanent national interests.[37]

From the CARICOM meeting, Obama traveled to Panama City to attend the seventh annual Summit of the Americas. While there, he made a bit of history when he met privately with Cuban president Raúl Castro, whose country had not had diplomatic or trade relations with the United States since the late 1950s. The two leaders explored ways to end the Cold War standoff originally triggered by a communist revolution that had taken place on the island two years before Obama was born. In March 2016, the US president traveled to Cuba for a state visit that seemed surreal to many who had watched the US embargo effectively isolate the Caribbean country for decades. The Obama administration had earlier laid the groundwork for the visit by, among other things, relaxing travel restrictions, reopening the US embassy in Havana, and dropping its designation of Cuba as a terrorism-sponsoring country. But even these historic measures seemed to pale in contrast to the sight of a US president shaking the hand of a Castro and addressing the Cuban people in Havana itself.

For many Black and mixed-race Cubans, who comprise a substantial portion of the island's population, the occasion was magical. Some affectionately referred to Obama as "el negro," or the Black guy, and hailed his arrival as a harbinger of progress to counter the widespread racial discrimination that still limited their opportunities and quality of life in the country. A few, like Alberto Gonzalez, a 44-year-old baker, deemed the visit a "revolution" for people of African descent everywhere. "Look at that family," he urged a reporter in reference to the Obamas. "Have you ever seen a more beautiful family?" During a March 22 speech, Obama spoke directly to Afro-Cubans and their aspirations by first recognizing their common history with Black Americans of enslavement. He also invoked Martin Luther King Jr.'s call to action in the "fierce urgency of now" and cited Nelson Mandela's lifelong struggle for racial equality and social justice. "And in Cuba, we want our engagement to help lift up the Cubans who are of African descent," Obama insisted, "who have proven there's nothing they cannot achieve when given the chance." For many Afro-Cubans, the statement was probably the most affirming that they had ever heard uttered by a US president, let alone a Black one. In the aftermath of Obama's visit, Cubans and others interpreted the improving relations as a positive sign of progress, though the continuing existence of the US detention facility at Guantánamo Bay still served as a reminder of the country's looming, hegemonic presence in the hemisphere. The thaw would be a slow, halting one, subject to lingering suspicions and possible reversals. Nonetheless, both countries seemed ready for a new kind of relationship, and Obama—and Raúl Castro—had acted boldly in seizing the moment.[38]

Issues of race and history came up again in Obama's interactions with Brazilian president Dilma Rousseff. At her invitation, he visited the South American country in 2011 and even traveled through a poverty-soaked favela, where Black residents marveled at the unusual sight of a person of their complexion in a high position of power. Obama had actually been a political and cultural phenomenon in Brazil since before his election, when several candidates for office there copied his campaign style and even adopted his name. However, he at least temporarily fell into disrepute once it was publicly disclosed in 2013 that the US National Security Agency had spied on Rousseff and other heads of state. Infuriated by the clandestine surveillance, the Brazilian president condemned the spying as a "breach of international law" before a meeting of the UN General Assembly in September. Two months later, she canceled a scheduled state visit to Washington, DC, despite Obama's entreaties.[39]

By June 2015, Rousseff had cooled enough to visit the White House and participate in a joint press conference with her US counterpart. As Obama had in Cuba, the Brazilian leader pointed out similarities between the history of her country and that of the United States, including the "blemish of slavery" and the evolving racial and cultural diversity, which she considered a "major asset." Obama, too, took the opportunity to recognize slavery's long shadow in the United States and complimented the recent decision of Gov. Nikki Haley to request the removal of the Confederate flag from the grounds of the South Carolina state capitol. The meeting of the two heads of state was notable primarily because of the importance and influence of their two large, populous nations and the sharp divergence of the leaders' future paths. Each had made history as the first Black president and the first woman president of their respective countries. However, Obama would leave office at the end of his two constitutionally limited terms; Rousseff would be impeached and removed from power in August 2016 for budget-related crimes. A subsequent run for a Senate seat in the Minas Gerais state in 2018 would also end badly for her, apparently concluding her career in public service. To the dismay of Rousseff and others, Brazil was swinging toward right-wing populism, a political trend that had already reached US shores.[40]

CHAPTER 13

Demographics and Destinies

FOUR DAYS BEFORE THE 2012 PRESIDENTIAL ELECTION, BARACK Obama received some very good news. According to the Bureau of Labor Statistics (BLS), the US economy, as of November 2, had 194,000 more jobs than in January 2009, when the president took office. The unemployment rate still hovered stubbornly at 7.9 percent; for African Americans, it was 13.3 percent. Further, more than 12 million people were still unemployed, 40 percent of whom had been without work for more than six months. However, in translating the BLS report into political shorthand, the administration was now able to present itself as a net "job creator," having presided over a nearly three-year employment expansion since the economy stopped shedding jobs in February 2010. Of course, behind the numbers was a more complicated picture.

On the positive side, the stock market continued to roar with the S&P 500 index up 75 percent since Obama entered the White House. Moreover, retail sales and housing starts were climbing, gas prices were falling, and the poverty rate had stabilized at 15.9 percent after rising every year since the start of the Great Recession in 2007. On the negative side, between 2010 and 2013 Blacks and Hispanics disproportionately lost more ground than whites according to a number of measurements, including median household wealth, median income, and homeownership rates. Since minority families collectively entered the economic downturn with fewer savings and stocks, they tended to neither have a monetary safety net to break their fall toward poverty nor hold wealth-producing equities when investment markets rebounded. Despite these glaring disparities, things could have been much worse for many. The auto bailout had saved hundreds of thousands of jobs, and antipoverty measures, such as expanded access to food stamps, Medicaid, tax credits, and housing vouchers, had prevented the poverty rate from dramatically escalating during the recession. Post-midterm gridlock in Washington had precluded further government stimulation of the economy, but by that time the economic contraction and monthly job losses had ended.[1]

Around the time of the November 2012 jobs report, President Obama reflected publicly on his first-term record and performance. During an interview, he expressed regret over not communicating more clearly to the American people the economic hazards that the country faced, as well as the fact that a recovery would be slow. At times, his administration had relied on its policy pronouncements and achievements to tell its story, just to find that the public's attention span and appetite for fine details were fickle and in short supply. The costs of such assumptions could be steep, such as the 2010 loss of the US House and legions of state and local offices. However, going into the presidential election, Obama had recouped some of the electoral goodwill that had gotten him elected four years earlier and seemed well positioned to campaign competitively against his Republican challenger, Mitt Romney.

Several surveys showed Obama polling in the 50 percent range in job approval just before Election Day on November 6, a meaningful threshold for presidents seeking a second term. It was also a notable improvement since the previous November, when his numbers were an average of six to ten points lower. As with the first campaign, a strong performance among minority voters would provide the margin of victory—or so the Obama campaign hoped. At the time, the president's approval rating among Black people was around 90 percent, and Hispanic respondents gave him a healthy 74 percent positive rating. These numbers would significantly offset his more lackluster 40 percent approval among white voters, which never fully recovered from the dip following Obama's comments about the Cambridge Police Department's treatment of Henry Louis Gates Jr. in 2009. In sum, African Americans, though still enduring disproportionate economic suffering, stuck with Obama, at least according to polls. The remaining question was whether they would show up at the ballot box in the robust numbers that they—along with Hispanics, Asians, young people, and other members of his winning coalition—had in 2008.[2]

In a campaign world in which it costs roughly a billion dollars to run for president, the stated support of voters is important but not decisive or even sufficient. Any serious bid for the White House requires persistent and targeted fundraising and strategic spending across multiple media markets for months at a time. Ever since his campaign for US senator in 2004, Obama had relied on a network of Black contributors who shared his values and could connect him with other potential donors. A substantial part of the money that he initially raised in the senatorial primary came from African American businesses and professionals, and much of the early radio and print coverage of his campaign emanated from Black media sources. By 2012, his reelection organization was able to employ this well-established formula to raise the funding necessary to finance an operation that would eventually approach ten figures in costs. The solo contributors, bundlers, and other campaign financiers comprised a royal class of African Americans whose income and assets easily placed them in the top 1 percent of US households. To name a few, there were Will and Jada Pinkett Smith, Kawanna Brown of Magic Johnson Enterprises, Lester N. Coney of Mesirow Financial, philanthropist Mattie McFadden-Lawson, and Mack Wilbourn, president of the Atlanta food management company Mack II. They were all part of the elite stratum of campaign contributors who helped make the Obama political brand possible and durable.

Running parallel to the Obama campaign's official fundraising efforts were super PACs such as 1911 United and Priorities USA Action. During the 2012 cycle, the latter became known for aggressively going after Mitt Romney with negative ads that portrayed him as a plutocratic corporate raider who had callously outsourced American jobs and profited from the resulting carnage. Priorities USA Action targeted swing states with its ad buys and produced commercials in Spanish to make sure that non-English-speaking Hispanic voters had access to its blistering critiques of the GOP challenger. As is also the case on the Republican side of the ad and money race, super PACs are the wraiths of the shadowy world of campaign finance, ethereal and hard to track but spectrally present and insidiously effective. Fed by dark money and loose accountability rules, they have a corrosive, distorting impact on the electoral process and potentially give individual donors outsized influence over candidates and their platforms. Such was the case when casino magnate Sheldon Adelson bankrolled the super PAC of GOP presidential contender Newt Gingrich with $20 million in contributions, thus allowing the candidate to linger in the 2012 primary race long after his political expiration date. Obama and especially Romney, who was more dependent on dark money for advertising, watched supportive super PACs do dirty work that was beneath their own campaigns but that ultimately complemented their presidential bids and messaging strategies.[3]

Once it was clear in May 2012 that Romney would be the Republican nominee, Obama and his team had to decide how best to run against him. Fortunately for them, there were a number of viable approaches, each with its own set of advantages that either cut close to the candidate's core identity or recast his putative strengths as liabilities. Actually, opposition researchers found that there was almost too much material to use against Romney and that they would have to focus and fine-tune their attacks for maximum effectiveness. As a political candidate, Romney presented himself as a corporate titan who understood business and economics and could thus bring the country completely out of its post-recession malaise. However, it was all too easy for the press and Obama's opposition researchers to locate workers who had been fired, their retirement benefits trimmed or eliminated, and their lives otherwise toppled by Romney's company Bain Capital. The private equity firm specialized in acquiring struggling businesses and putting them through debt-loaded stress tests that either killed them outright or gave them new life in often greatly shrunken and leaner form. In many cases, Romney and his investors profited even if an acquired company and affected employees suffered. The Republican candidate, who had unsuccessfully run for the GOP nomination in 2008, was unable to persuasively counter his image as a heartless corporate pillager. Largely unchallenged, Democratic campaign ads brutally transformed him into an unsavory caricature throughout the summer of 2012.

And then there was Romney the former Massachusetts governor and seasoned politician. His term (2003-2007) in the executive mansion of a blue state had required him to play toward the political center and to negotiate with a heavily Democratic legislature. He was moderate on many issues, including gay rights, abortion, and climate change, and he had succeeded in enacting a number of laws that would have been anathema to the national Republican Party, particularly as it moved further rightward. As he had prepared to run for the 2008 presidential nomination, Romney had revised his stance on a long list of issues, remaking himself into a hard-edged conservative in keeping with the ideological evolution of the nationwide GOP electorate. By the 2012 cycle, he had flipped on everything from his past support for immigration reform, gun control, and abortion rights to his previous opposition to the auto bailout and a constitutional ban on same-sex civil unions.

Romney's signature policy reversal was on health care. As governor, he had successfully pushed for universal health insurance, supporting a law that mandated that state residents acquire coverage. As a 2012 candidate, he denounced the individual mandate in the ACA—which was modeled after the Massachusetts bill—calling it an "unconscionable abuse of power." With so much backsliding on ideology and policy in so short a time, there was almost too much evidence for opponents to pick through in trying to portray Romney as an unprincipled hypocrite who could not be trusted with either the Republican nomination or the Oval Office. Spliced together with the opportunistic aggressiveness of his private equity work (or "vulture capitalism," as one GOP primary challenger called it), some campaign ads virtually made themselves. In several instances, Romney did himself no favors with unforced errors and gaffes, and his multiple expensive homes, overseas accounts, and reluctance to release tax returns further damaged his reputation and added to the evolving caricature.[4]

Finally, there was Mitt Romney the Mormon, devoted church elder, and family man. In political life, the candidate tended to emphasize the latter identity over the former one, and during the presidential campaign he seemed content to leave aside his membership in the Church of Jesus Christ of Latter-day Saints (LDS). His religious affiliation had always been available for scrutiny in the various senatorial, gubernatorial, and presidential races in which he ran. Yet it was rare for that part of his identity to be litigated in public, though it did register in some opinion polling. By the fall of 2012, several Black ministers in the South were strategizing ways to bring up Romney's faith among their congregations, some thinking it necessary to deflect lingering angst over Obama's endorsement of same-sex marriage in the spring. The president, however, made any campaign attacks on Romney's Mormonism off limits and personally avoided discussing the issue on the trail. In hindsight, it was really the only politically sensible course of action. Allowing a whisper campaign to flourish would have made the president appear small-minded and risked triggering a retaliatory revisiting of the falsehood that Obama was Muslim. Also, after some initial hesitation, Romney had repudiated a proposal by a super PAC to revive the Rev. Wright controversy, which would have been quite inconvenient in a tight race. In taking Romney's Mormonism off the table, Obama was simply returning the favor.

Notwithstanding moral qualms and political calculations, Obama did not need to raise the Mormon question. Such a line of attack would likely have muddled other parts of the Democratic messaging against Romney. Moreover, religious, non-Mormon Republicans were already vetting Romney's spiritual bona fides, sometimes in public and unflattering ways. The spectacle was odd to watch as avowedly evangelical Republicans attempted to reconcile themselves with a standard-bearer who was not evangelical or even Protestant. The dissonance made for many public moments of awkwardness and likely many interesting private exchanges. Aside from the thorny religion issue, Romney, well into the fall general campaign, was still prone to both incoming and self-inflicted damage. One example was his deficit-busting tax plan, which favored the wealthy and inadvertently vivified his plutocratic image. Another was the secretly recorded and publicly released video of him dismissing 47 percent of the US population as irresponsible moochers who felt entitled to government assistance. To be sure, even with these stumbles the presidential race tightened following the first debate on October 3, and Obama, the incumbent, was still saddled with a troubled economy. Not since 1940 had a president won reelection with a national unemployment rate as high as 7.9 percent. Nonetheless, Team Obama had created enough doubt about Romney to make it a race between two candidates and not just a referendum on the president's record.[5]

The daughter of Haitian immigrants, Ludmya "Mia" Bourdeau was born in Brooklyn, New York, in December 1975. Her family had fled political repression in their home country, and her parents hoped to give their two daughters a better life in the United States. After moving with her kin to Norwalk, Connecticut, Mia attended the University of Hartford, where she earned a degree in musical theater. Her older sister Cynthia had joined the LDS Church by this time, and Mia, too, was drawn to the teachings of the faith. In 1998, she married a Mormon missionary named Jason Love, and the couple settled in Saratoga Springs, a small town near Salt Lake City. After starting a family, Mia Love became involved in electoral politics and won a seat on the city council in 2003. Six years later, she was elected mayor, becoming the first Black woman to lead a Utah city.

This political feat, plus her ambitions, brought Love to the attention of the national Republican Party, which supported her run for a US House seat in 2012. It also brought her to the attention of GOP presidential candidate Mitt Romney, who called on her to vouch for his "likability" and competence at the Republican National Convention in August. "Barack Obama has had four years to turn our economy around and he has failed," Love proclaimed to a cheering, almost entirely white audience. "Mitt Romney has turned around countless companies, the Winter Olympics and a floundering state." Love raised nearly $2 million in her effort to unseat Rep. Jim Matheson of the Fourth Congressional District, and her campaign slogan, "Mother, Mayor, Leader, Gun Owner," evoked a Palinesque sensibility. But her political ascent plateaued, and she did not win the House seat in 2012. When Matheson decided not to run for reelection two years later, Love became the favorite to win the open position. She handily won both the Republican primary and the general election, becoming the first Black Republican woman ever to serve in Congress.[6]

Love was one of a relatively small number of Black members of the growing LDS faith in the United States. In some ways, her conversion experience and political conservatism were similar to the attributes of other Mormons but not necessarily reflective of the lives and values of Black LDS coreligionists around the country or even in the Salt Lake City area. The church itself had a deeply scarred history regarding race by the time Love discovered it. Its founding patriarchs, Joseph Smith and Brigham Young, supported slavery during the 1800s, and a ban against the ordination of Black priests stayed in place until 1978. Church doctrine condemned dark skin as spiritually unclean, thus institutionalizing racism in its wards. In the late twentieth century, the LDS leadership liberalized some of its policies, and missionaries reached out to Blacks and other minorities. Interestingly, Michigan governor George Romney, Mitt's father, was a prominent voice in efforts to steer the Mormon Church and the Republican Party toward an embrace of the Black freedom struggle of the 1960s. Concentrated primarily in western states like Utah, Idaho, and Wyoming, Mormons are an overwhelmingly white group, with Black people making up only 3 percent of their number by 2007. African Americans who find themselves attracted to the faith undoubtedly have to either ignore or otherwise make peace with the long history of LDS racism and exclusion. Mitt Romney's run for the White House against the first Black president probably caused many to think anew about the intersections of their racial and religious identities.

Around the Salt Lake City region, the seat of the LDS faith, African American Mormons were of different minds when it came to the 2012 presidential candidates. Paul Sleet, a computer systems analyst, endorsed Obama's reelection bid and characterized the first family as representing the church's values. Marguerite Driessen, a law professor at Brigham Young University, drew on LDS scripture to justify her intention to vote for the incumbent, telling a reporter that she, a liberal Black woman, had a duty "to elect people who will protect your liberties." Jerri A. Harwell, another professor and an unaffiliated voter, acknowledged that her Mormon faith was part of who she was but asserted that her racial identity was even more central and immutable. "I was born black; I was not born a member of the Church of Jesus Christ of Latter-day Saints," she related in an interview. "That's a choice, and I can undo that choice at any moment in time." Raised in Detroit and a member of the LDS faith since 1977, Harwell favored Obama as the better-qualified candidate and was not convinced that Romney could "relate to the common man." In particular, she was put off by Romney's reluctance to publicly disclose his income tax returns as he pursued the Republican presidential nomination.[7]

Unsurprisingly, not all Black Mormons in the Salt Lake City region were convinced that Obama deserved another term. Eddie Gist struggled with his election choices but leaned toward Romney. "It's tough because you've got the first black president, but he's running against a candidate who has the values I believe in," the 43-year-old LDS member opined. "I really can't go wrong either way." For Don

Harwell, the choice was clear. Unlike his wife, Jerri, the 66-year-old retiree and Mormon of almost thirty years was a convinced Romney voter. "I was raised in a time when people were responsible and accountable for self," he told a journalist in July. "People had respect for themselves, and they didn't expect welfare or anything for free." Although members of a conservative religious order, Black Mormons nationwide, especially those in urban areas and states more liberal than Utah, likely trended toward Obama and Democrats in their party affiliation. Still, like other voters, their electoral decisions were not made lightly and were significantly influenced by their values, experiences, and notions of self.[8]

Given partisan divisions among Black Mormons and their small numbers, the Romney campaign was aware that it would need to appeal to a broader range of African American voters in order to beat Obama. Even if the GOP candidate won every single Mormon vote in the country, that miracle alone could not carry him to victory in November. Romney's opening bid for Black support in the fall election came in July, when he was invited to speak to an NAACP convention in Houston. During his twenty-four-minute presentation, he talked positively about job creation and traditional marriage and negatively about the size of the deficit and the continuing existence of "non-essential programs like Obamacare." In essence, the speech was standard conservative fare. The crowd was polite, though generally tepid in its applause. It is likely that he convinced few of those present to vote for him. However, some probably gave him points for just showing up; Republican nominees George W. Bush and Robert Dole had declined invitations to attend the annual gathering in 2004 and 1996, respectively.[9]

Other Romney outreach included the organization of the Black Leadership Council, which was launched on September 5, the day before Barack Obama's scheduled acceptance speech at the DNC in Charlotte. With a twenty-one-person membership, the council included a number of well-known public figures, such as Sen. Tim Scott, Rep. Allen West, Florida lieutenant governor Jennifer Carroll,

Mayor Mia Love, and Artur Davis. By the latter half of the month, the group was prominently listed on the official campaign website, along with endorsements from Scott, West, and Carroll and a drop-down tab entitled "Former Obama Supporters for Romney." And then—nothing happened. According to West, the council never met, and Romney never called. Having promised that the group would help better connect him to "respected leaders" in Black communities, the candidate did not follow through. In a tight reelection campaign himself, West viewed the paper council as a missed opportunity to "actually show up" and place the GOP in contention for Black votes. In retrospect, the congressman may have realized that Romney was only halfheartedly invested in such a strategy.[10]

West and others would have been able to make more sense of Romney's fleeting gestures toward African American voters if they had looked more closely at the contemporary polling data and the election clock. Just before the Republican convention in late August, a much-reported NBC/WSJ poll showed the GOP candidate with zero support among Black respondents, compared to 94 percent who supported the Obama-Biden ticket. Along with being down four points overall against the incumbents (48 percent–44 percent), Romney and his VP running mate, Rep. Paul Ryan of Wisconsin, were losing among Latinx people by a two-to-one margin and among women and voters under 35 years of age by double digits. The good news for the Republican ticket: they were up among whites by thirteen points (53 percent–40 percent) and among rural voters and seniors by high single digits. With polling so dismal among minorities and especially Black voters, the Romney camp needed a high turnout among white Republican and independent voters if it planned to win the election with little to no outreach to African Americans, Hispanics, and other people of color. Put plainly, the simple racial math of the demographic obstacles that the campaign faced by late 2012 necessitated running up the white vote before the clock ran out on November 6.

The strategy was not necessarily an ill fit for the temperamentally staid Romney, who had in a few years' time politically transformed himself from a Rockefeller Republican into, in his words, a "severely conservative" presidential candidate. Back in his Bain Capital days, he had been criticized publicly for operating a "white boys club" that employed no Black people as of 1994, when he ran unsuccessfully for a US Senate seat. Shortly after entering the Massachusetts governor's mansion in 2003, he signed an executive order that dismantled the state's Office of Affirmative Action, infuriating local civil rights leaders. Even as he spoke before the NAACP in July 2012, his campaign's answer to the organization's inquiry concerning his stance on voter ID laws was simply, "Governor Romney believes that every legal vote should count." Thus, on matters of race, the candidate, at least in his past political incarnations, had not distinguished himself as especially enlightened, but he was by no means outside the GOP mainstream in terms of his record regarding African Americans.[11]

Romney's initial gut instinct in relation to competing against Obama for the White House did not appear to principally revolve around a race-based approach, though the southern strategy was, of course, available. Illustratively, in his 2010 book, *No Apology: The Case for American Greatness*, the candidate's attack angle against Obama was primarily ideological, with many pages dedicated to differences over the size and purpose of government as well as the appropriate management of foreign allies and enemies. Beyond a false suggestion that the president was moving the country toward socialism, the treatise was largely a political manifesto, the same genre as *The Audacity of Hope*, and did not overtly appeal to racial bias or grievances.[12]

Discouraging poll numbers and declining momentum can either bring out the best in a candidate or encourage their worst, most cynical impulses. Romney's campaign became smaller in its capacity and willingness to make a cross-racial appeal, eventually narrowing to a default consolidation of its base of mostly white, male, older, and rural voters. Around the time that he was polling at zero among Black voters, Romney decided to recognize the sixteenth anniversary of the Welfare Reform Act by misleadingly stating that the Obama administration had eliminated work requirements that some states sought to attach to public assistance eligibility. His remark was derivative of a larger Republican narrative concerning "makers" and "takers," particularly the notion that Democrats won elections by offering "free" things—for example, Medicaid, nutritional assistance, and unemployment insurance—to undeserving people. Further, the statement invoked long-standing racial stereotypes about welfare recipients. While most people on public assistance are white, many associate such programs with African Americans, who are disproportionately poor and, in the minds of some, more likely to abuse the system. Despite being debunked by multiple media outlets, Romney's comment reminded voters of Newt Gingrich's labeling of Barack Obama as the "food stamp president" back in January. Two days after he channeled the former House speaker, Romney made a second pronouncement that channeled another flamboyant Republican personality who trafficked in racist innuendo: Donald Trump.

At an August 24 campaign event, Romney raised the birther flag in the battleground state of Michigan. "Ann was born at Henry Ford hospital, I was born at Harper hospital," he proclaimed to a crowd in Commerce, referring to his and his wife's Detroit birthplaces. "No one has ever asked to see my birth certificate. They know that this is the place that we were born and raised." Romney's appeal to birtherism only made sense as an act of political desperation, though its invidious intent and impact should not be discounted. He had some time earlier conceded that the president was in fact born in the United States, and Trump had endorsed Romney back in the spring. Therefore, revisiting the canard so late in the game could only have been meant to firm up any remaining soft support among conservative voters who needed yet another birther reference to drive them to the ballot box. The Obama campaign, knowing how odious the false claim was to many of the president's supporters, called Romney out for failing to refute the "most strident voices in his party." With neither the welfare reform misstatement nor the birther flirtation paying any discernible dividends in the polls, the GOP candidate toned down both lines of attack, instead allowing appeals to race to stir freely in the climate that he, his campaign, and his party had already created.[13]

The whiteness of the Romney-era GOP was most clearly and starkly displayed at the Republican nominating convention. One observer likened the televised event to an Afrikaner Party gathering in apartheid South Africa. Although the comparison was not wholly apt, the racial homogeneity was striking. Of the 2,286 Republican delegates, only 47 (2.1 percent) were Black. This figure was a slight improvement over 2008 when only 38 (1.6 percent) of the delegates were Black. However, it was quite a step back from 2004 when the party appeared to be making some headway with the African American electorate by seating 167 (6.7 percent) Black delegates. The scarcity was even more noticeable in comparison with the DNC, which was held only days later, where African Americans comprised 26.2 percent of delegates, about twice their proportion of the general population. While attempts were made to make the GOP convention look more inclusive than it was, there was frankly little that could be done to camouflage the obvious. Speeches by Condoleezza Rice, Mia Love, and Artur Davis were well received and represented a good mix of past, present, and future Black officeholders in the party—or at least aspirants, in Davis's case. Yet offstage, the Republican Party was as white as it had ever been. In an ugly incident that underscored this uniformity, a couple of convention attendees perceived a Black CNN camerawoman as such a subhuman outsider that they felt comfortable pelting her with peanuts, exclaiming, "This is what we feed animals!" The offending men were ordered to leave the building, and GOP staffers issued a statement calling their behavior "inexcusable and unacceptable." Nevertheless, the show went on, and Romney, with his party united behind him, was given the nomination and officially anointed to take on Obama in November.[14]

The election was not nearly as close as many had assumed that it would be. Romney was actually ahead in some polls in October, but by Election Day the bottom had fallen out of his presidential hopes.

He did not experience the blowout that John McCain had in 2008, but he certainly did not fare much better. When all of the counting was done, Obama had beaten the Republican challenger 332-206 in the Electoral College, carrying more states and 5 million more popular votes. It was a decisive victory that was clear enough for election officials and press organizations to call before midnight.

As with any big campaign, a number of factors were behind Obama's triumph and Romney's defeat. Abiding the rightward march of his party, the GOP candidate came out of the long primary season with deeply conservative positions on abortion, immigration, health care, gun control, and a range of other issues. In cases where his stances on certain matters were less clear, he came across as vacillating and noncommittal, such as during debates when he would not disclose the specifics of a tax plan or a concrete proposal for entitlement reform. Such dodgy evasions played into what Romney himself called his image problem as the "flipping Mormon": the archetypal politician who would say and do anything in order to get elected. Furthermore, his waffling on all kinds of issues also made his background as a northeastern patrician and wily businessman less enticing in an age of anti–Wall Street protests, widening income inequality, and generalized economic anxiety. Hiding income tax returns and dismissing a large percentage of the population as morally irresponsible further tethered Romney to a sinister, cartoonish version of himself that he had helped to create. Additionally, Paul Ryan, despite his reputation as a virtuoso of conservative policymaking, brought no apparent electoral benefits to the ticket, as the incumbent president won the congressman's home state of Wisconsin by a seven-point margin.[15]

Similarly to 2008, the Obama team's ground game had been critical to its success. Investments in a nationwide campaign infrastructure once again paid off, and the organization further demonstrated its mastery of internet fundraising, social media advertising, electoral map analytics, early-voting mobilization, and old-fashioned person-to-person retail politics. Both Obama and his support staff stayed on message and were lucky not to have any Rev. Wright or 47 percent moments. The biggest unforeseen catastrophe was a hurricane that tore up the coastal Northeast just days before the election, but even it had a silver lining in that it allowed Obama to look and act presidential and above partisan politics as he visited storm-damaged areas. Gradually improving economic indicators, such as the solid jobs report of early November, certainly helped the president's reelection chances. At the end of the day, when compelled to make a choice, enough Americans were satisfied with seeing him at the helm for another term—or fearful enough of a switch to Romney—to suggest that the economic pain was not great enough to force the incumbent into retirement.[16]

Furthermore, the Obama campaign made the right kinds of appeals to the right kinds of voters. Core constituencies like African Americans, Hispanics, women, and young people did not abandon his coalition, and a critical mass of working-class white voters in crucial midwestern swing states supported him in sufficient numbers to deny Romney prizes like Ohio, Michigan, Wisconsin, and Iowa. If demographics were indeed destiny, the Republican candidate had gambled on winning the presidency by appealing to an ever-shrinking portion of the national electorate. It was a bet that ended badly for him and his party, which lost seats in both the US House and Senate.[17]

When Romney called the president to concede around midnight, he, too, had some sense of what he had just experienced as the losing candidate. He congratulated Obama on getting out "urban voters" in places like Cleveland and Milwaukee, employing an awkward euphemism for Black and other minority voters. But in essence, he was right: African Americans, Hispanics, and Asian Americans had supported the incumbent in a big way, providing the margin of victory. While Obama did well among women (55 percent) and those younger than 30 (60 percent), he excelled among nonwhite voters. Between 2008 and 2012, the minority share of the national electorate went from 26 to 28 percent, with 1.7 million more Black voters casting ballots alongside 1.4 million more Hispanics. The 2012 voter participation rate among Blacks (66 percent) actually surpassed that of whites (64 percent), which was two percentage points down from 2008 (equating to roughly 2 million votes). Obama won 93 percent of Black votes, 71 percent of Hispanic votes, 73 percent of Asian American votes, and 39 percent of non-Hispanic white votes, which combined to propel him to winning 51 percent of the national popular vote. Black women were especially involved in the 2012 electoral process, registering a voter participation rate nine percentage points higher than Black men.

In terms of political affiliation, the election confirmed the ongoing racial polarization of the parties. A Gallup poll conducted at the end of the year found that non-Hispanic whites accounted for 89 percent of respondents identifying as Republican, with Hispanics and Blacks comprising only 6 percent and 2 percent, respectively, of those claiming GOP membership. Only 60 percent of those identifying as Democrats were non-Hispanic whites, and African Americans accounted for 22 percent. Despite Romney's effort to turn out a greater share of the Republican (and largely white) vote, his campaign was swimming against the demographic tide that was washing over the country. Whether measured by births, deaths, age trends, or immigration patterns, the country was getting younger and browner. By contrast, the GOP, as gauged by its self-identified supporters and actual voters, was turning older and whiter. The racial schism reflected in the partisan schism was a troubling omen of a future when most issues, policies, elections, and outcomes would increasingly mirror the Black-white-brown divide. With demographers predicting a majority minority nation by around 2050, the implications for the parties and US society in general seemed clear, even decades ahead of the predicted eventuality. Whether winning or losing, both Obama's diversifying coalition and Romney's ever-whitening base were premonitions of opportunities and dangers to come.[18]

PART III.

THE BEST OF TIMES,
THE WORST OF TIMES

CHAPTER 14

Bamelot 2.0

FOR HIS SECOND PRESIDENTIAL TERM, BARACK OBAMA WAS sworn in twice: once on the constitutionally mandated date of January 20, 2013, which fell on a Sunday, and again the following day. The first ritual was a private affair in the Blue Room of the White House, administered by Chief Justice John G. Roberts Jr. The First Lady held her grandmother's Bible, upon which her husband placed his hand. The second swearing-in took place on the inaugural platform erected in front of the US Capitol Building. Before an estimated crowd of a million under a partly cloudy sky, the president this time placed his hand on two stacked Bibles—one belonging to President Abraham Lincoln and the other to Martin Luther King Jr.—and took the oath of office. His speech was hopeful and forward-looking. Among other references, he touched on slavery, evoking Lincoln's "house divided" metaphor and his desire that the American people "move forward together" after the Civil War. Obama went on to expansively discuss civil rights as including the struggles of African Americans, women, and LGBTQ people, and he reiterated the country's support for democracy across Asia, Africa, and the Middle East. In alluding to Dr. King's iconic "I Have a Dream" speech delivered on the National Mall fifty years earlier, Obama pointed out the need for the United

States to do more to protect the franchise. "Our journey is not complete until no citizen is forced to wait for hours to exercise the right to vote," he proclaimed, the long lines of November 6 still fresh in many minds. As wheelchair-seated Tuskegee Airmen and other honored guests looked on, Obama concluded his speech with waves to the cheering crowd, and mezzo-soprano Beyoncé Knowles launched another four years of his historic presidency with a soaring rendition of "The Star-Spangled Banner."[1]

Weeks before the inauguration, more than sixty civil rights, business and community leaders had met in the capital to plan for Obama's second term. The gathering was convened by Marc Morial, Benjamin Jealous, Al Sharpton, and others who sought to advance specific policies to address Black unemployment, health-care disparities, criminal justice reform, educational inequities, and voting rights. "The African-American community was disproportionately battered by the Great Recession, and has benefited the least from the fragile economic recovery," the leaders outlined in their agenda. They were particularly concerned about joblessness and the growing racial wealth gap, which they believed threatened "to relegate the black community to perpetual underclass status." Immediately following the election, Jealous in a BET interview had urged Obama to focus on job creation and workplace discrimination in order to alleviate a Black unemployment rate that was almost twice the national average. Morial, representing the National Urban League, had sent a letter to the White House with his ranked wish list, which called for a focus on jobs, education, and community safety. To be sure, a plethora of wish lists were in circulation following Obama's reelection, many of which were similar to ones that had been making the rounds since 2008. Emanating from civil rights groups, academicians, politicians, and media personalities, these agendas were diverse in tone, motivation, and feasibility. Some seemed to understand the limitations of executive power in the face of a divided government in Washington. Others assumed that Obama could get much more done through either executive orders or sheer force of will than was realistically possible.[2]

On one end of the spectrum were academicians, such as Professors Randall Kennedy and William Julius Wilson, both of Harvard University, who viewed Obama's record as promising thus far, if incomplete. They comprehended the racial funambulism that his position entailed, which Kennedy believed "was probably a virtual requirement" for a Black candidate facing a largely white electorate. Obama's steady temperament, especially regarding racial matters, made him, in Wilson's estimate, "the right president during these hard economic times because social tensions are indeed high." Some observers, such as political analyst Zerlina Maxwell, did not expect much change during the president's second term, given ongoing Republican control of the US House. However, she did want to see more advocacy for anti-poverty programs during the next four years, along with the nomination of an African American woman to the Supreme Court.[3]

Other Black commentators stuck different chords. Writer Ta-Nehisi Coates, while conceding that Obama was a "remarkable human being," hoped that Black people would get much more for their big turnout during the 2012 election than the "rhetoric of individual responsibility" and "targeted scorn" that he felt the president reserved for African Americans. Coates especially regretted what he perceived to be the administration's tepid response to the home foreclosure crisis and its overzealous enforcement of drug laws, both of which had caused great suffering for Black families. In the same vein, pastor Kevin R. Johnson of Bright Hope Baptist Church in Philadelphia pointed out the spike in Black unemployment during Obama's first term and demanded that he choose a more diverse Cabinet going forward. In response to Coates and Johnson, Jonathan Capehart of the *Washington Post* wrote that such critiques were "short sighted" and did not adequately take into consideration GOP obstructionism. He also believed that they understated the achievements of the Obama White House in terms of health care, increased educational funding, new banking regulations, and reduction of the sentencing disparity for various forms of cocaine possession.[4]

Along with the discourse concerning expectations of Obama's second term, the demographic texture of his second administration was a topic that was widely and often hotly scrutinized early on. To a certain degree, Obama, having won reelection with strong support from minorities and women, made himself vulnerable to withering criticism when in January he nominated a string of white men to lead the Departments of Defense, State, and the Treasury. Into the spring, the president faced carping commentaries from various women's, Hispanic, and Asian American groups demanding that he appoint officials who reflected the country's demographic makeup and the diverse coalition that had reelected him. No group was more vocal or insistent in this regard than African Americans, in particular the Congressional Black Caucus.

In a January interview, Rep. Charlie Rangel deemed the early racial and ethnic complexion of the second Obama administration "embarrassing as hell." He further suggested that the president, in his search for nominees from among his Harvard connections, had overlooked potential minority and female candidates. In March, CBC chair Marcia Fudge of Ohio reported having received calls from constituents questioning the perceived dearth of African American appointees. She wrote a letter to the president to stress that his personnel selections "have hardly been reflective of this country's diversity." A month later, Rep. Bennie Thompson was just as plainspoken about his concerns during a weekly address on the Black-owned American Urban Radio Networks. "Many of my colleagues and I are disturbed by the president's lack of attention to diversity in his Cabinet and administration," the Mississippi congressman asserted. "Neither I nor the Congressional Black Caucus will rest until African-Americans are represented throughout the administration." While their voices were perhaps representative, Rangel, Fudge, and Thompson did not speak for the entire forty-two-member CBC. Rep. Chaka Fattah of Pennsylvania pointed out in May that both Obama and Attorney General Eric Holder were high-ranking Black officials. He went on to emphasize that policy priorities were more important than personalities and that he was confident that the Cabinet would be more diverse once the president finished the nomination process. Notwithstanding the congressman's assurances, there was an audible clamor among the CBC for a clearer signal of intent from the White House concerning appointments.[5]

As the criticisms accumulated into the spring, Obama called for patience. "Until you've seen what my overall team looks like," he announced in early May, "it's premature to assume that somehow we're going backward. We're not going backwards, we're going forward." For the most part, Obama was as good as his word, even though the diversification process was spread over much of his second term. Aside from Eric Holder, Jeh Johnson was the most prominent African American man nominated by the president for a Cabinet position. An early supporter and fundraiser for Obama's 2008 campaign, Johnson served as the general counsel for the Department of Defense before being confirmed as secretary of the Department of Homeland Security in December 2013. He continued in this capacity until the end of the Obama presidency, overseeing US Customs and Border Protection, US Immigration and Customs Enforcement, the Federal Emergency Management Agency, the Secret Service, and the Coast Guard. Days before leaving office, Johnson approved a $24 million settlement of a long-litigated lawsuit brought against the Secret Service by a hundred Black agents who had endured varying degrees of job discrimination during the Clinton and George W. Bush administrations. Johnson considered the monetary redress as "simply the right thing to do," though his department acknowledged no wrongdoing or racial bias.[6]

In June 2013, Anthony Foxx, the mayor of Charlotte, was confirmed in a unanimous 100-0 Senate vote as secretary of transportation. A month later, B. Todd Jones, who had been serving in an acting capacity, was approved as director of the Bureau of Alcohol, Tobacco, Firearms and Explosives. He held this position until March 2015, when he resigned in the wake of criticism over the agency's handling of a proposed ban on armor-piercing bullets. In 2016, the Senate

confirmed John B. King Jr. as the secretary of education, replacing
the outgoing Arne Duncan, a Chicago neighbor of Obama and fellow
Harvard alum who had served in the role since 2009. A product of
New York public schools (and Harvard's Department of Government), King's background was one of hardship and triumph against
odds. He overcame the loss of both parents in childhood to become a
social studies teacher, the founder of a charter school, and eventually
the New York State education commissioner. Like Duncan, he was
not well liked by teachers unions for his support of Common Core
learning metrics and standardized testing. Thus, his appointment
was perceived as broadcasting the president's continuing willingness
to experiment with educational policy despite organized resistance.

Beyond Foxx, Jones, and King, several other Black men were
appointed to important offices during the second Obama term. These
individuals included Mel Watt (director of the Federal Housing
Finance Agency), Awenate Cobbina (special assistant to the president
and chief of staff for legislative affairs), Jay Williams (deputy director
of intergovernmental affairs), and Rob Nabors (White House deputy chief of staff). Quite significantly, General Lloyd Austin was
assigned to lead the US Central Command in March 2013, a portfolio
that covered twenty countries in the Middle East and Southwest Asia.
The West Point graduate remained at this post until his retirement
in April 2016.[7]

Prior to the 2012 election, Obama had considered nominating
UN ambassador Susan Rice to succeed Hillary Clinton as head of
the State Department. This appointment would have made her the
highest-ranking Black woman in the federal government. However,
after a deadly terrorist attack on the US diplomatic mission in Beng-
hazi, Libya, in September, Republicans in Congress sought to hold
Obama, Clinton, Rice, and others responsible for the violence and
its aftermath. In late November, ninety-seven GOP House members
wrote the president to express opposition to any plan to appoint Rice
as secretary of state. John McCain and Lindsey Graham stirred resistance in the Senate, which at the time had only a one-seat Democratic

majority. Rice understood the math and in mid-December bowed out of the nomination process, sparing herself what she thought would be a "lengthy, disruptive and costly" spectacle. The president did not press the matter but was angered by the "outrageous" treatment Rice had received from members of the Senate. In June 2013, he tapped Rice to succeed Tom Donilon as national security advisor, a position that did not require Senate confirmation. Rice served in this capacity until the end of the administration in January 2017.[8]

If she had been confirmed as secretary of state, Susan Rice would have been the second Black woman to fill the position; Condoleezza Rice had served as both State Department head and national security advisor during the George W. Bush administration. Notwithstanding GOP resistance to Susan Rice's nomination, a number of African American women did become Black firsts during the Obama presidency. In August 2013, Davita Vance-Cooks was unanimously confirmed as the first African American and first woman to lead the Government Publishing Office (formerly the Government Printing Office), which she had joined in 2004. Similarly, Carla Hayden, formerly the CEO of Enoch Pratt Free Library in Baltimore, was confirmed as librarian of Congress in September 2016, becoming the first Black person and first woman to hold that position. As the nation's chief librarian, she was responsible for 3,100 employees, more than 162 million collected items, and a nearly $650 million budget. In July 2014, Michelle Howard, a four-star admiral, was promoted to vice chief of naval operations, the first woman to reach that rank and the first African American to serve as second-in-command of that branch of the armed services. She followed in the footsteps of Marcia Anderson, who in 2011 was promoted to the rank of two-star army general, the first Black woman to achieve that distinction. In addition to these appointments and promotions, the Obama administration filled a number of high-profile West and East Wing positions with African American personnel. These staffers included Nicole Isaac (special assistant to the president for legislative affairs), Deesha Dyer (White House social secretary), Racquel Russell (deputy assistant to the president for urban policy and economic mobility), and Tonya Robinson (special assistant to the president for justice and regulatory policy).

Altogether, the percentage of African Americans in top decision-making positions in Obama's second term exceeded the percentage in such offices during the first term and matched the Black proportion of the general population (13 percent). Turnover led to some fluctuation in the numbers over time, but the administration made efforts to keep the percentage as stable as possible. As of July 2013, one survey of the administration revealed that white men held 48 percent of the top positions, white women held 26 percent, Hispanics filled 7 percent, and Asians were employed in 4 percent. Although the percentages of women and Hispanics were glaringly out of proportion with their numbers in the national population, these disparities were somewhat mitigated by the unprecedented gender and ethnic diversity represented in Obama's nominations to the federal judiciary. The CBC and other groups that had expressed initial disappointment with Obama over the demography of his administration were apparently satisfied with his various nominations over the second term, or at least their criticisms became fainter. Of course, there would be other occasions on which they would take him to task for an assortment of grievances—as well as come to his aid at just the right time.[9]

On a Thursday morning in late February 2014, Eric Holder experienced an arresting light-headedness and shortness of breath. A similar thing had happened to him several years earlier, but he had chosen to forgo medical treatment. This time, the attorney general, having just turned 63, took no chances and was taken by ambulance to the MedStar Washington Hospital Center for an evaluation. In short order, the symptoms passed, and Holder, who was lucid and good-humored the entire time, showed no other signs of distress. Finding no cause to admit him for further observation, the hospital released the attorney general, who took the rest of the day off and went home. Tall and fit, Holder was in good shape, and his health and wellness prospects were probably better than those of the average man his age. He did suffer from high blood pressure as well as chronic back pain, which was especially debilitating when he sat too long. Still, he played weekend basketball for exercise and routinely opted to take the five flights of steps to his office each morning. The heart attack scare, however, was a clarifying moment for him and his family. Sharon, his wife, tried to prevail on him to quit the Justice Department while they still had children at home and presumably before the stresses of the job—and his many enemies—led to a more severe test of his longevity. Holder, who had earlier in the month observed his fifth anniversary as the nation's chief law enforcement official, decided to stay on the job a bit longer but did so with a renewed sense of his own mortality and limitations.[10]

And then with a splash, he was back in the fray. Holder had become a fierce brawler during the Obama years, and he remained the best fighter on the president's team. He had survived multiple congressional grillings, the Fast and Furious debacle, contempt citations, and an impeachment threat and still appeared no worse for wear, aside from the recent emergency room visit. Predictably, his Republican foes continued to give him no quarter. On April 8, Holder was again summoned before the House Judiciary Committee to be browbeaten over the contempt vote and other matters, a kind of periodic drama that he, Hillary Clinton, Lisa Jackson, and other administration officials had learned to cope with over the past several years. A week later, Rep. Blake Farenthold of Texas proposed legislation to withhold the paychecks of federal officials found in contempt of Congress. Targeted at Holder directly, the effort went nowhere but did serve as a reminder of the GOP's disdain for the attorney general as a public official.

To say that such partisan conflict energized the attorney general would be overstating the case, especially given his high blood pressure and other health concerns. He would later admit, "I may have been cool in congressional hearings on the outside, but I was pissed off a lot of the time, too." Despite such dissembling, Holder did seem to relish rousing Black supporters with tales of how unfairly he and the president were being treated by Republicans. "What attorney general has ever had to deal with that kind of treatment?" he asked an audience at a National Action Network convention in New York in April. "What president has ever had to deal with that kind of treatment?" In an ABC interview in July, he named the "racial animus" that he detected in some of the GOP opposition, though he was careful to acknowledge that the nation had "made a great deal of progress" on civil rights and other matters over the previous fifty years. When Sarah Palin called for the president's impeachment for his handling of immigration policy, the attorney general characterized her as not "a particularly good vice presidential candidate" and "an even worse judge of who ought to be impeached and why." In the same interview, he also stood by his 2009 speech that had portrayed the American people as a "nation of cowards" when it came to forthrightly addressing matters of race, an assertion that had triggered a distracting controversy early in Obama's first term. By late 2014, Holder was looking for a graceful way to leave the stage of history without providing his enemies with an immediate cause to celebrate.[11]

On September 25, 2014, Holder announced his resignation as attorney general, pending the confirmation of a successor. His tenure in the job had been a long one, punctuated with notable achievements and protracted controversies. He continued as Justice Department head for another seven months, but the meaning and legacy of his historic stewardship of the agency were already discernible. Holder had been a strong advocate and protector of civil rights (especially in regard to voting), school desegregation, policing reform, and same-sex marriage. His guardianship of the franchise in particular, whether through litigation against voter suppression laws or the dispatching of personnel to provide security at polling sites, conferred on him virtual hero status among many African Americans, who were also thrilled by his outspokenness on behalf of social justice. While he rejected the notion proffered by one commentator that he was Barack Obama's unfiltered "Inner Nigger," the attorney general was less restrained in fighting congressional Republicans and other opponents and more candid in denouncing racial prejudice and discrimination than was his boss's style. Upon hearing the news of Holder's imminent departure, Rep. John Lewis lionized the attorney general as "the symbol of fairness, an embodiment of the best in the federal government." Likewise, Myrlie Evers-Williams, widow of the late civil rights leader Medgar Evers, considered no one a better ally of justice and civil rights than Holder. In a tearful ceremony at the White House, Obama labeled him the "people's lawyer" and attributed declines in the crime and incarceration rates to his work at the Justice Department.[12]

There were, of course, gray areas and ambiguities in Holder's record and even some blemishes that he came to regret. For example, he participated in the crafting of policies rationalizing the use of drone strikes against targets overseas, including Americans deemed to be threats to US national security. Furthermore, the Justice Department vigorously pursued officials who leaked classified information to journalists, even as some critics questioned the impact of such measures on civil liberties and freedom of the press. Although the pattern had been established prior to the Obama administration, the FBI became less diverse during Holder's leadership of the Justice Department, with the number of African American agents declining to less than 4.5 percent of the total by 2016. In his own estimate, the attorney general considered the government's failure to enact gun-control legislation, even in the face of mass murders of moviegoers, worshippers, and schoolchildren, to be the most regrettable thing that he witnessed during his watch.

One part of Holder's legacy over which he had more control had to do with the prosecution of financial crimes. To the dismay of many, during his six years as head of the Justice Department no individuals were prosecuted for the fraudulent mortgages and other corporate trickery that had led to the financial crisis and Great Recession. While some considered the decision an inexcusable dereliction of duty, there were reasons behind the department's caution and forbearance. Since the September 11, 2001, attacks, many of the resources of the agency, and the FBI especially, had been diverted away from financial crimes and toward antiterrorism efforts. Moreover, a series of overturned white-collar prosecutions made the Justice Department gun-shy about risking resources and reputations on uncertain pursuits, particularly since some courts tended to think of the rights of executives and corporations in expansive ways. In the absence of prosecutorial incentives, Holder and his lawyers opted for pursuing punitive settlements with culpable entities, such as JPMorgan Chase and Citigroup. This strategy netted the government billions of dollars in fines and made for sensational headlines but did little to curb the propensity for criminal conduct among some corporate officials. As a matter of course, those executives who were caught red-handed and decided to settle routinely paid the penalties with shareholder money, a maneuver that conveniently spared the culprits and their companies more thorough, litigation-driven scrutiny.

In July 2010, Congress had passed the Dodd-Frank Wall Street Reform and Consumer Protection Act, which addressed many of the financial abuses that had ruined the lives of millions of Americans. The legislation provided the Justice Department and other enforcement agencies with more tools for rooting out corporate corruption, as well as stronger safeguards against future malfeasance. Predictably, the financial services industry pushed back hard against the regulations, arguing that they were excessive and would hinder economic growth. Despite being bailed out to the tune of hundreds of billions of taxpayer dollars, some executives seemed to expect even more from politicians like Obama, whose presidential campaigns received more than $20 million in contributions from the securities and investment industry. Similarly to his approach to environmental policy, the president attempted to balance economic expansion and job creation with effective banking reform and consumer protections. In this case, his balancing act impressed neither the Occupy Wall Street protesters on the left nor the Tea Party rebels on the right. Republican lawmakers who had almost unanimously opposed the Dodd-Frank Act from the beginning added it to the list of laws that they hoped to repeal or water down once they won back the White House.

As the traffic cop caught in the middle, Holder was left to manage the onrushing lanes of bankers, regulators, politicians, demonstrators, and other interests while trying to avoid being flattened. It was dangerous, ugly work best done by a large group of responsible parties—such as Congress or the courts—among whom blame for mistakes could be more easily and evenly diffused. Unfortunately for him, Holder was not so lucky in his assignments. During a March 2013 appearance before the Senate Judiciary Committee, the attorney general expressed concern that prosecuting corporate wrongdoing too vigorously might damage the larger economy. In saying so, he was merely paraphrasing the White House's official position. However, in the midst of an ongoing home foreclosure crisis and other economic turmoil, the assertion came off as shockingly tone-deaf. Without delay, critics began to accuse Holder of giving a pass to Wall Street crooks who were presumably "too big to jail."[13]

Eric Holder's tenure at the Justice Department officially ended on April 23, 2015. On that day, his successor, Loretta Lynch, was confirmed on a 56-43 vote, with ten Republicans joining the majority. Born in North Carolina, the Harvard-trained lawyer had served two separate stints as the US attorney for the Eastern District of New York between 1999 and 2015. She was highly regarded for her work on bank fraud and civil rights cases, as well as her contributions to the International Criminal Tribunal, which prosecuted individuals suspected of participating in the Rwandan genocide of 1994. As a public official, Lynch was best known for her successful 1999 prosecution of New York policemen accused of brutalizing Haitian immigrant Abner Louima, a case that brought national attention to the problem of police misconduct. Fifty-five years old at the time of her nomination on November 8, 2014, Lynch would be the first Black female US attorney general. However, before accomplishing that feat, she had to endure a nearly unprecedented delay in the confirmation process, which to some was emblematic of Washington's dysfunction and to others reeked of bigotry.

In a gentlemen's agreement, the Democrats, who had just lost their Senate majority in the 2014 midterm elections, refrained from voting on the Lynch nomination before the new Republican majority was seated in January. The incoming Senate majority leader, Mitch McConnell, did not reciprocate by allowing Lynch a speedy, clean vote but instead tied her confirmation to the passage of an unrelated bill on human trafficking that included contentious abortion provisions. The Judiciary Committee approved her nomination on February 26, but McConnell put off the full Senate vote for almost two months. During that time, various protesters came to the capital to denounce the delay, including a group of Black women professionals, a contingent of Black men from around the country, and hunger strikers led by Al Sharpton. Sen. Richard Durbin of Illinois charged McConnell with compelling Lynch to "sit in the back of the bus" with his long postponement of the confirmation vote. The human trafficking bill was finally passed on April 22, and McConnell allowed a vote on the Lynch nomination the next day. The protracted process was longer than those involving the previous seven attorney general nominees combined. Obama called the more than 150-day wait "embarrassing" and "crazy," and Holder teased that the GOP, in its slowness to approve his successor, must "have discovered a new fondness for me." Lorenzo Lynch, the nominee's 83-year-old father, had a different, more generous take on the confirmation drama. Watching from the Senate gallery as his daughter made history, he could only think of how far the country had come. "The good guys won," he told reporters approvingly. "So all over this land good folks have stood in the right lane, in the right path."[14]

Former CBC chair Emanuel Cleaver thought that he had a good read of Barack Obama by the start of his second term. The two had sporadically clashed during the president's first four years in office, but the Missouri congressman and the vast majority of his caucus colleagues were supportive of Obama and his agenda when it counted most. The two men understood each other, as well as the fact that they, as a head of state and a House representative, had fundamentally different constituencies in terms of size, geography, demography, and often expectations and values. Cleaver still encountered people who believed that Obama, following reelection, would reveal his "real" self and radically change the trajectory of his presidency. But the congressman did not buy it; he did not expect the post-2012 Obama "to show up in a dashiki" or to be "some kind of reincarnation of Eldridge Cleaver or Huey Newton." The president could still surprise on occasion, such as the bold Osama bin Laden raid, the Al Green impression, and his bend-over-backward efforts to accommodate Republicans in budget negotiations, even as they moved the goal posts and threatened debt default and government shutdowns. Notwithstanding these episodes, Obama was not nearly as inscrutable as some had portrayed him. In fact, his even-keel temperament, pragmatic strategizing, and measured movements were entirely predictable in relation to most issues and circumstances.[15]

Obama met with the CBC membership at the White House on July 9, 2013. It was his first meeting with the group since May 2011. According to the accounts of the Oval Office and CBC chair Marcia Fudge, the ninety-minute meeting was cordial and productive, and a number of agenda items were discussed. Voting rights were of utmost concern in the wake of a recent US Supreme Court ruling that nearly had gutted the Voting Rights Act of 1965. The president promised to continue to fight for fair and equal access to the ballot in the face of efforts in some states to make voting more difficult. The group also discussed economic matters, including measures to address poverty, the high Black unemployment rate, and distressed neighborhoods. CBC members reminded Obama of the continuing need to support HBCUs and their students, along with the imperative to reform the immigration system in a fashion that benefited people of African and Caribbean descent. In turn, the president asked for the caucus's assistance in addressing gun violence and welcomed its expressed interest in further highlighting the benefits of the ACA. At the time, with the recent appointments of Anthony Foxx and Mel Watt, Fudge was personally content with the diversity of the administration. Considering the mix of personalities that comprised the CBC, surprisingly no outbursts or arguments appear to have transpired during the meeting, or at least not any that were noteworthy or disruptive enough to wind up in the media.[16]

Yet, as had been the case in the past, one needed only to wait a while to again witness a quarrel between the Obama White House and Black Congress. This time, the issue was judicial appointments. By most any measure, the president had an admirable record in terms of diversifying the federal bench. Before Republicans took over the Senate following the 2014 midterms, he had already surpassed all of his predecessors in the appointment of Blacks, Hispanics, Asians, and women to federal judgeships. As of April 2014, 42 percent of his confirmed nominees were women, 36 percent were racial or ethnic minorities, and eight appointees were openly gay. Analyzed by race and ethnicity alone, 18 percent of the total number of confirmed judges were Black, 12 percent were Hispanic, 7 percent were Asian, and 63 percent were white. By the time Obama left office three years later, the percentages of women and Blacks appointed during his two terms were the same, while 10 percent of nominees were Hispanic, 6 percent were Asian, and 37 percent were white men. Both of his confirmed Supreme Court nominees—Elena Kagan and Sonia Sotomayor—were women, and Sotomayor was Latina, the first ever.

It is possible that Obama would have put an even more diverse imprint on the courts before leaving office if his judicial nominations had not been routinely blocked by Republicans during the last two years of his presidency. There were, of course, critics who found other things to complain about, such as the high percentage of corporate lawyers and former prosecutors that the president nominated to the federal bench. But even these skeptics could not reasonably quibble with the effectiveness of his strategy to demographically diversify the stewards of the court system.[17]

The focal point of a dispute between selected CBC members and the president was his nomination of a slate of six candidates for federal judgeships in Georgia. Beyond the fact that only one of the nominees was African American in a state that was more than 30 percent Black, several of those named by Obama alarmed a number of caucus members. Court of Appeals judge Michael Boggs, a nominee for the Eleventh Circuit Court, had years earlier voted as a state representative to retain the Confederate battle flag design that was part of the Georgia state flag. Mark H. Cohen, whom Obama had advanced as a possible addition to the US District Court of Northern Georgia, had previously defended the state's strict voter ID law, which some believed had disproportionately impacted ballot access for minority citizens. The only Black nominee on the list, Eleanor L. Ross, was also recommended for the Northern Georgia District Court, though some Democrats harbored questions about her partisan loyalties. While the Obama administration tried to defend the controversial picks, it was not especially keen on any of the three candidates.

The problem that the president had faced in putting together his list of nominees was a procedural one, in which any US senator could negatively "blue slip" or hold up the confirmation of a federal judge nominated to serve in the lawmaker's home state. In this instance, in order to get his three favored choices—Julie E. Carnes, Leigh Martin May, and Jill A. Pryor—confirmed (that is, past the objections of Georgia GOP senators Saxby Chambliss and Johnny Isakson), the president had to nominate the other three: Boggs, Cohen, and Ross. Ever the practical strategist with a long view of events, Obama was used to such political horse trading and had learned since the 2010 loss of the House that clawing half a loaf from Republicans was a good day indeed. CBC members, on the other hand, saw the list of compromise candidates as an attempt to seat unprincipled people in high federal offices in a state with a long history of oppressing and excluding Black people.

Rep. David Scott, whose Thirteenth District cradled western and southern Atlanta, was the most vocal of the deal's critics. "You tell me, how can you have the Justice Department fighting the voter ID, voter suppression law in Texas and at the same time put on the court for life the man who defended that same law in Georgia?" the congressman queried in reference to the Cohen nomination. His articulated displeasure with the slate of candidates became more acidic by late February 2014 when he claimed that the president had been both disrespectful and dishonest in his handling of the nominations. Emanuel Cleaver, too, thought it best to fight the administration on the nominee list, believing that an unsuccessful resistance was better than acquiescence. Rep. G. K. Butterfield of North Carolina opined that the White House had given up too much leverage by accepting a package deal with three GOP-favored nominees. Having put forth the six candidates, the administration was in the unenviable position of having to defend them all, lest the list of judicial picks appear too much of a product of crass, quid pro quo politicking. Despite the White House's effort to mollify the opposition, the Boggs nomination was in serious trouble by May when Senate leader Harry Reid and Rep. John Lewis expressed discomfort with the nominee's past voting record on abortion and LGBTQ issues, in addition to his affinity for the Confederate flag. When the last of the Georgia nominees successfully passed through the Senate confirmation process in November, Boggs had been dropped from consideration. The next month, the White House announced that he would not be renominated.[18]

The scuffle over the judicial nominees was emblematic of the larger pattern of the president's engagement with the CBC. Interactions with individual members could sometimes run hot and cold, and on occasion words might be used that would have been best left unsaid. However, at the end of the day, the core relationship was one of mutuality and necessity for both parties, and neither could afford to be permanently estranged or uncooperative. Even in the midst of the most recent tensions, Obama was still endorsing people like John Conyers for reelection, and reliable standbys like James Clyburn defended the president on cable news shows against lingering impeachment threats from some House Republicans. When Obama met with the CBC again in February 2015 to discuss criminal justice reform, trade, and other matters, it was as much about acknowledging communal bonds and a sense of shared fate as it was about finding a way to get their agendas through a Congress that was now completely in the hands of Republicans. In a sense, they were a family in sentiment and expectations, with some relatives closer than others. But they all were also politicians with complicated loyalties and electoral obligations to a multitude of others beyond their circle in the capital.[19]

CHAPTER 15

A Second Wind

DURING HIS SECOND TERM, BARACK OBAMA WAS MORE WILLING to publicly discuss matters of race—and in more historically grounded and interpretively meaningful ways—than he had been during his first four years in office. Beyond his own moderate temperament and strategic pragmatism, several reasons were behind this gradual but decisive change. First, national reactions to a number of highly publicized police killings of Black people compelled him, as both president and a concerned citizen, to address the realities of racial profiling, institutional racism, and an assortment of other obstacles facing African Americans. Second, in the absence of congressional action, public attention naturally turned toward the White House for leadership in the form of policy proposals, executive orders, or other concrete steps. Third, with the economy slowly improving and the reelection campaign behind him, Obama was free to pursue agenda items that required the kind of political capital and sustained engagement that he had not been prepared to dedicate to them during his first term.

The administration's efforts to protect voting rights and to reform the criminal justice system, particularly in relation to policing and sentencing, were the clearest indications of his new willingness to take on issues that were deeply impacted by long-standing forms of racial discrimination, as well as to explicitly characterize these initiatives as being in the interest of racial equity and social justice. Along with these second-term motivations, Obama was undoubtedly acting with a view to his own legacy as a Black president—and not just a president who happened to be Black. That is, he understood that history's measuring stick would inevitably gauge how his eight years in office affected Black America, his most loyal constituency and the one in which he and the First Lady claimed abiding membership and kindred affinity.

The president's shift on race was neither absolute nor wholly divorced from his previous policy stances or his tendency to act within the realm of the politically possible and the electorally feasible. He was still convinced that Black suffering, white guilt, and resultant moral outrage were not sufficient drivers of a viable legislative agenda. In his view, loud calls for reparations and other racially targeted remedies were nonstarters for a US electorate that was ceding more power to a Republican Party that had shown little interest in addressing racial disparities or working with the White House on anything of consequence. Despite his own expressed hopefulness regarding race relations, his reading of the political climate was clear-eyed and sharpened by the cold, harsh light of US history and the last several years of his life fighting hyperpartisan battles. Furthermore, Obama's advocacy of individual agency, communal responsibility, and the merits of hard work never changed, and he was as critical of what he believed to be deadbeat fathers and cultural pathologies in his second term as he had been during his first.

Thus, according to the president's estimation, all of this could only lead to one set of answers: universalist policies with far-reaching support that aimed to help all Americans but that had the potential to disproportionately benefit the most needy and vulnerable. Whether legislation addressing health care, criminal justice, education, or job creation, this generalist approach, in his opinion, offered real value for Americans across the board, along with the consensus-building packaging and messaging necessary to get significant tasks accomplished.

In other words, such policies could fortify the national sense of community and encourage collective sacrifice on behalf of agreed-upon goals and in return for widely disseminated rewards. "I have much more confidence in my ability, or any president or leader's ability, to mobilize the American people around a multiyear, multibillion dollar investment to help every child in poverty in this country," he told an interviewer in October 2016, "than I [do] in being able to mobilize the country around providing a benefit specific to African Americans as a consequence of slavery or Jim Crow." To him, that was the simple political math of the matter, though "we can debate the justness of that."[1]

No program was more symbolic or pertinent to this aspect of Obama's policymaking ethos than the Affordable Care Act. It was his signature legislative achievement and, at least partly for that reason, his most controversial one, given the inflamed partisanship of the era. While pitched as a universalist solution to the national problem of 42 million uninsured Americans and escalating health-care costs, support for the law was skewed along racial and partisan lines. According to a November 2013 poll, only 16 percent of minorities surveyed thought that the ACA should be repealed, compared with 48 percent of white respondents. In April 2016, pollsters found that 64 percent of African Americans believed that the impact of the law had been "mostly positive," with 51 percent of Hispanics and only 31 percent of whites agreeing with that assessment. Another way of interpreting the racial divide regarding opinions of the ACA was to view it through a partisan lens. In the same poll, 78 percent of Democrats approved of the law, while only 9 percent of Republicans did. Among independents, 39 percent approved, and 48 percent disapproved. If the principal objective of the ACA was to insure more people more affordably, it was an incremental success. The implementation of the law was in early 2014, and the uninsured rate fell from a high of 18 percent in the third quarter of 2013 to 11.9 percent in the first quarter of 2015. During that period, the uninsured rate for Blacks and Hispanics declined 7.3 and 8.3 points, respectively, and for those in households earning less than $36,000 annually, the rate fell 8.7 points.[2]

The geopolitical dimensions of health-care coverage were among the most striking indicators of how the ACA affected various populations, especially after a 2012 US Supreme Court ruling allowed individual states the latitude to decline expanding Medicaid. The highest concentration of Black people acquiring health plans through the federally facilitated marketplace was in the South. For Hispanics, the highest concentrations were in the Southwest and Florida. However, since a large share of Black people lived in Republican-governed states that decided not to expand Medicaid under the original provisions of the ACA, they were unable to acquire insurance coverage. That is, they were caught between a rock and a hard place. Their incomes were too low to qualify them for subsidized plans on the health-care exchanges, and their state governors and/or legislatures forwent the option of making Medicaid more accessible, even as the federal government promised to defray nearly all of the additional costs. This coverage gap hit hardest the poorest people without dependent children (who would have qualified them for traditional Medicaid) and households hovering around the federal poverty line (which likely made them ineligible for ACA subsidies to pay for coverage on the exchanges). Rather than address this problematic feature of the law's implementation, US House Republicans instead voted dozens of times to repeal the ACA, knowing that such votes were entirely symbolic even after the GOP took control of the Senate following the 2014 midterms. In July of that year, congressional Republicans went as far as to vote to sue the president over the rollout and enforcement of the law's provisions.

While Democrats and the GOP tussled over the health-care law in Washington, DC, states such as Mississippi, with a 38 percent Black population that comprised 56 percent of its poor citizens, became case studies of how the intended impact of the ACA was stymied by the resistance of state governments. In 2013, the Deep South state had the largest percentage of poor and uninsured people in the nation. Residents such as 53-year-old Willie Charles Carter, indigent and without dependent children, qualified for neither ACA subsidies nor Medicaid. "I'm scared all the time," he told a reporter as he described post-surgery problems with a leg. "I just walk around here with faith in God to take care of me." Dr. H. Jack Geiger, a community physician and human rights activist who worked in Mississippi, saw a bitter irony in the rejection of Medicaid expansion by every Deep South state except Arkansas. "It is their populations that have the highest burden of illness and costs to the entire health care system," he observed just prior to the ACA's launch in 2014. Dr. Aaron Shipley, an African American physician who advocated for better health-care access for Black Mississippians, linked the dilemma to the state's legacy of racial oppression and antipathy toward the well-being of citizens of color. "If you look at the history of Mississippi, politicians have used race to oppose minimum wage, Head Start, all these social programs," he explained in an interview. "It's a tactic that appeals to people who would rather suffer themselves than see a black person benefit." Mississippi Republicans generally characterized their opposition to the law and its Medicaid expansion component as philosophical and economic, with some, like state senator Chris McDaniel, maintaining that being required to cover only 10 percent of the cost of the expansion was too high an expense for the state to bear. Not enhancing health-care access for Mississippians did, of course, carry its own price, such as the state's perennially dead-last ranking in infant mortality and life expectancy statistics.[3]

Through the end of Obama's term in office in 2017, Mississippi continued to have the highest number of nonelderly uninsured Black people of any US state. At 42 percent, the proportion was three times the national figure for African Americans and ten points higher than in Louisiana, the state with the second-highest percentage of Black people comprising the nonelderly uninsured. The District of Columbia, with its historically large Black population, also reported a high percentage of African Americans among its nonelderly uninsured, matching the Mississippi rate. However, the DC percentage represented only 9,800 individuals, which did not begin to approach the tally of such uninsured Black people in Texas, Florida, Georgia, and North Carolina, four states that alone accounted for almost 1.6

million of the 3.8 million nonelderly uninsured African Americans nationwide.[4]

The Obama administration also struggled with issues related to educational access and equity, and its reform efforts produced decidedly mixed anecdotal results. During the twenty-first century, the US school-age population became more racially diverse, while school districts and systems became more racially segregated. In 1997, white students comprised 64 percent of public school enrollees; by the fall of 2014, they accounted for just under 50 percent of such pupils, or 24.9 million. The fastest-growing enrollments were among Hispanic and Asian students, with their numbers reaching 12.9 million and 2.6 million, respectively. Black students remained a relatively stable segment of the public school population, with 7.7 million entering classrooms in the fall term of 2014. Behind these numbers, inequities abounded. The percentage of poor Black or Hispanic students attending K-12 public schools in which they comprised 75-100 percent of the population doubled between 2001 and 2014. Government-collected data revealed that such schools typically offered fewer math, science, and college preparatory classes than other schools and enrolled fewer students with preschool training. Other indicators of scholastic quality, including the staffing of predominantly minority schools with less-experienced and lower-paid teachers and the higher incidence of student suspensions and expulsions in such settings, were just as troubling. Related to this latter point, students who missed instructional time due to punitive removal from the learning environment were more likely to later have interactions with the juvenile justice system.

The racial bifurcation of student educational experiences could be clearly witnessed in the disproportionately high percentage of white students enrolled in K-12 private schools. By the first year of the Obama administration, these pupils made up 73 percent of this school population. Given that local school districts and states had a great deal of control over education funding and delivery, the US Department of Education largely fought an uphill battle against the resegregation of public schools and lingering legacies of racial discrimination. The administration was proactive in collecting data and launching incentive programs, such as the Race to the Top initiative, which encouraged school systems to address racial disparities and achievement gaps. Moreover, the Justice Department intervened in a number of school districts in the South and Southwest to enforce federal desegregation orders and to challenge the frequent summoning of law enforcement officials by school administrators to handle minor infractions by Black students. Additionally, in January 2015 the president unveiled a proposal to offer up to two years of free community college to "responsible students," a broad-stroke policy that fit well with his universalist method of governance. Despite these efforts, demographic shifts in public and private education systems proceeded apace, abetted by ongoing patterns of residential segregation, income inequality, and state and local policies that facilitated these trends.[5]

During his 2013 State of the Union (SOTU) address, Obama announced a plan to assist twenty of the most economically distressed towns around the country to improve education, job opportunities, housing, and public safety. He elaborated on the idea a year later and called for private-public partnerships that, among other things, offered tax credits to spur business investment and job creation in such communities, incentivized home developers to preserve and expand affordable housing, bolstered K-12 education and adult job-training programs, and financed transportation, infrastructure, and innovative policing strategies. The first five "promise zones" identified for the pilot program were San Antonio, Texas; Los Angeles, California; Philadelphia, Pennsylvania; southeastern Kentucky; and the Choctaw Nation of Oklahoma, and there were plans to announce the other fifteen over the next three years. The president promised to devote "intensive federal support at the local level" to realize each set of goals prioritized by the targeted communities and committed his administration to tracking outcomes. By June 2016, a total of twenty-two promise zones had been recognized, including Nashville, Tennessee; Atlanta, Georgia; San Diego, California; the Turtle Mountain Band of Chippewa Indians in North Dakota; and Puerto Rico's Ceiba, Fajardo, and Naguabo municipalities.[6]

During Obama's second term, this initiative amounted to a small-footprint approach to some significant and engrained problems of poverty, infrastructural deficiencies, and systemic discrimination and exclusion. The promise zones did create, in some cases, synergies and dynamics among federal agencies, the private sector, and local communities that produced some measurable outcomes. For example, college acceptance and enrollment rates in promise zones in San Antonio and Los Angeles improved markedly over just two years' time. Further, a $2.6 million Early Head Start–Child Care Partnership and Early Head Start Expansion grant from the US Department of Health and Human Services resulted in "improved fine motor and gross motor skills, and social, emotional, cognitive, and language development" among Choctaw students enrolled in the program. In St. Louis County, Missouri, a US Department of Labor grant of $5 million allowed workforce centers to support job-training and placement programs for young adults in the area. And in the South Carolina Low Country promise zone, which encompassed parts of six counties, a partnership with the Kronotex company secured a roughly $230 million commitment to build a fiberboard mill that was projected to create a hundred new jobs. Other locales reported similar initiatives, including Sacramento, which was designated a promise zone in 2015 and received a $2.7 million Jobs Plus grant from the US Department of Housing and Urban Development to defray the cost of job training and placement for several hundred public housing residents. When Obama left office in early 2017, the future of the promise zone program became uncertain. Still, there were cases in which local leadership—whether private industry, government, or citizens—provided enough of the motivation and resources necessary to propel many of the initiated projects forward beyond the president's time in office.[7]

Promise zones were a representative model of Obama's approach to both race and governance. The partnerships brought in public and private stakeholders and resources in pursuit of broadly construed policies that could disproportionately benefit the most underserved individuals and communities. It was the same operational paradigm behind the ACA, the stimulus package, and the earned income tax and child tax credits that the administration supported, as well as the president's proposals for a jobs bill, infrastructure revitalization, and criminal justice reform, none of which were ultimately enacted by Congress. Following the 2010 midterms and especially the 2014 loss of the Senate, Obama was largely reduced to executive orders and policy tweaks by regulatory agencies, which did not require congressional approval but could be undone by presidential successors or future legislation.

In his last two years in the White House, the president made some creative use of his limited authority, again packaging policies in universalist wrapping that actually helped the most desperate—and often Black—Americans the most. In 2014-2015, a series of executive directives and regulatory changes bolstered workers' rights and protections. One such enactment changed a rule to make millions more Americans eligible for extra overtime pay. Another regulation, issued by the National Labor Relations Board, made collective bargaining and unionization easier. Obama, via executive order, raised the minimum hourly wage for employees working on federal contracts and other projects to $10.10, a move that, in the president's words, "increases their morale and the productivity and quality of their work." Historically more dependent on public-sector employment than some other groups, African Americans likely benefited significantly from this wage increase, though their unemployment rate still hovered around 10 percent when the rule went into effect on January 1, 2015.[8]

According to his own pronouncements, Barack Obama wanted to do big things on criminal justice reform during his second term. The biases and inequities in the system had been apparent to him for many years, and his background as both a lawyer and community organizer in Chicago's South Side had offered him firsthand glimpses into how race and class shapes US justice. He believed that drug laws had visited a particularly harsh cycle of policing, criminalization, and incarceration on marginalized communities, with some sentencing guidelines allowing for or even mandating long prison stints that ruined lives, families, and whole regions of the country. In many instances, the burden of these laws fell heaviest on Black, brown, and impoverished people. "African-American kids and Latino kids are more likely to be poor and less likely to have the resources and the support to avoid unduly harsh penalties," Obama explained in an almost indignant tone during an early 2014 interview. "We should not be locking up kids or individual users for long stretches of jail time when some of the folks who are writing those laws have probably done the same thing." The president approved of the legalization of marijuana by states like Colorado and Washington, though these steps were incremental and did not address federal laws that still criminalized possession of a range of illicit substances. Following the 2014 midterms, he publicly acknowledged that the Republican-led Congress could not be counted on for "massive investment in urban communities," where many of the ravages of the War on Drugs had taken place. His increasingly candid assessment of the problems of the criminal justice system, along with the disparate racial and class implications, was matched with robust remedial actions that had been largely missing from his first term in office.[9]

In August 2013, the Justice Department announced a new initiative to reform policing, sentencing, and carceral practices. Entitled Smart on Crime, the plan called for the targeting of law enforcement and criminal justice resources toward high-need, high-impact areas and away from prosecuting offenses that did not meaningfully advance crime prevention, recidivism reduction, or public safety. It also offered local authorities more discretion in determining under what circumstances to pursue federal charges for certain crimes. The biggest proposed change was in the area of sentencing. With an eye to fairness and cost-effectiveness, Attorney General Holder declared that the Justice Department would revise its charging policy to eliminate "draconian mandatory minimum sentences" for nonviolent drug offenders who were not affiliated with "large-scale organizations, gangs, or cartels" and whose infractions were relatively minor. Such a shift in enforcement emphasis would direct low-level criminals toward shorter prison sentences or noncarceral penalties and treatment, reserving the harshest punishments for more serious criminals, including violent offenders.[10]

In making the system "smarter" in its preventative and humanitarian capacities, Holder asserted that his office would collaborate with the Department of Education and other agencies to disrupt the "school-to-prison pipeline," which criminalized a wide swath of student behaviors based on zero-tolerance disciplinary practices. The attorney general also urged greater use of alternatives to incarceration and the release of elderly prisoners who had served a substantial portion of their sentences and who were not convicted of violent crimes. In September, the administration called for prosecutors to refile charges in pending cases involving low-level federal drug crimes, with the added instruction to omit references to the quantity of illegal substances involved in order to avoid any otherwise applicable mandatory minimum sentencing laws.[11]

In April 2014, the US Sentencing Commission, an independent agency within the federal government, voted to lessen the penalties for most drug offenses. Three months later, the panel made the changes retroactive and applicable to almost 50,000 federal prisoners who were still serving sentences under the previous rules. Holder, who had originally asked the commission for more modest policy changes, supported its sweeping decision in the "interests of fairness" and public safety, given that there would be a one-year delay in implementation. Barring congressional legislation, which could block the new changes, the revised sentencing guidelines represented a major advancement of Holder's Smart on Crime plan.[12]

For the sizable number of nonviolent drug offenders serving time in federal prisons, the new policies signaled an almost revolutionary change in the way that the government handled certain kinds of crimes. Tens of thousands of inmates became instantly eligible to have multiple years shaved off their sentences. The short-term results of the policy amendments were striking. By the end of 2015, the number of federal prisoners fell from the 2013 all-time high of 219,298 to 205,723; in 2017, the population had declined to 185,617. Less dramatic decreases in the prison populations of selected states led to an overall decline in incarcerated people across the nation, though some locales and regions did not adopt substantive sentencing reforms. When Obama left office in 2017, Black people comprised 37 percent of the federal inmate population and 32 percent of all prisoners, although they accounted for only 12 percent of the adult US population. Between 2007 and 2017, Black incarceration rates had declined more rapidly than those of whites and Hispanics, traceable to factors such as the improving economy after 2010, declining crime rates, and the effects of the new sentencing laws. Still, at the end of 2017 the Black incarceration rate of 1,549 prisoners for every 100,000 adults was nearly six times that of whites and almost twice that of Hispanics. With Black people accounting for a plurality of the 1,489,363 US inmates at that time, the problem of racialized mass incarceration was still one of epic proportions. Nonetheless, the new sentencing guidelines and Justice Department policies did help engineer a slow but notable decrease in the Black inmate population and pointed toward new directions in the practice of criminal justice.[13]

During the last quarter of his presidency, Obama pressed his case for criminal justice reform further. In July 2015, he visited the El Reno Federal Correctional Institution in Oklahoma, becoming the first sitting president to tour such a facility. During his time at the prison, he met with six inmates convicted of drug offenses and listened to their stories and regrets. Two days earlier, he had attended an NAACP convention where he avidly supported, among other things, the Ban the Box movement, which called for employers to not require job applicants to disclose criminal backgrounds so early in the application process that otherwise qualified job seekers would be preemptively denied employment. At the end of the month, the administration announced that a limited number of inmates would soon be eligible to apply for federal student aid through the Second Chance Pell pilot program. The initiative would be funded independently of the existing Pell Grant system.

More reforms were promulgated the following year. In January, Obama adopted Justice Department recommendations to ban the use of solitary confinement to punish juvenile inmates or to penalize other prisoners accused of minor violations. The move was expected to affect approximately 10,000 federal inmates, who would be spared some of the negative psychological effects associated with prolonged isolation. Later that summer, the Justice Department addressed the privatization of federal incarceration, which had peaked in 2013 with nearly 30,000 inmates, or roughly 15 percent of the federal total, held in for-profit facilities. For decades, such arrangements had gradually transformed mass incarceration into a business that incentivized the constant streaming of convicted people into such institutions for the benefit of investors and at the expense of taxpayers. A government report found that private detention centers "compare poorly to our Bureau [of Prisons] facilities" and were neither cost-efficient nor satisfactory in terms of services, resources, or safety. Thus, in keeping with Holder's efforts to maximize resources and increase public trust in the criminal justice system, the bureau was directed to not renew concluded contracts with private prisons and to reduce the scope of existing ones.[14]

This whirlwind of proposals and actions related to sentencing, incarceration, and reentry was both consequential and legacy defining. Cumulatively, the recommended and implemented changes were the most far-reaching since the Violent Crime Control and Law Enforcement Act of 1994, which was at least partly responsible for the rise in prison populations. To further augment these policy changes, Obama and Holder decided to revisit the issue of clemency in an effort to devise a more expeditious method of deploying this most distinctive of executive powers. As discussed above, the president offered very little mercy during his first term to Americans convicted of federal crimes. In fact, his record of official forgiveness was virtually nonexistent, which had much to do with bureaucratic inertia and his own unwillingness to prioritize the matter. With only one commutation granted in four years, he had ranked the lowest of any chief executive since at least 1900 in this regard, and his approval of only twenty-three pardon applications placed him second only to George W. Bush as the least-generous president by this standard in more than a century. One observer noted that Obama's pardoning of two plump turkeys during Thanksgiving 2013 brought his total of forgiven fowl to ten, just one short of the number of people he had pardoned for drug-related crimes during his entire presidency. In hindsight, the derision was understandable, and the president suffered it needlessly. His clemency authority in federal cases was as close to absolute as any of his Article II powers under the Constitution, requiring neither congressional approval nor judicial review. Despite the life-altering force of his clemency pen, Obama ultimately decided not to wield this presidential prerogative to any appreciable degree during most of his years in the White House.

In a belated effort to improve this lackluster record, the Justice Department announced new guidelines in April 2014 that were meant to make thousands of people eligible for clemency. Petitioners would have to meet several criteria to earn consideration, and nothing was guaranteed. Those inmates who had served at least ten years in prison, were nonviolent, and were sentenced under old guidelines—including the pre-2010 cocaine laws that so severely penalized crack possession—were most likely to have their requests for clemency heard. To assist with the screening of the more than 30,000 inmates who would eventually seek review, the administration created Clemency Project 2014, which drew on government lawyers and outside groups to process applications. With volunteers from the American Civil Liberties Union, the American Bar Association, and the National Association of Criminal Defense Lawyers, the project appeared to be off to an auspicious start.

And then things went awry. Although the problem had been a foreseeable complication, lawyers had trouble getting court documents that were more than a decade old, making it hard to construct a case for clemency. Outside attorneys working pro bono could not gain access to privileged materials related to particular cases, and government lawyers complained—and at least one even resigned in frustration—about opaque decision-making at the Justice Department that resulted in overturned recommendations for clemency. The review process itself was multilayered and labyrinthine, requiring a recommendation from a US pardon attorney, then scrutiny from a deputy attorney general, followed by an assessment by the White House counsel, and finally approval from Obama. This system might have been workable for dozens or even a few hundred applications but not tens of thousands. The little progress that was made came to a near standstill as officials such as Deputy Attorney General Sally Yates were reduced to taking a "grocery bag of petitions home" each weekend in an attempt to break through the bottleneck. Ensnared in a problem largely of their own making, Obama and his staff were in the unenviable position of having invited prisoners to seek reconsideration of their sentences without first putting into place sufficient resources and a functioning infrastructure to handle the flood of requests.

A year after the launch of Clemency Project 2014, Obama still had the lowest pardon rate of any president in decades, and his commutation rate of 1.1 percent placed him just above Ronald Reagan and George W. Bush. If Obama's limited grants of mercy revealed any pattern at all, they simply confirmed that he and his advisors leaned toward older, safer candidates, with half of the pardons bestowed in his first six years in office going to recipients whose crimes were committed before 1989. Aside from this discernible motif, the president's clemency policy seemed as random and numerically irrelevant as ever.[15]

Obama would not act more boldly or urgently in regard to clemency until December 2015. According to one researcher, it was not unusual that the president would dispense mercy around Christmastime; indeed, 60 percent of his clemency grants occurred during the holidays. However, what was new was that Obama dramatically ramped up his exercise of his powers to bestow mercy for the remainder of his presidency. His use of commutations was particularly striking, and a new batch of approved applications was announced almost every month. Before the December 2015 commutations, Obama had officially shortened the sentences of only 89 people since taking office in January 2009. His December reduction of 95 sentences more than doubled that number in a single day. In March 2016, he shortened 61 sentences; he did the same for 58 more inmates in May and another 42 in June. On August 3, the president granted 214 commutations, the most conferred in one day since at least 1900. He closed the month with 111 more sentence reductions, again more than doubling his previous commutation tally in a single month's time. From there, Obama seemed to be in a race against time, nearly matching or topping his previous record with each passing month. He commuted 200 sentences in October and 153 in December, a month in which he also pardoned 78 people, thus more than doubling his previous sum of 70. As the first family prepared to turn the page on their White House years, Obama signed off on 209 commutations and 64 pardons on January 17, and then broke his own single-day commutation record two days later by reducing the sentences of 330 people.

Obama's about-face on clemency was extraordinary and historic. He could rightly boast about his crescendoing magnanimity, which he did in an article that appeared in his old journal, the *Harvard Law Review*, around the time that he left office. Much of the rejuvenated clemency effort was made possible by Obama's sheer force of will, sense of justice, and need for a positive criminal justice legacy, along with political timing that entailed few risks for unilateral presidential action and that offered abundant clarity concerning the improbability of congressional movement. The commutations especially hit the mark, freeing hundreds of people from life sentences, many of whom had been convicted for crack cocaine possession. Notwithstanding that his final commutation figure (1,715) placed him well ahead of the second-place presidential contender, Woodrow Wilson (1,366), the numbers alone did not capture all of the nuances and gray areas that were also at play.

Before the first big spike in sentence reductions in August 2016, most commutations were of the "time served" variety, which typically resulted in a prisoner's release in four months, unless such liberty was predicated on some condition, such as enrollment in a drug treatment program. Of the August commutations, almost 40 percent were of the "term" sort, which reduced only part of an inmate's sentence. For example, if a person had been convicted of a drug-related crime while wielding a gun or committing an assault, Obama's actions would have commuted the sentence related to the drug offense (in accordance with Justice Department guidelines) but left in place any prison time associated with the assault charge or gun crime. Parsing the sentences in this fashion allowed the president to provide relief for excessive drug sentences while not technically violating the administration's criterion that made violent offenses ineligible for commutation.[16]

In contrast to his fourth-place ranking among presidents regarding the sheer numbers of acts of clemency granted since 1900, Obama's rate of extending executive mercy was relatively low. He granted 1,927 clemency requests, including 212 pardons, out of a pool of 36,544 petitions, resulting in a 5.3 percent approval rate. This figure compared favorably only to the presidencies of George H. W. Bush (5.3 percent) and George W. Bush (1.8 percent). All other chief executives since 1900 had higher rates of granting such relief. To be sure, the scale of clemency requests during the Obama years was much higher than during any other presidency. From October 1, 2015, to September 30, 2016, alone, the administration took in 12,025 petitions for commutations and pardons, a larger number than any other president received during his entire time in office with the single exception of Franklin Roosevelt. Still, the exploding number of requests hardly excused the low rate of approvals, given that the White House and Justice Department had solicited applications from inmates eligible for consideration and had eight years to figure out a fair and efficient clemency policy and process.

There was no compelling reason for Obama to have limited his use of pardons and commutations as he waited for Republicans in

Congress to act on criminal justice reform. Their lack of interest in bipartisan policymaking and cooperation with the White House was unmistakably clear once the GOP captured the US House in 2010 and showed itself to be disagreeable about even the basic functions of government, such as raising the debt ceiling to avoid default. In the end, the president's generous use of his official powers of mercy during his last thirteen months in office illuminated a tragic irony. While his enhanced exercise of this executive prerogative demonstrated how much authority and latitude the Constitution had invested in him to address injustices in the penal system, it also signaled how unnecessarily harsh his first seven years in office had been for tens of thousands of inmates who arguably had deserved earlier consideration for clemency.

Obama occasionally placed a human face on his use of clemency powers by inviting people whom he had freed to the White House. It was both good optics for the administration and certainly a morale boost for those whom the president had offered a second chance. Obama did not abuse the system by pardoning well-connected, shady characters as Bill Clinton and others had done at the expense of their own reputations. He also avoided celebrity or show clemency, even in cases that may have merited his attention and that had attracted powerful supporters. Former boxing champion Jack Johnson never became a sympathetic enough figure in Obama's eyes to warrant a posthumous pardon, though Harry Reid, John McCain, and others pressed him for one through the last months of his presidency. Similarly, the conviction of Black nationalist Marcus Garvey on mail fraud charges in 1923 was allowed to stand for the duration of the Obama White House, despite the pleadings of his octogenarian son, the entreaties of several members of the CBC, and a petition containing thousands of signatures. Obama was not especially keen on pardons or posthumous displays of mercy and name clearing, so declining to take on the Johnson and Garvey cases was not out of line with his clemency practices. Nevertheless, the reluctance to act on these requests even in the last days of his presidency when any blowback would have been offset by bipartisan approbation (in the Johnson case) or the gratitude of almost an entire friendly nation (Jamaica, in Garvey's case) appeared overly cautious and, to some observers, rather petty.

As Obama left office, he constructed a list of unfinished business that still needed to be done regarding criminal justice. This unresolved agenda was published in his *Harvard Law Review* article and included aspirational tasks, such as passing sentencing reform, reducing gun violence, better identifying wrongful convictions, restoring the voting rights of felons, and using technology to enhance trust in law enforcement. The wish list was very much in keeping with his progressive, technocratic leanings, and these issues registered broad support among his Democratic base, including African Americans.

On the matter of the death penalty, which did not make his priorities list, Obama, like most Americans, was not against it "in theory," but he found its practice in the United States to be tainted by racial prejudice, erroneous convictions, and "gruesome and clumsy" application. By 2015, several polls showed that Black people as a group opposed capital punishment, a position that was informed by their overrepresentation on death rows across the country. Obama had previously charged the Justice Department with studying the death penalty, but its inquiry never resulted in any publicized recommendations or actions. When asked in October 2015 about the delayed review, the president was candid about his preoccupation with other issues beyond the sixty-two people—twenty-six of whom were Black— living with federal death sentences. "I got a lot of other things to do as well," he explained with a smile and a slightly defensive tone to Bill Keller of the Marshall Project, a nonprofit group devoted to criminal justice reform. Indeed, Obama was looking forward to two upcoming seasonal tasks. In November, he would participate in the obligatory pardoning of Abe, the Thanksgiving turkey. A month later, he would begin rolling out Christmastime commutations and pardons that would launch a historic clemency streak that would last until the final hours of his presidency.[17]

Overall, the Obama administration's record in the area of criminal justice was commendable and broadly impactful, albeit marked by significant gaps in progress and a limited applicability beyond federal jurisdictions. Since so many of the achievements occurred without the benefit of legislative backing, their durability was an open question once the president left office. This caveat especially applied to the future enforcement of existing consent decrees between the Justice Department and numerous police organizations around the country. Notwithstanding these uncertainties, the sentencing reforms acquired enough momentum to continue the reduction of the federal inmate population beyond 2017. Additionally, the nearly 2,000 acts of clemency granted by Obama could not be reversed, and the lives of the beneficiaries were thus permanently changed by his mercy.

For many Americans, voting was becoming harder and less convenient with each campaign cycle. Like other recent elections, the 2012 balloting was marred by a spectrum of problems both trifling and troubling. Many of the more alarming issues were related to either inadequate support at polling stations or purposeful efforts to depress voter turnout in some areas. Reports of previously registered voters being turned away from polls in predominantly Black districts in Pennsylvania emerged alongside tales of Tea Party groups interfering with people waiting in long lines to cast ballots in Georgia, Florida, and California. Vietnamese American voters found that too few interpreters had shown up to assist them at a polling place in South Philadelphia, and some decided to leave without casting a ballot. It is difficult to determine how many citizens eligible to register to vote were put off by new voter ID laws in various states that could require an appreciable investment of time, expense, and travel to achieve compliance. One study found that in the wake of North Carolina's decision to shift around early-voting places, African American voters on average had to travel farther to vote than the typical white voter, a discriminatory differential that decreased the electoral participation of registered Black voters by 0.5 percent for each one-tenth of a mile increase in distance to the polling station. Additionally, during the 2008 and 2012 election cycles, Black and Hispanic voters were much more likely than whites to be instructed to display photo identification before voting, to wait in lines for thirty minutes or longer, and to not receive requested absentee ballots.[18]

During his SOTU address in February 2013, Obama announced the establishment of a nonpartisan Presidential Commission on Election Administration to study ways to make voting more fair and accessible. The work would be led by Bob Bauer and Ben Ginsberg, the top attorneys for his and Mitt Romney's campaigns, respectively. An executive order issued in late March officially launched the effort, and the commission worked for the rest of the year to produce a report in January 2014. Of its several recommendations, most dealt with the logistics and technology of voting. The panel called for easier methods to register and to update voter profiles online, as well as more sharing of voter data between states in order to keep voter rolls accurate. Schools were identified as useful polling sites, and the commission recommended that students and teachers be allowed to take a day off at election time in the interest of security. The report also endorsed the establishment of voting times and methods beyond Election Day polling, including mail-in ballots and in-person early voting, which would ideally alleviate the long lines that plagued some locales. Along with making polling places more accessible to the disabled, the commission underscored the need for nationwide replacement and refurbishing of aging and defective voting machines, which could cause chaos in the event of generalized malfunctions or an especially close election that required a precise recount. As a to-do list for improving US elections, the report was reasonable and measured in its assessment and conclusions. However, in the interests of bipartisan comity, the commissioners had avoided prickly issues such as voter ID laws and recent court decisions that promised to affect access to the ballot far more extensively than decrepit voting equipment or missing wheelchair ramps at schools.[19]

The election commission and its report were important messaging from the White House regarding the necessity of protecting the franchise. But as things turned out, they were nothing more than that. US elections are always in the hands of fifty states and roughly 8,000 local jurisdictions, and many had neither the resources nor sense of urgency required to adopt the commission's recommendations. Furthermore, with a GOP-led House and a filibuster-prone Senate minority that were, at best, indifferent to working with the administration on voting rights or much else, action on this issue, despite the nonpartisan nature of the commission, was a remote possibility. Instead, the battle over voting rights continued to be fought primarily in the realm of the judiciary. In recent disputes, the courts had a mixed record on voter ID laws, gerrymandering, and other electoral matters. During the six years prior to the 2012 election, state courts had blocked voter ID laws in Missouri and Wisconsin, and federal judges had upheld such statutes in Indiana and South Carolina. In January 2013, the Supreme Court declined to overturn a consent decree that banned the RNC from targeting racial minorities with "ballot security" tactics that had the effect of intimidating voters and discouraging electoral participation. Predictably, the mandatory redistricting that took place after the 2010 Census triggered a new wave of litigation involving the fairness of electoral maps, spawning more political feuds that lasted well into the next decade.

The big case in the judicial pipeline was the *Shelby County, Ala. v. Holder* litigation, which had originated as a local challenge to the Voting Rights Act of 1965. In short, the county had sued to have sections 4(b) and 5 of the legislation declared unconstitutional, thus freeing selected states and municipalities with long histories of voting discrimination from having to clear proposed changes to voting laws with either the Justice Department or a federal court. The act had been upheld in district and appellate venues prior to the Supreme Court deciding to weigh in on the matter. In February 2013, the high court heard oral arguments in the case, which promised to have legal, political, and historic ramifications that reached far beyond the boundaries of Shelby County, Alabama.

Obama tried to get ahead of the brewing public anxiety over the challenge to the Voting Rights Act by going on a media offense. During an appearance on Sirius XM's *The Black Eagle* radio show, he explained that Americans would not lose their voting rights if part of the 48-year-old law was struck down. However, the government would be deprived of an important weapon designed to preemptively combat discriminatory policies enacted by states. "So generally speaking, you'd see less protection before an election with respect to voting rights," he told host Joe Madison. "People could keep on coming up with new schemes each election" to limit access to the franchise. The president's reserved assessment was in stark contrast to reactions to Justice Antonin Scalia's contention during oral arguments that the Voting Rights Act was a "racial entitlement" that was difficult to justify. John Lewis, having suffered grievous injury while demonstrating in support of passage of the law, labeled Scalia's remarks an "affront to all of what the civil rights movement stood for." Similarly, Benjamin Jealous of the NAACP warned during an interview, "those who would seek to use incendiary rhetoric from the bench of the Supreme Court should think twice about their place in history." Spencer A. Overton, a law professor at George Washington University, questioned whether the conservative justice was impartial enough to adjudicate cases involving voting discrimination, given his stated preconceptions.[20]

The most eloquent and powerful response to Scalia's remarks came from Desiline Victor, a 102-year-old North Miami woman of Haitian descent who had waited hours to vote in 2012. Her centenarian resilience drew national attention and earned her a seat as an honored guest at the SOTU address. In a March 12 open letter to Scalia, she courageously argued the case for the Voting Rights Act:

> During the early voting period in Florida last October, I went to my polling place early in the morning. The line was already

very long, and wait times were as high as six hours. I stood
for three hours before I started to get shaky on my feet. . . .
In addition, there were no poll workers available who could
help me in my native Kreyòl language, despite North Miami's
large Haitian community. I was told to come back later. I left.
But I was determined to vote, so I tried again. On my second
visit that night, I was happy when I finally cast my ballot. But
I was also upset. In this great nation why should anybody have
to stand in line for hours, and make two trips, to vote?

We need [to] make sure that all Americans can have their
voices heard—we need the Voting Rights Act. Justice Scalia,
the Voting Rights Act is not a racial entitlement. It is an important protection that helps all Americans exercise their right
to vote. It was put in place because, sadly, there are people in
this country who don't want everyone to have an equal voice
at the ballot box.

Victor, who would live through the entirety of the Obama presidency, had stated the case as plainly and forcefully as anyone could.
Black, female, immigrant, American—she checked all of the demographic boxes associated with the legendary struggles for suffrage in
the United States. Hers was an amicus brief like no other, but the
question was whether the court would listen to the words of such an
extraordinary elder.[21]

The Supreme Court decided *Shelby* along its ideological fault lines.
In a 5-4 verdict, the justices declared section 4(b) of the law unconstitutional, asserting that the list of fifteen states and regions covered by
the preclearance requirement in section 5 no longer reflected "current
conditions" and needed to be updated by Congress. Aside from the
fact that the House and Senate had voted overwhelmingly to renew
and strengthen the Voting Rights Act in 2006, the court proceeded
from the premise that the nature and geographical focuses of voting
discrimination had shifted significantly enough over the previous
five decades to justify dismantling a key portion of the law. Although

section 5 was left intact, it was instantly made unenforceable by the court's invalidation of section 4(b) and its roster of states and regions that needed to seek preclearance before changing voting laws. With this new ruling, the burden of proving a violation of voting rights fell on plaintiffs who could only make their cases *after* an alleged infringement had occurred, freeing states to enact all sorts of laws to alter voting requirements without first seeking federal approval. Viewed from another angle, the Voting Rights Act had allowed the Justice Department and other federal authorities to preemptively block more than 3,000 attempts to enact discriminatory voting measures between 1965 and 2013. With the *Shelby* decision, the government would be reduced to challenging such changes on a time-consuming, case-by-case basis, often after their enactment had already deprived voters of equal access to the ballot box.[22]

As the administration and others had feared, the Supreme Court's decision opened the floodgates. Within weeks, several Republican-controlled legislatures passed laws that amended voting practices and procedures. Lawmakers in North Carolina put forth one of the most comprehensive packages of restrictions, which included a voter ID requirement, a reduction in early-voting days, and a prohibition on registering to vote and casting an early ballot on the same day. The Ohio legislature adopted similar policies, as did Wisconsin lawmakers, who ended early voting on weekends. States like Arizona and Kansas went as far as to require proof of citizenship in the form of a birth certificate or passport prior to voting, a stipulation that was approved by a federal court. Republicans defended the new bevy of voting laws as being necessary for the standardization of the electoral process and to protect against scammers. It was an old argument that was still at odds with the exceedingly rare evidence of in-person voter fraud. More common than documented proof of such electoral shenanigans was the occasional GOP official, such as Buncombe County precinct chair Don Yelton, who let slip the actual reasons for supporting more restrictive voting laws. The new North Carolina voter ID bill was "going to kick the Democrats in the butt," he stated confidently during a televised interview in October 2013. "If it hurts a bunch of lazy blacks that want the government to give them everything, so be it." Even in a state whose government had been completely captured by Republicans, Yelton's comments were too much for the party establishment to abide publicly. Despite being subsequently pressured into resigning his post, Yelton remained unapologetic regarding his expressed sentiments.[23]

Beyond initially announcing that he was "deeply disappointed" by the *Shelby* decision, Obama tried to address the crisis on three different but parallel tracks. First, he huddled with a group of fifteen civil rights leaders at the White House and gave them a pep talk. He reportedly reminded the attendees that people who were around to witness the passage of the Voting Rights Act in the 1960s had endured a far worse racial climate than the present and that the Supreme Court's decision was not beyond fixing. He told the group to relay any local violations of voting rights to federal authorities and stressed his commitment to seeking a bipartisan legislative remedy for the damage done by *Shelby*. Next, Obama instructed the Justice Department to continue aggressively defending equal access to the franchise, which Holder did with alacrity. In July, the attorney general filed a lawsuit against Texas over its new law, drawing on surviving sections of the Voting Rights Act to halt the state's actions. He, along with the NAACP and the League of Women Voters, also sued North Carolina over its restrictive legislation. With polls showing that a majority of Americans disapproved of the *Shelby* ruling, Holder and allies waged battle across the legal terrain as well as in the court of public opinion.

The administration was encouraged by some early successes, though these were accompanied by some setbacks. In October 2014, federal courts blocked a voter ID law from taking effect in Wisconsin, and the Arkansas Supreme Court did the same just days later. Also during October, the US Supreme Court upheld two provisions of the North Carolina law and declined a request to overturn the Texas photo ID requirement. Coming so close to the midterm elections, the late-hour decisions caused confusion among voters, who were unsure of what credentials to bring to the polls. To make matters more perplexing, several states had included on their ballots proposals to either tighten or loosen voting requirements. Holder, anticipating trouble, arranged to send monitors to eighteen states to guard against voting rights violations. His agency also coordinated with the FBI and US attorneys' offices to address any irregularities that might occur.

Wholly predictably by this point in US political history, a smorgasbord of polling-site mix-ups, misplaced registrations, misinformation, and other problems awaited voters who ventured to the ballot box on November 4. Voters in North Carolina, which had cut early voting by seven days, were told that they could not cast ballots if they went to the wrong polling station. In Georgia, hundreds of individuals, many of them first-time voters, called a hotline to inquire whether their registration had been processed, a requirement for voting. In Kansas, 22,000 people were denied the opportunity to vote since they could not readily prove their citizenship. Moreover, in Texas, which had become a flashpoint in the struggle over voting rights, people were turned away at the polls on account of a voter ID law that had been affirmed by the US Supreme Court less than three weeks earlier. Some critics of the new voting restrictions claimed that part of their purpose was to discourage people from voting by creating inconveniences and sowing confusion. Whatever the intentions of their authors, the effects were clear enough for all to see. The 2014 turnout figure ended up being the lowest of any midterm election since 1942.[24]

Along with strategizing with civil rights activists and deploying Justice Department resources, Obama attempted to motivate Congress to address the fallout from *Shelby*. However, if the executive branch was resolute and the judiciary more ambivalent concerning the need to address the implications of the Supreme Court decision, lawmakers in the Senate and the House, particularly Republicans, were decidedly uninterested in the issue. A Senate Judiciary Committee meeting scheduled for July 17, 2013, attracted only two GOP members. Bipartisan legislation proposed by Sen. Patrick J. Leahy (D-VT) and Rep. Jim Sensenbrenner (R-WI) the following January went nowhere as a number of states enacted restrictions ahead of the midterms. With the return of the Senate to Republican control in 2015, Sen. Charles Grassley of Iowa, the new Judiciary Committee chair, refused to act on any proposal to undo the Supreme Court's dismantling of the preclearance clause of the Voting Rights Act, asserting that there was no need for such a fix. Rep. Bob Goodlatte, Grassley's GOP counterpart in the House, echoed his thinking. In desperation, congressional Democrats, led by the CBC, tried to attach a voting rights proposal to an Interior Department spending bill but were ultimately unable to compel Republicans to act. With full control of Congress and a presidential election season on the horizon, GOP lawmakers saw little urgency in revisiting *Shelby*; after all, it was state legislatures dominated by their party that had so hurriedly implemented new voting restrictions in the immediate aftermath of the court decision. Any revival of preclearance formulas would have been anathema to these new measures.[25]

Until the end of his presidency, Obama continued to press for congressional action on voting rights. On the occasion of the fiftieth anniversary of the Selma demonstrations, he called for Congress to honor the sacrifices of civil rights activists by fortifying the Voting Rights Act. To counterbalance the power of moneyed interests in the electoral system, he also suggested that the United States follow the lead of some other countries and make voting mandatory, which would compel more young, lower-income, and minority voters to participate in elections. With both houses of Congress in the hands of unsympathetic Republicans and the courtroom struggle against voting restrictions making slow, uneven progress, Obama was largely left with using the bully pulpit to try to inspire, cajole, and shame the opposition into action. It was, of course, a losing strategy, given the implacable nature of the resistance, but it was all that he could do as the hours ran short on his White House tenure.

Attorney General Holder maintained his vigilance in protecting voting rights, as did his successor, Loretta Lynch. Holder was particularly supportive of the enfranchisement of felons, who are legally prevented from casting ballots in most states. Despite having served their sentences, Americans with criminal records have been routinely locked out of the political process long after release, experiencing an often permanent form of second-class citizenship that brings into question the rehabilitative principle behind the correctional system. The burden of this disfranchisement falls disproportionately on African Americans, who have suffered from such citizenship erasure from the state-level backlash against Reconstruction in the late nineteenth century to the current War on Drugs. During the last year of the Obama administration, some progress was made regarding the restoration of voting rights for convicted felons, with both Maryland and Virginia reopening the ballot box to these Americans. Still, as many as 5.8 million people remain disfranchised due to state laws that continue to punish them post-incarceration. This population of disfranchised individuals continues to climb in number in direct correlation with the nation's ongoing failure to overhaul its prison-centric criminal justice system.[26]

The 2016 election was the first presidential cycle not covered by the Voting Rights Act's preclearance requirements since President Lyndon B. Johnson was in office. Just days before the November 8 balloting, courts were still attempting to clarify and affirm voting procedures in various states that had been muddled by the raft of voter ID laws and other measures that were birthed by the *Shelby* decision. Justice Department personnel again fanned out across dozens of jurisdictions to monitor the voting, though the agency's enforcement powers had been curtailed by the weakening of the Voting Rights Act. And like clockwork, the same problems that had appeared in other recent elections again proliferated across the country. Tellingly, the most disturbing scenarios arose in swing states like North Carolina, Ohio, and Pennsylvania whose legislatures had strenuously endeavored to adopt more restrictive voting procedures and qualifications. In the long run, the election would be memorable for reasons beyond lengthy lines, equipment glitches, understaffed polling sites, and deceptive messaging. It had revealed just how frighteningly vulnerable the system was to malignant forces and regressive atrophy.[27]

CHAPTER 16

"If I Had a Son"

TRAYVON MARTIN WAS THE QUINTESSENTIAL AMERICAN TEEN-
ager. Tall and lean, he liked sports, hanging out with friends, and
visiting relatives. He lived in the Miami area with his father, Tracy
Martin, who drove trucks for a living. His parents had divorced in
1999, but Trayvon's mother, Sybrina Fulton, a Miami-Dade government employee, lived close by, and his brother, Jahvaris, attended
Florida International University. Similar to other 17-year-old boys,
Trayvon probably sank too much time into video games, watching
sitcom reruns, and calling and texting his girlfriend. School was a
mixed bag for him, though he was mechanically inclined and known
to be respectful toward teachers. He found chemistry tough, disliked
the lunch menu, and on one occasion was suspended for reportedly
possessing a small quantity of marijuana. Aside from such scrapes,
Trayvon looked forward to his junior prom at Dr. Michael M. Krop
Senior High School, when an evening of friends, music, and dancing
would carry him through this much-talked-about rite of passage.
Trayvon liked planes and hoped to fix and fly them someday; his
Gmail inbox was already percolating with SAT and other college-
related messages, including invitations to visit Saint Leo University,
located north of Tampa. His parents wanted him to have a wealth of

experiences beyond South Florida and exposed him to skiing, snow-boarding, horseback riding, and a Broadway musical during a summer trip to New York. According to Tracy Martin, his boy "still had a lot of kid in him" despite the occasional mellow moment spent listening to R&B, rap, or gospel music streaming through earbuds. Several years after the fact, Tracy could still vividly recall how a 9-year-old Trayvon had pulled him from a house fire, thus saving his life. The feat officially made the youth his father's "main man" and "hero," bonding the two even closer together.

On February 26, 2012, Tracy and Trayvon visited the former's fiancée in the Retreat at Twin Lakes, a gated community in Sanford some 250 miles from Miami. Trayvon had been there several times before and had made friends among some of the local boys with whom he played football. It was a Sunday, likely a quiet day in the neighborhood, and after dinner, Trayvon had an appetite for something sweet. Around 6:30 p.m., he ventured by foot to a local store and bought a bag of Skittles candy and a bottle of iced tea. It was a winter evening, and twilight caught him before he made his way back home. The dropping temperature was noticeable even through his hooded sweatshirt, which had become damp with falling rain.

And then the stranger appeared. He followed Trayvon prior to their direct encounter, and the boy, sensing danger, tried to flee. The man, shorter but heavier than Trayvon, caught up with him and apparently engaged the youth verbally before physically assaulting him. Trayvon yelled for help and demanded that the man go away and get off him. Against the backdrop of the teenager's pleas and screams, neighbors called 911 for emergency assistance. Suddenly, a single gunshot cracked loudly through the night air, silencing the youth's cries. When the police arrived, they found 28-year-old George Zimmerman, a resident of the Retreat, standing near Trayvon, who was face down and motionless. Officers could not revive the boy, who had suffered a bullet wound to the chest. In a 911 call made just prior to the fatal skirmish, Zimmerman had claimed that the boy was a "real suspicious guy," was "up to no good or he's on drugs or something," and had "something in his hands." When Trayvon had fled in fear, Zimmerman gave chase, even though the 911 dispatcher explicitly told him not to do so. Following the shooting, Zimmerman maintained that he had killed the teenager in self-defense. Law enforcement officials found the rationale persuasive and consistent with the state's Stand Your Ground law, which allows for the use of deadly force to protect oneself and others even when retreat is a viable option for avoiding conflict. After several hours of questioning, Zimmerman was allowed to return home later that night. Trayvon Martin's body, unidentified at the time, was delivered to the Volusia County medical examiner's office.

When Trayvon did not come home that Sunday evening, his father called the police. A plainclothes detective came by with a picture of his son's body for identification purposes, and, according to Tracy Martin, "from that point, our nightmare [began]." Questions about the killing and the police response to it went unanswered for weeks, and the press showed little initial interest in the story. Desperate for justice for their son, Trayvon's parents accepted pro bono representation from Benjamin Crump, a Tallahassee-based civil rights lawyer, and worked with a publicist to tell their boy's story. Growing pressure from civil rights activists and national media reports compelled state and local officials to focus on the case. On March 22, the city commission voted "no confidence" in Police Chief Bill Lee, who temporarily stepped down from his position to allow an investigation to proceed without being overshadowed by his previous handling of the killing and its aftermath. Later that day, Gov. Rick Scott announced the appointment of a new prosecutor to investigate the case. As Zimmerman, the confirmed shooter who had still not been charged with a crime, quietly quit his job and moved out of the Retreat neighborhood, protests stirred around the country, and many people demanded federal action. A month after his death, Trayvon Martin had gone from unknown Black teen to iconic symbol of a twenty-first-century civil rights movement, his boyish, hoodie-wreathed face becoming as familiar as his teenage relatability, poignantly epitomized by his evening trip to the store for Skittles and iced tea.[1]

From the vantage point of the White House, the Trayvon Martin case included a number of combustible elements that needed to be handled with care. The local investigation was ongoing, and President Obama was reluctant to weigh in too forcefully lest he jeopardize the Florida process and any federal inquiry that might take place. Of course, there was the matter of race. Zimmerman, who claimed Hispanic (white and Peruvian) heritage, had killed an unarmed Black teen in a locale freighted with a long history of racial injustice and continuing tensions. To step too fast or firmly into the situation might inflame an already fraught set of circumstances, much like what had occurred in 2009 when Obama criticized the Cambridge Police Department for arresting Henry Louis Gates Jr. for "breaking into" his own house. The president's poll numbers among whites had never quite recovered from that moment of candor, and he had learned the lesson of not placing gut-level impulses too far ahead of political calculations.

The politics in this case, too, were clear. Not only could a conflagration around race be damaging in an election year, but Florida, of all swing states, needed to be protected from GOP encroachment. Obama had won the state's twenty-seven electoral votes by less than three percentage points in 2008, and it was quite conceivable that Mitt Romney would fare better in November 2012. To win Florida again, Obama needed a healthy turnout of Black and Hispanic voters, along with enough young and female voters to make up for the likelihood that Republicans would overperform among white conservatives in the South. With all of these considerations hovering overhead, press secretary Jay Carney conveyed the White House's official position on the Martin case on March 20, confirming that the administration had expressed condolences to the teenager's family, was monitoring developments via the Justice Department, and was "not going to wade into a local law-enforcement matter."[2]

What Obama offered the nation, by way of Carney, was a lawyer's brief, a scholar's abstract, which was understandably cautious from a political or legal perspective but glaringly unsuited to the leadership moment that now faced his White House. The statement disappointed many as too detached and removed from the anger and pain that the killing of an unarmed, unoffending teenager should rightly arouse, especially from an African American man occupying the country's highest office. Some pointed out that Obama was fully capable of capturing and articulating the national zeitgeist when he so desired, a quality that had helped to get him elected in the first place. Thus, they were dismayed when he hesitated in a situation that seemed so ripe for a display of his formidable oratorical talents. "Obama is perfectly willing to give a sermon to black men on Father's Day about what they need to be doing," political analyst and blogger Yvette Carnell coolly observed after the Carney remarks, "but totally incapable of advocating for a black boy who was murdered in the street while carrying only Skittles and iced tea." Such sentiments became generalized to the point that significant pressure built for Obama to personally address the Martin tragedy. According to Valerie Jarrett, the president was visibly shaken by the boy's death and wanted to speak out publicly but was steered clear by aides who only saw land mines and traps that might politically ensnare him. Perhaps sensing history's gaze, Obama wanted a chance to redo the bland statement that Carney had given on his behalf and instructed David Plouffe to arrange for a reporter to ask him about the Martin case during a press conference on March 23.[3]

Mike Viqueira of NBC soft-pitched the question during the Friday media event, and Obama swung for the fences. The president called for a thorough investigation into "every aspect" of the death of Trayvon Martin and the use of federal, state, and local resources to determine what had occurred. He urged the nation to empathize with the trauma that the boy's parents were experiencing, as well as their expectation that the situation be investigated "with the seriousness that it deserves." Obama appealed to the mothers and fathers of the country, asserting, "When I think about this boy, I think about my own kids." And most important, he spoke directly to Tracy Martin and Sybrina Fulton with the kind of compassion and empathy that only he, a Black president, could offer in this moment. "My main message is to the parents of Trayvon Martin," he proclaimed with accentuated clarity. "If I had a son, he'd look like Trayvon." In hindsight, it was probably the most perfectly fitting thing that Obama said publicly at any time during his entire eight years in office. He rose to the occasion, placing warm, calming hands on a grieving family that was trying to express its pain through mature, dignified advocacy on behalf of their deceased young son. And they appreciated what Obama did, and what only he could do. "We'd like to thank the President and the millions of people from around the world who have shown their support for Trayvon," the parents conveyed in an email, almost audibly exhaling. "We are all working together to not only get justice for Trayvon, but also to ensure that this kind of senseless tragedy doesn't happen to another child."[4]

Despite the president's statement and the various efforts to achieve justice in the Martin case, some of the worst anguish was yet to come. On July 13, 2013, George Zimmerman was acquitted of second-degree murder and manslaughter, indictments that could have resulted in significant prison time. Across the country, outraged citizens took to the streets and to social media to decry the verdict, and an NAACP petition calling for the Justice Department to file civil rights charges gathered more than 275,000 signatures in a matter of hours. As he had a year earlier, Obama defaulted to the language of caution and conciliation, proposing "calm reflection" on the tragic chain of events and a national meditation over whether "we're doing all we can to stem the tide of gun violence that claims too many lives." Eric Holder, speaking at an NAACP gathering in Orlando on July 16, reiterated the president's sentiments and encouraged "respectful, responsible dialogue" in the wake of the jury decision. The US attorney general had previously launched an investigation into the Martin killing but warned that it would be a challenge to bring a federal hate-crime case against Zimmerman based on the available evidence. During his Orlando appearance, Holder did criticize Stand Your Ground laws that allowed for the use of lethal violence in the face of avoidable threats, though Zimmerman had not invoked the Florida statute in his courtroom defense.[5]

Obama's mindful caution, while arguably warranted by the ongoing federal investigation, provoked mixed reactions. Columnist Keli Goff of The Root.com urged the chief executive to realize that "he is a black president, and not just an American president who happens to be black and subsequently has a responsibility to speak for those black Americans who cannot speak for themselves." Goff's colleague David Swerdlick took issue with her critique, insisting that as president, Obama was duty bound to uphold the US criminal justice system "with all its attendant flaws," as well as jury verdicts, even if he did not agree with them. Members of the CBC were particularly vocal about the case and the White House responses. "It's not unusual for the president to avoid 'black' and 'race' and 'poverty,'" Rep. Charlie Rangel contended, "but we're pretty much satisfied with his statement as it relates to the Zimmerman verdict." Congresswoman Gwen Moore of Wisconsin readily pardoned Obama for not "put[ting] a dashiki on" and raising a "black power fist" but called on him to "level the playing field to make sure that African-Americans have the same opportunities." Bobby Rush, who had defeated Obama for a US House seat back in 2000, wanted the president to "speak more forthrightly" about the case and favored a continuing discussion of the issues raised by the tragedy and its aftermath. Still in shock over the verdict days later, Sybrina Fulton stated in a July 18 interview that she wanted the administration to probe her son's death as thoroughly as possible. In her view, the Florida jury had failed her son in not recognizing that "this was a teenager just trying to get home," not some burglar or other lawbreaker whose actions may have warranted an intervention. "This is sending out a terrible message to young teenagers," she warned, with a somber Tracy Martin seated at her side.[6]

Later that evening, Obama met with senior aides to discuss the developing media narrative and public expectations following the July 13 verdict. He had talked with friends and family members about the case, and Sharpton and others were pressing him for a more robust response to what many believed to be a miscarriage of justice.

The following afternoon during a White House press conference, the president elaborated on his statement of a few days earlier, commending the parents of Trayvon Martin for their "incredible grace and dignity" and positing that the slain youth "could have been me thirty-five years ago." He went on to describe Black experiences, including his own, with racial profiling and how many African Americans viewed the Florida case on a historical continuum of "racial disparities in the application of our criminal laws—everything from the death penalty to enforcement of our drug laws." In acknowledging that young Black men were overrepresented among perpetrators, victims, and those convicted of violent crimes, Obama emphasized that Black people tended to place such statistics in a historical context and view them through the lens of their lived reality of poverty, racial discrimination, violent environmental conditions, and resultant communal dysfunction.

To address some of the issues bound up in the Martin case, Obama called for the Justice Department to work with state and local officials to provide better training for law enforcement agencies in order to mitigate the distrust that many in the public harbored toward the police. He also called for a reexamination of Stand Your Ground laws and other policies that encouraged the kind of conflict that had led to Trayvon Martin's death. Additionally, he supported a "long-term project" to "bolster and reinforce our African American boys," an endeavor that he had discussed several times with his wife, Michelle. With an optimistic flourish, Obama ended his statement by stressing that race relations were improving with every new generation, even if the United States was not yet a "post-racial society." He challenged other leaders "to encourage the better angels of our nature, as opposed to using these episodes to heighten divisions."[7]

The president's follow-up statement of July 19 received more favorable reviews than his earlier comments on the verdict. Illustratively, Anthea Butler, a professor of religion at the University of Pennsylvania, called Obama's commentary a " 'balm in Gilead' that will help many," and CBC chair Marcia Fudge deemed it courageous enough to make her proud. Sybrina Fulton and Tracy Martin issued a message of appreciation for the public support that they had received, with special gratitude directed toward the White House. "President Obama sees himself in Trayvon and identifies with him," the parents stated approvingly. "This is a beautiful tribute to our boy." Despite such reactions, the president's words did not allay the anger of those who viewed the Florida ruling as an insufferable affront. A host of artists—including Rod Stewart, Madonna, Stevie Wonder, Jay-Z, Kanye West, and Rihanna—endorsed a proposed boycott of the Sunshine State, resolving not to perform there unless its Stand Your Ground law was overturned. African American public opinion was almost entirely on the side of these celebrity protesters, with 86 percent of those polled expressing disapproval of the not-guilty verdict, compared with only 31 percent of whites who disagreed with the court's finding. Announced in February 2015, the Justice Department's decision to not pursue federal charges due to insufficient evidence of a racial motivation behind the fatal shooting hardly calmed matters, though Holder did disclose plans to ask Congress to lower the evidentiary threshold for prosecuting civil rights cases.[8]

Resentment and anger over the Trayvon Martin tragedy and the failure to convict Zimmerman simmered for years and was stoked further by a number of widely reported killings of Black men and boys by law enforcement officials and others during the remainder of the Obama presidency. The Martin case was singular in its public resonance mostly because so many people could see their own children in the biography of the slain teenager. In an era of cyberbullying, school shootings, mass incarceration, and epidemic drug addiction, Trayvon was anybody's son, everybody's child, just trying to get home. And the deadly randomness of Trayvon's encounter with George Zimmerman was eminently relatable. Whether on the way to or from work, school, or play, many struggled with the gnawing possibility that they could be victimized, however arbitrarily and undeserved, at any time by violent people acting on stereotyped profiles and a warped sense of mission. Though the likelihood of victimization might be low in most contexts, the sheer possibility was still terrifying and aroused a consuming, generalized fear across some communities. Thus, beyond being a child caught in the cross hairs of an ill-intentioned adult, Trayvon was a sympathetic stand-in for anyone who had ever looked over their shoulder at night, hoping not to catch a glimpse of a stranger trailing too closely behind them.

Several months before the jury verdict in the Zimmerman trial, another incident involving the death of a young person seized national attention. Fifteen-year-old Hadiya Pendleton lived in Chicago, attended King College Prep High School, located only a mile from the Obamas' home in the city, and was a majorette in the band. Similar to Trayvon Martin, she was a typical twenty-first-century teenager: she liked Fig Newtons, was style-conscious about her lip gloss, and enjoyed spending time with friends. Hadiya had been to Washington, DC, recently with a group of her classmates, having been invited to perform at the 2013 inauguration. It had been a high point in her young life and gave her much to talk about when she returned to the Windy City. Unfortunately, her budding journey through adolescence was derailed by a case of mistaken identity, an epidemic of gang violence, and the ready availability of firearms in the nation's third-largest metropolis. On January 29, Hadiya, while surrounded by friends in Harsh Park in the Kenwood neighborhood, was shot by 18-year-old Michael Ward, who had mistaken the group for gang members. Two others were wounded in the gunfire; Hadiya perished from her injuries.

The details of Hadiya Pendleton's death were of the sort that aroused as much bewilderment and fury as they did agony and despair. To be sure, Chicago was plagued by such violence, and Hadiya was only one of the forty people killed that month, making it the deadliest January in the city in more than a decade. Rahm Emanuel, formerly the White House chief of staff, had been mayor since May 2011 but had proved incapable of reversing the escalating trend in gun deaths and subsequently lost much of the confidence of Black residents in particular. During his first full year in office in 2012, Chicago had endured more than 500 homicides, making it the murder capital of the country. Nationally, Black children and teenagers comprised 45 percent of the young people who lost their lives to gun violence in 2008 and 2009, though they made up only 15 percent of the youth population. During those same years, gunfire claimed more lives of African American males between the ages of 15 and 19 than any other cause. In 2011, almost 1,700 Black people under 22 years of age were killed in the United States, compared with the 469 Americans who died during military service in Afghanistan that year. Against this dismal background, the upward, admirable trajectory of Hadiya's experiences made her abbreviated life all the more tormenting to both her loved ones and sympathetic strangers alike. Perhaps most distressing, the girl's murder and so many others like it stirred no national urgency or coordinated sense of purpose that could be channeled toward addressing the lethal mix of guns, gangs, drugs, poverty, and hopelessness that made such killings disturbingly frequent.

Word of the Chicago tragedy reached Michelle Obama in the White House, prompting her to contact the family and to request to attend Hadiya's funeral. The First Lady met privately with several of Hadiya's relatives and classmates just prior to the February 9 service, consoling the grieving attendees and personalizing the handwritten message that her husband had sent expressing condolences and promising to "work as hard as we can to end this senseless violence." To spur legislative movement on gun control, President Obama invited the slain girl's parents, Nathaniel Pendleton and Cleopatra Cowley, to his State of the Union address in early February, recognizing them in his speech and demanding congressional action on firearms. The president also met privately with them to express his sympathy. In common with many other parents, the Obamas could feel the dispiriting sadness pulsating through Hadiya's premature death and funeral. She had died almost literally outside of their Chicago home and at only 15, almost the same age as their daughter Malia.[9]

A month before Hadiya's passing, the president had traveled to Newtown, Connecticut, to meet with the parents of almost two dozen first-graders who had been gunned down in a school massacre. He wept openly as the cascading parental grief soaked him in sorrow, and he would later remember the mass killing as the worst day of his presidency. Notwithstanding these ghastly atrocities and heartrending memorials, which became morose fixtures of the Obama years in the White House, federal lawmakers refused to pass gun reform laws. Lobbying organizations such as the National Rifle Association, which exercised considerable electoral muscle in local, state, and federal elections, brooked no retreat from an expansive reading of the Second Amendment. Risking a bludgeoning in fundraising and attack ads, it was indeed a rare GOP legislator—or even Democrat in some southern and western states—who dared cross the group and its pro-gun agenda. Thus, for all his power to wage war or to pursue peace abroad, Obama found the Congress immovable in its opposition to even minor measures that might curb gun violence and limit access to firearms. Subsequently, he and the First Lady were reduced to sending prayers and giving hugs to mourning survivors in lieu of the passage and implementation of laws that might have halted some of the gunfire and trauma.[10]

In the wake of the climbing death toll in Chicago, Jesse Jackson Sr. publicly counseled Obama to return to his hometown in order to help remedy the crisis of gun violence that had gripped the city. As part of a larger push to inspire legislative action, the president visited the beleaguered metropolis on February 15. During a speech, he implored Congress to pass a bill that required universal background checks for gun buyers and that banned assault-style rifles and high-capacity magazines. "There was something profound and uniquely heart-breaking and tragic about a group of 6-year-olds being killed," Obama told an audience at Hyde Park Academy High School. "But last year there were 443 murders with a firearm on the streets of this city and 65 of those victims were 18 and under; so that's the equivalent of a Newtown every four months." The fear and frustration sparked by this violent status quo was dramatized by a protest of Chicago morticians in March 2013. Driving their hearses slowly through the city for all to see, the funeral home directors sought to graphically convey the message that, as one lamented, "We're burying too many of our young people." In April, Michelle Obama returned to the city to further advocate for a gun-control bill, but it would soon die in the US Senate. During her visit with high school students, she was alarmed to find so many of them preoccupied with the possibility of untimely death, either their own or someone else's.[11]

The number of murders in Chicago actually dropped substantially over the next two years. An improving economy and a declining national crime rate were partially responsible for the positive trend, though the lower numbers proved unsustainable as homicides in Chicago spiked again in the last year of the Obama presidency. Left with only his office pen, Obama did sign an executive order in January 2016 that mandated that gun sellers acquire a federal license and subject potential buyers to background checks, regardless of the location of the sale. Aside from this measure, his legacy and that of the Congress and the country during this period were little more than rhetorical in terms of gun reform.[12]

Something was rotten in the city of Ferguson, Missouri. Nestled in the northeastern section of St. Louis County, the municipality was first established as a depot on the North Missouri Railroad line before being incorporated as the town of Ferguson Station in 1894. During the twentieth century, it served as the headquarters of Emerson Electric Company and grew to a moderate size, though it remained largely in the shadow of its sprawling neighbor St. Louis to the south. As a middling settlement in a midwestern border state, there was nothing especially remarkable about Ferguson, with the exception of the racial metamorphosis that it underwent during the latter part of the twentieth century. Strictly segregated in a fashion that preserved white political, economic, and spatial supremacy, the city was less than 1 percent Black in 1970. Following the demolition of public housing in St. Louis, more Black people moved out into the nearby suburbs, resulting in a gradual transformation of the demography of those areas. By 1980, Ferguson was 14 percent Black; twenty years later, African Americans made up just over half of its residents. In 2010, Blacks accounted for 67 percent of the population of 21,203, with whites having declined to 29 percent of the inhabitants. Much of the demographic shift had resulted from whites moving back to a gentrifying St. Louis or to outer-ring suburbs as Blacks moved to inner-ring areas like Ferguson. This was a distinctly twenty-first-century version of racial segregation and white flight in which whitening central cities were surrounded by darkening suburbs that were encircled by even whiter exurbs.[13]

In this reshuffling of residents, neighborhoods, and geopolitical assumptions, power relations were much slower to change. In fact, Ferguson was a prime example of how patterns of racial privilege and exclusion can become engrained, regardless of where people live and work. Statistics tell part of the story of inequality and polarization. In 2014 when the national Black unemployment rate tapered off to less than 11 percent, Black people in Ferguson were contending with an estimated rate that approached 16 percent, while less than 7 percent of the city's white residents could not find jobs. Similarly, the estimated poverty rate among African Americans was almost three times the white rate of roughly 10 percent, a disparity that was also reflected in homeownership. In Ferguson, Black families were principally renters; 84 percent of households lived under leasing arrangements in 2010. White families were primarily homeowners, controlling almost half of the city's "owner-occupied housing units" despite collectively representing less than a third of the municipality's population. These disparities, in some form or another, were long-standing and were consistent with the racial inequities that could be found all over Missouri and the rest of the country. Like other locales, Ferguson was a product of its history, institutional dynamics, and migratory streams, and no one could reasonably expect it not to reflect these realities.[14]

What was also noteworthy about Ferguson were the systems of control and exploitation that held it together and perpetuated its racial order. The local government and affiliated agencies were demographically unrepresentative, repressive, and predatory in the starkest of ways. A substantial part of the city's revenues were raised through overzealous and discriminatory policing and judicial practices that disproportionately targeted African Americans. According to a 2013 report issued by the office of the Missouri attorney general, Ferguson police officers were almost two times as likely to stop and arrest Black drivers than white ones, even though the former were less likely to be found possessing contraband. Additionally, a US Justice Department investigation concluded in 2015 that local police personnel routinely violated the First and Fourth Amendments as evinced by their interference with the right to freedom of expression, their stopping and arresting of citizens without reasonable suspicion or probable cause, and their recurrent resort to excessive force. In abetting these constitutional transgressions, the Ferguson Municipal Court often levied inordinate fines for minor offenses and dispensed arrest warrants for those who would not or could not pay such expenses.[15]

The Justice Department inquiry uncovered clear evidence that police and municipal officials stereotyped and intentionally discriminated against Black residents of the city, handing down a version of justice that was indelibly tainted by racism and malice. Just as stunning as the bias itself was the racial configuration of the institutions that oversaw and perpetuated it. In 2014, Ferguson's Republican mayor, James Knowles III, was white, as were five of its six city council members, notwithstanding the fact that the municipality's population was two-thirds Black. The police force was even more racially skewed, with whites holding fifty positions on its fifty-three-member force.[16]

It is likely that this Jim Crow–style, midwestern-flavored colonialism would not have come to the attention of the Justice Department or the country more generally if there had not been a triggering incident that made Ferguson an international flashpoint. On August 9, 2014, around noon, Michael Brown, an 18-year-old Black youth, was shot to death in the middle of a public street by Darren Wilson, a white police officer. Details of the encounter would remain contested and unsettled across the varying accounts of eyewitnesses.

Wilson claimed that Brown had approached him and tried to take his service pistol, which resulted in a struggle. Dorian Johnson, an acquaintance of the teenager who was present during the confrontation, later stated that Wilson had initiated the melee, grabbing Brown by the throat before drawing his weapon. Johnson, along with other observers, also asserted that Brown's hands were raised in surrender when Wilson opened fire. What was clear from subsequent reports and inquiries was that the officer shot the teenager at least six times and from a distance too far to leave gunpowder burns on the victim's skin or clothing. To make matters worse, the police department and other responding agencies were in no rush to remove the teen's dead body from the center of Canfield Drive, allowing him to lie there only partially covered for four hours.[17]

The Saturday midday shooting and its immediate aftermath drew a crowd from the adjacent apartment complex and elsewhere. The flagrant nature of the killing—committed in the open air of a public thoroughfare—and the long delay in dignifying Brown's corpse with a timely examination and removal ignited passions. Curious and shocked bystanders eventually gave way to incensed demonstrators who took to the streets to demand an explanation for what had occurred along with an acknowledgment of responsibility. Over the next twenty-four hours, dozens of people were arrested on an array of charges that included assault, burglary, and theft. As video footage out of Ferguson illuminated the rolling disaster confronting local authorities, the Obama administration issued a statement on the White House website expressing "deepest condolences" for the family of Michael Brown and requesting that Americans honor him "through reflection and understanding." The message confirmed that the Justice Department was investigating the killing in tandem with Ferguson officials and was ready to "direct resources to the case as needed." The statement was the kind of measured, nonjudgmental offering that had become formulaic for the White House when faced with a troubling situation; a more forceful and substantive response would follow only when the crisis did not abate and threatened to consume the media cycle. In this case, the tensions and protests in Ferguson did not dissipate; instead, an escalation ensued.[18]

According to Valerie Jarrett, Obama, who had been vacationing in Martha's Vineyard when Ferguson began to spiral, was "horrified" by news reports of a boiling insurrection in a midwestern city. While the Trayvon Martin case had led to spirited demonstrations and high-decibel outrage across social media, it had not precipitated a civil conflagration that threatened to consume an entire municipality of tens of thousands of people. After his August 12 statement landed with a thud and quickly floated off into the White House archives, Obama decided to deliver televised remarks from Massachusetts two days later. This time, he was more urgent and specific in his plans for action as Ferguson erupted in flames.

The president reaffirmed that the Justice Department had launched an independent investigation into the killing of Michael Brown and was consulting with local authorities to ensure the safety of peaceful protests. He called for a transparent investigation by Ferguson officials and mentioned that he had expressed concerns about the heightening conflict to Gov. Jay Nixon, who was planning a visit to the city. Obama spoke sympathetically about the slain teenager and his death under "heartbreaking and tragic circumstances." And somewhat predictably, the president did his trademark tightrope walk, taking to the high wire to carefully tread the chasm between the protesters and the police. "There is never an excuse for violence against police, or for those who would use this tragedy as a cover for vandalism or looting," he emphatically stated, adding, "there's also no excuse for police to use excessive force against peaceful protests, or to throw protesters in jail for lawfully exercising their First Amendment rights." For good measure, Attorney General Holder echoed Obama's comments in a separate statement, adding that he was troubled by the use of military armaments and vehicles by the Ferguson Police Department (FPD) to counter public demonstrations.[19]

The president's incremental approach to the unfolding emergency was prudent, given the known information and variables. It

was consistent with a managerial style that valued strategic movement and consensus-building, with any necessary adjustments being
rooted squarely in practicality and realizable objectives. According to
one poll, 60 percent of African American respondents agreed with
Obama's handling of the Ferguson situation, well above the 35 percent
of whites who approved. Moderate and steady, his statecraft did not,
of course, satisfy everyone, especially those who equated leadership
with swift and decisive action.

Ja'Mal Green, a Chicago-based activist affiliated with the Black
Lives Matter movement, probably captured the sentiments of many
in his generational cohort when he critiqued Obama's middle-of-the-
road gestures toward Ferguson police officials and demonstrators.
"He is trying to walk a neutral line and he wants to please both
sides," Green told a reporter. "You need to pick your time when you
fight for home or you'll just have everybody hate you." Sherrilyn Ifill,
president of the NAACP Legal Defense Fund, wanted the administration to lead an effort to improve the training of police officers in
order to avoid incidents like the Ferguson tragedy, but she did not
believe that waiting for the president to speak on matters of race was
itself a necessary end. "I think we have to be careful," she warned,
"we don't become addicted to the habit of saying, 'what will President Obama say.'" Al Sharpton, who had become a confidant of the
president, deemed some of the criticism of Obama "well-intentioned"
but understood his hesitancy to speak too candidly about ongoing
investigations. During the Ferguson crisis, the reverend served as an
unofficial but vital liaison between the Brown family, community
leaders, and the White House, conveying messages that facilitated
coordination of local and federal planning.[20]

Following Obama's televised statement, Gov. Nixon assigned the
state highway patrol to guard duty in Ferguson. The troopers replaced
the local police department, which had further lost the confidence of
the populace by approaching protesters with military weaponry, teargas canisters, and rounds of rubber bullets, images that were broad-
cast around the world and that kindled protests from Miami to Los

Angeles. Capt. Ronald S. Johnson, an African American officer in the Missouri Highway Patrol, was tasked with pursuing a new strategy of conciliation. He ordered his contingent to remove their teargas masks to avoid the appearance of imminent offensive action, and he marched and mingled with protesters, listening to their versions of events.

Notwithstanding Johnson's efforts, violence broke out again on Sunday evening, August 17. Police and protesters exchanged volleys, the former—including the state patrol and city of St. Louis officers—firing teargas and some of the latter responding with Molotov cocktails. The new round of hostilities was in part provoked by the FPD, which had recently released video purporting to show Michael Brown stealing merchandise from a convenience store minutes before his death. The circulated footage was denounced as a smear by the Brown family and others who felt that it hardly justified the teenager's killing, especially since Wilson could not have known about it before he confronted Brown. As groups of predominantly Black protesters raged against the perceived abuses of the city's government and police force, approximately fifty white demonstrators clustered near Busch Stadium in downtown St. Louis. Dressed in blue shirts that read "I stand by you, Darren Wilson," their vigil on behalf of the man who had killed Michael Brown was a vivid reminder of how divided the county—and indeed, the country—was over issues of race, policing, and justice.[21]

In the wake of these outbursts of violence, Obama and the Justice Department increased pressure on Ferguson officials while simultaneously reaching out further to the Black community there and elsewhere. The FBI dispatched forty agents across the neighborhood near the site of Michael Brown's death to interview witnesses and collect information. At the request of the teenager's family, Holder ordered another autopsy, this time performed by a federal medical examiner. On Monday, Obama announced that he was sending the attorney general to Ferguson later in the week, a move that was applauded by many of the 1,000 Black civil rights leaders, community activists, and others with whom Holder and Jarrett had held conference calls during the previous several days. The president also previewed an upcoming White House evaluation of the practice of outfitting local police departments with military-style weapons and equipment, a practice that had accelerated after the September 11 attacks but had not been closely tracked or scrutinized for effectiveness or accountability. Ever aware that he faced several constituencies and sometimes conflicting interests when he spoke publicly, Obama attempted to smooth the ground for Holder's visit with empathetic signals directed toward both the African American community and law enforcement. He acknowledged discriminatory treatment of Black people by the criminal justice system that needed to be addressed, along with the imperative that better police training be prioritized. He also pointed out the dangers of police work and that an attack on law officers "only serves to raise tensions and stir chaos." Just before his trip to Ferguson, Holder in a *St. Louis Post-Dispatch* column reiterated the president's remarks, defending the right to peacefully protest while "condemning actions of looters, vandals and others seeking to inflame tensions and sow discord."[22]

Holder's time in Ferguson was brief but impactful. In addition to connecting with Captain Johnson and members of the FBI and Justice Department on the ground, he interacted with local residents to hear their concerns. One of his most important meetings was with the teen's parents, Michael Brown Sr. and Lezley McSpadden; in a reverential gesture, the attorney general journeyed to the site of their son's death. Holder's presence in Ferguson was both symbolic and therapeutic. Conflicts between protesters and the police were deescalating, calming down in frequency and belligerence. Furthermore, some understood Holder's appearance in the city as a direct stand-in for Obama. "Having the attorney general visit the site of an ongoing investigation is extra rare," explained Cornell William Brooks, the national NAACP president. "The U.S. government's pursuit of justice for this family is huge." Holder, conscious of the significance of his visible involvement in the affairs of the troubled city, left with a flourish, one that Obama would hardly have matched under the circumstances. "I am the attorney general of the United States," he informed a group of college students. "But I am also a Black man."[23]

Back in Washington, DC, Holder on September 4 announced the start of an investigation into the FPD, which would be separate from the various inquiries into the killing of Michael Brown. During his encounters with Black residents in Ferguson, he had heard enough about discriminatory municipal policies and practices to warrant a closer look. Although Obama never made his way to the city, he comprehended the importance of developments there to the arc of his presidency. In a speech before the UN General Assembly on September 24, he referenced the killing of Michael Brown as an indication of continuing "racial and ethnic tensions" in the country. "I realize that America's critics will be quick to point out that at times we too have failed to live up to our ideals, that America has plenty of problems within our own borders," the president conceded. "This is true."[24]

After two months of tense calm, Ferguson exploded again on November 24 when a grand jury composed of nine whites and three Blacks declined to indict Darren Wilson for the killing of Michael Brown. Some demonstrators took to the streets peacefully, blocking traffic on Interstate 44 and demanding justice. Others set businesses and police cars alight and were not cowed by the arrival of 2,200 National Guardsmen or the plumes of teargas that polluted the night air. Fearing a contagion of rebellion, the St. Louis Lambert International Airport forbade the landing of incoming planes, and area school districts announced the cancellation of classes for the following day. News of the jury decision fueled protests across the country as people took to the streets of St. Louis, Philadelphia, Oakland, Cleveland, and other cities. When daylight broke again over Ferguson, sixty-one people had been arrested, many charged with trespassing and burglary. At least eighteen individuals were treated for injuries at local hospitals.

In a late evening statement from the White House briefing room, the president called on citizens to respect the grand jury's judgment, reminding listeners that the country was based on the rule of law. He went on to acknowledge that the decision had disappointed some, yet he expressed optimism over how far the nation had come in terms of race relations. His upbeat tone, however, was not without more somber notes. "But what is also true," he maintained as fiery images of Ferguson dominated the night's news cycle, "is that there are still problems, and communities of color aren't just making these problems up." In a separate communication, Holder stressed that his department's investigations into Michael Brown's death and questionable police practices were ongoing and independent of local inquiries. He, too, urged protesters to not resort to violence and for law enforcement officials to respect peaceful demonstrations, sentiments repeated in a statement issued by the crestfallen Brown family. Local protests during the next evening were less tumultuous and confrontational, despite scattered hotspots around the country. Nonetheless, images of the burning city of Ferguson were now emblazoned in the popular consciousness, epitomized by widely circulated videos of protesters chanting "Hands Up, Don't Shoot," words that became a rallying cry against police misconduct across the nation.[25]

In January 2015, the Justice Department announced that it had not managed to gather sufficient evidence to charge Darren Wilson with a crime related to the killing of Michael Brown, given the high standards of proof required to justify federal indictments and prosecutions in such cases. The decision was anticlimactic; few had realistically expected Wilson, who had resigned from the FPD, to be federally charged. Even with compelling evidence and credible eyewitnesses, it is notoriously difficult to prosecute police officers in any US court, let alone in instances like this one in which so many conflicting accounts and lingering questions still remained.

In March, the Justice Department's investigation of police abuses in Ferguson did bear fruit with the release of a report uncovering institutionalized and systemic discrimination against Black residents of the city. As mentioned above, the police department and the courts were shown to have disproportionately preyed on local African Americans to finance the municipal budget, resulting in dubious arrests and exorbitant fines for often minor offenses. The municipal administration and its agencies had also violated an array of constitutional amendments related to excessive use of force, unwarranted stops and searches, and suppression of free speech rights. During a March 6 town hall at historically Black Benedict College in Columbia, South Carolina, the president was candid about the findings, describing the judicial and policing practices of Ferguson as an "oppressive and abusive situation" that would need to be addressed or else the city would face federal litigation. Holder, who had traveled to South Carolina with Obama, deemed the conclusions of the investigation "appalling" and promised that his department was "prepared to use all of the powers that we have . . . to ensure that the situation changes there," including the possible disbanding of the FPD.[26]

Negotiations over a settlement agreement between the federal government and Ferguson officials began after the investigation's findings were released and continued into the next year. By this time, the Justice Department under Holder had launched similar probes into at least twenty other municipalities and police departments suspected of various forms of misconduct and was overseeing no fewer than fourteen consent decrees aimed at reforming law enforcement procedures and practices. In the Ferguson case, Holder pressed for a number of reforms, including prohibiting arrests without probable cause; curbing the unjustified employment of weapons such as stun guns, batons, and pepper spray; forbidding retaliation against citizens for "exercising their right to witness, observe, record, comment on, or protest police activity"; and requiring the use of body-worn and in-car cameras by police personnel. Additionally, the police department would be mandated to provide its services "free from unlawful bias or discrimination," to better train officers and review their performance, and to implement a community-engagement plan to enhance trust and cooperation between law enforcement agencies and citizens. The proposed agreement further directed the Ferguson Municipal Court to prioritize public safety over generating revenue. Such a change in mission and purpose would require the institution to cease imposing fines on the indigent and those who failed to appear for a court date, to make policies more transparent, and to initiate a comprehensive amnesty program designed to eliminate or reduce existing and pending unjust legal and financial burdens against defendants. Finally, the Justice Department's plan provided for the appointment of an independent monitor to supervise the enactment and progression of the agreement.[27]

On February 9, 2016, the Ferguson City Council balked. In a 6-0 vote, the members repudiated the agreement, claiming that it was too expensive and requesting new terms. Within twenty-four hours, the Justice Department filed a civil rights lawsuit against the city, highlighting its well-documented record of constitutional violations and other misdeeds. At a press conference, Attorney General Loretta Lynch confirmed the resolve of the US government to hold the city accountable for its criminal justice practices. Sensing an expensive, losing fight against federal authorities, the unity of the city council started to crack. On March 14, the Justice Department sent a memo to state court administrators across the country advising them to consider alternatives to incarceration for indigent defendants unable to pay fines. "The consequences of the criminalization of poverty are not only harmful," Lynch declared in a statement, "they are far-reaching." While the communiqué did not single out the Ferguson abuses, it did make clear that the government stood ready to pursue cases against state officials and agencies whose overreliance on fines and imprisonment violated federal law. Perhaps taking the memo as yet another sign of the futility of their resistance, the Ferguson council members relented and unanimously endorsed the consent decree the following day.[28]

The lessons of Ferguson, as well as progress toward racial reconciliation and equity, were hard won and complicated. The nearly all-white police department, which had been such a potent symbol of repression and exclusion, hired its first African American chief in May 2016 and gradually began to diversify its ranks. While Mayor

James Knowles won reelection in 2017, the city council became more reflective of the local population, with three Black members in its ranks in 2019. By that time, a nine-member Civilian Review Board had been established to handle complaints alleging police misconduct, and a Human Rights Commission, appointed by the mayor and city council, was empaneled to investigate, among other things, claims of discrimination in housing, employment, and public accommodations. These reforms amounted to a kind of progress but of a limited sort. Racial disparities in wealth, homeownership, and employment remained, as did legacies of segregation and communal atrophy. Of US cities with 10,000 or more residents, Ferguson led the country in the proportion of Black men between the ages of 25 and 54 who were missing from daily life, resulting in a ratio of 60 Black men to every 100 Black women in that age cohort. Three years after the death of Michael Brown, familiar patterns of white flight continued, with African Americans becoming an even larger percentage of the population. Still haunted by the events of 2014, the small midwestern city, with one foot in a tragic past and the other striding toward an uncertain future, plodded along the narrow path that its history and geography had carved between the metropolis of St. Louis and the outlying exurbs.[29]

For the Obama administration, Ferguson was a unique case study in crisis management. This racial convulsion was very different from the Gates ruckus in 2009 or the Sherrod brouhaha of 2010. Even the Trayvon Martin case was distinct from Ferguson, insofar as the boy's death had not resulted in burning cities or any racialized taking of sides in regard to which constituencies supported or opposed the lethal methods of the police. To a much greater degree than those episodes, the political heat radiating from Ferguson could be readily felt at the White House, and its implications were as clear as the midnight flames that lashed the Missouri sky. The racial profiling, random stops, bogus courts, ridiculous fines, and lily-white police force—it had all gone too far. And with the public killing of a Black teenager in the middle of a street in a Black neighborhood, a critical mass of people were no longer content with waiting for the slow-turning wheels of the law to address long-standing municipal malfeasance and police aggression. To be sure, there were many places like Ferguson with long, sordid histories of racial discrimination and disfranchisement that had lasted into the present, and any of them could have exploded after a precipitating tragedy or indignity. But it turned out to be Ferguson, Missouri, that blew up during Obama's watch, and thus it was his crisis to address.

Overall, the president was true to form: initially cautious yet incrementally amplifying his administration's response as the first reaction proved insufficient. In this case, his more active agenda concerning criminal justice merged with a growing willingness to take on matters of race, leading to a more substantive policy and executive response than would have likely been the case during his first term in office. The quick launch of an investigation into the Michael Brown killing and police abuses, dramatized by Holder's visit and Obama's more frank rhetoric, set a tone of urgency and determination. Furthermore, the forceful pursuit of consent decrees in Ferguson and elsewhere, coupled with the administration's other efforts toward criminal justice reform, projected a seriousness of effort concerning racial justice that many had not believed Obama capable of until actually witnessing it. Ferguson was an important battle in the administration's broader struggle for deep cultural, institutional, and structural change in US life regarding issues of race. As became more starkly evident over time, the president had largely been spared the kind of attention-focusing, regional-turned-national eruptions that Ferguson ended up being. His fortunes, as well as those of the country, noticeably shifted during his second term.

Attorney General Loretta Lynch had a jarring first week on her new job. In fact, her welcome was a blast of flames, teargas, and sirens from a smoldering metropolis that was almost visible from her DC office in the Robert F. Kennedy Department of Justice Building. Just moments after she was sworn in to lead the agency on April 27, 2015,

President Obama met with Lynch to discuss a meltdown in Balti-more, Maryland, some forty miles away. On April 12, Freddie Gray, a 25-year-old African American man, had been arrested by police and placed in the back of a van. It was unclear why he was detained, though officers at the scene later claimed that he had tried to flee after making eye contact and that he was discovered to be carrying a knife. In any event, Gray, fitted with handcuffs and leg shackles, was not secured in the van with a seat belt in accordance with Baltimore Police Department (BPD) policy. When Gray was retrieved from the van less than an hour later, he was suffering from injuries reminiscent of a devastating car crash. His spinal cord was nearly severed and his voice box smashed. News of the arrest and the grave damage to Gray spread, and some commentators surmised that he had been subjected to a "rough ride": a reckless form of extralegal punishment meted out to suspects being transported by police. If that was indeed the case, it was not the first time a captive passenger had faced mortal danger in BPD custody. In separate incidents in 2004 and 2005, two men were critically wounded during police van rides. Similar to Gray, both men were Black and suffered varying degrees of paralysis. Unlike him, they both survived; Gray lapsed into a coma and died on April 19.

Over the next two weeks, outrage over Gray's arrest and death propelled protests in Baltimore and elsewhere. For the first time since 1968, the National Guard was called out to stabilize the city after a particularly eventful night of demonstrations on April 27—the day of Gray's funeral—that resulted in burning buildings, incinerated cars, looting, arrests, and injuries. By this juncture, the urban terrain resembled a veritable war zone with the attendant military presence and destruction. Baltimore, a predominantly African American city, had a Black mayor, state's attorney, and city council president. Its police commissioner, Anthony W. Batts, was also Black, as were al-most half of the force's officers. These racial dynamics, however, did not quell the mounting pressure on local and state officials to act, especially after the various violations of police protocol during the

Gray arrest were disclosed to the public. On May 1, the city of Baltimore's state's attorney, Marilyn Mosby, announced charges against six officers—three Black and three white—involved in Gray's arrest and death. Three weeks later, grand jury proceedings led to indictments ranging from illegal arrest and assault to involuntary manslaughter and murder. Over the next year, however, the government's case fell apart mostly due to a prosecutorial inability to marshal evidence and construct a case that could secure convictions. Mosby accused the BPD of obstructing her investigation, an explanation that likely satisfied few.[30]

Attorney General Lynch visited the city days after Mosby announced her intention to pursue charges against the officers involved in the Gray affair. During her stay, she met with members of the deceased man's family, Mayor Stephanie Rawlings-Blake, law enforcement officials, and community leaders. After returning to Washington, Lynch launched an investigation into possible patterns of police misconduct in Baltimore. At least in this matter, there was plenty of evidence to make a case. Since 2011, more than a hundred individuals had won judgments or settlements involving allegations of police brutality and civil rights abuses. During these years, the city of Baltimore paid approximately $5.7 million to satisfy claims against BPD officers accused of beating suspects. If anything, there seemed to be too much evidence of ongoing police malfeasance, which raised the question of why it had been allowed to go unchecked for so long.

The findings of the Justice Department's investigation were released in August 2016, less than a month after Mosby dropped the last charges against the officers in the Gray case. The report's conclusions were as disturbing as anything that the agency had found in its probes of metropolitan police departments around the country. The uncovered illegalities and malpractice included unconstitutional stops, searches, and arrests that disproportionately targeted African Americans; excessive use of force against citizens, including people with mental disabilities, juveniles, and nonthreatening individuals;

and a failure to implement policies that enhanced training, accountability, data collection and analysis, and community policing strategies. Rather than resist the conclusions and recommendations of the
Justice Department, the BPD entered into a consent decree in January 2017 that was much the same as the one that the city council of
Ferguson finally had accepted a year earlier. The agreement called for,
among other things, an end to illegal stops and arrests, better systems
of accountability, the enactment of measures to build community
trust, and oversight of reform efforts by an independent monitor.[31]

Baltimore was not simply an East Coast version of Ferguson. The
port city was thirty times more populous, its government and many
of its affiliated agencies were run by African Americans, and its police
force was 48 percent Black. However, Baltimore was very much like
Ferguson in terms of its municipal culture, which institutionalized
racial bias, unconstitutional practices, and police impunity. Unfortunately, the two cities were not alone in regard to the prevalence of
civil rights violations and police misconduct. By the end of Obama's
two terms in office, an overly long list of Black individuals were
killed under wrongful or otherwise questionable pretenses by law
enforcement officers. Each occurrence spurred new demonstrations
of varying intensity and duration, as well as pressure on the administration to address the deadly pattern with substantive policies and
concrete actions.

The Midwest was the scene of several such incidents. In April 2014,
Dontre Hamilton, a 31-year-old Milwaukee man, was shot 14 times
by Officer Christopher Manney, who had responded to a complaint
about a man sleeping in a public park. Six months later, 17-year-
old Laquan McDonald was killed by Chicago policeman Jason Van
Dyke. A video recording of the encounter showed the teenager, who
was apparently holding a small knife, walking away from approaching law enforcement officers; Van Dyke proceeded to shoot him 16
times. Cleveland, with a population that was more than 50 percent
Black, had been the site of two police killings that appalled many
who heard about them. In November 2012, Timothy Russell and

Malissa Williams were killed after allegedly leading local police on a twenty-two-mile, high-speed car chase. The pair died in a barrage of 137 bullets, 49 of which were fired by Officer Michael Brelo, who distinguished himself from his colleagues by standing on the hood of the car and firing repeatedly at the occupants through the windshield. Perhaps most tragic of all, 12-year-old Tamir Rice was shot to death by Officer Timothy Loehmann in November 2014 as the boy played with a pellet gun near a recreation center. Video revealed that Rice was shot dead within three seconds of the arrival of the police car, hardly enough time for him to receive an order, let alone to comply with it. Adding insult to injury, the city of Cleveland filed a posthumous claim against the boy's estate to recoup $500 for the cost of his ultimately futile ride in an ambulance.[32]

Three incidents in northern and southern states in 2014 and 2015 became causes célèbres in the growing public outcry over the deaths of unarmed African Americans while either in confrontations with or in the custody of police officers. In July 2014, Eric Garner, a 43-year-old father, was choked to death on the streets of Staten Island while being arrested for selling loose cigarettes. His last words, "I can't breathe," were caught on a widely distributed video of the killing and became part of the cultural lexicon of activists protesting police violence nationwide. In April of the following year, Walter Scott was shot five times from behind as he fled on foot during a traffic stop in Charleston, South Carolina. Officer Michael Slager initially claimed that he had killed Scott in self-defense, but a cellphone video made by a bystander captured the policeman firing at the unarmed man's back and subsequently placing his stun gun next to the slain man's body. In July, Sandra Bland was stopped for failing to activate a turn signal while changing lanes in Prairie View, Texas. State trooper Brian Encinia saw fit to arrest the 28-year-old woman and have her confined to the Waller County jail, where she was found hanged to death in her cell three days later. Attorney General Lynch summarized a common sentiment when she stated in an interview that the incident "highlights the concern of many in the Black community that a routine

stop for many of the members of the Black community is not handled
with the same professionalism and courtesy that other people may
get from the police." Bland's death was officially ruled a suicide, a
conclusion that some of her friends and family members contested.[33]

In most of the instances described above, no one was ever convicted for the killings. In relation to the deaths of Michael Brown,
Dontre Hamilton, Tamir Rice, Eric Garner, and Sandra Bland, no
indictments were issued by grand juries, and subsequent federal investigations did not result in charges against the officers involved.
Several of the cases did lead to civil litigation that was resolved with
multimillion-dollar settlements. For example, the city of Cleveland
settled a lawsuit in the Rice killing for $6 million, and New York City
agreed to pay $5.9 million to address a wrongful death claim filed by
the family of Eric Garner. These payments were the closest thing to
justice that came out of these tragedies. In some cases, the police officers involved remained employed long after the killings took place,
and police unions and some public officials went out of their way to
proclaim their innocence or to praise their lethal deeds.[34]

In a world more interconnected than ever before, news of the
US epidemic of police shootings, accompanied by a plethora of disturbing images, virally circled the globe and attracted unflattering
attention. Days after the killing of Michael Brown in the streets of
Ferguson, UN secretary-general Ban Ki-moon issued a statement
urging US authorities to respect the rights of protesters to peacefully
assemble and to express themselves in accordance with "U.S. and
international standards in dealing with demonstrators." A year later
during the aftermath of the killing of Freddie Gray, the UN Human
Rights Council endorsed a blistering report that included 348 recommendations for improving the human rights record of the United
States. Among other identified problem areas, the document suggested that US officials "continue to vigorously investigate recent cases
of alleged police-led human rights abuses against African-Americans
and seek to build improved relations and trust between U.S. law
enforcement and all communities around the U.S."[35]

To the chagrin of the White House and other official entities, in-dividual foreign governments also chided the country for its rampant police misconduct. In a holiday message on Twitter on December 24, 2014, Ayatollah Ali Khamenei, supreme leader of Iran, tweeted, "It's expected that followers of #Jesus follow him in his fight against arrogants and in his support for the oppressed. #BlackLivesMatter." If the Iranian message could be dismissed as opportunistic carping, the July 2016 travel warning issued by the Bahamian Ministry of Foreign Affairs and Immigration was more concerning. Having ob-served the "recent tensions in some American cities over shootings of young black males by police officers," the Caribbean nation advised its citizens—and especially "young males"—in the United States "to exercise extreme caution in affected cities in their interactions with the police." To a country and a president that were used to advocating for human rights around the world, the role reversal must have been both awkward and humbling.[36]

From the events of Ferguson and New York through developments in Baltimore and Cleveland, the Obama administration tried to keep up with the frenetic pace of police killings, fiery demonstrations, and heated public discourse, which increasingly controlled and saturated the media cycle. By the Ferguson upheaval of late 2014, the president and the Justice Department had learned that racial fissures in many communities were too deep and unstable to justify a wait-and-see, gradualist approach to every crisis. Such cautious pragmatism was beginning to look like resignation born of confusion and/or a lack of policy and principle, a leadership look that Obama could scarcely afford, nor was it natural to him. In sending Holder to Ferguson and Lynch to Baltimore, he indicated that criminal justice reform would be prioritized as a legacy-defining issue during his last two years in office, and he applied the resources of his administration accordingly. He also recalibrated his own pronouncements to signal the new shift in direction. Against the backdrop of consent degrees, adjustments to sentencing guidelines, burgeoning use of clemency powers, and other measures, Obama used his advocacy of criminal justice reform as a platform to focus the country's attention on the broader issues of institutional racism and systemic injustices.

In the wake of the Ferguson tremors in September 2014, the president pointed out how minority youths "feel targeted by law enforcement—guilty of walking while black or driving while black, judged by stereotypes that fuel fear and resentment and hopelessness." He also emphasized the "significant racial disparities" that continued to define drug sentences and the use of the death penalty, and a general sense that "the justice system treats people of different races unequally." When a Staten Island grand jury declined in December to indict the police officers who killed Eric Garner, Obama told a White House audience that on the issue of criminal justice reform, "I'm not interested in talk; I'm interested in action." Days later, he stated in a BET interview that his administration would shortly be implementing the recommendations of a new task force on policing and that he was prepared to deny funding to locales that resisted the suggested improvements.[37]

During his 2015 SOTU address, Obama, in search of a middle ground for purposes of cooperation, appealed to a new Republican Congress for action. "We may have different takes on the events of Ferguson and New York," he conceded in reference to the social turmoil surrounding the deaths of Michael Brown and Eric Garner. "But surely we can understand a father who fears his son can't walk home without being harassed. Surely we can understand the wife who won't rest until the police officer she married walks through the front door at the end of his shift." In calling for a bipartisan effort to fix the criminal justice system, the president undoubtedly understood that with full GOP control of the federal legislature and the next presidential campaign cycle about to start, congressional movement on any of his policy priorities was unlikely. Indeed, his statements were probably meant to prime the public for more executive action on criminal justice matters than to arouse the conscience of a Republican-led Congress.[38]

Obama's rhetoric in the midst of protests over the arrest and death of Freddie Gray in April pushed his criminal justice agenda further along vectors of race, government policy, and societal responsibility. The day after Gray's funeral, the president wove the strands together during a White House appearance, explicitly calling for transformative changes in American life and race relations.

> Without making any excuses for criminal activities that take place in these communities, what we also know is that if you have impoverished communities that have been stripped away of opportunity, where children are born into abject poverty; they've got parents—often because of substance-abuse problems or incarceration or lack of education themselves—can't do right by their kids; . . . it's more likely that those kids end up in jail or dead, than they go to college. In communities where there are no fathers who can provide guidance to young men; communities where there's no investment, and manufacturing has been stripped away; and drugs have flooded the community, and the drug industry ends up being the primary employer for a whole lot of folks—in those environments, if we think that we're just going to send the police to do the dirty work of containing the problems that arise there without as a nation and as a society saying what can we do to change those communities, to help lift up those communities and give those kids opportunity, then we're not going to solve this problem. . . .
>
> If we are serious about solving this problem, then we're going to not only have to help the police, we're going to have to think about what can we do—the rest of us—to make sure that we're providing early education to these kids; to make sure that we're reforming our criminal justice system so it's not just a pipeline from schools to prisons; so that we're not rendering men in these communities unemployable because of a felony record for a nonviolent drug offense; that we're making investments so that they can get the training they need to find jobs. . . .

But if we really want to solve the problem, if our society really wanted to solve the problem, we could. It's just it would require everybody saying this is important, this is significant— and that we don't just pay attention to these communities when a CVS burns, and we don't just pay attention when a young man gets shot or has his spine snapped. We're paying attention all the time because we consider those kids our kids, and we think they're important. And they shouldn't be living in poverty and violence.[39]

One journalist called Obama's statement, delivered during a joint press conference with Japanese prime minister Shinzo Abe, "the best public 15 minutes of his presidency." Considering the rhetorical trajectory of his two terms, no previous public commentary on race quite measured up to this one in candor, earnestness, or exasperation. It was not a new Obama, though it was a newly revealed President Obama. Readers could have gleaned some of this kind of thinking from his pre–White House ruminations, especially as chronicled in *Dreams from My Father* and, to a lesser degree, *The Audacity of Hope*. The observant journalist perhaps captured best the revelatory but true-to-previous-form character of the Rose Garden statement, noting, "Suddenly, [Obama] seemed exactly himself, power speaking truth."[40]

As president, Obama felt obligated both to support law enforcement officers and to do his best to deescalate violence and tensions between the police and citizens. It was all, of course, part of the tightrope walking that he was required to perform as chief executive, navigating conflicting constituencies with centrist prose and strategic pragmatism. Moreover, upholding police work and the rule of law was part of his job as he understood it, even as he sought to refashion the criminal justice system to be less criminal and more just. Notwithstanding criticism from various quarters that characterized him as not being supportive enough, Obama proved to be a stalwart ally of the law enforcement community. During his watch, the Justice Department generally backed an expansive interpretation of police discretion in Supreme Court cases, even in litigation involving excessive use of force. Throughout his presidency, Obama roundly condemned attacks on police personnel, including fatal shootings of multiple officers in separate incidents in New York, Dallas, and Baton Rouge by gunmen seeking vengeance for police-involved killings of Black men. Three weeks after fires raged in Baltimore, he signed a bill that created a system of national alerts to assist law enforcement officers in distress. On occasion, Obama could appear to pander too much to law enforcement interests, which sometimes provoked vocal reactions. Rather predictably, when the president used the term "thugs"—an expression that Mayor Rawlings-Blake also employed—to describe those whom he suspected of taking advantage of the anger in Baltimore to loot and cause additional mayhem, CBC members and others took him to task for applying the label too generally and for using a word that had negative racial connotations.[41]

In its attempts to improve policing practices, the Obama administration tried to collect better data to determine the scope and nature of the problems. Somewhat surprisingly, no federal policy required state and local law enforcement agencies to keep use-of-force statistics by race, and the official data that were available were gathered on a strictly voluntary basis by police departments. Some media organizations and public interest groups did create their own databases of traffic stops, police applications of deadly force, and lawsuit settlements. However, no government entity was charged with tracking police killings, particularly by race, and thus there was no definitive or even generally accepted tally of such fatalities. Nonetheless, the anecdotal data published in various reputable venues were troubling.

For example, between 2013 and 2015, about 30 percent of people killed by police nationally were Black, more than twice the African American proportion of the general population. Moreover, from 1999 to 2016, ninety Black people on average died in police chases annually, a rate that was twice as high as expected given their percentage of the US populace. In terms of financial compensation for law enforcement misconduct, the ten cities with the largest police departments paid a cumulative $1.02 billion between 2010 and 2014 to resolve complaints related to "beatings, shootings, and wrongful imprisonment." The amount paid in 2014 alone was $248.7 million. In April of that year, the Justice Department announced plans to create the National Initiative for Building Community Trust and Justice for the purpose of collecting and analyzing racial data on police stops, searches, arrests, and case outcomes. In October 2016, the department reported that it would begin the collection of information on police shootings and other use-of-force incidents the following year, using federal statistical models to assist local police departments in their efforts to track violent encounters.[42]

Several days after the body of Freddie Gray was interred in a Baltimore County cemetery, the report of the President's Task Force on 21st Century Policing was released. Obama had commissioned the document in the midst of the Ferguson crisis and had asked Philadelphia police commissioner Charles H. Ramsey and Professor Laurie O. Robinson of George Mason University to cochair the endeavor. The group offered dozens of recommendations to improve police work, many of which were designed to change both the culture and practice of policing. The more salient suggestions focused on building community trust, refining data collection techniques, more transparent policies, independent investigations of police use of force and deaths in police custody, and more consistent and standardized training of law enforcement personnel. Drawing on many of the report's ideas, subsequent consent decrees became the operational embodiments of the task force's work, providing the surest means for the federal government to influence and track changes in the policies and practices of law enforcement agencies. To signal the president's seriousness concerning the implementation of the task force's proposals, the Justice Department announced the availability of more than $100 million in grants to help police departments pursue projects related to the report's recommendations. To further demonstrate his commitment to meaningful criminal justice reform, Obama affirmed that he would end the transfer of military-style equipment, including grenade launchers, armored vehicles, and weaponized aircraft, to local police departments, a move aimed at diminishing antagonism between law enforcement and marginalized communities.[43]

As he contemplated the contours of a revamped criminal justice system, Obama became absorbed by possibilities to address the myriad obstacles that stymied the success of male youths of color and led many into early encounters with police, courts, and prisons. His inspiration and sense of urgency came from several sources, including the Trayvon Martin tragedy, Obama's own fatherless background, and successful mentoring programs in Chicago and elsewhere. To actuate these budding ideas, Obama launched the My Brother's Keeper (MBK) initiative in February 2014 during a White House ceremony. Among the audience of mostly African American and Hispanic young men were a number of prominent supporters and well-wishers, including Colin Powell, Magic Johnson, Rahm Emanuel, New York mayor Michael Bloomberg, and the parents of both Trayvon Martin and Jordan Davis, two Black teenagers who had been killed in separate incidents in Florida. MBK was billed as an interagency proposition that would first empanel a task force, led by White House Cabinet secretary Broderick D. Johnson, to come up with recommendations for action over the next ninety days. The group's specific charge was to identify "evidence-based" interventions that could address issues such as "access to early childhood supports; grade school literacy; pathways to college and a career . . . ; access to mentoring services and support networks; and interactions with the criminal justice system and violent crime." It was also tasked with recommending "improvements to Federal policies, regulations, and programs that apply to boys and young men of color."[44]

As he inaugurated the task force, Obama offered a more personal take on its mission. "I didn't have a dad in the house," he told the assembled young people and stakeholders. "I made excuses. Sometimes I sold myself short." Carefully balancing individual responsibility with an appeal for public empathy, he counseled the youngsters to expect to work hard for life's rewards, and he reminded other listeners that "some Americans . . . have had the odds stacked against them in uni-que ways that require unique solutions." Partnering with entities such as the Annie E. Casey Foundation, Bloomberg Philanthropies, and the Ford Foundation, the MBK initiative received funding commit-ments of $200 million spread over five years. Additional multimillion-dollar pledges from AT&T, the Emerson Collective and its Silicon Valley partners, and the Citi Foundation came in over the summer.[45]

The task force's ninety-day update came in late May. Unsurpris-ingly, its recommendations for assisting minority youths were heavy on education, mentoring, and criminal justice reform. The report called for better childcare, "pre-school for all," and initiatives to close gaps in reading proficiency by third grade. Schools with high dropout rates were singled out as warranting special attention, and the task force advanced a "cradle-to-college-to-career approach" to supporting youths of color that would supplant the more familiar school-to-prison pipeline, which doomed many boys to early failure and stig-matization. On the topic of criminal justice, the report suggested designating violence as a public health issue and addressing it as such. It also advocated reform of the juvenile justice system to allow for alternatives to incarceration and recommended removing obstacles to the reintegration of ex-offenders into community life. A year after the release of the task force's recommendations, Obama announced the establishment of a nonprofit organization, My Brother's Keeper Alliance, which, capitalized with $80 million in initial donor contri-butions, would take up the mantle of the original initiative. "This will remain a mission for me and for Michelle not just for the rest of my presidency but for the rest of my life," the president declared before a Bronx audience. Up to that point in his White House tenure, Obama had made virtually no public commitments regarding how he intended to spend his years beyond the presidency.[46]

As a testament to both its visibility and perceived momentum, MBK stirred other expectations that eventually powered critiques of its mission and shortcomings. Just as the president's task force re-leased its update in May 2014, a public petition, first appearing on the website of the African American Policy Forum, called for the White

House to also focus attention on the "complex lives of Black women and Black girls." Signed by more than 200 Black men, the document pointed out gender violence, wage discrimination, and exclusion from the professions as issues facing African American women that required as much of a governmental and societal response as troubles afflicting Black males. The petition also cautioned Obama about relegating the Black condition to a "culture of pathology" framework that held Black men largely responsible for their educational, unemployment, and carceral problems. The following month, a letter signed by more than a thousand women of color further pushed the demand to include women and girls in the administration's initiatives, though the signatories applauded MBK's "move beyond colorblind approaches to race-specific problems."[47]

Apparently—and somewhat inexplicably—caught off guard by the criticism, the White House convened a July meeting with a number of scholars, activists, and others who had taken exception to MBK and its male-focused agenda. Surrogates Valerie Jarrett, Broderick Johnson, and Al Sharpton attended the gathering and managed to smooth out some of the more jagged differences. One attendee, Melanie Campbell, chief executive of the Black Women's Roundtable, thought that the meeting was a "good start," though it undoubtedly raised expectations of subsequent action. In late September at a CBC awards dinner, the president rather defensively reminded the audience that he had two daughters and was thus sensitive to issues facing Black women. He also highlighted the existence of the White House Council on Women and Girls, which, in his words, "has for years been working on issues affecting women and girls of color." The reassurances seemed enough for the moment, and the intensity of the controversy subsided. In the end, it was another lesson learned publicly by the funambulist in chief, who had slipped on yet another shaky tightrope despite arguably the best of intentions.[48]

One of the by-products of the Trayvon Martin case and the widely reported killings of Black people by law enforcement officers was the rise of a national grassroots movement that became a mouthpiece for protests against these recurring tragedies. Initially consisting of spontaneous nodes of activism that sprang up in response to specific instances of police violence, increasingly interconnected and engaged networks of activists gave voice to elaborate agendas for addressing the larger racial, structural, and systemic issues behind perceived injustices. Similar to the Tea Party rebellion and the Occupy Wall Street demonstrations, protests against police killings took advantage of social media, especially Twitter and Facebook, to create dynamic information relays and vast webs of user-participants. Internet posts, videos, tweets, and hashtags launched emergent issues and events into cycles of viral reportage, instantaneously creating communities of sentiment and deep archives of commentaries and images. Groups with names like Black Youth Project, Hands Up United, and Ferguson Action took to the streets and smartphones to publicize developments as they occurred and to strategize responses. The swift ascent of these activist formations in the national discourse and even global consciousness was made possible by the seamless mating of ubiquitous twenty-first-century digital technology with youth militancy and idealism. Once mobilized, these social justice coalitions fueled iterative patterns of messaging, organizing, and protesting that amplified both the power of the media of choice and the urgency of the articulated demands.

The best-known group to materialize from this cluster of activism was the Black Lives Matter (BLM) movement, which gained its name and momentum when three Black women—Patrisse Cullors, Alicia Garza, and Opal Tometi—started using the Twitter hashtag #BlackLivesMatter in the wake of the acquittal of George Zimmerman. As an organizational expression of mass outrage and resistance, BLM was decentralized and diffused, with no recognized national leadership or codified agenda. Many activists believed that this arrangement was best; such openness seemingly allowed for the spontaneous development of local leadership and agendas. Also, if the movement remained dynamic and at least nominally democratic in structure and ethos, some thought that it could possibly deter external interests from co-opting its vital energies or steering its more prominent volunteers

toward the professional careerism so embedded in the nonprofit sector. Despite apprehensions and precautions, moneyed individuals and
groups did appear, including the George Soros and Ford Foundations.
Some prospective sponsors were genuinely drawn to the progressive
policy potential of BLM. Others imagined the movement's sprawling
branches of activists and workers as vehicles for their own projects.
From BLM's inception onward, conservative forces in media and
politics responded to it in a variety of ways, ranging from perverse
fascination to avowed revulsion. Most commonly, such critics wrote
off the movement as antipolice and racially chauvinistic because of its
demand for greater respect for Black life in the United States.

Regularly pressed to more clearly state their beliefs and objectives,
BLM activists produced successive documents and websites that were
probably meant to be less authoritative than simply indicative of
generally held opinions in the movement. In the summer of 2016, a
consortium of allied groups published *A Vision for Black Lives: Policy
Demands for Black Power, Freedom, & Justice*. This declaration called
for, among other things, economic justice, independent Black political power, communal self-determination, reparations, and an "end
to the war on black people." Other listed demands were the abolition
of the death penalty, the demilitarization of police agencies, an end
to the privatization of criminal justice, and the cessation of various
forms of discrimination against Black youths, LGBTQ individuals,
ex-offenders, and immigrants. Many of these policy proposals were
versions of 1960s Black protest doctrines and literature (such as the
Ten-Point Program of the Black Panther Party), retrofitted for the
societal conditions and media ecology of the new century. However,
what was decidedly different were the actors; a generational shift in
the leadership of civil rights activism was occurring, inspired by its
own set of demands, strategies, battlefields, and martyrs. This cultural
realignment was not merely reflective of the Joshua generation coming into its own. Instead, it was a millennial awakening that forthrightly identified its own Emmett Till in the hoodie-wearing Trayvon
Martin and its own Watts and Detroit uprisings in the incandescent
ashes of Ferguson and Baltimore.[49]

Barack Obama was publicly sympathetic to the BLM movement and its crusading fervor against police violence and racial oppression in general. While his favorable impressions were often tempered by laudatory comments about the "overwhelming majority" of law enforcement officers who he believed were "doing the right thing," his admiration for the activists seemed genuine. Perhaps recalling the anti-apartheid demonstrations and community organizing of his youth, Obama actually appeared energized by some of the idealism and, as he put it, "righteous anger" that he discerned in BLM members. "It's thanks in large part to the activism of young people like many of you, from Black Twitter to Black Lives Matter," he told a crowd at Howard University's commencement in May 2016, "that America's eyes have been opened—white, Black, Democrat, Republican—to the real problems, for example, in our criminal justice system." On a number of occasions, Obama reached out to some of the more visible BLM personalities, such as Brittany Packnett, who agreed to serve on his Task Force on 21st Century Policing. Similarly, in the wake of shootings of police officers in Baton Rouge and Dallas, he spoke well of BLM protesters in an effort to debunk rumors insinuating their culpability in the deaths of law enforcement officials. He even admonished police agencies to be "respectful of the frustrations people in these communities feel, and not just dismiss their protests and complaints."[50]

Despite the president's outreach and sympathy, not all of the young activists reciprocated the gestures. Aislinn Pulley, a member of Black Lives Matter Chicago, declined a February 2016 invitation to the White House to meet with a cross-generational cohort of civil right leaders. She considered the event no more substantive than a "photo opportunity" for Obama and thus not worth her time. In July, activists, including Erica Garner, the daughter of the late Eric Garner, complained about an ABC town hall meeting with the president that did not allow much time for the kind of dialogue that some had hoped would occur. BLM founder Patrisse Cullors wanted to see more of a "truth-and-reconciliation process" that would have laid bare the country's problems of race and criminal justice, instead of what she deemed a "curated event for ABC to quell protesters and organizers." Sometimes, the criticisms from activists frustrated Obama, since it often revealed, in his view, a "lack of awareness" of the limits of his power as head of only one branch of government. Nonetheless, while he might boil with annoyance or even mumble to himself words that might otherwise have caused a media frenzy if stated audibly, the president typically allowed the young people their say, no matter how seemingly off base. "Usually I'd just smile," he later told an interviewer with a laugh. In hindsight, it was a reasonable concession for him to make to the voices of the next generation. After all, their time had come.[51]

CHAPTER 17

The Measure of a President

THE GREAT RECESSION OFFICIALLY ENDED IN JUNE 2009 WHEN a budding economic expansion slowly began to register in gross domestic product (GDP) figures and other data. The eighteen-month plummet had been the longest descent into fiscal misery since the stock market crash of 1929 signaled the advent of the Great Depression, a churning, spiraling plunge into darkness that did not bottom out for almost four years. The recovery from the twenty-first-century recession was gradual and halting, with spikes in unemployment, home foreclosures, wealth loss, and other economic indicators occurring years after the business cycle had technically shifted toward positive territory. But the pain of the downturn and the relief of the expansion were experienced by Black America in quite different degrees compared to how others were affected by these developments. That is, African Americans collectively endured more economic injuries, fell into a deeper fiscal trough, and were slower to make progress toward the next peak due to the distance of their initial fall and historical and societal factors that continued to impede their climb.

In March 2015, the national unemployment rate was 5.5 percent, a real improvement over the 7.9 percent figure that haunted the country on the eve of the 2012 presidential election. However, for Blacks, who had traditionally coped with a rate that was twice that of whites, employment statistics were a reminder of how differently many of them experienced the US economy and its cyclical gyrations. Almost six years after the Great Recession had officially concluded, Black unemployment stood at 10.1 percent, substantially higher than the Latinx figure (6.8 percent), more than double that of whites (4.7 percent), and triple that of Asians (3.2 percent). Parsed along geographic lines, Black unemployment was lowest in Virginia (7.4 percent) and highest in Washington, DC (15.8 percent). Yet even the relatively low Virginia rate was more than a percentage point above the state (Tennessee) with the highest rate of white unemployment. In fact, the Black unemployment rate was higher than 10 percent in forty-two states during the first quarter of 2015, figures that were similar to those marking the worst of the overall national unemployment rate during the entirety of the recession and its aftermath. Many factors were behind these differentials, including hiring discrimination and regional patterns of economic decline and recovery. Also, Black people disproportionately occupied zones of the economy that were slower to recuperate following the recession, such as the public sector, which continued to struggle to replace the teachers, post office workers, bus drivers, and other employees who were hard hit by contracting state budgets.[1]

Exacerbating these employment trends was a racial wage gap that had grown wider over the previous several decades. In 2016, Black male workers earned on average only 70 percent of the hourly wage of their white male counterparts, in contrast to 80 percent in 1979. For Black women in the labor force, the fall was steeper, with their average hourly wage dropping from 95 percent to 82 percent of the wage of their white female counterparts over the same period. Some of the differences in income could again be attributed to the relative distribution of Black workers across various job markets. In the burgeoning high-tech industry, Blacks accounted for only 7 percent of employees in 2016, and Hispanics and women were similarly underrepresented in these fields at 8 percent and 36 percent of the workforce, respectively. As with other employment areas with stark racial and gender imbalances, Silicon Valley's preponderance of white men at its highest ranks—coupled with an overrepresentation of Asian men—was partly related to issues of resources, training, and pipelines. For example, three-quarters of US public schools did not offer the computer science classes that were essential to grooming students for careers in technology, a structural gap in the educational system that replicated inequalities in both access and income. Wage inequities played out in other areas as well. The Democratic Party, so reliant on minority voters for its electoral viability, spent less than 2 percent of its consultant fees on minority-owned firms during the 2010 and 2012 election cycles. In common with GOP operations, Black, Latinx, and Asian staffers were paid on average less than white employees were, though some of this differential was related to minority staffers not being well represented among the higher-paying jobs in communications, polling, and data analysis.[2]

Beyond unemployment and the job market, the second decade of the twenty-first century was notable for other crises that were unfurling across Black America. The opioid epidemic, which had heretofore disproportionately ravaged rural white communities, was beginning to take firm root in cities with sizable African American populations. Fentanyl, a synthetic pain reliever, and other drugs were responsible for escalating overdose deaths among Black people in urban counties, with a 41 percent jump in such deaths among African Americans in 2016 alone, the highest surge among any racial or ethnic group. The Centers for Disease Control and Prevention reported that the overdose mortality affected Black people in the 45- to 64-year age range most severely, a macabre analogue to the gun violence epidemic that so devastated younger age cohorts.

Additionally, in a world that was getting warmer and more precarious due to a rolling climate change catastrophe, Black communities were especially susceptible to environmental hazards, both natural and man-made. In a September 2016 report, the US Commission on Civil Rights, an independent fact-finding agency of the federal government, charged the EPA with not doing enough to protect marginalized communities from a spectrum of dangers. These environmental perils included the tendency of corporate polluters and others to locate waste disposal facilities in or near minority, sovereign tribal, and low-income areas, along with a lack of government research into the possible effects of coal ash lagoons and coal plants on the drinking water of these communities. The commission's study found that the civil rights office of the EPA had never officially charged any entity with discrimination nor had it even casually enforced the Title VI provisions of the 1964 Civil Rights Act, which endowed the agency with formidable tools to address environmental injustices of various kinds.[3]

The Obama presidency can be measured in a fashion that renders a quantitative portrait of the eight years, though such modeling obscures many deeper nuances and other factors operating beneath the mathematical surface. On the positive side, a host of metrics changed for the better during Obama's tenure in the White House. Measured from January 2009, when the president took office, to the election of his successor in November 2016, the national unemployment rate went from 7.8 percent to 4.6 percent, GDP growth climbed from −5.4 percent to +3.2 percent, the consumer confidence index rose from 37.4 to 107.1, and 11.3 million jobs were created, representing 75 consecutive months of employment gains. The Dow Jones industrial index, a measure of stock market valuation, nearly tripled during these eight years, cresting at 18,332.74 on Election Day 2016 from 7,949.09 on Inauguration Day 2009. Part of this roaring equity appreciation was due to a revived US auto industry, which had nearly collapsed during the recession. General Motors stock was worth a mere seventy-five cents a share in May 2009, but it was valued at $35.15 per share by January 3, 2017, an increase of almost 4,700 percent. There was more good news in the realm of health care. When Obama took office, 49 million Americans were uninsured; in 2015, this number had fallen to 29.8 million. By the end of his presidency, thirty-one states and Washington, DC, were participating in Medicaid expansion, which complemented the coverage provided to millions of others through the ACA health-care exchanges.

Other quantitative measurements of Obama's two terms were a bit less impressive, despite some having mixed or debatable meanings. While the $590 billion federal budget deficit for fiscal year 2016 was sharply down from the $1.4 trillion shortfall of fiscal year 2009, the national debt had ballooned to $19.9 trillion by December 2016, up from 10.6 trillion in January 2009. Moreover, the number of Americans receiving food assistance between 2009 and 2015 jumped from 33 million to 46 million, but such aid helped stabilize the number of people in poverty at around 43 million during those six years. Median household income climbed ever so slightly from $54,988 to $56,516 during this period, a reflection of stagnant wage growth and widening income inequality. A traditional gauge of wealth and financial sturdiness, homeownership rates declined 4 percent during the Obama years, from 67.3 to 63.5 percent. To compound the troublesome nature of nearly static household incomes and homeownership rates, both college tuition and student loan debt showed no signs of plateauing during the second decade of the century, the latter increasing from an average of $24,000 in 2009 to more than $30,000 in 2015.

Other data generated during the Obama presidency captured patterns of conflict at home and abroad. Between January 2009 and December 2016, US troop levels in Iraq and Afghanistan decreased dramatically, with service personnel deployed in the former country down from 139,500 to 5,200 and reduced in the latter nation from 34,400 to 9,800. Neither instance of curtailed deployments signaled victory. Iraq remained a cauldron of flammable political and sectarian hostilities, and the Taliban insurgency in Afghanistan continued to be nearly as formidable as it had been when US soldiers were first sent there in 2001. On the home front, hate crimes, as defined and tallied by the Justice Department, were largely consistent in number from 2012 to 2015, with an annual average of 5,763 events. This figure, like the higher 2009 total of 6,604, was almost certainly an undercount because of the number of unreported incidents.[4]

In and of itself, a statistical profile of the Obama presidency is not a sufficient assessment of his effectiveness, achievements, and limitations over the eight-year period. The numbers neither account for, in any holistic fashion, the myriad individual experiences, impressions, and interpretations of his time in office nor the similarly immeasurable variables behind the quantitative data and their meaning across broad swaths of the population. Other layers of information, both numerical and qualitative, allow for the ascription of further texture and character to the longitudinal trend lines, assisting in the construction of a more complex and detailed portrait of the Obama years, especially as they related to Black America.

For example, opinions concerning race relations, criminal justice, Obama's job performance, and other matters were regularly captured in polling data that provide some insight into national and subgroup attitudes at various points in his presidency. During the 2008 election campaign, almost 60 percent of African Americans polled thought that race relations were poor, but this number was reduced by half upon Obama's victory. In the aftermath of protests in Baltimore in April 2015, 61 percent of Americans surveyed considered race relations generally bad; following the Charleston church massacre two months later, the negative sentiment among Black respondents reached 68 percent. In August 2016, 82 percent of African Americans considered anti-Black racism to be widespread, in contrast to 66 percent of Hispanic respondents and 56 percent of whites surveyed. By October, polls revealed that 57 percent of Blacks and 40 percent of whites believed that race relations had grown worse over the course of the Obama presidency. Furthermore, three-quarters of surveyed African Americans felt that the criminal justice system favored whites, and a similar proportion had a favorable view of the Black Lives Matter movement, compared to 38 percent of whites who shared this opinion.

Despite discouraging survey data regarding race relations and other issues, Obama's approval ratings reached a crescendo at the twilight of his presidency. A month before the 2016 election, his assessment stood at a healthy 55 percent approval nationally, with his job performance receiving a positive endorsement from 85 percent of Blacks, 68 percent of Hispanics, and 47 percent of whites polled. For the duration of his time in the White House, Gallup's weekly polling of presidential approval reported only three weeks—one each in January 2012, February 2014, and March 2014—in which Obama's rating among Black people was lower than 80 percent. From January through September 2016, the weekly average was 89 percent. As he left office and his presidency trailed off into history, racial divisions continued to mark how various Americans viewed his achievements and significance. According to one survey, 76 percent of Black respondents believed that history would judge Obama as "above average or outstanding" as a head of state; only 38 percent of whites concurred. African Americans (60 percent) were also more likely than Hispanics (38 percent) or whites (31 percent) to agree that the Obama presidency had "made progress on the problems facing the nation." Considering the long-standing unevenness in his approval ratings when viewed across racial groups, it is not surprising that Obama's transition into the history books was characterized by a similar perceptual racialization of his legacy and meaning.[5]

Against the backdrop of the quantitative metrics, more subjective, long-view evaluations of Obama's presidency began to appear following his reelection. Several Black historians weighed in publicly as early as January 2015 as part of a *New York Magazine* questionnaire-based project that encapsulated the opinions of fifty-three scholars. While not yet benefiting from historical hindsight derived from observing the entirety of Obama's White House tenure, their appraisals did highlight notable patterns of change and continuity that appeared to be integral to the two-term presidency.

For example, Crystal Feimster of Yale University considered Obama's work on behalf of girls and women to be among his most important legacies. From the appointment of two women as US Supreme Court justices to efforts to combat wage discrimination and sexual assault, she believed that this "commonly overlooked" part of his administration's agenda would warrant greater future recognition.

Annette Gordon-Reed of Harvard posited that the election of an African American to the presidency, as well as the related reality of a Black first family, had inestimable implications for how young people thought about their own life possibilities. Moreover, she appreciated Obama's historical sensibilities and his inclination toward patience and strategic caution. In a similar vein, Thomas Holt of the University of Chicago asserted that Obama the politician and public figure had reoriented the trajectory of Black leadership, requiring future national figures to build constituencies both within the African American community and across interracial coalitions. In the realm of foreign policy, Holt believed that drone warfare and the growth of the national security state were "the most unfortunate legacy of the Obama presidency" because they established controversial precedents for successors. Like Feimster, emerita professor Nell Painter noted the progressivism of the ACA, but in common with her other colleagues, she was struck by how much racism, obstructionism, and mean-spirited "craziness" had been directed toward Obama.[6]

In the waning months of the Obama presidency, an assortment of public commentaries streamed out of Black academia, with some offering laudatory takes on the two terms while others were more critical. Randall Kennedy of Harvard interpreted the resilient Black support for Obama as a sign of gratitude for his debunking of negative images of African American men. By providing a model of a "serious, competent, dignified male politician," he defied stereotypes, all the more so by having a professional Black spouse. Kennedy's Harvard colleague Henry Louis Gates Jr., who had made so much news early in the Obama presidency, gave the chief executive high marks for a list of achievements, including the ACA, the auto bailout, financial reform, and rapprochement with Cuba. "I mean, the man did a lot!" Gates exclaimed in a November 2016 interview, adding that Obama would be remembered as "a symbol of openness, of tolerance, cosmopolitanism." Sociologist William Julius Wilson, who had known Obama since the 1980s, understood him to be a unifying figure during a time of extreme societal angst over the economy and other matters. Although he thought that the president could have better articulated his first-term accomplishments, Wilson considered Obama's administration—aside from its rhetorical focus on the middle class—to be the most beneficial for lower-income families since the Great Society programs of the Lyndon Johnson presidency. "I just feel like things would have been a lot worse if he hadn't been president," the professor told a reporter in December 2015 as he recounted his contentment with the 2009 stimulus package and the ACA.[7]

Michael Eric Dyson, a veteran of discursive wars over Obama's presidency long before it ended in January 2017, could be harsh in his critique of the chief executive. In his estimate, Obama had not used the bully pulpit forcefully enough to lead the nation in discussions about race and was too slow in diversifying his second-term administration. These perceived shortcomings were in addition to the fact that the president did not appoint a Black woman to the Supreme Court. Furthermore, Dyson was especially put off by what he saw as the incongruence between the strong African American electoral support for Obama and the president's unwillingness to be held accountable on issues concerning race. Still, in spite of his dismay, Dyson, a professor and Baptist minister, could be eloquent and generous in both his orations and his writings, and he did not let his conflicted reading of Obama's policies and symbolism preclude him from occasionally giving credit. "President Obama is an extraordinary figure who has done some good things in bad times, and some great things under impossible circumstances," he wrote in a *New York Times* article in June 2016. "Mr. Obama's presence in office has reflected our most helpful embrace of change, even as it throws light on the deeply entrenched bigotry that could reverse such changes."[8]

Such acclamation, albeit drenched in a heavy dose of caveats, was hard to find in some other academic quarters. Eddie S. Glaude Jr., a professor of religion at Princeton University, was damning in his assessment of the Obama administration in his 2016 book, *Democracy in Black*. Not only had Obama, in his reasoning, "sold black America the snake oil of hope and change" in 2008 and 2012, but

African Americans had suffered cruelly under a "post-black liberal" president who was too quick to counsel "personal responsibility and accountability" as solutions to the persistence of racism. Glaude's grim, blanket portrayal of African American life during the Obama presidency—"things have gotten worse"—was at odds with some of the empirical data on unemployment, health-care coverage, incarceration rates, high school graduation rates, and other matters. However, the sense of distress in many quarters of the country was still quite palpable at the end of Obama's time in office, and observers like Glaude did capture some of the visceral despair that was not remedied during the period.[9]

Other academicians had their own language for describing the era. In a June 2015 interview, Cornel West was characteristically candid and colorful in his assessment of the Obama presidency, declaring that Obama was the "first niggerized black president," allegedly too timid and calculating to challenge white supremacy. By this time, West, in his trademark black suit and salt-and-pepper afro, was campaigning for Vermont senator Bernie Sanders, who was seeking the Democratic presidential nomination. "What I love about Brother Bernie is he's a brother of integrity and honesty and decency," the professor enthusiastically proclaimed at a September rally at historically Black Benedict College. In almost the exact same words, he had spoken effusively about the presidential ambitions of a certain other US senator, though that seemed a lifetime ago.[10]

While some castigated Obama for not being more of an activist in chief, prominent civil rights figures and representatives of such organizations understood the nature of his duties as president, even as they sometimes pressed him for more attention and action. Al Sharpton, who over time became a vital link between Black activists and the White House, respected the administrative role in which the presidency cast Obama, as did Jesse Jackson, who enjoyed far less access to the Oval Office. The two-time presidential candidate avoided equating Obama with historical figures, such as Martin Luther King Jr., or construing him as part of any prophetic tradition, emphasizing instead Obama's constitutional duties as head of state. "What we needed from Dr. King was motivation and vision," Jackson asserted in a 2013 interview. "What we need from the president is appropriation and legislation." In its 2017 postmortem of the Obama presidency, the National Urban League offered a generally favorable evaluation of the previous eight years, citing declines in Black unemployment and uninsured rates and increases in the high school graduation rate and average wages. Notwithstanding these advances, the organization noted "missed opportunities and outright failures" during the Obama years, including little to no progress on gun reform, urban investment, or home foreclosures. Overall, the civil rights group rated the Obama administration "excellent," its second-highest grade.[11]

Years after the Obama presidency ended, NAACP president Cornell William Brooks had largely fond memories of it, although he could still cite "points of frustration." In a 2020 interview with me, he expressed admiration for the chief executive's character, intellect, transparency, and accomplishments, including his actions to save the US and world economies, his "evolution" on marriage equality and LGBTQ rights, and the passage of the ACA. Brooks had hoped for more progress on criminal justice reform, which he believed was stymied by congressional inaction. Further, he thought that the administration could have pushed harder for voting rights legislation in the wake of the devastating impact of the *Shelby Co. v. Holder* verdict. Aside from an additional disappointment regarding Obama's decision not to nominate a Black woman for the US Supreme Court, Brooks was generous in his assessment of the Obama years. He was even humorous in recollecting one meeting with the president in which his bona fides as signifier in chief were on full display. "After walking past pictures of George Washington and other figures hanging on the wall," the activist recalled about a journey to the White House, "I will always remember Obama dapping up the brothers around the table." According to Brooks, the white staff members reacted to the handshakes and banter as if they were routine for Obama when greeting Black acquaintances in such settings.[12]

Other individuals who interacted with Obama during his presidency also made note of his demeanor and style and years later were able to vividly recall his private temperament and approach to governance. Rep. James Clyburn of the CBC made a distinction between Obama the individual and Obama the chief executive. He characterized his personal relationship with the president as "very positive," while their working relationship was entirely transactional, just as Clyburn's interactions had been with the Bush and Clinton administrations. Following her service as director of the White House Domestic Policy Council, Melody Barnes remembered how Obama had encouraged a rigorous work ethic among West Wing staffers, with his own assiduity serving as a model. "Everyone does not need to be in the Oval Office all the time," Barnes recalled Obama asserting on at least one occasion, even though the storied power center has always been an irresistible magnet for the most awestruck and ambitious of White House personnel. Sharpton, who spent many hours with the president over the course of the eight years, was intrigued by the incessant operation of Obama's mental gears. "Even during light moments, there's a heaviness about him," the clergyman reflected in a memoir. "He always seems to be looking at the bigger picture, a step or two beyond everyone else." Despite the burdens of the presidency, Marc Morial, who often attended Oval Office meetings with Sharpton, considered Obama a "cool customer" and an "emotionally grounded person." The president was "all business" in how he managed meetings and, according to Morial, preferred to preside over a "methodical conversation where everyone had a chance to say what they had to say" before he weighed in with a response.[13]

During his presidential campaign and first term in office, Obama expended much time and energy on cultivating the hip-hop and rap communities. As mentioned earlier, most of these interactions were cultural signifying designed to firm up his electoral coalition. However, a few relationships were enduring, and Obama's own meaning to rappers and others remained noteworthy throughout his tenure in the White House. Artists like Common and T.I. viewed the symbolism of an African American president as one of Obama's most salient legacies. "As a black man, I know that he has represented black people in a beautiful way," Common rhapsodized in a January 2017 interview, adding, "[Obama] provided the scope of what a black man can be . . . how much depth and intelligence and resolve and courage and compassion and strength and humanity we have as black people." Like so many others, Crooked I, a rapper from Long Beach, found the Obama presidency most notable for the unyielding resistance of Republicans to the Democrat's agenda. "I've never seen a person of power get treated like that," he declared in a CNN interview. "That would have never happened to a white president." In describing GOP obstructionism, Ice Cube, an Obama contemporary, likened the president to "the black kid at the white school that don't nobody want to play with." For this reason, Ice Cube did not fault Obama for not accomplishing more while in office but instead credited him with doing "the best job that a man in his position can do under the circumstances."[14]

Other rappers chimed in during the last months of the Obama White House. Jeezy (formerly Young Jeezy) was initially disappointed by the lack of progress on issues such as criminal justice reform but applauded the "beginning of some type of slight change" by the time of Obama's final push for new policing and sentencing policies in the last quarter of his presidency. Vic Mensa, a Chicago native, offered an assessment that took on Obama's balancing of race and various constituencies. In a 2017 interview, he conceded that the president could not primarily represent Black people, but Mensa still believed that Obama "could have been a lot more vocally sympathetic" to issues facing African Americans. In particular, he thought that the president reached out more to law enforcement officers than to those who were the victims of police misconduct. Interestingly, Lizzo, a Detroit artist, was less preoccupied with scrutinizing Barack Obama and his legacy than she was with deciphering the significance of his wife. "A bar has been raised by Michelle Obama for what we expect out of the First Lady," the 29-year-old rapper and singer proclaimed as the first family prepared to depart the White House. "She's like the Beyoncé of first ladies. . . . If people don't like Obama, they love Michelle." With a Gallup favorability rating of 68 percent when she became a private citizen again on January 20, 2017, Michelle Obama remained an inspiration to many who had witnessed her master her White House role over the course of a decade.[15]

Other voices in the worlds of sports, entertainment, and literature offered their assessments of the Obama years in their own unique ways. NBA all-star Kobe Bryant attributed more politically aware locker rooms to the influence of Obama, who encouraged athletes not only to be concerned about societal problems but to think more deeply about how to constitutionally bring about change. Consistent with his lightheartedly irreverent style, comedian Chris Rock drew on a basketball analogy to measure the Obama presidency. "Everybody wanted Michael Jordan, right? We got Shaq," he claimed in late 2014. "That's not a disappointment. . . . It's still a Hall of Fame career." In the aftermath of the 2016 election, writer Ta-Nehisi Coates meditated on the substance and image of Obama in an *Atlantic* article entitled "My President Was Black." Impressed by Obama's moral compass and ability to maneuver around and across racial boundaries, he was less enamored of his abiding faith in the core decency of white America. Coates believed that the president's multiracial background and experiences had been as much a blind spot as an advantage in relation to his understanding of the US condition. "[Only] a black man with that same biography could underestimate his opposition's resolve to destroy him," he wrote dourly. This observation undoubtedly benefited from hindsight and was not so clear earlier in Obama's tenure, yet it seemed starkly affirmed by the rightward lurch of the national electorate and the arresting outcome of the November 2016 vote.[16]

For the millions of African Americans among whom Obama's approval rating typically hovered between 80 and 90 percent, there were just as many unique anecdotes about his presidency and its meaning as there were Black people who had witnessed his terms in office. Their individual voices could register euphoria, admiration, and gratitude concerning his achievements, as well as shock, disappointment, and fury regarding his perceived shortcomings. Much depended on the happenings of the moment and Obama's relative positioning and reaction to them. Overall and in keeping with his consistently high poll numbers among his most loyal constituency, it seems reasonable to conclude that Black America discerned lasting value in his two terms in the White House, even as Black people's collective circumstances did not improve at the rate that many would have liked.

Encounters and interviews with African Americans from various walks of life captured some of the contemporaneous thinking about the Obama presidency. For Loretta Augustine-Herron, who had worked with Obama during his community organizer days in 1980s Chicago, the mere election of a Black man to the nation's highest office was life altering. "If he never did anything else for African-Americans, just the fact that he occupies the White House, it lets us see ourselves in a different light," she told an interviewer in January 2017. "We see a chance for us to fit into the United States society in a way we've never fit in." Glennon Threatt, an Alabama public defender, concurred with this sentiment. "What he has done is shown that a black man can be a successful president and a successful husband and a successful father," Threatt opined at the end of the eight years; he found the feat "extraordinary." Russell Singleton, a 64-year-old shoeshine station manager in Chicago, found the Obama presidency a bit too miraculous to see it repeated anytime soon. "I don't think that I'll see another black president in my lifetime and I'll say in the younger generation's lifetime," he mused in March 2016, before adding, "They won't allow us to have the reins again. It's a big prize and they hold onto it dearly." His opinion was both a testament to the truly historic achievement of a two-term presidency by Obama and a recognition of the relentless forces that had arrayed themselves so implacably against his legislative agenda and even the idea of a Black head of state.[17]

While Obama's electoral coalition trended younger, 75-year-old Yancy Jones of Inglewood, California, was as determined a member of the 93 percent of the Black electorate that helped reelect the president as anyone. Over the intervening years between elections, he had watched bitterly as concerted efforts were made nationwide to make voting less accessible, a disfranchisement strategy that his parents had fought against during an earlier time. Having recently suffered a stroke that impaired his speech and diminished his stamina, Jones struggled to get to the polls in November 2012. However, he managed to make his way, Bible and cane in hand, to the voting booth and never doubted that he would. "I'm proud of the man," he said of Obama hours after casting his ballot. "He fought the good fight against all odds. He got Bin Laden and he kept his head high when people were attacking and doubting him. That's a hero in my book, and you don't find many of them anymore." For Jones, casting a ballot for Obama was a solemn duty in the face of an existential threat to voting rights. As discussed earlier, this view was shared by 102-year-old Desiline Victor who, an entire continent away in Miami, was concurrently making a similar trek to the polls to daringly challenge the country to live up to the promise of its creed.[18]

In the wake of his second inauguration in early 2013, Barack Obama characterized his presidency as "both the best of times and worst of times for the African-American community." In his usual temperate, pensive tone, he contended that hard-working Black people, when given the opportunity, could now achieve things in life that would not have been possible a generation earlier. Yet aside from this progress, the president conceded that the aftershocks of the Great Recession had left "a whole lot of people in a whole lot of communities" in ongoing economic straits. Despite polls that sometimes suggested otherwise, Obama was not convinced that the country had grown more racially divided during his watch. Even in the midst of the Ferguson turmoil in late 2014, he attributed strife between law enforcement and Black communities to long-standing tensions that were sometimes dramatically captured in opinion polls following widely reported incidents. In ruminating publicly about his presidency, one regret that he shared on a few occasions related to the failure of his administration, especially in its early years, to clearly articulate its policy objectives to the American people, as opposed to assuming that the nation would simply follow the Oval Office's lead. "I think a certain arrogance crept in," he admitted during a November 2015 interview, "in the sense of thinking as long as we get the policy ready, we didn't have to sell it." Brutal midterm elections in 2010 and 2014 taught hard lessons on this score that ended up severely constricting his party's legislative wherewithal and his presidential legacy.[19]

In his approach to governance, Obama remained convinced that the universalist approach was the only viable methodology available to a president tasked with leading the entirety of the American people. While he understood the arguments of some African American leaders and other commentators concerning the perceived need to explicitly target ameliorative policies toward the most distressed populations, he was never persuaded of either the electoral or administrative efficacy of such a strategy. During a conversation with occasional critic Michael Eric Dyson, Obama made his case plain.

> [My approach] is based not only on how I think I should govern as president—meaning I've got to look out for all Americans, and do things based on what will help people across the board who are vulnerable and who need help. But it's also based on a very practical political reality that some of my African American critics don't have to worry about because they've just got a different role to play. I've got to put together coalitions that allow me to get legislation through a House or a Senate that results in a bill on my desk that I can sign into law. I have to appropriate dollars for any program which has to go through ways and means committees, or appropriations committees, that are not dominated by folks who read Cornel West or listen to Michael Eric Dyson. . . .
>
> I don't always have the luxury of speaking prophetically or in theory. . . . I've got the job of governing and delivering to the people who desperately need help.[20]

It was a straightforward argument that benefited from a realistic understanding of executive branch powers, existing political realities, and the limits and perils of any advocacy of a race-based agenda by a president dependent on interracial (and predominantly white) electoral and governing coalitions. Nonetheless, proponents of targeted remedies remained vocal and persistent throughout the Obama tenure, apparently convinced that the rectitude of their cause superseded any quibbles concerning its political or legislative practicality.

In a September 2016 interview with presidential historian Doris Kearns Goodwin, Obama offered a concise, colorful take on his White House years that meshed well with his growing tendency to more openly discuss race. At the time, he was occupied with clemency requests, lingering international obligations, campaigning for Democratic candidates, and embedding his policy legacy as deeply and irreversibly as possible into the country's DNA. However, he was still acutely aware of the novelty of his most fascinating and enduring accomplishment, which would stand the test of time no matter what happened once he left Washington. "I'm named Barack Hussein Obama. I'm African American. And I've been elected twice to this office with the majorities of the American people," he confidently told Goodwin in respond to a question about governing in the cacophonous, attention-jarring internet age. "So something is working." Caught off guard by his candor, the historian could only utter words of agreement as their laughter reverberated through the Oval Office.[21]

CHAPTER 18

The Pendulum Swings Back

MITT ROMNEY'S LOSS IN THE 2012 PRESIDENTIAL ELECTION sparked much fretting and second-guessing among Republicans. Some observers pointed to the skillful employment of data-driven voter outreach by the Obama campaign as a critical factor affecting the outcome, while others blamed Romney's defeat on a long primary season that had forced him too far rightward to compete effectively for the undecided political center during the general election. Along with concerns about Romney's image as an aloof patrician and corporate raider, one of the most commonly cited reasons for the GOP candidate's trouncing by Obama was the party's declining appeal among the ever-diversifying electorate that decides US elections. Since 1992, when whites comprised 87 percent of voters, their share had dropped steadily during each presidential cycle. In 2008, they comprised 74 percent of the electorate; in 2012, 72 percent. Romney had succeeded in running up historically high margins among white voters, receiving 59 percent of their ballots, the highest proportion won by any presidential nominee since 1988. However, his electoral prospects suffered from notable underperformances among Blacks, Hispanics, Asians, women, young people, and other groups that again propelled Obama to victory.

Conservative pundits who had not publicly taken issue with Romney's flagrant appeals to white voters during the campaign were quick to point out the shortcomings of the strategy as he became a footnote in US political history. Columnist George Will criticized the Republican candidate for his hard-core "self-deportation" stance on immigration, a position that helped cap his support among Hispanics at less than 30 percent. Former Arkansas governor and GOP presidential contender Mike Huckabee called Republicans' lack of a viable plan for attracting voters of color "pathetic," especially since, in his view, such people should naturally gravitate toward the party's free-market policies and social conservatism. Fox News host Bill O'Reilly put Romney's defeat in stark terms that seemed to presume that a particular kind of white political dominance was now in eclipse. "The demographics are changing," he reckoned within hours of the vanquishing of Romney. "It's not a traditional America anymore."[1]

Hoping to avoid a similar electoral disaster in 2016, RNC chair Reince Priebus commissioned a study of the causes of the GOP's troubles. Colloquially known as an "autopsy" report, the document largely confirmed what was already known about the party's inferior digital operations, the limits of its elite-friendly prescriptions for reviving the economy, its creeping nativism, and its controversial support for restricting access to birth control and other reproductive services, which some would derisively refer to as the GOP's "war on women." In March 2013, Priebus promised to dedicate $10 million toward rehabilitating the Republican brand among marginalized communities that had been alienated by much of the party's messaging during the 2012 campaign. Rather than addressing any problems inherent to the appeal of conservative principles and policies among minority voters, Priebus and the RNC concluded that the GOP's electoral dilemma was mainly related to a failure to actively court people of color.[2]

Prominent Black Republicans generally shared Priebus's view but were quick to highlight how the tone and behavior of various GOP politicians and media personalities had diminished the party's allure among minorities, women, and other segments of the electorate. In her usual circumspect manner of critiquing the party, Condoleezza Rice contended that conservative orthodoxies on issues such as fiscal responsibility, school choice, and military spending were widely popular. Nevertheless, she believed that the party had sent "mixed messages" on issues related to women and immigration. Furthermore, in the face of ongoing demographic changes, the GOP needed an "even bigger tent" to accommodate a more diverse voting-age population. A week after Romney's defeat, former RNC chair Michael Steele stressed the rhetorical timbre and demographic elements behind the 2012 election outcome. "Cut the crap out and recognize your message is tone deaf to voters and your brand isn't as strong as it once was," he entreated in an interview. "50,000 Hispanics are turning 18 every month, and what is the party going to do about that?" Colin Powell, who had endorsed Barack Obama in 2008 and 2012, criticized the intolerance that he believed was ascendant in the GOP and would eventually lead to its irrelevance. "There are certain elements within the party which go out of their way to demonize people who don't look like the way they'd like them to look like, or came from some other place," the former secretary of state asserted in a televised interview in February 2014. "And I think the party has to deal with this." By the Republican National Convention in July 2016, Powell had tuned out the party altogether, declining to attend the Cleveland gathering or to watch it on television.[3]

Rather ironically, as the Republican Party became more tribal and insular, a number of Black conservatives took the opportunity to hitch their political fortunes to the GOP as it prepared for the 2016 election season. Ben Carson, a renowned surgeon, became one of the most well known of these political players. Raised in a poverty-stricken Detroit tenement by a divorced mother, he managed to surmount a rough childhood to win admission into Yale University and then the University of Michigan Medical School, from which he graduated in 1977 with an MD. Carson went on to have a distinguished career as director of pediatric neurosurgery at Johns Hopkins Hospital, where he became the first person to separate conjoined twins. Politically, he described himself as a "flaming liberal" in college, but he became more conservative as he achieved greater professional success. A Seventh-day Adventist, Carson came to embrace a strong belief in "personal responsibility and hard work," and by the time President George W. Bush awarded him the Medal of Freedom in 2008, Carson sounded more like a traditional conservative than the progressive of his earlier years. As late as 2013, he was still a registered independent, but by then he was convinced that churches and the private sector could do a better job of addressing issues such as poverty and health care than could government agencies and programs. In July of that year, Carson retired at age 61. "I want to quit while I'm at the top of my game," he told an adoring crowd at the annual Conservative Political Action Conference, "and there are many more things that could be done." Indeed, whispers of a presidential run had been swirling for months, and Carson had done little to quiet them.[4]

For all intents and purposes, Ben Carson's political career began on February 7, 2013. He was tapped to give the keynote address at the National Prayer Breakfast, an annual gala held in Washington and attended by a who's who of the nation's elite and a sprinkling of foreign dignitaries. With the US president sitting only feet away on the same stage, Carson took full advantage of the spotlight. He excoriated the "moral decay" and "fiscal irresponsibility" that he viewed as destroying the country, comparing the situation to the circumstances that led to the collapse of the Roman Empire. Between biblical parables and paeans to US nationalism, he was particularly critical of the ACA, which he thought inserted too much governmental control into the lives and health-care choices of citizens. As possible solutions to a tax code and a medical system that he found inefficient, he proposed implementing a flat tax based on biblical tithing along with health savings accounts that would privatize and shift medical expenses more squarely toward consumers.

Visibly annoyed, Obama rarely smiled or applauded during Carson's time at the podium and conspicuously looked down and away for almost a full minute as the surgeon lectured the audience about alternatives to the ACA and other progressive policies. After the event, Carson claimed that he had not been "particularly political" in his presentation, but such a characterization was belied by the reaction of the conservative commentariat, which immediately took the speech as a proclamation of electoral intent. "I love this guy!" Rush Limbaugh effused as he aired excerpts of the speech on his radio show. The day after the prayer breakfast, the *Wall Street Journal* published an editorial entitled "Ben Carson for President." Whatever his motives, Carson was now a rising star in American conservatism and was on his way to becoming a name in Republican politics.[5]

Carson declared his candidacy for the Republican presidential nomination in May 2015. He had been flirting with the idea for more than two years by that time, and thus the announcement came as no surprise. What was a bit unexpected, however, was both his penchant for off-color commentaries and his unpreparedness to engage in deep policy discussions beyond health-care matters. Some of Carson's views on international affairs were simply mistaken, such as when he suggested that China was militarily involved in the Syrian civil war. Other positions were the stuff of sci-fi movies and fringe conspiracy theories, including his warning that terrorists might seek to explode a nuclear weapon high above the earth "in our exoatmosphere and destroy our electric grid." Even his references to biblical scripture could raise eyebrows, such as his contention that the Egyptian pyramids were constructed to store grain as opposed to holding the remains of dead pharaohs.[6]

Although mild-mannered and soft-spoken, Carson was not averse to either making crude analogies or evoking darker subject matter to make a point. Even before his official campaign announcement, he had compared the United States to Nazi Germany, arguing that political correctness had stifled the ability of Americans "to say what they believe." When he found it necessary to graphically denounce some liberal boogeymen, he evoked comparisons to antebellum times. "I have to tell you Obamacare is, really I think, the worst thing that's happened in this nation since slavery," he told the audience of the

Values Voter Summit in October 2013, hyperbole that he also applied to abortion. Carson's popularity among Republicans was not hurt by his coarse references to race, including his questioning of the president's identity. It was a pastime in which he, like so many previous Obama opponents, could apparently not refrain from indulging. "He's an 'African' American. He was, you know, raised white," Carson stated in an interview in early 2016. "So, for him to, you know, claim that, you know, he identifies with the experience of black Americans, I think, is a bit of a stretch."[7]

Carson's remarks sat well with Republican primary voters, who liked both the rough edges of his speeches and debate performances and his impeccable professional credentials. As a Black conservative, his needling of Obama was, for many partisans, an added bonus, especially after Carson declared that he had never faced racism in the GOP, thus implying that Republican attacks on the president had nothing to do with race. Although he did briefly ride high in the candidate preference polls, Carson was ultimately ill equipped to satisfy the electoral hunger and political fantasies of the Republican Party of the period. While not nearly as bombastic and blatantly self-promoting as Herman Cain, the retired neurosurgeon was just as new to political campaigning, and it showed in various ways. His campaign organization suffered from disorganization, neglect, and serial staff turnover as early as the summer of 2015, long before the Iowa caucuses. Moreover, Carson's policy prescriptions were largely in line with those of the other sixteen candidates running for the Republican nomination, a symmetry that hardly distinguished the low-key, bespectacled physician from the pack. His fellow candidates included sitting US senators and governors with long records of public service, and several, including Sen. Marco Rubio of Florida, Gov. John Kasich of Ohio, and Gov. Scott Walker of Wisconsin, represented swing states that the party needed to carry in November 2016. To be sure, GOP voters were susceptible to an outsider candidate with a populist rallying cry and an ethnonationalist appeal that spoke to the party's tribal moment and promised to disrupt the Washington status quo. Yet Carson offered none of this, nor could he have. After a dismal fifth-place delegate count in the Super Tuesday primaries on March 1, he announced the suspension of his bid for the presidency the following day.[8]

Barack Obama lost little sleep over the presidential ambitions of Ben Carson. In the raucous Republican primary campaign, which included more than its share of sudden shifts in fortunes, vicious intraparty squabbles, and outright buffoonery, it was easy to find both humor and lowbrow entertainment value in much of what transpired. Still, the president remained fully aware that a lot of the pontificating, posturing, and bickering was actually about him as GOP voters tried to determine who among the large, unwieldy field of Republican candidates was best able to win a general election and dismantle as much of his legacy as possible. Until the final quarter of his tenure in office, Obama typically downplayed, at least in public, the racially tinged portion of the GOP opposition against him, choosing to portray expressed differences and fevered attacks as primarily ideological and political. However, by 2015, Obama was more likely than ever to identify racial animosity among his conservative opponents, just as he was given to more candid acknowledgments of institutional racism and structural discrimination. "I think if you are talking about the specific virulence of some of the opposition directed towards me," he ruminated in a December interview, "that may be explained by the particulars of who I am." This admission was not a new revelation on Obama's part but instead a lucid understanding of the nature of his enemies and the upcoming struggle over his legacy. Similarly, when the president joined Twitter in May 2015, the torrent of racist abuse that greeted him was a vivid reminder that the Tea Party slanders, birtherism, and white supremacist rhetoric and machinations of the previous six years had been injected deep into the bloodstream of the body politic, poisoning both the civic culture and the legislative possibilities of his "hope and change" presidency.[9]

To succeed Obama and safeguard his accomplishments, Democratic primary voters chose Hillary Rodham Clinton as their 2016 standard-bearer. She had faced stiff competition from Vermont senator Bernie Sanders for the presidential nomination but prevailed after it became clear that the self-avowed democratic socialist had not bothered to build a solid campaign organization among the southern Black voters whom the Clintons had cultivated for literally decades. Obama campaigned vigorously for his former secretary of state, reminding audiences of the stakes involved in the election and encouraging a strong turnout at the polls. During a September appearance at a CBC gala, he stated that he would take it as a "personal insult" if the African American community did not mobilize to protect his legacy and the policy gains of the previous seven years. According to opinion polls and interviews of prospective Black voters, Obama's prodding was needed.

While African Americans overwhelmingly favored Clinton over her GOP rival, Donald Trump, many were less than enthusiastic in their support. Some of the hesitancy had to do with the Clinton brand, which had not fully recovered from various scandals and from the centrist policies of the 1990s, which had delivered "welfare reform" and a crime bill that, respectively, frayed the social safety net and increased the momentum behind mass incarceration. Also, the 2008 presidential primaries were still a fresh memory for many Black voters, who could still recall some of the less savory campaign strategies of the Clintons. By the fall of 2016, Hillary Clinton was saying the necessary things about criminal justice reform, federal aid for struggling communities, protecting the ACA, and other policy matters to convince both Obama and vital parts of his electoral coalition that she would provide at least continuity on most issues if elected. Despite this reassurance, she remained disturbingly unpopular just weeks before the election, with a favorability rating of only 38 percent, according to Gallup.[10]

As Obama's campaign staffers had reminded him when he was contemplating a vice presidential running mate, choosing Hillary Clinton for any purpose or task necessarily meant enduring the presence of her husband, Bill Clinton. Following the bitter primary battles of 2008, Obama and the former president had, at best, a tolerable relationship built primarily on political expedience. In the transactional, tight spots of electoral politics, Bill Clinton had come through for Obama, particularly at nominating conventions, and the president had come through for Hillary, such as giving her a national platform—and valuable foreign policy experience—as secretary of state and supporting her 2016 presidential bid. In April 2014, former president Clinton even told a talk-show host that he enjoyed being known as the "first Black president" and that he and his wife had "done everything we could to support him [Obama]." Nonetheless, Bill Clinton occasionally showed himself capable of undermining the real first Black president in decidedly irritating ways.[11]

In the midst of the 2012 campaign, the former president publicly praised Mitt Romney's work at Bain Capital and deemed his "sterling business career" as qualifying him to serve as president. Further, during a chat at the annual Clinton Global Initiative meeting in New York, Clinton was overheard offering the GOP candidate tips for improving his stage presence in debates with Obama. Four years later, the former president called the ACA a "crazy system" that was neither affordable nor efficient. After Democratic critics chastised him for giving the Republican presidential candidate an additional line of attack against his wife and Obama, Clinton backpedaled and lauded the health-care law for doing a "world of good." In spite of such barbs, the Obamas publicly characterized the relationship between the two presidents as "terrific" and "easy," even though Barack Obama had reportedly whispered to an aide in 2011 that he could only take the former president "in doses" following an awkward round of golf. As late as July 2014, former Democratic presidential candidate Bill Richardson was still convinced that Bill Clinton had not forgiven him for endorsing Obama during the 2008 primaries, a grudge that seemed to him "unusually long." In the gritty world of zero-sum politics, it was all par for the course. In this case, such maneuvering, indirection, and quid pro quos were the price of safeguarding Obama's legacy and emblazoning Hillary Clinton's name in the history books as the first woman president.[12]

Donald Trump had talked about running for president since the late 1980s, when a number of conservatives, hoping to spruce up the GOP image following the White House exit of the 77-year-old Ronald Reagan, had unsuccessfully tried to convince him to jump into the New Hampshire primary. Still most at home among New York skyscrapers and Atlantic City casinos, Trump did not give in to the temptation for another three decades, though he theatrically teased presidential bids during nearly every cycle, even as late as 2011. However, the now-legendary roasting that he suffered at the hands of Barack Obama during the White House Correspondents' Association dinner that year was more than enough to scare him away from the campaign trail, despite the fact that lingering aftereffects of the recession had left the president vulnerable to a challenge. Instead, Trump bided his time and decided to throw his hat into the ring four years later. The glitzy announcement was made in June 2015 at Trump Tower in New York City. It was as self-adoring and imperious as many would have expected, given his penchant for media spectacles and narcissistic displays. Trump's opening jabs at illegal immigration, and especially his characterization of Mexicans as rapists and drug dealers, were a preview of the campaign to come. Unbeknown to observers at the time, his candidacy marked a fateful rupture in both the Republican Party and the trajectory of US politics.

Ideologically, Trump was truly a mixed bag, and he swapped out doctrinal flavors and policy ingredients as the notion struck him. Some of his stated plans were warmed-over Republican orthodoxy, including tax cuts, school-choice options, enhanced military spending, and repeal of the ACA. Other elements carried a whiff of big-government affinities, such as his pledges to preserve Social Security, Medicare, and Medicaid and "to undertake a massive rebuilding of infrastructure." In relation to foreign policy, Trump was leery of the world and suspicious of protracted engagements with both allies and foes. To the chagrin of neoconservatives, he was routinely critical of seemingly interminable Middle Eastern wars started by George W. Bush, and to the dismay of multilateralists, he promised to renege on various international agreements, such as the Iran nuclear deal negotiated by Barack Obama.

In nearly all things, Trump offered simple solutions to difficult, even intractable problems, wrapped in the flourish of a showman and the bombast of a demagogue. In his view, unwanted immigration across the southern border could be halted with a great wall, which Mexico could be compelled to finance. Likewise, trade disputes with China could be remedied with tariffs and other instruments of economic warfare, which would show the world that the United States would no longer be pushed around or taken for granted by either friend or foe. As described in his 2015 book, *Crippled America: How to Make America Great Again*, the country had fallen behind and lost the luster that had been emblematic of some idyllic past. Americans deserved, in his words, a leader "with a proven track record in business who understands greatness, someone who can rally us to the standard of excellence we once epitomized and explain what needs to be done." Facing a world of ruthless competitors and rampant foul play not unlike the cutthroat New York real-estate market that had honed his own stratagems and cynicism, Trump declared that "America needs to start winning again" and that he held the keys to its resurgence.[13]

Based on his four colorful decades in public life, it was easy to dismiss Trump as a punchline. But this reading was too simplistic and underestimated his canny understanding of the political moment and his ability to exploit it. Years of cultivating a celebrity persona in New York tabloids and as the executive host of a reality TV show had groomed him for the klieg lights and melodrama of electoral politics. By the 2016 campaign, he was able to commandeer the incessant 24/7 media cycle and regularly bend it—and in particular the premium that media placed on inflammatory scoops—to his will in a manner that very few politicians could. Despite his personal wealth, Trump was a master at conjuring and articulating grievances, which he coated with the rhetoric of populist nationalism and economic angst. Just as important, he spoke directly to the fears of a white working class that was horrified by the demographic churn that the country was undergoing, as well as its implications for future power relations between racial and ethnic groups.

During the campaign, Trump served up a robust menu of national enemies and foreign aliens who allegedly threatened American culture, identity, jobs, security, and lives. Whether it was Mexicans crossing the Rio Grande, Muslims coming from Asia and Africa, or cheap Chinese labor that had supposedly maimed the US manufacturing sector, he painted a ghastly picture of US decline and pointed at foreigners and people of color as the culprits. It was the southern strategy internationalized for the twenty-first century with a more concentrated potency than anything that the Tea Party had been able to conjure. To put it plainly, Trump's proposals for a border wall, a Muslim ban, and "yellow peril" protectionism embodied a grotesque apotheosis of decades of Republican deceits aimed at melding the racial loyalty of white voters—regardless of their actual class interests—to a party increasingly captured by wealthy corporate donors.

Aside from their bad-faith pandering to certain segments of the electorate, there was a crucial difference between conventional GOP strategies and Trump's campaign methods. The New York businessman was far more interested in burnishing his own brand and its profitability than in the political fortunes of the Republican Party. Animated by such narrow motives, he was more than willing to aggrandize his own position by soiling the GOP's reputation and its ruling elites—represented by his primary challengers and congressional leaders—with a toxic sludge of grandstanding, name-calling, and bald-faced lies. According to Trump's narrative, these Republican gatekeepers had deluded the masses with promises of rising wages, comfortable retirements, and continuing global dominance as they themselves became richer and more entrenched by betting the country's future on globalism, unchecked immigration, and free trade. "I have joined the political arena so that the powerful can no longer beat up on people that cannot defend themselves," Trump declared during the Republican National Convention in July 2016 that officially nominated him as the party's general election candidate. "Nobody knows the system better than me, which is why I alone can fix it. . . . I am your voice." By this time, Trump had managed to convince millions of GOP voters to support him personally, beyond the imperatives of partisan affiliation. Party allegiance had become a secondary consideration, merely a vehicle for realizing a Trump presidency and its fantastical vision of a restored American glory.[14]

Unlike traditional Republican messaging on matters of race, which was usually coded and sometimes plausibly deniable, Trump openly fanned white racial biases and fears for his own political advantage. It was a strategy that heightened his appeal in some quarters but often to the embarrassment of party officials, who found themselves having to disavow extremist elements that were inspired by Trump's rhetoric. David Duke, a former KKK grand dragon and occasional candidate for various offices, publicly threw his support behind the businessman during the Republican primaries. "Voting for these people, voting against Donald Trump at this point is really treason to your heritage," Duke announced on his radio show as he counseled listeners against supporting Hispanic presidential candidates Marco Rubio and Ted Cruz. After Trump won the nomination, Duke decided to run for a US Senate seat in Louisiana, reasoning, "The climate of this country has moved in my direction." As late as November 2016, the endorsements of white supremacists were still coming in, and the Republican nominee rarely did anything to discourage them. A KKK newspaper prominently featured Trump's campaign slogan, "Make America Great Again," in a banner headline and expressed support for his message. In this instance, Trump's staff did denounce the KKK and "hate in any form." Nevertheless, the publication listed stopping "white genocide" as its primary goal, and Trump had retweeted a message associated with the Twitter handle @WhiteGenocideTM back in January, which seemed to belie his campaign's expressed aversion to white supremacist motifs.[15]

Viewed in a global context, Trump's campaign for the US presidency was part of a larger political shift toward the far right and authoritarianism that was occurring in several countries. Whether spawned by immigration crises, paralyzing political dysfunction, or escalating inequalities of all sorts, these emergent social forces posed critical challenges to both democratic governance and the democratic ideal itself. In some societies, the political center could no longer hold, and the void was increasingly filled by opportunistic demagogues who would have previously been considered too extreme to govern. In their moments of turmoil and weakness, such societies had become susceptible to figures who offered pat remedies to complicated dilemmas and who attacked long-established institutions—including the courts, the press, and even the rule of law itself—as the causes of societal ills. As power became invested in a single individual or faction, traditional notions of right and left, conservative and liberal could not be neatly applied, since the rule by authoritarians was not always ideological but instead personal and even tribal. Thus, the rise of Norbert Hofer in Austria, Marine Le Pen in France, Rodrigo Duterte in the Philippines, and Jair Bolsonaro ("Trump of the tropics") in Brazil was not especially striking for each one's ideological, partisan, or institutional particularities. Instead, the developments were noteworthy because these political personalities had attracted the national gaze by meticulously stoking popular passions on socially combustible issues—such as immigration, crime, ethnonationalism, and race—as an end in itself.

This worldwide trend was apparent during the 2016 US election cycle. Andrew Anglin, founder of the neo-Nazi website the *Daily Stormer*, saw the telltale pattern and took comfort in it. He applauded Trump's stated plan to deport Mexicans upon his entering the White House and appreciated his "willingness to call them out as criminal rapists, murderers and drug dealers." When the Republican candidate hesitated to repudiate the likes of David Duke or retweeted white nationalist imagery, Anglin understood the gestures as purposeful outreach to those of his ilk. "Our Glorious Leader and ULTIMATE SAVIOR has gone full wink-wink-wink to his most aggressive supporters," he posted on his website, evoking classical fascist tropes to describe Trump's candidacy. At the time, it was too early to discern what Trump would do with actual power, but his inclinations and impulses were on full display and attracted devotees from the dark periphery of the political spectrum.[16]

The racial tribalism that Trump cultivated among Republican voters was notably advanced by his use of the current president as a foil. Obama was the face of the browning of the United States that many of Trump's supporters loathed. He was a stand-in for all of the racial others whom Trump construed as jeopardizing the (white) American future, whether Mexicans from the South, Muslims from the East, or urban Blacks in US cities. While he deemed Obama an "awful president" for his policy positions, at least some of Trump's disdain was personal and related to the years of stinging criticism that the president had leveled against him, the 2011 correspondents' dinner, and his current campaigning on behalf of Hillary Clinton. Trump's embrace of birtherism was, of course, political and personal, serving both as a launching pad for his electoral aspirations and as a gnawing insinuation that Obama's presence in the Oval Office could never be legitimate.

As he proved on many occasions, Trump tended to carry perceived personal insults and grudges around like so much baggage and could rarely refrain from lashing out at those who had offended him. And like Obama, he could go for the jugular with startling effectiveness, though he was not the long-view planner that the president had shown himself to be. Trump could think tactically, a skill that he no doubt learned in business endeavors. Yet his attention span was too short to attend to the fine details of everyday affairs—except when it came to petty fights and resentments—or the interlocking intricacies of a grand strategy. In engaging Trump in any fashion, one was left with dealing with scattershot, contradictory, and sometimes nonsensical behaviors and discourse, which could be self-defeating for him even as he typically sought to advance his personal interests above all else. His campaigning during the general election season consistently confirmed his penchant for inconsistency, artifice, and drama, particularly as he sought to deal with Obama and the African American electorate.

The exigencies of electoral math compelled Trump to reach out to Black people after he secured the GOP nomination in July. He did not need to win the Black vote, but he did need to do better than the 6 percent of African American ballots won by Mitt Romney, especially in selected swing states. In his opening gambit, Trump roundly criticized Obama for not delivering for African Americans on issues related to employment, education, and the "disastrous conditions in so many of our inner cities." In positioning himself as an alternative to Obama and his would-be Democratic successor, Hillary Clinton, Trump dissonantly asked Black voters during his speeches before almost entirely white audiences, "What do you have to lose?" Drawing on a nineteenth-century presidential reference, the Republican nominee reminded observers that he represented the party of Lincoln, a deployment of a well-worn slavery-era trope that still occasionally cropped up in US political discourse. During a late October speech in Charlotte, North Carolina, Trump evoked a twentieth-century president in his call for a "new deal for Black America"—before immediately proceeding to advocate for a border wall that he claimed would protect African Americans from job competition with illegal immigrants. For all of his jumbled, halfhearted efforts to attract Black voters, Trump continued to register in the single digits in polls. Subsequently, just days before the election, his support among Black people was no more impressive than what Mitt Romney or John McCain had been able to muster.[17]

Just as he made last-minute attempts to court Black voters, Trump duplicitously cast them as villains, a time-honored GOP strategy aimed at peeling a few African American votes away from the Democratic Party while consolidating the white Republican base. In August, he proclaimed his full-throated support for voter ID laws right after a North Carolina statute was struck down by a federal appellate court for its "racially discriminatory intent." The following month, he called for the nationalization of stop-and-frisk laws, even though such statutes had been found to be unconstitutional racial profiling in places like his native New York City. Representative of Trump's transparently disingenuous bid for Black votes was his announcement in September that he no longer believed that Barack Obama was born outside of the United States. The concession appeared purely political in motivation and indicated just how desperate he was to at least temporarily shake the birther label as he tried to cobble together a viable electoral coalition. Sensing vulnerability, Clinton demanded that Trump apologize to Obama for his years-long perpetuation of the smear. CBC chair G. K. Butterfield denounced Trump as a "disgusting fraud" who never would have attacked a white politician with such venomous aspersions. In the end, it is unlikely that Trump's new stance on the president's nativity affected many of his GOP supporters. An August poll revealed that 41 percent of registered Republicans still believed that Obama was not born in the United States, and another 31 percent expressed doubts. The survey results were a stark reminder of how effective Trump's birther crusade had been in spreading falsehoods about Obama's citizenship.[18]

In campaigning for Clinton, Obama typically portrayed Trump as ignorant, unqualified, and temperamentally unsuited for the presidency. Like so many others, he assumed that the mere juxtaposition of the politically inexperienced reality TV showman alongside a two-term US senator, former secretary of state, and past First Lady was enough of an unflattering comparison to steer most Americans clear of the GOP candidate. In explaining Trump's rise in US politics, Obama charged the Republican establishment with making his candidacy possible through its acquiescence to and sometimes avid cultivation of nativism, Islamophobia, and racial prejudice (including birtherism) among voters. Trump was the culmination of these ideological tendencies in the GOP, which were inflamed by a reactionary backlash against the country's evolving racial and ethnic diversity. Moreover, Obama attributed Trump's ascendance to an economic recovery that had been slow and uneven. In some instances, the forces of globalization, automation, and inequality had ravaged entire communities, and many of those displaced by machines, downsizing, or outsourcing were left in tenuous socioeconomic positions. In his pledges to fix all of the problems of the US working class through trade wars, Muslim bans, border walls, and other panaceas, Trump, in Obama's view, made false promises that were not only impossible to keep but cynically offered in the first place. Worse still, the Republican candidate had weaponized the fears and biases of the disaffected for the sole purpose of stirring up electoral support that was largely predicated on Americans' skepticism about the future—and each other.[19]

At least a few of Barack Obama's worst fears about the 2016 election did not come to pass. Based on some of Trump's campaign rhetoric, the president had reason to believe that the Republican nominee might question the legitimacy of a Clinton victory. Such a failure to concede the race would not only bring into doubt the election results but could potentially damage public faith in US democracy and its foundational institutions and most sacred rites. To forestall such a scenario, White House officials had planned to have an array of Republican congresspeople, former presidents, and previous Cabinet-level appointees come forward to publicly affirm the election outcome. The administration also made preparations to reveal information gathered by the intelligence community that showed that Russian agents, hackers, social media trolls, and other actors had meddled in the election to support Trump at the expense of Clinton. Up until that time, Obama and his staff had refrained from publicizing the known extent of Russian interference in the election, apparently hoping to avoid the appearance of unduly intervening in a campaign that they believed Clinton was poised to win. As things turned out, trotting out Republican officials to validate the election results proved unnecessary. Furthermore, the administration ultimately chose not to immediately disclose the Russian infiltration of the election, though ongoing investigations later revealed disturbing details regarding the scope of Moscow's tampering and manipulation. The November balloting was, of course, marred by the long lines, voting machine malfunctions, and other problems that were all-too-common fixtures of US elections, but the rampant fraud that Trump and some other Republicans warned of never materialized.[20]

Officially decided in the early morning hours of November 9, Trump beat Clinton by the slimmest of margins across three swing states—Michigan, Wisconsin, and Pennsylvania—which was enough to win the Electoral College vote and thus the presidency. Similarly to Romney and McCain before him, Trump overperformed among non-Hispanic whites, garnering 57 percent of their votes. He did even better among whites without college degrees and managed to carry the college-educated white vote by four percentage points over Clinton. Men and voters over 65 years of age cast 52 percent of their ballots for Trump, and as expected he swept rural areas. Like Obama, Clinton's strength was with minorities, women, the college educated, urbanites, and younger Americans. She received 89 percent of the Black vote, 66 percent of the Hispanic vote, 55 percent of ballots cast by people younger than 30, and 54 percent of the women's vote. While she lost too many battleground states to overtake Trump in the Electoral College, Clinton prevailed in the popular vote by a margin of nearly 3 million ballots, winning 48.5 percent of the total votes cast.

There were many reasons behind Clinton's loss, though it is difficult to weigh the relative importance of each. Going into the general election season, the Clinton brand had been tarnished by assorted scandals, the most recent of which involved a secret email server that she had relied on during her time as secretary of state. Clinton fatigue had plagued portions of the electorate since the 1990s and afflicted both the 2008 election cycle and the 2016 one. American voters are not inherently averse to political dynasties, as illustrated by the decades of electoral success enjoyed by the Kennedys and the Bushes.

Still, Hillary Clinton did not benefit from any lingering affinity for her surname, her centrism, or her previous public service, and it is probable that her gender played a role in driving down her likability and electability among some voters.

To be sure, Clinton was able to stitch together much of Obama's winning coalition. However, the Black turnout rate appeared to have declined between 5 and 10 percent from its 2012 level; this alone was enough to cost her the election. Other factors were at play as well. Third-party candidates, including Jill Stein of the Green Party and Libertarian Gary Johnson, likely drew votes away from both Clinton and Trump and were crucial determinants in narrowly decided swing states. Documented efforts by Russian operatives to use Facebook, Twitter, and other media to dissuade Black voters and others from supporting Clinton undoubtedly had an impact, as did the announcement by FBI director James Comey just days before the election that his agency was reopening an investigation into the former secretary of state's emails. As in 2008, the seeming inevitability of a Clinton victory militated against it, and Trump proved to be a more relentless and cunning campaigner than many observers had imagined. Ultimately, shifting demographics, the Obama coalition, and her opponent's many foibles were not enough to send Clinton back to the White House. The pendulum that had swung forward to make an Obama presidency possible was now swinging backward to usher in the era of Trump.[21]

Black public reactions to the election outcome generally ranged from shock and anger to sadness and fear. Van Jones, a CNN commentator and former Obama White House official, was visibly distraught as he contemplated the meaning of a Trump presidency. "How do I explain this to my children?" he wondered on air, having raised them not to resort to the bullying and bigotry that Trump had just dumped in abundant quantities into US electoral politics. During an appearance on *Saturday Night Live*, comedian Dave Chappelle soberly wished the president-elect luck but made a request in return. "I'm going to give him a chance," he told the studio audience. "And we, the historically disenfranchised, demand that he give us one, too." David A. Love, writing for the online news site TheGrio.com, was slightly less charitable in his message to Trump and his supporters. "America, say hello to President Trump," he wrote in an editorial that suggested that GOP voters had lied to pollsters, thus leading to an Election Day surprise. "And you can thank white folks for this mess."[22]

The idea that Trump's election represented a white backlash against the historic presidency of Barack Obama held sway in some quarters. Harvard professor Randall Kennedy mused years later that he had mistakenly assumed that a Trump presidency was not possible in the twenty-first century. "If you put Obama next to his successor, you see a declension in character, in knowledge, in every significant way that you want to talk about leadership," he posited in a 2020 interview with me. Yet, as unlikely as it seemed, Trump had triumphed in the campaign, duly becoming Obama's successor. Rev. Dr. Stanley Fuller of Baltimore made the point even more sharply. The Obama presidency "made more of a difference to Caucasians than it did to us, for different reasons," the African American clergyman asserted in an interview with me. "Donald Trump is only president because Barack Hussein Obama was president. . . . That they would select a substandard individual was because an above average African American was in the office and handled it. I'm clear about that."[23]

Somewhat out of tune with the prevailing African American mood, minister Louis Farrakhan of the Nation of Islam celebrated the Trump victory as the needed inducement for Blacks to separate from whites and seek a land of their own elsewhere. "The white man is going to push. He's putting in place the very thing that will limit the freedom of others," the Muslim leader declared at a New Jersey event in December. "My message to Mr. Trump: Push it real good. Push it so good that black people say, 'I'm outta here. I can't take it no more.'" Farrakhan's response to the election was certainly a minority opinion among African Americans. Nonetheless, he was probably right in his assumption that many Black people anticipated a Trump administration that would not be concerned about their rights and freedoms.[24]

The NAACP issued a conciliatory statement on the day after the election but let it be known that it had not forgotten the troubling tone of the campaign. As head of the country's oldest civil rights organization, President Cornell William Brooks congratulated Trump on his victory and offered to work with him on matters of mutual concern, notwithstanding that "the 2016 campaign has regularized racism, standardized anti-Semitism, de-exceptionalized xenophobia, and mainstreamed misogyny." If the new administration fell short on supporting the NAACP's notions of liberty and justice, Brooks promised that his organization would be "in its face." A week after the election, the leadership of the Black Lives Matter Global Network announced a redoubling of its efforts to end state violence against African Americans in the wake of the "election of a white supremacist to the highest office in American government." The group's public statement anticipated a Trump administration bent on inflicting "death, disenfranchisement, and deportations" and called for more civic engagement as a means of countering the supposedly imminent assault. Like many Black people, Alabama resident George Rudolph saw primarily regressive undertones in the election outcome. His wife, Sarah, had been grievously wounded in the KKK bombing of a Black church in Birmingham in 1963, which further inclined him to frame Trump's victory in historical terms. "It looks like we are going back to the back of the bus," the 65-year-old Vietnam veteran told a reporter. He seemed resigned to seeing only darker days ahead.[25]

Beyond the disparate reactions of Black individuals and organizations, outrage over the election exploded across every region of the country. Thousands took to the streets of Chicago, New York, Philadelphia, Austin, Atlanta, San Francisco, and other cities to protest the voting results. Some chanted "Trump's a racist," "Impeach Trump," or "Abolish the Electoral College," while others lit fires, blocked thoroughfares, and vandalized property. Individuals and groups pleased with the outcome of the election also let their feelings be known.

Freshmen at Wake Forest University in North Carolina stormed out of their dormitory in the early morning hours following Trump's win and gleefully hurled racial epithets across the private campus. Two students in York County, Pennsylvania, marched through the halls of their high school with a picture of Trump as someone cried "White Power!" In Minnesota, Moses Karngbaye was horrified to discover graffiti in the bathroom of his high school that read "#Go Back to Africa" and "Make America Great Again." Within just eight days of the November 8 vote, the Southern Poverty Law Center tallied more than 700 incidents of harassment and intimidation related to the election, with a plurality (206) directed at immigrants and the second-highest number (151) targeting Black people.

Asked during a televised November 13 interview to respond to the turmoil generated by his victory, Trump initially dismissed the "very small amount" of hatred and conflict that had raged across the nation for the past several days. Pressed further by the interviewer, the president-elect looked into the camera and demanded that the perpetrators of violence and mischief "stop it." Trump's call for calm neither quieted the country nor made Americans any more optimistic about the future. One poll conducted after Election Day revealed that 46 percent of respondents expected race relations to get worse following Trump's win. Of the African Americans surveyed, 74 percent predicted worse relations, compared to 43 percent of whites.[26]

As protests, hate crimes, and social media wars consumed the country, the news of Trump's triumph hit the White House hard. One staffer likened the executive mansion to a "funeral home" replete with long faces and an enervating silence. Obama, aware that all eyes were on him, appeared subdued before his team, trying hard not to crack at a time when they needed his usual equanimity. "So, what happened?" the president asked Cody Keenan, a speechwriter, as he tried to process the idea of Donald Trump as his successor. Obama had not prepared well for such a reality and thus found himself searching for whispers of hope amid a howling wind of defeat. For his public face and upcoming pronouncements to the American people, he settled on committing to do his part to ensure a peaceful transfer of power and to encourage his fellow citizens, particularly young people, to remain optimistic and engaged. His first priority was to fortify Americans' faith in their democracy, despite the facts that Trump had lost the popular vote and that Russian meddling on his behalf would cast a long shadow over the legitimacy of his election. When asked by Keenan whether he wanted to reassure the world regarding the days to come, Obama paused. "No," he replied. "I don't think that I'm the one to tell them that."[27]

The president's evolving answer to that query ("What happened?") centered on Trump, Clinton, and himself. As he had maintained during the campaign, the GOP candidate was not an aberration that had sprung up in full bloom without historical roots or partisan nurturing. Instead, Trump was entirely a creature of a Republican Party that had for at least a generation cultivated racial bigotry, anti-immigrant passions, Islamophobia, and other ugliness for the sake of political gain. According to Obama, the novelty of Trump was that he was able to crystallize these strands of GOP ideology and politicking into a single campaign that was flamboyant and media savvy enough to attract sustained attention yet simple and direct enough for anyone to understand. "What surprised me," the president acknowledged days after the election, "was the degree to which those tactics and rhetoric completely jumped the rails." He was especially disappointed that establishment Republicans, such as John Boehner, had not moved to check the extreme elements—the Tea Party rebels, the conspiracy theorists, and eventually Trump—that were gradually taking over their party. It was a kind of comeuppance for a GOP leadership that had been too shortsighted in its quest for power and dominance to realize the self-destructive course that it was plotting. However, at this junction, Obama could hardly have found any pleasure in the arresting implications of Republican voters being so disconnected from their party leadership that they were willing to take a gamble on electing a candidate whom Obama had once labeled a "carnival barker."[28]

Although he had campaigned widely for Hillary Clinton, Obama also considered her a factor in her own demise. One could argue that the 2016 election was a rerun of Clinton being Clinton. Just like in 2008, she was too entitled to the nomination, too cautious and unimaginative to know when to move from the center, too organizationally inflexible to spend more time campaigning in shaky midwestern swing states, and too reliant on credentials and past story lines. Obama, however, was careful not to explicitly criticize Clinton for losing to the likes of Donald Trump. Such carping was not his style, and he knew that Democratic infighting was the last thing needed in the face of unified Republican control of the White House and the Congress. Nonetheless, he hinted clearly at the nominee's shortcomings.

In a post-election interview, Obama complimented the young people who had assisted his campaigns and served in his administration. "If you look at the data from the election," he observed, "if it were just young people who were voting, Hillary would have gotten 500 electoral votes." Instead, she underperformed among key parts of the Obama coalition, especially when it came to Black voters, who could not get quite as excited about her as they had been about Obama. In the same interview, he noted that Clinton was not able to attract the support of working-class whites in the same way that he had in 2008 and 2012. He politely chalked it up to the influence of conservative media like Fox News and the inability of Democrats to clearly articulate their policy prescriptions and achievements. But he also pointed out that Clinton had failed to perform the basic due diligence of showing up, a mistake that cost her precious votes in Michigan, for example, where Trump's margin of victory was fewer than 11,000 votes. "Part of it is also Democrats not working at a grass-roots level, being in there, showing up, making arguments," Obama said of the recent election results. "And when we're on the ground we do well. This is why I won Iowa."[29]

Along with theorizing about Trump's win and Clinton's defeat, Obama tried to assess the election results relative to his own appearance on history's stage. Like many others, he had assumed that the

United States would eventually elect a president of color, given the demographic trends of the twenty-first century. Yet in hindsight, he opined that he may have been as much as two decades too early in winning the office. In his estimate, a significant portion of the country's population was not quite prepared for a Black president, and they had thus not been successful in processing such a reality, even during nearly a decade of an Obama White House. Subsequently, when Trump emerged promising to "make America great again" and appealing to yesteryear notions of racial normalcy, nearly half of the electorate was amenable to such a proposal.

Obama's speculation regarding his historical timing was a self-deprecating supposition that did not quite match the known facts. His margins in the Electoral College and popular vote in two consecutive elections had been too significant to write off as a mistake or poor timing, not to mention that he had succeeded in getting reelected in the midst of economic conditions that by all rights should have crushed his bid for a second term. He had activated voters and segments of society that had never been given to civic participation and inspired them to show up in record numbers in two different election cycles. Thus, it was not so much that he was historically out of place as a Black president, but instead that his formula for success was not easily replicated, at least not by Hillary Clinton. At the time, Obama could only take cold comfort in this singular accomplishment, especially when it was followed by the depressing task of having to pass the White House keys to a nemesis such as Trump. Nonetheless, most US voters had shown (twice) that they were ready for a Black commander in chief. In a less modest moment, Obama openly claimed in December that he would have beaten Trump if he had been allowed to run for a third term, an assertion that seemed to belie his fretting over history's clock.[30]

After congratulating him in a 3:30 a.m. call and extending an invitation to meet, Obama hosted Trump in the White House on Thursday, November 10. Surrounded by reporters and illuminated by incessant camera flashes, the two men sat together to signal the forthcoming transfer of power. In perhaps the most awkward and surreal moment of his twenty-year career in electoral politics, Obama seemed alert and congenial, making eye contact with Trump, who appeared much more anxious and out of his element. They exchanged handshakes and platitudes as the moment seemed to require, with the Republican calling his predecessor a "very good man" and the Democrat telling the next occupant of the White House, "if you succeed, the country succeeds." The two met privately for ninety minutes, during which Obama broached issues such as health care, counterterrorism policy, and the process for filling Cabinet positions. He later reported to his staff that Trump's knowledge of these matters was rudimentary at best, about the same depth as he had shown during the presidential debates in the fall. The niceties lasted for about a month, with both men calling for calm and national reconciliation. Obama's staff proceeded to make transition arrangements with the incoming team, and Trump in early December claimed that he was taking some of the president's appointment recommendations "very seriously."[31]

And then Trump started tweeting again. On December 28, the same day that he reported that he had a "very, very good talk" with Obama by phone, the president-elect turned to Twitter to contend that he was doing his "best to disregard the many inflammatory President O statements and roadblocks." Trump was not specific in his allegations, and he claimed later that day that the two staffs were still cooperating "very well." One source of irritation for the Republican may have been the beginnings of a "deep dive" investigation into Russian intervention in the US election, which Obama had announced earlier that month. Intelligence agencies had already collected incriminating evidence that Vladimir Putin's government and its operatives had sought to sway the election, and some of the leads implicated a number of members of the Trump campaign and the incoming administration who had established questionable contacts with various Russian actors. Before departing the White House in late January, Obama ordered that information about Moscow's cyberattack and disinformation campaign be spread across as many agencies as possible. The stated aim was to counter future efforts by Russians and others to interfere in US elections and to leave a clear trail of evidence for intelligence officials to follow as they pursued investigations into the foreign meddling. Another goal was to proactively anticipate the likelihood that the incoming Trump administration would not be keen on investigating claims of Russian interference that might taint his election victory or even jeopardize his presidency. Without public prodding and incontrovertible evidence embedded throughout the government, it was entirely conceivable that Trump and his partisans, once in power, would dismiss the entire episode as "fake news" and as a "witch hunt" orchestrated by Democrats still smarting from Clinton's defeat.[32]

On January 20, 2017, the Obamas prepared to leave the White House in as dignified a manner as they had arrived eight years earlier. Their gracious reception by the Bush family in 2008—even after Obama had just won an election by running against much of the Republican's legacy—served as a model for how they would receive their successors. In the morning, the first couple had coffee and tea with the Trumps before accompanying them to the Capitol for the inauguration. As George W. Bush had done upon departing the White House in 2009, Barack Obama, in one of his last acts in the Oval Office, left a handwritten letter in the Resolute Desk for the next chief executive. His message acknowledged the "great good fortune" that being a president entailed and advised Trump to assist hard-working American families to be successful in their efforts to get ahead. Obama also alluded to the "indispensable" nature of US leadership around the globe and the need to maintain the international relations "upon which our own wealth and safety depend." In thinking about the turmoil and lingering questions surrounding the 2016 election, he called on Trump to be a champion of democracy, its institutions, and the rule of law. "Regardless of the push and pull of daily politics," Obama wrote, "it's up to us to leave those instruments of our democracy at least as strong as we found them." Trump later expressed gratitude for Obama's gesture, telling an interviewer that the 275-word note was "complex" and "thoughtful." As developments soon revealed, the new president turned out to be more of a challenge to democratic norms and the international order than a protector of these things.[33]

Following the swearing-in of the forty-fifth president, the Obamas were taken to Joint Base Andrews in Prince George's County, Maryland. In the cavernous hangar there, they were greeted by nearly 2,000 administration officials and well-wishers. The former president's words of encouragement were brief, and he and Michelle spent about half an hour wading through the crowd for last hugs and farewells. Holding hands, the couple then boarded an awaiting Boeing 747, joining several friends and aides for a vacation flight to Palm Springs, California. As they taxied onto the runway and then soared into the partly cloudy skies above, Eric Holder, snapping pictures from the crowd, could only shake his head. The eight-year journey that he had just witnessed still seemed unbelievable, though he had personally experienced most of it at his departing friend's side as attorney general. Contemplating the national journey ahead probably evoked a similar incredulity but for entirely different reasons.[34]

From the air, Michelle Obama could see both the life that she had left and the new one ahead. While there had been many occasions for smiles and even laughter, being First Lady had been difficult. As she recalled later, there had been no margin for error, no room for slipups, and no grace period for navigating the learning curve. As a Black woman, she needed to be perfect or as close to flawless as possible, since, in her words, "people will measure everyone of our race, of our gender by what we do." It was a hard, if not impossible, expectation to live up to, but her husband's disposition and temperament had been instrumental in helping her cope. She continued to be amazed by his "practiced calm" as the world seemed to close in on them during the financial crisis, the Tea Party mania, the midterm losses, and Trump's election victory.[35]

At times, Michelle had allowed herself to vent in public, such as during the 2016 campaign when she called out Trump's birther lies, his audiotaped boasts about groping women, and his overall unsuitability to lead the country. Still, she was much more likely to face the challenges of her time in the White House with focused resolve and quiet grace than to engage in any public displays of anger or self-pity. When it was revealed that the 2016 convention speech of Melania Trump had lifted several lines from Michelle's 2008 oration at the DNC, the First Lady did not take the Republican candidate's wife to task for the plagiarism. Instead, she later welcomed the incoming First Lady to the White House and offered her advice about surviving the public glare and pressures to come. While she wore it well, it was still all too much. Now, finally out of the bubble and thousands of feet above it, Michelle let go. As the 747 carried her to her new post-presidency world, she cried like a woman who had suddenly discovered her true self again—a good, long, cleansing cry with life-affirming tears.[36]

Donald Trump's first days in the White House were marked by protests and upheaval. Less than twenty-four hours after the inauguration, coordinated women's marches and other demonstrations materialized in cities around the world to denounce the new president, his rhetoric, and his stated policy agenda. In Washington, DC, half a million people gathered to express their disapproval, as did approximately 250,000 in Chicago and more than 100,000 in New York, the latter shouting their way past Trump Tower on Fifth Avenue in a boisterous show of disdain. Abroad, tens of thousands met in London's Trafalgar Square in solidarity with their US counterparts, and thousands of others demonstrated at the Eiffel Tower in Paris. In Prague's Wenceslas Square, protesters paraded with pictures of the new US president and Vladimir Putin, reminding the world of Russia's pro-Trump intervention in the 2016 election. Similar mass marches occurred in Boston, Los Angeles, Philadelphia, Mexico City, Sydney, and Berlin.

Although Barack Obama was not on the ballot in 2016, Trump had, since his first flirtations with birtherism several years earlier, positioned himself as the anti-Obama. This messaging was not only rhetorical and stylistic but was also aimed at the policy record of the Obama administration. Upon assuming the Oval Office, Trump immediately sought to overturn or neutralize a number of his predecessor's regulatory actions related to environmental protections, workers' rights, financial reforms, internet privacy, gun policy, and abortion. The Justice Department under Attorney General Jeff Sessions moved to stiffen penalties for nonviolent drug offenses, which threatened criminal justice reforms that Obama had vigorously pursued during his last years in office. Additionally, Trump's Housing and Urban Development secretary, former presidential candidate Ben Carson, led the administration's efforts to weaken Obama-era initiatives to reduce housing segregation. With a zeal that was appreciated by carbon-producing industries, the EPA proceeded to reverse fuel efficiency standards designed to combat global warming, and the Trump administration approved the Keystone XL oil pipeline, which Obama had refused to authorize. On the international front, Trump repudiated the Trans-Pacific Partnership trade agreement, rejected the Paris climate accord, and abandoned a multilateral nuclear nonproliferation pact with Iran.

From Obama's perspective, if there was a bright spot in Trump's assault on his legacy, it was undoubtedly the multiple failures of the Republican-controlled Congress to repeal the ACA. Furthermore, if there was a positive legislative achievement that Obama could credit to the Trump administration, it was the signing in 2018 of the bipartisan First Step Act, which, despite the more draconian posture of Sessions's Justice Department, further liberalized sentencing guidelines for federal inmates. Despite these developments, Trump seemed to purposefully look for ways to overturn Obama's legacy, no matter the issue or its relative importance. In one of his typical attempts at one-upmanship, Trump acceded to requests to pardon boxing champion Jack Johnson, an act of posthumous clemency that Obama had repeatedly declined to grant. In another effort to undo Obama's work, the Trump Treasury Department delayed the issuance of twenty-dollar bills imprinted with Harriet Tubman's likeness until at least 2028, twelve years after the currency redesign had been originally approved by the Obama administration.[37]

Beyond simply being predicated on rescinding Obama's achievements, Trump's appeal was also based on the not-so-subtle understanding among many of his supporters that he would champion white racial grievances and stem the tide of demographic change in the United States. Toward these ends, he pushed early on for the erection of a southern border wall, the implementation of a Muslim ban, and the ending of temporary protected status for Haitian refugees. In a January 2018 outburst before lawmakers in the Oval Office, he made it clear that his purpose was to reverse the browning of the United States, an objective that animated much of his voter base. "Why do we want all these people from shithole countries coming here?" he reportedly queried in reference to African and Haitian immigrants. His stated preference was for more immigrants from places like Norway, an overwhelmingly white country. While his indelicate statement stirred a protracted controversy in the capital and in the media, his approval rating remained relatively stable in the polls, particularly among self-identified Republicans who largely supported his stances on matters of race.[38]

Trump's desire to whiten the United States was easily observable in how he populated his administration. Seventeen of his initial twenty-four top Cabinet appointees were white men, and he hired non-Hispanic whites to serve in 88 percent of the more than a thousand midlevel political positions filled during his first nine months in office. Trump's nominations to the federal judiciary revealed a similar preference, with white men constituting 74 percent of his nominees, women comprising 19 percent, and nonwhite women making up just 2 percent. These figures were a significant departure from Obama's nominees: white men were only 37 percent of his appointees, women were almost at parity (42 percent), and 15 percent were nonwhite women. To many, Trump's language, actions, and governing style confirmed the worst of their fears: his administration had unleashed a racial backlash against a diversifying United States. One February

2018 poll showed that a majority of Americans considered his policies bad for Muslims and Hispanics, and most believed that Black people continued "to face disadvantages to getting ahead in the U.S." Fifty-seven percent of respondents considered Trump a racist, including more than 80 percent of African Americans polled.[39]

It did not appear that Trump was much bothered by being labeled a racist, nor did the appellation seem to affect his approval rating in polls, which hovered around 40 percent on average. Other un-flattering qualities, such as his unprecedented penchant for telling mistruths, also did not prove to be a disability for him among GOP partisans, even though the *Washington Post* attributed more than 26,000 "false or misleading claims" to him by mid-October 2020, or roughly 19 on average for each day of his presidency. Trump exaggerated or outright lied about things big and small, including the size of the crowd that attended his inauguration and his claim that Obama had tapped phones in Trump Tower, a charge that was disproved by Trump's own Justice Department and FBI. The divisive racial rhetoric and policies, along with the prolific lying, were not so much accidental defects of his presidency but rather intended features of it.[40]

Trump's tenure in the Oval Office was also marked by his insatiable need to project strength and to win at any costs, even if it meant breaking norms, rules, and institutional constraints designed to prevent presidential abuses of power. Aside from apparent violations of the emolument clause of the Constitution and various conflicts of interest, Trump's entire term in office was overshadowed by scandal and investigations. A special prosecutor's report did not definitively find that he had purposely conspired with Russians to subvert the 2016 election, but it did detail several efforts by the president to obstruct justice. In late 2019, the White House was rocked by the public disclosure that Trump and selected officials and aides had tried to coerce the government of Ukraine to investigate the president's political opponents by withholding congressionally approved military assistance. With each passing day, a House-led inquiry, now in the hands of a post-midterm Democratic majority, discovered more documents and testimony that seemed to warrant ever-stronger rebukes of the president's actions. Trump, defiant, isolated, and increasingly unconcerned with consequences, fell back on his support base, regularly riling it up with loud dismissals of the investigations as a lynching and as an attempted coup by Democrats who still had not digested the results of the 2016 election.[41]

On December 18, 2019, Trump became the third US president to be impeached, in this instance on charges of abuse of power and obstruction of Congress. After a two-week trial with a predictably partisan outcome, he was acquitted on both counts in February 2020 by a Republican-led Senate still under the stewardship of majority leader Mitch McConnell. Going into the presidential election cycle, the political atmosphere was charged with a kind of danger and uncertainty that the US republic had seldom faced in its more than 230-year history. Worse still, it was impossible to tell how long the system could continue to endure the severe stress test that the Trump presidency had proven itself to be.[42]

Epilogue

LIFE AFTER THE WHITE HOUSE WAS EVENTFUL FOR THE OBAMAS.
Malia started college at Harvard in the fall of 2017, leaving only
Sasha, sixteen, at home with the former first couple. To avoid dis-
rupting their younger daughter's high school experience, Barack and
Michelle Obama decided to stay in the DC area until at least her
graduation. They moved only two miles northwest of their former
residence at 1600 Pennsylvania Avenue, settling in an 8,200-square-
foot, nine-bedroom mansion in the Kalorama neighborhood, close
to Embassy Row on Massachusetts Avenue. Originally built in the
1920s and now priced at $8.1 million, the Tudor-style home was more
than spacious enough to host friends from out of town or to entertain
local acquaintances.

When not enjoying their new abode, the couple traveled widely
to decompress from eight years of White House life, occasionally
roaming in rich and famous circles that featured the likes of Oprah
Winfrey, Tom Hanks, Bruce Springsteen, David Geffen, and Richard Branson. In March 2017, the Obamas joined the ranks of the
wealthiest stratum of Americans, signing book deals with Penguin
Random House valued at $65 million. For the publisher, it was an
extraordinary gamble for a handful of future works, but given the

worldwide popularity and fascinating life stories of the two authors, it was hard to imagine the bet not paying off. Supplementing these earnings, the former president routinely commanded as much as $400,000 for invited speeches, and Michelle could bring in at least half as much for similar appearances. A 2018 arrangement with the streaming service Netflix provided the Obamas with an additional venue for producing and sponsoring a range of media content, as well as a powerful vehicle for maintaining the Obama brand. Barack Obama in particular proved to be a savvy tastemaker and social influencer by regularly releasing lists of his favorite books and songs, a practice that instantly increased sales for the lucky authors and artists and kept his own name in the cultural mainstream and public consciousness.[1]

Beyond writing another memoir, Obama spent much of his time after the White House years planning his presidential center. He selected Jackson Park in Chicago as the site of construction and envisioned a sprawling twenty-acre campus that would include a library, museum, archive, foundation, community garden, and academic resources. The total cost was estimated to range between $500 million and $1 billion and would require years of fundraising and networking. Unforeseen resistance from neighborhood and environmental groups concerned about the economic and ecological impacts of the center stalled construction, even as the Obamas, in a show of goodwill and personal investment, donated $2 million of their own money to underwrite a summer jobs program in the South Side community. Even before they left the White House, the Obamas had worked in earnest to bring the project to fruition, cultivating allies and supporters in government and the larger Chicago community. In December 2020, a federal review was completed that seemingly cleared the way for construction to begin the following year, though other assessments of the center's environmental impact were ongoing.[2]

During his first years as a private citizen, the former president was careful not to publicly weigh in too often regarding the performance of his successor. Bush had extended him this courtesy after leaving the

White House in 2009, and Obama, in turn, extended it to Trump. Moreover, he likely wanted to minimize the opportunities for the new president to use him as a foil for distracting Americans from the many controversies that engulfed the Trump administration. As he had shown over the previous several years, Trump was not above stoking his base with attacks on Obama, which often took on a racial character in the context of his broader appeal to white aggrievement. Only when Trump's actions involved especially high stakes did the former president feel compelled to raise his voice in opposition. For example, Obama denounced Trump's decision to abandon the Paris climate agreement and his withdrawal of the United States from the Iran nuclear deal. When the Republican president fumbled in his response to a deadly neo-Nazi rally in Charlottesville, Virginia, in August 2017, Obama tweeted a Nelson Mandela quote: "No one is born hating another person because of the color of his skin or his background or his religion." During a visit to South Africa in July 2018 to mark the hundredth anniversary of the anti-apartheid leader's birth, Obama further critiqued Trump's presidency. He castigated "strongman politics" that weakened institutions and extinguished the vital energies of democracy. Without naming his GOP successor, he excoriated the "utter loss of shame among political leaders when they're caught in a lie and they just double down and lie some more." Such references to Trump became more frequent and explicit as the 2020 campaign season dawned.[3]

While in Africa, Barack Obama decided to attend to part of his biography and identity by making another journey to Kenya. When he was there three years earlier, he had promised that he would return. This time, his half sister Auma had convinced him to make the journey to mark the opening of a sports and training center that she had founded in Kogelo. Prior to making the trip to his father's home district, Obama met with President Kenyatta and opposition leader Raila Odinga in Nairobi and complimented them for working together to settle a dispute over the prior year's presidential election. Following a brief stay in the capital, Obama ventured to Siaya County under tight security. As expected, he was met with the adulation of adoring Kenyans as he passed by murals of his likeness and bars that served "Obama brew." At the dedication ceremony for Auma's center, he was joined by Granny Sarah, who was visibly moved by the encounter. Now 96 and using a wheelchair, she had lived long enough to see again her stepgrandson, now a private citizen. It was enough good fortune to warrant a celebration. Helping the matriarch to her feet, Auma started swaying, and so did Sarah, and then Barack. Before an amused crowd, they laughed and danced in the land of his father, whose youthful dreams and unquenchable wanderlust had made the moment possible.[4]

More so than earlier cohorts, the 2020 Democratic presidential candidates were a diverse group of more than twenty contenders. Several people of color (three African Americans, two Asian Americans, and a Hispanic American) were in the running, along with six women and one openly gay man. In common with other minority candidates, the Black aspirants, including New Jersey senator Cory Booker and late entrant Deval Patrick, a former Massachusetts governor, never quite gathered the momentum that some of their candidacies seemed to initially promise, with a few lingering into the new year with only marginal support. Notwithstanding their political and biographical similarities to Obama, none of these nomination contenders catalyzed the public imagination in the ways that the Illinois senator had more than a decade earlier. With both Booker and Patrick bowing out of the race by the New Hampshire primary in February, the possibility of electing a Black president in 2020 fizzled well before the campaign calendar shifted to more diverse states, such as South Carolina and Nevada, later that month.[5]

Of the 2020 candidates, US senator Kamala Harris of California, a former state attorney general and San Francisco prosecutor, had appeared to be the one cut most clearly from Obama's mold. The biracial daughter of Jamaican and Indian immigrants, she was just left of center politically and learned early in life how to navigate demographic boundaries. With an eye on the important primary state of South Carolina, she made an early pitch to concretize her racial bona fides with Black voters in no uncertain terms. "I'm black, and I'm proud of being black," Harris declared in an interview in early 2019. "I was born black. I will die black, and I'm not going to make excuses for anybody because they don't understand." Her emphatic racial signifying sounded closer to Barack Obama leaving the White House in 2017 than campaigning for it in 2008 and was an indication of the importance of drawing early African American support during the Democratic primaries. Lagging in the polls just weeks ahead of the Iowa caucuses, the California senator's unfocused campaign messaging and fundraising woes served her poorly. In a stunning reversal of her earlier momentum, Harris was compelled to exit the race for the White House in December 2019. Unbeknown to anyone at the time, her ambitions were not completely thwarted. She would in due course have a second wind.[6]

As early as 2018, Obama had begun meeting separately with a number of the presidential candidates in his office in the World Wildlife Fund building in Washington's West End. He was circumspect about publicly disclosing the details of these sessions and carefully maintained a detached neutrality. Only after former vice president Joe Biden surged to the top of the field during the spring primaries did Obama endorse the presumptive nominee. In a move that proved historic and demonstrated the clout of African American voters in the Democratic Party, Biden selected Kamala Harris as his running mate, making her the first Black woman to receive the VP nomination of a major political party. The selection of Harris seemed all the more consequential during a summer of discontent when protests once again blazed across the country in the wake of yet another well-publicized rash of police killings of unarmed Black people.

Unlike any election cycle in recent memory, a gnawing uncertainty loomed over the 2020 process as the outbreak of a coronavirus pandemic abbreviated the primary season, elevated unemployment to Great Depression levels, and caused more than 200,000 deaths in the United States alone by the time of the first presidential debate in late September. The implications for the November election of the unprecedented health crisis and the attendant economic damage unfolded over several months as voters prepared for a Trump-Biden matchup that would feature Obama in a starring role. In early October, Trump disclosed on Twitter that he had tested positive for the coronavirus, and he eventually required hospitalization as part of his treatment. Given Trump's refusal to wear a protective mask even at crowded campaign events, his diagnosis was less a surprise than a morbid counterpoint to months of his downplaying the plague's severity.[7]

Having campaigned as an Obama-Biden Democrat who would restore integrity to the White House and normalcy to the nation, Biden soundly defeated Trump in the general election. His historic tally of more than 81 million votes placed him well ahead of Trump's 74 million, and he won the Electoral College vote by the same 306-232 margin that Trump had garnered in 2016. In many ways, the election was similar to recent presidential contests and featured long-established partisan coalitions and voting patterns. Biden excelled among minorities, women, college graduates, urban and suburban voters, and people under 45 years of age. Like Democratic candidates before him, his regional strength lay mostly in the East and West, and he also won Upper Midwest swing states that Hillary Clinton had narrowly lost four years earlier. In contrast, Trump managed to largely reconstruct his base electorate of 2016, winning most white, male, older, rural, and non-degreed voters. Furthermore, he enjoyed solid support across southern and midwestern states. However, the president lost the crucial swing states of Michigan, Wisconsin, and Pennsylvania, which had ensured his victory four years earlier, as well as the Sunbelt states of Arizona and Georgia, with their increasingly diverse electorates. If there was a silver lining for the GOP in Trump's defeat, it was in the incremental improvement in his showing among minority voters. Compared to his 2016 performance, the president augmented his share of African American (12 percent), Hispanic (32 percent), and Asian (34 percent) electoral support, a shift that will no doubt preoccupy Democratic strategists for years to come.[8]

After his November 3 trouncing at the polls, Trump flailed wildly and dangerously for weeks. Instead of conceding defeat, he tried to delegitimize the election by falsely claiming that mail-in ballots, voting machines, and recounts had all been rigged against him, although down-ballot Republicans overall did well in the election. In his daily tweets to his tens of millions of Twitter followers, he raged against poll workers, governors, and judges who resisted his assault on US democracy. Well into December, Trump and his allies filed scores of progressively outlandish lawsuits in an unprecedented effort to overturn Biden's decisive win. For weeks after Trump's defeat, Republican powerbrokers, including Senate majority leader Mitch McConnell, remained reluctant to publicly challenge his fictions and authoritarian impulses, a craven reticence that undoubtedly emboldened the large numbers of Republicans in Congress, in statehouses, and among the general public who openly supported Trump's attempts to reverse the election results.[9]

All of this devious scheming, desperate maneuvering, and rank cowardice might have been oddly amusing had the threat to US democratic principles and institutions not been so grave. In one especially chilling reminder of the existential risks to the constitutional system, many Americans found it terrifyingly surreal to learn that Trump had conferred with confidants in the White House in December about the possibility of using the military to derail the coming transfer of power.[10] Against this backdrop of incessant machinations and unseemly drama, the Electoral College officially confirmed Biden's win on December 14.

Breakthroughs in vaccine research offered a bit of good news for the lame-duck president, but by the end of 2020 coronavirus-related deaths had spiked to well over 300,000 US fatalities, underscoring the cost of Trump's initial failure to implement an effective federal response to the pandemic. Similar to how his presidency began, it ended with a months-long invasive cyberattack by Russian operatives on American companies and government agencies, including the Departments of Homeland Security, Energy, and the Treasury. Characteristically hesitant to criticize Vladimir Putin or his government's actions no matter how hostile, Trump took to Twitter to baselessly blame the Chinese for the espionage, even as US intelligence officials and his own secretary of state, Mike Pompeo, singled out Moscow as the culprit. "The cyberattack is far greater in the Fake News Media than in actuality," Trump tweeted on December 19. "I have been fully briefed and everything is well under control." His spurious assurances were of little comfort to Americans as they again witnessed the unspooling damage of a Russian offensive against their institutions and national security. Trump's ongoing penchant for misstatements and false claims escalated in his final weeks in office, further eroding public trust in government, elections, science, and even previously agreed-upon truths.[11]

As some had expected, the Trump administration concluded on a particularly appalling note. Acting on his incendiary tweets and other pronouncements calling for mass demonstrations in Washington to contest his electoral defeat, a frenzied mob of Trump supporters gathered on January 6—the day that Congress was scheduled to formally count the Electoral College votes—and stormed the Capitol Building, forcing a postponement of the session and a lockdown of the complex. Televised images of overwhelmed police officers clashing with belligerent rioters, some of whom made their way into the Senate Chamber and congressional offices, seemed from an alternative universe. Whether simply the venting of partisan passions gone awry or the last gasp of a bungled coup attempt orchestrated from the White House itself, the scenes were outrageous and conjured visions of a kind of political turmoil that typically plagues less durable governments in less stable countries. Rattled by the violence, several foreign nations called on the Trump administration to allow for a peaceful transfer of power, a hallmark of US democracy. "Shocking scenes in

Washington, D.C.," NATO chief Jens Stoltenberg tweeted as images of the besieged Capitol Building circulated around the globe. "The outcome of this democratic election must be respected."[12]

Having instructed his supporters to "show strength" by marching on Congress, Trump was slow to respond to the insurrection, even as other Republican officials, including Vice President Mike Pence, called for a cessation of the violence. The president eventually released a one-minute video address that encouraged the rioters at the Capitol Building to go home; however, he again falsely asserted to his supporters that "we had an election that was stolen from us." Initially caught flat-footed, even though Trump had called for the demonstrations several days earlier, the Capitol Police, assisted by the National Guard and other agencies, slowly regained control of the Capitol grounds and began enforcing a 6:00 p.m. citywide curfew that had been announced earlier by Mayor Muriel Bowser. The failure of various law enforcement and military agencies to provide adequate protection for the Capitol prior to the invasion resulted in firings and investigations in the immediate aftermath of the insurrection. Not wholly without reason, some speculated that the lax security arrangements at the Capitol Building on January 6 were not coincidental but instead indicated a level of coordinated dereliction that implicated the Trump administration, the Capitol Police, and several congressional officials.[13]

As night fell, members of Congress, who had been hurriedly evacuated when the mob breached the premises, resumed the ceremonial counting of Electoral College votes, a process that was prolonged by futile GOP challenges to the electoral vote tallies of Arizona and Pennsylvania. Fortunately, none of the legislators had been injured in the earlier invasion of their workplace. The same, however, could not be said of US institutions, which were bruised and battered after years of antidemocratic assaults from foreign and domestic sources.[14]

Trump's failure to reverse the election outcome by either lawful or extralegal means triggered acute repercussions during his last days in office. Twitter, which had arguably enabled his denigration of US democracy over the previous four years, permanently suspended his personal account on January 8 "due to the risk of further incitement of violence." It was a significant blow to Trump's ability to instantly communicate with his massive following, though it came much too late to lend credibility to Twitter's claim that it had been "transparent around our policies and their enforcement" concerning Trump's ongoing abuse of its platform. Cracks in GOP support for the president widened in the wake of the insurrection, and several officials, including transportation secretary Elaine Chao and education secretary Betsy DeVos, resigned in protest over Trump's countenancing of mob rule. Many Republicans in Congress condemned the January 6 rampage that ultimately resulted in five deaths, and a few even pinned blame on Trump. Alaska senator Lisa Murkowski, however, was an exception among GOP legislators: she publicly called for Trump's immediate departure. "I want him to resign. I want him out," she told reporters in her Capitol Hill office. "He has caused enough damage." Despite having intimately witnessed years of White House scandals and intrigues as vice president, Mike Pence resisted demands for the activation of the Twenty-Fifth Amendment, which could have—with the consent of a majority of the Cabinet—at least temporarily relieved Trump of presidential authority. Even as Trump publicly excoriated Pence for not attempting to illegally derail the electoral vote counting in Congress, the vice president decided against intervening on behalf of the country to end his boss's tenure prior to 12:00 p.m. on January 20.[15]

If Pence and other administration officials intended to simply wait out the crisis until Inauguration Day, others, incensed by the brazen attack on the Capitol, felt compelled to act. On January 8, House speaker Nancy Pelosi, Trump's most powerful and seasoned foe in Washington, publicly disclosed that she had discussed the "unstable president" with top Pentagon officials in an effort to limit his access to the nuclear codes. She also announced that the House would proceed with a second impeachment of Trump for "inciting violence against the Government of the United States." Predictably falling along mostly partisan lines, the House's 232-197 vote on January 13 in favor of impeachment was both symbolic and substantive. The congressional indictment marked Trump's record with a unique stain, distinguishing him as the only US president to be impeached twice, and both rebukes occurred in a single term. In recess until January 19, the Senate—split 50-50 between Democrats and Republicans and still under Mitch McConnell's control until Inauguration Day—signaled that it would not proceed with a trial prior to Trump leaving office as constitutionally required on January 20. Though Pelosi considered Trump an immediate threat to US democracy, she did not press the issue and instead waited until after the inauguration to transmit the impeachment article to the Senate. Spared the ignominy of early removal from office, Trump's legal troubles were likely just beginning as he left the White House for the final time, since the two impeachments highlighted charges and allegations for which he might still be criminally liable. Notoriously litigious himself, much of Trump's post-presidency life will probably be spent fending off federal and state indictments related to a range of alleged offenses committed before and during his White House years.[16]

Surprising no one, Trump boycotted the inauguration of Joe Biden, a decision that the incoming president considered a "good thing." During the period between his election and his swearing-in, Biden was measured in his responses to Trump's efforts to stay in power. As courts, statehouses, and ultimately Congress reaffirmed his status as president-elect, Biden, a center-left Democrat with an affable manner, steadily gathered advisors and deployed his transition team, which often found the outgoing administration to be uncooperative. In the fraught moment of the Capitol Building invasion, Biden made an in-person press statement that seemed all the more presidential since it preceded Trump's own videotaped response to the crisis. In candid terms, Biden condemned the lawlessness as bordering on sedition and stressed the fragility of US democracy in the overheated political climate. Further sharpening the contrast between himself and his predecessor, he called on Trump to "step up" in the midst of the chaos and mob action in order to fortify the rule of law and the public's faith in its application. As Barack Obama had done when he announced his bid for the presidency in Springfield, Illinois, fourteen years earlier, Biden quoted Abraham Lincoln and called for peace and mutual respect even in a time of bitter division—for the sake of the American experiment in republican government, the "last best hope of earth." It was the kind of hopeful appeal for unity and civility that no one had heard from a US president in quite some time.[17]

Following his heavily guarded inauguration, Biden began his term with the thinnest of Democratic majorities in the Senate—where Vice President Kamala Harris will be called upon to cast tie-breaking votes—and the House. Politically, he could have been in a far worse position, but it was still hard to imagine a time when the nation as a whole was more sick, impoverished, vulnerable, and flat-out exhausted than when it entered 2021. The Trump era was indeed over, but what lay ahead was hardly discernible to those who had survived the rolling crises of the previous four years.

Conversations with my elderly relative, first referenced in the preface, about the 2016 and 2020 presidential election campaigns, were almost as intriguing as they were back in 2008 when we both tried to imagine a Black first family. Now in his 80s, my family member reverted back to form. Having only voted in 2008 and 2012, he swore off voting in the 2016 election until the very last moment, though he was a bit more driven to vote against Trump four years later. "It doesn't matter which one wins," he flatly told me during the 2016 cycle. "They won't get anything done, at least not for Black people." I could only view his words as a not-too-unreasonable interpretation of at least a portion of the Obama presidency, as much as doing so made me uncomfortable. History and historians have only now begun to judge the Obama White House years in their entirety, and we will continue to do so for generations. Nonetheless, my elderly relative is likely not alone in his early conclusions, despite their simplicity.

On the positive side of the ledger, the two-term Obama presidency accomplished much. Many of these achievements directly benefited African Americans and their communities, as well as the broader population. The stimulus package, auto bailout, and other emergency measures saved millions from the free-falling joblessness and poverty that would have accompanied an actual depression, though the Black unemployment rate spiked to nearly 17 percent during 2010-2011 and remained notably higher than the national average during Obama's tenure. The Affordable Care Act, Obama's signature legislative triumph, measurably reduced the Black uninsured rate, and hard-won enhancements of unemployment benefits, nutritional assistance, Pell Grants, and tax credits fortified a fraying social safety net. Largely through the Justice Department, the administration stood firmly behind voting rights, school desegregation, LGBTQ equality, reproductive rights, and criminal justice reform. New fuel efficiency standards, green energy initiatives, and the Paris climate agreement promised to slow the ravages of climate change, though the Trump administration made strenuous efforts to undo some of these policies. Quite significantly, powerful symbolism merged with real efforts at diversity to make the Obama administration unique as well as unprecedented. His Cabinet, West Wing, and judicial appointments mirrored the demographic texture of the country more than the racial and gender profiles of earlier administrations, and the optics of a Black first family in the White House was of incalculable importance in the eyes of many Americans and others around the world.

In the sphere of international affairs, Obama's record was decidedly mixed. As he had promised during the 2008 campaign, he succeeded in reducing US troop deployments abroad, especially in Iraq and Afghanistan. But the Arab Spring and its reversals seemed to have genuinely caught him off guard and left him torn between either supporting the new rebels or abiding the allied autocrats. In Africa, the administration mitigated much suffering in places like Liberia, yet the independence of South Sudan failed to resolve a long-standing East African dilemma, which turned out to require more attention, resources, and patience than anyone had anticipated. In the Caribbean, rapprochement with Cuba created diplomatic openings that had not previously existed during Obama's lifetime, and the US response to the 2010 earthquake in Haiti was humane and substantive. Regarding rivalries among the great powers, geopolitical maneuvers against China and Russia failed to rein in the former's economic penetration of Africa or the latter's willingness to destabilize Western democracies, including the United States. Additionally, the emergence of the ISIS terrorist group in the Middle East and the increasing US reliance on armed drones in counterinsurgency operations raised questions about both the efficacy and ramifications of US policies abroad.

For many Black critics on the left, perceived shortcomings of the Obama administration had as much to do with style, degree, and timing as with any unbridgeable differences over discernible motives or desired outcomes. Slow, cautious responses to police violence in places like Ferguson and Baltimore were emblematic of a managerial ethos that prized pragmatic movement and informed incrementalism over nearly all else. Such a philosophy was behind Obama's universalist methodology regarding big, transformative policies, which were often moderated further by his tendency to be keenly concerned about balancing complex and divergent interests among various constituencies. Occasionally, this governance approach did provide disproportionately greater benefits to the most vulnerable, as in the case of the ACA and drug sentencing reform, even though some of the president's critics pressed him for more targeted remedies to address historical discrimination and ongoing racial disparities.

There were, of course, some policies and actions that reflected poorly on the administration, and history's judgment will likely not find soft words for characterizing them. For instance, Obama's reluctance to exercise his clemency powers until the last quarter of his presidency represented an uncommon lapse of empathy. Moreover, the administration's hesitancy to pursue the white-collar rogues responsible for the countless toxic mortgages and other chicanery that led to the financial crisis and its attendant human suffering is difficult to excuse. Although it stoked the ire of the CBC and other stakeholders, the White House fumbling over HBCU loan rules was more readily attributable to some Ivy League myopia and unfamiliarity with these minority-serving institutions and their student bodies than to any ill intent. Furthermore, a willingness to countenance authoritarians, warmongers, and kleptocrats in Africa and elsewhere had much to do with the tough tradeoffs between principle and practice that such policy environments required, notwithstanding that US goals can be greatly sullied by the means employed to reach them.

On the issue of immigration, Obama arguably had good intentions and wanted Congress to pass a comprehensive reform bill. Such legislation would have concretized temporary measures such as his 2012 executive order that allowed some undocumented individuals to remain in the country. However, the president's efforts to put off some removals while deporting millions of other unauthorized immigrants earned him the suspicions of an increasingly nativist GOP and the reputation of "deporter in chief" among some Hispanic and other constituencies. In the end, immigration policy was a politically polarizing issue, and the xenophobic appeals of Donald Trump and others made a bipartisan resolution a remote possibility.[18]

Wedged between two Republicans whom history is not likely to elevate very high on its list of best presidents, Barack Obama left office popular among most Americans, and especially among Black people. He had accomplished something that many previously believed unachievable and had been reelected with Electoral College and popular vote margins that were increasingly rare in US presidential races. Mildly wizened by his years in the Oval Office, Obama has now quietly slipped into the roles of senior statesman and cultural icon, though his vaunted political talents are still occasionally brought to bear on behalf of others on the campaign trail.

Obama's latest memoir, *A Promised Land*, was published only days after the 2020 election. Though excessively detailed with the tedium and minutiae of governing, the book radiates confidence regarding the nation's future. But the volume also is tempered by a wisdom that comes from experiencing hard-won successes, dispiriting reversals, and unintended consequences. Like many Americans, Obama views the Trump presidency as a dire cautionary tale, and he recognizes that "no single election will settle" the issues that so fiercely divide the country. Yet writing in the midst of a pandemic, nationwide protests, and a near economic collapse, Obama still holds fast to a belief in the "possibility of America" and "our experiment in democracy." Just as he did when he made his improbable bid for the presidency, Obama expressly places his faith in the younger generation of Americans whose future is tied to the promises and perils of the new century. Ever the pragmatic realist, he continues to see and write about "the world as it is." This newest meditation—though filtered through the harrowing hindsight of the last four years—reads much the same as the aspirational mantra of hope and change that Obama is best known for. And as one might expect by this point in his journey, he makes no apologies for his enduring optimism.[19]

ACKNOWLEDGMENTS

AS WITH MY PREVIOUS PROJECTS, THERE IS NOT ENOUGH INK or paper to adequately thank all of the people who inspired and facilitated my work on this book. Various individuals at the University of North Carolina at Chapel Hill were supportive in ways that warrant my eternal gratitude. Colleagues in the Department of African, African American, and Diaspora Studies have provided me with a wonderful intellectual community. I am especially thankful to Eunice Sahle and Reginald Hildebrand for making possible my return to Chapel Hill and for being such great people. The UNC History Department has also been supportive of my career and work, as have the Institute for the Arts and Humanities (special thanks to Michele Berger and the fall 2017 faculty fellows for their feedback and encouragement), the College of Arts and Sciences, the Office of the Provost, the UNC library system, and several other individuals and organizations, including Indiana University at Bloomington. A number of additional colleagues have assisted me during my professional journey and merit recognition here: John Bodnar, Kevin K. Gaines, Michael Gomez, J. Lee Greene, William J. Moses, Colin Palmer, Patricia Schechter, and Richard B. Turner.

The staff members at Johns Hopkins University Press were a delight to work with. The draft manuscript benefited significantly from the keen eye and editorial talents of Laura Davulis, who understood the book's potential right from the start of our collaboration. Expert copyediting by Merryl A. Sloane helped further hone the manuscript into a book that I am proud to share with the world. My literary agent, Kevin O'Connor, has been the most stalwart, reliable, and upbeat advocate that an author could hope for, and I look forward to working together on future projects. I would also like to express my heartfelt appreciation for my family and their genuine care for my well-being and work. Special gratitude goes to my wife, Alfreda, who doubles as my most valued reader.

I am indebted to the Obama administration officials, congresspeople, civil rights leaders, clergy members, academicians, and others who shared their thoughts and experiences with me via interviews and correspondence. Like so many other researchers, I also owe a debt of gratitude to the legions of journalists, scholars, bloggers, digital archivists, government staffers, professional photographers, amateur videographers, and others who have been instrumental to the documentation and preservation of twenty-first-century history, politics, and culture. The internet has made their vital work more accessible than ever, and all future studies of the Obama presidency and its times will surely benefit, as I have, from these sources and the 24/7 multimedia coverage of this era.

NOTES

CHAPTER 1. WANDERERS AND DREAMERS

1. Meriwether, *Proudly We Can Be Africans*; Julius K. Nyerere, "One-Party Government," in Asante and Abarry, *African Intellectual Heritage*, 555-558.
2. Obama, *Dreams from My Father*, 9; Firstbrook, *The Obamas*; Shachtman, *Airlift to America*, 5-6; Jacobs, *The Other Obama*.
3. Jackie Robinson, Harry Belafonte, and Sidney Poitier were among the roughly 8,000 people who helped fund the scholarships. "Obama Overstates Kennedys' Role in Helping His Father," *Mercury News* (San Jose, CA), May 28, 2008, http://www.mercurynews.com/2008/03/29/obama-overstates-kennedys-role-in-helping-his-father/; Shachtman, *Airlift to America*, 5-8.
4. Rachel L. Swarns, "Words of Obama's Father Still Waiting to Be Read by His Son," *New York Times*, June 18, 2016, http://www.nytimes.com/2016/06/19/nyregion/letters-by-and-about-barack-obamas-father.html; Schmitt, *Demographic Statistics of Hawaii*, 120-121.
5. Nordyke, "Blacks in Hawai'i."
6. Jacobs, *The Other Obama*, 116.
7. Obama, *Dreams from My Father*, 125-126, 422; Jacobs, *The Other Obama*, 120-121; Shachtman, *Airlift to America,* 9.
8. Obama, *Dreams from My Father*, 126; Department of Health, State of Hawaii, "Certificate of Live Birth" (Barack Hussein Obama II, 61 10641), https://obamawhitehouse.archives.gov/sites/default/files/rss_viewer/birth-certificate-long-form.pdf; Jenny Neyman, "Obama Baby Sitter Awaits New Era—Soldotna Woman Eager for Former Charge's Reign," *Redoubt Reporter* (Soldotna, AK), Jan. 20, 2009, http://redoubtreporter.blogspot.com/2009/01/obama-baby-sitter-awaits-new-era.html; Jonathan Martin,

"Obama's Mother Known Here as 'Uncommon,'" *Seattle Times*, Apr. 8, 2008, https://www.seattletimes.com/seattle-news/politics/obamas-mother-known-here-as-uncommon/; Shachtman, *Airlift to America*, 10. One report states that Obama Sr. never mentioned Ann and Barack Jr. in his scholarship applications. Swarns, "Words of Obama's Father." For biographies of Barack Obama that focus primarily on his pre-presidential life, see Garrow, *Rising Star*; Maraniss, *Barack Obama*; Remnick, *The Bridge*; Mendell, *Obama*.

9. Janny Scott, "The Young Mother Abroad," *New York Magazine*, Apr. 24, 2011, 32; Scott, *A Singular Woman*; Obama, *Dreams from My Father*, xii, 29, 50-51; Obama, *A Promised Land*, 6.

10. In his autobiography, Obama used the pseudonym "Coretta" to protect the privacy of Joella Edwards, who has since gone on record with her recollections. Obama, *Dreams from My Father*, 58-62, 75; Alice Dewey and Geoffrey White, "Ann Dunham: A Personal Reflection," reproduced from *Anthropology News*, Nov. 2008, 20, https://web.archive.org/web/201006 10025012/http://www.anthropology.hawaii.edu/News/Announcements /Dunham/dunham.html; Nordyke, "Blacks in Hawai'i," 242; Jackie Calmes, "On Campus, Obama and Memories," *New York Times*, Jan. 3, 2009, A11.

11. Obama, *Dreams from My Father*, 63-71, 128; Jacobs, *The Other Obama*, 171-177, 225-230.

12. Obama, *Dreams from My Father*, 70-71, 129; Obama, *The Audacity of Hope*, 2-3, 205; Obama, *And Then Life Happens*, 158-160; Obama, *A Promised Land*, 7-8.

13. Jon Meacham, "On His Own," *Newsweek*, Sept. 1, 2008, 31; Philip Galanes, "Barack Obama and Bryan Cranston on the Roles of a Lifetime," *New York Times*, May 6, 2016, http://www.nytimes.com/2016/05/08/fash ion/barack-obama-bryan-cranston-table-for-three.html.

14. The quotations in the paragraphs that follow are from Obama, *Dreams from My Father*, 82, 124, 134-135, unless otherwise noted.

15. Obama, *The Audacity of Hope*, 10.

16. Diane Salvatore, "The Obamas," *Ladies' Home Journal*, Sept. 2008, 128, 131.

17. *Michelle Obama: A Portrait of the First Lady*, 21-23; Rosalind Rossi, "The Woman behind Obama," *Chicago Sun-Times*, Jan. 20, 2007, https://web .archive.org/web/20080215230648/http://www.suntimes.com/news/metro /221458%2CCST-NWS-mich21.article; Jeffrey Ressner, "Michelle Obama Thesis Was on Racial Divide," *Politico*, Feb. 23, 2008, https://www.politico .com/story/2008/02/michelle-obama-thesis-was-on-racial-divide-008642; Peter Slevin, "Michelle Obama, Race and the Ivy League," *Politico*, Mar. 26, 2015, https://www.politico.com/magazine/story/2015/03/michelle -obama-princeton-harvard-116390; Rachel L. Swarns and Jodi Kantor, "In First Lady's Roots, a Complex Path from Slavery," *New York Times*, Oct. 8, 2009, http://www.nytimes.com/2009/10/08/us/politics/08genealogy.html;

Swarns, *American Tapestry*, 1-2; Rachel L. Swarns, "Meet Your Cousin, the First Lady: A Family Story, Long Hidden," *New York Times*, June 17, 2012, 1, 19; Benilde Little, "Michelle Obama in High Cotton," in Chambers, *The Meaning of Michelle*, 22.

18. Richard Wolffe, "Barack's Rock," *Newsweek*, Feb. 25, 2008, 26, 30-32; *Michelle Obama: A Portrait of the First Lady*, 22.

19. In *The Audacity of Hope*, Obama stated that he met Michelle Robinson in the summer of 1988 at the Sidley & Austin law firm, but this assertion is mistaken. He did not enter Harvard Law School until the fall of 1988, and Michelle Obama's book and other sources place their first meeting in the summer of 1989. Obama, *The Audacity of Hope*, 327-328; Liza Mundy, "When Michelle Met Barack," *Washington Post*, Oct. 5, 2008, http://www .washingtonpost.com/wp-dyn/content/story/2008/10/03/ST2008100 302144.html; Wolffe, "Barack's Rock," 31; Obama, *Becoming*, 102-103.

20. Michael R. Dove, "Dreams from His Mother," *New York Times*, Aug. 10, 2009, https://www.nytimes.com/2009/08/11/opinion/11dove.html; Obama, *Dreams from My Father*, 439-442; Obama, *Becoming*, 160.

21. Richard Wolffe, "Who Is Michelle Obama?," *Newsweek*, Feb. 16, 2008, https://www.newsweek.com/who-michelle-obama-94161; "Obama Named First Associate Dean of Student Services," *University of Chicago Chronicle* 15.19 (June 6, 1996), http://chronicle.uchicago.edu/960606/obama.shtml; "Michelle Obama Appointed Vice President for Community and External Affairs at the University of Chicago Hospitals," University of Chicago, May 9, 2005, https://www.uchicagomedicine.org/forefront/news/2005 /may/michelle-obama-appointed-vice-president-for-community-and -external-affairs-at-the-university-of-chic; Obama, *Dreams from My Father*, 93, 270.

22. Law School, University of Chicago, "Statement regarding Barack Obama," University of Chicago Law School, accessed May 30, 2019, https://www .law.uchicago.edu/media; Toobin, *The Oath*, 28-30.

23. Jo Becker and Christopher Drew, "Pragmatic Politics, Forged on the South Side," *New York Times*, May 11, 2008, 18-19.

24. David Jackson and Ray Long, "Obama Knows His Way around a Ballot," *Chicago Tribune*, Apr. 3, 2007, https://web.archive.org/web/200810110540 57/http://www.chicagotribune.com/news/politics/obama/chi-0704030ba ma-ballot-archive%2C0%2C5693903.story; "Election Results for 1996 General Election, Illinois Senate, District 13," Chicago Democracy Project, accessed May 31, 2019, http://chicagodemocracy.org/ElectionResults .jsp?election=crdd_general,gis_entity_crdd_1996_General_Election,il _sen_13; episode 2 of "Making Obama," Feb. 15, 2018; Obama, *Dreams from My Father*, 144-248.

25. Jackie Calmes, "Statehouse Yields Clues to Obama," *Wall Street Journal*, Feb. 23, 2007, https://web.archive.org/web/20080918032039/http://online .wsj.com/public/article/SB117219748197216894-Sn60V_4KLQHp_xz7CjY

Luyjv3Jg_20070324.html; Amy Clark, "Obama Record May Be Gold Mine for Critics," Associated Press, Jan. 17, 2007, https://www.cbsnews.com/news/obama-record-may-be-gold-mine-for-critics/; Peter Slevin, "Obama Forged Political Mettle in Illinois Capitol," *Washington Post*, Feb. 9, 2007, http://www.washingtonpost.com/wp-dyn/content/article/2007/02/08/AR2007020802262.html.

26. Janny Scott, "In Illinois, Obama Proved Pragmatic and Shrewd," *New York Times*, July 30, 2007, https://www.nytimes.com/2007/07/30/us/politics/30obama.html.

27. Eli Saslow, "From Outsider to Politician," *Washington Post*, Oct. 9, 2008, http://www.washingtonpost.com/wp-dyn/content/article/2008/10/08/AR2008100803890_4.html; episode 4 of "Making Obama," Mar. 1, 2018.

28. Obama taunt quoted in Michael Ciric, "State Senator Ricky [*sic*] Hendon Resigns! But, Who Knew Obama Was an Ass-Kicking Stud?," *Chicago Now*, Feb. 24, 2011, http://www.chicagonow.com/chicago-political-commentary/2011/02/state-senator-ricky-hendon-resigns-but-who-knew-obama-was-an-ass-kicking-stud/. Also see Saslow, "From Outsider to Politician."

29. Obama, *The Audacity of Hope*, 2-3; Obama, *A Promised Land*, 71; Michael Weisskopf, "How He Learned to Win," *Time*, May 19, 2008, 28; "Bobby L. Rush," in *Biographical Directory of the United States Congress*, accessed June 2, 2019, http://bioguide.congress.gov/scripts/biodisplay.pl?index=r000515; Ted Kleine, "Is Bobby Rush in Trouble?," *Reader* (Chicago), Mar. 16, 2000, https://www.chicagoreader.com/chicago/is-bobby-rush-in-trouble/Content?oid=901745.

30. Two decades later, Obama would characterize his run for Rush's seat as one of the more "stupid" decisions he had made in public life. Obama, *A Promised Land*, 36-37. Also see Weisskopf, "How He Learned to Win," 28; Kleine, "Is Bobby Rush in Trouble?"; episode 4 of "Making Obama," Mar. 1, 2018.

31. Obama, *Becoming*, 151, 183; Obama, *The Audacity of Hope*, 340; Obama, *A Promised Land*, 35-36, 70.

32. Becker and Drew, "Pragmatic Politics"; Obama, *A Promised Land*, 42-45.

33. Neither Barack Obama nor his campaign organizations were ever charged with any legal wrongdoing related to Tony Rezko. McClelland, *Young Mr. Obama*, 235; Weisskopf, "How He Learned to Win," 30; Wolffe, *Renegade*, 253; Christopher Drew and Michael McIntire, "An Obama Patron and Friend until an Indictment," *New York Times*, June 14, 2007, https://www.nytimes.com/2007/06/14/us/politics/14rezko.html; Natasha Korecki, "Onetime Obama Donor Tony Rezko Released to Halfway House," *Chicago Sun-Times*, July 7, 2015, https://chicago.suntimes.com/2015/7/7/18470092/onetime-obama-donor-tony-rezko-released-to-halfway-house; Mackenzie Weinger, "Former Obama Fundraiser Sentenced," *Politico*, Nov. 22, 2011, https://www.politico.com/story/2011/11/former-obama-fundraiser-sentenced-068935.

34. Weisskopf, "How He Learned to Win," 26-30; Monica Davey, "As Quickly as Overnight, a Democratic Star Is Born," *New York Times*, Mar. 18, 2004, https://www.nytimes.com/2004/03/18/us/as-quickly-as-overnight-a-demo cratic-star-is-born.html; Noam Scheiber, "Race against History," *New Republic*, May 31, 2004, https://newrepublic.com/article/67604/race-against -history-0.

35. Barack Obama, "The Audacity of Hope" (speech), July 27, 2004, Boston, MA, reprinted in Dionne and Reid, *We Are the Change We Seek*, 5-13; Obama, *A Promised Land*, 52.

36. "Ryan Drops Out of Senate Race in Illinois," CNN, June 25, 2004, http:// www.cnn.com/2004/ALLPOLITICS/06/25/il.ryan/; "Election Results" (2004), CNN, accessed June 3, 2019, http://www.cnn.com/ELECTION /2004/pages/results/states/IL/S/01/index.html; Obama, *The Audacity of Hope*, 18, 209-213.

37. "President Barack Obama" (US Senate voting record), accessed June 3, 2019, https://www.govtrack.us/congress/members/barack_obama/400 629; "Barack Obama," *Biographical Dictionary of the United States Congress*, accessed June 3, 2019, http://bioguide.congress.gov/scripts/biodisplay .pl?index=o000167; "Committee Assignments: Barack Obama, US Senator for Illinois," accessed June 3, 2019, https://web.archive.org/web/2006 1209190827/http://obama.senate.gov/committees/.

38. According to Obama, Senate colleagues such as Harry Reid and Ted Kennedy raised the prospect of a presidential bid with him as early as 2006. Obama, *A Promised Land*, 66-70, 77-78. Also see Suskind, *Confidence Men*, 125-126.

39. Becker and Drew, "Pragmatic Politics"; Evan Thomas et al., "How He Did It," *Newsweek*, Nov. 17, 2008, 40; Mendell, *Obama*, 382.

40. Jarrett, *Finding My Voice*, 132-133.

CHAPTER 2. JOSHUA RISING

1. Rick Pearson and Ray Long, "Obama: I'm Running for President," *Chicago Tribune*, Feb. 10, 2007, https://www.chicagotribune.com/nation-world/chi-0 70210obama-pearson1-story-story.html; "Obama Launches Presidential Bid," BBC News, Feb. 10, 2007, http://news.bbc.co.uk/2/hi/americas/6349081.stm.

2. Pearson and Long, "Obama: I'm Running for President"; Sarson, *Barack Obama*, 284-287.

3. Suskind, *Confidence Men*, 125-126; Obama, *The Audacity of Hope*, 244-249; David Leonhardt, "A Free-Market-Loving, Big-Spending, Fiscally Conservative Wealth Redistributionist," *New York Times Magazine*, Aug. 24, 2008, 28-35, 52-54.

4. Rachel L. Swarns, "Obama's Path on Preferences, Race and Class," *New York Times*, Aug. 3, 2008, A1, A16; Obama, *The Audacity of Hope*, 68, 244; Dahlia Lithwick, "A Complicated Record on Race," *Newsweek*, Apr. 7, 2008, 34-35.

5. "Barack on This Week with George Stephanopoulos," YouTube, accessed Dec. 4, 2020, https://www.youtube.com/watch?v=vGpjFh5Izkc.

6. Lithwick, "Complicated Record on Race," 34-35.

7. Jeff Zeleny and Jim Rutenberg, "A Delegator, Obama Picks when to Take Reins," *New York Times*, June 16, 2008, http://www.nytimes.com/2008/06/16/us/politics//16manage.html; Jodi Kantor, "Barack Obama, Forever Sizing Up," *New York Times*, Oct. 2008, WK1, 4-5; Doris Kearns Goodwin, "Barack Obama and Doris Kearns Goodwin: The Ultimate Exit Interview," *Vanity Fair*, Sept. 21, 2016, http://www.vanityfair.com/news/2016/09/barack-obama-doris-kearns-goodwin-interview; Michael Powell, "Deliberative in a Manic Game," *New York Times*, June 4, 2008, A18; Evan Thomas et al., "How He Did It," *Newsweek*, Nov. 17, 2008; Alter, *The Promise*, 297-298.

8. Debra J. Dickerson, "Colorblind," *Salon*, Jan. 22, 2007, http://www.salon.com/2007/01/22/obama_161/; Alim and Smitherman, *Articulate while Black*, 22-23.

9. Obama, *A Promised Land*, 122-124. Also see Peter Wallsten, "Obama Struggles to Balance African Americans' Hopes with Country's as Whole," *Washington Post*, Oct. 28, 2012, http://www.washingtonpost.com/politics/decision2012/obama-after-making-history-has-faced-a-high-wire-on-racial-issue/2012/10/28/d8e25ff4-1939-11e2-bd10-5ff056538b7c_story.html.

10. "Obama, Clinton Speeches in Selma, Alabama" (transcript), CNN, Mar. 4, 2007, www.cnn.com/TRANSCRIPTS/0703/04/le.02.html; Reid, *Fracture*, 139-140. The Joshua-Moses analogy was first mentioned to Obama during a talk with Otis Moss III, the ministerial successor to Jeremiah Wright at Trinity United Church of Christ.

11. Todd S. Purdum, "The Comeback Id," *Vanity Fair*, June 4, 2008, https://www.vanityfair.com/news/2008/07/clinton200807; Barack Obama, "What I Am Opposed to Is a Dumb War" (speech), Oct. 2, 2002, Chicago, IL, reprinted in Dionne and Reid, *We Are the Change We Seek*, 1-4.

12. Obama, *The Audacity of Hope*, 34-35; Obama, *Dreams from My Father*, ix–x; Obama, *A Promised Land*, 87, 125; Thomas et al., "How He Did It," 41; Jeffrey M. Jones, "Analysis of Support for Barack Obama," Gallup, Oct. 24, 2007, http://www.gallup.com/poll/102337/Analysis-Support-Barack-Obama.aspx.

13. Todd and Gawiser, *How Barack Obama Won*, 70-74; "Entrance Polls: Iowa," CNN, Jan. 3, 2008, http://www.cnn.com/ELECTION/2008/primaries/results/epolls/#IADEM; Sylvester Monroe and Bryan Monroe, "Obama Victory Surprises, Inspires Nation," *Jet*, Jan. 21, 2008, 10, 62-63; Chris Liddell-Westefeld, "Obama: 'They Said This Day Would Never Come,'" *Crooked Media*, Jan. 3, 2018, https://crooked.com/article/said-day-never-come/.

14. Against Democratic Party rules, Michigan held a primary contest on January 15 in which Obama's name did not appear on the ballot. Clinton won the vote, but the Democratic National Committee Rules and By-laws Committee later reduced each Michigan delegate's vote by half.

The same was done in regard to Florida, which also held an unauthorized primary vote on January 18. Todd and Gawiser, *How Barack Obama Won*, 61, 101-107, 113-123; Avi Zenilman and Amie Parnes, "DNC Panel Agrees to Seat Mich., Fla.," *Politico*, May 31, 2008, https://www.politico.com /story/2008/05/dnc-panel-agrees-to-seat-mich-fla-010732.

15. Halperin and Heilemann, *Game Change*, 218-219.

16. Thomas et al., "How He Did It," 61-63; Balz and Johnson, *Battle for America 2008*, 165-166.

17. In a 2020 interview with me, Clyburn disclosed that Bill Clinton contacted him a few weeks after that late-night phone call to apologize for his behavior and accusations. Clyburn interview; Clyburn, *Blessed Experiences*, 3-4, 7; Jackie Calmes, "Clinton's Road to Second Place," *Wall Street Journal*, June 4, 2008, https://www.wsj.com/articles/SB121252558317842545.

18. "Bill Clinton Race Remarks about Obama 2008," ElectionWallDotOrg .mp4, YouTube, accessed June 4, 2019, https://www.youtube.com/watch ?v=DctowDg1pMk; "Barack Obama Interview: Complete Transcript," ABC News, Feb. 3, 2008, https://abcnews.go.com/ThisWeek/story?id= 4197507&page=1; Lee and Morin, "Using the 2008 Presidential Election."

19. Kate Phillips, "More Finger Wagging from a Miffed Bill Clinton," *New York Times*, Apr. 23, 2008, https://www.nytimes.com/2008/04/23/us/poli tics/23bill.html; Balz and Johnson, *Battle for America 2008*, 167; Thomas et al., "How He Did It," 62; Roger Simon, "Jackson to Dems: Play Nice," *Politico*, Feb. 20, 2008, http://www.politico.com/story/2008/02/jackson -to-dems-play-nice-008606; Kevin Cirilli, "Bill Clinton's 8 Digs at Obama," *Politico*, Sept. 5, 2012, https://www.politico.com/story/2012/09/bill-clintons -8-digs-at-obama-080728; Ryan Lizza, "Bill vs. Barack," *New Yorker*, Apr. 28, 2008, https://www.newyorker.com/magazine/2008/05/05/bill-vs-barack.

20. Purdum, "Comeback Id"; Cobb, *Substance of Hope*, 92; Lizza, "Bill vs. Barack."

21. Jeffrey M. Jones, "Obama Gaining among Middle-Aged, Women, Hispanics," Gallup, Feb. 19, 2008, http://www.gallup.com/poll/104428/Obama-Gaining-Among-MiddleAged-Women-Hispanics.aspx.

22. Margaret Ramirez, "Farrakhan Sings Obama's Praises," *Chicago Tribune*, Feb. 25, 2008, https://www.chicagotribune.com/news/ct-xpm-2008-02-25 -0802240188-story.html; Claude A. Clegg III, "'You're Not Ready for Farrakhan': The Nation of Islam and the Struggle for Black Political Leadership, 1984-2000," in Johnson and Stanford, *Black Political Organizations*, 99-131.

23. A photograph of US senator Barack Obama, minister Louis Farrakhan, and others, smiling and posing, did exist at the time of the 2008 primaries. The photographer, Askia Muhammad, had taken the image at a Congressional Black Caucus event in 2005, but subsequently decided to suppress the image until 2018 so that Obama would not be politically damaged by it. According to Muhammad, he made arrangements to provide a copy to Leonard Farrakhan, the minister's son-in-law, after the CBC gathering. Ernie Suggs, "Suppressed Photo of Obama, Farrakhan Might Have Derailed 2008 Campaign," *Atlanta Journal-Constitution*, Feb. 7, 2018, https://www

.ajc.com/news/local/suppressed-photo-obama-farrakhan-might-have-derail
ed-2008-campaign/Jnrh8LRoW3DY6lYXZLIDSN/; Vinson Cunningham,
"The Politics of Race and the Photo That Might Have Derailed Obama,"
New Yorker, Jan. 28, 2018, https://www.newyorker.com/culture/annals-of
-appearances/the-politics-of-race-and-the-photo-that-might-have-derailed
-obama; Rowan Morrison, "The Photo That Never Saw the Light of Day:
Obama with Farrakhan in 2005," *Talking Points Memo*, Jan. 25, 2018, https:
//talkingpointsmemo.com/livewire/photo-of-obama-louis-farrakhan-to
-be-released.

24. Ramirez, "Farrakhan Sings Obama's Praises"; Will Thomas, "Ohio Democratic Debate on MSNBC: Highlights, Video," *Huffington Post*, Mar. 28,
2008 (updated Dec. 6, 2017), https://www.huffingtonpost.com/2008/02
/26/ohio-democratic-debate-on_n_88495.html; Wolffe, *Renegade*, 250.

25. Wolffe, *Renegade*, 167-168; Jeremiah Wright, "America's Chickens Coming
Home to Roost" (sermon), YouTube, accessed June 4, 2019, https://www
.youtube.com/watch?v=UUtZNQoREFA; Lisa Miller, "Trying Times for
Trinity," *Newsweek*, Mar. 24, 2008, 50.

26. Miller, "Trying Times for Trinity," 50; Obama, *Dreams from My Father*, 280-
286, 440; Obama, *The Audacity of Hope*, 356-357; Obama, *A Promised Land*,
119-120; Obama, *Becoming*, 262-263.

27. Jodi Kantor, "Disinvitation by Obama Is Criticized," *New York Times*, Mar.
6, 2007, http://www.nytimes.com/2007/03/06/us/politics/06obama.html;
Thomas et al., "How He Did It," 67; Obama, *Becoming*, 262-263; Halperin
and Heilemann, *Game Change*, 235; Miller, "Trying Times for Trinity," 50;
Plouffe, *The Audacity to Win*, 224-225.

28. Thomas B. Edsall, "Pastor's Remarks Spark Debate about Obama Campaign," *Huffington Post*, Mar. 28, 2008 (updated May 25, 2011), https://
www.huffpost.com/entry/pastors-remarks-spark-deb_n_91749; Miller,
"Trying Times for Trinity," 50; Plouffe, *The Audacity to Win*, 224-225;
Obama, *A Promised Land*, 116.

29. Plouffe, *The Audacity to Win*, 212-213; Obama, *A Promised Land*, 140-143.

30. The quotations in the paragraphs that follow are from Barack Obama, "We
the People in Order to Form a More Perfect Union" (speech), Philadelphia,
PA, Mar. 18, 2008 (in possession of author); "Obama Speech: 'A More Perfect Union,'" YouTube, accessed June 5, 2019, https://www.youtube.com
/watch?v=pWe7wTVbLUU.

31. "Obama and Wright Controversy Dominate News Cycle," Pew Research
Center, Mar. 27, 2008, http://pewresearch.org/pubs/777/obama-wright
-news-interest; Frank Newport, "Clinton Supporters Believe Wright Is
Relevant to Campaign," Gallup, May 5, 2008, https://news.gallup.com/
poll/107020/clinton-supporters-believe-wright-relevant-campaign.aspx.
For accounts and analyses of the Wright controversy and Obama's speech,
see Reid, *Fracture*, 167-176; Dyson, *Black Presidency*, 86-117; Cobb, *Substance of Hope*, 16-35; Tiffany R. Patterson, "Barack Obama and the Politics of Anger," in Gidlow, *Obama, Clinton, Palin*, 26-38; Walker and

Smithers, *The Preacher and the Politician*, 24-51; Kloppenberg, *Reading Obama*, 203-215.

32. Bill Moyers, "The Journal: Reverend Jeremiah Wright," PBS, Apr. 25, 2008, https://www.pbs.org/moyers/journal/04252008/watch.html; Halperin and Heilemann, *Game Change*, 245-246.

33. "Faith, Social Justice and Public Service," C-SPAN, Apr. 28, 2008, https://www.c-span.org/video/?205074-1/faith-social-justice-public-service; "Reverend Wright at the National Press Club" (transcript), *New York Times*, Apr. 28, 2008, https://www.nytimes.com/2008/04/28/us/politics/28text-wright.html; Thomas et al., "How He Did It," 72.

34. More than a decade later, Valerie Jarrett would still claim to not fully understand Jeremiah Wright's reaction to Obama's race speech. "To me, it didn't make any sense that Barack's pastor was willing to be responsible for his defeat," she wrote in a memoir. "Why would he try to ruin the chance for the first black man—and his parishioner—to be elected president?" Jarrett, *Finding My Voice*, 151; Wolffe, *Renegade*, 183; Balz and Johnson, *Battle for America 2008*, 211; Rich Schapiro, "Rev. Jeremiah Wright Claims President Obama 'Threw Me under the Bus' in Letter to African Aid Group," *New York Daily News*, May 18, 2010, https://www.nydailynews.com/news/politics/rev-jeremiah-wright-claims-president-obama-threw-bus-letter-african-aid-group-article-1.447986.

35. Kathy Kiely and Jill Lawrence, "Clinton Makes Case for Wider Appeal," ABC News, May 9, 2008, https://abcnews.go.com/Politics/Vote2008/story?id=4809356&page=1; "Black, White, and Shades of Gray," *Newsweek*, June 2, 2008, 29.

36. Thomas et al., "How He Did It," 66, 84.

37. Jarrett, *Finding My Voice*, 137; Wolffe, *Renegade*, 144-145.

38. Thomas et al., "How He Did It," 48; Obama, *A Promised Land*, 105; Lisa Miller, "Obama's Other Pastor," *Newsweek*, Oct. 13, 2008, 50.

39. "Andrew Young Says Obama Lacks Experience to Be President, Bill Clinton 'as Black as Barack,'" Fox News, Dec. 10, 2007, https://foxnews.com/story/andrew-young-says-obama-lacks-experience-to-be-president-bill-clinton-as-black-as-barack; Halperin and Heilemann, *Game Change*, 199.

40. Paul Farhi, "Tavis Smiley Will Cut Ties with Joyner Radio Show," *Washington Post*, Apr. 12, 2008, http://www.washingtonpost.com/wp-dyn/content/article/2008/04/11/AR2008041103056.html; Tavis Smiley, "Regarding the Tom Joyner Morning Show," *Huffington Post*, Apr. 11, 2008 (updated May 25, 2011), https://www.huffpost.com/entry/regarding-the-tom-joyner_b_96325.

41. Matt Bai, "What Would a Black President Mean for Black Politics?," *New York Times Magazine*, Aug. 10, 2008, 36; Balz and Johnson, *Battle for America 2008*, 167-168.

42. Thomas et al., "How He Did It," 62; Kevin Chappell, "Obama Dawns as Democrats' Hope to Win White House," *Jet*, May 26, 2008, 8-10; Russell Berman, "Rangel Leads N.Y. Delegation in Endorsing Obama," *New York*

Sun, June 6, 2008, https://www.nysun.com/new-york/rangel-leads-ny-dele
gation-in-endorsing-obama/79456/; David A. Hollinger, "Obama, Blackness, and Postethnic America," *Chronicle Review*, Feb. 29, 2008, B8; Ray-
mond Hernandez, "A New Campaign Charge: You Supported Clinton,"
New York Times, July 1, 2008, https://www.nytimes.com/2008/07/01/us/
politics/01dems.html; Reid, *Fracture*, 163-167.

43. Gwen Ifill, "The Obamas: Portrait of an American Family," *Essence*, Sept.
2008, 156.

44. Julie Bosman, "Obama Calls for More Responsibility from Black Fathers,"
New York Times, June 16, 2008, http://www.nytimes.com/2008/06/16/us
/politics/16obama.html; Ifill, "The Obamas," 156; Perry Bacon Jr., "Jackson Incident Revives Some Blacks' Concerns about Obama," *Washington
Post*, July 11, 2008, http://www.washingtonpost.com/wp-dyn/content
/article/2008/07/10/AR2008071002812.html.

45. Jonathan Alter, "The Obama Dividend," *Newsweek*, Mar. 31, 2008, 37;
Obama, "We the People" (speech); Obama, *The Audacity of Hope*, 244-245;
"Barack Obama Answers Your Questions," MTV, Nov. 2, 2008, http://
www.mtv.com/news/articles/1598409/barack-obama-answers-your-que
stions.jhtml; Bosman, "Obama Calls for More Responsibility"; David Remnick, "Going the Distance," *New Yorker*, Jan. 27, 2014, 53.

46. During the 1990s, Jackson served as the "shadow senator" for the District
of Columbia, a largely symbolic position created by the city council to
lobby Congress for DC statehood. Richard L. Berke, "Washington Talk;
Behind-the-Scenes Role for a 'Shadow Senator,'" *New York Times*, Mar.
27, 1991, https://www.nytimes.com/1991/03/27/us/washington-talk-behind
-the-scenes-role-for-a-shadow-senator.html; James M. Smallwood, "Jesse
Jackson: Run, Jesse, Run!," in Glasrud and Wintz, *African Americans and
the Presidency*, 112-126.

47. Roddie A. Burris, "Jackson Slams Obama for 'Acting White,'" *State* (SC),
Sept. 19, 2007, reprinted in *Politico*, https://www.politico.com/story/2007
/09/jackson-slams-obama-for-acting-white-005902; Simon, "Jackson to
Dems"; "Jesse Jackson Makes Crude Remarks about Obama on Fox
News," YouTube, July 9, 2008, https://www.youtube.com/watch?v=TQl
_6buUggM; Bacon, "Jackson Incident Revives Some Blacks' Concerns";
"Jackson Apologizes for 'Crude' Obama Remarks," CNN, July 9, 2008,
http://www.cnn.com/2008/POLITICS/07/09/jesse.jackson.comment/.

48. Bacon, "Jackson Incident Revives Some Blacks' Concerns"; "Jackson Apologizes for 'Crude' Obama Remarks."

49. Allison Samuels, "At Arm's Length," *Newsweek*, July 21, 2008, 34; "Jackson
Apologizes for 'Crude' Obama Remarks"; "American Morning" (transcript), CNN, July 10, 2008, http://transcripts.cnn.com/TRANSCRIPTS
/0807/10/ltm.02.html.

50. "Why Jesse Jackson Hates Obama's Guts!," *National Enquirer*, July 15, 2008,
https://www.nationalenquirer.com/celebrity/why-jesse-jackson-hates-oba
mas-guts/; "Operation PUSH Documents Financial Ties with Jackson
Lover," CNN, Feb. 1, 2001, http://edition.cnn.com/2001/US/02/01/jack

son.money/index.html; "Mother Wants Jesse Jackson to 'Be a Father' to Illegitimate Child," CNN, Aug. 16, 2001, http://www.cnn.com/2001/US /08/16/jackson.mistress/index.html.

51. Among those receiving 1 percent of the Gallup poll's tally were Maya Angelou, Colin Powell, Louis Farrakhan, Bill Cosby, Tavis Smiley, and Cornel West. Lydia Saad, " 'Black Spokesman' Title Still Up for Grabs," Gallup, July 14, 2008, http://www.gallup.com/poll/108805/black-spokesman-title -still-graps.aspx; Samuels, "At Arm's Length," 34; episode 2 of "Making Obama," Feb. 15, 2018; Obama, *A Promised Land*, 16-18.

52. Wolffe, "Barack's Rock," 28; Ifill, "The Obamas," 214.

53. Ifill, "The Obamas," 153, 155; Thomas et al., "How He Did It," 65-66; Obama, *Becoming*, 259-262; Obama, *A Promised Land*, 134.

54. Obama, *Becoming*, 262, 264-265; Wolffe, "Barack's Rock," 29; "Remarks by the First Lady at Tuskegee University Commencement [abridged]," Tuskegee University, Tuskegee, AL, May 9, 2015, in Felix and Measom, *Michelle Obama*, 78; Mitch Kachun, "Michelle Obama, the Media Circus, and America's Racial Obsession," in Gidlow, *Obama, Clinton, Palin*, 39-49; Obama, *A Promised Land*, 133.

55. Allison Samuels, "What Michelle Means to Us," *Newsweek*, Dec. 1, 2008, 29-30; Ifill, "The Obamas," 153, 155, 214; O'Brien, *Secret Lives*, 295.

56. Jeff Zeleny, "First Black to Lead the Ticket for a Major Party," *New York Times*, June 4, 2008, A1, A19; Adam Nagourney and Mark Leibovich, "Clinton Ends Campaign with Clear Call to Elect Obama," *New York Times*, June 8, 2008; Clinton, *Hard Choices*, 2-4; Alex Johnson, "Obama Expects GOP to Attack His Patriotism," NBC News, June 4, 2008, http://www.nbcnews.com/id/24973823.

57. Karen Tumulty, "The Mistakes She Made," *Time*, May 19, 2008, 24-25.

58. Patrick Healy and Michael Luo, "A Senate Stalwart Who Bounced Back," *New York Times*, Aug. 24, 2008, 20; Adam Nagourney and Jeff Zeleny, "Obama Selects Biden Adding Foreign Expertise to Ticket," *New York Times*, Aug. 24, 2008, 22; Biden, *Promises to Keep*; "Biden's Description of Obama Draws Scrutiny," CNN, Feb. 9, 2007, https://www.cnn.com /2007/POLITICS/01/31/biden.obama/; Adam Nagourney, "Biden Unwraps '08 Bid with an Oops!," *New York Times*, Feb. 1, 2007, https:// www.nytimes.com/2007/02/01/us/politics/01biden.html; Plouffe, *The Audacity to Win*, 288-289; Levingston, *Barack and Joe*, 38-46; Obama, *A Promised Land*, 162-165.

59. Thomas et al., "How He Did It," 91.

CHAPTER 3. THE PENDULUM SWINGS FORWARD

1. James Surowiecki, "The Widening Racial Wealth Divide," *New Yorker*, Oct. 10, 2016, http://www.newyorker.com/magazine/2016/10/10/the-widening -racial-wealth-divide; David J. Lynch, "First Black President Can't Help Blacks Stem Wealth Drop," *Bloomberg*, Sept. 4, 2012, https://www.bloom berg.com/news/articles/2012-09-05/first-black-president-can-t-help-blacks

-stem-wealth-drop; Barbara Ehrenreich and Dedrick Muhammad, "The Recession's Racial Divide," *New York Times*, Sept. 13, 2009, 17; Jesse Washington, "Blacks' Economic Gains Wiped Out in Downturn," Associated Press, July 10, 2011, http://www.nbcnews.com/id/43645168/ns/business -eye_on_the_economy/t/blacks-economic-gains-wiped-out-downturn/; Josh Boak, "For Minorities, Pain Is Severe Decade after Housing Peaked," Associated Press, June 20, 2016, https://apnews.com/b8ceee210bb344e68 bebe95ab73faf5a; Richard Fry, "In a Recovering Market, Homeownership Rates Are Down Sharply for Blacks, Young Adults," Pew Research Center, Dec. 15, 2016, http://www.pewsocialtrends.org/2016/12/15/in-a-recovering -market-homeownership-rates-are-down-sharply-for-blacks-young-adults/; Frey, *Diversity Explosion*, 111-113; Sugrue, *Not Even Past*, 105-106; Timothy Williams, "As Public Sector Sheds Jobs, Blacks Are Hit Hardest," *New York Times*, Nov. 28, 2011, http://www.nytimes.com/2011/11/29/us/as-public -sector-sheds-jobs-black-americans-are-hit-hard.html; Perry Bacon Jr., "Black Unemployment: Decline in Government Jobs Hurts African -Americans," TheGrio.com, May 4, 2012, https://thegrio.com/2012/05 /04/black-unemployment-decline-in-government-jobs-hurts-african -americans/.

2. Sabrina Tavernise, "Black Americans See Gains in Life Expectancy," *New York Times*, May 8, 2016, http://www.nytimes.com/2016/05/09/health /blacks-see-gains-in-life-expectancy.html; Nell Irwin, Claire Cain Miller, and Margot Sanger-Katz, "America's Racial Divide, Charted," *New York Times*, Aug. 19, 2014, http://www.nytimes.com/2014/08/20/upshot/amer icas-racial-divide-charted.html; Centers for Disease Control and Prevention, "HIV Surveillance—United States, 1981-2008."

3. Justin Wolfers, David Leonhardt, and Kevin Quealy, "1.5 Million Missing Black Men," *New York Times*, Apr. 20, 2015, https://www.nytimes.com/in teractive/2015/04/20/upshot/missing-black-men.html; Irwin, Miller, and Sanger-Katz, "America's Racial Divide, Charted."

4. Irwin, Miller, and Sanger-Katz, "America's Racial Divide, Charted"; National Coalition on Black Civic Participation, *Black Women in the United States, 2014*.

5. Frey, *Diversity Explosion*, 17, 107, 115, 122.

6. Frey, *Diversity Explosion*, 114; Smith, *Black Mosaic*, 8-9, 203; Monica Anderson, "A Rising Share of the U.S. Black Population Is Foreign Born," Pew Research Center, Apr. 9, 2015, https://www.pewsocialtrends.org/2015/04 /09/a-rising-share-of-the-u-s-black-population-is-foreign-born/.

7. Wolffe, *Renegade*, 24-25; Melissa Harris, "Executive Profile: Martin Nesbitt, the First Friend," *Chicago Tribune*, Jan. 21, 2013, https://www.chi cago tribune.com/business/ct-biz-0121-executive-profile-nesbitt-20130 121-story.html.

8. Balz and Johnson, *Battle for America 2008*, 321-322; Kevin Chappell, "A Moment in History," *Jet*, Sept. 15, 2008, 16, 18, 28; Barack Obama, "Change Happens" (speech), Aug. 28, 2008, Denver, CO, reprinted in Dionne and Reid, *We Are the Change We Seek*, 70-87.

9. Alex Johnson, "Obama Expects GOP to Attack His Patriotism," NBC News, June 4, 2008, http://www.nbcnews.com/id/24973823.

10. Jonathan Chait, "The Color of His Presidency," *New York Magazine*, Apr. 4, 2014, http://nymag.com/news/features/obama-presidency-race-2014-4/.

11. Frank Rich, "The Terrorist Barack Hussein Obama," *New York Times*, Oct. 12, 2008, WK10; Evan Thomas et al., "How He Did It," *Newsweek*, Nov. 17, 2008, 107-108; Halperin and Heilemann, *Game Change*, 354-427; Wolffe, *Renegade*, 271; Obama, *A Promised Land*, 168-170, 194-195; Kara Spak, "Bill Ayers to Retire from UIC," *Chicago Sun-Times*, Aug. 5, 2010, https://web.archive.org/web/20100921124812/http://www.suntimes.com /news/metro/2570004,ayers-to-retire-080510.article.

12. "John Lewis, Invoking George Wallace, Says McCain and Palin 'Playing with Fire,'" *Politico*, Oct. 11, 2008, https://www.politico.com/blogs/jon athanmartin/1008/John_Lewis_invoking_George_Wallace_says_McCain _and_Palin_playing_with_fire.html.

13. Thomas et al., "How He Did It," 108; "Sarah Mania! Sarah Palin's Greatest Hits," YouTube, accessed June 15, 2019, https://www.youtube.com /watch?v=NrzXLYA_e6E; "Palin Defends Terrorist Comment against Obama," YouTube, accessed June 15, 2019, https://www.youtube.com /watch?v=Y8aGOOvyE2U; "Hate at McCain and Palin Rallies: People Yelling Kill Him!," YouTube, accessed June 15, 2019, https://www .youtube.com/watch?v=jw303y77MaA; "N-Word Yelled at Sarah Palin Rally," YouTube, accessed June 15, 2019, https://www.youtube.com /watch?v=oB-8DOvJuAg; "The McCain-Palin Mob," YouTube, accessed June 15, 2019, https://www.youtube.com/watch?v=KjxzmaXAg9E.

14. Tim Shipman "Sarah Palin Blamed by the US Secret Service for Death Threats against Barack Obama," *Telegraph* (London), Nov. 8, 2008, http:// www.telegraph.co.uk/news/worldnews/sarah-palin/3405336/Sarah-Palin -blamed-by-the-US-Secret-Service-for-death-threats-against-Barack-Obama .html; Thomas et al., "How He Did It," 110.

15. Michelle, Malia, and Sasha Obama were given the code names "Renaissance," "Radiance," and "Rosebud," respectively. Obama, *Becoming*, 286; Rich, "Terrorist Barack Hussein Obama"; Thomas et al., "How He Did It," 40; Krissah Thompson, "The Leading Lady," *Essence*, Oct. 2011, 134.

16. "The New Dynamics of Protecting a President: Most Threats against Obama Issued Online," *Washington Post*, Oct. 8, 2014, https://www.wash ingronpost.com/politics/the-new-dynamics-of-protecting-a-president-most -threats-against-obama-issued-online/2014/10/07/a525ef6c-4b11-11e4-891d -713f052086a0_story.html.

17. "ATF: Plot by Skinheads to kill Obama Is Foiled," Associated Press, Oct. 27, 2008, http://www.nbcnews.com/id/27405681/ns/politics-decision_08/t /atf-plot-skinheads-kill-obama-foiled/; "2 Held in Obama Effigy Hanging on Ky. Campus," Associated Press, Oct. 30, 2008, http://www.nbcnews .com/id/27463694/ns/us_news-crime_and_courts/t/held-obama-effigy -hanging-ky-campus/; Larry Altman, "Lynched Effigy of Obama Comes Down in Redondo Beach after Complaints," *Mercury News* (San Jose, CA),

Oct. 30, 2008, http://www.mercurynews.com/politics/ci_10856986; "Officials Outraged by Coffin Bearing Anti-Obama Sticker," *News and Record* (Greensboro, NC), Nov. 2, 2008, B5; Rick Jervis, "Fires at Black Churches Raise Concern," *USA Today*, June 30, 2015 (updated July 1, 2015), http://www.usatoday.com/story/news/2015/06/30/black-churches-fires-charleston-shooting/29516267/; Dan Barry, "Up from the Ashes, a Symbol That Hate Does Not Win," *New York Times*, Sept. 25, 2011, https://www.nytimes.com/2011/09/26/us/church-rebuilds-after-2008-election-night-arson.html; "Obama Rejects Supremacist Threat," Special Broadcasting Service (Sydney, Australia), Aug. 23, 2013 (last modified), https://www.sbs.com.au/news/obama-rejects-supremacist-threat.

18. Balz and Johnson, *Battle for America 2008*, 373; "Transcript: McCain Concedes Presidency," CNN, Nov. 5, 2008, http://edition.cnn.com/2008/POLITICS/11/04/mccain.transcript/; "Senator John McCain Election Night Speech," YouTube, accessed June 16, 2019, https://www.youtube.com/watch?v=NvgqRKYapU8.

19. "Legal Bills Swayed Palin, Official Says," *New York Times*, July 5, 2009, https://www.nytimes.com/2009/07/06/us/06palin.html.

20. Lydia Saad, "Blacks, Postgrads, Young Adults Help Obama Prevail," Gallup, Nov. 6, 2008, http://www.gallup.com/poll/111781/Blacks-Postgrads-Young-Adults-Help-Obama-Prevail.aspx; Tom Rosentiel, "Inside Obama's Sweeping Victory," Pew Research Center, Nov. 5, 2009, http://pewresearch.org/pubs/1023/exit-poll-analysis-2008; Todd and Gawiser, *How Barack Obama Won*, 29-37; "National Urban League Report on 'The Hidden Swing Voters: Impact of African-Americans in 2012,'" UnityFirst.com, July 23, 2012, https://unityfirst.com/2012/national-urban-league-report-on-the-hidden-swing-voters-impact-of-african-americans-in-2012/.

21. For an insightful study of the effectiveness of the Obama campaign's organizing efforts, see McKenna and Han, *Groundbreakers*. Also see Todd and Gawiser, *How Barack Obama Won*, 27; Andy Barr, "Obama to Make Run at Arizona," *Politico*, Oct. 31, 2008, https://www.politico.com/story/2008/10/obama-to-make-run-at-arizona-015127; Andrew Rasiej and Micah L. Sifry, "The Web: 2008's Winning Ticket," *Politico*, Nov. 12, 2008, https://www.politico.com/story/2008/11/the-web-2008s-winning-ticket-015520.

22. Frank Newport, "Americans See Obama Election as Race Relations Milestone," Gallup, Nov. 7, 2008, http://www.gallup.com/poll/111817/Americans-See-Obama-Election-Race-Relations-Milestone.aspx.

23. John Lewis, "The Warriors of Peace," *Newsweek*, commemorative inaugural edition (2009), 103-106; Van R. Johnson II to President Obama, n.d., in Walton et al., *Letters to President Obama*.

24. Henry Louis Gates Jr., "Integration at the Top," and Annette Gordon-Reed, "Jefferson's Vision," both in *Newsweek*, commemorative inaugural edition (2009), 64, 116, 121.

25. Alice Walker, "White House Advice," *Newsweek*, commemorative inaugural edition (2009), 106, 108.

26. Marsalis and Sykes quoted in "What Obama Means to Me," *Newsweek*, commemorative inaugural edition (2009), 124, 127; Allison Samuels, "Audacity of Hoping," *Newsweek*, Feb. 2, 2009, 38.

27. Samuels, "Audacity of Hoping," 38.

28. Allison Samuels, "What Michelle Means to Us," *Newsweek*, Dec. 1, 2008, 29-30.

29. Samuels, "Audacity of Hoping," 40; "Martin Luther King III DNC Speech: Text," *Huffington Post*, Sept. 28, 2008 (updated May 25, 2011), https://www .huffpost.com/entry/martin-luther-king-iii-dn_n_122258; William Branigin and Philip Rucker, "Obama Commemorates MLK Day with Service," *Washington Post*, Jan. 19, 2009, http://www.washingtonpost.com/wp-dyn /content/article/2009/01/19/AR2009011901189.html.

30. "Inaugural Address," Jan. 20, 2009, in Obama, *Public Papers*, 1:1-4; "Complete List of Obama's 10 Official Inaugural Balls," *Los Angeles Times*, Jan. 8, 2009, https://latimesblogs.latimes.com/washington/2009/01/obama-in augur-1.html; "Obamas Dance, Celebrate at Inaugural Balls," CNN, Jan. 21, 2009, http://www.cnn.com/2009/POLITICS/01/20/inauguration.balls /index.html.

CHAPTER 4. BAMELOT

1. Grove, *Inside the White House*, 9-15, 27-28, 147; Asch and Musgrove, *Chocolate City*, 16-151.

2. Keckley, *Behind the Scenes*; "Blacks Who Slept at the White House," *Ebony*, Sept. 1988, 66, 68, 70; Harlan, *Booker T. Washington*, 304-324; Grove, *Inside the White House*, 152, 223, 232, 234, 236, 331; Weiss, *Whitney M. Young, Jr.*, 142-148; Gittinger and Fisher, "LBJ Champions the Civil Rights Act of 1964"; Kirk, *Music at the White House*, 118-120, 232, 245; Robert Yoon, "Michael Jackson's Meeting with the Gipper," CNN, June 26, 2009, http:// politicalticker.blogs.cnn.com/2009/06/26/when-jackson-met-reagan/; "President Ronald Reagan Hosts Michael Jackson at the White House," YouTube, accessed June 19, 2019, https://www.youtube.com/watch?v=XE mj9MTqoGk.

3. After his presidency, Barack Obama described the living quarters of the White House as "less a home than an extended series of suites in a boutique hotel, complete with a gym, pool, tennis court, movie theater, salon, bowling alley, and medical office." Obama, *A Promised Land*, 252. Also see "The President's Desk," White House Museum, accessed Jan. 22, 2020, http://www.whitehousemuseum.org/furnishings/resolute-desk.htm; Grove, *Inside the White House*, 43, 90-91; Monkman, *White House*, 15, 265; White House Historical Association, *White House*, 98; "Churchill Out, Martin Luther King In: First Glimpse at President Obama's Revamped and Thoroughly Modern Oval Office," *Daily Mail* (London), Sept. 1, 2010, http:// www.dailymail.co.uk/news/article-1307752/Churchill-Martin-Luther-King -President-Obama-revamps-Oval-Office.html.

4. David Remnick, "Going the Distance," *New Yorker*, Jan. 27, 2014, 44, 47; Rhodes, *World as It Is*, xi; Obama, *Becoming*, 287-288; *President Obama: A Day in the Life of America's Leader*, 94-99; Obama, *A Promised Land*, 228, 327; Kessler, *First Family Detail*, 37.

5. Grove, *Inside the White House*, 92-93; Obama, *The Audacity of Hope*, 43-44.

6. Michael Lewis, "Obama's Way," *Vanity Fair*, Oct. 2012, 263-264; Krissah Thompson, "The Nine Important Things Michelle Obama and Oprah Said Last Night," *Washington Post*, June 15, 2016, http://www.washington post.com/news/arts-and-entertainment/wp/2016/06/15/the-nine-impor tant-things-michelle-obama-and-oprah-said-last-night.

7. Grove, *Inside the White House*, 89-90; Shailagh Murray, "The Busy Life of Obama Scheduler Alyssa Mastromonaco," *Washington Post*, Dec. 22, 2008, http://www.washingtonpost.com/wp-dyn/content/article/2008/12/21/AR 2008122102491.html; *President Obama: A Day in the Life of America's Leader*, 36-46.

8. Suzy Khimm, "Rob Nabors Is the Man behind Many Political Deals," *Washington Post*, Dec. 10, 2012, http://www.washingtonpost.com/lifestyle/style /rob-nabors-is-man-behind-many-political-deals/2012/12/10/2a039878-4264 -11e2-8e70-e1993528222d_story.html; "Full Text of Bill Daley's Announcement," *Politico*, Jan. 27, 2011, https://www.politico.com/story/2011/01/full -text-of-bill-daleys-announcement-048318; Jake Tapper, "Jay Carney Picked as New White House Press Secretary," ABC News, Jan. 27, 2011, https:// abcnews.go.com/Politics/president-obama-taps-jay-carney-press-secretary -deparle/story?id=12780593; Barnes interview; White House Task Force on Childhood Obesity, *Solving the Problem of Childhood Obesity*; Mike Allen, "Melody Barnes Leaving White House," *Politico*, Oct. 20, 2011, https:// www.politico.com/story/2011/10/melody-barnes-leaving-white-house-066 458; Robin Givhan, "White House Task Force Issues Report on Fighting Childhood Obesity," *Washington Post*, May 12, 2010, http://www.washing-tonpost.com/wp-dyn/content/article/2010/05/11/AR2010051101792.html; Frances Romero, "Energy Czar: Carol Browner," *Time*, Dec. 2, 2008, http://content.time.com/time/specials/packages/article/0,28804,1863062 _1863058_1866567,00.html; Scott Wilson, "White House Deputy Chief of Staff Mona Sutphen Has a World of Experience," *Washington Post*, Apr. 14, 2009, http://www.washingtonpost.com/wp-dyn/content/article/2009 /04/13/AR2009041302968.html; "Executive Profile Mona K. Sutphen," *Bloomberg*, June 20, 2019, https://www.bloomberg.com/research/stocks /private/person.asp?personId=49946381&privcapId=12828188.

9. "The Meteoric Rise of the State Department's Susan Rice," *Journal of Blacks in Higher Education* 20 (Summer 1998), 40-41; "Obama's Cabinet Ambassador to the United Nations—Susan Rice (Announced)," *RealClearPolitics*, Dec. 1, 2008, https://www.realclearpolitics.com/lists/cabinet/rice.html; Edith M. Lederer, "Trusted Obama Adviser Susan Rice Is First African -American Woman Named to be US Envoy to UN," Associated Press, Dec. 1, 2008, https://web.archive.org/web/20081205165303/http://www

.startribune.com/nation/35326694.html; " 'At the Heart of the UN's Work':
An Interview with Ambassador Susan Rice," *Huffington Post*, May 14, 2013,
https://www.huffpost.com/entry/at-the-heart-of-the-uns-w_b_2856901;
"Ambassador Ron Kirk," White House, accessed June 16, 2019, https://
obamawhitehouse.archives.gov/blog/author/ambassador-ron-kirk; Joseph
J. Schatz, "U.S. Trade Rep Kirk Set to Exit," *Politico*, Jan. 23, 2013, https://
www.politico.com/story/2013/01/ron-kirk-to-step-down-as-trade-represen
tative-086587.

10. "Biography of Lisa P. Jackson," US Environmental Protection Agency, accessed June 16, 2019, https://archive.epa.gov/epa/aboutepa/biography-lisa
-p-jackson.html; "The EPA Is Not the Villain," *Newsweek*, Dec. 6, 2010,
14; Juliet Eilperin, "EPA Head Jackson to Resign Post," *Washington Post*,
Dec. 27, 2012, http://www.washingtonpost.com/national/health-science
/epa-head-jackson-to-resign-post/2012/12/27/50637f50-4fda-11e2-8b49-646
75006147f_story.html; John M. Broder, "E.P.A. Chief Set to Leave: Term
Fell Shy of Early Hope," *New York Times*, Dec. 27, 2012, https://www.ny
times.com/2012/12/28/science/earth/lisa-p-jackson-of-epa-to-step-down
.html; Clare Foran and Mike Magner, "Former EPA Administrator Lisa
Jackson Is Back in the Spotlight," *National Journal* (reprinted in the *Atlantic*), Sept. 10, 2013, https://www.theatlantic.com/politics/archive/2013/09
/former-epa-administrator-lisa-jackson-is-back-in-the-spotlight/444858/.

11. "Biography of the 18th US Surgeon General 2009-2013: Regina M. Benjamin, MD, MBA," accessed June 20, 2019, http://reginabenjamin.net
/about/; "Senate Confirms Regina Benjamin as Surgeon General," *Senatus*,
Oct. 29, 2009, https://senatus.wordpress.com/2009/10/29/senate-confirms
-regina-benjamin-as-surgeon-general/; Gardiner Harris, "A Doctor from
the Bayou," *New York Times*, July 13, 2009, https://www.nytimes.com/2009
/07/14/health/policy/14surgeon.html; Desiree Hunter and Lauran Neer-
gaard, "Regina Benjamin, Obama's Pick for Surgeon General," Associated
Press, May 25, 2011, https://web.archive.org/web/20160303224833/http://
www.huffingtonpost.com/2009/07/13/regina-benjamin-obamas-pi_n_230
547.html; "Surgeon General: Don't Let Hair Get in the Way" (interview
transcript), NPR, Aug. 8, 2012, https://www.npr.org/2012/08/08/158419580
/surgeon-general-dont-let-hair-get-in-the-way; "Regina Benjamin to Step
Down as Surgeon General after 4 Years," Associated Press, June 12, 2013,
http://thegrio.com/2013/06/12/regina-benjamin-to-step-down-as-surgeon
-general-after-4-years/; Madison Park, "Obama's Trainer: Busy People Can
Exercise, Too," CNN, Dec. 23, 2011, http://www.cnn.com/2011/12/23
/health/obama-fitness-trainer/index.html; Obama, *A Promised Land*, 290
-291, 539-540; Bill Simmons, "President Obama and Bill Simmons: The
GQ Interview," *GQ*, Nov. 17, 2015, http://www.gq.com/story/president
-obama-bill-simmons-interview-gq-men-of-the-year; Jodi Kantor, "Leaving Obama's Shadow, to Cast One of His Own," *New York Times*, Nov. 10,
2011, https://www.nytimes.com/2011/11/11/us/politics/reggie-love-is-leaving
-obamas-shadow-to-cast-his-own.html; Judy Kurtz, "Obama Still Chews

Nicorette to Cut Smoking Urge," TheHill.com, Oct. 21, 2015, https://the
hill.com/blogs/in-the-know/in-the-know/257647-obama-still-chews-nico
rette-to-cut-smoking-urge; Nikki Schwab, "Obama Still Chewing Nicotine
Gum," *U.S News & World Report*, June 12, 2014, https://www.usnews.com
/news/blogs/washington-whispers/2014/06/12/obama-still-chewing-nico
tine-gum.

12. Jesse Lee, "Van Jones to CEQ," White House, Mar. 10, 2009, https://oba
mawhitehouse.archives.gov/blog/2009/03/10/van-jones-ceq; Joseph Williams, "The Return of Van Jones," *Politico*, Nov. 26, 2011, http://www.po-
litico.com/news/stories/1111/69083.html; Emily Schultheis, "Van Jones
Reflects on 'Rough Exit,'" *Politico*, July 7, 2010, http://www.politico.com
/news/stories/0710/39476.html; Van Jones, "Introducing the 'American
Dream' Movement," *Huffington Post*, Feb. 22, 2011 (updated May 25, 2011),
https://www.huffpost.com/entry/american-dream-movement_b_826477;
Brian Steinberg, "Jay-Z to Guest on CNN's Launch of 'The Van Jones
Show,'" *Variety*, Jan. 19, 2018, https://variety.com/2018/tv/news/van-jones
-cnn-jay-z-1202669241/.

13. In an exchange with me years later, Desirée Rogers was charitable in her reflection on her White House years. "I think my team and I were able to
create wonderful experiences at the WH that reinforced the spirit of the
Obama Presidency. They [the first family] brought inclusion, diversity,
grace and a wonderful respect for all America has to offer both intellectually and culturally." Rogers interview. Also see Rachel Swarns, "Atop
Capital's Guest Lists, an Outsider," *New York Times*, Dec. 19, 2008, ST12;
Obama, *A Promised Land*, 542; Jason Horowitz, Spencer Hsu, and Roxanne Roberts, "The Party Crashers: Turmoil in the White House," *Washington Post*, Dec. 21, 2009, http://www.washingtonpost.com/wp-dyn/con
tent/article/2009/12/20/AR2009122002668.html; "White House Social Secretary Desiree Rogers to Step Down," *Chicago Sun-Times*, Feb. 26, 2010,
https://chicago.suntimes.com/news/2010/2/26/18538949/white-house-social
-secretary-desiree-rogers-to-step-down; Jeremy W. Peters, "Desirée Rogers,
Post Crash," *New York Times*, Oct. 3, 2010, 1, ST10; Jason Horowitz,
"White House Announces Resignation of Social Secretary Desirée Rogers,"
Washington Post, Feb. 27, 2010, http://www.washingtonpost.com/wp-dyn
/content/article/2010/02/26/AR2010022603734_pf.html; Kessler, *First Family Detail*, 220-223; Sydney Ember and Nicholas Fandos, "Pillars of Black
Media, Once Vibrant, Now Fighting for Survival," *New York Times*, July 2,
2016, https://www.nytimes.com/2016/07/03/business/media/black-owned
-media-companies-struggle-to-adapt-to-a-digital-world.html.

14. Jarrett, *Finding My Voice*, 5-39; Jeffrey Bartholet and Daniel Stone, "A Team
of Expatriates," *Newsweek*, Jan. 26, 2009, 52; Richard Wolffe, "Barack's
Rock," *Newsweek*, Feb. 25, 2008, 32; Richard Wolffe, "Who Is Michelle
Obama?," *Newsweek*, Feb. 16, 2008, https://www.newsweek.com/who
-michelle-obama-94161.

15. Evan Thomas et al., "How He Did It," *Newsweek*, Nov. 17, 2008, 67, 71; Robert Draper, "Obama's BFF," *New York Times Magazine*, July 26, 2009, 34, 36-37; Obama, *A Promised Land*, 115; Jo Becker, "The Other Power in the West Wing," *New York Times*, Sept. 2, 2012, 16.

16. Al Sharpton had high praise for Jarrett in his 2013 memoir. "Let me just say that in the more than four decades I've been in public life, I don't think I've met anyone who had more integrity in their dealings with me than Valerie Jarrett. She never told me she was going to do something that she didn't do. . . . Her degree of sincerity and truthfulness is truly rare in public life." Sharpton, *Rejected Stone*, 183. Also see Becker, "The Other Power," 16; Draper, "Obama's BFF," 30-37, 46-47; Noam Scheiber, "The Obama Whisperer," *New Republic*, Nov. 9, 2014, http://www.newrepublic.com/article /120170/valerie-jarrett-obama-whisperer; Morial, *Gumbo Coalition*, 126; George E. Condon Jr. and Jim O'Sullivan, "Has Obama Done Enough for Black Americans?," *National Journal*, Apr. 5, 2013, https://www.the atlantic.com/politics/archive/2013/04/has-president-obama-done-enough -for-black-americans/274699/.

17. Draper, "Obama's BFF," 30-37, 46-47; Becker, "The Other Power," 16; Jarrett, *Finding My Voice*, 175. According to his 2020 memoir, Obama did not grasp the damage being inflicted on office morale by Rahm Emanuel and other senior male staffers until Valerie Jarrett informed him. The concerns of the women staffers were brought to the men's attention, and Obama recalled that Emanuel and others "were surprised and chastened and vowed to do better." Obama, *A Promised Land*, 537.

18. Glenn Thrush, "The Survivor," *Politico*, July–Aug. 2014, http://www.poli tico.com/magazine/story/2014/06/the-survivor-108018_full.html; "Holder Faces Grilling on Marc Rich Pardon," CNN, Feb. 8, 2001, https://web .archive.org/web/20120302160328/http://articles.cnn.com/2001-02-08/jus tice/pardon.probe.03_1_evasion-and-illegal-oil-marc-rich-pincus-green?_s =PM:LAW; Peter Baker and Matt Apuzzo, "Shared Vision, Varying Styles," *New York Times*, Aug. 19, 2014, http://www.nytimes.com/2014/08/20/us /holder-and-obama-differ-in-approach-to-underlying-issues-of-missouri-un rest.html; A. James Memmott, "Obama Picks Caroline Kennedy, Holder, Johnson to Lead VP Search," *Muckety*, June 5, 2008, https://web.archive .org/web/20080701235153/http://news.muckety.com/2008/06/05/obama -picks-caroline-kennedy-eric-holder-to-join-johnson-in-vp-search/3221.

19. Thrush, "The Survivor"; Josh Gerstein, "Eric Holder: Black Panther Case Focus Demeans 'My People,'" *Politico*, Mar. 1, 2011, https://www.politico .com/blogs/under-the-radar/2011/03/eric-holder-black-panther-case-focus -demeans-my-people-033839; Obama, *A Promised Land*, 585; Charlie Savage, "Lightning Rod for G.O.P. Defies Thunderbolts," *New York Times*, Dec. 18, 2011, 1, 29.

20. Office of the Inspector General, US Department of Justice, *Review of ATF's Operation Fast and Furious*; Richard A. Serrano, "Emails Show Top Justice

Department Officials Knew of ATF Gun Program," *Los Angeles Times*, Oct. 3, 2011, https://www.latimes.com/nation/la-xpm-2011-oct-03-la-na-atf -guns-20111004-story.html; Charlie Savage, "Agent Who Supervised Gun-Trafficking Operation Testifies on His Failings," *New York Times*, July 26, 2011, https://www.nytimes.com/2011/07/27/us/politics/27guns.html; Richard A. Serrano, "Kenneth Melson, Who Oversaw ATF's Fast and Furious, Steps Down," *Los Angeles Times*, Aug. 30, 2011, https://www.latimes.com /archives/la-xpm-2011-aug-30-la-pn-atf-director-resign-20110830-story.html.

21. Sharyl Attkisson, "Attorney General Holder Subpoenaed for Documents in ATF Gunwalker Fast and Furious Case," CBS News, Oct. 14, 2011, https:// www.cbsnews.com/news/attorney-general-holder-subpoenaed-for-docu ments-in-atf-gunwalker-fast-and-furious-case/; Charlie Savage, "House Panel's Vote Steps Up Partisan Fight on Gun Inquiry," *New York Times*, June 20, 2012, http://www.nytimes.com/2012/06/21/us/obama-claims-exec utive-privilege-in-gun-case.html; Terry Frieden and Deirdre Walsh, "Issa: Holder Must Turn Over Documents or Face Contempt Vote," CNN, June 19, 2012, https://web.archive.org/web/20120708233608/http://articles.cnn .com/2012-06-19/politics/politics_holder-contempt_1_issa-contempt-vote -holder?_s=PM:POLITICS; "Final Vote Results for Roll Call 441," US House of Representatives, June 28, 2012, http://clerk.house.gov/evs/2012 /roll441.xml; Danielle Weisberg, "House of Rep. Holds AG Eric Holder in Contempt," NBC News, June 28, 2012, http://www.msnbc.com/the-last -word/house-rep-msna39936; Seung Min Kim, "Dems Treat Contempt with Contempt," *Politico*, June 28, 2012, https://www.politico.com/story /2012/06/dems-treat-contempt-with-contempt-077996; "No Criminal Pro-secution of Holder for Contempt," CNN, July 6, 2012, http://www.cnn .com/2012/06/29/politics/holder-contempt/index.html; Josh Gerstein, "House Panel Sues Holder over Fast and Furious Docs," *Politico*, Aug. 12, 2012, http://www.politico.com/blogs/under-the-radar/2012/08/report-house -to-sue-holder-monday-over-fast-and-furious-131898.html; Terry Frieden, " 'Fast and Furious' Report Slaps 14 at Justice, ATF," CNN, Sept. 19, 2012, https://www.cnn.com/2012/09/19/us/us-fast-furious-report/index.html.

22. Jake Miller, "Federal Judge Reopens 'Fast and Furious' Controversy," CBS News, Aug. 21, 2014, https://www.cbsnews.com/news/federal-judge-reopens -fast-and-furious-controversy/; Josh Gerstein, "Judge Upends Settlement in Fast and Furious Documents Case," *Politico*, Oct. 22, 2018, https://www .politico.com/story/2018/10/22/fast-and-furious-documents-case-926645; "Mexico: News of Another US Gun-Tracking Program Stirs Criticism," *Los Angeles Times*, Oct. 6, 2011, https://latimesblogs.latimes.com/world_now /2011/10/mexico-wide-receiver-reaction-guns-weapons-left-right.html.

23. Thrush, "The Survivor"; Joy-Ann Reid, "Eric Holder, George Lucas among CBC Foundation Gala Honorees," TheGrio.com, Sept. 22, 2012, http:// thegrio.com/2012/09/22/eric-holder-george-lucas-honorees-at-cbc-founda tion-gala/; Ben Smith, "Obama Will Keep His 'Heat Shield,' " *Buzzfeed*,

Jan. 9, 2013, http://www.buzzfeed.com/bensmith/obama-will-keep-his
-heat-shield.

CHAPTER 5. PRESIDENT OF THE ENTIRE UNITED STATES

1. David Von Drehle, "Honor and Effort: What President Obama Achieved in Eight Years," *Time*, Dec. 22, 2016, http://time.com/4616866/barack-oba ma-administration-look-back-history-achievements/; "Economic Rescue Swiftly Signed into Law," Agence France-Presse, Oct. 3, 2008, https://web .archive.org/web/20120429172133/http://afp.google.com/article/ALeqM5 h4oyrrEcqeJEeVRgcrDXB7egD02A; Jeremy Pelofsky and John Crawley, "Bush Throws Lifeline to Auto Industry," Reuters, Dec. 19, 2008, https:// www.reuters.com/article/us-autos-bailout/bush-throws-lifeline-to-auto-in dustry-idUSTRE4BI34F20081219; Obama, *A Promised Land*, 297-301; David Cho, "At Geithner's Treasury, Key Decisions on Hold," *Washington Post*, May 18, 2009, http://www.washingtonpost.com/wp-dyn/content/art icle/2009/05/17/AR2009051702268.html.

2. Sean J. Savage, "The First Hundred Days: FDR and Obama," in Watson et al., *Obama Presidency*, 92, 95; US Equal Employment Opportunity Commission, "Equal Pay Act of 1963 and Lilly Ledbetter Fair Pay Act of 2009," accessed June 20, 2019, https://www.eeoc.gov/eeoc/publications/brochure-eq ual_pay_and_ledbetter_act.cfm; Obama, *A Promised Land*, 234; Mark Memmott, "As Flag Is Put Away, America's Mission in Iraq Symbolically Ends," NPR, Dec. 15, 2011, https://www.npr.org/sections/thetwo-way/2011/12/15 /143753891/as-flag-is-put-away-americas-mission-in-iraq-symbolically-ends; Robert Pear, "House Passes Spending Bill, and Critics Are Quick to Point Out Pork," *New York Times*, Feb. 25, 2009, https://www.nytimes.com/2009 /02/26/us/politics/26spend.html; Omnibus Appropriations Act, 2009; "President Obama Signs Landmark National Service Legislation," Corporation for National and Community Service, Apr. 21, 2009, https://www .nationalservice.gov/newsroom/press-releases/2009/president-obama-signs -landmark-national-service-legislation; "Edward M. Kennedy Serve America Act One Year Later," Corporation for National and Community Service, Apr. 2010, https://www.nationalservice.gov/sites/default/files/docu ments/10_0421_saa_implementation.pdf.

3. Drehle, "Honor and Effort"; Oberlander, "Long Time Coming"; Office of the Legislative Counsel, US House of Representatives, *Compilation of Patient Protection and Affordable Care Act*; Kimberly Amadeo, "2010 Patient Protection & Affordable Care Act Summary," *Balance*, June 20, 2019, https://www.thebalance.com/2010-patient-protection-affordable -care-act-3306063; Megan Brenan, "Approval of the Affordable Care Act Falls Back below 50%," Gallup, Nov. 30, 2018, https://news.gallup.com /poll/245057/approval-affordable-care-act-falls-back-below.aspx; Dhrumil Mehta, "Does Trying to Repeal Obamacare *Actually* Increase Its Appeal?,"

FiveThirtyEight.com, Mar. 29, 2019, https://fivethirtyeight.com/features
/does-trying-to-repeal-obamacare-actually-increase-its-appeal/; Paul Starr,
"Achievement with Credit: The Obama Presidency and Inequality," in
Zelizer, *Presidency of Barack Obama*, 53-57.

4. George W. Bush issued 291 executive orders, Bill Clinton issued 364, and
Ronald Reagan issued 381. National Archives, "Executive Orders," *Federal
Register*, accessed June 30, 2019, https://www.federalregister.gov/presidential
-documents/executive-orders; National Archives, "Executive Orders Disposition Tables," *Federal Register*, accessed June 30, 2019, https://www.ar
chives.gov/federal-register/executive-orders/clinton.html; National Archives,
"Reagan Executive Orders Disposition Tables," *Federal Register*, accessed
June 30, 2019, https://www.archives.gov/federal-register/executive-orders
/reagan.html; Milkis and Nelson, *American Presidency*, 476; Rudalevige,
"Contemporary Presidency"; "Embryonic Stem Cell Research," Association of American Medical Colleges, accessed June 30, 2019, https://www
.aamc.org/advocacy/research/74440/embryonicstemcellresearch.html;
Julia Preston and John H. Cushman Jr., "Obama to Permit Young Migrants
to Remain in U.S.," *New York Times*, June 15, 2012, https://www.nytimes
.com/2012/06/16/us/us-to-stop-deporting-some-illegal-immigrants.html.

5. Lydia Saad, "At 100 Days, Obama Approval Broad as Well as Deep," Gallup, Apr. 29, 2009, https://news.gallup.com/poll/118054/100-days-obama
-approval-broad-deep.aspx; Lydia Saad, "Blacks Far More Satisfied with U.S.
under Obama," Gallup, Nov. 2, 2008, https://news.gallup.com/poll/124037
/blacks-far-more-satisfied-u.s.-obama.aspx.

6. April Ryan interview quoted in Michael A. Fletcher, "Obama, Civil Rights
Leaders Discuss Improving Conditions for Black America," *Washington
Post*, Feb. 10, 2010, http://www.washingtonpost.com/wp-dyn/content/art
icle/2010/02/10/AR2010021003200.html; Zenitha Prince, "Muffled Black
Criticisms Reflect Racial Pride, Pragmatism," *Afro-American* (Washington, DC), Mar. 20, 2010, http://www.afro.com/muffled-black-criticisms
-reflect-racial-pride-pragmatism/.

7. Obama interviews with Joe Madison and Tom Joyner quoted in Carol E.
Lee and Abby Phillip, "With Black Voters, Obama Gets More Personal,"
Politico, Oct. 11, 2010, http://www.politico.com/news/stories/1010/43385
.html. Also see "Remarks at a Rally for Governor Martin J. O'Malley in
Bowie, Maryland," Oct. 7, 2010, in Obama, *Public Papers*, 2:1529-1535; Ri-
chard Prince, "Johnson Publishing Co. Expects New Strategy in January,"
TheRoot.com, Sept. 10, 2010, https://journalisms.theroot.com/johnson
-publishing-co-expects-new-strategy-in-january-1790883610.

8. Bureau of Labor Statistics, US Department of Labor, "Unemployment
Holds Steady for Much of 2016 but Edges Down in the Fourth Quarter,"
Mar. 2017, https://www.bls.gov/opub/mlr/2017/article/unemployment
-holds-steady-for-much-of-2016-but-edges-down-in-fourth-quarter.htm;
Frank Newport, "Blacks' Approval of President Obama Remains High,"
Gallup, Dec. 15, 2014, https://news.gallup.com/poll/180176/blacks-appro

val-president-obama-remains-high.aspx; Gary C. Jacobson, "Legislative Success and Political Failure: The Public's Reaction to Barack Obama's Early Presidency," in Pfiffner and Davidson, *Understanding the Presidency*, 183; Skocpol, *Obama and America's Political Future*, 54; Suskind, *Confidence Men*, 334-335; Jann Wenner, "Obama in Command," *Rolling Stone*, Oct. 14, 2010, 39.

9. Sam Youngman and Michael O'Brien, "Obama Describes Midterm Losses as a 'Shellacking' by Republicans," TheHill.com, Nov. 3, 2010, https://the hill.com/blogs/blog-briefing-room/news/127511-obama-said-election-under scores-that-he-has-to-do-a-better-job; Liz Halloran, "Obama Humbled by Election 'Shellacking,'" NPR, Nov. 3, 2010, https://www.npr.org/templates /story/story.php?storyId=131046118; Dan Balz, "The GOP Takeover in the States," *Washington Post*, Nov. 13, 2010, http://www.washingtonpost.com /wp-dyn/content/article/2010/11/13/AR2010111302389.html.

10. "Election Center" (2010 voting data), CNN, accessed July 2, 2019, http:// www.cnn.com/ELECTION/2010/results/polls/#USH00p1; Mark H. Lopez, "Dissecting the 2010 Electorate," Pew Research Center, Apr. 26, 2011, https://www.pewhispanic.org/2011/04/26/ii-dissecting-the-2010-electorate /; "Black Lawmakers in South Lose Influence," *New York Times*, Nov. 20, 2011, 16.

11. "Republicans Capture Control of the House, CNN Projects," CNN, Nov. 3, 2010, http://www.cnn.com/2010/POLITICS/11/03/election.house/.

12. "The President's Agenda and the African American Community," White House, Nov. 2011, https://obamawhitehouse.archives.gov/sites/default/files /af_am_report_final.pdf; Joseph Williams, "W.H. Makes Its Case to Black Voters," *Politico*, Dec. 5, 2011, http://www.politico.com/news/stories/1211 /69752.html.

13. "The President's Agenda and the African American Community"; Valerie Jarrett, "Commemorating National Black HIV/AIDS Awareness Day," White House, Feb. 7, 2012, https://obamawhitehouse.archives.gov/blog /2012/02/07/commemorating-national-black-hivaids-awareness-day; White House Office of National AIDS Policy, *National HIV/AIDS Strategy for the United States*; White House Office of National AIDS Policy, *National HIV/AIDS Strategy: Federal Implementation Plan*; Gardiner Harris, "Obama to Face Reckoning in New Orleans over Katrina Promises," *New York Times*, Aug. 26, 2015, http://www.nytimes.com/2015/08/27/us/politics/obama-to -face-reckoning-in-new-orleans-over-katrina-promises.html; Tom Bassing, "Black Farmers' Quest for Justice Draws to Close," Reuters, May 5, 2012, https://uk.reuters.com/article/us-usa-farmers-settlement/black-farmers -quest-for-justice-draws-to-a-close-idUKBRE8440EA20120505; "Establishment of the White House Office of Urban Affairs," Executive Order 13503, *Federal Register*, Feb. 19, 2009, https://www.federalregister.gov/documents /2009/02/24/E9-4068/establishment-of-the-white-house-office-of-urban -affairs; "Sparking Community Revitalization," White House, accessed July 5, 2019, https://obamawhitehouse.archives.gov/issues/urban-and-economic

-mobility/community-revitalization; Ryan Holeywell, "Whatever Happened to the Office of Urban Affairs?," *Governing*, Mar. 29, 2013, https://www.gov erning.com/blogs/fedwatch/gov-federal-office-of-urban-affairs-still-exist .html; Danielle Schlanger, "Obama's Urban Affairs Office Brings Hope but Not Much Change," *Huffington Post*, July 26, 2013, https://www.huffpost .com/entry/white-house-office-of-urban-affairs_n_3654660.

14. "Remarks on Signing an Executive Order concerning Historically Black Colleges and Universities," Feb. 26, 2010, in Obama, *Public Papers*, 1:303-305; Abby Phillip, "Obama Hails Nation's Black Colleges," *Politico*, Sept. 13, 2010, http://www.politico.com/news/stories/0910/42071.html; William Jawando, "Recognizing What Historically Black Colleges and Universities Mean to America," White House, Feb. 28, 2010, https://obamawhitehouse .archives.gov/blog/2010/02/28/recognizing-what-historically-black-colleges -and-universities-mean-america.

15. Lauren V. Burke, "Obama and the Congressional Black Caucus: Allies and Foes," TheRoot.com, Oct. 30, 2016, https://www.theroot.com/obama-and -the-congressional-black-caucus-allies-and-fo-1790857469; Lawrence Ross, "Scold-in-Chief? The Love-Hate Relationship between HBCUs and President Obama," TheRoot.com, May 18, 2016, https://www.theroot.com /scold-in-chief-the-love-hate-relationship-between-hbcu-1790855361; Clyburn interview.

16. Stephanie Brown, "HBCU Alums: Your Opportunity," Barack Obama website, Sept. 18, 2012, http://www.barackobama.com/african-americans/; Jenee D. Harris, "New Morehouse Pres a 'Trusted Voice' to Obama," TheRoot.com, Nov. 14, 2012, http://www.theroot.com/buzz/new-morehouse -pres-trusted-voice-obama; Valerie Jarrett, "President Obama Names New Leadership to the White House Initiative on Historically Black Colleges and Universities," White House, Sept. 12, 2013, https://obamawhitehouse .archives.gov/blog/2013/09/12/president-obama-names-new-leadership -white-house-initiative-historically-black-colle; White House Initiative on Historically Black Colleges and Universities, US Department of Education, "The Passing of Executive Director Dr. George Cooper," accessed July 6, 2019, https://sites.ed.gov/whhbcu/2015/07/20/the-passing-of-executive-di rector-dr-george-cooper/.

17. "Commencement Address at Morehouse College in Atlanta, Georgia," May 19, 2013, in Obama, *Public Papers*, 1:465-471; Barack Obama, "You See, Change Requires More than Righteous Anger" (speech), May 7, 2016, Washington, DC, reprinted in Dionne and Reid, *We Are the Change We Seek*, 285-302; "President Obama Delivers the Commencement Address at Howard University," YouTube, accessed June 26, 2019, https://www.you tube.com/watch?v=_K4MctEmkmI.

18. US Department of Education, "Fact Sheet: Obama Administration Investments in Historically Black Colleges and Universities," Oct. 24, 2016, https:// www.ed.gov/news/press-releases/fact-sheet-obama-administration-invest ments-historically-black-colleges-and-universities; US Department of Education, "Programs: Title III Part B, Strengthening Historically Black Col-

leges and Universities Program," Sept. 16, 2016, https://www2.ed.gov/pro
grams/iduestitle3b/funding.html; Postsecondary National Policy Institute,
"Issue Primers: Historically Black Colleges and Universities (HBCUs)," June
17, 2019, https://pnpi.org/historically-black-colleges-and-universities-hbcus/.
19. Sam Dillon, "U.S. Urges Creativity by Colleges to Gain Diversity," *New
York Times*, Dec. 2, 2011, http://www.nytimes.com/2011/12/03/education
/us-urges-campus-creativity-to-gain-diversity.html.
20. Dillon, "U.S. Urges Creativity by Colleges"; Peter Schmidt, "Obama Administration Gives Colleges Broad Leeway on Affirmative Action," *Chronicle of Higher Education*, Dec. 2, 2011, http://www.chronicle.com/article
/Obama-Administration-Gives/130008; "President Obama Signs New Initiative to Improve Educational Outcomes for African Americans," White
House, July 26, 2012, https://obamawhitehouse.archives.gov/the-press
-office/2012/07/26/president-obama-signs-new-initiative-improve-educa
tional-outcomes-africa.
21. "Brief for the United States as Amicus Curiae Supporting Respondents," in
the case *Abigail Noel Fisher v. University of Texas at Austin, et al.*, University
of Texas, Aug. 2012, https://utexas.app.box.com/s/gmydtcyj15lak37atf8u7yeqo
ucsokwm; Tal Kopan, "White House Backs Affirmative Action in Higher
Ed," *Politico*, Aug. 13, 2012, https://www.politico.com/blogs/under-the-ra
dar/2012/08/white-house-backs-affirmative-action-in-higher-ed-132020.
22. Robert Barnes, "Supreme Court Sends Texas Affirmative Action Plan Back
for Further Review," *Washington Post*, June 24, 2013, https://www.washing
tonpost.com/politics/supreme-court-sends-texas-affirmative-action-plan-
back-for-further-review/2013/06/24/62707a22-dcde-11e2-9218-bc2ac7cd44
e2_story.html; Jocelyn Samuels and Catherine E. Lhamon to College or
University President, Sept. 27, 2013, http://www2.ed.gov/about/offices/list
/ocr/letters/colleague-201309.html; Adam Lipsak, "Supreme Court Upholds
Affirmative Action Program at University of Texas," *New York Times*, June
23, 2016, https://www.nytimes.com/2016/06/24/us/politics /supreme-court
-affirmative-action-university-of-texas.html; Robert Barnes, "Supreme Court
Upholds University of Texas Affirmative-Action Admissions," *Washington
Post*, June 23, 2016, https://www.washingtonpost.com/politics/courts_law
/supreme-court-upholds-university-of-texas-affirmative-action-admissions
/2016/06/23/513bcc10-394d-11e6-8f7c-d4c723a2becb_story.html.
23. "Read the Full Transcript of TIME's Conversation with President Obama
and Misty Copeland," *Time*, Mar. 14, 2016, https://time.com/4254551/pres
ident-obama-misty-copeland-transcript/; Edmund Sanders, "So Alike and
Yet So Different," *Los Angeles Times*, July 17, 2008, https://www.latimes
.com/archives/la-xpm-2008-jul-17-fg-obamadad17-story.html.
24. Julie Hirschfeld Davis and Nicholas Fandos, "Malia Obama Rebels, Sort
of, by Choosing Harvard," *New York Times*, May 1, 2016, https://www.ny
times.com/2016/05/02/us/politics/malia-obama-rebels-sort-of-by-choosing
-harvard.html; Max Larkin and Mayowa Aina, "Legacy Admissions Offer
an Advantage—and Not Just at Schools like Harvard," NPR, Nov. 4, 2018,
https://www.npr.org/2018/11/04/663629750/legacy-admissions-offer-an

-advantage-and-not-just-at-schools-like-harvard; Scott Jaschik, "Harvard's Admitted Class Has Record Share of Asian Americans," *Inside Higher Ed*, Apr. 1, 2019, https://www.insidehighered.com/admissions/article/2019/04/01/share-asian-americans-hits-record-high-harvards-class-admitted; Peter Arcidiacono, Josh Kinsler, and Tyler Ransom, "Legacy and Athlete Preferences at Harvard," National Bureau of Economic Research, Working Paper No. 26316, Sept. 2019, https://www.nber.org/papers/w26316.pdf.

25. For an insightful discussion of mass incarceration in the United States, see Alexander, *New Jim Crow*, 2-14. Also see "Growth in Federal Prison System Exceeds States'," Pew Research Center, Jan. 22, 2015, http://www.pewtrusts.org/en/research-and-analysis/fact-sheets/2015/01/growth-in-federal-prison-system-exceeds-states; US Department of Education, "Report: Increases in Spending on Corrections Far Outpace Education," July 7, 2016, https://www.ed.gov/news/press-releases/report-increases-spending-corrections-far-outpace-education; Matt Ferner, "New Report Details Devastating Effects of Mass Incarceration on the U.S.," *Huffington Post*, May 2, 2016, https://www.huffpost.com/entry/effects-mass-incarceration_n_5727b6abe4b0b49df6ac0e00; Eric Goode, "Incarceration Rates for Blacks Have Fallen Sharply, Report Shows," *New York Times*, Feb. 28, 2013, A12; Executive Office of the President of the United States, *Economic Perspectives on Incarceration*; Antonovics and Knight, *New Look at Racial Profiling*; Anwar, Bayer, and Hjalmarsson, "Impact of Jury Race in Criminal Trials."

26. Alexander, *New Jim Crow*, 2-14, 173-208.

27. "Setting the Stage for a Second Term," *Time*, Dec. 31, 2012–Jan. 7, 2013, 88.

28. Josh Gerstein, "President Obama Backing Off Strict Crime Policy," *Politico*, Sept. 11, 2010, https://www.politico.com/story/2010/09/obama-backing-off-strict-crime-policy-042004; "U.S. Sentencing Commission Votes to Make Crack/Powder Cocaine Sentencing Reforms Retroactive," Drug Policy Alliance, June 29, 2011, http://www.drugpolicy.org/news/2011/06/us-sentencing-commission-votes-make-crackpowder-cocaine-sentencing-reforms-retroactive; White House, *Promoting Responsible Fatherhood*.

29. Bush, *Decision Points*, 105.

30. Dafna Linzer and Jennifer LaFleur, "Presidential Pardons Heavily Favor Whites," ProPublica, Dec. 3, 2011, http://www.propublica.org/article/shades-of-mercy-presidential-forgiveness-heavily-favors-whites; Josh Gerstein, "Obama Denies Batch of Pardons," *Politico*, Oct. 28, 2010, https://www.politico.com/story/2010/10/obama-denies-batch-of-pardons-044285; "The Quality Of Mercy, Strained," *New York Times*, Jan. 6, 2013, 10; Kari Huus, "President Obama 'Stingy' on Pardons, Says Clemency Expert," MSNBC, May 8, 2012, http://usnews.msnbc.msn.com/_news/2012/05/08/11585277-president-obama-stingy-on-pardons-says-clemency-expert?lite; Margaret Colgate Love, "Time to Pardon People as Well as Turkeys, Mr. President," *Washington Post*, Nov. 12, 2010, http://www.washingtonpost.com/wp-dyn/content/article/2010/11/11/AR2010111106093.html; Melissa Harris-Perry, "An Open Letter to a Pardoned Turkey" (transcript), NBC News, Nov. 24, 2012, http://www.nbcnews.com/video/mhp/49948073; Alan Silverleib, "Par-

don for Black Boxer Jailed for Interracial Dating Waits on Obama," CNN, Oct. 19, 2009, http://www.cnn.com/2009/POLITICS/10/19/boxer.pardon /index.html; Zack Burgess, "Why Won't Obama Pardon Jack Johnson?," TheGrio.com, Dec. 10, 2010, http://thegrio.com/2010/12/20/why-wont -obama-pardon-jack-johnson/; Andrew Miga, "Lawmakers Seek Pardon for Boxing Champ," Associated Press, Mar. 5, 2013, https://www.starad vertiser.com/2013/03/05/sports/lawmakers-seek-pardon-for-boxing-champ/; David A. Love, "There's No Excuse for Not Pardoning Jack Johnson," TheGrio.com, Mar. 6, 2013, https://thegrio.com/2013/03/06/theres-no -excuse-for-not-pardoning-jack-johnson/; James Ford, "The Final Fight: Why a Pardon for Jack Johnson Is Problematic, but Essential," PIX11 TV, Dec. 16, 2016, https://pix11.com/2016/12/16/the-final-fight-why-a-pardon -for-jack-johnson-is-problematic-but-essential/.

31. Josh Gerstein, "Obama's Drug-Sentencing Quagmire," *Politico*, Jan. 5, 2015, https://www.politico.com/story/2015/01/barack-obama-drug-sentencing-pol icy-113954; Roger Simon, "How a Murderer and Rapist Became the Bush Campaign's Most Valuable Player," *Baltimore Sun*, Nov. 11, 1990, https:// www.baltimoresun.com/news/bs-xpm-1990-11-11-1990315149-story.html.

32. Thurber, *Republicans and Race*, 385; "Democrats Charge G.O.P. Poll Watch Today Will Harass the Negroes and the Poor," *New York Times*, Nov. 3, 1964, https://www.nytimes.com/1964/11/03/archives/democrats-charge-gop-poll -watch-today-will-harass-the-negroes-and.html.

33. Joy-Ann Reid, "NAACP Blasts GOP's 'Withering Attacks on Voting Rights,'" TheGrio.com, Aug. 28, 2012, https://thegrio.com/2012/08/28/naacp-blasts -gops-withering-attacks-on-voting-rights/; Barbara Liston, "In Florida, Black Churches Scramble to Get Early Voters to Polls," Reuters, Oct. 27, 2012, https://www.reuters.com/article/us-usa-campaign-florida/in-florida- black-churches-scramble-to-get-early-voters-to-polls-idUSBRE89Q0D720 121027; Michael Isikoff, "RNC Cuts Ties with Firm over Voter Fraud Alle- gations," NBC News, Sept. 27, 2012, http://firstread.nbcnews.com/_news /2012/09/27/14126789-rnc-cuts-ties-with-firm-over-voter-fraud-allegations ?lite; Luke Johnson, "Obama for America Files Motion to Enforce Early Voting in Ohio," *Huffington Post*, Sept. 5, 2012, https://www.huffpost.com /entry/early-voting-ohio-obama-for-america_n_1858586; US District Court, Southern District of Ohio, *Obama for America, et al., v. Jon Husted, et al.*; Dan Burns, "Supreme Court Denies Ohio Request to Curtail Early Vot- ing," Reuters, Oct. 17, 2012, https://readersupportednews.org/news-section 2/341-193/14024-supreme-court-denies-ohio-request-to-curtail-early-voting; Lauren Fox, "Ohio Sees Fierce Fight over Voter Rolls," *U.S. News & World Report*, Oct. 19, 2012, https://www.usnews.com/news/articles/2012/10/19 /ohio-sees-fierce-fight-over-voter-roles.

34. Lise Olsen, "'Dead' Voter Controversy Raises Even More Concern," *Hous- ton Chronicle*, Oct. 3, 2012, http://www.chron.com/news/politics/article /Dead-voter-controversy-raises-even-more-concern-3913984.php.

35. Gaskins and Iyer, *Challenge of Obtaining Voter Identification*; Jon C. Rogow- ski and Cathy J. Cohen, "Black and Latin Youth Disproportionately

Affected by Voter Identification Laws in the 2012 Election," BlackYouth-Project.com, accessed June 30, 2019, http://research.blackyouthproject.com /files/2013/03/voter-ID-laws-feb28.pdf; US Government Accountability Office, *Elections*; Halimah Abdullah, "As Election Day Nears, Voter ID Laws Still Worry Some, Encourage Others," CNN, Oct. 12, 2012, https:// www.cnn.com/2012/10/12/politics/voter-laws-update/index.html; Emily Schultheis, "Voter ID Laws to Have Smaller Impact," *Politico*, Oct. 25, 2012, https://www.politico.com/story/2012/10/voter-id-laws-to-have-small er-impact-on-election-082893; Charlie Savage, "Federal Court Blocks Voter ID Law in South Carolina, but Only for Now," *New York Times*, Oct. 10, 2012, https://www.nytimes.com/2012/10/11/us/politics/court-blocks-south -carolina-voter-id-law-for-now.html.

36. Pete Yost and Ramit Plushnick-Mastic, "Eric Holder Calls Voter ID a Modern 'Poll Tax' at NAACP Convention," Associated Press, July 10, 2012, http: //thegrio.com/2012/07/10/eric-holder-calls-voter-id-a-modern-poll-tax-at -naacp-convention/#; Melissa Noel, "Congressional Black Caucus Launches Voter Protection Initiative," TheGrio.com, Sept. 26, 2012, http://thegrio.com /2012/09/26/congressional-black-caucus-launches-voter-protection-initia tive/; Susan Saulny, "Obama Looks to Rally Blacks in North Carolina," *New York Times*, Oct. 9, 2012, http://www.nytimes.com/2012 /10/10/us/politics /black-support-for-obama-uncertain-in-2012.html; Susan Saulny, "With Less Time for Voting, Black Churches Redouble Their Efforts," *New York Times*, Oct. 28, 2012, https://www.nytimes.com/2012/10/29/us/politics/black-chu rches-in-florida-urge-congregations-to-vote.html; Joy-Ann Reid, "African-Americans Voting Early in Large Numbers, Campaign Says," The Grio.com, Oct. 30, 2012, http://thegrio.com/2012/10/30/african-americans-early-voting -in-record-numbers/.

37. Susan Cornwell, "Refile—Complaints about Voter IDs, Ballots, Long Lines in Elections," Reuters, Nov. 6, 2012, https://www.reuters.com/article/usa -campaign-voting/refile-complaints-about-voter-ids-ballots-long-lines-in -us-election-idUSL1E8M67M320121106; Mackenzie Weinger, "Al Gore: Voter Suppression like 'Racist Jim Crow Tactics,'" *Politico*, Nov. 6, 2012, https://www.politico.com/blogs/media/2012/11/al-gore-voter-suppression -like-racist-jim-crow-tactics-148722; "Remarks at an Election Victory Celebration in Chicago, Illinois," Nov. 7, 2012, in Obama, *Public Papers*, 2:1768.

38. Derek T. Dingle, "Oval Office Interview with President Barack Obama," *Black Enterprise*, Aug. 7, 2012, https://www.blackenterprise.com/president -obama-interview-small-business-unemployment-exclusive/.

CHAPTER 6. DANCING WITH THE CAUCUS

1. US House of Representatives, "Creation and Evolution of the Congressional Black Caucus," History, Art and Archives, accessed July 10, 2019, https://history.house.gov/Exhibitions-and-Publications/BAIC/Historical

-Essays/Permanent-Interest/Congressional-Black-Caucus/; US House of Representatives, "Black-American Members by Congress, 1870–Present," History, Art and Archives, accessed Dec. 9, 2020, https://history.house .gov/Exhibitions-and-Publications/BAIC/Historical-Data/Black-American -Representatives-and-Senators-by-Congress/; Congressional Black Caucus, "The Congressional Black Caucus Agenda for the 109th Congress," accessed July 10, 2019, https://web.archive.org/web/20051230080634/http:// www.house.gov/watt/cbc/cbcpriorities.htm.

2. Emanuel Cleaver II, "Obama Will Be the First Black President, Not the Black President First," *Washington Post*, Dec. 17, 2008, http://www.was hingtonpost.com/wp-dyn/content/article/2008/12/16/AR2008121602478 .html.

3. Glenn Thrush and Patrick O'Connor, "CBC to Obama: Don't Forget Us," *Politico*, Feb. 24, 2009, https://www.politico.com/story/2009/02/cbc-to -obama-dont-forget-us-019216; Alter, *The Promise*, 56.

4. Todd J. Gillman, "Black Caucus Meets Chief from Its Ranks," *Dallas Morning News*, Feb. 27, 2009, http://www.pressreader.com/usa/the-dallas-morn ing-news/20090227/281629596176043.

5. Silla Brush, "Black Caucus Tells Obama You've Done Too Little for African-Americans," TheHill.com, Dec. 3, 2009, https://thehill.com/homenews /administration/70353-black-caucus-tells-obama-youve-done-too-little-for -african-americans-; Brady Dennis, Zachary A. Goldfarb, and Neil Irwin, "Obama Faces Congressional Anger about Economy," *Washington Post*, Nov. 20, 2009, http://www.washingtonpost.com/wp-dyn/content/article/2009 /11/19/AR2009111903167_pf.html; Lauren V. Burke, "Obama and the Congressional Black Caucus: Allies and Foes," TheRoot.com, Oct. 30, 2016, https://www.theroot.com/obama-and-the-congressional-black-caucus-allies -and-fo-1790857469; David Jackson, "Obama Rejects Congressional Black Caucus Criticism," *USA Today*, Dec. 3, 2009, http://content.usatoday.com /communities/theoval/post/2009/12/obama-rejects-congressional-black -caucus-criticism-/1.

6. Lisa Lerer and Nia-Malika Henderson, "CBC: Obama Not Listening," *Politico*, Mar. 11, 2010, https://www.politico.com/story/2010/03/cbc-obama -not-listening-034239; "Obama to Black Leaders: Fire Up against GOP Surge," NBC News, Sept. 18, 2010, http://www.nbcnews.com/id/392509 50/ns/politics-decision_2010/t/obama-black-leaders-fire-against-gop-surge/; Joseph Williams, "CBC Talks Jobs with Obama," *Politico*, May 12, 2011, https://www.politico.com/story/2011/05/cbc-talks-jobs-with-obama-054 889.

7. "Remarks at the Congressional Black Caucus Foundation Phoenix Awards Dinner," Sept. 24, 2011, in Obama, *Public Papers*, 2:1123-1127; "Congressional Black Caucus Foundation Phoenix Awards Dinner," YouTube, accessed July 1, 2019, https://www.youtube.com/watch?v=swlaZJ2RbBw.

8. Joseph Williams, "Obama to CBC: 'Can't Stop Marching,'" *Politico*, Sept. 24, 2011, https://www.politico.com/story/2011/09/obama-to-cbc-cant-stop

-marching-064350; David Goldstein, "Black Caucus Head Treads Line between Criticizing, Supporting Obama," McClatchy Newspapers, Sept. 19, 2011, https://www.mcclatchydc.com/news/politics-government/article246 99058.html; Mark Smith, "Obama Tells Blacks to 'Stop Complainin' and Fight," Associated Press, Sept. 29, 2011, https://newpittsburghcourier.com /2011/09/29/obama-tells-blacks-to-stop-complainin-and-fight/; Nicholas Ballasy, "CBC Chairman: African Americans Would 'March on the White House' if Obama Wasn't Black," *Daily Caller*, Jan. 24, 2012, https://daily caller.com/2012/01/24/cbc-chairman-african-americans-would-march-on -the-white-house-if-obama-wasnt-black/; Joseph Williams, "Obama Reopens Rift with Black Critics," *Politico*, Sept. 29, 2011, https://www.poli tico.com/story/2011/09/obama-reopens-rift-with-black-critics-064680.

9. Jennifer Epstein, "Waters: Tea Party Can Go to Hell," *Politico*, Aug. 22, 2011, https://www.politico.com/story/2011/08/waters-tea-party-can-go-to -hell-061828; Mackenzie Weinger, "Waters: Obama Remarks 'Curious,'" *Politico*, Sept. 26, 2011, https://www.politico.com/story/2011/09/waters -obama-remarks-curious-064405.

10. Joseph Williams, "Obama Learns Perils of Roiling Waters," *Politico*, Oct. 20, 2011, https://www.politico.com/story/2011/10/obama-learns-perils-of -roiling-waters-066418; Sabrina Tavernise and Helene Cooper, "A Dedication to King, and the Work Yet to Do," *New York Times*, Oct. 16, 2011, https://www.nytimes.com/2011/10/17/us/memorial-of-martin-luther-king -jr-dedicated-in-washington.html; Frank Newport, "Blacks' Approval of President Obama Remains High," Gallup, Dec. 15, 2014, https://news .gallup.com/poll/180176/blacks-approval-president-obama-remains-high .aspx; California Secretary of State, "Supplement to the Statement of Vote: Counties by Congressional District for United States President" (2008), accessed July 12, 2019, https://elections.cdn.sos.ca.gov/sov/2008-general /ssov/6-pres-by-congress.pdf; California Secretary of State, "Supplement to the Statement of Vote: Counties by Congressional District for President" (2012), accessed July 12, 2019, https://elections.cdn.sos.ca.gov/sov /2012-general/ssov/pres-by-congress.pdf; California Secretary of State, "United States Representative" (2008), accessed July 12, 2019, https:// elections.cdn.sos.ca.gov/sov/2008-general/23_34_us_reps.pdf; California Secretary of State, "United States Representative" (2012), accessed July 12, 2019, https://elections.cdn.sos.ca.gov/sov/2012-general/12-us-reps.pdf.

11. Sharpton quoted in Williams, "Obama Reopens Rift with Black Critics." Also see L. Douglas Wilder, "Obama's CBC Speech Wide of Mark," *Politico*, Sept. 27, 2011, http://www.politico.com/news/stories/0911/64530 .html; "Top Black Lawmaker Urges Obama to Focus on African-American Jobs," CNN, Aug. 19, 2011, http://www.cnn.com/2011/POLITICS/08/18 /michigan.maxine.waters.obama/index.html.

12. BET interview in "Dr. Emmett Miller's Son Interviews President Obama 2011," YouTube, accessed July 2, 2019, https://www.youtube.com/watch?v=A K7hlYZAk1A. Also see Williams, "Obama Reopens Rift with Black Critics."

13. Alex Isenstadt, "CBC Draws Fire for Obama Criticism," *Politico*, Nov. 2, 2011, https://www.politico.com/story/2011/11/cbc-draws-fire-for-obama -criticism-067386; George E. Condon Jr. and Jim O'Sullivan, "Has Obama Done Enough for Black Americans?," *National Journal*, Apr. 5, 2013, https:// www.theatlantic.com/politics/archive/2013/04/has-president-obama-done -enough-for-black-americans/274699/; Alex Isenstadt, "Obama Endorses Conyers," *Politico*, Feb. 10, 2012, https://www.politico.com/blogs/david -catanese/2012/02/obama-endorses-conyers-114174.

14. Isenstadt, "CBC Draws Fire"; Jennifer Epstein, "Waters to Obama Aide: Say 'Black,'" *Politico*, Aug. 23, 2011, https://www.politico.com/story/2011 /08/waters-to-obama-aide-say-black-061912; Glenn Thrush and Joseph Williams, "Black Leaders Turn Up Heat on Obama," *Politico*, Aug. 30, 2011, https://www.politico.com/story/2011/08/black-leaders-turn-up-heat -on-obama-062284; Ben Pershing, "Ethics Panel Says Rep. Laura Richard-son Broke Federal Law, Obstructed Probe," *Washington Post*, Aug. 1, 2012, https://www.washingtonpost.com/blogs/2chambers/post/ethics-panel-says -rep-laura-richardson-broke-federal-law-obstructed-probe/2012/08/01/gJQ AfoFNPX_blog.html; "Janice Hahn Wins 44th Congressional District," *Los Angeles Times*, Nov. 7, 2012, https://latimesblogs.latimes.com/california -politics/2012/11/janice-hahn-44th-congressional-district-win.html.

15. David Kocieniewski, "Rangel Inquiry Finds Evidence beyond Dispute," *New York Times*, Nov. 15, 2010, https://www.nytimes.com/2010/11/16/nyregion /16rangel.html; "Obama to Black Leaders: Fire Up against GOP Surge"; Paul Kane and David A. Fahrenthold, "House Censures Rep. Charles Rangel in 333-79 vote," *Washington Post*, Dec. 3, 2010, http://www.wash ingtonpost.com/wp-dyn/content/article/2010/12/02/AR2010120201626 .html; Alex Isenstadt, "Rangel's Love for Obama Unrequited," *Politico*, June 25, 2012, https://www.politico.com/story/2012/06/rangels-love-for -obama-unrequited-077821.

16. Isenstadt, "Rangel's Love for Obama Unrequited"; "Rangel's Challenger Concedes in Close NY Primary," Associated Press, July 9, 2012, https:// news.yahoo.com/rangels-challenger-concedes-close-ny-primary-1835266 73.html; "U.S. House: New York District 13 (Rangel vs. Schley)," CNN, Dec. 10, 2012, http://www.cnn.com/election/2012/results/state/NY/house /13/.

17. Isenstadt, "CBC Draws Fire."

18. Jeff Coen, Rick Pearson, and David Kidwell, "Blagojevich Arrested: Fitz-gerald Calls It a 'Political Corruption Crime Spree,'" *Chicago Tribune*, Dec. 10, 2008, https://www.chicagotribune.com/news/chi-rod-blagojevich-1209 -story.html; Ray Long and Rick Pearson, "Impeached Illinois Gov. Rod Blagojevich Has Been Removed from Office," *Chicago Tribune*, Jan. 30, 2009, https://www.chicagotribune.com/news/chi-blagojevich-impeach ment-removal-story.html; John Bresnahan, "Jackson Cited Deal for Obama Seat," *Politico*, Dec. 2, 2011, https://www.politico.com/story/2011/12/jackson -cited-deal-for-obama-seat-069620; Andrew Greiner, "Jesse Jackson Jr.

Wins Reelection from Mayo Clinic," NBC Chicago, Oct. 24, 2012 (updated Nov. 7, 2012), https://www.nbcchicago.com/blogs/ward-room/Jesse-Jackson-Jr-Wins-Reelection-175717941.html.

19. Carla K. Johnson, "Rep. Jesse Jackson Jr. Home from Mayo Clinic after Depression Treatment," TheGrio.com, Sept. 8, 2012, http://thegrio.com/2012/09/08/rep-jesse-jackson-jr-home-from-mayo-clinic-after-depression-treatment; Michael Isikoff, "Rep. Jesse Jackson Jr. under Federal Investigation over Alleged Financial Improprieties," NBC News, Oct. 12, 2012, http://openchannel.nbcnews.com/_news/2012/10/12/14399883-rep-jesse-jackson-jr-under-federal-investigation-over-alleged-financial-improprities?lite; Kevin Cirilli, "Report: Rep. Jackson in Plea Talks," Politico, Nov. 9, 2012, https://www.politico.com/story/2012/11/report-rep-jackson-in-plea-talks-083631; Greiner, "Jesse Jackson Jr. Wins Reelection"; Henry C. Jackson and Sophia Tareen, "Ethics Trouble Not over for Jesse Jackson Jr.," Associated Press, Nov. 23, 2012, https://www.seattletimes.com/seattle-news/politics/trouble-not-over-for-jesse-jackson-jr/; James Rowley, "Jesse Jackson Jr. Resigns Seat in Congress Citing Federal Probe," Bloomberg, Nov. 22, 2012, https://www.bloomberg.com/news/articles/2012-11-21/jackson-resigns-from-u-s-congress-citing-probe-of-his-conduct; Monica Davey, "A Family Business in Disarray," New York Times, Nov. 25, 2012, ST1; Katherine Skiba and Marina Villeneuve, "Both Jacksons Get Prison Terms: He'll Serve First," Chicago Tribune, Aug. 14, 2013, https://www.chicagotribune.com/news/breaking/chi-jesse-jackson-jr-sentence-20130814-story.html; Kim Janssen, "Jesse Jackson Jr. to Judge: Let Me Sell the Home where My Wife and Kids Live," Chicago Tribune, Mar. 1, 2018, https://www.chicagotribune.com/news/ct-met-jackson-divorce-0302-chicago-inc-20180301-story.html; Patrick O'Connell, "Jesse Jackson Jr., Sandi Jackson Reach Settlement in Contentious Divorce Case," Chicago Tribune, Apr. 13, 2018, https://www.chicagotribune.com/news/breaking/ct-met-jackson-divorce-settlement-20180413-story.html.

20. Jake Sherman, "Carson: Tea Party Wants Blacks 'Hanging on a Tree,'" Politico, Aug. 31, 2011, https://www.politico.com/story/2011/08/carson-tea-party-wants-blacks-hanging-on-a-tree-062396; Jennifer Epstein, "Clyburn: Obama Faces Racism," Politico, May 26, 2011, https://www.politico.com/story/2011/05/clyburn-obama-faces-racism-055753; Wallsten, "Obama Struggles to Balance African Americans' Hopes"; Joyce Jones, "Congressional Black Caucus Wins Five, Loses Two," BET.com, Nov. 8, 2012, https://www.bet.com/news/features/vote-2012/news/politics/2012/11/08/congressional-black-caucus-wins-five-loses-two.amp.html.

21. Jesse J. Holland, "Record Numbers of Black Candidates Seeking Office," Associated Press, Oct. 16, 2014, http://lawattstimes.com/index.php?option=com_content&view=article&id=2578:record-number-of-black-candidates-seeking-office; Jonathan Martin, "Black Pols Stymied in Obama Era," Politico, Apr. 29, 2013, https://www.politico.com/story/2013/04/black-pols-stymied-in-obama-era-090727.

CHAPTER 7. MAN ON A TIGHTROPE

1. Lisa Miltler, "Skip Gates's Next Big Idea," *Newsweek*, Apr. 18, 2011, 42-45; Milton J. Valencia, "Sergeant, Gates Both to Blame, Report Says," *Boston Globe*, July 1, 2010, http://archive.boston.com/news/local/massachusetts /articles/2010/07/01/sergeant_gates_both_to_blame_report_says/; "Charge Dropped against Harvard Scholar," *Washington Times*, July 22, 2009, https:// www.washingtontimes.com/news/2009/jul/22/charge-dropped-against-black -harvard-scholar/; Cambridge Police Department (MA), Incident Report No. 9005127, July 16, 2009, https://s.wsj.net/public/resources/documents /GatesPoliceReport.pdf; Ogletree, *Presumption of Guilt.*

2. "The President's News Conference," July 22, 2009, in Obama, *Public Papers*, 2:1152-1153; "Obama: Police Acted 'Stupidly' in Scholar Arrest," YouTube, accessed July 6, 2019, https://www.youtube.com/watch?v=LZYsW_PxWAM.

3. "'Disgraceful': Cops Angry after Obama Slams Arrest of Black Scholar," Fox News, July 24, 2009 (updated Jan. 14, 2015), https://www.foxnews.com/story /disgraceful-cops-angry-after-obama-slams-arrest-of-black-scholar; Jarrett, *Finding My Voice*, 211-212; "Invite Pookie for a Beer" (editorial), July 2009, cited in Malveaux, *Are We Better Off?*, 176; Helene Cooper and Abby Good-nough, "Over Beers, No Apologies, but Plans to Have Lunch," *New York Times*, July 30, 2009, https://www.nytimes.com/2009/07/31/us/politics/310 bama.html.

4. David Alexander, "Obama More Bartender than Mediator at Beer Summit," Reuters, July 30, 2009, https://www.reuters.com/article/us-obama-race/oba ma-more-bartender-than-mediator-at-beer-summit-idUSTRE56U0KN200 90731; Jamelle Bouie, "The Professor, the Cop, and the President," *Slate*, Sept. 21, 2016, https://slate.com/news-and-politics/2016/09/the-henry-louis-gates -beer-summit-and-racial-division-in-america.html; "Obama's Ratings Slide across the Board," Pew Research Center, July 30, 2009, https://www.people -press.org/2009/07/30/obamas-ratings-slide-across-the-board/; "Obama Weekly Job Approval by Demographics.09102016" (.xlsx), Sept. 21, 2016, https://www.evernote.com/shard/s4/client/snv?noteGuid=0953576f-5e23-4a 3a-9cf3-747c21679e09&noteKey=eec113a6a1858d85&sn=https%3A%2F%2F www.evernote.com%2Fshard%2Fs4%2Fsh%2F0953576f-5e23-4a3a-9cf3-747c 21679e09%2Feec113a6a1858d85&title=Obama%2BWeekly%2BJob%2BAppr oval%2Bby%2BDemographics; Dan Kopf, "Obama's Approval Rating from His First Day to His Last, in Charts," *Quartz*, Jan. 20, 2017, https://qz.com /889644/obamas-approval-rating-from-his-first-day-to-his-last-in-charts/.

5. Jarrett, *Finding My Voice*, 211-212; Obama, *A Promised Land*, 397; Dyson, *Black Presidency*, 13-14.

6. Sarah Wheaton, "N.A.A.C.P. Backtracks on Official Accused of Bias," *New York Times*, July 20, 2010, https://www.nytimes.com/2010/07/21/us/21sherr od.html; "USDA Employee Says She Was Forced Out," *USA Today*, July 21, 2010, 6A.

7. Clyburn quoted in Noam Scheiber, "The Obama Whisperer," *New Republic*, Nov. 9, 2014, http://www.newrepublic.com/article/120170/valerie-jarrett -obama-whisperer; Spooner quoted in Rick Hampson, "Racial Politics Take a New Turn," *USA Today*, July 22, 2010, 1A, 2A.

8. Wheaton, "N.A.A.C.P. Backtracks on Official Accused of Bias"; "USDA Employee Says She Was Forced Out"; Sheryl Gay Stolberg, "Persistent Issue of Race Is in the Spotlight, Again," *New York Times*, July 23, 2010, A13; "NAACP 'Snookered' over Video of Former USDA Employee," CNN, July 21, 2010, http://edition.cnn.com/2010/POLITICS/07/20/agriculture .employee.naacp/.

9. Shirley Sherrod filed a defamation lawsuit against Andrew Breitbart over the edited video, which was confidentially settled in 2015. Tierney Sneed, "Ex-USDA Official Settles Her Lawsuit over Breitbart Video That Got Her Fired," *Talking Points Memo*, Oct. 1, 2015, https://talkingpointsmemo.com /muckraker/sherrod-breitbart-lawsuit-settle; Joseph Williams, "Shirley Sherrod Returns to the USDA," *Politico*, May 14, 2011, https://www.politico .com/story/2011/05/shirley-sherrod-returns-to-the-usda-054970; Peter Wallsten, "Obama Struggles to Balance African Americans' Hopes with Country's as Whole," *Washington Post*, Oct. 28, 2012, http://www.washington post.com/politics/decision2012/obama-after-making-history-has-faced-a -high-wire-on-racial-issue/2012/10/28/d8e25ff4-1939-11e2-bd10-5ff056538b 7c_story.html.

10. Sherrod, *Courage to Hope*, 21-22.

11. Stolberg, "Persistent Issue of Race"; Dyson, *Black Presidency*.

12. Fredrick Harris, "Still Waiting for Our First Black President," *Washington Post*, June 1, 2012, https://www.washingtonpost.com/opinions/still-waiting -for-our-first-black-president/2012/06/01/gJQARsT16U_story.html; Fredrick Harris, "The Price of a Black President," *New York Times*, Oct. 28, 2012, 1, 9; Harris, *Price of the Ticket*, 183-189.

13. Kennedy interview; Kennedy, *Persistence of the Color Line*, 32-33.

14. Patrick Gavin, "West: President Obama's 'No Messiah,'" *Politico*, July 26, 2010, https://www.politico.com/click/stories/1007/west_obamas_no_mes siah.html; Andrew Goldman, "Cornel West Flunks the President," *New York Times Magazine*, July 24, 2011, 11; Chris Hedges, "The Obama Deception: Why Cornel West Went Ballistic," *Truthdig*, May 16, 2011, https:// www.truthdig.com/articles/the-obama-deception-why-cornel-west-went -ballistic/.

15. Hedges, "Obama Deception"; Jesse Washington, "Blacks' Economic Gains Wiped Out in Downturn," Associated Press, July 10, 2011, http://www.nbc news.com/id/43645168/ns/business-eye_on_the_economy/t/blacks-econo mic-gains-wiped-out-downturn/; Joyce Jones, "Cornel West and Tavis Smiley Launch Nationwide Poverty Tour This Weekend," BET.com, Aug. 5, 2011, https://www.bet.com/news/national/2011/08/05/cornell-west-and -tavis-smiley-launch-nationwide-poverty-tour-this-weekend.html; Cornel West, "Dr. King Weeps from His Grave," *New York Times*, Aug. 25, 2011,

https://www.nytimes.com/2011/08/26/opinion/martin-luther-king-jr-would
-want-a-revolution-not-a-memorial.html.

16. Wallsten, "Obama Struggles to Balance African Americans' Hopes"; Hedges, "Obama Deception."

17. Alter, *The Center Holds*, 272-273.

18. Glenn Thrush and Joseph Williams, "Black Leaders Turn Up Heat on Obama," *Politico*, Aug. 30, 2011, https://www.politico.com/story/2011/08 /black-leaders-turn-up-heat-on-obama-062284; Joyce Jones, "Obama Discusses Jobs and the Economy with BET News," BET.com, Sept. 26, 2011, https://www.bet.com/news/politics/2011/09/26/obama-discusses-jobs-and -the-economy-in-an-exclusive-sit-down-with-bet.html; Morial interview; Morial, *Gumbo Coalition*, 52, 128.

19. Allison Samuels, "The Black War over Obama," *Newsweek*, Aug. 22-29, 2011, 14-15; Thrush and Williams, "Black Leaders Turn Up Heat on Obama"; Al Sharpton, "In Case You Missed the Memo: Obama Has Been Fighting for Black America," TheGrio.com, June 7, 2012, https://thegrio.com/2012/06 /07/in-case-you-missed-the-memo-the-first-black-president-has-been -fighting-for-you/; Melissa Harris-Perry, "Cornel West v. Barack Obama," *Nation*, May 17, 2011, https://www.thenation.com/article/cornel-west-v -barack-obama/.

20. "Cornel West Calls Barack Obama 'a Disastrous Response to a Catastrophe,'" *Huffington Post*, May 2, 2012 (updated Oct. 18, 2012), https://www .huffpost.com/entry/cornel-west-mitt-romney_n_1471061; "The Poverty Tour 2.0," *Tavis Talks*, July 30, 2012, http://www.tavistalks.com/tavis -smiley-and-cornel-west-take-%E2%80%9C-poverty-tour-20%E2%80%9 D-battleground-states; "The Poverty Tour 2.0," YouTube, accessed July 7, 2019, https://www.youtube.com/watch?v=d3-Rm8lYDDw; Jodi Kantor, "For First Black President, a Complex Calculus of Race," *New York Times*, Oct. 21, 2012, 1; Cord Jefferson, "Commentary: Why a Poverty Tour Now?," BET.com, Sept. 7, 2012, https://www.bet.com/news/features/vote-2012 /news/politics/2012/09/07/commentary-why-a-poverty-tour-now.html; "Cornel West: Obama a 'Rockefeller Republican in Blackface,'" TheRoot .com, Nov. 11, 2012, https://www.theroot.com/cornel-west-obama-a-repub lican-in-blackface-1790894082.

21. Jim Norman, "Americans' Support for Affirmative Action Programs Rises," Gallup, Feb. 27, 2019, https://news.gallup.com/poll/247046/americans -support-affirmative-action-programs-rises.aspx; Obama, *The Audacity of Hope*, 247.

22. Julie Mason, "Obama's MLK Moment," *Politico*, Oct. 14, 2011, https://www .politico.com/story/2011/10/obamas-mlk-moment-065936; "John Lewis Medal of Freedom," YouTube, accessed July 7, 2019, https://www.youtube .com/watch?v=MRT8I1GmE_E.

23. White House visitor records show that a person or people with the name Jesse L. Jackson visited the residence three times during 2009-2010, apparently on tours. Neither the name nor any variations of it appear in visitor

logs for 2011 and 2012. "White House Visitor Records" (.csv spreadsheets), White House, https://obamawhitehouse.archives.gov/21stcenturygov/tools /visitor-records; Mason, "Obama's MLK Moment"; Tim Mak, "On Employment, Black Leaders Press Obama," *Politico*, Sept. 2, 2011, https://www .politico.com/story/2011/09/on-unemployment-black-leaders-press-obama -062574; Molly Ball, "Jackson: Obama Not Tough Enough," *Politico*, July 29, 2011, https://www.politico.com/story/2011/07/jackson-obama-not-tough -enough-060268; Byron Tau, "Jackson: Trump Birth Talk Is Race 'Code,'" *Politico*, Apr. 26, 2011, https://www.politico.com/blogs/ben-smith/2011/04 /jackson-trump-birth-talk-is-race-code-035326; Jesse Jackson, "Obama Has Worked for All Americans," *Chicago Sun-Times*, Oct 30, 2012, http://www .suntimes.com/news/jackson/16032905-452/obama-has-worked-for-all-amer icans.html; Rev. Jesse L. Jackson Sr., "Obama Has Worked for All Americans," Institute of the Black World 21st Century, Nov. 1, 2012, https://ibw21 .org/commentary/obama-has-worked-for-all-americans/.

24. Dan Gilgoff, "Across Country, Black Pastors Weigh In on Obama's Same-Sex Marriage Support," CNN, May 13, 2012, http://religion.blogs.cnn.com /2012/05/13/across-country-black-pastors-weigh-in-on-obamas-same-sex -marriage-support/; Joseph Williams, "Black Voters Divided on Gay Marriage," *Politico*, May 10, 2012, https://www.politico.com/story/2012/05 /black-voters-remain-divided-on-gay-marriage-076133; Jones and Cox, *Religion, Values, and Experiences*, 22, 28-29; Timothy Stewart-Winter, "The Gay Rights President," in Zelizer, *Presidency of Barack Obama*, 95-110; Peter Baker and Rachel L. Swarns, "After Obama's Decision on Marriage, a Call to Pastors," *New York Times*, May 13, 2012, https://www.nytimes .com/2012/05/14/us/politics/on-marriage-obama-tried-to-limit-risk.html.

25. "Civil Rights Leaders Commend Obama's Gay Marriage Stance," TheGrio .com, May 12, 2012, https://thegrio.com/2012/05/12/civil-rights-leaders -commend-obamas-gay-marriage-stance/; "NAACP Passes Resolution in Support of Marriage Equality," NAACP, May 20, 2012, https://www.naacp .org/latest/naacp-passes-resolution-in-support-of-marriage-equality/.

26. "Clyburn Seeks 'National Policy' Legalizing Same-Sex Marriage," MSNBC, May 14, 2012, http://nbcpolitics.msnbc.msn.com/_news/2012/05/14/11699 232-clyburn-seeks-national-policy-legalizing-same-sex-marriages; "U.S.A.— South Carolina Representative James Clyburn Seeks 'National Policy' Legalizing Same-Sex Marriages," ActUp.org, May 14, 2012, http://actup .org/news/usa-south-carolina-rep-clyburn-seeks-national-policy-legalizing -same-sex-marriages/; Patrick Gavin, "Booker: Obama Wrestled with Heart," *Politico*, May 10, 2012, https://www.politico.com/story/2012/05 /booker-obama-wrestled-with-heart-076153.

27. Gilgoff, "Across Country, Black Pastors Weigh In"; Nichols interview; Peter Wallsten, "Black Church Leaders Try to Inspire Congregants to Vote for Obama," *Washington Post*, Sept. 3, 2012, https://www.washingtonpost .com/politics/black-church-leaders-try-to-inspire-congregants-to-vote-for -obama/2012/09/03/136b2da0-f3f0-11e1-892d-bc92fee603a7_story.html.

28. Gilgoff, "Across Country, Black Pastors Weigh In"; John Blake, "Complexity in Black Church Relations to Obama's Gay Marriage Announcement," CNN, May 11, 2012, https://www.cnn.com/2012/05/11/us/complexity-in -black-church-reactions-to-obamas-gay-marriage-announcement-reveal /index.html.

29. Gilgoff, "Across Country, Black Pastors Weigh In"; Dan Merica, "Black Pastors Group Launches Anti-Obama Campaign around Gay Marriage," CNN, July 31, 2012, http://religion.blogs.cnn.com/2012/07/31/black-pas tors-group-launches-anti-obama-campaign-around-gay-marriage/; "Black Pastors Coalition Wants Holder Impeached over Gay Marriage Issue," United Press International, Feb. 25, 2014, https://www.upi.com/Top_News /US/2014/02/25/Black-pastors-coalition-wants-Holder-impeached-over -gay-marriage-issue/90981393339564/.

30. Lonnae O'Neal Parker, "Black Preacher Spreads the Word . . . against Obama," *Washington Post*, Nov. 4, 2012, https://www.washingtonpost .com/politics/decision2012/black-preacher-spreads-the-word—against -obama/2012/11/04/c9899928-26d6-11e2-9972-71bf64ea091c_story.html.

31. "Obama Nominates Out Gay Black Judge to Federal Bench," *Buzzfeed*, Nov. 14, 2012, https://www.buzzfeednews.com/article/chrisgeidner/oba ma-nominates-out-gay-black-judge-to-federal-ben; *Obergefell v. Hodges*, Supreme Court of the United States blog, accessed July 7, 2019, https:// www.scotusblog.com/case-files/cases/obergefell-v-hodges/; Kristen Holmes, "Obama Nominates Openly Gay Man to Lead Army," CNN, Sept. 18, 2015, https://www.cnn.com/2015/09/18/politics/eric-fanning -secretary-of-the-army/index.html; "U.S. Senate Backs Fanning as Army Secretary," Reuters, May 17, 2016, http://news.trust.org item /20160517212821-g837v.

CHAPTER 8. PITCHFORKS, DAGGERS, AND CARNIVAL BARKERS

1. Jon Meacham, "A Conversation with Barack Obama: What He's Like Now," *Newsweek*, May 25, 2009, 36-43; Doris Kearns Goodwin, "Barack Obama and Doris Kearns Goodwin: The Ultimate Exit Interview," *Vanity Fair*, Sept. 21, 2016, http://www.vanityfair.com/news/2016/09/barack-obama -doris-kearns-goodwin-interview.

2. Rep. Joe Wilson's words came back to haunt him. During a town hall meeting in Aiken, South Carolina, in 2017, pro-Obamacare audience members mocked the congressman with the chant "You lie!" as he declared his commitment to repealing the health-care law. Phil Helsel, "Rep. Joe Wilson's 'You Lie' Line Used against Him at Contentious Town Hall," NBC News, Apr. 11, 2017, https://www.nbcnews.com/politics/politics-news/rep-joe-wil son-s-you-lie-line-used-against-him-n745426; Michael A. Fletcher, "A Question of Racism," *Undefeated*, June 1, 2016, https://theundefeated.com/featu res/a-question-of-racism/; "Rep. Wilson Shouts, 'You Lie' to Obama during

Speech," CNN, Sept. 10, 2009, http://www.cnn.com/2009/POLITICS/09/09/joe.wilson/; "GOP Rep. to Obama: 'You Lie!,'" YouTube, accessed July 10, 2019; https://www.youtube.com/watch?v=qgce06Yw2r0; Carl Hulse, "House Rebukes Wilson for Shouting 'You Lie,'" *New York Times*, Sept. 15, 2009, https://www.nytimes.com/2009/09/16/us/politics/16wilson.html; Ta-Nehisi Coates, "'The Filter . . . Is Powerful': Obama on Race, Media, and What It Took to Win," *Atlantic*, Dec. 20, 2016, https://www.theatlantic.com/politics/archive/2016/12/ta-nehisi-coates-obama-transcript/510965/.

3. Jonathan Bernstein, "Happy Hour Roundup: New Report Confirms GOP Obstructionism Is Unprecedented," *Washington Post*, May 3, 2013, https://www.washingtonpost.com/blogs/plum-line/wp/2013/05/03/happy-hour-roundup-new-report-confirms-gop-obstructionism-is-unprecedented; Glenn Kessler, "When Did McConnell Say He Wanted to Make Obama a 'One-Term President'?," *Washington Post*, Sept. 25, 2012, https://www.washingtonpost.com/blogs/fact-checker/post/when-did-mcconnell-say-he-wanted-to-make-obama-a-one-term-president/2012/09/24/79fd5cd8-0696-11e2-afff-d6c7f20a83bf_blog.html. Years after he left the White House, Obama still had an impression of Mitch McConnell's Machiavellianism. "What McConnell lacked in charisma or interest in policy he more than made up for in discipline, shrewdness, and shamelessness—all of which he employed in the single-minded and dispassionate pursuit of power." Obama, *A Promised Land*, 245–246.

4. Chris Cillizza and Aaron Blake, "The Tea Party, the Debt Ceiling and John Boehner's Conundrum," *Washington Post*, July 12, 2011, https://www.washingtonpost.com/blogs/the-fix/post/the-tea-party-the-debt-ceiling-and-john-boehners-conundrum/2011/07/11/gIQAZMESAI_blog.html; Binyamin Appelbaum and Eric Dash, "S. & P. Downgrades Debt Rating of U.S. for the First Time," *New York Times*, Aug. 5, 2011, https://www.nytimes.com/2011/08/06/business/us-debt-downgraded-by-sp.html; Jodi Kantor, "Change Comes: After 4 Years, Friends See Shifts in the Obamas," *New York Times*, Jan. 20, 2013, 16.

5. Glenn Thrush and Donovan Slack, "The Race Issue Rises Again," *Politico*, Feb. 6, 2012, https://www.politico.com/story/2012/02/the-race-issue-rises-again-072485; Donovan Slack, "Jan Brewer: Obama 'Didn't Feel I Treated Him Cordially,'" *Politico*, Jan. 25, 2012, https://www.politico.com/blogs/politico44/2012/01/jan-brewer-obama-didnt-feel-i-treated-him-cordially-112328; Morgan Whitaker, "Obama Gets Warmer Greeting from Brewer on Phoenix Tarmac," MSNBC, Aug. 6, 2013, http://www.msnbc.com/politicsnation/obama-gets-warmer-greeting-brewer; Yvonne Wingett Sanchez, "Brewer Calls Obama Offensive on CNN, Defends Trump's Comments," *Arizona Republic*, June 26, 2016, https://www.azcentral.com/story/news/politics/politicalinsider/2016/06/26/brewer-calls-obama-offensive-defends-trumps-comments-cnn/86406294/.

6. Halimah Abdullah, "Obama Interrupted: Disrespectful or Latest in 'Era of Incivility'?," CNN, June 15, 2012, https://www.cnn.com/2012/06/15/politics/obama-interrupted/index.html; "TheGrio Editorial: Disrespect Is the

Story, Not Neil Munro," TheGrio.com, June 16, 2012, https://thegrio.com /2012/06/16/thegrio-editiorial-disrespect-is-the-story-not-neil-munro/; Coates, "The Filter . . . Is Powerful"; Keith Coffman, "Shot Fired into Obama Campaign Office in Denver," Reuters, Oct. 12, 2012, https://www .chicagotribune.com/nation-world/ct-xpm-2012-10-12-sns-rt-us-usa-cam paign-denver-gunshotbre89c02f-20121012-story.html; Dorkys Ramos, "Secret Service Visits Man Who Hanged Obama Effigy as Halloween Decoration," BET.com, Oct. 25, 2012, http://www.bet.com/news/national/20 12/10/25/secret-service-visits-man-who-hanged-obama-effigy-as-halloween -decoration.html.

7. Zachary Courser, "The Tea Party at the Election," in Pfiffner and Davidson, *Understanding the Presidency*, 292, 304; Skocpol, *Obama and America's Political Future*, 53-54; Sherman, *Loudest Voice in the Room*, 330-337; Suskind, *Confidence Men*, 334-335; Jann Wenner, "Obama in Command," *Rolling Stone*, Oct. 14, 2010, 39; Tom Rosentiel, "No Decline in Belief That Obama Is a Muslim," Pew Research Center, Apr. 1, 2009, https:// www.pewresearch.org/2009/04/01/no-decline-in-belief-that-obama-is-a -muslim/; Obama, *A Promised Land*, 405, 672.

8. Existing video of the spitting incident involving Emanuel Cleaver is subject to interpretation, and it is possible that the protester in question inadvertently sprayed the congressman while shouting. "Tea Party, Dems Row over N-Word Video 'Evidence,'" CBS News, Apr. 13, 2010, https://www .cbsnews.com/news/tea-party-dems-row-over-n-word-video-evidence; "Health Bill Opponents Heckle Top Dems," Associated Press, Mar. 20, 2010, https://www.nbcnews.com/id/wbna35965961.

9. Jacobson, "Legislative Success and Political Failure," 183; Alter, *The Center Holds*, 20; Kate Zernike and Megan Thee-Brenan, "Poll Finds Tea Party Backers Wealthier and More Educated," *New York Times*, Apr. 14, 2010, https://www.nytimes.com/2010/04/15/us/politics/15poll.html; "Health Bill Opponents Heckle Top Dems"; Gary Gerstle, "Civic Ideals, Race, and Nation in the Age of Obama," in Zelizer, *Presidency of Barack Obama*, 272-276; Jacobson, "Legislative Success and Political Failure," 183-184; Ian Gray, "Tea Party Election Results: Conservative Movement of 2010 Takes Pounding in 2012," *Huffington Post*, Nov. 7, 2012, https://www.huffpost.com/entry /tea-party-election-results_n_2084506.

10. Tracie Rozhon, "Fred C. Trump, Postwar Master Builder of Housing for Middle Class, Dies at 93," *New York Times*, June 26, 1999, https://www .nytimes.com/1999/06/26/nyregion/fred-c-trump-postwar-master-builder -of-housing-for-middle-class-dies-at-93.html; Michael Kranish and Robert O'Harrow Jr., "Inside the Government's Racial Bias Case against Donald Trump's Company, and How He Fought It," *Washington Post*, Jan. 23, 2016, https://www.washingtonpost.com/politics/inside-the-governments-racial -bias-case-against-donald-trumps-company-and-how-he-fought-it/2016 /01/23/fb90163e-bfbe-11e5-bcda-62a36b394160_story.html; David W. Dunlap, "1973: Meet Donald Trump," *New York Times*, July 30, 2015, https:// www.nytimes.com/times-insider/2015/07/30/1973-meet-donald-trump.

11. Alexander Burns, "Donald Trump's Instinct for Racially Charged Rhetoric, before His Presidential Bid," *New York Times*, July 31, 2015, https://www .nytimes.com/2015/08/01/nyregion/trumps-instinct-for-racially-charged-rhe toric-before-his-presidential-bid.html; Michael Wilson, "Trump Draws Criticism for Ad He Ran after Jogger Attack," *New York Times*, Oct. 23, 2002, https://www.nytimes.com/2002/10/23/nyregion/trump-draws-criti cism-for-ad-he-ran-after-jogger-attack.html; "Donald Trump: Central Park Five Settlement Is a 'Disgrace,'" *New York Daily News*, June 21, 2014, https:// www.nydailynews.com/new-york/nyc-crime/donald-trump-central-park -settlement-disgrace-article-1.1838467%0A; German Lopez, "Donald Trump's Long History of Racism, from the 1970s to 2019," *Vox*, Aug. 13, 2020, https://www.vox.com/2016/7/25/12270880/donald-trump-racist -racism-history.

12. Kranish and Fisher, *Trump Revealed*, 290-291; Maureen Dowd, "When Hillary and Donald Were Friends," *New York Times Magazine*, Nov. 2, 2016, https://www.nytimes.com/2016/11/06/magazine/when-hillary-and-donald -were-friends.html; "Trump Endorses McCain," CNN, Sept. 18, 2008, http://politicalticker.blogs.cnn.com/2008/09/18/trump-endorses-mccain/; Trump, *Too Much and Never Enough*; Maureen Dowd, "Trump Fired Up," *New York Times*, Dec. 23, 2006, https://www.nytimes.com/2006/12/23 /opinion/23dowd.html.

13. Fox Butterfield, "Trump Urged to Head Gala of Democrats," *New York Times*, Nov. 18, 1987, https://www.nytimes.com/1987/11/18/us/trump-urged -to-head-gala-of-democrats.html; Donald J. Trump, "What I Saw at the Revolution," *New York Times*, Feb. 19, 2000, https://www.nytimes.com /2000/02/19/opinion/what-i-saw-at-the-revolution.html; Shannon Travis, "Was He Ever Serious? How Trump Strung the Country Along, Again," CNN, May 17, 2011, http://edition.cnn.com/2011/POLITICS/05/16/trump .again/index.html.

14. Kyle Cheney, "No, Clinton Didn't Start the Birther Thing: This Guy Did," *Politico*, Sept. 16, 2016, https://www.politico.com/story/2016/09/birther -movement-founder-trump-clinton-228304; Poniewozik, *Audience of One*, 164-167.

15. According to conservative conspiracy theorist James O'Keefe, in 2013 Trump encouraged him to find a way to "get inside Columbia [University]" in order to access Obama's undergraduate records. O'Keefe, *American Pravda*, 1-2. Also see "Whoopi Goldberg, Donald Trump Spar over Obama on 'The View,'" *Wall Street Journal*, Mar. 24, 2011, https://blogs.wsj.com/speakeasy /2011/03/24/donald-trump-discusses-president-obama-on-the-view/; Jack Mirkinson, "Whoopi Goldberg Explodes at Donald Trump about Obama's Birth Certificate on 'The View,'" *Huffington Post*, Dec. 6, 2017, https:// www.huffpost.com/entry/whoopi-goldberg-donald-trump-obama-birth -certificate_n_839927; Lopez, "Donald Trump's Long History"; Obama, *A Promised Land*, 672-675.

16. Alter, *The Center Holds*, 40-41; Barack Obama to Loretta J. Fuddy, Apr. 22, 2011, and Loretta J. Fuddy to the Honorable Barack Obama, Apr. 25, 2011,

White House, https://obamawhitehouse.gov/sites/default/files/rss_viewer/birth-certificate-correspondence.pdf; "President Obama Provides His Birth Certificate to the Press," YouTube, accessed July 11, 2019, https://www.youtube.com/watch?v=QM2GJn6hpJE; "Barack Obama Releases Birth Certificate, Donald Trump 'Proud,'" YouTube, accessed July 11, 2019, https://www.youtube.com/watch?v=dnkQ9TABCFM.

17. "Remarks at the White House Correspondents' Association Dinner," Apr. 30, 2011, in Obama, *Public Papers*, 1:478-480; "C-SPAN: President Obama at the 2011 White House Correspondents' Dinner," YouTube, accessed July 12, 2019, https://www.youtube.com/watch?v=n9mzJhvC-8E; Obama, *A Promised Land*, 690-692; Maggie Haberman and Alexander Burns, "Donald Trump's Presidential Run Began in an Effort to Gain Stature," *New York Times*, Mar. 12, 2016, https://www.nytimes.com/2016/03/13/us/politics/donald-trump-campaign.html.

18. Justin Sink, "Reggie Love: Obama Wanted 'Impromptu Press Conference' on Birth Certificate," TheHill.com, Aug. 14, 2013, https://thehill.com/blogs/blog-briefing-room/news/317137-love-obama-wanted-impromptu-press-conference-on-birth-certificate; Alter, *The Center Holds*, 40; Jennifer Epstein, "Obama Laughs Off Trump's Offer," *Politico*, Oct. 24, 2012, https://www.politico.com/blogs/politico44/2012/10/obama-laughs-off-trumps-offer-147154; Lymari Morales, "Obama's Birth Certificate Convinces Some, but Not All, Skeptics," Gallup, May 13, 2011, https://news.gallup.com/poll/147530/obama-birth-certificate-convinces-not-skeptics.aspx; Similoluwa Ojurongbe, "Kansas Considers Removing Obama from Ballot in November," TheGrio.com, Sept. 14, 2012, https://thegrio.com/2012/09/14/kansas-considers-removing-obama-from-ballot-in-november/; "Obama to Appear on Kansas Ballot after 'Birther' Challenge Dropped," CNN, Sept. 17, 2012, http://politicalticker.blogs.cnn.com/2012/09/17/obama-to-appear-on-kansas-ballot-after-birther-challenge-dropped/; Obama, *Becoming*, 352-353.

19. To add another wrinkle of complication to Barack Obama's ancestry and racial identity, researchers for Ancestry.com claimed in 2012 that they had genetically traced his mother, Ann Dunham, to a progenitor named John Punch, an African who had been enslaved in early colonial Virginia. "Ancestry.com Discovers President Obama Related to First Documented Slave in America," Ancestry.com, July 30, 2012, www.ancestrycdn.com/legacy/my-content/offer/us/obama_bunch/pdf/press_release_final.pdf; Sheryl Gay Stolberg, "Obama Has Ties to Slavery Not by His Father but His Mother, Research Suggests," *New York Times*, July 30, 2012, https://www.nytimes.com/2012/07/30/us/obamas-mother-had-african-forebear-study-suggests.html; Carrie Budoff Brown, "Trip May Help Obama Back Home," *Politico*, May 24, 2011, https://www.politico.com/story/2011/05/trip-may-help-obama-back-home-055458; "President Barack Obama," White House, https://obamawhitehouse.archives.gov/administration/president-obama; David Remnick, "Obama Reckons with a Trump Presidency," *New Yorker*, Nov. 18, 2016, https://www.newyorker.com/magazine

/2016/11/28/obama-reckons-with-a-trump-presidency; Coates, "The Filter . . . Is Powerful."

20. Christopher Ingraham, "The Ugly Truth about Hate Crimes—in 5 Charts and Maps," *Washington Post*, June 18, 2015, https://www.washingtonpost.com/news/wonk/wp/2015/06/18/5-charts-show-the-stubborn-persistence-of-american-hate-crime/; Mark Potok, "The Year in Hate and Extremism," Southern Poverty Law Center, Mar. 4, 2013, https://www.splcenter.org/fighting-hate/intelligence-report/2013/year-hate-and-extremism; Daniel Trotta, "U.S. Army Battling Racists within Its Ranks," Reuters, Aug. 21, 2012, https://www.reuters.com/article/usa-wisconsin-shooting-army/u-s-army-battling-racists-within-its-own-ranks-idUSL2E8JHO6K20120821; Office of Intelligence and Analysis, US Department of Homeland Security, *Rightwing Extremism*; Jeff Zeleny and Jim Rutenberg, "Officials Say They Saw a Spike in Threats against Obama Early in His Term," *New York Times*, Dec. 6, 2009, 27, 32.

21. Zeleny and Rutenberg, "Officials Say They Saw a Spike in Threats," 27, 32; Kessler, *First Family Detail*, 55–57; Feinman, *Assassinations, Threats, and the American Presidency*, 181; Brandi Kruse, "Secret Service Says Number of Threats against President 'Overwhelming,'" MyNorthwest.com (Seattle, WA), Aug. 27, 2012, https://mynorthwest.com/33700/secret-service-says-number-of-threats-against-president-overwhelming/.

22. Stephen A. Crockett Jr., "Man Who Planned to Kill President Obama Sentenced to Death," TheRoot.com, May 14, 2014, https://www.theroot.com/man-who-planned-to-kill-president-obama-sentenced-to-de-1790875697; John Hult, "'No One Else Will Be Harmed': McVay Sentenced to Death," *Argus Leader* (Sioux Falls, SD), Apr. 14, 2014 (updated Apr. 15, 2014), https://www.argusleader.com/story/news/crime/2014/04/14/death-sentencing-trial-hands-jury/7707659/; Naeesa Aziz, "North Carolina Man Arrested after Threatening to Kill Obama on Twitter," BET.com, Sept. 7, 2012, https://www.bet.com/news/national/2012/09/07/north-carolina-man-arrested-after-threatening-to-kill-obama-on-twitter.html; Western District of North Carolina, US Attorney's Office, "Charlotte Man Is Sentenced to Six Months in Prison for Making Threats against the President on Twitter," May 29, 2013, https://www.justice.gov/usao-wdnc/pr/charlotte-man-sentenced-six-months-prison-making-threats-against-president-twitter; Don Terry, "Alabama Man Pleads Guilty to Threatening Obama on Twitter," *Salon*, Mar. 20, 2013, https://www.salon.com/2013/03/20/alabama_man_pleads_guilty_to_threatening_obama_on_twitter_partner/; Robbie Brown, "140 Characters Spell Charges and Jail," *New York Times*, July 2, 2013, https://www.nytimes.com/2013/07/03/us/felony-counts-and-jail-in-140-characters.html; Eric Tucker, "Police Probe Threats to First Lady," Associated Press, July 13, 2012, https://www.montereyherald.com/2012/07/13/police-probe-threats-to-first-lady/.

23. Emily le Coz, "U.S. Man Pleads Guilty to Sending Ricin to Obama, Two Others," Reuters, Jan. 17, 2014, https://news.yahoo.com/u-man-pleads-guilty-sending-ricin-obama-two-021953593.html; "Missouri Man Charged with Threatening to Shoot President Obama," Reuters, Mar. 17, 2015,

https://www.reuters.com/article/us-usa-crime-missouri-threats-idUSKBN0
ME05F20150318; Steven Nelson, "Slingshot Owner Convicted of Threats
to Kill Obama," *U.S. News & World Report*, Jan. 13, 2016, https://www.us
news.com/news/articles/2016-01-13/wisconsin-man-convicted-of-threats-to
-kill-obama; "The New Dynamics of Protecting a President: Most Threats
against Obama Issued Online," *Washington Post*, Oct. 8, 2014, https://www
.washingtonpost.com/politics/the-new-dynamics-of-protecting-a-president
-most-threats-against-obama-issued-online/2014/10/07/a525ef6c-4b11-11e4
-891d-713f052086a0_story.html.

24. Ed Henry, "Plot to Assassinate Obama Foiled in Turkey," CNN, Apr. 6,
2009, http://www.cnn.com/2009/POLITICS/04/06/turkey.assassination
.plot/index.html; "Man Sentenced after Plotting to Kill President," *News
and Observer* (Raleigh, NC), July 14, 2012; "Ulugbek Kodirov Jailed 16 Years
for Plot to Assassinate President Obama," Thomson Reuters, July 13, 2012,
https://www.pri.org/stories/2012-07-13/ulugbek-kodirov-jailed-16-years-plot
-assassinate-president-obama.

25. Carol D. Leonnig, "Secret Service Fumbled Response after Gunman Hit
White House Residence in 2011," *Washington Post*, Sept. 27, 2014, https://
www.washingtonpost.com/politics/secret-service-stumbled-after-gunman
-hit-white-house-residence-in-2011/2014/09/27/d176b6ac-442a-11e4-b437
-147368204804_story.html; Josh Gerstein, "White House Shooter Gets 25
Years," *Politico*, Mar. 31, 2014, https://www.politico.com/blogs/under-the
-radar/2014/03/white-house-shooter-gets-25-years-186074; Obama, *Becoming*,
353-354; Michael Lewis, "Obama's Way," *Vanity Fair*, Oct. 2012, 263-264.

26. "White House Fence-Jumper Made It Far Deeper into Building than Previously Known," *Washington Post*, Sept. 29, 2014, https://www.washington
post.com/politics/white-house-fence-jumper-made-it-far-deeper-into-build
ing-than-previously-known/2014/09/29/02efd53e-47ea-11e4-a046-120a8a855
cca_story.html; Richard Reeve, "Omar J. Gonzalez, Accused White House
Fence-Jumper, Identified as Army Veteran Who Served in Iraq," Associated
Press, Sept. 21, 2014, https://wjla.com/news/local/omar-j-gonzalez-accused
-white-house-fence-jumper-identified-as-army-veteran-who-served-in-iraq
-10735; Jeff Mason, "U.S. Secret Service Investigates after Man Jumps White
House Fence, Reaches Doors," Reuters, Sept. 20, 2014, https://www.reu
ters.com/article/us-usa-whitehouse-security/u-s-secret-service-investigates
-after-man-jumps-white-house-fence-reaches-doors-idUSKBN0HE2J520
140921; "Secret Service Agents Interviewed White House Intruder before
Breach," Associated Press, Sept. 23, 2014, https://www.theguardian.com
/world/2014/sep/23/secret-service-agents-interview-white-house-intruder;
Jack Date, Whitney Lloyd, and Ariane de Vogue, "White House Fence
Jumper Omar Gonzalez Had 800 Rounds of Ammo in Car, Prosecutors
Say," ABC News, Sept. 22, 2014, https://abcnews.go.com/Politics/white
-house-fence-jumper-omar-gonzalez-arrested-july/story?id=25678693.

27. Eileen Sullivan and Alicia A. Caldwell, "Secret Service Chief Quits due to
Security Lapses," Associated Press, Oct. 2, 2014, https://www.thedailytimes
.com/news/secret-service-chief-quits-due-to-security-lapses/article_f6d965d

8-c87b-585e-8fd7-c9d2b225ab7d.html; Peter Baker, "Some Blacks See Secret Service as Flawed Shield for the President," *New York Times*, Oct. 2, 2014, https://www.nytimes.com/2014/10/03/us/politics/in-secret-services-missteps-blacks-sense-a-flawed-shield-for-the-president.html; "White House Intruder Indicted," Associated Press, Sept. 30, 2014, https://www.politico.com/story/2014/09/white-house-intruder-indicted-111482; Ian Simpson, "White House Fence Jumper Sentenced to 17 Months in Prison," Reuters, June 16, 2015, https://www.businessinsider.com/r-white-house-fence-jumper-senten ced-to-17-months-minus-time-served-2015-6; Obama, *A Promised Land*, 542; Michael S. Schmidt, "A Deterrent at the White House for Fence Jumpers," *New York Times*, July 1, 2015, https://www.nytimes.com/politics/first-draft/2015/07/01/a-deterrent-at-the-white-house-for-fence-jumpers/.

28. The 2013 law also provides Secret Service protection for the children of presidents until age 16. Kevin Liptak, "Obama Signs Bill, Gets Secret Service Protection for Life," CNN, Jan. 10, 2013, http://politicalticker.blogs.cnn.com/2013/01/10/obama-signs-bill-gets-secret-service-protection-for-life/; Obama, *A Promised Land*, 137-138; Kessler, *First Family Detail*, 40-41.

CHAPTER 9. GUESS WHO'S COMING TO TEA

1. Thurber, *Republicans and Race*, 3.
2. Rigueur, *Loneliness of the Black Republican*, 305; Farrington, *Black Republicans*, 230; Fields, *Black Elephants in the Room*; Laura Rozen, "Powell Defends Obama Afghan Policies," *Politico*, Nov. 17, 2010, https://www.politico.com/story/2010/11/powell-defends-afghan-policies-045196; "Colin Powell Endorses Barack Obama for President," CBS News, Oct. 25, 2012, https://www.cbsnews.com/news/colin-powell-endorses-barack-obama-for-president/; "Rice: Obama Foreign Policy 'Lacking,'" *Politico*, June 26, 2012, https://www.politico.com/story/2012/06/rice-obama-foreign-policy-lacking-077832; Jennifer Steinhauer, "Black Hopefuls Pick This Year in G.O.P. Races," *New York Times*, May 4, 2010, https://www.nytimes.com/2010/05/05/us/politics/05blacks.html.
3. "Life of the Party," *New York Times Magazine*, Jan. 2, 2011, 11; "WEST, Allen (1961–)," *Biographical Dictionary of the United States Congress*, accessed July 15, 2019, http://bioguide.congress.gov/scripts/biodisplay.pl?index=W000807; Anthony Man and David Fleshler, "Allen West Defeats Ron Klein," *Sun Sentinel* (Deerfield Beach, FL), Nov. 3, 2010, https://www.sun-sentinel.com/news/fl-xpm-2010-11-03-fl-election-us-congress-20101102-story.html; Steinhauer, "Black Hopefuls Pick This Year in G.O.P. Races"; Peter D. Klingman, "Race and Faction in the Public Career of Florida's Josiah T. Walls," in Rabinowitz, *Southern Black Leaders*, 59-78; Beth Sullivan, "African-American Congressman-Elect: Tea Party Is about Principles, Not Racism," Fox News, Nov. 6, 2010 (updated Dec. 23, 2015), https://www.foxnews.com/politics/african-american-congressman-elect-tea-party-is-about-principles-not-racism.

4. Marin Cogan, "CBC: Black Republicans Welcome," *Politico*, Nov. 9, 2010, https://www.politico.com/story/2010/11/cbc-black-republicans-welcome-04 4886; Marin Cogan, "West: Congressional Black Caucus Is 'Monolithic,'" *Politico*, Nov. 15, 2010, https://www.politico.com/story/2010/11/west-black -caucus-is-monolithic-045133; Jennifer Epstein, "West: I'll Lead You off 'Plantation,'" *Politico*, Aug. 18, 2011, https://www.politico.com/story/2011 /08/west-ill-lead-you-off-plantation-061627; Jennifer Epstein, "Waters Responds to West Comments," *Politico*, Aug. 19, 2011, https://www.politico .com/story/2011/08/waters-responds-to-west-comments-061652; Reid J. Epstein, "Rep. West Considers Quitting CBC," *Politico*, Aug. 31, 2011, https://www.politico.com/story/2011/08/rep-west-considers-quitting-cbc -062414; David Goldstein, "Black Caucus Head Treads Line between Criticizing, Supporting Obama," McClatchy Newspapers, Sept. 19, 2011, https:// www.mcclatchydc.com/news/politics-government/article24699058.html.

5. M. J. Lee, "West: Food Stamp President a 'Fact,'" *Politico*, Jan. 23, 2012, https://www.politico.com/story/2012/01/west-newt-right-on-foodstamp -prez-071814; M. J. Lee, "West Fills Hummer, Blames Obama," *Politico*, Feb. 23, 2012, https://www.politico.com/story/2012/02/west-fills-hummer -blames-obama-073218; M. J. Lee, "Reince Priebus: I Won't Toss West in a 'Ditch,'" *Politico*, July 4, 2012, https://www.politico.com/story/2012/07 /priebus-i-wont-toss-west-in-a-ditch-078115; M. J. Lee, "West: Social Security Disability Is 'Slavery,'" *Politico*, July 9, 2012, https://www.politico.com /story/2012/07/rep-west-socsec-is-modern-slavery-078223; "Congressman West Condemns the Attack on the Sovereign Soil of Our Nation," CongressNewsletter.com, Sept. 12, 2012, http://west.congressnewsletter.net /mail/util.cfm?gpiv=2100094262.35481.109&gen=1.

6. Matt Sedensky, "West Wants Ballots, Voting Machines Impounded," Associated Press, Nov. 7, 2012, https://www.yahoo.com/news/west-wants-ballots -voting-machines-impounded-221021617—election.html; Frank Thorp, "Congressman Says 80 Fellow Lawmakers Are Communists," MSNBC, Apr. 11, 2012, http://firstread.msnbc.msn.com/_news/2012/04/11/11144072 -congressman-says-80-fellow-lawmakers-are-communists.

7. Lizette Alvarez, "Race in New District Is New Test for a G.O.P. Firebrand," *New York Times*, July 19, 2012, http://www.nytimes.com/2012/07/20/us/poli tics/allen-west-faces-challenge-in-new-florida-district.html; Jennifer Bendery, "Patrick Murphy Reveals Strategy for Beating Allen West: Allen West," *Huffington Post*, Aug. 15, 2012, https://www.huffpost.com/entry/patrick -murphy-allen-west_n_1777302; Michael McAuliff, "Patrick Murphy, Disgusted Ex-Republican, Pushes Bipartisan Caucus as Democrat in Congress," *Huffington Post*, Mar. 6, 2013, https://www.huffpost.com/entry/patrick -murphy-bipartisan_n_2814094; Kevin Robillard, "Allen West Demands Recount," *Politico*, Nov. 7, 2012, https://www.politico.com/story/2012/11 /allen-west-demands-recount-083476; Alex Isenstadt, "West Concedes to Patrick Murphy," *Politico*, Nov. 20, 2012, https://www.politico.com/story /2012/11/west-concedes-to-patrick-murphy-084068; "Fox News Channel

Signs Former U.S. Representative Allen West to Contributor Role," Fox News, May 16, 2013, http://press.foxnews.com/2013/05/fox-news-channel-signs-former-u-s-representative-allen-west-to-contributor-role/; Zack Budryk, "NRA Board Member Allen West Urges CEO LaPierre to Step Down," TheHill.com, May 14, 2019, https://thehill.com/regulation/lobbying/443686-nra-board-member-allen-west-urges-ceo-lapierre-to-step-down.

8. Zev Chafets, "Tea for Tim," *Newsweek*, Nov. 15, 2010, 38 40; "SC Elects Black GOP Congressman: 1st since 2003," Associated Press, Nov. 2, 2010, http://www.washingtonpost.com/wp-dyn/content/article/2010/11/02/AR2010110207838.html; Marin Cogan, "S.C.'s Scott: Tea Party Talent Scout," *Politico*, Aug. 27, 2011, https://www.politico.com/story/2011/08/scs-scott-tea-party-talent-scout-062168; Caroline May, "Tim Scott: First Black Republican Elected to Congress from the South since Reconstruction," *Daily Caller*, Nov. 2, 2010, http://dailycaller.com/2010/11/02/tim-scott-first-black-republican-elected-to-congress-from-the-south-since-reconstruction; "Biography: US Senator Tim Scott Serving South Carolina," accessed July 16, 2019, https://web.archive.org/web/20170710055714/https://www.scott.senate.gov/about-me/biography#; "SC State House 117—R Primary," Our Campaigns, accessed Nov. 8, 2019, https://www.ourcampaigns.com/RaceDetail.html?RaceID=438595.

9. Chafets, "Tea for Tim," 38-41; "Statewide Results" (2010), South Carolina State Election Commission, accessed July 17, 2019, http://www.enr-scvotes.org/SC/19077/40477/en/summary.html; "Election 2010," *New York Times*, Dec. 10, 2010, https://www.nytimes.com/elections/2010/results/primaries/south-carolina/runoff.html; "MURRAY, George Washington (1853-1926)," in *Biographical Directory of the United States Congress*, accessed July 17, 2019, http://bioguide.congress.gov/scripts/biodisplay.pl?index=M001106; Bill Turque, "Rep. Tim Scott of South Carolina to Be First Black Republican Senator since 1978," *Washington Post*, Dec. 17, 2012, https://www.washingtonpost.com/politics/rep-tim-scott-of-south-carolina-to-be-first-black-republican-senator-since-1978/2012/12/17/cdd1db44-4878-11e2-ad54-580638ede391_story.html; David Eldridge, "Rep. Scott: Proud of Obama, but He's Failed," *Washington Times*, Aug. 25, 2011, http://www.washingtontimes.com/news/2011/aug/25/rep-scott-proud-obama-hes-failed/; Cogan, "CBC: Black Republicans Welcome"; Jennifer Steinhauer and Jeff Zeleny, "Tim Scott to Be Named for South Carolina Senate Seat, Republicans Say," *New York Times*, Dec. 17, 2012, https://thecaucus.blogs.nytimes.com/2012/12/17/tim-scott-to-be-named-for-empty-south-carolina-senate-seat-republicans-say/; Tim Alberta, " 'God Made Me Black on Purpose,' " *Politico*, Mar.–Apr. 2018, https://www.politico.com/magazine/story/2018/03/16/senator-tim-scott-black-republican-trump-profile-217237.

10. Cain, *This Is Herman Cain!*, 117, 123.

11. Cain, *This Is Herman Cain!*, 1; Kate Zernike, "A G.O.P. Hopeful Gathers Momentum as More Voters Like What They Hear," *New York Times*, June 5, 2011, 18, 23; Joshua Green, "Herman Cain, the GOP Wild Card," *Atlantic*, Mar. 2011, https://www.theatlantic.com/magazine/archive/2011

/03/herman-cain-the-gop-wild-card/308367/; Hao Li, "Herman Cain 2012: The Story of a Self-Made Man," *International Business Times*, May 21, 2011, https://www.ibtimes.com/herman-cain-2012-story-self-made-man-285259; Steve Jordan, "Cain: The Godfather's Years," *Omaha World Herald*, Oct. 11, 2011, https://archive.is/20130130200355/http://www.omaha.com/article/20 111011/NEWS01/710119907/0#selection-1747.0-1747.27.

12. Thomas M. Hoenig, "Herman Cain's Service as a Director of the Federal Reserve Bank of Kansas City," Federal Reserve Bank of Kansas City, May 26, 2011, https://web.archive.org/web/20110617100029/http://www.kansas cityfed.org/publicat/newsroom/2011pdf/press.release.05.26.11.pdf; Sheryl Gay Stolberg, "Cain, Now Running as Outsider, Came to Washington as Lobbyist," *New York Times*, Oct. 23, 2011, 1, 20; Green, "Herman Cain, the GOP Wild Card"; Byron York, "Herman Cain Sounds Off on Race, a Debate Win, and the Need to Simplify Government," *Washington Examiner*, May 15, 2011, https://www.washingtonexaminer.com/herman-cain-sounds -off-on-race-a-debate-win-and-the-need-to-simplify-government; "Tea Party Favorite Herman Cain Joins 2012 GOP Race," Fox News, May 21, 2011 (up-dated Dec. 23, 2015), https://www.foxnews.com/politics/tea-party-favorite -herman-cain-joins-2012-gop-race.

13. Cain, *This Is Herman Cain!*, 179, 183-184; York, "Herman Cain Sounds Off"; T. A. Frank, "'I Still Don't Plan on Going to Any Political-Correctness School,'" *New York Times Magazine*, Nov. 13, 2011, 28, 30; Michael Daly and David A. Graham, "Citizen Cain," *Newsweek*, Oct. 24, 2011, 26-34.

14. Rich Mitchell, "Herman Cain Responds to Obama Budget," CDN, Apr. 13, 2011, https://www.conservativedailynews.com/2011/04/herman-cain-re sponds-to-obama-budget/; Sean J. Miller, "Herman Cain: Liberals Cry 'Racism' for Attacks on Obama," TheHill.com, Feb. 11, 2011, https://the hill.com/blogs/ballot-box/gop-presidential-primary/143625-herman-cain -liberals-cry-racism-for-attacks-on-obama-; Zernike, "G.O.P. Hopeful Gathers Momentum"; "Candidate Herman Cain Releases Music Video," YouTube, accessed July 16, 2019, https://www.youtube.com/watch?v=An woyWeQvyc; Conor Friedersdorf, "How Herman Cain Succeeds in Spite of Racism," *Atlantic*, June 30, 2011, https://www.theatlantic.com/politics /archive/2011/06/how-herman-cain-succeeds-in-spite-of-racism/241260/; Juana Summers, "Jackson Blasts 'Plantation' Comments," *Politico*, Sept. 30, 2011, https://www.politico.com/story/2011/09/jackson-blasts-plantation -comments-064841; Alex Seitz-Wald, "Herman Cain Goes Birther: Obama Must 'Prove He Was Born in the United States,'" ThinkProgress, Mar. 31, 2011, https://thinkprogress.org/herman-cain-goes-birther-obama-must -prove-he-was-born-in-the-united-states-def200f76882/; York, "Herman Cain Sounds Off"; Alexander Burns, "Herman Cain: Impeaching Obama Would Be 'a Great Thing,'" *Politico*, Aug. 17, 2011, https://www.politico.com /story/2011/08/cain-impeaching-obama-would-be-a-great-thing-061518.

15. Miller, "Herman Cain: Liberals Cry 'Racism' for Attacks on Obama"; "Candidate Herman Cain Releases Music Video"; Daly and Graham, "Citizen Cain," 34; Caitlin McDevitt, "Harry Belafonte Calls Herman a 'Bad Apple,'"

Politico, Oct. 10, 2011, https://www.politico.com/blogs/click/2011/10/harry-belafonte-calls-herman-cain-a-bad-apple-039867.

16. Andrew Rafferty and Mark Murray, "Cain Says His Race Will Help the GOP: But Is He Right?," MSNBC, Nov. 22, 2011, http://firstread.msnbc.msn.com/_news/2011/11/22/8953778-cain-says-his-race-will-help-the-gop-but-is-he-right?; "More Right Wing Delusional Thinking," Mikeb302000 (blog), accessed July 19, 2019, http://mikeb302000.blogspot.com/2011/11/more-right-wing-delusional-thinking.html.

17. Anna Palmer et al., "Exclusive: 2 Women Accused Cain of Inappropriate Behavior," *Politico*, Oct. 30, 2011, https://www.politico.com/story/2011/10/exclusive-2-women-accused-cain-of-inappropriate-behavior-067194; Jonathan Martin et al., "Herman Cain Accused by Two Women of Inappropriate Behavior," *Politico*, Oct. 31, 2011, https://www.politico.com/news/stories/1011/67194_Page3.html; Shannon McCaffrey, "Supporting Cain, GOP Base Evokes Thomas Hearings," *Seattle Times*, Nov. 1, 2011, https://www.seattletimes.com/seattle-news/politics/supporting-cain-gop-base-evokes-thomas-hearings/.

18. Juana Summers and Maggie Haberman, "Cain Fights Back against Affair Claims," *Politico*, Nov. 29, 2011, https://www.politico.com/story/2011/11/cain-fights-back-against-affair-claims-069252; Joseph Straw and Bill Hutchinson, "Who Is Ginger White? Herman Cain's Alleged Mistress Is Single Mom and Unemployed Former Businesswoman," *New York Daily News*, Nov. 29, 2011, https://www.nydailynews.com/news/politics/ginger-white-herman-cain-alleged-mistress-single-mom-unemployed-businesswoman-article-1.983794; Aaron Gould Sheinin, "Woman Claims 13-Year Affair with Herman Cain," *Atlanta Journal-Constitution*, Aug. 10, 2012, https://www.ajc.com/news/local/woman-claims-year-affair-with-herman-cain/koivGLCyYPFUHAKfjNfurN/ ; Brian Ross, Cindy Galli, and Lee Ferran, "Newest Cain Accuser Has History of Financial Trouble," ABC News, Nov. 28, 2011, https://abcnews.go.com/Blotter/herman-cain-denies-affair-allegation/story?id=15042918.

19. Juana Summers, "Cain Bows Out," *Politico*, Dec. 3, 2011, https://www.politico.com/story/2011/12/cain-bows-out-069698; Robert Traynham, "Herman Cain's Presidential Run: A Setback [for] Black Conservatives?," TheGrio.com, Dec. 3, 2011, https://thegrio.com/2011/12/03/herman-cains-presidential-run-a-setback-black-conservatives/.

20. M. J. Lee, "Cain to Mitt Romney: Pick West for VP," *Politico*, Apr. 9, 2012, https://www.politico.com/story/2012/04/cain-to-mitt-pick-west-for-vp-074961; Mackenzie Weinger, "West: 'Willing and Ready' to Be VP," *Politico*, Mar. 6, 2012, https://www.politico.com/story/2012/03/west-willing-and-ready-to-be-vp-073660; Rodney Ho, "Fox News Hires Herman Cain as Contributor," *Atlanta Journal-Constitution*, Feb. 16, 2013, https://www.ajc.com/entertainment/fox-news-hires-herman-cain-contributor/4G1BmYxn4IuovAxBXqVFPN/; Molly Crane-Newman and Nancy Dillon, "Admitted Herman Cain Ex-Mistress Ready to Describe His Privates to Senate Committee if He Doesn't Withdraw from Fed Board Consideration,"

New York Daily News, Apr. 18, 2019, https://www.nydailynews.com/news/national/ny-herman-cain-accusers-call-for-recusal-from-fed-board-consideration-20190418-uy3l2yxqyvcfjan4sdfteqnvxq-story.html.

21. "Lieutenant Governor: Michael S. Steele," *Maryland Manual On-Line: A Guide to Maryland and Its Government*, accessed July 20, 2019, https://msa.maryland.gov/msa/mdmanual/08conoff/ltgov/former/html/msa13921.html; Michael Sokolove, "Why Is Michael Steele a Republican Candidate?," *New York Times Magazine*, Mar. 26, 2006, https://www.nytimes.com/2006/03/26/magazine/326steele.html; "Michael Steele on Civil Rights," OnTheIssues, accessed July 20, 2019, http://www.issues2000.org/Domestic/Michael_Steele_Civil_Rights.htm.

22. "Steele: Obama Wasn't Vetted because He's Black," CNN, May 22, 2009, http://politicalticker.blogs.cnn.com/2009/05/22/steele-obama-wasnt-vetted-because-hes-black/.

23. Steele, *Right Now*, 25, 35-36, 155-156; Office of Intelligence and Analysis, US Department of Homeland Security, *Rightwing Extremism*; "Steele Blasts 'Right-Wing Extremist' Label," Fox News, Apr. 20, 2009 (updated Jan. 27, 2017), https://www.foxnews.com/transcript/steele-blasts-right-wing-extremist-label.

24. Andy Barr, "Steele: No Reason for Black GOP Base," *Politico*, Apr. 21, 2010, https://www.politico.com/story/2010/04/steele-no-reason-for-black-gop-base-036171.

25. Alter, *The Center Holds*, 182; Lucia Graves, Ryan Grim, and Elise Foley, "Black GOP Official Resigns, Citing Arizona Tea Party Threats," *Huffington Post*, May 25, 2011, https://www.huffpost.com/entry/anthony-miller-resigns-giffords-threats_n_808116; Jon Terbush, "Michael Steele Joins MSNBC as Political Analyst," *Talking Points Memo*, May 23, 2011, https://talkingpointsmemo.com/news/michael-steele-joins-msnbc-as-political-analyst.

26. Howard Fineman, "Part of Something Larger," *Newsweek*, Feb. 25, 2008, 33; US House of Representatives, "Davis, Artur," History, Art and Archives, accessed July 20, 2019, https://history.house.gov/People/Detail/12579; Todd and Gawiser, *How Barack Obama Won*, 167.

27. US House of Representatives, "Davis, Artur"; Josh Kraushaar, "Sparks Trounces Davis with Black Voters," *Politico*, June 2, 2010, https://www.politico.com/story/2010/06/sparks-trounces-davis-with-black-voters-038042; Gwen Ifill, "Artur Davis and the Rebuke of Obama," *National Journal*, Aug. 17, 2012, http://www.nationaljournal.com/columns/gwens take/artur-davis-and-the-rebuke-of-obama-20120817; "Three Maps That Explain the Artur Davis Switch," *Slate*, Aug. 16, 2012, https://slate.com/news-and-politics/2012/08/three-maps-that-explain-the-artur-davis-switch.html; Mary Orndorff Troyan, "Alabama Republicans Embrace Davis as Speaker at GOP Convention," *Birmingham News*, Aug. 17, 2012 (updated Jan. 14, 2019), https://www.al.com/sweethome/2012/08/alabama_republicans_embrace_da.html; Artur Davis, "I Should Have Supported Voter ID Law," Recovering Politician, Oct. 21, 2011, http://therecoveringpolitician.com/contributors/adavis/artur-davis-i-should-have-supported-voter-id-law; Caryn

Freeman, "Ex-Democrat Artur Davis Says Obama Has Taken Us 'Backward' on Fox News," TheGrio.com, May 31, 2012, https://thegrio.com/2012/05/31/ex-democrat-artur-davis-says-obama-has-taken-us-backwards-on-fox-news/; Zerlina Maxwell, "Why Artur Davis Is Wrong: Republicans Squandered Any Black Good Will," TheGrio.com, June 20, 2012, https://thegrio.com/2012/06/20/why-artur-davis-is-wrong-republicans-squandered-any-black-good-will/; Ashley Killough, "Congressional Black Caucus Blasts Artur Davis over Party Switch," CNN, Aug. 28, 2012, http://politicalticker.blogs.cnn.com/2012/08/28/congressional-black-caucus-blasts-artur-davis-over-party-switch/; Mackenzie Weinger, "Artur Davis Hits Back over CBC Letter," *Politico*, Aug. 28, 2012, https://www.politico.com/story/2012/08/artur-davis-hits-back-over-cbc-letter-080297.

28. Brian Lyman, "Todd Strange Wins 3rd Term as Montgomery Mayor," *Montgomery Advertiser*, Aug. 25, 2015, https://www.montgomeryadvertiser.com/story/news/politics/southunionstreet/2015/08/25/todd-strange-wins-third-term—montgomery-mayor/32373407/; Maggie Astor, "Seven Ways Alabama Has Made It Harder to Vote," *New York Times*, June 23, 2018, https://www.nytimes.com/2018/06/23/us/politics/voting-rights-alabama.html; Andrew J. Yawn, "Feeling Blue: Democrats Deny Artur Davis," *Montgomery Advertiser*, Oct. 20, 2015, https://www.montgomeryadvertiser.com/story/news/2015/10/16/feeling-blue-democrats-deny-artur-davis/73932654/.

CHAPTER 10. SIGNIFIER IN CHIEF

1. Kate Andersen Brower, "The Secret Lives of Hillary and Bill in the White House," *Politico*, Apr. 7, 2015, https://www.politico.com/magazine/story/2015/04/clinton-white-house-the-residence-excerpt-116706_Page2.html; Kate Andersen Brower, "The Permanent White House Staff Is, Understandably, on Edge about the 2016 Presidential Race," *Vanity Fair*, Apr. 10, 2016, https://www.vanityfair.com/news/2016/04/white-house-staff-on-edge-2016-presidential-race.

2. Brower, *The Residence*, 10–11; Mary J. Blige, "Real Love," in *What's the 411?* (Uptown Records and MCA Records, 1992).

3. Jennifer Epstein, "Inside Obama's 50th-Birthday Bash," *Politico*, Aug. 5, 2011, https://www.politico.com/story/2011/08/inside-obamas-50th-birthday-bash-060722; Jodi Kantor, "For First Black President, a Complex Calculus of Race," *New York Times*, Oct. 21, 2012, 22.

4. Al Green later expressed gratitude for Obama's singing of his song and gave the president a B+ for his effort. Tim Mak, "Al Green: Prez Gets a B+," *Politico*, May 5, 2012, https://www.politico.com/blogs/click/2012/05/al-green-prez-gets-a-b-122543; "Obama Sings Let's Stay Together at Apollo," YouTube, accessed Dec. 10, 2020, https://www.youtube.com/watch?v=ooQI3_K7w_g; Caitlin McDevitt, "Obama Sings, Al Green Sales Spike," *Politico*, Jan. 27, 2012, https://www.politico.com/blogs/click/2012/01/obama-sings-al-green-sales-spike-112554; Obama, *A Promised Land*, 542–543;

Caitlin McDevitt, "Obama Invited to Perform on 'American Idol,'" *Politico*, Jan. 31, 2012, https://www.politico.com/blogs/click/2012/01/obama-in vited-to-perform-on-american-idol-112895; Byron Tau, "Obama Sings, Hopes Voters Swoon," *Politico*, Feb. 22, 2012, https://www.politico.com/story/2012 /02/obama-sings-hopes-voters-swoon-073182; "Remarks at PBS's 'In Performance at the White House: Red, White, and Blues,'" Feb. 21, 2012, in Obama, *Public Papers*, 1:188-189.

5. In addition to the massacre at Mother Emanuel, the FBI also investigated several mysterious fires at Black churches across the South in late June 2015. Rick Jervis, "Fires at Black Churches Raise Concern," *USA Today*, July 1, 2015, https://www.usatoday.com/story/news/2015/06/30/black-churches -fires-charleston-shooting/29516267/; "Dylann Roof's Journal," *Post and Courier* (Charleston, SC), Dec. 9, 2016, https://bloximages.newyork1.vip .townnews.com/postandcourier.com/content/tncms/assets/v3/editorial/c /5f/c5f6550c-be72-11e6-b869-7bdf860326f5/584b525a792e0.pdf.pdf; "Dylann Roof Authored a Horrifyingly Racist Manifesto," *Mother Jones*, June 20, 2015, https://www.motherjones.com/politics/2015/06/alleged-charleston -shooter-dylann-roof-manifesto-racist/; Ralph Ellis et al., "Shooting Suspect in Custody after Charleston Church Massacre," CNN, June 18, 2015, https://www.cnn.com/2015/06/18/us/charleston-south-carolina-shooting /index.html; Tanya Somanader, "President Obama Delivers a Statement on the Shooting in South Carolina," White House, June 18, 2015, https:// obamawhitehouse.archives.gov/blog/2015/06/18/latest-president-obama -delivers-statement-shooting-south-carolina; Barack Obama, "Amazing Grace" (eulogy), June 26, 2015, reprinted in Dionne and Reid, *We Are the Change We Seek*, 267-277; Dyson, *Black Presidency*, 255-271; Kevin Sack and Alan Blinder, "Anguish, Rage and Mercy as Dylann Roof Is Sentenced to Death," *New York Times*, Jan. 11, 2017, https://www.nytimes.com/2017/01 /11/us/dylann-roof-sentencing.html; Julie Hirschfeld Davis, "'Long and Genuine' Hugs: Shooting Victims' Relatives Recall Obama's Empathy," *New York Times*, June 16, 2016, https://www.nytimes.com/2016/06/17/us/politics /obama-orlando-shooting.html.

6. Caitlin McDevitt, "Ice-T Says Rap Got Obama Elected," *Politico*, June 14, 2012, https://www.politico.com/blogs/click/2012/06/ice-t-says-rap-got-oba ma-elected-126136; Erik Nielson, "Obama's Honeymoon with Hip Hop Is Over," *New Republic*, Jan. 23, 2013, https://newrepublic.com/article/112118 /the-honeymoon-over-obama-and-hip-hop; "Obamas Dance, Celebrate at Inaugural Balls," CNN, Jan. 21, 2009, http://www.cnn.com/2009/POLI TICS/01/20/inauguration.balls/; Evan Thomas, Holly Bailey, and Jonathan Darman, "Here We Go Again," *Newsweek*, Aug. 11, 2008, 34, 36; Evan Thomas et al., "How He Did It," *Newsweek*, Nov. 17, 2008.

7. Jann Wenner, "Obama in Command," *Rolling Stone*, Oct. 14, 2010, 46; Amie Parnes, "W.H. Hosts Common after All," *Politico*, May 11, 2011, https:// www.politico.com/click/stories/1105/despite_outrage_common_performs_at _w_h_.html; "Remarks at the White House Correspondents' Association

Dinner," Apr. 28, 2012, in Obama, *Public Papers*, 1:533; Caitlin McDevitt, "Will Smith Happy to Pay More Taxes," *Politico*, May 8, 2012, https://www.politico.com/blogs/click/2012/05/will-smith-happy-to-pay-more-taxes-122736; M. J. Lee, "Jay-Z: Obama Can Tax Me," *Politico*, Dec. 9, 2011, https://www.politico.com/story/2011/12/jay-z-obama-can-tax-me-070176; Caitlin McDevitt, "Jay-Z Still on Team Obama," *Politico*, May 14, 2012, https://www.politico.com/blogs/click/2012/05/jay-z-still-on-team-obama-123436; Vivyan Tran, "Kanye Raps: 'Mitt Romney Don't Pay No Tax,'" *Politico*, Sept. 13, 2012, https://www.politico.com/blogs/click/2012/09/kanye-raps-mitt-romney-dont-pay-no-tax-135475; Kyle Harvey, "Hip-Hop Community Reacts to Obama's Re-Election," TheGrio.com, Nov. 7, 2012, https://thegrio.com/2012/11/07/hip-hop-community-reacts-to-obamas-re-election/.

8. Nielson, "Obama's Honeymoon with Hip Hop Is Over."

9. Chuck Creekmur, "Nicki Minaj Receives Death Threats over Mitt Romney Rap Line," AllHipHop, Sept. 4, 2012, https://allhiphop.com/news/nicki-minaj-receives-death-threats-over-mitt-romney-rap-line-_OoPs1MUaUW9kynNKHsX9w/; Reggie Ugwu, "Nicki Minaj Responds to President Barack Obama over Romney Rap," BET.com, Sept. 11, 2012, https://www.bet.com/news/music/2012/09/11/nicki-minaj-responds-to-president-obama-over-romney-rap.html.

10. Belafonte, *My Song*; Danielle Cadet, "Harry Belafonte: If Mitt Romney Is Elected, 'We're in for a Terrible, Terrible Future,'" *Huffington Post*, Oct. 24, 2012, https://www.huffpost.com/entry/harry-belafonte-mitt-romney-obama-election_n_1972499; Allison Samuels, "Black Hollywood Weighs Whether to Support Obama a Second Time," *Newsweek*, Jan. 23, 2012, https://www.newsweek.com/black-hollywood-weighs-whether-support-obama-second-time-64303; Ashley Killough, "Samuel L. Jackson: 'Wake the F*** Up' for Obama," CNN, Sept. 27, 2012, http://politicalticker.blogs.cnn.com/2012/09/27/samuel-l-jackson-wake-the-fk-up-for-obama/; Mark Shanahan and Meredith Goldstein, "Behind the Curtain, Obama Going Places around the Vineyard," *Boston Globe*, Aug. 22, 2011, http://archive.boston.com/ae/celebrity/articles/2011/08/22/behind_the_curtain_obama_going_places_around_the_vineyard/.

11. Caitlin McDevitt, "Will Ferrell and Friends Defend Obama," *Politico*, Oct. 23, 2011, https://www.politico.com/blogs/click/2011/10/will-ferrell-and-friends-defend-obama-040214; "Chris Rock on Obama: 'Being the First Black ANYTHING Sucks,'" *Huffington Post*, July 12, 2012, https://www.huffpost.com/entry/chris-rock-obama-being-the-first-black-anything-sucks_n_1669222; statement by Yolanda Adams, Barack Obama website, accessed Apr. 25, 2012, http://www.barackobama.com/african-americans; "Mary J. Blige on POTUS' Grade: 'I Would Give Him an A because He's a Human Being Who Got Tossed a Lot of Mess,'" CNN, Sept. 6, 2012, http://cnnpressroom.blogs.cnn.com/2012/09/06/mary-j-blige-on-potus-grade-i-would-give-him-an-a-because-hes-a-human-being-that-got-tossed-a-lot-of-mess/; "THR Emmy Roundtable: 6 Drama Actresses on Death Threats, Post-Baby

Auditions," *Hollywood Reporter*, May 29, 2013, http://www.hollywoodreport er.com/news/scandals-kerry-washington-kate-mara-558887; Chris Wither-spoon, "Star Jones: 'If You Have a Vagina, Brown Skin and a Brain, I Don't See How You Endorsed Romney," TheGrio.com, Nov. 14, 2012, https:// thegrio.com/2012/11/14/star-jones-if-you-have-a-vagina-brown-skin-and -a-brain-i-dont-see-how-you-endorsed-romney/; Stacey Dash, "Vote for Romney. The only choice for your future," Twitter, Oct. 7, 2012, 2:32 p.m., https://twitter.com/staceydash/status/255012859363352576; "Stacey Dash 'Shocked' by 'Fury' over Her Romney Support," *USA Today*, Oct. 10, 2012, https://www.usatoday.com/story/entertainment/2012/10/10/clueless-stacey -dash-shocked-by-romney-support-fury/1624013/.

12. "Stepping Up for O," *Page Six*, Jan. 4, 2012, https://pagesix. com/2012/01/04/stepping-up-for-o; Kevin Cirilli, "Spike Lee: Barack Obama Is 'Not Perfect,'" *Politico*, Aug. 10, 2012, https://www.politico.com/blogs /click/2012/08/spike-lee-barack-obama-is-not-perfect-131674; Leigh Munsil, "Obama Fundraises at BET Chair's Home," *Politico*, Apr. 27, 2012, https:// www.politico.com/blogs/politico44/2012/04/obama-fundraises-at-bet-chairs -home-121906; Nancy Dillon, "Secret Service, Los Angeles County Sher-iff's Deputies Check Security at Will Smith and Jada Pinkett Smith Estate ahead of Michelle Obama Fundraiser," *New York Daily News*, Oct. 23, 2012, https://www.nydailynews.com/news/election-2012/security-checks-jada -pinkett-smith-estate-obama-fundraiser-article-1.1190212; Kia Makarechi, "Jay-Z & Beyoncé's Obama Fundraiser: Hip Hop's Royal Couple Will Host President at 40/40 Club," *Huffington Post*, Sept. 11, 2012, https://www.huff post.com/entry/jay-z-beyonce-obama-fundraiser_n_1874623; Donovan Slack, "Obama: Jay-Z and I Have a Lot in Common," *Politico*, Sept. 18, 2012, https://www.politico.com/blogs/politico44/2012/09/obama-jay-z -and-i-have-a-lot-in-common-135954.

13. Robert Draper, "Can the Democrats Catch Up in the Super-PAC Game?," *New York Times Magazine*, July 5, 2012, https://www.nytimes.com/2012/07 /08/magazine/can-the-democrats-catch-up-in-the-super-pac-game.html; Alexander Burns, "Morgan Freeman Gives $1 Million to Obama Super PAC," *Politico*, July 19, 2012, https://www.politico.com/blogs/burns-haber man/2012/07/morgan-freeman-gives-1-million-to-obama-super-pac-129427.

14. Sinbad quoted in Ta-Nehisi Coates, "My President Was Black," *Atlantic*, Jan.–Feb. 2017, https://www.theatlantic.com/magazine/archive/2017/01/my -president-was-black/508793/. Also see Caitlin McDevitt, "Chris Rock: I Love 'Our Zebra President,'" *Politico*, June 7, 2012, https://www.politico .com/blogs/click/2012/06/chris-rock-i-love-our-zebra-president-125537; "Morgan Freeman: No Black President for U.S. Yet," NPR, July 3, 2012, https://www.npr.org/2012/07/05/156212527/morgan-freeman-no-black -president-for-u-s-yet.

15. Colleen Curtis, "Watch: The Tuskegee Airmen Visit the White House," White House, Feb. 3, 2012, https://obamawhitehouse.archives.gov/blog /2012/02/03/watch-tuskegee-airmen-visit-white-house; Jennifer Epstein,

"Obama Reflects on Black History," *Politico*, Feb. 22, 2012, https://www
.politico.com/story/2012/02/obama-reflects-on-black-history-073168;
"Obama Signs Bill Sending Bust of Frederick Douglass to Capitol's Emancipation Hall," TheGrio.com, Sept. 22, 2012, https://thegrio.com/2012
/09/22/obama-signs-bill-sending-bust-of-frederick-douglass-to-capitols
-emancipation-hall/; "President Obama Designates Five New National
Monuments," White House, Mar. 25, 2013, https://obamawhitehouse
.archives.gov/the-press-office/2013/03/25/president-obama-designates
-five-new-national-monuments.

16. Matt Compton, "Rosa Parks Has a Permanent Place in the US Capitol,"
White House, Feb. 27, 2013, https://obamawhitehouse.archives.gov/blog
/2013/02/27/rosa-parks-has-permanent-place-us-capitol; Suzanne Gamboa,
"Rosa Parks Statue Unveiled at Capitol," Associated Press, Feb. 27, 2013,
https://www.realclearpolitics.com/articles/2013/02/27/rosa_parks_statue
_unveiled_at_capitol_117189.html; "Remarks at the Dedication Ceremony
for a Statue Honoring Rosa Parks at the United States Capitol," Feb. 27,
2013, in Obama, *Public Papers*, 1:149-150; "Remarks at the 'Let Freedom
Ring' Ceremony Commemorating the 50th Anniversary of the March on
Washington for Jobs and Freedom," Aug. 28, 2013, in Obama, *Public Papers*,
2:974-978; Jesse J. Holland, "Obama Asks for $50 Million to Restore Civil
Rights Sites," Associated Press, Feb. 4, 2015, https://www.apnews.com/789
84e8a031841dd9c9643d8136fd44f; Gregory Korte, "Anti-Slavery Activist
Harriet Tubman to Replace Jackson on $20 Bill," *USA Today*, Apr. 21, 2016,
https://www.usatoday.com/story/news/politics/2016/04/20/report-lew-con
sidered-anthony-10-bill/83274530/; Mary Clare Jalonick, "Obama Signs
Bill to Review Civil Rights–Era Killings," Associated Press, Dec. 16, 2016,
https://www.pbs.org/newshour/politics/obama-signs-bill-review-civil-rights
-era-killings.

17. Megan Slack, "President Obama and the First Lady Mark the Beginning
of Kwanzaa," White House, Dec. 27, 2011, https://obamawhitehouse
.archives.gov/blog/2011/12/27/president-obama-and-first-lady-mark
-beginning-kwanzaa.

18. Kantor, "For First Black President"; Josh Gerstein, "Art Sends Rare W.H.
Message on Race," *Politico*, Aug. 24, 2011, https://www.politico.com/story
/2011/08/art-sends-rare-wh-message-on-race-061677.

19. Donovan Slack, "Obama: Michelle Was Teasing Leno, Not Gabby," *Politico*, Aug. 15, 2012, https://www.politico.com/blogs/politico44/2012/08/oba
ma-michelle-was-teasing-leno-not-gabby-132163; Ken Thomas, "Jordan,
NBA Players to Raise Money for Obama," Associated Press, Aug. 7, 2012,
https://www.courant.com/sdut-jordan-nba-players-to-raise-money-for
-obama-2012aug07-story.html; Donovan Slack, "Obama's Celebrity $up-
port," *Politico*, Sept. 21, 2012, https://www.politico.com/blogs/politico
44/2012/09/obamas-celebrity-upport-136352; Todd Johnson, "NBA Players Past and Present Star in New Ad Backing Barack Obama," TheGrio
.com, Oct. 8, 2012, https://thegrio.com/2012/10/08/nba-players-past-and

-present-star-in-new-ad-backing-barack-obama/; "HoopsHype.com NBA Campaign Donors," HoopsHype, Aug. 21, 2012, http://hoopshype.com/campaign.htm; Al Weinberg, "Obama Talks Hoops in NYC, Dunks Rep. Todd Akin," NBC News, Aug. 24, 2012, http://firstread.nbcnews.com/_news/2012/08/22/13422335-obama-talks-hoops-in-nyc-dunks-rep-todd-akin; Karin Tanabe, "Charles Barkley Calls GOP Field 'Idiots,'" *Politico*, Dec. 21, 2011, https://www.politico.com/blogs/click/2011/12/charles-barkley-calls-gop-field-idiots-108391.

20. Vivyan Tran, "Obama Meets with Athletes," *Politico*, Jan. 28, 2013, https://www.politico.com/gallery/obama-meets-with-athletes?slide=0; Greta Van Susteren, "Did You See What Hank Aaron Said about President Obama?," Fox News, Sept. 22, 2012, https://gretawire.foxnewsinsider.com/2012/09/22/did-you-see-what-hank-aaron-said-about-president-obama/; Magic Johnson, "Insurance That's High Quality and Affordable? Now That's a Slam Dunk," White House, Jan. 15, 2014, https://obamawhitehouse.archives.gov/blog/2014/01/15/insurance-thats-high-quality-and-affordable-now-thats-slam-dunk; Justin Sink, "Slam Dunk? LeBron Joins O-Care Push," The Hill.com, Mar. 14, 2014, https://thehill.com/blogs/blog-briefing-room/news/200838-slam-dunk-lebron-james-joins-obamacare-push; David Hudson, "LeBron James Wants You to #GetCovered," White House, Mar. 14, 2014, https://obamawhitehouse.archives.gov/blog/2014/03/14/lebron-james-wants-you-getcovered; Caitlin McDevitt, "Dennis Rodman: 'I'm Doing Obama's Job,'" *Politico*, May 10, 2013, https://www.politico.com/blogs/click/2013/05/dennis-rodman-im-doing-obamas-job-163688; Kim Hjelmgaard, "Obama Defends Kaepernick's National Anthem Protest," *USA Today*, Sept. 5, 2016, https://www.usatoday.com/story/sports/nfl/2016/09/05/obama-defends-kaepernicks-national-anthem-protest/89879478/.

21. "President Obama: Woods' Golf Game 'on Another Planet,'" Golf Channel, Feb. 21, 2013, https://www.golfchannel.com/news/president-obama-tiger-woods-golf-game-another-planet; Obama, *A Promised Land*, 540; "President Obama Plays Pick-Up Basketball with Scottie Pippen, Staff," TheGrio.com, Nov. 6, 2012, https://thegrio.com/2012/11/06/president-obama-plays-pick-up-basketball-with-scottie-pippen-staff/; Charles Woodson, "Commentary: We Can't Let Up in This Election," BET.com, Nov. 5, 2012, http://www.bet.com/news/features/vote-2012/news/sports/2012/11/commentary-we-can-t-let-up.html.

CHAPTER 11. RENAISSANCE WOMAN

1. Obama, *Becoming*, 284, 291; Jodi Kantor, "For First Black President, a Complex Calculus of Race," *New York Times*, Oct. 21, 2012, 22; Obama, *A Promised Land*, 221–222, 287–288.

2. Lois Romano, "White House Rebel," *Newsweek*, June 13–20, 2011, 51; Allison Samuels, "What Michelle Obama Must Do Now," *Newsweek*, Oct. 23, 2009, https://www.newsweek.com/what-michelle-obama-must-do-now

-81263; Daniel Nasaw, "Barack Obama Meets Coffins of Soldiers Killed in Afghanistan," *Guardian* (US edition), Oct. 29, 2009, https://www.theguardian.com/world/2009/oct/29/barack-obama-soldiers-dover-base; Obama, *A Promised Land*, 440-441; David Nakamura and Craig Whitlock, "Obama Pays His Respects to Slain Troops at Dover Air Force Base," *Washington Post*, Aug. 9, 2011, https://www.washingtonpost.com/blogs/44/post/president-obama-to-pay-his-respects-to-troops-at-dover-air-force-base/2011/08/09/gIQA2Aak4I_blog.html.

3. Romano, "White House Rebel," 50; Colleen Curtis, "First Lady Michelle Obama Welcomes Students to a Blues Workshop at the White House," White House, Feb. 22, 2012, https://obamawhitehouse.archives.gov/blog/2012/02/22/first-lady-michelle-obama-welcomes-students-blues-workshop-white-house; "Remarks by the First Lady at the African Methodist Episcopal Church Conference," White House, June 28, 2012, https://obamawhitehouse.archives.gov/the-press-office/2012/06/28/remarks-first-lady-african-methodist-episcopal-church-conference; Jennifer Epstein, "First Lady Bemoans Culture of African Americans Aspiring to Be 'a Baller or a Rapper,'" *Politico*, May 17, 2013, https://www.politico.com/blogs/politico44/2013/05/first-lady-bemoans-culture-of-african-americans-aspiring-to-be-a-baller-or-a-rapper-164266; Jennifer Steinhauer, "Michelle Obama Edges into a Policy Role on Higher Education," *New York Times*, Nov. 12, 2013, A16; Donovan Slack, "First Lady Michelle Obama Highlights Civil Rights Legacy at Greensboro Commencement," *Politico*, May 12, 2012, https://www.politico.com/blogs/politico44/2012/05/first-lady-michelle-obama-highlights-civil-rights-legacy-at-greensboro-commencement-123257.

4. Mark Landler, "Helpings of Energy and Cheer for the Trail," *New York Times*, Feb. 10, 2012, https://www.nytimes.com/2012/02/11/us/politics/michelle-obama-injects-optimism-into-campaign.html; "Jimmy Fallon vs. Michelle Obama in Let's Move Fitness Challenge," YouTube, accessed July 23, 2019, https://www.youtube.com/watch?v=Cc6ES0-JFfE; Darlene Superville, "White House South Lawn Becomes First Lady's Grassy Stage," Associated Press, Jan. 1, 2016, https://www.bostonglobe.com/news/nation/2016/01/01/white-house-south-lawn-becomes-first-lady-grassy-stage/VICfpNwYbFIengoOKcgkjK/story.html; Hadas Gold, "Michelle Obama Releasing Rap Album (but She Doesn't Sing)," *Politico*, Aug. 13, 2013, https://www.politico.com/blogs/politico44/2013/08/michelle-obama-releasing-rap-album-but-she-doesnt-sing-170422; David Jackson, "Michelle Obama Launches School Exercise Program," *USA Today*, Feb. 28, 2013, https://www.usatoday.com/story/theoval/2013/02/28/michelle-obama-lets-move-active-schools/1954137/; Jose Del Real, "Michelle Obama Rips Shutdown, Defends Obamacare," *Politico*, Oct. 25, 2013, https://www.politico.com/story/2013/10/michelle-obama-rips-shutdown-defends-obamacare-098867; Kathleen Hennessey, "Embracing New Labels, First Lady Jumps into Food Fight," *Chicago Tribune*, Feb. 27, 2014, http://www.chicagotribune.com/news/politics/la-pn-obama-food-20140227,0,4217309.story; Helena Bottemiller

Evich, "Michelle Obama Gets Her Way on Nutrition Labels," *Politico*, May 20, 2016, https://www.politico.com/story/2016/05/flotus-labeling -crusade-223398.

5. Tom Rosentiel, "Michelle Obama's Strong Personal Image," Pew Research Center, Jan. 21, 2010, https://www.pewresearch.org/2010/01/21/michelle -obamas-strong-personal-image/; Jeffrey M. Jones, "Michelle Obama Remains Popular in U.S.," Gallup, May 30, 2012, https://news.gallup.com /poll/154952/michelle-obama-remains-popular.aspx; Alyssa Brown, "Michelle Obama Maintains Positive Image," Gallup, Mar. 3, 2014, https:// news.gallup.com/poll/167696/michelle-obama-maintains-positive-image .aspx; Alexis Garrett Stodghill, "Michelle Obama Is Now the Most Televised First Lady in History," TheGrio.com, Apr. 23, 2012, https://thegrio .com/2012/04/23/michelle-obama-found-to-be-the-most-televised-first-lady -in-history/; Andrea Reiher, "*Forbes* 2013 100 Most Powerful Women Full List: Beyonce, Sofia Vergara and More Influential Women," *Screener*, May 23, 2013, http://screenertv.com/news-features/forbes-2013-100-most-power ful-women-full-list-beyonce-sofia-vergara-and-more-influential-women/; "Eleanor Roosevelt Is Top U.S. First Lady, Survey Says," Reuters, Feb. 15, 2014, https://www.reuters.com/article/us-usa-poll-firstladies/eleanor-roose velt-is-top-u-s-first-lady-survey-says-idUSBREA1E0ZB20140215.

6. Kevin Cirilli, "Twitter: Michelle's Speech Tops Mitt's," *Politico*, Sept. 5, 2012, https://www.politico.com/story/2012/09/twitter-michelle-speech-tops-mitts -080717; Kate Andersen Brower, "Michelle Obama along with Ann Romney Fuel Husbands' Coffers," *Bloomberg*, Sept. 18, 2012, https://www.bloom berg.com/news/articles/2012-09-19/michelle-obama-along-with-ann-romney -fuel-husbands-coffers; Jennifer Epstein, "Michelle Obama Shoots Down '16 Talk," *Politico*, May 29, 2012, https://www.politico.com/story/2012/05 /michelle-obama-shoots-down-16-talk-076822.

7. Vanessa Evans, "First Lady Seeks Oprah's Support for President Obama's Second Term," Yahoo! News, Apr. 25, 2011, https://news.yahoo.com/s/ac/2 0110425/pl_ac/8364091_first_lady_seeks_oprahs_support_for_president _obamas_second_term; Colleen Curtis, "First Lady Michelle Obama Celebrates Maya Angelou at BET Honors," White House, Jan. 16, 2012, https:// obamawhitehouse.archives.gov/blog/2012/01/16/first-lady-michelle-obama -celebrates-maya-angelou-bet-honors; Nekesa Mumbi Moody, "Michelle Obama Declares 'Black Girls Rock!,'" Associated Press, Mar. 29, 2015, https://apnews.com/47e0909ec8dc46af92aa4f063902de78; "Michelle Obama Gives an Inspirational Speech at Black Girls Rock!," YouTube, accessed July 23, 2019, https://www.youtube.com/watch?v=p-Hv85-ILl4.

8. Donna Owens, "On Mother's Day, Black Women Hail Michelle Obama: America's 'First Mom,'" TheGrio.com, May 13, 2012, https://thegrio.com/20 12/05/13/on-mothers-day-black-women-salute-first-mom-michelle-obama/; Peter Slevin, "How Michelle Obama Became a Singular American Voice," *Washington Post*, Dec. 12, 2016, https://www.washingtonpost.com/graphics /national/obama-legacy/michelle-obama-biography.html.

9. Eric Wilson, "Michelle Obama's Dress in High Definition," *New York Times*, Sept. 5, 2012, https://www.nytimes.com/2012/09/06/fashion/michelle-obamas-dress-in-high-definition.html; Tiffanie Darke, "It's Official: Michelle Is World's Best Dressed," *Times* (London), Mar. 10, 2013, https://www.thetimes.co.uk/article/its-official-michelle-is-worlds-best-dressed-05s v73r833b; Slevin, *Michelle Obama*, 274-278.

10. Writer Cormac O'Brien places Eleanor Roosevelt's height at six feet. O'Brien, *Secret Lives*, 294. See also Shayanne Gal, Pat Ralph, and Samantha Lee, "The Height Differences between All the US Presidents and First Ladies," *Business Insider*, Feb. 18, 2019, https://www.businessinsider.com/us-president-first-lady-height-differences-2018-7; Obama, *Becoming*, 264; Katherine Boyle, "Michelle Obama's Rosy Tracy Reese Dress Seals an Enduring Partnership," *Washington Post*, Sept. 5, 2012, https://www.washingtonpost.com/lifestyle/style/michelle-obamas-rosy-tracy-reese-dress-seals-an-enduring-partnership/2012/09/05/d19c98fc-f76c-11e1-8b93-c4f4ab1c8d13_story.html; Slevin, *Michelle Obama*, 274-278; Terry McMillan, "With Grace, First Lady Makes History," *Politico*, Nov. 20, 2013, https://www.politico.com/story/2013/11/with-unapologetic-grace-first-lady-makes-history-100100. *Times of India* quoted in Heather Timmons, "First Lady's Dance Moves Woo Indian Crowds," *New York Times*, Nov. 8, 2010, https://www.nytimes.com/2010/11/09/world/asia/09michelle.html.

11. "Michelle Obama on Ditching Her Bangs: 'It's Hard to Make Speeches with Hair in Your Face!,'" *Huffington Post*, Aug. 16, 2013, https://www.huffpost.com/entry/michelle-obama-no-more-bangs_n_3762185; "Read the Full Transcript of TIME's Conversation with President Obama and Misty Copeland," *Time*, Mar. 14, 2016, https://time.com/4254551/president-obama-misty-copeland-transcript/; Philip Galanes, "Barack Obama and Bryan Cranston on the Roles of a Lifetime," *New York Times*, May 6, 2016, http://www.nytimes.com/2016/05/08/fashion/barack-obama-bryan-cranston-table-for-three.html; Krissah Thompson, "Michelle Obama's Posterior again the Subject of a Public Rant," *Washington Post*, Feb. 4, 2013, https://www.washingtonpost.com/lifestyle/style/michelle-obamas-posterior-again-the-subject-of-a-public-rant/2013/02/04/c119c9a8-6efb-11e2-aa58-243de81040ba_story.html.

12. Thompson, "Michelle Obama's Posterior"; Allie Malloy and Sunlen Serfaty, "Michelle Obama Says She Was Held to Different Standard in '08 Campaign due to Her Race," CNN, May 11, 2015, https://www.cnn.com/2015/05/09/politics/michelle-obama-commencement-tuskegee-university/index.html; Mackenzie Weinger, "Sensenbrenner Sorry for 'Big Butt' Quip," *Politico*, Dec. 22, 2011, https://www.politico.com/story/2011/12/sensenbrenner-sorry-for-big-butt-quip-070788; Slevin, *Michelle Obama*, 291-292; Althea Legal-Miller, "Michelle Obama Undressed: Lost in Translation or Just Racist?," Clutch Magazine Online, Aug. 27, 2012, reprinted in *Philadelphia Sun*, Sept. 3, 2012, https://www.philasun.com/week-in-review/michelle-obama-undressed-lost-in-translation-or-just-racist/.

13. Obama, *Becoming*, x.

14. Breanna Edwards, "PETA Goes after Michelle Obama on Easter Egg Roll," TheRoot.com, Apr. 17, 2014, https://www.theroot.com/peta-goes-after-michelle-obama-on-easter-egg-roll-1790875365; Peter Wallsten, "Michelle Obama Confronts Protester, Threatens to Leave Fundraiser," *Washington Post*, June 4, 2013, https://www.washingtonpost.com/news/post-politics/wp/2013/06/04/michelle-obama-confronts-protester-threatens-to-leave-fundraiser/; Lucy McCalmont, "Michelle Obama: Talk about Race," *Politico*, May 19, 2014, https://www.politico.com/story/2014/05/michelle-obama-race-brown-v-board-of-education-106784; Knuckey and Kim, "Evaluations of Michelle Obama as First Lady"; Julie Hirschfeld Davis, "Yes, Slaves Did Help Build the White House," *New York Times*, July 26, 2016, https://www.nytimes.com/2016/07/27/us/politics/michelle-obama-white-house-slavery.html; Obama, *Becoming*, 397.

15. Romano, "White House Rebel," 48; Krissah Thompson, "Michelle Obama's Washington," *Washington Post*, Sept. 25, 2013, http://www.washingtonpost.com/wp-srv/special/lifestyle/michelle-obamas-washington/; Jennifer Steinhauer, "A First Lady at 50, Finding Her Own Path," *New York Times*, Jan. 17, 2014, A1, A15; Katherine Skiba, "Michelle Obama's 50th: 'Such a Fun, Fun Party,'" *Chicago Tribune*, Jan. 19, 2014, https://www.chicagotribune.com/news/breaking/chi-michelle-obama-50th-birthday-party-2014 0119-story.html.

16. Jodi Kantor, "The First Marriage," *New York Times Magazine*, Nov. 1, 2009, 44-53, 58, 60, 62; Obama, *A Promised Land*, 268, 287, 544-545; "Michelle Obama's Dream Job: Being Beyoncé," TheGrio.com, May 25, 2012, https://thegrio.com/2012/05/25/michelle-obamas-dream-job-being-beyonce/; *President Obama: A Day in the Life of America's Leader*, 123; Sandra Sobieraj Westfall, "'I've Got to Be Me,'" *People*, June 4, 2012, 94-98; Rachel Weiner, "Michelle Obama Accidentally Calls Herself 'Busy Single Mother,'" *Washington Post*, Apr. 4, 2013, https://www.washingtonpost.com/news/post-politics/wp/2013/04/04/michelle-obama-accidentally-calls-herself-busy-single-mother/; Eun Kyung Kim, "President Obama: At Times, Michelle Has Felt like a Single Mom," *Today*, Apr. 24, 2013, https://www.today.com/news/president-obama-times-michelle-has-felt-single-mom-1B9514851.

17. Oprah Winfrey, "Michelle Obama Is Still Optimistic," *Elle*, Nov. 12, 2018, https://www.elle.com/culture/career-politics/a24788222/michelle-obama-november-2018/; *Michelle Obama: A Portrait of the First Lady*, 55; Amie Parnes, "'First Grandma' Embraces Life in D.C.," *Politico*, Sept. 12, 2011, https://www.politico.com/story/2011/09/first-grandma-embraces-life-in-dc-061719; "Obama Attends Daughter's Basketball Game," Associated Press, Mar. 9, 2013, https://apnews.com/article/d612948bbf3344ab87c8abf4fa11045e; O'Brien, *Secret Lives*, 295; Amy DuBois Barnett, "Mom in Chief," *Ebony*, May 2012, 109; "Sasha & Malia Obama Receive Dating Advice from Their Watchful Dad," Reuters, Dec. 20, 2013, https://www.huffpost.com/entry/obama-girls-get-dating-advice_n_4483938; Slevin, *Michelle Obama*, 281-282; Krissah Thompson, "The Nine Important Things Michelle Obama and

Oprah Said Last Night," *Washington Post*, June 15, 2016, http://www.washing
tonpost.com/news/arts-and-entertainment/wp/2016/06/15/the-nine-impor
tant-things-michelle-obama-and-oprah-said-last-night; Obama, *A Promised
Land*, 221.

18. Obama, *Becoming*, 353; Holmes, *Faith of the Postwar Presidents*, 312; Jennifer
Epstein, "Oh Come All Ye Faithful?," *Politico*, Dec. 24, 2014, https://www.po
litico.com/story/2014/12/president-barack-obama-religion-113791; "Evergreen
Chapel at Camp David," About Camp David, Aug. 19, 2010, https:/ about
campdavid.blogspot.com/2010/08/evergreen-chapel-at-camp-david.html.

CHAPTER 12. THE BLOOD OF AFRICA

1. Ofeibea Quist-Arcton, "Africa Celebrates Barack Obama's Victory," NPR,
Nov. 5, 2008, https://www.npr.org/templates/story/story.php?storyId=966
43771; Michael D. Shear, "In Mandela, Obama Found a Beacon Who Inspired from Afar," *New York Times*, June 27, 2013, https://www.nytimes.com
/2013/06/28/world/africa/mandela-obama-africa.html; Maurice Possley, "Activism Blossomed in College," *Chicago Tribune*, Mar. 30, 2007, https://www
.chicagotribune.com/nation-world/chi-0703291042mar30-archive-story.html.
Though an admirer of Mandela, Obama had less flattering things to say
about those who succeeded him in the South African government. "By all
accounts," Obama recollected in his 2020 memoir, "much of the goodwill
built up through Mandela's heroic struggle was being squandered by corruption and incompetence under [African National Congress] leadership, leaving large swaths of the country's black population still mired in poverty and
despair." Obama, *A Promised Land*, 337.

2. "World Citizens Prefer Obama to McCain by More than 3-to-1," Gallup,
Oct. 28, 2008, https://news.gallup.com/poll/111253/world-citizens-prefer
-obama-mccain-more-than-3to1.aspx; Ian T. Brown and Bob Tortora, "Sub-
Saharan Africans More Approving of U.S. Leadership," Gallup, Aug. 3,
2009, https://news.gallup.com/poll/121994/sub-saharan-africans-approv
ing-leadership.aspx; Jenny Marlar, "U.S. Leadership Approval Still High
in 10 African Nations," Gallup, Sept. 22, 2010, https://news.gallup.com
/poll/143189/leadership-approval-high-african-nations.aspx; Julie Ray, "U.S.
Leadership Losing Some Status in Key Countries," Gallup, Apr. 19, 2012,
https://news.gallup.com/poll/153929/leadership-losing-status-key-countries
.aspx; Richard Wike, "Wait, You Still Don't Like Us?," *Foreign Policy*, Sept.
19, 2012, https://foreignpolicy.com/2012/09/19/wait-you-still-dont-like-us/.

3. Obama, *The Audacity of Hope*, 319.

4. "Remarks to the Ghanaian Parliament in Accra," July 11, 2009, in Obama,
Public Papers, 2:1087-1092; Peter Baker, "Obama Tells a Rapt Africa of Need
for Responsibility and Reform," *New York Times*, July 12, 2009, 1, 10.

5. Toby Thompkins, "The Obama Effect: Ghana Reacts to the President's
First Visit," *Ebony*, Oct. 2009, 76-80, 83; Jeffrey Gettleman, "Welcome
Back, Son: Now Don't Forget Us," *New York Times*, July 12, 2009, WK3.

6. Zeleza, "Obama's Africa Policy," 170-171; Jacob Dlamini, "A Hyphenated Legacy? Obama's Africa Policy," in Zelizer, *Presidency of Barack Obama*, 227-245; Sahle, *World Orders, Development and Transformation*, 215.

7. Nicholas Kulish, "After Obama's Visit, an Electric Moment for Tanzania Lingers," *New York Times*, July 2, 2013, https://www.nytimes.com/2013/07/03/world/africa/after-obamas-visit-an-electric-moment-for-tanzania-lingers.html.

8. White House, *U.S. Strategy toward Sub-Saharan Africa*.

9. "Statement on the Presidential Election in Cote d'Ivoire," Oct. 28, 2010, in Obama, *Public Papers*, 2:1692-1693; "The Ivory Coast Votes for President after Years of Turmoil," CNN, Oct. 31, 2010, http://www.cnn.com/2010/WORLD/africa/10/31/ivory.coast.election/index.html; "Obama Dangled White House Visit to Ease Ivorian Row," Reuters, Dec. 9, 2010, https://www.reuters.com/article/us-ivorycoast-obama/obama-dangled-white-house-visit-to-ease-ivorian-row-idUSTRE6B86E220101209; "Obama Joins African Leaders in Pressing Gbagbo to Step Aside in Ivory Coast," *Guardian* (US edition), Dec. 8, 2010, https://www.theguardian.com/global-development/2010/dec/08/ivory-coast-elections-obama-letter; "President Obama's Message to the People of Cote D'Ivoire," White House, Mar. 25, 2011, https://obamawhitehouse.archives.gov/blog/2011/03/25/president-obama-s-message-people-cote-d-ivoire; "Remarks following a Meeting with President John Evans Atta Mills of Ghana," Mar. 8, 2012, in Obama, *Public Papers*, 1:273-274; Grant T. Harris, "President Obama Meets with Leaders of Sierra Leone, Senegal, Malawi, and Cape Verde," White House, Mar. 28, 2013, https://obamawhitehouse.archives.gov/blog/2013/03/28/president-obama-meets-leaders-sierra-leone-senegal-malawi-and-cape-verde.

10. Mark Landler, "In Obama's Praise of Mandela, a Nudge to Africa," *New York Times,* Dec. 13, 2013, https://www.nytimes.com/2013/12/14/world/africa/in-obamas-praise-of-mandela-a-nudge-to-africa.html; Michael D. Shear, Nicholas Kulish, and Lydia Polgreen, "Rare Visit Underscores Tangles in Obama's Ties to Africa," *New York Times*, June 26, 2013, https://www.nytimes.com/2013/06/27/world/africa/rare-visit-underscores-tangles-in-obamas-ties-to-africa.html; Adam Nossiter, "U.S. Engages with an Iron Leader in Equatorial Guinea," *New York Times*, May 30, 2011, https://www.nytimes.com/2011/05/31/world/africa/31guinea.html; Colum Lynch, "Exclusive: Rwanda Revisited," *Foreign Affairs*, Apr. 5, 2015, https://foreignpolicy.com/2015/04/05/rwanda-revisited-genocide-united-states-state-department/; Zeleza, "Obama's Africa Policy," 173.

11. Zeleza, "Obama's Africa Policy," 173; Peter Baker, "Obama, on China's Turf, Presents U.S. as a Better Partner for Africa," *New York Times*, July 29, 2015, https://www.nytimes.com/2015/07/30/world/africa/obama-on-chinas-turf-presents-us-as-a-better-partner-for-africa.html; Peter Apps, "With Multiple Missions, U.S. Military Steps Up Africa Focus," Reuters, June 27, 2013, https://www.reuters.com/article/uk-usa-africa-military/with-multiple-missions-u-s-military-steps-up-africa-focus-idUKBRE95Q1F120130627; Nicholas

Kulish and Michael D. Shear, "In Tanzania, Obama Calls for a Partnership with Africa to Aid Its Economy," *New York Times*, July 1, 2013, https://www .nytimes.com/2013/07/02/world/africa/obama-tanzania-visit.html; Shear, Kulish, and Polgreen, "Rare Visit Underscores Tangles"; "Data: China-Africa Trade," China Africa Research Initiative, Johns Hopkins University, accessed July 28, 2019, http://www.sais-cari.org/data-china-africa-trade; Office of the US Trade Representative, "Africa," accessed July 28, 2019, https: //ustr.gov/countries-regions/africa.

12. "Remarks at George Washington University," Dec. 1, 2011, in Obama, *Public Papers*, 2:1498-1500; "Obama Touts $3B in Pledges to Help Feed Africa," TheGrio.com, May 21, 2012, https://thegrio.com/2012/05/21/obama-touts -3b-in-pledges-to-help-feed-africa/; "Fact Sheet: Power Africa," White House, June 30, 2013, https://obamawhitehouse.archives.gov/the-press-office/2013 /06/30/fact-sheet-power-africa; Mark Felsenthal and Jeff Mason, "Obama Seeks to Build Africa Business Ties on Tanzania Stop," Reuters, July 1, 2013, https://www.reuters.com/article/uk-obama-tanzania/obama-seeks-to-build -africa-business-ties-on-tanzania-stop-idUKBRE9600J420130701; Pilita Clark, "Barack Obama's Power Africa Initiative Makes Slow Progress," *Financial Times*, July 24, 2016, https://www.ft.com/content/96dac28a -49c9-11e6-8d68-72e9211e86ab; Power Africa, *Annual Report 2019*.

13. Kirk Semple, "Liberians in New York 'Jubilant' at Expulsion Reprieve," *New York Times*, Mar. 21, 2009, https://www.nytimes.com/2009/03/22/nyregion /22liberians.html; Helene Cooper, "Liberian President Pleads with Obama for Assistance in Combating Ebola," *New York Times*, Sept. 12, 2014, https:// www.nytimes.com/2014/09/13/world/africa/liberian-president-pleads-with -obama-for-assistance-in-combating-ebola.html.

14. Cooper, "Liberian President Pleads with Obama"; Justin Sink, "Obama at CDC Warns Ebola Outbreak 'Spiraling out of Control,'" TheHill.com, Sept. 16, 2014, https://thehill.com/policy/healthcare/217920-obama-ebola -outbreak-spiraling-out-of-control; Jonathan Paye and Maria Cheng, "Liberia President Praises US for Ebola Help Pledge," Associated Press, Sept. 17, 2014, https://www.theherald-news.com/2014/09/18/liberia-leader-praises-u-s -for-ebola-help-pledge/a4fxuts/; Helene Cooper, "Liberia's President Urges U.S. to Continue Ebola Aid," *New York Times*, Feb. 27, 2015, https://www .nytimes.com/2015/02/28/world/africa/liberias-president-urges-us-to-contin ue-ebola-aid.html; Norimitsu Onishi, "Last Known Ebola Patient in Liberia Is Discharged," *New York Times*, Mar. 6, 2015, A4; Gregg Zoroya, "U.S. to Leave as Ebola Rates Plummet," *USA Today*, Feb. 5, 2015, 1A; Rice, *Tough Love*, 401-407; Joint and Coalition Operational Analysis, *Operation United Assistance*; World Health Organization, "Liberia"; *President's Malaria Initiative*.

15. Scott Straus, "Darfur and the Genocide Debate," *Foreign Affairs*, Jan.–Feb. 2005, https://www.foreignaffairs.com/articles/sudan/2005-01-01/darfur-and -genocide-debate; Alex de Waal, "Darfur's Deep Grievances Defy All Hopes for an Easy Solution," *Guardian* (US edition), July 25, 2004, https://www

.theguardian.com/society/2004/jul/25/internationalaidanddevelopment.vol untarysector; Kevin Peraino, "Sorry, Sudan," *Newsweek*, Oct. 4, 2010, 39-42.

16. "Remarks at a United Nations Ministerial Meeting on Sudan in New York City," Sept. 24, 2010, in Obama, *Public Papers*, 2:1429-1431; Jesse Lee, "President Obama in Ministerial Meeting on Sudan: 'The Fate of Millions,'" White House, Sept. 24, 2010, https://obamawhitehouse.archives.gov/blog /2010/09/24/president-obama-ministerial-meeting-sudan-fate-millions; Maggie Fick, "Over 99 Pct in Southern Sudan Vote for Secession," Associated Press, Jan. 30, 2011, https://usatoday30.usatoday.com/news/topstories/2011 -01-30-2052877353_x.htm; "Readout of the President's Call with Former South African President Thabo Mbeki about Sudan," White House, Oct. 29, 2010, https://obamawhitehouse.archives.gov/the-press-office/2010/10 /29/readout-presidents-call-with-former-south-african-president-thabo -mbeki-; Jeffrey Gettleman, "Bashir Wins Election as Sudan Edges toward Split," *New York Times*, Apr. 26, 2010, https://www.nytimes.com/2010/04 /27/world/africa/27sudan.html; "Salva Kiir: South Sudan's President in a Cowboy Hat," BBC News, June 21, 2018, https://www.bbc.com/news/world -africa-12107760; "U.S. Pledges up to $50 Million Urgent Aid for South Sudan," Reuters, May 19, 2014, https://www.reuters.com/article/us-usa -southsudan-aid/u-s-pledges-up-to-50-million-urgent-aid-for-south-sudan -idUSBREA4I0X020140519; Julie Pace and Darlene Superville, "Obama Pushes for End to Crippling Crisis in South Sudan," Associated Press, July 29, 2015, https://lasentinel.net/obama-pushes-for-end-to-crippling-crisis -in-south-sudan.html; Somini Sengupta, "U.S. Push for South Sudan Arms Embargo Falls Short at U.N.," *New York Times*, Dec. 23, 2016, https://www .nytimes.com/2016/12/23/world/africa/south-sudan-genocide-arms-embargo -united-nations.html.

17. "Remarks at a United Nations Meeting on Libya in New York City," Sept. 20, 2011, in Obama, *Public Papers*, 2:1086-1088; Joe Sterling and Greg Botelho, "Clinton Demands Arab Spring Nations Protect Embassies, Halt Violence," CNN, Sept. 16, 2012, https://www.cnn.com/2012/09/14/world /meast/embassy-attacks-main/index.html; "Sudan Rejects Addition of Marines at US Embassy," NBC News, Sept. 15, 2012, http://www.msnbc.com /msnbc/sudan-rejects-addition-marines-us; Michael R. Gordan and Eric Schmitt, "Attacks Raise Question of U.S. Forces in Africa," *New York Times*, Nov. 4, 2012, 1, 4; Lolita C. Baldor, "Hagel Orders Airlift for Central African Republic," Associated Press, Dec. 9, 2013, https://www.ksl.com/article /27961731/hagel-orders-airlift-for-central-african-republic; Charlie Savage and Thom Shanker, "U.S. Drug Fight Turns to Africa, Gangs' New Hub," *New York Times*, July 22, 2012, 1, 8; Charles Hoskinson and Josh Gerstein, "Obama Will Deploy Troops to Africa," *Politico*, Oct. 14, 2011, https://www .politico.com/story/2011/10/obama-will-deploy-troops-to-africa-065989; Jeffrey Gettleman, "In Vast Jungle, U.S. Troops Aid in Search for Kony," *New York Times*, Apr. 29, 2012, https://www.nytimes.com/2012/04/30/world/ africa/kony-tracked-by-us-forces-in-central-africa.html; Pamela Constable,

"White House to Send Specialists to Help Recover Abducted Nigerian Schoolgirls," *Washington Post*, May 6, 2014, https://www.washingtonpost .com/local/protesters-plan-morning-rally-to-demand-nigerian-authorities -take-action-to-rescue-girls/2014/05/06/c3408bba-d514-11e3-8a78-8fe5032 2a72c_story.html; Peter Baker, "Nigeria's New President, Hoping to Host Obama, Visits White House Instead," *New York Times*, July 20, 2015, https:// www.nytimes.com/2015/07/21/world/africa/nigerias-new-president-hoping -to-host-obama-visits-white-house-instead.html; Adam Nossiter, "Boko Haram Helped by U.S. Policies, Nigerian President Says," *New York Times*, July 23, 2015, https://www.nytimes.com/2015/07/24/world/africa/muham-madu-buhari-says-us-should-arm-nigeria-against-boko-haram.html; Jamie Crawford, "U.S. Deploys Troops to Africa," CNN, Oct. 14, 2015, https:// www.cnn.com/2015/10/14/politics/united-states-troops-cameroon-africa /index.html; "U.S. Is Cutting Aid to Rwanda," *New York Times*, July 22, 2012, 10; Indyk, Lieberthal, and O'Hanlon, *Bending History*, 250-251.

18. Craig Whitlock, "U.S. Expands Secret Intelligence Operations in Africa," *Washington Post*, June 13, 2012, https://www.washingtonpost.com/world /national-security/us-expands-secret-intelligence-operations-in-africa/2012 /06/13/gJQAHyvAbV_story.html; Craig Whitlock and Greg Miller, "U.S. Assembling Secret Drone Bases in Africa, Arabian Peninsula, Officials Say," *Washington Post*, Sept. 20, 2011, https://www.washingtonpost.com/world /national-security/us-building-secret-drone-bases-in-africa-arabian-penin sula-officials-say/2011/09/20/gIQAJ8rOjK_story.html; Craig Whitlock, "Drone Base in Niger Gives U.S. a Strategic Foothold in West Africa," *Washington Post*, Mar. 21, 2013, https://www.washingtonpost.com/world/national -security/drone-base-in-niger-gives-us-a-strategic-foothold-in-west-africa /2013/03/21/700ee8d0-9170-11e2-9c4d-798c073d7ec8_story.html; Justin Sink, "U.S. Reaches Lease Deal on Sole African Base," TheHill.com, May 5, 2014, https://thehill.com/policy/defense/205202-us-reaches-lease-deal-on -sole-african-base; Craig Whitlock, "Pentagon Set to Open Second Drone Base in Niger as It Expands Operations in Africa," *Washington Post*, Sept. 1, 2014, https://www.washingtonpost.com/world/national-security/penta gon-set-to-open-second-drone-base-in-niger-as-it-expands-operations-in -africa/2014/08/31/365489c4-2eb8-11e4-994d-202962a9150c_story.html; Jim Miklaszewski, "American Hostage in Somalia Rescued by US Navy SEALs in Overnight Raid," MSNBC, Jan. 25, 2012, https://www.hiiraan.com/news 4/2012/jan/22348/american_hostage_in_somalia_rescued_by_us_navy_seals _in_overnight_raid.aspx; "Somali Islamists Offer 10 Camels as Bounty for Obama," CNN, June 9, 2012, https://www.cnn.com/2012/06/09/world /africa/somalia-al-shabaab-bounties/index.html; "Somali al-Shabab Camel Reward for Barack Obama 'Absurd,'" BBC News, June 11, 2012, https:// www.bbc.com/news/world-africa-18394703; Ernesto Londoño and Scott Wilson, "U.S. Strikes al-Shabab in Somalia and Captures Bombing Suspect in Libya," *Washington Post*, Oct. 6, 2013, https://www.washingtonpost

.com/world/national-security/us-navy-seals-raid-al-shabab-leaders-somalia
-home-in-response-to-nairobi-attack/2013/10/05/78f135dc-2e0c-11e3-8ade-a1
f23cda135e_story.html; Philip Ewing, "U.S. Kills Somali Terrorist Leader,"
Politico, Sept. 5, 2014, https://www.politico.com/story/2014/09/al-shabab
-terror-leader-killed-ahmed-godane-110632; Juliet Eilperin and Kevin Sieff,
"Despite Economic Gains, Obama's Work in Africa Is Unfinished," *Washington Post*, July 28, 2015, https://www.washingtonpost.com/world/on-his
-trip-to-east-africa-obama-confronts-new-gains-old-stalemates/2015/07
/28/7c6b98fd-a631-4e99-a144-bd0f1ecef743_story.html; Mark Mazzetti,
Jeffrey Gettleman, and Eric Schmitt, "In Somalia, U.S. Escalates a Shadow
War," *New York Times*, Oct. 16, 2016, https://www.nytimes.com/2016/10/16
/world/africa/obama-somalia-secret-war.html; Helene Cooper, "U.S. Strikes
in Somalia Kill 150 Shabab Fighters," *New York Times*, Mar. 7, 2016, https://
www.nytimes.com/2016/03/08/world/africa/us-airstrikes-somalia.html.

19. In Yemen in late 2011, two separate US-orchestrated drone strikes killed
Anwar al-Awlaki and his 16-year-old son, Abdulrahman al-Awlaki, both
US citizens. In response to lawsuits, the Obama administration asserted
that it had acted legally in defending the United States against terrorist
attacks. Matt Spetalnick, "Obama: Americans Deserve to Know More
about Drone War," Reuters, Feb. 14, 2013, https://www.reuters.com/arti
cle/us-obama-drones/obama-americans-deserve-to-know-more-about
-drone-war-idUSBRE91E03U20130215; Laura Kasinof, "Strikes Hit Yemen
as Violence Escalates in Capital," *New York Times*, Oct. 15, 2011, https://
www.nytimes.com/2011/10/16/world/middleeast/yemeni-security-forces
-fire-on-protesters-in-sana.html; Jessica Yellin, Gabriella Schwarz, and
Jennifer Hyde, "Obama Revealed: The Man, the President," CNN, Sept.
4, 2012, https://www.cnn.com/2012/09/04/politics/obama-revealed/index
.html; Doris Kearns Goodwin, "Barack Obama and Doris Kearns Goodwin: The Ultimate Exit Interview," *Vanity Fair*, Sept. 21, 2016, http://www
.vanityfair.com/news/2016/09/barack-obama-doris-kearns-goodwin-inter
view; Ta-Nehisi Coates, "'Better Is Good': Obama on Reparations, Civil
Rights, and the Art of the Possible," *Atlantic*, Dec. 21, 2016, https://www
.theatlantic.com/politics/archive/2016/12/ta-nehisi-coates-obama-transcript
-ii/511133/; Charlie Savage, Eric Schmitt, and Mark Mazzetti, "Obama Expands War with Al Qaeda to Include Shabab in Somalia," *New York Times*,
Nov. 27, 2016, https://www.nytimes.com/2016/11/27/us/politics/obama
-expands-war-with-al-qaeda-to-include-shabab-in-somalia.html.

20. Alyssa Brown and Frank Newport, "In U.S., 65% Support Drone Attacks
on Terrorists Aboard," Gallup, Mar. 25, 2013, https://news.gallup.com/poll
/161474/support-drone-attacks-terrorists-abroad.aspx; Juliana Menasce
Horowitz, "The Day after: Obama Triumph Sobered by Unmet Global
Expectations," Pew Research Center, Nov. 26, 2012, https://www.pewre
search.org/global/2012/11/26/the-day-after-obama-triumph-sobered-by
-unmet-global-expectations/.

21. "Drone Warfare," Bureau for Investigative Journalism, accessed July 30, 2019, https://www.thebureauinvestigates.com/projects/drone-war; Jeremy Scahill, "The Assassination Complex," *Intercept*, Oct. 15, 2015, https://the intercept.com/drone-papers/the-assassination-complex/; Kathryn Olmsted, "Terror Tuesdays: How Obama Refined Bush's Counterterrorism Policies," in Zelizer, *Presidency of Barack Obama*, 215-220.

22. Obama, *A Promised Land*, 352-354, 427.

23. Benjamin Aciek Machar, "Kenyan Politics," in Bangura, *Assessing Barack Obama's Africa Policy*, 212-213; "ICC Postpones Kenyan President's Trial to February," CNN, Oct. 31, 2013, https://www.cnn.com/2013/10/31/world /kenya-icc-trial-postponed/index.html.

24. Donovan Slack, "W.H. Urges Peaceful Acceptance of Kenyan Election Results," *Politico*, Mar. 30, 2013, https://www.politico.com/blogs/politico44 /2013/03/wh-urges-peaceful-acceptance-of-kenyan-election-results-160541; Shear, Kulish, and Polgreen, "Rare Visit Underscores Tangles"; Simon Ndonga, "Kenya Not Bothered by Obama's Snub—Ruto," Capital FM (Nairobi, Kenya), June 30, 2013, https://www.capitalfm.co.ke/news/2013 /06/kenya-not-bothered-by-obamas-snub-ruto/.

25. Grant Harris and Shannon Green, "Reinforcing the U.S.-Africa Partnership," White House, Mar. 30, 2015, https://obamawhitehouse.archives.gov /blog/2015/03/30/reinforcing-us-africa-partnership; Peter Baker, "Kenya Trip Takes Obama Back to a Complex Part of Himself," *New York Times*, July 22, 2015, https://www.nytimes.com/2015/07/23/world/africa/africa -trip-takes-obama-back-to-a-complex-part-of-himself.html; Edward-Isaac Dovere, "Obama's Most Dangerous Trip Yet," *Politico*, July 25, 2015, https:// www.politico.com/story/2015/07/obama-kenya-visit-security-120586; Peter Baker and Marc Santora, "Obama Arrives in Kenya, on Personal and Official Journey," *New York Times*, July 24, 2015, https://www.nytimes.com/20 15/07/25/world/africa/obama-arrives-in-kenya-on-personal-and-official- journey.html; Edward-Isaac Dovere, "When Obama Met Kenyatta," *Politico*, July 25, 2015, https://www.politico.com/story/2015/07/when-barack -obama-met-kenyatta-120623; Julie Pace, "Gay Rights Clash: Obama, African Host Are at Odds," Associated Press, June 27, 2013, https://news.yahoo .com/gay-rights-clash-obama-african-host-odds-193249657.html; Obama, *Dreams from My Father*, 214-216; Peter Baker and Marc Santora, "Obama in Kenya: An Upbeat Tone, but Notes of Discord, Too," *New York Times*, July 25, 2015, https://www.nytimes.com/2015/07/26/world/africa/in-kenya-oba ma-hails-africas-growth-and-potential.html; Grant Harris and Stephen Pomper, "Further U.S. Efforts to Protect Human Rights in Uganda," White House, June 19, 2014, https://obamawhitehouse.archives.gov/blog/2014/06 /19/further-us-efforts-protect-human-rights-uganda; Tonny Onyulo, "Kenyans Greet Obama with Wish List for Change," *USA Today*, July 24, 2015, https://www.usatoday.com/story/news/world/2015/07/24/kenyans-greet -obama-wish-list-change/30622843/; Jeff Mason and Edith Honan, "Obama Chides Kenya on Gay Rights, Ready for Closer Security Work," Reuters, July 25, 2015, https://www.reuters.com/article/obama-africa-kenya/update

-4-obama-chides-kenya-on-gay-rights-ready-for-closer-security-work-idUS
L5N10504J20150725.

26. Quist-Arcton, "Africa Celebrates Barack Obama's Victory"; Josphat Kasire
and Tom Odula, "Granny Obama, Kenya Celebrate White House Win," Associated Press, Nov. 7, 2012, https://news.yahoo.com/granny-obama-kenya
-celebrate-white-house-win-134621039.html; Brian Ross, Megan Chuch-
mach, and Martha Raddatz, "Osama bin Laden Wanted to Kill President
Obama," ABC News, May 13, 2011, https://abcnews.go.com/Blotter/osama
-bin-laden-wanted-kill-president-obama/story?id=13595181; Louise Lief,
"Obama Step-Grandma on Women's Rights," TheRoot.com, Sept. 28,
2012, https://www.theroot.com/obama-step-grandma-on-womens-rights
-1790893468; Jason Horowitz, "Amid Politics, Obama Drifted Away from
Kin," *New York Times*, Apr. 22, 2014, A16; Tonny Onyulo, "Obama's Struggling Ancestral Kenya Village Misses Him—and Cashing In on His Presidency," *USA Today*, Sept. 5, 2017, https://www.usatoday.com/story/news
/world/2017/09/02/obamas-struggling-ancestral-kenya-village-misses-him
-and-cashing-his-presidency/581838001/.

27. Rodrique Ngowi, "Obama Uncle in Mass. Wins New Deportation Hearing," Associated Press, Dec. 4, 2012, https://news.yahoo.com/obama-uncle
-mass-wins-deportation-hearing-211304992.html; "Massachusetts: Obama
Uncle Avoids Deportation," Associated Press, Dec. 3, 2013, https://www
.nytimes.com/2013/12/04/us/massachusetts-obama-uncle-avoids-deporta-
tion.html; Tom Curry, "White House Reverses Story on Obama Living
with Kenyan Uncle in the 1980s," NBC, Dec. 5, 2013, https://www.nbc
news.com/politics/politics-news/white-house-reverses-story-obama-living
-kenyan-uncle-1980s-flna2D11702082.

28. Horowitz, "Amid Politics, Obama Drifted"; Katharine Q. Seelye, "Zeituni
Onyango, 61, Obama's Aunt from Kenya," *New York Times*, Apr. 9, 2014,
A19; Obama, *Dreams from My Father*, 306; Denise Lavoie, "Zeituni Onyango: Obama Aunt Who Stayed in US Illegally, Dead at 61," Associated
Press, Apr. 8, 2014, https://www.courant.com/sdut-obama-aunt-who-stayed
-in-us-illegally-dies-at-61-2014apr08-story.html; Jacobs, *The Other Obama*,
153-154.

29. Quist-Arcton, "Africa Celebrates Barack Obama's Victory"; Duncan Miriri,
"Obama's Brother Plans to Vote for Trump," Reuters, July 25, 2016, https://
www.reuters.com/article/us-usa-election-obama-idUSKCN10518K; Tonny
Onyulo and Hellen Wagaluka, "Obama's Half Brother Supports Donald
Trump," *USA Today*, Sept. 22, 2016, 9A; Elizabeth Chuck, "Donald Trump
Invites Barack Obama's Half-Brother, Malik, to Final 2016 Debate," NBC
News, Oct. 19, 2016, https://www.nbcnews.com/news/us-news/donald
-trump-invites-barack-obama-s-half-brother-malik-final-n668966.

30. Curry, "White House Reverses Story"; Horowitz, "Amid Politics, Obama
Drifted"; Obama, *Dreams from My Father*, 299-442; Rachel L. Swarns,
"Words of Obama's Father Still Waiting to Be Read by His Son," *New
York Times*, June 18, 2016, http://www.nytimes.com/2016/06/19/nyregion
/letters-by-and-about-barack-obamas-father.html.

31. "Fact Sheet: Obama Administration Accomplishments in Sub-Saharan Africa," White House, June 14, 2012, https://obamawhitehouse.archives.gov /the-press-office/2012/06/14/fact-sheet-obama-administration-accomplish ments-sub-saharan-africa; David Nakamura and Sudarsan Raghavan, "Ahead of Obama's Visit, Africans Feel He Hasn't Lived Up to Promises," *Washing ton Post*, June 25, 2013, https://www.washingtonpost.com/politics/ahead -of-obamas-visit-africans-feel-he-hasnt-lived-up-to-promises/2013/06/25 /35258712-d8f4-11e2-a9f2-42ee3912ae0e_story.html; President Barack Obama, "Africa's Progress Is Good for America," TheRoot.com, July 23, 2015, https:// www.theroot.com/africa-s-progress-is-good-for-america-1790860603; Jackie Burns, "White House Hosts Visiting Young African Leaders," White House, Oct. 25, 2012, https://obamawhitehouse.archives.gov/blog/2012/10 /25/white-house-hosts-visiting-young-african-leaders; Ben Rhodes, "500 of Africa's Most Promising Young Leaders Arrive for the First Washington Fellowship," White House, June 21, 2014, https://obamawhitehouse.archives .gov/blog/2014/06/21/500-africa-s-most-promising-young-leaders-arrive -first-washington-fellowship; Andrew Siddons, "Washington Meeting of African Leaders Opens to Protests," *New York Times*, Aug. 5, 2014, A11; Garrett Brinker, "President Obama Speaks at the U.S.-Africa Business Forum," White House, Aug. 5, 2014, https://obamawhitehouse.archives.gov/blog /2014/08/05/president-obama-speaks-us-africa-business-forum; Jonathan Topaz, "Obama's Africa Toast Gets 'Personal,'" *Politico*, Aug. 6, 2014, https:// www.politico.com/story/2014/08/obama-toast-slavery-africa-leaders-summit -109754; Kevin Liptak, "5 Reasons Obama's Africa Leaders' Summit Matters," CNN, Aug. 5, 2014, https://www.cnn.com/2014/08/04/politics/white -house-africa-summit/index.html; Eric Bradner, "Obama Touts Africa Deals," *Politico*, Aug. 5, 2014, https://www.politico.com/story/2014/08/ obama-invest-14b-africa-109718.
32. Siddons, "Washington Meeting of African Leaders," A11; "Remarks at the United States–Africa Leaders Summit Dinner," Aug. 5, 2014, in Obama, *Public Papers*, 2:1073-1074.
33. Topaz, "Obama's Africa Toast"; Megan Slack, "President Obama Visits Senegal," White House, June 27, 2013, https://obamawhitehouse.archives.gov /blog/2013/06/27/president-obama-visits-senegal; Pace, "Gay Rights Clash."
34. Michelle Obama, "FLOTUS Travel Journal: Visiting Goree Island," White House, June 27, 2013, https://obamawhitehouse.archives.gov/blog/2013/06 /27/flotus-travel-journal-visiting-goree-island; Obama, *Becoming*, 160.
35. Helene Cooper, "Obama Pledges Aid to Haiti," *New York Times*, Jan. 14, 2010, https://www.nytimes.com/2010/01/15/us/15prexy.html; Kolbe, "Mortality, Crime and Access to Basic Needs"; "Magnitude 7.0—Haiti Region," US Geological Survey, Jan. 12, 2010, https://web.archive.org/web/20100115 110510/http://earthquake.usgs.gov/earthquakes/eqinthenews/2010/us2010r ja6/#details.
36. "Rights Groups Call for Pause in Deportations to Haiti," *New York Times*, Feb. 6, 2011, 20; Steven Forester, "Even after Obama's Immigration Policy

Change, Haitian Families' Dreams Deferred," TheGrio.com, June 18, 2012, https://thegrio.com/2012/06/18/even-after-obamas-immigration-policy -change-haitian-families-dreams-deferred/; "Implementation of Haitian Family Reunification Parole Program," *Federal Register*, Dec. 18, 2014, https://www.federalregister.gov/documents/2014/12/18/2014-29533/imple mentation-of-haitian-family-reunification-parole-program; Geneva Sands, "Trump Admin Ends Family-Based Reunification Programs for Haitians and Filipino World War II Vets," CNN, Aug. 2, 2019, https://www.cnn .com/2019/08/02/politics/trump-end-two-family-reunification-programs /index.html.

37. Matt Spetalnick, "In Jamaica, Obama Seeks to Reassert U.S. Leadership in Caribbean," Reuters, Apr. 8, 2015, https://www.reuters.com/article/us-usa -caribbean/in-jamaica-obama-seeks-to-reassert-u-s-leadership-in-caribbean -idUSKBN0N002K20150409; Matt Spetalnick, "Update 2—Obama Touts Clean Energy in Bid to Restore U.S. Leadership in Caribbean," Reuters, Apr. 9, 2015, https://uk.reuters.com/article/usa-caribbean/update-2-obama -touts-clean-energy-in-bid-to-restore-u-s-leadership-in-caribbean-idUKL2N 0X625520150409; Mark Weisbrot, "Obama Should Put an End to Extreme Austerity in Jamaica," Al Jazeera America, Apr. 8, 2015, http://america.alja zeera.com/opinions/2015/4/obama-should-put-an-end-to-extreme-austerity -in-jamaica.html; Jim Kuhnhenn, "White House Notebook: Nuttin' but Love for Obama in Jamaica," Associated Press, Apr. 9, 2015, http://www.msn bc.com/msnbc/white-house-notebook-nuttin-love-obama-jamaica; "Com- rade Obama? Portia Gets Political Bounce from US President," *Gleaner* (Kingston, Jamaica), Apr. 11, 2015, http://jamaica-gleaner.com/article/lead -stories/20150412/comrade-obama-portia-gets-political-bounce-us-president.

38. Kevin Liptak and Jim Acosta, "Barack Obama and Raul Castro Meet, Launch New Era of U.S.-Cuba Ties," CNN, Apr. 12, 2015, https://www .cnn.com/2015/04/11/politics/panama-obama-castro-meeting/index.html; "Steps Obama Has Taken to Ease US Restrictions on Cuba," Associated Press, Mar. 20, 2016, https://www.dailyherald.com/article/20160320/news /303209985; Bernadette Meehan, "Rescission of Cuba as a State Sponsor of Terrorism," White House, May 29, 2015, https://obamawhitehouse.archives .gov/blog/2015/05/29/rescission-cuba-state-sponsor-terrorism; Michael Weissenstein, "For Black Cubans, Obama Visit a Source of Pride," Asso- ciated Press, Mar. 20, 2016, https://www.detroitnews.com/story/news/world /2016/03/20/black-cubans-obama-visit-source-pride/82045854/; Damien Cave, "Cuba Says It Has Solved Racism: Obama Isn't So Sure," *New York Times*, Mar. 23, 2016, https://www.nytimes.com/2016/03/24/world/americas /obamaurges-raised-voices-incubas-husheddiscussions-ofrace.html; "Watch President Obama's Full Speech to Cubans from Havana," YouTube, ac- cessed Aug. 3, 2019, https://www.youtube.com/watch?v=CXRxEBLEUc4.

39. Oliveira-Monte, *Barack Obama Is Brazilian*, 88, 91-92, 121-122; "Remarks in Rio de Janeiro, Brazil," Mar. 20, 2011, in Obama, *Public Papers*, 1:259-263; Alexei Barrionuevo and Jackie Calmes, "President Underscores Similarities

with Brazilians, but Sidesteps One," *New York Times*, Mar. 20, 2011, https://www.nytimes.com/2011/03/21/world/americas/21brazil.html; Obama, *A Promised Land*, 662-663.

40. Eugene Scott, "Brazilian President: Our Countries Share Fight against 'Blemish of Slavery,'" CNN, July 1, 2015, https://www.cnn.com/2015/07/01/politics/brazilian-president-discusses-overcoming-slavery/index.html; Catherine E. Shoichet and Euan McKirdy, "Brazil's Senate Ousts Dilma Rousseff in Impeachment Vote," CNN, Sept. 1, 2016, https://www.cnn.com/2016/08/31/americas/brazil-rousseff-impeachment-vote/index.html; "Brazil's Former Leader Rousseff Fails in Bid for Senate Seat," EWN, Oct. 8, 2018, https://ewn.co.za/2018/10/08/brazil-s-former-leader-rousseff-fails-in-bid-for-senate-seat.

CHAPTER 13. DEMOGRAPHICS AND DESTINIES

1. Steve Hargreaves, "Obama Now a Job Creator," CNN, Nov. 2, 2012, https://money.cnn.com/2012/11/02/news/economy/obama-jobs-report/; Julie Hirschfeld Davis, "Obama First since FDR Re-Elected with 7.9% Joblessness," *Bloomberg*, Nov. 7, 2012, https://www.bloomberg.com/news/articles/2012-11-07/obama-defies-history-on-economy-wins-with-coalition-vote; Bishaw, *Poverty: 2000 to 2012*; Bureau of Labor Statistics, US Department of Labor, "Labor Force Statistics from the Current Population Survey," accessed Aug. 4, 2019, https://data.bls.gov/timeseries/lns14000006; Rakesh Kochhar and Richard Fry, "Wealth Inequality Has Widened along Racial, Ethnic Lines since End of Great Recession," Pew Research Center, Dec. 12, 2014, https://www.pewresearch.org/fact-tank/2014/12/12/racial-wealth-gaps-great-recession/; Paul Tough, "The Birthplace of Obama the Politician," *New York Times Magazine*, Aug. 19, 2012, 30-31.

2. "The RD Interview with President Barack Obama," *Reader's Digest*, Nov. 2012, 166-173; "Obama Weekly Job Approval by Demographics.09102016" (.xlsx) Sept. 21, 2016, https://www.evernote.com/shard/s4/client/snv?noteGuid=0953576f-5e23-4a3a-9cf3-747c21679e09&noteKey=eec113a6a1858d85&sn=https%3A%2F%2Fwww.evernote.com%2Fshard%2Fs4%2Fsh%2F0953576f-5e23-4a3a-9cf3-747c21679e09%2Feec113a6a1858d85&title=Obama%2BWeekly%2BJob%2BApproval%2Bby%2BDemographics; "January 2017 Political Survey," Pew Research Center, Jan. 4-9, 2017, assets.pewresearch.org/wp-content/uploads/sites/5/2017/01/19114252/01-19-17-2017-Political-outlook-topline-for-release.pdf; "Presidential Approval Ratings—Barack Obama," Gallup, accessed Aug. 4, 2019, https://news.gallup.com/poll/116479/barack-obama-presidential-job-approval.aspx; Brett LoGiurato, "Obama's Approval Rating Is Soaring at Exactly the Right Time," *Business Insider*, Nov. 4, 2012, https://www.businessinsider.com/obama-approval-rating-polls-rasmussen-50-percent-gallup-2012-11; "Washington Post–ABC News Poll," *Washington Post*, accessed Aug. 4, 2019, https://www.washingtonpost.com/wp-srv/politics/polls/postabcpoll_20121102.html; Frank Newport, "Blacks' Approval of President Obama Remains High," Gallup, Dec. 15, 2014, https://

news.gallup.com/poll/180176/blacks-approval-president-obama-remains
-high.aspx; Frank Newport, "Hispanics' Approval of Obama Down since
'12," Gallup, Sept. 26, 2014, https://news.gallup.com/poll/177404/hispanics
-approval-obama-down.aspx.

3. Obama, *The Audacity of Hope*, 240; Donovan Slack, "Obama Camp Identifies More Bundlers," *Politico*, Mar. 2, 2013, https://www.politico.com/blogs
/politico44/2013/03/obama-camp-identifies-more-bundlers-158294; "Obama
for America and Obama Victory Fund 2012 Volunteer Fundraisers," Obama
Biden.com, accessed Mar. 2, 2013, http://www.obamabiden.com/volunteer
-fundraisers-q4.html; Allison Samuels, "Black Hollywood Weighs Whether
to Support Obama a Second Time," *Newsweek*, Jan. 23, 2012, https://www
.newsweek.com/black-hollywood-weighs-whether-support-obama-second
-time-64303; Dave Levinthal, "New Super PAC Backs Obama," *Politico*, Jan.
1, 2012, https://www.politico.com/story/2012/01/new-super-pac-1911-uni
ted-backs-obama-070987; Zerlina Maxwell, "Bill Burton behind the Super
Pac That Succeeded: Priorities USA," TheGrio.com, Nov. 14, 2012, https://
thegrio.com/2012/11/14/bill-burton-behind-the-super-pac-that-succeeded
-priorities-usa/; Robert Draper, "The Price of Power," *New York Times Magazine*, July 8, 2012, 22, 38; Mayer, *Dark Money*; Abby Phillip and Dave Levinthal, "Adelson Tally to Gingrich: $20M," *Politico*, Apr. 21, 2012, https://www
.politico.com/story/2012/04/gingrich-camp-mired-in-debt-075418; Steven
Bertoni, "Billionaire Sheldon Adelson Says He Might Give $100M to Newt
Gingrich or Other Republican," *Forbes*, Feb. 21, 2012, https://www.forbes
.com/sites/stevenbertoni/2012/02/21/billionaire-sheldon-adelson-says-he
-might-give-100m-to-newt-gingrich-or-other-republican/#5511a0bd4400;
Chris Cillizza and Aaron Blake, "How Super PACs Are Saving Mitt Romney," *Washington Post*, July 24, 2012, https://www.washingtonpost.com
/blogs/the-fix/post/how-super-pacs-are-saving-mitt-romney/2012/07/23/gJ
QA1zKX5W_blog.html.

4. Axelrod, *Believer*, 456–457; Alter, *The Center Holds*, 207–208, 231; "Mitt Romney's Election Campaign Insults Voters," *Washington Post*, Nov. 2, 2012,
https://www.washingtonpost.com/opinions/mitt-romneys-election-cam
paign-insults-voters/2012/11/02/69fcc1fc-2428-11e2-9313-3c7f59038d93_story
.html; Maggie Haberman, "Obama's Win: 12 Takeaways," *Politico*, Nov. 7,
2012, https://www.politico.com/story/2012/11/12-takeaways-from-obamas
-win-083462; Mark Halperin, "All the Right Moves . . . and Some Wrong
Ones," *Time*, Nov. 19, 2012, 27–28; M. J. Lee, "Palin: Mitt Needs Bain Show
& Tell," *Politico*, Jan. 12, 2012, https://www.politico.com/story/2012/01/palin
-mitt-needs-bain-show-tell-071364; Glen Johnson, "Romneycare May Come
Back to Haunt Mitt on Health Issue," Associated Press, Mar. 27, 2010,
https://www.deseretnews.com/article/700019894/Romneycare-may-come
-back-to-haunt-Mitt-on-health-issue.html; Ashley Parker, "Having Opposed Auto Bailout, Romney Now Takes Credit for Rebound," *New York
Times*, May 8, 2012, https://thecaucus.blogs.nytimes.com/2012/05/08/hav
ing-opposed-auto-bailout-romney-now-takes-credit-for-rebound; Miranda
Blue and Ryan Kelly, "Romney's Nuances on Gay Issue," PolitiFact, Oct. 5,

2007, https://www.politifact.com/truth-o-meter/article/2007/oct/05/rom neys-nuances-gay-issues/; Erika Riggs, "A Look at Mitt Romney's Homes," *Portland Press Herald* (Maine), Jan. 30, 2012, https://www.pressherald.com /2012/01/30/a-look-at-mitt-romneys-homes/; "Obama 'Romney Singing' Ad 2012," YouTube, accessed Aug. 5, 2019, https://www.youtube.com/watch?v =pd1AXQyKY6k.

5. Peter Wallsten, "Black Church Leaders Try to Inspire Congregants to Vote for Obama," *Washington Post*, Sept. 3, 2012, https://www.washingtonpost .com/politics/black-church-leaders-try-to-inspire-congregants-to-vote-for -obama/2012/09/03/136b2da0-f3f0-11e1-892d-bc92fee603a7_story.html; "The Esquire/Yahoo! News Voter Poll," *Esquire*, Oct. 10, 2012, https://www.es quire.com/news-politics/a16168/esquire-yahoo-news-poll-1112/; Michael D. Shear, "Romney Condemns Ad Proposal Using Reverend Wright," *New York Times*, May 17, 2012, https://www.nytimes.com/2012/05/18/us/politics /romney-condemns-ad-proposal-using-rev-jeremiah-wright.html; Balz, *Collision 2012*, 5-6; Laurie Goodstein, "The Theological Differences behind Evangelical Unease with Romney," *New York Times*, Jan.14, 2012, https:// www.nytimes.com/2012/01/15/us/politics/evangelical-christians-unease-with -romney-is-theological.html; Jonathan Merritt, "Analysis: The Unexpected Evangelical Silence on Mitt Romney's Mormonism," Religion News Service, June 11, 2012, https://religionnews.com/2012/06/11/analysis-the-unexpected -evangelical-silence-on-mitt-romneys-mormonism/.

6. Robert Gehrke and Matt Canham, "Mia Love: From Dreams of Broadway to Capitol Hill," *Salt Lake Tribune*, Oct. 9, 2012, https://archive.sltrib.com /article.php?id=55031749&itype=CMSID; Mia Love, "Romney's the Man We Need at the Helm," *USA Today*, Aug. 31, 2012, https://www.pressreader .com/usa/usa-today-international-edition/20120904/page/7; "Mia Love's 2012 Republican National Convention Speech," *Washington Post*, Nov. 5, 2014, https://www.washingtonpost.com/video/politics/mia-loves-2012-re publican-national-convention-speech/2014/11/05/3bdaafc4-64f8-11e4-ab86 -46000e1d0035_video.html; Danielle Ryan, "Mia Love Concedes Tight Race to Jim Matheson," *Los Angeles Times*, Nov. 7, 2012, https://www.la times.com/politics/la-xpm-2012-nov-07-la-pn-mia-love-concedes-congres sional-race-20121107-story.html; Robert Gehrke, "Utahn Mia Love Makes History as First Black Republican Woman in Congress," *Salt Lake Tribune*, November 6, 2014, https://archive.sltrib.com/article.php?id=1783406&i type=CMSID.

7. Mika Gilmore, "Mitt Romney and the Ghosts of Mormon History," *Rolling Stone*, Oct. 25, 2012, 62-68; Harris and Bringhurst, *Mormon Church and Blacks*, 1; "A Portrait of Mormons in the U.S.," Pew Research Center, July 24, 2009, https://www.pewforum.org/2009/07/24/a-portrait-of-mormons-in -the-us/; Susan Saulny, "Black Mormons and the Politics of Identity," *New York Times*, May 22, 2012, https://www.nytimes.com/2012/05/23/us/for -black-mormons-a-political-choice-like-no-other.html; Donna Owens, "For Black Mormons, Presidential Race Brings New Attention," TheGrio.com,

July 10, 2012, https://thegrio.com/2012/07/10/for-black-mormons-presiden tial-race-brings-new-attention/; Harwell interview.

8. Owens, "For Black Mormons, Presidential Race Brings New Attention."

9. "Mormons," Religious Landscape Study (2014), Pew Research Center, accessed Aug. 6, 2019, https://www.pewforum.org/religious-landscape-study /religious-tradition/mormon/; Juana Summers, "Mitt at NAACP: Booed on Health Care," *Politico*, July 11, 2012, https://www.politico.com/story /2012/07/mitt-at-naacp-booed-on-health-care-078387; "2012 NAACP Convention—Mitt Romney," YouTube, accessed Aug. 6, 2019, https://www .youtube.com/watch?v=VspxfjfQ6Zo; Brian Todd, "President Clashes with Civil Rights Group," CNN, July 13, 2004, http://www.cnn.com/2004/US /07/12/Bush.NAACP/index.html; Michael A. Fletcher and Gary Younge, "Dole Declines NAACP Offer to Give Speech at Convention," *Washington Post*, July 9, 1996, https://www.washingtonpost.com/archive/politics /1996/07/09/dole-declines-naacp-offer-to-give-speech-at-convention/0fd b5b10-9a93-449e-8f23-2a0ce2e7ab5b/.

10. The drop-down tabs for the Black Leadership Council and Former Obama Supporters for Romney were added to the campaign website by September 19, 2012. "Romney for President Announces Black Leadership Council," MittRomney.com, Sept. 5, 2012, http://www.mittromney.com/news/press /2012/09/romney-president-announces-black-leadership-council; John Avlon, "Allen West Slams Mitt Romney, Republican Approach to Minority Voters," *Daily Beast*, Mar. 15, 2013 (updated July 12, 2017), https://www .thedailybeast.com/allen-west-slams-mitt-romney-republican-approach-to -minority-voters.

11. Mark Murray, "NBC/WSJ Poll: Heading into Conventions, Obama Has Four-Point Lead," NBC News, Aug. 21, 2012, http://firstread.nbcnews.com /_news/2012/08/21/13399788-nbcwsj-poll-heading-into-conventions-obama -has-four-point-lead?lite; Ashley Parker and Michael D. Shear, "To Boos and Polite Applause, Romney Speaks to the N.A.A.C.P.," *New York Times*, July 11, 2012, https://thecaucus.blogs.nytimes.com/2012/07/11/to-boos-and -polite-applause-romney-speaks-to-the-n-a-a-c-p; "Romney—I Was a Severely Conservative Governor," YouTube, accessed Aug. 6, 2019, https:// www.youtube.com/watch?v=DI8PlTtM7DU; Edward Mason, "Romney's Diversity Record Could Prove Awkward," *Atlantic*, Mar. 1, 2012, https:// www.theatlantic.com/politics/archive/2012/03/romneys-diversity-record -could-prove-awkward/253426/; Trip Gabriel, "Romney Makes a Push for Black Voters," *New York Times*, July 10, 2012, https://www.nytimes.com/2012 /07/11/us/politics/romney-courts-black-vote-an obama-strength-in-08.html.

12. Romney, *No Apology*, 26-28, 31.

13. Perry Bacon Jr., "Is Welfare a Wedge Issue for Mitt Romney?," TheGrio.com, Aug. 23, 2012, https://thegrio.com/2012/08/23/is-welfare-a-wedge-issue-for -mitt-romney/; "Obama to Appear on Kansas Ballot after 'Birther' Challenge Dropped," CNN, Sept. 17, 2012, http://politicalticker.blogs.cnn.com /2012/09/17/obama-to-appear-on-kansas-ballot-after-birther-challenge-drop

ped/; Perry Bacon Jr., "Why Is Mitt Romney Talking about Birth Certificates?," TheGrio.com, Aug. 24, 2012, https://thegrio.com/2012/08/24/why-is-mitt-romney-talking-about-birth-certificates/; "Romney Campaign Rally in Commerce, Michigan," C-SPAN, Aug. 24, 2012, https://www.c-span.org/video/?307749-1/romney-campaign-rally-commerce-michigan; Ben Craw and Zachary D. Carter, "Paul Ryan: 60 Percent of Americans Are 'Takers,' Not 'Makers,'" *Huffington Post*, Oct. 5, 2012, https://www.huffpost.com/entry/paul-ryan-60-percent-of-a_n_1943073.

14. Alter, *The Center Holds*, 290; Bositis, *Blacks and the 2012 Republican National Convention*; Bositis, *Blacks and the 2012 Democratic National Convention*; Rosalind S. Helderman and Jon Cohen, "As Republican Convention Emphasizes Diversity, Racial Incidents Intrude," *Washington Post*, Aug. 29, 2012, https://www.washingtonpost.com/politics/2012/08/29/b9023a52-f1ec-11e1-892d-bc92fee603a7_story.html; Fleur Delacour, "Brew Interview: CNN Camerawoman Speaks Out!," WitchesBrewOnline.com, Aug. 30, 2012, http://witchesbrewonline.com/2012/08/brew-exclusive-cnn-camerawoman-speaks-out/; "Two People Removed from RNC after Taunting Black Camera Operator," CNN, Aug. 29, 2012, http://politicalticker.blogs.cnn.com/2012/08/29/two-people-removed-from-rnc-after-taunting-black-camera-operator/; Sean Sullivan, "CNN Camerawoman: I'm 'Not Surprised' by Peanut-Throwing," *Washington Post*, Aug. 30, 2012, https://www.washingtonpost.com/news/post-politics/wp/2012/08/30 cnn-camerawoman-im-not-surprised-by-nuts-incident/.

15. Peter Hamby, "Analysis: Why Romney Lost," CNN, Nov. 7, 2012, https://www.cnn.com/2012/11/07/politics/why-romney-lost/index.html; Davis, "Obama First since FDR Re-Elected"; Haberman, "Obama's Win: 12 Takeaways"; D'Elia and Norpoth, "Winning with a Bad Economy"; Halperin, "All the Right Moves"; *Mitt*, directed by Whiteley.

16. Hamby, "Analysis: Why Romney Lost"; Haberman, "Obama's Win: 12 Takeaways."

17. "How the Race Was Won," *USA Today*, Nov. 7, 2012, http://usatoday30.usatoday.com/news/graphics/elections-2012/how-race-was-won/index.html.

18. Rhodes, *World as It Is*, 191; Axelrod, *Believer*, 477; Frank Newport, "Democrats Racially Diverse; Republicans Mostly White," Gallup, Feb. 8, 2013, https://news.gallup.com/poll/160373/democrats-racially-diverse-republicans-mostly-white.aspx; "How the Race Was Won"; Mark Hugo Lopez and Paul Taylor, "Latino Voters in the 2012 Election," Pew Research Center, Nov. 7, 2012, https://www.pewhispanic.org/2012/11/07/latino-voters-in-the-2012-election/; Paul Taylor and D'Vera Cohn, "A Milestone en Route to a Majority Minority Nation," Pew Research Center, Nov. 7, 2012, https://www.pewsocialtrends.org/2012/11/07/a-milestone-en-route-to-a-majority-minority-nation/; John McCormick, "Blacks Made History Surpassing White Voter Turnout Rates," *Bloomberg*, May 9, 2013, https://www.bloomberg.com/news/articles/2013-05-08/blacks-made-history-surpassing-white-voter-turnout-rates; File, *Diversifying Electorate*; "Most Children Younger than

Age 1 Are Minorities, Census Bureau Reports," US Census Bureau, May 17, 2012, https://www.census.gov/newsroom/releases/archives/population/cb12 -90.html; Jeffrey S. Passel, Gretchen Livingston, and D'Vera Cohn, "Explaining Why Minority Births Now Outnumber White Births," Pew Research Center, May 17, 2012, https://www.pewsocialtrends.org/2012/05/17 /explaining-why-minority-births-now-outnumber-white-births/; Carol Morello and Ted Mellnik, "White Deaths Outnumber Births for First Time," *Washington Post*, June 13, 2013, https://www.washingtonpost.com /local/white-deaths-outnumber-births-for-first-time/2013/06/13/3bb1017c-d 388-11e2-a73e-826d299ff459_story.html; D'Vera Cohn, "It's Official: Minority Babies Are the Majority among the Nation's Infants, but Only Just," Pew Research Center, June 23, 2016, https://www.pewresearch.org/fact-tank/2016 /06/23/its-official-minority-babies-are-the-majority-among-the-nations -infants-but-only-just/.

CHAPTER 14. BAMELOT 2.0

1. Jackie Calmes, "Obama Sworn in for 2nd Term, This Time Quietly," *New York Times*, Jan. 21, 2013, https://www.nytimes.com/2013/01/21/us/politics /president-obama-inauguration.html; "Presidential Inaugurations and the Bible: Barack Obama," Museum of the Bible, accessed Aug. 8, 2019, https:// www.museumofthebible.org/book-minute/presidential-inaugurations-and -the-bible-barack-obama; "Barack Obama: Complete Presidential Inauguration 2013: *The New York Times*," YouTube, accessed Aug. 8, 2019, https:// www.youtube.com/watch?v=Hwqz2TPv3y8; Paige Lavender, "Obama Inauguration Bible: President, John Roberts Inscribe Traveling King Family Bible," *Huffington Post*, Jan. 21, 2013, https://www.huffpost.com/entry/oba ma-inauguration-bible_n_2523130; Byron Tau, "Crowd Shrinks by Nearly Half for 2nd Inaugural," *Politico*, Jan. 21, 2013, https://www.politico.com /blogs/politico44/2013/01/crowd-shrinks-by-nearly-half-for-2nd-inaugural -154825; "Inaugural Address," Jan. 21, 2013, in Obama, *Public Papers*, 1:45- 48; Larry Margasak, "Tuskegee Airmen Honored Guests at Inaugural," Associated Press, Jan. 21, 2013, https://news.yahoo.com/tuskegee-airmen-honor ed-guests-inaugural-192712691—politics.html.
2. Sheila Stewart, "Sharpton, Leaders Deliver Black Agenda for Obama's Second Term," NewsOne.com, Dec. 4, 2012, https://newsone.com/2095116 /sharpton-leaders-deliver-black-agenda-for-obamas-second-term/; Jonathan P. Hicks, "Obama's Second Term Should Focus on Jobs, Black Leaders Insist," BET.com, Nov. 7, 2012, https://www.bet.com/news/features /vote-2012/news/politics/2012/11/07/obama-s-second-term-should-focus -on-jobs-black-leaders-insist.html.
3. Susan Saulny, "Among Blacks, Pride Is Mixed with Expectations for Obama," *New York Times*, Jan. 20, 2013, https://www.nytimes.com/2013 /01/21/us/politics/blacks-see-new-patience-and-high-expectations-for -obama.html; Zerlina Maxwell, "What Can Black America Expect from

a New Obama Term?," TheGrio.com, Nov. 7, 2012, https://thegrio.com/2012/11/07/what-can-black-america-expect-from-a-2nd-obama-term/.

4. Ta-Nehisi Coates, "How the Obama Administration Talks to Black America," *Atlantic*, May 20, 2013, https://www.theatlantic.com/politics/archive/2013/05/how-the-obama-administration-talks-to-black-america/276015/; Jonathan Capehart, "Obama Can't Win with Some Black Critics," *Washington Post*, May 21, 2013, https://www.washingtonpost.com/blogs/post-partisan/wp/2013/05/21/obama-cant-win-with-some-black-critics/.

5. Jennifer Epstein, "Obama Diversity Disappoints Again," *Politico*, May 5, 2013, https://www.politico.com/story/2013/05/obama-diversity-disappoints-again-090922; Kevin Cirilli, "Rangel Hits Obama on Diversity," *Politico*, Jan. 10, 2013, https://www.politico.com/story/2013/01/charlie-rangel-hits-obama-on-diversity-086005; Eleanor Clift, "Congressional Black Caucus Is Unhappy with Obama's Cabinet Picks," *Daily Beast*, Mar. 22, 2013, https://www.thedailybeast.com/congressional-black-caucus-is-unhappy-with-obamas-cabinet-picks; Deborah Barfield Berry, "Lawmaker Raps Obama for Lack of Diversity in Top Posts," *USA Today*, Apr. 10, 2013, https://www.usatoday.com/story/news/politics/2013/04/10/thompson-chides-obama-diversity/2071979/; Jonathan Martin, "Black Pols Stymied in Obama Era," *Politico*, Apr. 29, 2013, https://www.politico.com/story/2013/04/black-pols-stymied-in-obama-era-090727.

6. Epstein, "Obama Diversity Disappoints Again"; Gillespie, *Race and the Obama Administration*, 95-112; Carrie Dann, "Obama Lauds DHS Pick Jeh Johnson as 'Cool and Calm Leader,'" NBC News, Oct. 18, 2013, https://www.nbcnews.com/politics/politics-news/obama-lauds-dhs-pick-jeh-johnson-cool-calm-leader-flna8C11418565; Carol D. Leonnig, "Secret Service Agrees to Pay $24 Million in Decades-Old Race-Bias Case Brought by Black Agents," *Washington Post*, Jan. 17, 2017, https://www.washingtonpost.com/politics/secret-service-agrees-to-pay-24-million-to-settle-decades-old-race-bias-case-brought-by-black-agents/2017/01/17/b386006e-dd23-11e6-ad42-f3375f271c9c_story.html.

7. Tim Devaney, "ATF Director Steps Down after Bullet Ban Controversy," TheHill.com, Mar. 20, 2015, https://thehill.com/regulation/administration/236423-atf-chief-to-step-down; "Education Secretary Approved," Associated Press, Mar. 14, 2016, https://www.nytimes.com/2016/03/15/us/education-secretary-approved.html; Michael Grunwald, "Obama vs. Teachers Unions: It's Still On," *Politico*, Oct. 2, 2015, https://www.politico.com/agenda/story/2015/10/obama-vs-teachers-unions-its-stilll-on-000264; Kate Taylor, "MaryEllen Elia Named New York State Education Commisioner," *New York Times*, May 26, 2015, https://www.nytimes.com/2015/05/27/nyregion/maryellen-elia-named-new-york-state-education-commissioner.html; "John B. King, Jr., Secretary of Education—Biography," US Department of Education, accessed Aug. 9, 2019, https://www2.ed.gov/news/staff/bios/king.html; Jonathan Zimmerman, "Education in the Age of Obama: The Paradox of Consensus," in Zelizer, *Presidency of Barack Obama*, 119-121;

Keli Goff, "Obama's 2nd-Term Team Diversifies," TheRoot.com, Apr. 1, 2013, https://www.theroot.com/obamas-2nd-term-team-diversifies-1790884598.

8. Jeff Duncan et al. to President Barack Obama, Nov. 19, 2012, http://jeffdun can.house.gov/sites/jeffduncan.house.gov/files/Rep.%20Duncan%20Letter %20to%20President%20Obama%20on%20Ambassador%20Susan%20Rice %20%2811.19.12%29.pdf; Laurie Ure, "Republicans Increase Pressure on Obama over Rice," CNN, Nov. 20, 2012, https://www.cnn.com/2012/11 /20/politics/benghazi-house-letter/; Susan E. Rice to President Barack Obama, Dec. 13, 2012, http://i2.cdn.turner.com/cnn/2012/images/12/13 /ser.letter.pdf; "Susan Rice Withdraws from Consideration as Secretary of State," CNN, Dec. 14, 2012, https://www.cnn.com/2012/12/13/politics /rice-withdraws-secretary-of-state/index.html; Rice, *Tough Love*, 306-332; Steve Holland and Mark Felsenthal, "Obama Picks Loyalist Susan Rice as National Security Advisor," Reuters, June 5, 2013, https://www.reuters .com/article/us-obama-security-rice/obama-picks-loyalist-susan-rice-as -national-security-adviser-idUSBRE9540MM20130605.

9. Josh Hicks, "Davita Vance-Cooks Confirmed as First Female and African American Public Printer," *Washington Post*, Aug. 2, 2013, https://www.wash ingtonpost.com/news/federal-eye/wp/2013/08/02/davita-vance-cooks-con firmed-as-first-female-and-african-american-public-printer/; Vance-Cooks interview; Mario Trujillo, "Obama Nominates First Black, Female Librarian of Congress," TheHill.com, Feb. 24, 2016, https://thehill.com/policy/tech nology/270598-obama-nominates-first-black-female-librarian-of-congress; Nicholas Fandos, "New Librarian of Congress Offers a History Lesson in Her Own Right," *New York Times*, Sept. 14, 2016, https://www.nytimes .com/2016/09/15/us/librarian-of-congress-carla-hayden.html; "Navy Has Its First Female Four-Star Admiral," Associated Press, July 1, 2014, https://www .washingtonexaminer.com/navy-has-its-first-female-four-star-admiral; Car- rie Healey, "Navy Names First Female 4-Star Admiral," TheGrio.com, Dec. 16, 2013, https://thegrio.com/2013/12/16/navy-names-first-female-4-star-ad miral/; Brett Barrouquere, "Army Promotes Highest-Ranking Black Woman," Associated Press, Sept. 30, 2011, https://www.phillytrib.com/news/army -promotes-highest-ranking-black-woman/article_669484b8-7e52-50d9 -ba65-ab60295f1cc7.html; Helena Andrews-Dyer, "Deesha Dyer Named the New White House Social Secretary," *Washington Post*, Apr. 16, 2015, https:// www.washingtonpost.com/news/reliable-source/wp/2015/04/16/deesha-dyer -is-the-new-white-house-social-secretary/; Goff, "Obama's 2nd-Term Team Diversifies"; Emily Heil and Al Kamen, "Obama's Second-Term Cabinet: Few Women, Minorities," *Washington Post*, May 2, 2013, https://www.wash ingtonpost.com/blogs/in-the-loop/post/obamas-second-term-cabinet-fewer -women-minorities/2013/05/02/439c962c-b32f-11e2-9a98-4be1688d7d84 _blog.html; Brian Resnick and Brian McGill, "White Males Are a Minor- ity among Top Obama Administration Officials," *Atlantic*, July 19, 2013, https://www.theatlantic.com/politics/archive/2013/07/white-males-are-a -minority-among-top-obama-administration-officials/454542/.

10. "Holder Hospitalized and Released after Shortness of Breath," NBC News, Feb. 27, 2014, https://www.nbcnews.com/news/us-news/holder-hospitalized -released-after-shortness-breath-n40186; Josh Gerstein, "Eric Holder Discharged from Hospital," *Politico*, Feb. 28, 2014, https://www.politico.com /story/2014/02/attorney-general-eric-holder-hospitalized-104039; Glenn Thrush, "The Survivor," *Politico*, July–Aug. 2014, http://www.politico.com /magazine/story/2014/06/the-survivor-108018_full.html.

11. Mario Trujillo, "Holder Says GOP Treats Him Differently," TheHill.com, Apr. 10, 2014, https://thehill.com/blogs/blog-briefing-room/news/203174 -holder-what-attorney-general-has-ever-had-to-deal-with-that; Shadee Ashtari, "Blake Farenthold Introduces Bill to Withhold Eric Holder's Paycheck," *Huffington Post*, Apr. 17, 2014, https://www.huffpost.com/entry /blake-farenthold-eric-holder-paycheck_n_5161891; Nia-Malika Henderson, "Eric Holder Explains His (and Obama's) 'Cool' Demeanor," *Washington Post*, Feb. 9, 2015, https://www.washingtonpost.com/news/the-fix /wp/2015/02/09/eric-holder-explains-his-and-obamas-cool-demeanor/; Seung Min Kim, "Holder Blasts Palin over Impeachment Call," *Politico*, July 13, 2014, https://www.politico.com/blogs/politico-now/2014/07/holder -blasts-palin-over-impeachment-call-192002; Justin Sink, "Holder Sees 'Racial Animus' in Opposition," TheHill.com, July 13, 2014, https://the hill.com/blogs/blog-briefing-room/news/212082-holder-sees-racial-animus -in-opposition.

12. Nedra Pickler, "Holder Resigning: Attorney General Backed Rights," Associated Press, Sept. 25, 2014, https://apnews.com/71f05d22e0e14afd83521170f 41d2e81; Nirvi Shah and Maggie Severns, "Education, Segregation and the W.H.," *Politico*, May 17, 2014, https://www.politico.com/story/2014/05 /brown-board-of-education-barack-obama-106781; Rich Benjamin, "Obama's Safe, Overrated and Airy Speech," *Salon*, July 20, 2013, https://www.salon .com/2013/07/19/obamas_safe_overrated_and_airy_speech/; "Remarks on the Resignation of Attorney General Eric H. Holder, Jr.," Sept. 25, 2014, in Obama, *Public Papers*, 2:1231-1234; Dyson, *Black Presidency*, 233-234; David Nather, "Holder's Real Legacy," *Politico*, Sept. 25, 2014, https://www.politi co.com/story/2014/09/eric-holder-legacy-111330.

13. Pickler, "Holder Resigning"; Devlin Barrett, "Same Issues to Greet Eric Holder's Successor as Attorney General," *Wall Street Journal*, Sept. 25, 2014, https://www.wsj.com/articles/u-s-attorney-general-eric-holder-to-step-down -1411656836; Josh Gerstein, "Comey Vows Fight as FBI Minority Agent Numbers Slip," *Politico*, May 16, 2016, https://www.politico.com/blogs /under-the-radar/2016/05/james-comey-fbi-minority-agents-223234; Eisinger, *Chickenshit Club*, xvii–xx; Thrush, "The Survivor"; Timothy M. Phelps, "Atty. Gen. Eric Holder Reinvigorated to Pursue His Goals," *Los Angeles Times*, Feb. 15, 2014, https://www.latimes.com/nation/la-xpm-2014 -feb-15-la-na-holder-profile-20140216-story.html; Obama, *A Promised Land*, 292; C. Eugene Emery Jr., "Hillary Clinton: Barack Obama Set New Wall Street Fundraising Record when He First Ran for President," PolitiFact,

Mar. 7, 2016, https://www.politifact.com/truth-o-meter/statements/2016 /mar/07/hillary-clinton/hillary-clinton-barack-obama-set-new-wall-street-f/; "Sen. Barack Obama—Illinois," Center for Responsive Politics, accessed Aug. 11, 2019, https://www.opensecrets.org/members-of-congress/summary ?cid=N00009638&cycle=CAREER; Peter Nicholas and Daniel Lippman, "Wall Street Is Still Giving to President," *Wall Street Journal*, July 3, 2012, https://www.wsj.com/articles/SB10001424052702303933404577500081074098 5338; Philip Bump, "How 'Dodd-Frank' Is Becoming the New 'Obamacare,'" *Washington Post*, Oct. 30, 2014, https://www.washingtonpost.com/news /the-fix/wp/2014/10/30/how-dodd-frank-is-becoming-the-new-obamacare/; Alan Rappeport, "Bill to Erase Some Dodd-Frank Banking Rules Passes in House," *New York Times*, June 8, 2017, https://www.nytimes.com/2017/06 /08/business/dealbook/house-financial-regulations-dodd-frank.html; Nather, "Holder's Real Legacy."

14. Aruna Viswanatha and Roberta Rampton, "Obama Picks Brooklyn Prosecutor Lynch for Attorney General," Reuters, Nov. 7, 2014, https://www .reuters.com/article/us-usa-justice-lynch/obama-picks-brooklyn-prosecutor -lynch-for-attorney-general-idUSKBN0IR1RR20141108; Stephanie Clifford, "Loretta Lynch, a Nominee for Attorney General, Is Praised for Substance, Not Flash," *New York Times*, Nov. 8, 2014, https://www.nytimes .com/2014/11/09/us/politics/in-line-to-be-attorney-general-loretta-lynch -at-home-in-glare.html; Athena Jones, "Democrats Refuse to Take Back Charges of Racism over Lynch Nom," CNN, Mar. 21, 2015, https://www .cnn.com/2015/03/19/politics/loretta-lynch-nomination-racism-democrats /index.html; Seung Min Kim and Burgess Everett, "Loretta Lynch Supporters Stage Hunger Strike to Urge Confirmation," *Politico*, Apr. 15, 2015, https://www.politico.com/story/2015/04/loretta-lynch-supporters-hunger -strike-confirmation-116994; "Campaign to 'Confirm Lynch Fast': Women Civil Rights Leaders Join National Action Network in Launching Fast to Confirm Loretta Lynch as Attorney General after Historic Delay," National Action Network, Apr. 15, 2015, https://nationalactionnetwork.net /featured/campaign-to-confirm-lynch-fast-women-civil-rights-leaders-join -national-action-network-in-launching-fast-to-confirm-loretta-lynch-as -attorney-general-after-historic-delay/; Seung Min Kim, "Obama: Lynch Delay 'Embarrassing,'" *Politico*, Apr. 17, 2015, https://www.politico.com /story/2015/04/barack-obama-delaying-loretta-lynch-vote-embarrassing -gop-117081; Athena Jones, "Black Women, Lynch Supporters Confront McConnell Aide," CNN, Apr. 17, 2015, https://www.cnn.com/2015/04/15 /politics/loretta-lynch-mitch-mcconnell nomination/index.html; Sari Horwitz, "Race Creeps into Debate over Stalled Nomination for Attorney General," *Washington Post*, Apr. 17, 2015, https://www.washingtonpost.com/ world/national-security/race-creeps-into-stalled-vote-on-nominee-for-attor ney-general/2015/04/17/0a7cec24-e51a-11e4-b510-962fcfabc310_story.html; Athena Jones, "Black Men Descend on the Capitol to Push for Big 'Yes' Vote on Lynch," CNN, Apr. 22, 2015, https://www.cnn.com/2015/04/22

/politics/loretta-lynch-vote-black-support/index.html; Athena Jones, "Loretta Lynch Makes History," CNN, Apr. 27, 2015, https://www.cnn.com /2015/04/23/politics/loretta-lynch-attorney-general-vote/index.html; Michael Hirsh, "What Made Loretta Lynch's Father See Red," *Politico*, Apr. 23, 2015, https://www.politico.com/story/2015/04/what-made-loretta-lynchs -father-see-red-117308.

15. George E. Condon Jr. and Jim O'Sullivan, "Has Obama Done Enough for Black Americans?," *National Journal*, Apr. 5, 2013, https://www.theatlantic .com/politics/archive/2013/04/has-president-obama-done-enough-for -black-americans/274699/.

16. Jennifer Epstein, "After Gripes, Congressional Black Caucus Says Meeting with Obama Satisfied," *Politico*, July 9, 2013, https://www.politico.com /blogs/politico44/47?tab=most-read; "Readout of the Congressional Black Caucus' Meeting with President Obama," CBC, July 9, 2013, https://cbc .house.gov/news/documentsingle.aspx?DocumentID=117; "Readout of the President's Meeting with the Congressional Black Caucus," White House, July 9, 2013, https://obamawhitehouse.archives.gov/the-press-office/2013 /07/09/readout-president-s-meeting-congressional-black-caucus; Nedra Pickler, "Black Caucus Expressing No Hard Feelings for Obama," Associated Press, July 9, 2013, https://apnews.com/cd4be8f32f2842bea312797 e734d4f51.

17. John Gramlich, "Trump Has Appointed a Larger Share of Female Judges than Other GOP Presidents, but Lags Obama," Pew Research Center, Oct. 2, 2018, https://www.pewresearch.org/fact-tank/2018/10/02/trump-has -appointed-a-larger-share-of-female-judges-than-other-gop-presidents -but-lags-obama/; Catherine Lucey and Meghan Hoyer, "Trump Choosing White Men as Judges, Highest Rate in Decades," Associated Press, Nov. 13, 2017, https://www.apnews.com/a2c7a89828c747ed9439f60e4a89193e; Mike Dorning, "Obama Irks Allies in Judge Picks as Diversity Hits Record," *Bloomberg*, Apr. 24, 2014, https://www.bloomberg.com/news/articles/2014 -04-24/obama-irks-allies-in-judge-picks-as-diversity-hits-record; David A. Love "President Obama's Mixed Record of Minority Judicial Appointees," TheGrio.com, Feb. 6, 2014, https://thegrio.com/2014/02/06/president -obamas-mixed-record-of-minority-judicial-appointees/.

18. Jonathan Allen, "Civil Rights Leaders to Hit Obama," *Politico*, Dec. 23, 2013, https://www.politico.com/story/2013/12/civil-rights-leaders-to-hit-obama -on-judges-101473; Mike Lillis, "Black Lawmakers to Go after Obama," TheHill.com, Jan. 26, 2014, https://thehill.com/homenews/house/196385 -black-lawmakers-to-go-after-obama-at-presser; Mike Lillis, "Amid Pushback, Jarrett to Meet Black Democrats on Obama's Judicial Picks," TheHill.com, Feb. 5, 2014, https://thehill.com/homenews/house/197481 -jarrett-to-meet-cbc-on-judges; "The Complicated History of the Voter ID Law in Georgia," TheGrio.com, Apr. 3, 2012, https://thegrio.com/2012/04 /03/the-complicated-history-of-the-voter-id-law-in-georgia/; "Rep. David Scott: President Obama Shows 'Disrespect' with Judicial Nominees," TheGrio.com, Feb. 27, 2014, https://thegrio.com/2014/02/27/rep-david

-scott-president-obama-shows-disrespect-with-judicial-nominee/; Molly
K. Hooper, "Dem. Lawmaker: White House Is Being 'Dishonest,'"
TheHill.com, Feb. 28, 2014, https://thehill.com/video/house/199504-dem
-lawmaker-white-house-is-being-dishonest; Carl Hulse, "Post-Filibuster,
Obama Faces New Anger over Judicial Choices," *New York Times*, Feb. 28,
2014, A1; Lauren French, "Lewis Opposes Boggs Nomination," *Politico*, May
19, 2014, https://www.politico.com/story/2014/05/john-lewis-michael-boggs
-oppose-judge-nomination-georgia-106839; Peter Sullivan, "Obama Drops
Nominee Opposed by CBC," TheHill.com, Dec. 31, 2014, http://thehill
.com/blogs/blog briefing-room/228303-obama-drops-controversial-nominee
-opposed-by-black-caucus.
19. Justin Sink, "Obama Endorses Conyers for Reelection," TheHill.com, May
15, 2014, https://thehill.com/blogs/ballot-box/house-races/206256-obama
-endorses-conyers-for-reelection; Kendall Breitman, "Clyburn: GOP Will
Try to Impeach President Obama," *Politico*, Nov. 12, 2014, https://www
.politico.com/story/2014/11/rep-jim-clyburn-gop-impeach-obama-112789;
Jim Kuhnhenn, "Obama Makes Trade Pitch to Congressional Black Caucus," Associated Press, Feb. 10, 2015, https://apnews.com/f1b9471b5ab14119
88d9c212a252abab.

CHAPTER 15. A SECOND WIND

1. Jon Hurdle and Peter Baker, "Despite 'Enormous Strides,' Minorities Still
Face Barriers, President Says," *New York Times*, Aug. 23, 2013, https://www
.nytimes.com/2013/08/24/us/politics/despite-strides-minorities-still-face
-barriers-obama-says.html; Perry Bacon Jr., "In Wake of Police Shootings, Obama Speaks More Bluntly about Race," NBC News, Jan. 3, 2015,
https://www.nbcnews.com/politics/barack-obama/wake-police-shootings
-obama-speaks-more bluntly-about-race-n278616; "Remarks at the 'Let
Freedom Ring' Ceremony Commemorating the 50th Anniversary of the
March on Washington for Jobs and Freedom," Aug. 28, 2013, in Obama,
Public Papers, 2:974–978; Ta-Nehisi Coates, "'Better Is Good': Obama on
Reparations, Civil Rights, and the Art of the Possible," *Atlantic*, Dec. 21,
2016, https://www.theatlantic.com/politics/archive/2016/12/ta-nehisi
-coates-obama-transcript-ii/511133/.
2. Alex Roarty, "Poll: Minorities Provide Bulk of Support for Obamacare,"
Atlantic, Nov. 21, 2013, https://www.theatlantic.com/politics/archive/2013
/11/poll-minorities-provide-bulk-of-support-for-obamacare/435993/; Jessica
C. Smith and Carla Medalia, "Health Insurance Coverage in the United
States: 2014," US Census Bureau, Sept. 16, 2015, https://www.census.gov
/library/publications/2015/demo/p60-253.html; "More Americans Dis-
approve than Approve of Health Care Law," Pew Research Center, Apr. 27,
2016, https://www.people-press.org/2016/04/27/more-americans-disapprove
-than-approve-of-health-care-law/; Jenna Levy, "U.S. Uninsured Rate Continues to Fall," Gallup, Mar. 10, 2014, https://news.gallup.com/poll/167798
/uninsured-rate-continues-fall.aspx; Jenna Levy, "In U.S., Uninsured Rate

Dips to 11.9% in First Quarter," Gallup, Apr. 13, 2015, https://news.gallup
.com/poll/182348/uninsured-rate-dips-first-quarter.aspx.

3. The House Republicans filed their lawsuit against the president on November 21, 2014. It ultimately had no impact on the implementation or enforcement of the ACA. Michael R. Crittenden and Colleen McCain Nelson, "House Votes to Authorize Boehner to Sue Obama," *Wall Street Journal*, July 30, 2014, https://www.wsj.com/articles/house-votes-to-authorize-bodhner-to-sue-obama-1406760762; Lauren French and Josh Gerstein, "House Files Obamacare Lawsuit," *Politico*, Nov. 21, 2014, https://www.politico.com/story/2014/11/house-files-obamacare-lawsuit-113089; US Department of Health and Human Services, *Health Insurance Marketplace*; Sabrina Tavernise and Robert Gebeloff, "Millions of Poor Are Left Uncovered by Health Law," *New York Times*, Oct. 3, 2013, A1, A18; Phil McCausland, "Residents Suffer as Mississippi and 13 Other States Debate Medicaid Expansion," NBC News, Nov. 4, 2019, https://www.nbcnews.com/news/us-news/residents-suffer-mississippi-13-other-states-debate-medicaid-expansion-n1075661; "The State of US Health, 1990-2016: Burden of Diseases, Injuries, and Risk Factors among US States," JAMA Network, Apr. 10, 2018, https://jamanetwork.com/journals/jama/fullarticle/2678018; Ryan Sit, "Mississippi Has the Highest Infant Mortality Rate and Is Expected to Pass the Nation's Strictest Abortion Bill," *Newsweek*, Mar. 19, 2018, https://www.newsweek.com/mississippi-abortion-bill-strictest-infant-child-health-851178.

4. "Distribution of the Nonelderly Uninsured by Race/Ethnicity" (2017), Henry J. Kaiser Family Foundation, accessed Aug. 14, 2019, https://www.kff.org/uninsured/state-indicator/distribution-by-raceethnicity-2/?current Timeframe=0&sortModel=%7B%22colId%22:%22Location%22,%22sort %22:%22asc%22%7D.

5. Jens Manuel Krogstad and Richard Fry, "Dept. of Ed. Projects Public Schools Will Be 'Majority-Minority' This Fall," Pew Research Center, Aug. 18, 2014, https://www.pewresearch.org/fact-tank/2014/08/18/u-s-public-schools-expected-to-be-majority-minority-starting-this-fall/; "Expansive Survey of America's Public Schools Reveals Troubling Racial Disparities," US Department of Education, Mar. 21, 2014, https://www.ed.gov/news/press-releases/expansive-survey-americas-public-schools-reveals-troubling-racial-disparities; Motoko Rich, "Analysis Finds Higher Expulsion Rates for Black Students," *New York Times*, Aug. 24, 2015, https://www.nytimes.com/2015/08/25/us/higher-expulsion-rates-for-black-students-are-found.html; US Government Accountability Office, *K-12 Education*; Smith and Harper, *Disproportionate Impact of K-12 School Suspension*; Nirvi Shah and Maggie Severns, "Education, Segregation and the W.H.," *Politico*, May 17, 2014, https://www.politico.com/story/2014/05/brown-board-of-education-barack-obama-106781; David Hudson, "The President Proposes to Make Community College Free for Responsible Students for 2 Years," White House, Jan. 8, 2015, https://obamawhitehouse.archives.gov/blog/2015/01/08/president-proposes-make-community-college-free-responsible-students-2-years.

6. Obama quote from "Fact Sheet: President Obama's Promise Zones Initiative," White House, Jan. 8, 2014, https://obamawhitehouse.archives.gov/the-press -office/2014/01/08/fact-sheet-president-obama-s-promise-zones-initiative.

7. "Address before a Joint Session of the Congress on the State of the Union," Feb. 12, 2013, in Obama, *Public Papers*, 1:97-106; Tom Curry, "Obama Makes Pitch for 'Promise Zones' to Boost Depressed Areas," NBC News, Jan. 9, 2014, https://www.nbcnews.com/politics/politics-news/obama-makes-pitch -promise-zones-boost-depressed-areas-flna2D11889282; "Obama Adminis- tration Announces Final Round of Promise Zone Designations to Expand Access to Opportunity in Urban, Rural and Tribal Communities," White House, June 6, 2016, https://obamawhitehouse.archives.gov/the-press-off ice/2016/06/06/obama-administration-announces-final-round-promise-zone -designations; Tyrone R. Williams, "Another Voice: Promise Zone Helps Transform Challenged Neighborhoods," *Sacramento Business Journal*, June 21, 2019, https://www.bizjournals.com/sacramento/news/2019/06/21/another -voice-promise-zone-helps-transform.html.

8. Noam Scheiber, "As His Term Wanes, Obama Champions Workers' Rights," *New York Times*, Aug. 31, 2015, https://www.nytimes.com/2015/09/01/busi ness/economy/as-his-term-wanes-obama-restores-workers-rights.html; "Exe- cutive Order—Minimum Wage for Contractors," White House, Feb. 12, 2014, https://obamawhitehouse.archives.gov/the-press-office/2014/02/12 /executive-order-minimum-wage-contractors; Bureau of Labor Statistics, US Department of Labor, "Labor Force Statistics from the Current Popu- lation Survey," accessed Aug. 4, 2019, https://data.bls.gov/timeseries/lns 14000006.

9. David Remnick, "Going the Distance," *New Yorker*, Jan. 27, 2014, 40-61; James Oliphant, "Obama Faces Up to Policy Limits on U.S. Urban Ills," Reuters, Apr. 29, 2015, https://www.reuters.com/article/us-usa-police-balti more-obama-policy/obama-faces-up-to-policy-limits-on-u-s-urban-ills-id USKBN0NK0BC20150429.

10. Sari Horwitz, "Holder Seeks to Avert Mandatory Minimum Sentences for Some Low-Level Drug Offenders," *Washington Post*, Aug. 12, 2013, https:// www.washingtonpost.com/world/national-security/holder-seeks-to-avert -mandatory-minimum-sentences-for-some-low-level-drug-offenders/2013 /08/11/343850c2-012c-11e3-96a8-d3b921c0924a_story.html; Charlie Savage, "Justice Dept. Seeks to Curtail Stiff Drug Sentences," *New York Times*, Aug. 12, 2013, https://www.nytimes.com/2013/08/12/us/justice-dept-seeks -to-curtail-stiff-drug-sentences.html; "The Attorney General's Smart on Crime Initiative," US Department of Justice, Mar. 9, 2017, https://www .justice.gov/archives/ag/attorney-generals-smart-crime-initiative.

11. Charlie Savage, "U.S. Orders More Steps to Curb Stiff Drug Sentences," *New York Times*, Sept. 20, 2013, A6; Horwitz, "Holder Seeks to Avert Man- datory Minimum Sentences"; Savage, "Justice Dept. Seeks to Curtail Stiff Drug Sentences."

12. Matt Apuzzo, "New Rules Permit Early Release for Thousands of Drug Of- fenders," *New York Times*, July 18, 2014, https://www.nytimes.com/2014

/07/19/us/new-rule-permits-early-release-for-thousands-of-drug-offenders
.html; Ryan J. Reilly, "An Obscure Commission Just Voted to Shorten the
Sentences of 46,000 Federal Drug Offenders," *Huffington Post*, July 18, 2014,
https://www.huffpost.com/entry/drug-sentencing-retroactivity_n_5600121.

13. Federal Bureau of Prisons, "Statistics," accessed Aug. 20, 2019, https://www
.bop.gov/about/statistics/population_statistics.jsp; Bronson and Carson, *Prisoners in 2017*; Carson, *Prisoners in 2018*; John Gramlich, "The Gap between
the Number of Blacks and Whites in Prison Is Shrinking," Pew Research
Center, Apr. 30, 2019, https://www.pewresearch.org/fact-tank/2019/04/30
/shrinking-gap-between-number-of-blacks-and-whites-in-prison/.

14. Although he instructed the Office of Personnel Management to forgo inquiring about criminal records early in the hiring process for federal jobs,
Obama declined to "ban the box" outright for employers filling federal contracts. Instead, he awaited a congressional fix that would carry more weight
and permanency than an executive order. Peter Baker, "Obama Takes Steps
to Help Former Inmates Find Jobs and Homes," *New York Times*, Nov. 2,
2015, https://www.nytimes.com/2015/11/03/us/obama-prisoners-jobs-housing
.html; Halimah Abdullah, "Obama Visits Prison in Push for Reforms,"
NBC News, July 16, 2015, https://www.nbcnews.com/news/us-news/obama
-set-visit-oklahoma-prison-push-criminal-justice-reform-n393056; Obama,
"President's Role," 847–848; "Remarks by the President at the NAACP Conference," White House, July 14, 2015, https://obamawhitehouse.archives.gov
/the-press-office/2015/07/14/remarks-president-naacp-conference; Nick Anderson, "Feds Announce New Experiment: Pell Grants for Prisoners," *Washington Post*, July 31, 2015, https://www.washingtonpost.com/news/grade
-point/wp/2015/07/31/feds-announce-new-experiment-pell-grants-for-pri
soners/; Barack Obama, "Why We Must Rethink Solitary Confinement,"
Washington Post, Jan. 25, 2016, https://www.washingtonpost.com/opinions
/barack-obama-why-we-must-rethink-solitary-confinement/2016/01/25/29
a361f2-c384-11e5-8965-0607e0e265ce_story.html; Deputy Attorney General
Sally Q. Yates, Memorandum for the Acting Director, Federal Bureau of
Prisons, Aug. 18, 2016, https://assets.documentcloud.org/documents/302
7877/Justice-Department-memo-announcing-announcing.pdf.

15. Josh Gerstein, "Holder: W.H. to Widen Drug Clemency," *Politico*, Apr. 21,
2014, https://www.politico.com/story/2014/04/eric-holder-barack-obama
-drug-clemency-105865; Julia Edwards and Aruna Viswanatha, "U.S. Justice
Department Announces Clemency Review of Drug Offenders," Reuters,
Apr. 23, 2014, https://www.reuters.com/article/us-usa-justice-clemency/u-s
-justice-department-announces-clemency-review-of-drug-offenders-idUS
BREA3M1CR20140423; Crouch, "Barack Obama and the Clemency Power";
Ryan J. Reilly, "Obama Has Pardoned Almost as Many Turkeys as Drug
Offenders," *Huffington Post*, Nov. 27, 2013, https://www.huffpost.com/en
try/obama-pardons_n_4345849; Matt Apuzzo, "Justice Dept. Starts Quest
for Inmates to Be Freed," *New York Times*, Jan. 30, 2014, https://www.ny
times.com/2014/01/31/us/politics/white-house-seeks-drug-clemency-can

didates.html; Philip Rucker, "Obama Grants Pardons to 17 People for Non-violent Offenses," *Washington Post*, Mar. 1, 2013, https://www.washington post.com/politics/obama-grants-pardons-to-17-people-for-nonviolent-offen ses/2013/03/01/1932107e-82bf-11e2-a350-49866afab584_story.html; US De-partment of Justice, "Clemency Statistics," accessed Aug. 21, 2019, https:// www.justice.gov/pardon/clemency-statistics; Gregory Korte, "Obama Ac-cused of Shirking Pardon Duties," *USA Today*, Feb. 4, 2015, 1A; Leah Li-bresco, "Obama Begins to Catch Up with Clemency Pleas," FiveThirtyEight .com, Mar. 31, 2015, https://fivethirtyeight.com/features/obama-begins-to -catch-up-with-clemency-pleas/; Sari Horwitz, "Lack of Resources, Bureau-cratic Tangles Have Bogged Down Obama's Clemency Efforts," *Washing-ton Post*, May 6, 2016, https://www.washingtonpost.com/politics/courts _law/lack-of-resources-bureaucratic-tangles-have-bogged-down-obamas -clemency-efforts/2016/05/06/9271a73a-1202-11e6-93ae-50921721165d_story .html; Peter Baker, "Obama Plans Broader Use of Clemency to Free Non-violent Drug Offenders," *New York Times*, July 3, 2015, https://www.ny times.com/2015/07/04/us/obama-plans-broader-use-of-clemency-to-free -nonviolent-drug-offenders.html; Josh Gerstein, "Obama's Drug-Sentenc-ing Quagmire," *Politico*, Jan. 5, 2015, https://www.politico.com/story/2015 /01/barack-obama-drug-sentencing-policy-113954.

16. Franklin Roosevelt, elected to the presidency four times, holds the record for the most acts of presidential clemency, numbering 3,796. US Depart-ment of Justice, "Clemency Statistics"; John Gramlich and Kristen Bialik, "Obama Has Used Clemency Power More Often than Any President since Truman," Pew Research Center, Jan. 20, 2017, https://www.pewresearch.org /fact-tank/2017/01/20/obama-used-more-clemency-power/; Gregory Korte, "Obama Grants 95 Christmastime Pardons and Commutations," *USA Today*, Dec. 19, 2015, https://www.usatoday.com/story/news/nation/2015/12/18 /obama-commutations-pardons/77565676/; Sari Horwitz and Ann E. Mari-mow, "President Obama Grants Early Release to 61 More Federal Drug Offenders," *Washington Post*, Mar. 30, 2016, https://www.washingtonpost .com/world/national-security/president-obama-grants-early-release-to-61 -more-federal-drug-offenders/2016/03/30/7256bb60-f683-11e5-8b23-538270 a1ca31_story.html; Kevin Liptak, "Obama Shortens Sentences for More Drug Offenders," CNN, May 5, 2016, https://www.cnn.com/2016/05/05 /politics/obama-commutations-sentencing-reform/index.html; Greg Clary, "Obama Commutes Sentences for Dozens of Drug Offenders," CNN, June 3, 2016, https://www.cnn.com/2016/06/03/politics/obama-drug-offenders -prison-sentences/index.html; Neil Eggleston, "President Obama Com-mutes the Sentences of 214 Additional People," White House, Aug. 3, 2016, https://obamawhitehouse.archives.gov/blog/2016/08/03/president-obama -commutes-sentences-214-additional-people; "Obama Cuts Short the Sen-tences of 111 Federal Inmates," Associated Press, Aug. 30, 2016, https://www .chicagotribune.com/nation-world/ct-obama-commutes-drug-sentences -20160830-story.html; Gregory Korte, "For Obama, a Shift in Clemency

582   NOTE TO PAGE 370

Strategy," *USA Today*, Sept. 15, 2016, https://www.usatoday.com/story/news
/politics/2016/09/15/obama-shift-clemency-strategy/90255992/; Neil Eggleston, "102 Second Chances," White House, Oct. 6, 2016, https://obama
whitehouse.archives.gov/blog/2016/10/06/102-second-chances; Lydia
Wheeler and Jordan Fabian, "Obama Commutes Sentences of 98 Inmates,"
TheHill.com, Oct. 27, 2016, https://thehill.com/regulation/administration
/303125-obama-commutes-sentences-of-inmates; Kevin Freking, "Obama
Pardons 78, Shortens the Sentence for 153," Associated Press, Dec. 19, 2016,
https://www.apnews.com/91a2af333a0b41f99f9372ab3c3053c1; Neil Eggleston, "President Obama Has Now Granted More Commutations than Any
President in This Nation's History," White House, Jan. 17, 2017, https://
obamawhitehouse.archives.gov/blog/2017/01/17/president-obama-has-now
-granted-more-commutations-any-president-nations-history; Neil Eggleston,
"The Reinvigoration of the Clemency Authority," White House, Jan. 19,
2017, https://obamawhitehouse.archives.gov/blog/2017/01/19/reinvigoration
-clemency-authority; Obama, "President's Role," 837.
17. Gramlich and Bialik, "Obama Has Used Clemency"; Natalie Villacorta,
"Harry Reid, John McCain Push for Boxer Pardon," *Politico*, Feb. 13, 2014,
https://www.politico.com/story/2014/02/jack-johnson-pardon-harry-reid
-john-mccain-103485; Harper Neidig, "Reid, McCain Urge Obama to Pardon Former Boxer Jack Johnson," TheHill.com, July 2, 2016, https://the
hill.com/blogs/blog-briefing-room/news/286361-reid-mccain-urge-obama
-to-pardon-former-heavyweight-champ-jack; DeNeen L. Brown, "Obama
Leaves White House without Pardoning Black Nationalist Marcus Garvey,"
Washington Post, Jan. 21, 2017, https://www.washingtonpost.com/local
/obama-leaves-white-house-without-pardoning-black-nationalist-marcus
-garvey/2017/01/20/d8b6f044-d906-11e6-9a36-1d296534b31e_story.html;
Obama, "President's Role," 855-865; "Less Support for Death Penalty, Especially among Democrats," Pew Research Center, Apr. 16, 2015, https://
www.people-press.org/2015/04/16/less-support-for-death-penalty-especially
-among-democrats/; US Department of Justice, "Clemency Statistics";
Gillespie, *Race and the Obama Administration*, 89-94; Andrew Dugan, "Solid
Majority Continues to Support Death Penalty," Pew Research Center, Oct.
15, 2015, https://news.gallup.com/poll/186218/solid-majority-continue-sup
port-death-penalty.aspx; "List of Federal Death-Row Prisoners," Death Penalty Information Center, accessed Aug. 21, 2019, https://deathpenaltyinfo
.org/state-and-federal-info/federal-death-penalty/list-of-federal-death-row
-prisoners; Kathleen Hennessey, "Where's Death Penalty in Push for Criminal Justice Overhaul?," Associated Press, Nov. 26, 2015, https://apnews
.com/f9b47f7d72d541ab829670545744524f; "Exclusive: Obama Calls the
Death Penalty 'Deeply Troubling,'" Marshall Project, Oct. 23, 2015, https://
www.themarshallproject.org/2015/10/23/watch-obama-discuss-death-penalty
-racial-profiling-with-the-marshall-project; "Watch Obama Pardon Turkey
'Abe' for Thanksgiving," YouTube, accessed Aug. 21, 2019, https://www.you
tube.com/watch?v=kAViObmYzAk.

18. Jason Cherkis, "Election Problems Included Confusion, Intimidation, Untrained Poll Workers," *Huffington Post*, Nov. 12, 2012, https://www.huffpost .com/entry/election-problems-confusion-intimidation_n_2095384; Sobel, *High Cost of "Free" Photo Voter Identification*; Anderson, *One Person, No Vote*, 119; Daniel Weeks, "Why Are the Poor and Minorities Less Likely to Vote?," *Atlantic*, Jan. 10, 2014, https://www.theatlantic.com/politics /archive/2014/01/why-are-the-poor-and-minorities-less-likely-to-vote /282896/.

19. "Address before a Joint Session of the Congress on the State of the Union," Feb. 12, 2013, in Obama, *Public Papers*, 1:105; Pam Fessler, "Obama Forms Presidential Commission to Study Voting Problems," NPR, Mar. 28, 2013, https://www.npr.org/sections/itsallpolitics/2013/03/28/175605639/obama -forms-presidential-commission-to-study-voting-problems; Jackie Calmes, "U.S. Panel Suggests Ways to Reduce Voting Delays," *New York Times*, Jan. 23, 2014, A18; Presidential Commission on Election Administration, *American Voting Experience*.

20. David G. Savage, "Supreme Court Denies RNC Bid to End Voter Fraud Consent Decree," *Los Angeles Times*, Jan. 14, 2013, https://www.latimes.com /world/la-xpm-2013-jan-14-la-pn-supreme-court-rnc-voter-fraud-20130114 -story.html; *Shelby County, Ala. v. Holder*, 679 F. 3d 848 (2012), Leagle.com, accessed Aug. 23, 2019, https://www.leagle.com/decision/infco20120518150; Justin Sink, "Obama Calms Fears over Supreme Court Action on Voting Rights," TheHill.com, Feb. 22, 2013, https://thehill.com/blogs/blog-brief ing-room/news/284361-obama-calms-fears-over-supreme-court-action-on -voting-rights; Darlene Superville, "Obama: Keep Key Voting Rights Act Provision," Associated Press, Feb. 22, 2013, https://www.washingtonexam iner.com/obama-keep-key-voting-rights-act-provision; Amy Davidson Sorkin, "In Voting Rights, Scalia Sees a 'Racial Entitlement,'" *New Yorker*, Feb. 28, 2013, https://www.newyorker.com/news/amy-davidson/in-voting-rights -scalia-sees-a-racial-entitlement; Liz Goodwin, "Civil Rights Leaders Outraged over Scalia's 'Racial Entitlement' Argument," Yahoo! News, Feb. 28, 2013, https://www.yahoo.com/news/blogs/ticket/civil-rights-leaders-out raged-over-scalia-racial-entitlement-172338534—election.html.

21. Ryan J. Reilly, "Desiline Victor, Obama's 102-Year-Old Voter, 'Shocked' by Scalia's 'Racial Entitlement' Remark," *Huffington Post*, Mar. 18, 2013, https:// www.huffpost.com/entry/desiline-victor-obamas-10_n_2901246; Carli Teproff, "Woman Who Earned Praise from Obama after Waiting in Line for Hours to Vote Dies at 106," *Miami Herald*, Oct. 2, 2017, https://www .miamiherald.com/news/local/obituaries/article176489296.html.

22. Darren Samuelsohn and Josh Gerstein, "Voting Rights Provision Struck Down," *Politico*, June 26, 2013, https://www.politico.com/story/2013/06 /supreme-court-voting-rights-act-ruling-093324; *Shelby County, Ala. v. Holder*, 133 S. Ct. 2612 (2013), Leagle.com, accessed Aug. 23, 2019, https:// www.leagle.com/decision/insco20130625e09; Berman, *Give Us the Ballot*, 283, 303-304, 311.

23. Charlie Savage, "Justice Dept. Poised to File Lawsuit over Voter ID Law," *New York Times*, Sept. 30, 2013, A11, A15; Steven Yaccino and Lizette Alvarez, "New G.O.P. Bid to Limit Voting in Swing States," *New York Times*, Mar. 29, 2014, https://www.nytimes.com/2014/03/30/us/new-gop-bid-to-limit-voting-in-swing-states.html; Michael Wines, "The Student Vote Is Surging: So Are Efforts to Suppress It," *New York Times*, Oct. 24, 2019, https://www.nytimes.com/2019/10/24/us/voting-college-suppression.html; Melanie Eversley, "N.C. Republican Activist Resigns after Voter ID Remarks," *USA Today*, Oct. 25, 2013, https://www.usatoday.com/story/news/politics/2013/10/24/north-carolina-yelton-resigns/3184993/.

24. Robert Barnes, "Supreme Court Stops Use of Key Part of Voting Rights Act," *Washington Post*, June 25, 2013, https://www.washingtonpost.com/politics/supreme-court-stops-use-of-key-part-of-voting-rights-act/2013/06/25/26888528-dda5-11e2-b197-f248b21f94c4_story.html; Reid J. Epstein and Jennifer Epstein, "Obama: VRA Decision 'Small-Bore Stuff Compared to Lynching,' " *Politico*, July 29, 2013, https://www.politico.com/blogs/politico44/2013/07/obama-vra-decision-small-bore-stuff-compared-to-lynching-169443; Sam Baker, "Voting Rights Challenge in Texas Opens Up New Obama-GOP Fight," TheHill.com, July 25, 2013, https://thehill.com/homenews/administration/313583-dojs-texas-challenge-likely-for-other-states-; Savage, "Justice Dept. Poised to File Lawsuit," A11, A15; Gary Langer, "Many Criticize Voting Rights Ruling; Partisan Splits on Gay Marriage Continue," ABC News, July 3, 2013, https://abcnews.go.com/blogs/politics/2013/07/many-criticize-voting-rights-ruling-partisan-splits-on-gay-marriage-continue/; Adam Liptak, "Courts Strike Down Voter ID Laws in Wisconsin and Texas," *New York Times*, Oct. 9, 2014, https://www.nytimes.com/2014/10/10/us/politics/supreme-court-blocks-wisconsin-voter-id-law.html; Andrew Demillo, "Arkansas High Court Strikes Down Voter ID Law," Associated Press, Oct. 16, 2014, https://www.inquirer.com/philly/news/nation_world/20141016_Arkansas_high_court_strikes_down_voter_ID_law.html; Curtis Skinner, "Supreme Court Denies Request to Block Texas Voter ID Law," Reuters, Oct. 18, 2014, https://www.reuters.com/article/us-usa-court-texas-election/supreme-court-denies-request-to-block-texas-voter-id-law-idUSKCN0I708Z20141018; Josh Gerstein, "Supreme Court OKs North Carolina Voting Changes," *Politico*, Oct. 8, 2014, https://www.politico.com/blogs/under-the-radar/2014/10/supreme-court-oks-north-carolina-voting-changes-196787; "North Carolina NAACP v. McCrory," Brennan Center for Justice, May 15, 2017, https://www.brennancenter.org/legal-work/north-carolina-naacp-v-mccrory-amicus-brief; Hayley Munguia, "Voter ID Laws Are Now in 17 More States than They Were in 2000," FiveThirtyEight.com, Oct. 31, 2014, https://fivethirtyeight.com/features/voter-id-laws-are-now-in-17-more-states-than-they-were-in-2000/; Ben Kamisar, "Holder Sends Poll Watchers to 18 States," TheHill.com, Nov. 3, 2014, https://thehill.com/blogs/blog-briefing-room/news/222682-justice-to-send-monitors-to-18-states; Erik Eckholm and Richard Fausset, "Voters

Report Problems in a Number of States as New Limits Take Effect," *New York Times*, Nov. 5, 2014, P8; Trip Gabriel and Manny Fernandez, "Voter Laws Scrutinized for Impact on Midterms," *New York Times*, Nov. 19, 2014, A13, A16.

25. Priya Anand, "Many Republican No-Shows on VRA," *Politico*, July 17, 2013, https://www.politico.com/story/2013/07/many-republican-no-shows-on-vra-094383; Michael A. Memoli, "Bipartisan Group Begins Effort to Restore Parts of Voting Rights Act," *Chicago Tribune*, Jan. 16, 2014, https://www.chicagotribune.com/la-pn-bipartisan-group-voting-rights-act-20140116-story.html; Mike Lillis, "Republicans Slam Brakes on Voting Rights Bill," TheHill.com, Aug. 1, 2015, https://thehill.com/homenews/house/249959-republicans-slam-brakes-on-voting-rights-bill; Mike Lillis, "Dems Float Compromise Linking Confederate Flag to Voting Rights," TheHill.com, July 16, 2015, https://thehill.com/homenews/house/248222-dems-float-compromise-linking-confederate-flag-to-voting-rights.

26. Edward-Isaac Dovere, "Obama Honors 'Sacrifice in the Face of Wanton Violence,'" *Politico*, Mar. 7, 2015, https://www.politico.com/story/2015/03/obama-honors-sacrifice-in-the-face-of-wanton-violence-115858; Holly Yan, "Obama: Maybe It's Time for Mandatory Voting," CNN, Mar. 19, 2015, https://www.cnn.com/2015/03/19/politics/obama-mandatory-voting/index.html; Holloway, *Living in Infamy*; Pete Williams, "It's Time to Let Felons Vote, Holder Says," NBC News, Feb. 11, 2014, http://www.nbcnews.com/news/us-news/its-time-let-felons-vote-holder-says-n26906; Sheryl Gay Stolberg and Erik Eckholm, "Virginia Governor Restores Voting Rights to Felons," *New York Times*, Apr. 22, 2016, https://www.nytimes.com/2016/04/23/us/governor-terry-mcauliffe-virginia-voting-rights-convicted-felons.html.

27. Michael Wines, "As ID Laws Fall, Voters See New Barriers Rise," *New York Times*, Oct. 25, 2016, https://www.nytimes.com/2016/10/26/us/elections/voter-id-laws.html; Julia Harte, "Justice Department to Monitor Tuesday's Election in 28 States," Reuters, Nov. 7, 2016, https://www.reuters.com/article/us-usa-election-monitors-idUSKBN1321YW; Michael Wines, "After a Fraught Election, Questions over the Impact of a Balky Voting Process," *New York Times*, Nov. 12, 2016, https://www.nytimes.com/2016/11/13/us/politics/voter-registration-election-2016.html.

CHAPTER 16. "IF I HAD A SON"

1. Bryon Tau, "Obama: 'If I Had a Son, He'd Look like Trayvon,'" *Politico*, Mar. 23, 2012, https://www.politico.com/blogs/politico44/2012/03/obama-if-i-had-a-son-hed-look-like-trayvon-118439; Lane DeGregory, "Trayvon Martin's Killing Shatters Safety within Retreat at Twin Lakes in Sanford," *Tampa Bay Times*, Mar. 26, 2012, https://www.tampabay.com/news/humaninterest/trayvon-martins-killing-shatters-safety-within-retreat-at-twin-lakes-in/1221799/; Audra D. S. Burch and Laura Isensee, "Trayvon Martin: A Typical Teen Who Loved Video Games, Looked Forward to Prom," *Miami*

Herald, May 19, 2012, https://www.miamiherald.com/news/state/florida
/trayvon-martin/article1939761.html; Daniel Trotta, "Trayvon Martin:
Before the World Heard the Cries," Reuters, Apr. 3, 2012, https://www
.reuters.com/article/us-usa-florida-shooting-trayvon/trayvon-martin-
before-the-world-heard-the-cries-idUSBRE832oUK20120403; Deborah
Acosta, "What Trayvon Martin's Tweets Say about Him," *Miami Herald*,
Apr. 9, 2012, https://www.mcclatchydc.com/news/crime/article24727540
.html; "Trayvon Martin Shooting Death—Initial Police Reports and '911'
Call Transcript," *Chicago Tribune*, Mar. 27, 2012, https://blogs.chicago
tribune.com/news_columnists_ezorn/2012/03/trayvon-martin-shooting
-death-initial-police-reports.html; "Trayvon Martin 911 Call—Enhanced
Audio—Justice for Trayvon," YouTube, accessed Sept. 1, 2019, https://
www.youtube.com/watch?v=2KfiGcGhyjY.

2. Joseph Williams, "Black Leaders Press W.H. on Martin," *Politico*, Mar. 22,
2012, https://www.politico.com/story/2012/03/black-leaders-press-wh-on
-fla-shooting-074385.

3. Williams, "Black Leaders Press W.H. on Martin"; Jarrett, *Finding My Voice*,
275–276.

4. Jarrett, *Finding My Voice*, 275–276; Jamil Smith, "Obama: 'If I Had a Son,
He'd Look like Trayvon,'" msnbc.com, Mar. 23, 2012, https://www.msnbc
.com/melissa-harris-perry/obama-if-i-had-son-hed-look-t-msna35978;
"Obama: If I Had a Son He'd Look like Trayvon Martin," YouTube, accessed Dec. 23, 2020, https://www.youtube.com/watch?v=Yt_g5JPdP8Y.

5. Dan Merica, "Obama Says Martin's Death a Tragedy, Asks Nation to
Respect Call for Calm," CNN, July 15, 2013, https://www.cnn.com/2013
/07/14/politics/obama-zimmerman/index.html; Ruby Cramer, "275,000
People Have Already Signed NAACP Call for Civil Rights Charges against
George Zimmerman," *Buzzfeed*, July 14, 2013, https://www.buzzfeednews
.com/article/rubycramer/more-than-55000-people-have-already-signed
-naacp-call-for-ci; Emanuella Grinberg, "Anger, Sadness but 'Little Surprise' over Zimmerman Verdict," CNN, July 14, 2013, https://www.cnn
.com/2013/07/13/justice/zimmerman-verdict-reax/index.html; Jordy Yager
and Daniel Strauss, "Holder Attacks 'Stand Your Ground' Laws for Sowing 'Dangerous Conflict,'" TheHill.com, July 17, 2013, https://thehill.com
/video/administration/311461-holder-slams-stand-your-ground-law-in-wake
-of-zimmerman-ruling; Pete Williams and Tracy Connor, "Holder Speaks
Out against 'Stand Your Ground' Laws after Zimmerman Verdict," NBC
News, July 17, 2013, https://www.nbcnews.com/news/us-news/holder-speaks
-out-against-stand-your-ground-laws-after-zimmerman-flna6C10654061.

6. Keli Goff, "Obama Fails Black America and Trayvon," TheRoot.com, July
14 2013, https://www.theroot.com/obama-fails-black-america-and-trayvon
-1790884852; David Swerdlick, "Obama's Response to the Verdict Was
Right," TheRoot.com, July 15, 2013, https://www.theroot.com/obamas
-response-to-the-verdict-was-right-1790897304; Edward-Isaac Dovere,
"Obama Keeps Quiet on Race—Again," *Politico*, July 16, 2013, https://

www.politico.com/story/2013/07/obama-keeps-quiet-on-race-again-094
250; "Trayvon Martin's Mom Speaks Out on Verdict," CBS News, July 18,
2013, https://www.cbsnews.com/video/trayvon-martins-mom-speaks-out
-on-on-verdict-i-was-stunned/.

7. Obama quotes in "Remarks on the Verdict in *State of Florida v. George Zimmerman*," July 19, 2013, in Obama, *Public Papers*, 2:824-827; Glenn Thrush
and Carrie Budoff Brown, "Obama Weighs In on Race, Reluctantly," *Politico*, July 19, 2013, https://www.politico.com/story/2013/07/obama-weighs
-in-on-race-reluctantly-094495.

8. Anthea Butler, "The Speech We've Been Waiting For," *Politico*, July 19, 2013,
https://www.politico.com/story/2013/07/opinion-anthea-butler-barack
-obama-speech-094501; "July 21: Rick Snyder, Marc Morial, Marcia Fudge,
Tavis Smiley, Charles Ogletree, Michael Steele, Jennifer Granholm, David
Brooks, Chuck Todd" (transcript), NBC News, July 21, 2013, http://www
.nbcnews.com/id/52534530/ns/meet_the_press-transcripts/t/july-rick-snyder
-marc-morial-marcia-fudge-tavis-smiley-charles-ogletree-michael-steele-jen
nifer-granholm-david-brooks-chuck-todd/; Christine Armario, "Obama's
Remarks on Race Resonate with Many," Associated Press, July 20, 2013,
https://news.yahoo.com/obamas-remarks-race-resonate-many-025342716.
html; Justin Sink, "Report: Jay Z, Kanye West, Rolling Stones Join Wonder's Florida Boycott," TheHill.com, July 22, 2013, https://thehill.com/blogs
/blog-briefing-room/news/312559-report-kanye-west-rolling-stones-join
-stevie-wonders-florida-boycott; James Arkin, "Poll: Racial Split on Zimmerman Verdict," *Politico*, July 23, 2013, https://www.politico.com/story
/2013/07/george-zimmerman-trial-verdict-racial-split-poll-094604; Julia
Edwards, "U.S. Won't File Charges against George Zimmerman in Trayvon
Martin Death," Reuters, Feb. 24, 2015, https://www.reuters.com/article
/usa-florida-zimmerman-idUSL1N0VY28X20150224; Peter Williams, "Attorney General Holder to Call for Lower Bar in Civil Rights Prosecutions,"
NBC News, Feb. 27, 2015, https://www.nbcnews.com/news/us-news/at
torney-general-holder-call-lower-bar-civil-rights-prosecutions-n313856.

9. "Address before a Joint Session of the Congress on the State of the Union,"
Feb. 12, 2013, in Obama, *Public Papers*, 1:105; Tracy Connor and Andrew
Rafferty, "Two Charged with Murder in Hadiya Pendleton Shooting," NBC
News, Feb. 11, 2013, http://usnews.nbcnews.com/_news/2013/02/11/16930
158-two-charged-with-murder-in-hadiya-pendleton-shooting; Trymaine Lee,
"Two Gang Members Charged in Murder of Hadiya Pendleton," NBC
News, Feb. 12, 2013, https://www.msnbc.com/msnbc/two-gang-members
-charged-murder-hadiya-msna18772; Leah Hope, Eric Horng, and Megan
Hickey, "Mickiael Ward Found Guilty in Hadiya Pendleton Murder Trial,"
ABC7Chicago.com, Aug. 23, 2018, https://abc7chicago.com/mickiael-ward
-found-guilty-in-hadiya-pendleton-murder-trial/4038551/; "Chicago Was
Nation's Murder Capital in 2012: FBI," NBCChicago.com, Sept. 20, 2013,
https://www.nbcchicago.com/blogs/ward-room/chicago-fbi-homicide-report
-224396461.html; DeWayne Wickham, "Gun Violence Threatens Young

Blacks," *USA Today*, Feb. 11, 2013, https://www.usatoday.com/story/opinion/2013/02/11/dewayne-wickham-on-blacks-and-gun-violence/1906819/.

10. Philip Rucker, "Michelle Obama Mourns Slain Teenager at Chicago Funeral," *Washington Post*, Feb. 9, 2013, https://www.washingtonpost.com/politics/michelle-obama-heads-to-chicago-for-slain-teenagers-funeral/2013/02/09/418a9ea4-716e-11e2-8b8d-e0b59a1b8e2a_story.html; Donovan Slack, "Photo: Obama Meets the Pendletons," *Politico*, Feb. 13, 2013, https://www.politico.com/blogs/politico44/2013/02/photo-obama-meets-the-pendletons-156947; Jodi Kantor, "Change Comes: After 4 Years, Friends See Shifts in the Obamas," *New York Times*, Jan. 20, 2013, 1, 16.

11. Renita D. Young, "Chicago Marchers Urge Obama to Come Home to Address Gun Violence," Reuters, Feb. 2, 2013, https://www.reuters.com/article/us-usa-crime-chicago/chicago-marchers-urge-obama-to-come-home-to-address-gun-violence-idUSBRE91200X20130203; Rebekah Metzler, "President Obama Visits Chicago to Push for Gun Reforms," Reuters, Feb. 15, 2013, https://www.usnews.com/news/articles/2013/02/15/president-obama-visits-chicago-to-push-for-gun-reforms; Justin Sink, "Michelle Obama: Gun Violence Has Children Fearing Death Every Day," TheHill.com, May 3, 2013, https://thehill.com/blogs/blog-briefing-roo/news/297647-michelle-obama-gun-violence-makes-schoolchildren-fear-death-daily; Jonathan P. Hicks, "Chicago Gun Violence Prompts Protests from Morticians," BET.com, Mar. 12, 2013, https://www.bet.com/news/national/2013/03/12/chicago-gun-violence-prompts-protests-from-morticians.html.

12. "Tracking Chicago Homicide Victims," *Chicago Tribune*, Aug. 26, 2013, https://www.chicagotribune.com/news/breaking/ct-chicago-homicides-data-tracker-htmlstory.html; Ryan J. Foley and Eric Tucker, "Obama's Move on Guns May Have Only Modest Effect on Violence," Associated Press, Jan. 5, 2016, https://www.staugustine.com/news/2016-01-05/obamas-move-guns-may-have-only-modest-effect-violence.

13. "Moving Ferguson Forward," City of Ferguson, accessed Sept. 4, 2019, http://www.fergusoncity.com/141/City-History; Richard Rothstein, "The Making of Ferguson," Economic Policy Institute, Oct. 15, 2014, https://www.epi.org/publication/making-ferguson/; Pamela Engel, "These Maps of St. Louis Segregation Are Depressing," *Business Insider*, Aug. 15, 2014, https://www.businessinsider.com/colin-gordon-maps-white-flight-in-st-louis-2014-8; "Profile of General Population and Housing Characteristics: 2010" (Ferguson, MO), US Census Bureau, accessed Dec. 24, 2020, https://data.census.gov/cedsci/table?q=Profile%20of%20General%20Population%20and%20Housing%20Characteristics%3A%202010%20ferguson%20missouri&tid=ACSDP5Y2010.DP05.

14. "Poverty Status in the Past 12 Months, 2010-2014" (Ferguson, MO), US Census Bureau, accessed Dec. 24, 2020, https://data.census.gov/cedsci/table?q=Poverty%20Status%20in%20the%20Past%202012%20Months,%202010-2014%20Ferguson%20city,%20Missouri&g=1600000US2923986&tid=ACSST5Y2014.S1701&hidePreview=false; "Employment Status: 2014"

(Ferguson, MO), US Census Bureau, accessed Dec. 24, 2020, https://data
.census.gov/cedsci/table?q=Employment%20Status,%202014%20Ferguson
%20city,%20Missouri&g=1600000US2923986&tid=ACSST5Y2014.S230
1&hidePreview=false; "Demographic Characteristics for Occupied Housing Units, 2010" (Ferguson, MO), US Census Bureau, accessed Dec. 24,
2020, https://data.census.gov/cedsci/table?q=General%20Housing%20
Characteristics%202010%20Ferguson,%20Missouri&g=1600000US2923
986&tid=ACSST5Y2010.S2502&hidePreview=false; Bureau of Labor Statistics, US Department of Labor, "Labor Force Statistics from the Current Population Survey," accessed Aug. 4, 2019, https://data.bls.gov/time
series/lns14000006.

15. Office of the Missouri Attorney General, "2013 Vehicle Stops Executive
Summary," accessed Dec. 19, 2020, https://ago.mo.gov/home/vehicle-stops
-report/2013-executive-summary.

16. Eric Tucker, "U.S. Justice Dept. Announces Probe of Ferguson Police,"
Associated Press, Sept. 4, 2014, https://www.phillytrib.com/u-s-justice
-dept-announces-probe-of-ferguson-police/article_2676feec-ed6f-5670
-bd96-9eeccef20413.html; Office of Public Affairs, US Department of
Justice, "Justice Department Announces Findings of Two Civil Rights
Investigations in Ferguson, Missouri," Mar. 4, 2015, https://www.justice
.gov/opa/pr/justice-department-announces-findings-two-civil-rights
-investigations-ferguson-missouri; Office of Public Affairs, US Department of Justice, "Justice Department Files Lawsuit to Bring Constitutional Policing to Ferguson, Missouri," Feb. 10, 2016, https://www.jus
tice.gov/opa/pr/justice-department-files-lawsuit-bring-constitutional
-policing-ferguson-missouri; Jesse Washington, "Strong DOJ Response
to Ferguson Seeks Truth, Calm," Associated Press, Aug. 18, 2014, https://
www.apnews.com/aa374d7060784b81b6bd587fe7a5fa78.

17. Julie Pace, "Obama Steps into Another Racially Charged Incident," Associated Press, Aug. 15, 2014, https://apnews.com/195b483d018944f4878723
81b8c6185c; DeNeen L. Brown, Emily Wax-Thibodeaux, and Jerry Markon,
"Justice Department Orders New Autopsy: Violence Erupts in Streets Once
Again," *Washington Post*, Aug. 18, 2014, https://www.washingtonpost.com
/politics/state-of-emergency-declared-in-missouri-amid-renewed-tensions
-over-browns-death/2014/08/17/65e9836c-25c9-11e4-8593-da634b334390_
story.html; David Hunn and Kim Bell, "Why Was Michael Brown's Body
Left There for Hours?," *St. Louis Post-Dispatch*, Sept. 14, 2014, https://www
.stltoday.com/news/local/crime-and-courts/why-was-michael-brown-s-body
-left-there-for-hours/article_0b73ec58-c6a1-516e-882f-74d18a4246e0.html.

18. Benjamin Goad, "Holder Opens Federal Probe of Slain Teen," TheHill.com,
Aug. 11, 2014, https://thehill.com/regulation/administration/214879-holder
-opens-federal-probe-of-slain-teen; "Statement on the Death of Michael
Brown, Jr.," Aug. 12, 2014, in Obama, *Public Papers*, 2:1099.

19. "Remarks in Edgartown, Massachusetts," Aug. 14, 2014, in Obama, *Public
Papers*, 2:1099-1101; Bill Simmons, "President Obama and Bill Simmons:
The GQ Interview," *GQ*, Nov. 17, 2015, http://www.gq.com/story/president

-obama-bill-simmons-interview-gq-men-of-the-year; Glenn Thrush, "Revved Up," *Politico*, Aug. 21, 2014, https://www.politico.com/magazine/story/2014 /08/al-sharpton-obama-race-110249.

20. Perry Bacon Jr., "Should Obama Do More on Ferguson and Other Racial Issues?," NBC News, Aug. 14, 2014, https://www.nbcnews.com/storyline /michael-brown-shooting/should-obama-do-more-ferguson-other-racial -issues-n180921; Michael D. Shear and Yamiche Alcindor, "Jolted by Deaths, Obama Found His Voice on Race," *New York Times*, Jan. 14, 2017, https:// www.nytimes.com/2017/01/14/us/politics/obama-presidency-race.html; Edward-Isaac Dovere, "Under Obama, Racial Hope, No Change," *Politico*, Aug. 24, 2014, https://www.politico.com/story/2014/08/barack-obama-racial -tensions-ferguson-missouri-110288.

21. John Schwartz, Michael D. Shear, and Michael Paulson, "New Tack on Un-rest Eases Tension in Missouri," *New York Times*, Aug. 14, 2014, https://www .nytimes.com/2014/08/15/us/ferguson-missouri-police-shooting.html; Brown, Wax-Thibodeaux, and Markon, "Justice Department Orders New Autopsy."

22. Brown, Wax-Thibodeaux, and Markon, "Justice Department Orders New Autopsy"; Washington, "Strong DOJ Response to Ferguson"; David Naka-mura and Katie Zezima, "Top Obama Advisors Tell African American Leaders That Justice Will Prevail in Ferguson," *Washington Post*, Aug. 20, 2014, https://www.washingtonpost.com/politics/top-obama-advisors-tell -african-american-leaders-that-justice-will-prevail-in-ferguson/2014/08 /19/67983100-27d5-11e4-958c-268a320a60ce_story.html; "Remarks on the Situation in Iraq and Ferguson, Missouri, and an Exchange with Reporters," Aug. 18, 2014, Obama, *Public Papers*, 2:1103-1109; Matt Apuzzo and Mi-chael S. Schmidt, "In Washington, Second Thoughts on Arming Police," *New York Times*, Aug. 23, 2014, https://www.nytimes.com/2014/08/24/us /in-washington-second-thoughts-on-arming-police.html; Jim Kuhnhenn, "Obama: Time to Review Local Police Militarization," Associated Press, Aug. 18, 2014, https://apnews.com/article/2ee37e78ee374667aba01094e5 2db138; Eric H. Holder Jr., "From Eric Holder: A Message to the People of Ferguson," *St. Louis Post-Dispatch*, Aug. 20, 2014, https://www.stltoday .com/news/local/from-eric-holder-a-message-to-the-people-of-ferguson /article_ea8b7358-67a3-5187-af8c-169567f27a0d.html.

23. Jonathan P. Hicks, "Commentary: Eric Holder's Huge Imprint in Fergu-son," BET.com, Aug. 21, 2014, https://www.bet.com/news/politics/2014/08 /21/commentary-eric-holder-s-huge-imprint-in-ferguson.amp.html.

24. Tucker, "Justice Dept. Announces Ferguson Police Probe"; "Remarks to the United Nations General Assembly in New York City," Sept. 24, 2014, in Obama, *Public Papers*, 2:1214-1220; Jennifer Epstein and Josh Gerstein, "Obama: U.S. Has Own Racial Tensions," *Politico*, Sept. 24, 2014, https:// www.politico.com/story/2014/09/obama-ferguson-un-address-111290.

25. Jim Salter and David A. Lieb, "Brown Family Blasts Prosecutor's Handling of Case," Associated Press, Nov. 25, 2014, https://oklahoman.com/article/53 70180/brown-family-blasts-prosecutors-handling-of-case; "Remarks on the

Situation in Ferguson, Missouri, and an Exchange with Reporters," Nov. 24, 2014, in Obama, *Public Papers*, 2:1526-1528; Monica Davey and Julie Bosman, "Protests Flare after Ferguson Police Officer Is Not Indicted," *New York Times*, Nov. 24, 2014, https://www.nytimes.com/2014/11/25/us/ ferguson-darren-wilson-shooting-michael-brown-grand-jury.html; Justin Sink, "Holder: Civil Rights Charges Still Possible," TheHill.com, Nov. 24, 2014, https://thehill.com/blogs/blog-briefing-room/news/225265-holder -civil-rights-charges-still-possible; "Ferguson Shooting: Protests Spread across US," BBC News, Nov. 26, 2014, https://www.bbc.com/news/world-us -canada-30203526.

26. Kevin Johnson and Yamiche Alcindor, "U.S. Set to Clear Ferguson Officer," *USA Today*, Jan. 22, 2015, 1A; David Nather, "Obama on Ferguson: 'They Weren't Just Making It Up,'" *Politico*, Mar. 6, 2015, https://www.politico .com/story/2015/03/obama-ferguson-reaction-doj-115839.

27. Tucker, "Justice Dept. Announces Ferguson Police Probe"; US District Court, Eastern District of Missouri, *United States of America v. the City of Ferguson*.

28. Office of Public Affairs, US Department of Justice, "Justice Department Files Lawsuit to Bring Constitutional Policing to Ferguson, Missouri," Feb. 10, 2016, https://www.justice.gov/opa/pr/justice-department-files -lawsuit-bring-constitutional-policing-ferguson-missouri; Matt Apuzzo, "Department of Justice Sues Ferguson, Which Reverses Course on Agree-ment,"*New York Times*, Feb. 10, 2016, https://www.nytimes.com/2016/02 /11/us/politics/justice-department-sues-ferguson-over-police-deal.html; Eric Tucker, "Justice Dept.: States Shouldn't Jail over Fine Nonpayment," Associated Press, Mar. 14, 2016, https://www.apnews.com/e0908189c79 14665a59c95ba36ceod3a; John Eligon, "Ferguson Approves a Federal Plan to Overhaul Police and Courts," *New York Times*, Mar. 15, 2016, https:// www.nytimes.com/2016/03/16/us/ferguson-approves-a-federal-plan-to -overhaul-police-and-courts.html.

29. See links for "City Council," "Civilian Review Boards," and "Human Rights Commission" on City of Ferguson website, accessed Sept. 8, 2019, https:// www.fergusoncity.com/; Ron Mott, "Three Years after Michael Brown's Death, Has Ferguson Changed?," NBC News, Aug. 9, 2017, https://www .nbcnews.com/storyline/michael-brown-shooting/three-years-after-michael -brown-s-death-has-ferguson-changed-n791081; Justin Wolfers, David Leon-hardt, and Kevin Quealy, "1.5 Million Missing Black Men," *New York Times*, Apr. 20, 2015, https://www.nytimes.com/interactive/2015/04/20/upshot/mis sing-black-men.html. On June 2, 2020, Ella Jones, a member of the Fergu-son City Council, was elected mayor of the city, becoming the first African American to hold that office. The following day, former president Barack Obama posted a tweet that referred to Jones's election as "a reminder of the difference politics and voting can make in changing who has the power to make real change in a community like Ferguson with a history of blatant discriminatory law enforcement practices." Mark Schlinkmann, "Ferguson

Picks Ella Jones as First African American and First Woman Mayor," *St. Louis Post-Dispatch*, June 3, 2020, https://www.stltoday.com/news/local/govt-and -politics/ferguson-picks-ella-jones-as-first-african-american-and-first-woman -mayor/article_4fcddeed-9586-571c-b88a-bbcae3c71f70.html; Barack Obama, Twitter, June 3, 2020, 11:04 a.m., https://twitter.com/BarackObama/status /1268196826374647808.

30. David Hudson, "President Obama Meets with U.S. Attorney General Loretta Lynch," White House, Apr. 27, 2015, https://obamawhitehouse .archives.gov/blog/2015/04/27/president-obama-meets-us-attorney-general -loretta-lynch; David A. Graham, " 'Rough Rides' and the Challenges of Improving Police Culture," *Atlantic*, Apr. 27, 2015, https://www.theatlantic .com/politics/archive/2015/04/the-rough-ride-and-police-culture/391538/; Oliver Laughland and Jon Swaine, "Six Baltimore Officers Suspended over Police-Van Death of Freddie Gray," *Guardian* (US edition), Apr. 20, 2015, https://www.theguardian.com/us-news/2015/apr/20/baltimore-officers -suspended-death-freddie-gray; Holly Yan and Dana Ford, "Baltimore Riots: Looting, Fires Engulf City after Freddie Gray's Funeral," CNN, Apr. 28, 2015, https://www.cnn.com/2015/04/27/us/baltimore-unrest/index.html; Lacey Johnson, "Thousands March in Baltimore to Protest Black Man's Death," Reuters, Apr. 25, 2015, https://www.reuters.com/article/usa-police -baltimore/thousands-march-in-baltimore-to-protest-black-mans-death -idINKBN0NG0VU20150425; Tom Foreman Jr. and Amanda Lee Myers, "Baltimore on Edge: National Guardsmen Take Up Positions," Associated Press, Apr. 28, 2015, https://www.thestate.com/news/nation-world/national /article19786302.html; Scott Malone and Ian Simpson, "Six Baltimore Offi- cers Charged in Death of Gray, One with Murder," Reuters, Apr. 30, 2015, https://www.reuters.com/article/us-usa-police-baltimore-idUSKBN0NL1 GO20150501; Moore, *Five Days*, xxv–xxviii; Catherine E. Shoichet, "Fred- die Gray Death: Grand Jury Indicts Police Officers," CNN, May 21, 2015, https://www.cnn.com/2015/05/21/us/baltimore-freddie-gray-death-officers -indicted/index.html; Sheryl Gay Stolberg and Jess Bidgood, "All Charges Dropped against Baltimore Officers in Freddie Gray Case," *New York Times*, July 27, 2016, https://www.nytimes.com/2016/07/28/us/charges-dropped -against-3-remaining-officers-in-freddie-gray-case.html.

31. Sari Horwitz, "Justice Department to Launch Federal Investigation of Balti- more Police," *Washington Post*, May 7, 2015, https://www.washingtonpost .com/world/national-security/justice-department-to-launch-federal-investi gation-of-baltimore-police/2015/05/07/b3a422da-f4d4-11e4-b2f3-af5479e6 bbdd_story.html; Mark Puente, "Undue Force," *Baltimore Sun*, Sept. 28, 2014, http://data.baltimoresun.com/news/police-settlements/; Civil Rights Division, US Department of Justice, *Investigation of the Baltimore City Po- lice Department*; Office of Public Affairs, US Department of Justice, "Justice Department Reaches Agreement with City of Baltimore to Reform Police Department's Unconstitutional Practices," Jan. 12, 2017, https://www.jus tice.gov/opa/pr/justice-department-reaches-agreement-city-baltimore-re form-police-department-s.

32. Todd Richmond, "Milwaukee Police Reforms Sought after Shooting," Associated Press, Dec. 23, 2014, https://www.greenbaypressgazette.com/story /news/2014/12/23/milwaukee-police-reforms-sought-after-dontre-hamilton -shooting/20826495/; Don Babwin and Sophia Tareen, "Protesters to Target Chicago Shopping Area on Black Friday," Associated Press, Nov. 25, 2015, https://www.dailyherald.com/article/20151125/news/311259979; Police Accountability Task Force, *Recommendations for Reform*; Mark Gillespie, "Ohio Patrolman Acquitted in 2 Deaths amid 137-Shot Barrage," Associated Press, May 23, 2015, https://www.policeone.com/legal/articles/855 4669-Ohio-patrolman-acquitted-in-2-deaths-amid-137-shot-barrage/; US District Court, Northern District of Ohio, *United States of America v. City of Cleveland*; Ashley Fantz, Steve Almasy, and Catherine E. Shoichet, "Tamir Rice Shooting: No Charges for Officers," CNN, Dec. 28, 2015, https://www.cnn.com/2015/12/28/us/tamir-rice-shooting/index.html; Phil Helsel, "Cleveland Wants Tamir Rice Estate to Pay $500 Ambulance Bill," NBC News, Feb. 10, 2016, https://www.nbcnews.com/news/us-news/cleve land-wants-tamir-rice-estate-pay-500-ambulance-bill-n516281.

33. Barbara Goldberg and Sebastien Malo, "NY Policeman Not Indicted in Chokehold Death; U.S. Justice Sets Probe," Reuters, Dec. 3, 2014, https:// www.reuters.com/article/us-usa-new-york-chokehold/ny-policeman-not -indicted-in-chokehold-death-u-s-justice-sets-probe-idUSKCN0JH2B I20141203; J. David Goodman, "Eric Garner Case Is Settled by New York City for $5.9 Million," *New York Times*, July 13, 2015, https://www.nytimes .com/2015/07/14/nyregion/eric-garner-case-is-settled-by-new-york-city-for -5-9-million.html; Meg Kinnard, "White Ex-Cop Gets 20 Years in Prison for Fatal Shooting," Associated Press, Dec. 7, 2017, https://www.detroit news.com/story/news/nation/2017/12/07/north-charleston-police-shoot ing/108394934/; K. K. Rebecca Lai et al., "Assessing the Legality of Sandra Bland's Arrest," *New York Times*, July 22, 2015, https://www.nytimes.com /interactive/2015/07/20/us/sandra-bland-arrest-death-videos-maps.html; Emmarie Huetteman, "Lynch Says Death in Police Custody Highlights Fears among Blacks," *New York Times*, July 26, 2015, https://www.nytimes .com/2015/07/27/us/politics/lynch-says-death-in-custody-highlights-fears -among-blacks.html.

34. Illustratively, Daniel Pantaleo, the officer who strangled Eric Garner to death in July 2014, remained employed by the NY Police Department for more than five years after the fatal encounter. He was eventually fired in August 2019 following a ruling by a police administrative judge charging that Pantaleo had violated the department's ban on chokeholds. Ashley Southall, "Daniel Pantaleo, Officer Who Held Eric Garner in Chokehold, Is Fired," *New York Times*, Aug. 19, 2019, https://www.nytimes.com/2019 /08/19/nyregion/daniel-pantaleo-fired.html; Mark Gillespie, "Cleveland Settles Lawsuit over Tamir Rice Shooting for $6M," Associated Press, Apr. 25, 2016, https://www.onlineathens.com/national-news/2016-04-25/cleve land-settles-lawsuit-over-tamir-rice-shooting-6m; Goodman, "Eric Garner Case Is Settled"; Puente, "Undue Force."

35. "U.N. Chief Calls for Protection of Rights in Missouri Protests," Reuters, Aug. 18, 2014, https://www.reuters.com/article/us-usa-missouri-shooting-un /u-n-chief-calls-for-protection-of-rights-in-missouri-protests-idUSKBN0G I1MF20140818; Jamil Dakwar, "UN Issues Scathing Assessment of US Human Rights Record," American Civil Liberties Union, May 15, 2015, https:// www.aclu.org/blog/human-rights/human-rights-and-criminal-justice/un -issues-scathing-assessment-us-human-rights.

36. Salma Abdelaziz, "Iran's Supreme Leader Vilifies U.S. Police on Twitter, Says #BlackLivesMatter," CNN, Dec. 30, 2014, http://www.cnn.com/2014/12 /29/world/meast/ayatollah-tweet-abdelaziz/index.html; "Ministry of Foreign Affairs and Immigration Issues Travel Advisory for Bahamians Traveling to United States of America," Ministry of Foreign Affairs and Immigration (Bahamas), July 8, 2016, https://mofa.gov.bs/ministry-of-foreign -affairs-and-immigration-issues-travel-advisory-for-bahamians-traveling -to-united-states-of-america/.

37. Darlene Superville, "Obama: Mistrust of Police Corroding America," Associated Press, Sept. 28, 2014, https://www.apnews.com/90b1d78db5424a2 6bac82618dff9d9cb; "Remarks at the Congressional Black Caucus Foundation Phoenix Award Dinner," Sept. 27, 2014, in Obama, *Public Papers*, 2:1242-1243; Tanya Somanader, "President Obama Delivers a Statement on the Grand Jury Decision in the Death of Eric Garner," White House, Dec. 3, 2014, https://obamawhitehouse.archives.gov/blog/2014/12/03/president -obama-delivers-statement-grand-jury-decision-death-eric-garner; "Remarks at the White House Tribal Nations Conference," Dec. 3, 2014, in Obama, *Public Papers*, 2:1559-1560; Joyce Jones, "BET Exclusive: Obama Talks Race, Racism and How Far America Has to Go," BET.com, Dec. 8, 2014, https:// www.bet.com/news/politics/2014/12/08/in-bet-exclusive-obama-talks-race -and-racism.html.

38. "Remarks by the President in State of the Union Address," White House, Jan. 20, 2015, https://obamawhitehouse.archives.gov/the-press-office/2015 /01/20/remarks-president-state-union-address-January-20-2015.

39. "Remarks by President Obama and Prime Minister Abe of Japan in Joint Press Conference," White House, Apr. 28, 2015, https://obamawhitehouse .archives.gov/the-press-office/2015/04/28/remarks-president-obama-and -prime-minister-abe-japan-joint-press-confere.

40. Nedra Pickler, "Obama: Police Must Hold Officers Accountable for Wrongdoing," Associated Press, Apr. 29, 2015, https://baltimore.cbslocal.com/2015 /04/29/obama-police-must-hold-officers-accountable-for-wrongdoing/; Michael Daly, "The Most Honest 15 Minutes of Obama's Presidency," *Daily Beast*, Apr. 28, 2015 (updated July 12, 2017), https://www.thedailybeast.com /the-most-honest-15-minutes-of-obamas-presidency.

41. Matt Apuzzo and Adam Liptak, "Holder's Team, in Balancing Act, Often Aligns with the Police," *New York Times*, Apr. 22, 2015, A15; Colleen Long and Jennifer Peltz, "AP Sources: Cops' Killer Angry at Chokehold Death," Associated Press, Dec. 21, 2014, https://www.apnews.com/132d998fa3044e8

4be53d09efbdc950b; Joel Achenbach et al., "Five Police Officers Were Killed by a Lone Attacker, Authorities Say," *Washington Post*, July 9, 2016, https://www.washingtonpost.com/news/morning-mix/wp/2016/07/08/like -a-little-war-snipers-shoot-11-police-officers-during-dallas-protest-march -killing-five/; Ashley Fantz and Steve Visser, "Baton Rouge Shooting: 3 Officers Dead; Shooter Was Missouri Man, Sources Say," CNN, July 18, 2016, https://www.cnn.com/2016/07/17/us/baton-route-police-shooting /index.html; "Obama Signs Bill Creating Nationwide Alert System for Police," Associated Press, May 19, 2015, https://apnews.com/f7dd4dcf3f824b 2d8324173bd00d66be; Mike Lillis, "Black Lawmakers Push Back on Obama over 'Thugs,'" TheHill.com, May 1, 2015, https://thehill.com/homenews /house/240807-black-lawmakers-push-back-on-obama-over-thugs.

42. "Holder Calls for Better Data on Police Use of Force," PBS, Jan. 15, 2015, https://www.pbs.org/newshour/politics/holder-calls-better-data-police-use -force; Reuben Fischer-Baum and Carl Bialik, "Blacks Are Killed by Police at a Higher Rate in South Carolina and the U.S.," FiveThirtyEight.com, Apr. 8, 2015, https://fivethirtyeight.com/features/blacks-are-killed-at-a -higher-rate-in-south-carolina-and-the-u-s/; Thomas Frank, "Black People Are Three Times Likelier to Be Killed in Police Chases," *USA Today*, Dec. 1, 2016, https://www.usatoday.com/pages/interactives/blacks-killed-police -chases-higher-rate/; Zusha Elinson and Dan Frosch, "Police-Misconduct Costs Soar," *Wall Street Journal*, July 16, 2015, A1, A16; Benjamin Goad, "DOJ to Spend $4.75M Studying Race," TheHill.com, Apr. 28, 2014, https://thehill.com/regulation/204556-doj-to-spend-475-million-for-data -collection-on-race-arrests; Eric Lichtblau, "Justice Department to Track Use of Force by Police across U.S.," *New York Times*, Oct. 13, 2016, https:// www.nytimes.com/2016/10/14/us/justice-department-track-police-shooting -use-force.html; National Initiative for Building Community Trust and Justice, accessed Dec. 19, 2020, https://trustandjustice.org/.

43. In an interview with me, task force cochair Laurie Robinson recalled President Obama as being notably immersed in the group's work, even to the point of conducting one particularly probing session with members in a manner that she found reminiscent of a "graduate seminar." Favorably comparing Obama's attentiveness to that of her less-engaged university students, she marveled, "And here the leader of the free world, I thought to myself, is taking notes, and I thought, 'Wow, that's special!'" Robinson interview. Also see Nedra Pickler and Eric Tucker, "Obama: 'Now Is the Moment' for Police to Make Changes," Associated Press, Mar. 3, 2015, https://www.semi ssourian.com/story/2171639.html; President's Task Force on 21st Century Policing, *Final Report*; Nedra Pickler, "Obama Restricts Police Military Gear, Says It Can Alienate," Associated Press, May 18, 2015, https://apnews.com /10785eac6d3e4c26a1baed8f0d796b48.

44. "Remarks on the My Brother's Keeper Initiative," Feb. 27, 2014, in Obama, *Public Papers*, 1:190-196; Jesse J. Holland, "Obama Plan Aims to Improve Odds for Minority Boys," Associated Press, Feb. 27, 2014, https://www.ap

news.com/d67733c667f74f41b5eeb51247760576; Joyce Jones, "Obama to Help Set Chicago Boys on Path toward Becoming Men," BET.com, Feb. 15, 2013, https://www.bet.com/news/national/2013/02/15/obama-helps-set -chicago-boys-on-path-toward-becoming-men.html; Valerie Jarrett and Broderick Johnson, "My Brother's Keeper: A New White House Initiative to Empower Boys and Young Men of Color," White House, Feb. 27, 2014, https://obamawhitehouse.archives.gov/blog/2014/02/27/my-brother-s -keeper-new-white-house-initiative-empower-boys-and-young-men-color; Michael D. Shear, "Obama Starts Initiative for Young Black Men, Noting Statistics and His Own Experience," *New York Times*, Feb. 28, 2014, A11, A14; "Presidential Memorandum—Creating and Expanding Ladders of Opportunity for Boys and Young Men of Color," White House, Feb. 27, 2014, https://obamawhitehouse.archives.gov/the-press-office/2014/02/27/presiden tial-memorandum-creating-and-expanding-ladders-opportunity-boys-.

45. Shear, "Obama Starts Initiative for Young Black Men"; David Hudson, "My Brother's Keeper: 90 Days In," White House, May 30, 2014, https://obama whitehouse.archives.gov/blog/2014/05/30/my-brothers-keeper-90-days; Cameron Brenchley, "President Obama at My Brother's Keeper Town Hall: 'America Will Succeed if We Are Investing in Our Young People,'" White House, July 21, 2014, https://obamawhitehouse.archives.gov/blog /2014/07/21/president-obama-my-brother-s-keeper-town-hall-america-will -succeed-if-we-are-investi.

46. Hudson, "My Brother's Keeper: 90 Days In"; Brenchley, "President Obama at My Brother's Keeper Town Hall"; Peter Baker, "Obama Finds a Bolder Voice on Race Issues," *New York Times*, May 4, 2015, https://www.nytimes .com/2015/05/05/us/politics/obama-my-brothers-keeper-alliance-minorities .html; Edward Wyckoff Williams, "My Brother's Keeper Sets Its Sights on Mentoring, with Help from Magic Johnson," TheRoot.com, May 30, 2014, https://www.theroot.com/my-brother-s-keeper-sets-its-sights-on-mentoring -with-1790875847; Trymaine Lee, "Obama's My Brother's Keeper Initiative Takes Crucial Next Step," MSNBC, May 30, 2014, http://www.msnbc.com /msnbc/next-steps-my-brothers-keeper.

47. "Letter of 250+ Concerned Black Men and Other Men of Color Calling for the Inclusion of Women and Girls in 'My Brother's Keeper,'" African American Policy Forum, May 30, 2014, http://aapf.org/recent/2014/05/an -open-letter-to-president-obama; Nia-Malika Henderson, "1,000 Women of Color Want Women and Girls Included in 'My Brother's Keeper,'" *Washington Post*, June 18, 2014, https://www.washingtonpost.com/blogs/she-the -people/wp/2014/06/18/1000-women-of-color-want-women-and-girls -included-in-my-brothers-keeper/.

48. Nia-Malika Henderson, "White House Meets with Activists Calling for Gender Equity in My Brother's Keeper," *Washington Post*, July 15, 2014, https://www.washingtonpost.com/blogs/she-the-people/wp/2014/07/15 /white-house-meets-with-activists-calling-for-gender-equity-in-obamas -my-brothers-keeper-program/; "Remarks at the Congressional Black

Caucus Foundation Phoenix Award Dinner," Sept. 27, 2014, in Obama, *Public Papers*, 2:1242-1243.

49. For an informative overview of the Black Lives Matter movement and its various incarnations and offshoots, see Ransby, *Making All Black Lives Matter*. Also see Gene Demby, "The Birth of a New Civil Rights Movement," *Politico*, Dec. 31, 2014, https://www.politico.com/magazine/story /2014/12/ferguson-new-civil-rights-movement-113906; Laura Barrón-López, "Why the Black Lives Matter Movement Doesn't Want a Singular Leader," *Politico*, July 22, 2020, https://www.politico.com/news/2020/07/22/black -lives-matter-movement-leader-377369; Taylor, *From #BlackLivesMatter to Black Liberation*, 176-181; Char Adams, "A Movement, a Slogan, a Rallying Cry: How Black Lives Matter Changed America's View on Race," NBC News, Dec. 29, 2020, https://www.nbcnews.com/news/nbcblk/movement -slogan-rallying-cry-how-black-lives-matter-changed-america-n1252434; Shannon Luibrand, "How a Death in Ferguson Sparked a Movement in America," CBS News, Aug. 7, 2015, https://www.cbsnews.com/news/how -the-black-lives-matter-movement-changed-america-one-year-later/; Elizabeth Day, "#BlackLivesMatter: The Birth of a New Civil Rights Movement," *Guardian* (US edition), July 19, 2015, https://www.theguardian.com /world/2015/jul/19/blacklivesmatter-birth-civil-rights-movement; Trymaine Lee, "Black Lives Matter Releases Policy Agenda," NBC News, Aug. 1, 2016, https://www.nbcnews.com/news/us-news/black-lives-matter-releases-policy -agenda-n620966; Movement for Black Lives, *A Vision for Black Lives: Policy Demands for Black Power, Freedom, & Justice*, accessed Dec. 16, 2018, https://policy.m4bl.org/wp-content/uploads/2016/07/20160726-m4bl -Vision-Booklet-V3.pdf; "Vision for Black Lives," M4BL.org, accessed Dec. 25, 2020, https://m4bl.org/policy-platforms/.

50. Darlene Superville, "Obama Defends Black Lives Matter Movement," Associated Press, Oct. 23, 2015, https://www.pbs.org/newshour/politics/obama -defends-black-lives-matter-movement; Barack Obama, "You See, Change Requires More than Righteous Anger" (speech), May 7, 2016, Washington, DC, reprinted in Dionne and Reid, *We Are the Change We Seek*, 285-302; Toluse Olorunnipa and Justin Sink, "Obama Urges a 'Thoughtful' Tone amid Protests in the U.S.," Bloomberg, July 10, 2016, https://www.bloom berg.com/news/articles/2016-07-10/as-nation-boils-over-obama-urges -thoughtful-tone-in-protests.

51. Kathleen Hennessey, "Black Leaders: Supreme Court Standoff a Civil Rights Issue," Associated Press, Feb. 18, 2016, https://www.columbian.com/news /2016/feb/18/black-leaders-supreme-court-standoff-a-civil-rights-issue/; Breanna Edwards, "BLM Activists Speak on 'Manipulative,' 'Disingenuous' Town Hall on Race," TheRoot.com, July 15, 2016, https://www.theroot .com/blm-activists-speak-on-manipulative-disingenuous-t-1790856058; Ta-Nehisi Coates, "My President Was Black," *Atlantic*, Jan.–Feb. 2017, https://www.theatlantic.com/magazine/archive/2017/01 my-president -was-black/508793/.

CHAPTER 17. THE MEASURE OF A PRESIDENT

1. David A. Love, "The Latest Unemployment Numbers Are Great if You're Not Black," TheGrio.com, Mar. 7, 2015, https://thegrio.com/2015/03/07 /latest-unemployment-numbers-blacks-african-american/; Valerie Wilson, "So Far, the Black Unemployment Rate Has Only Recovered in States Where It Was Highest before the Great Recession," Economic Policy Institute, May 6, 2015, https://www.epi.org/publication/so-far-the-black -unemployment-rate-has-only-recovered-in-states-where-it-was-highest -before-the-great-recession/; "U.S. Business Cycle Expansions and Contractions," National Bureau of Economic Research, accessed Sept. 21, 2019, https://www.nber.org/cycles/; Patricia Cohen, "Public-Sector Jobs Vanish, Hitting Blacks Hard," *New York Times*, May 24, 2015, https:// www.nytimes.com/2015/05/25/business/public-sector-jobs-vanish-and -blacks-take-blow.html.

2. Mary C. Daly, Bart Hobijn, and Joseph H. Pedtke, "Disappointing Facts about the Black-White Wage Gap," Federal Reserve Bank of San Francisco, Sept. 5, 2017, https://www.frbsf.org/economic-research/publications /economic-letter/2017/september/disappointing-facts-about-black-white -wage-gap/; Mike Snider, "EEOC: More Diversity Needed in Tech Hiring," *USA Today*, May 18, 2016, https://www.usatoday.com/story/tech/news /2016/05/18/eeoc-more-diversity-needed-tech-hiring/84532454/; Jose Del-Real, "Dem Party Hires Few Minority Firms," *Politico*, June 25, 2014, https://www.politico.com/story/2014/06/dem-party-hires-few-minority -firms-108284; Tim Mak, "Democrats Are Stiffing Minority Political Consultants," *Daily Beast*, June 27, 2014 (updated July 12, 2017), https://www .thedailybeast.com/democrats-are-stiffing-minority-political-consultants; Tim Mak, "Democrats Pay Black Staffers 30% Less," *Daily Beast*, Aug. 11, 2014 (updated Apr. 14, 2017), https://www.thedailybeast.com/democrats -pay-black-staffers-30-less.

3. Josh Katz and Abby Goodnough, "The Opioid Crisis Is Getting Worse, Particularly for Black Americans," *New York Times*, Dec. 22, 2017, https:// www.nytimes.com/interactive/2017/12/22/upshot/opioid-deaths-are-spread ing-rapidly-into-black-america.html; Timothy Cama, "EPA Blasted over Lack of Protection of Minorities," TheHill.com, Sept. 23, 2016, https://the-hill.com/policy/energy-environment/297503-civil-rights-commission -blasts-epa-on-protecting-minorities; US Commission on Civil Rights, *Environmental Justice*.

4. Mark Murray, "Then vs. Now: A Statistical Look at Obama's Presidency," NBC News, Dec. 5, 2016, https://www.nbcnews.com/politics/first-read /then-vs-now-statistical-look-obama-s-presidency-n692181; Eli Watkins, Caroline Kenny, and Sophie Tatum, "44 Ways to Judge the Obama Era," CNN, Jan. 19, 2017, https://www.cnn.com/2017/01/18/politics/obama -presidency-statistics/index.html; "Hate Crime," Uniform Crime Reporting (FBI), accessed Sept. 21, 2019, https://ucr.fbi.gov/hate-crime.

5. For an interesting analysis of a sampling of Black attitudes and opinions regarding the Obama presidency, see Gillespie, *Race and the Obama Administration*, 163-189. Also see Dalia Sussman, "Negative View of U.S. Race Relations Grows, Poll Finds," *New York Times*, May 4, 2015, https://www.nytimes.com/2015/05/05/us/negative-view-of-us-race-relations-grows-poll-finds.html; Kevin Sack and Megan Thee-Brenan, "Poll Finds Most in U.S. Hold Dim View of Race Relations," *New York Times*, July 23, 2015, https://www.nytimes.com/2015/07/24/us/poll-shows-most-americans-think-race-relations-are-bad.html; Jennifer Agiesta, "Most Say Race Relations Worsened under Obama, Poll Finds," CNN, Oct. 5, 2016, https://www.cnn.com/2016/10/05/politics/obama-race-relations-poll/index.html; Jeffrey M. Jones, "Six in 10 Americans Say Racism against Blacks Is Widespread," Gallup, Aug. 17, 2016, https://news.gallup.com/poll/194657/six-americans-say-racism-against-blacks-widespread.aspx; Jennifer Agiesta, "Obama Approval Hits New High," CNN, Oct. 5, 2016, https://www.cnn.com/2016/10/06/politics/obama-approval-rating-new-high/index.html; "Obama Weekly Job Approval by Demographics.09102016" (.xlsx), Sept. 21, 2016, https://www.evernote.com/shard/s4/client/snv?noteGuid=0953576f-5e23-4a3a-9cf3-747c21679e09&noteKey=eec113a6a1858d85&sn=https%3A%2F%2Fwww.evernote.com%2Fshard%2Fs4%2Fsh%2F0953576f-5e23-4a3a-9cf3-747c21679e09%2Feec113a6a1858d85&title=Obama%2BWeekly%2BJob%2BApproval%2Bby%2BDemographics; "Obama Leaves Office on High Note, but Public Has Mixed Views of Accomplishments," Pew Research Center, Dec. 14, 2016, https://www.people-press.org/2016/12/14/obama-leaves-office-on-high-note-but-public-has-mixed-views-of-accomplishments/.
6. Jonathan Chait, "The Obama History Project," *New York Magazine*, Jan. 11, 2015, http://nymag.com/intelligencer/2015/01/53-historians-on-obamas-legacy.html.
7. Randall Kennedy, "Did Obama Fail Black America?," *Politico*, July–Aug. 2014, https://www.politico.com/magazine/story/2014/06/black-president-black-attorney-general-so-what-108017; Matt Wilstein, "Henry Louis Gates, Jr.: Trump Makes Reagan 'Look like a Liberal on Race Relations,'" *Daily Beast*, Nov. 15, 2016, https://www.thedailybeast.com/henry-louis-gates-jr-trump-makes-reagan-look-like-a-liberal-on-race-relations; William Julius Wilson, "The Right President Returns," TheRoot.com, Jan. 24, 2013, https://www.theroot.com/the-right-president-returns-1790895011; Molly Lanzarotta, "William Julius Wilson on Poverty and Inequality," Harvard Kennedy School, Nov. 9, 2012, https://www.hks.harvard.edu/news-events/publications/insight/social/william_julius_wilson; Hillel Italic, "At 80, W. J. Wilson, Scholar of Race and Class, Looks Ahead," Associated Press, Dec. 29, 2015, https://www.apnews.com/bd4157cb90ed41ca96f18aaedc7e4d64.
8. Michael Eric Dyson, "Barack Obama, the President of Black America?," *New York Times*, June 24, 2016, https://www.nytimes.com/2016/06/26/opinion/sunday/barack-obama-the-president-of-black-america.html; Dyson, *Black Presidency*, 117, 156.

9. Glaude, *Democracy in Black*, 7-8, 155; US Bureau of Labor Statistics, "Great Recession, Great Recovery? Trends from the Current Population Survey," *Monthly Labor Review*, Apr. 2018, https://www.bls.gov/opub/mlr/2018 /article/great-recession-great-recovery.htm; Jenna Levy, "In U.S., Uninsured Rate Dips to 11.9% in First Quarter," Gallup, Apr. 13, 2015, https://news .gallup.com/poll/182348/uninsured-rate-dips-first-quarter.aspx; John Gramlich, "The Gap between the Number of Blacks and Whites in Prison Is Shrinking," Pew Research Center, Apr. 30, 2019, https://www.pewresearch .org/fact-tank/2019/04/30/shrinking-gap-between-number-of-blacks-and -whites-in-prison/; "Data: U.S. Graduation Rates by State and Student Demographics," *Education Week*, Dec. 7, 2017 (updated Jan. 29, 2019), https://www.edweek.org/ew/section/multimedia/data-us-graduation-rates -by-state-and.html.

10. Ian Schwartz, "Cornel West on Obama: 'The First Black President Has Become the First Niggerized Black President,'" *RealClearPolitics*, June 22, 2015, https://www.realclearpolitics.com/video/2015/06/22/cornel_west_on_obama _the_first_black_president_has_become_the_first_niggerized_black_presi dent.html; John Wagner and Vanessa Williams, "Cornel West Joins Bernie Sanders on the Campaign Trail in South Carolina," *Washington Post*, Sept. 12, 2015, https://www.washingtonpost.com/politics/cornel-west-joins-bernie -sanders-on-the-campaign-trail-in-south-carolina/2015/09/12/bc9b4236-58c2 -11e5-b8c9-944725fcd3b9_story.html.

11. Jonathan Allen, "Obama and King," *Politico*, Aug. 24, 2013, https://www .politico.com/story/2013/08/barack-obama-and-martin-luther- king-jr-095866; Peter Baker, "President, Not Preacher, but Speaking More on Race," *New York Times*, Aug. 27, 2013, https://www.nytimes.com/2013/08/28/us/politics/president-not-preacher -but-speaking-more-on-race.html; National Urban League, *Obama Administration Scorecard*.

12. Brooks interview.

13. Clyburn interview; Barnes interview; Sharpton, *Rejected Stone*, 193; Morial interview.

14. John Eligon, "T.I. Writes Open Letter to Barack Obama: 'Your Legacy Will Live On,'" *New York Times*, Jan. 6, 2017, https://www.nytimes.com/2017 /01/06/arts/music/tip-ti-harris-open-letter-barack-obama.html; Kendall Breitman, "Ice Cube: No One Plays with Obama," *Politico*, June 17, 2014, https://www.politico.com/story/2014/06/ice-cube-obama-time-interview -107934; Deena Zaru and Brenna Williams, "Barack Obama's Evolution in 10 Years of Hip-Hop Lyrics," CNN, Aug. 14, 2017, https://www.cnn .com/2017/01/18/politics/obama-legacy-hip-hop-lyrics/index.html.

15. Zaru and Williams, "Barack Obama's Evolution"; Justin McCarthy, "President Obama Leaves White House with 58% Favorable Rating," Gallup, Jan. 16, 2017, https://news.gallup.com/poll/202349/president-obama-leaves -white-house-favorable-rating.aspx.

16. Ben Strauss, "What Kobe Bryant Misses Most about Obama," *Politico*, June 6, 2017, https://www.politico.com/magazine/story/2017/06/06/what-kobe

-bryant-misses-most-about-obama-215233; Emily Greenhouse, "Why Chris Rock and Ta-Nehisi Coates (Sort of) Forgive Obama His Flaws," *Bloomberg*, Dec. 5, 2014, https://www.bloomberg.com/news/articles/2014-12-05/why -chris-rock-and-tanehisi-coates-sort-of-forgive-obama-his-flaws; Ta-Nehisi Coates, "My President Was Black," *Atlantic*, Jan.–Feb. 2017, https://www.the atlantic.com/magazine/archive/2017/01/my-president-was-black/508793/.

17. Sharon Cohen and Deepti Hajela "Obama Racial Legacy: Pride, Promise, Regret and Deep Rift," Associated Press, Jan. 4, 2017, https://www.apnews .com/29b24a7985a442d8b890261da99cad86; Yamiche Alcindor, "Proud of Obama's Presidency, Blacks Are Sad to See Him Go," *New York Times*, Mar. 12, 2016, https://www.nytimes.com/2016/03/13/us/politics/proud-of-obamas -presidency-blacks-are-sad-to-see-him-go.html.

18. Allison Samuels, "Black Voters Turn Out in Big Numbers for Obama," *Daily Beast*, Nov. 6, 2012 (updated July 14, 2017), http://www.thedaily beast.com/articles/2012/11/06/black-voters-turn-out-in-big-numbers-for -obama.html.

19. "Obama Calls Today 'Best of Times and Worst of Times' for Blacks," TheGrio.com, Feb. 21, 2013, https://thegrio.com/2013/02/21/obama-calls -today-best-of-times-and-worst-of-times-for-blacks/; "Transcript: President Obama's Full NPR Interview," NPR, Dec. 29, 2014, https://www .npr.org/2014/12/29/372485968/transcript-president-obamas-full-npr-inter view; Bill Simmons, "President Obama and Bill Simmons: The GQ Interview," *GQ*, Nov. 17, 2015, http://www.gq.com/story/president-obama-bill -simmons-interview-gq-men-of-the-year.

20. Dyson, *Black Presidency*, 161-162.

21. Doris Kearns Goodwin, "Barack Obama and Doris Kearns Goodwin: The Ultimate Exit Interview," *Vanity Fair*, Sept. 21, 2016, http://www.vanityfair .com/news/2016/09/barack-obama-doris-kearns-goodwin-interview.

CHAPTER 18. THE PENDULUM SWINGS BACK

1. Dylan Byers and Mackenzie Weinger, "Media: GOP Must Expand Base," *Politico*, Nov. 7, 2012, https://www.politico.com/story/2012/11/media-gop -must-expand-base-083446.

2. Steve Phillips, "What about White Voters?," Center for American Progress, Feb. 5, 2016, https://www.americanprogress.org/issues/race/news/2016/02 /05/130647/what-about-white-voters/; Maggie Haberman, "RNC: Voters See GOP as 'Scary,'" *Politico,* Mar. 18, 2013, https://www.politico.com/ story/2013/03/rnc-report-gop-scary-out-of-touch-088974; Republican National Committee, *Growth and Opportunity Project*; "Face the Nation Transcripts, Mar. 17, 2013: Ryan, Klobuchar, Priebus," CBS News, Mar. 17, 2013, https://www.cbsnews.com/news/face-the-nation-transcripts-march-17-2013 -ryan-klobuchar-priebus/; College Republican National Committee, *Grand Old Party for a Brand New Generation*.

3. Kevin Cirilli, "Condi: GOP Sent 'Mixed Messages,'" *Politico*, Nov. 9, 2012, https://www.politico.com/story/2012/11/condi-gop-sent-mixed-messages

-083627; Bobby Cervantes, "Steele: 2012 Process Was 'Tortured,'" *Politico*, Nov. 12, 2012, https://www.politico.com/story/2012/11/steele-2012-process -was-tortured-083714; "Colin Powell: 'Some Elements' of GOP 'Demonize' Minorities," NBC News, Feb. 7, 2014, https://www.nbcnews.com/politics /elections/colin-powell-some-elements-gop-demonize-minorities-n25021; Patrick Healy, Yamiche Alcindor, and Jeremy W. Peters, "Black Republicans See a White Convention, Heavy on Lectures," *New York Times*, July 19, 2016, https://www.nytimes.com/2016/07/20/us/politics/black-republicans-convention.html.

4. Steve Kilar, "Dr. Ben Carson Announces His Retirement, Hints at Political Future," *Baltimore Sun*, Mar. 17, 2013, https://www.baltimoresun.com/health /bs-xpm-2013-03-17-bs-md-carson-at-cpac-20130316-story.html; Trip Gabriel, "Neurosurgeon's Speeches Have Conservatives Dreaming of 2016," *New York Times*, Mar. 20, 2013, https://www.nytimes.com/2013/03/21/us /politics/dr-benjamin-carson-obama-critic-have-conservatives-dreaming -of-2016.html; Carson, *Gifted Hands*; Carson, *America the Beautiful*; Aaron Blake, "Ben Carson Announces Retirement, Feeds Presidential Speculation," *Washington Post*, Mar. 16, 2013, https://www.washingtonpost.com/news /post-politics/wp/2013/03/16/ben-carson-lets-say-you-magically-put-me -in-the-white-house/.

5. Jason Zengerle, "What if Sarah Palin Were a Brain Surgeon?," *GQ*, Mar. 24, 2015, https://www.gq.com/story/ben-carson-tea-party; "Dr. Benjamin Carson's Speech at the National Prayer Breakfast," YouTube, accessed Oct. 5, 2019, https://www.youtube.com/watch?v=KpiryahOspY; Kari Rea, "Dr. Ben Carson for President? 'I'll Leave That Up to God,'" ABC News, Feb. 17, 2013, https://abcnews.go.com/blogs/politics/2013/02/dr-ben-carson-for -president-ill-leave-that-up-to-god/; "Ben Carson for President," *Wall Street Journal*, Feb. 8, 2013, https://www.wsj.com/articles/SB10001424127887323 4522045782923023582078 28.

6. Bill Barrow, "Ben Carson Says 'No Path Forward' in His Bid for White House,"Associated Press, Mar. 2, 2016, https://apnews.com/6b6e2002d32 14b249ba0a900f50d6e1b; Zack Beauchamp, "Ben Carson Warned Debate Viewers about EMPs—a Threat That Only Exists in Action Movies," *Vox*, Jan. 14, 2016, https://www.vox.com/2016/1/14/10773716/gop-debate-2016 -fox-business-emp; Gregory Krieg, "Carson's Theory: Egypt's Pyramids Stored Grain," CNN, Nov. 5, 2015, https://www.cnn.com/2015/11/05/pol itics/ben-carson-pyramids-grain/index.html.

7. Elias Isquith, "Ben Carson: America Today Is 'Very Much like Nazi Germany,'" *Salon*, Mar. 13, 2014, https://www.salon.com/2014/03/12/ben_car son_america_today_is_very_much_like_nazi_germany/; Mark Murray, Chuck Todd, and Carrie Dann, "First Read: The Pressure's on Jeb Bush before Wednesday's Debate," NBC News, Oct. 26, 2015, https://www .nbcnews.com/meet-the-press/first-read-pressures-jeb-bush-wednesdays- debate-n451481; "Dr. Ben Carson Says Obamacare Is 'Worst Thing since Slavery,'" TheGrio.com, Oct. 11, 2013, https://thegrio.com/2013/10/11 /dr-ben-carson-says-obama-is-worst-thing-since-slavery/; Eugene Scott

and Theodore Schleifer, "Ben Carson Defends Saying Obama Was 'Raised White,'" CNN, Feb. 23, 2016, https://www.cnn.com/2016/02/23/politics /ben-carson-barack-obama-raised-white/index.html; Robert Costa and Philip Rucker, "Ben Carson's Campaign Faces Turmoil amid Staff Exits and Super PAC Rivalry," *Washington Post*, June 5, 2015, https://www.wash ingtonpost.com/politics/ben-carsons-campaign-faces-turmoil-after-staff -exits-and-super-pac-chaos/2015/06/05/ceo8f9b2-0ba8-11e5-a7ad-b430f c1d3f5c_story.html.

8. Barrow, "Ben Carson Says 'No Path Forward,'"; Scott and Schleifer, "Ben Carson Defends Saying Obama Was 'Raised White.'"

9. Jennifer Epstein, "Obama: Gridlock Not because of Race," *Politico*, Aug. 28, 2013, https://www.politico.com/blogs/politico44/2013/08/obama-gridlock -not-because-of-race-171387; David Badash, "'Hello N*gger': Conservatives Welcome President Obama to Twitter," New Civil Rights Movement, May 19, 2015, https://www.thenewcivilrightsmovement.com/2015/05/1_hello_n _gger_conservatives_welcome_president_obama_to_twitter/; Julie Hirsch- feld Davis, "Obama's Twitter Debut, @POTUS, Attracts Hate-Filled Posts," *New York Times*, May 21, 2015, https://www.nytimes.com/2015/05/22/us /politics/obamas-twitter-debut-potus-attracts-hate-filled-posts.html; "Video and Transcript: NPR's Interview with President Obama," NPR, Dec. 21, 2015, https://www.npr.org/2015/12/21/460030344/video-and-transcript-nprs -interview-with-president-obama.

10. Obama's remarks at the CBC gala quoted in M. J. Lee, Dan Merica, and Jeff Zeleny, "Obama: Would Be 'Personal Insult' to Legacy if Black Voters Don't Back Clinton," CNN, Sept. 17, 2016, https://www.cnn.com/2016 /09/17/politics/obama-black-congressional-caucus/index.html. Also see "Obama, Clinton Making First Joint Campaign Appearance," Associated Press, July 5, 2016, https://www.toledoblade.com/Politics/2016/07/05/ Obama-Clinton-making-first-joint-campaign-appearance.html; Gabriel Debenedetti, "Obamas Combine Forces with the Clintons to Fend Off Trump," *Politico*, Nov. 7, 2016, https://www.politico.com/story/2016/11 /obama-clinton-trump-philadelphia-230917; Jonathan Martin, "Young Blacks Voice Skepticism on Hillary Clinton, Worrying Democrats," *New York Times*, Sept. 4, 2016, https://www.nytimes.com/2016/09/05/us/politics /young-blacks-voice-skepticism-on-hillary-clinton-worrying-democrats .html; Errin Haines Whack, "Activists Split as Clinton Makes Push for Black Millennials," Associated Press, Oct. 28, 2016, https://apnews.com /337e465bcb264f029e9cd31cdda512e9; Jeffrey M. Jones, "Hillary Clinton Favorable Rating at New Low," Gallup, Dec. 19, 2017, https://news.gallup .com/poll/224330/hillary-clinton-favorable-rating-new-low.aspx.

11. Seema Mehta, "Bill Clinton on Being the First Black President, and Aliens Too," *Chicago Tribune*, Apr. 3, 2014, https://www.chicagotribune.com /entertainment/la-pn-bill-clinton-jimmy-kimmel-20140403-story.html.

12. Byron Tau, "Bill Clinton: Mitt Romney's Business Record 'Sterling,'" *Po- litico*, May 31, 2012, https://www.politico.com/blogs/politico44/2012/05 /bill-clinton-mitt-romneys-business-record-sterling-124980; Patrick Healy

and Amy Chozick, "To Avert Repeat of 2008 Clinton Team Hopes to Keep Bill at His Best," *New York Times*, Mar. 28, 2015, https://www.nytimes.com /2015/03/29/us/politics/to-avert-repeat-of-2008-clinton-team-hopes-to-keep -bill-at-his-best.html; Nancy Cook and Brianna Ehley, "Bill Clinton's Obamacare Remarks Put Hillary on the Hot Seat," *Politico*, Oct. 4, 2016, https://www.politico.com/story/2016/10/bill-clinton-obamacare-crazy-229 100; Alexandra Jaffe, "Bill Clinton Attempts to Clarify Scathing Obama- care Comments," NBC News, Oct. 4, 2016, https://www.nbcnews.com /politics/2016-election/bill-clinton-attempts-clarify-scathing-obamacare -comments-n659411; "Obama & the Road Ahead: The *Rolling Stone* Inter- view," *Rolling Stone*, Nov. 8, 2012, 42; Byron Tau, "FLOTUS Touts 'Easy' Relationship with the Clintons," *Politico*, Sept. 6, 2012, https://www.polit ico.com/blogs/politico44/2012/09/flotus-touts-easy-relationship-with-the -clintons-134752; Halperin and Heilemann, *Double Down*, 61; Paul Singer, "Bill Richardson: Bill Clinton Still Mad about 2008 Obama Endorsement," *USA Today*, July 18, 2014, https://www.usatoday.com/story/news/politics /onpolitics/2014/07/18/bill-richardson-bill-clinton-still-mad-about-2008 -obama-endorsement/81211288/.

13. Fox Butterfield, "Trump Urged to Head Gala of Democrats," *New York Times*, Nov. 18, 1987, https://www.nytimes.com/1987/11/18/us/trump-urged -to-head-gala-of-democrats.html; "Here's Donald Trump's Presidential An- nouncement Speech," *Time*, June 16, 2015, https://time.com/3923128/donald -trump-announcement-speech/; Richard Eisenberg, "Social Security: Where Clinton and Trump Stand," Next Avenue, Aug. 8, 2016, https://www.next avenue.org/social-security-trump-clinton-stnd/; Trump, *Crippled America*, xii–xv.

14. Jenna Johnson, "Trump Calls for 'Total and Complete Shutdown of Mus- lims Entering the United States,'" *Washington Post*, Dec. 7, 2015, https:// www.washingtonpost.com/news/post-politics/wp/2015/12/07/donald-trump -calls-for-total-and-complete-shutdown-of-muslims-entering-the-united -states/; Nicholas Confessore, "How the G.O.P. Elite Lost Its Voters to Donald Trump," *New York Times*, Mar. 28, 2016, https://www.nytimes.com /2016/03/28/us/politics/donald-trump-republican-voters.html; Liu and Jacobson, "Republican Candidates' Positions on Donald Trump"; Belcher, *Black Man in the White House*, 178–179; "Full Text: Donald Trump 2016 RNC Draft Speech Transcript," *Politico*, July 21, 2016, https://www.politico .com/story/2016/07/full-transcript-donald-trump-nomination-acceptance -speech-at-rnc-225974.

15. Andrew Kaczynski, "David Duke Urges His Supporters to Volunteer and Vote for Trump," *Buzzfeed*, Feb. 25, 2016, https://www.buzzfeednews.com /article/andrewkaczynski/david-duke-urges-his-supporters-to-volunteer -and-vote-for-tr; Melinda Deslatte, "Ex-KKK Leader David Duke Runs for Senate: 'My Time Has Come,'" Associated Press, July 22, 2016, https:// apnews.com/8ef9762cc2fe4ccfa059c2d9beb9dc43; Christina Coleburn, "Donald Trump on Racist Endorsement: 'I Don't Know Anything about David Duke,'" NBC News, Feb. 29, 2016, https://www.nbcnews.com

/politics/2016-election/donald-trump-racist-endorsement-i-don-t-know
-anything-about-n527576; Peter Holley, "KKK's Official Newspaper Supports Donald Trump for President," *Washington Post*, Nov. 2, 2016, https://
www.washingtonpost.com/news/post-politics/wp/2016/11/01/the-kkks
-official-newspaper-has-endorsed-donald-trump-for-president/; Nicholas
Confessore, "For Whites Sensing Decline, Donald Trump Unleashes Words
of Resistance," *New York Times*, July 13, 2016, https://www.nytimes.com
/2016/07/14/us/politics/donald-trump-white-identity.html; Donald J.
Trump, Twitter, Jan. 22, 2016, 10:51 a.m., https://twitter.com/realDonald
Trump/status/690562515500032000.

16. Kim Hjelmgaard, "Donald Trump's Populist Wave Sweeps through Europe,"
USA Today, Nov. 13, 2016, https://www.usatoday.com/story/news/world
/2016/11/13/donald-trump-victory-hailed-europe-populists/93580556/; Griff
Witte, Emily Rauhala, and Dom Phillips, "Trump's Win May Be the Beginning of a Global Populist Wave," *Washington Post*, Nov. 13, 2016, https://
www.washingtonpost.com/world/trumps-win-may-be-just-the-beginning
-of-a-global-populist-wave/2016/11/13/477c3b26-a6ba-11e6-ba46-53db57f0
e351_story.html; Confessore, "For Whites Sensing Decline, Donald Trump
Unleashes."

17. Trump, *Crippled America*, 132; Lauren Victoria Burke, "Is Trump Right? A
Look at What Obama's Done for Black Community," NBC News, Aug. 4,
2015, https://www.nbcnews.com/news/nbcblk/donald-trump-right-what
-obamas-done-black-america-n403881; Danny Freeman, "Trump to African-
American Voters: What Do You Have to Lose?," NBC News, Aug. 19, 2016,
https://www.nbcnews.com/politics/2016-election/trump-african-american
-voters-what-do-you-have-lose-n634816; Emily Stephenson, "Trump Calls
Democrats 'Party of Slavery' in Minority Outreach Effort," Reuters, Aug.
31, 2016, https://www.reuters.com/article/us-usa-election-trump-minorities
/trump-calls-democrats-party of slavery-in-minority-outreach-effort-idUS
KCN1160Co; Ali Vitali, "Donald Trump Outlines His 'New Deal for Black
America,'" NBC News, Oct. 26, 2016, https://www.nbcnews.com/politics
/2016-election/donald-trump-outlines-his-new-deal-black-america-n673566.

18. Louis Nelson, "Trump: Without ID Law, Voters Will Vote '15 Times' for
Clinton," *Politico*, Aug. 9, 2016, https://www.politico.com/story/2016/08
/donald-trump-voter-id-law-fraud-226832; Brentin Mock, "How Police Are
Using Stop-and-Frisk Four Years after a Seminal Court Ruling," CityLab,
Aug. 18, 2017, https://www.citylab.com/equity/2017/08/stop-and-frisk-four
-years-after-ruled-unconstitutional/537264/; David A. Graham, "Trump's
'Voter Suppression Operation' Targets Black Voters," *Atlantic*, Oct. 27,
2016, https://www.theatlantic.com/politics/archive/2016/10/trumps-black
-voter-dilemma/505586/; Jill Colvin and Jonathan Lemire, "Reversing
Course, Trump Admits Obama Was Born in the US," Associated Press,
Sept. 16, 2016, https://www.apnews.com/61f7085d848248cd98410027d33
f2101; Nick Gass and Louis Nelson, "Clinton: Trump Owes Apology to
Obama, Americans over Birther Claims," *Politico*, Sept. 16, 2016, https://
www.politico.com/story/2016/09/clinton-trump-apology-birther-obama

-228274; Jesse J. Holland, "Many Black Voters Skeptical at Trump's Birther About-Face," Associated Press, Sept. 16, 2016, https://www.apnews.com/45 99cd40851a444d940e4254a3e6b373; Lauren V. Burke, "Obama and the Congressional Black Caucus: Allies and Foes," TheRoot.com, Oct. 30, 2016, https://www.theroot.com/obama-and-the-congressional-black-caucus-allies -and-fo-1790857469; Josh Clinton and Carrie Roush, "Poll: Persistent Partisan Divide over 'Birther' Question," NBC News, Aug. 10, 2016, https:// www.nbcnews.com/politics/2016-election/poll-persistent-partisan-divide -over-birther-question-n627446. According to later news investigations, the Trump campaign used Facebook ads and data analytics to target Black people and try to discourage them from voting altogether in 2016. "Revealed: Trump Campaign Strategy to Deter Millions of Black Americans from Voting in 2016," Channel 4 News (London), Sept. 28, 2020, https:// www.channel4.com/news/revealed-trump-campaign-strategy-to-deter -millions-of-black-americans-from-voting-in-2016.

19. Gregory Korte, " 'They're Shocked!': Obama Mocks GOP Establishment for Handling of Trump," *USA Today*, Mar. 11, 2016, https://www.usatoday .com/story/news/politics/onpolitics/2016/03/11/theyre-shocked-obama -mocks-gop-establishment-handling-trump/81670924/; Stephen Collinson, "Obama Takes on Trump with Tough Talk," CNN, Aug. 6, 2016, https:// www.cnn.com/2016/08/05/politics/obama-trump-unprecedented-presiden tial-takedowns/index.html; Doris Kearns Goodwin, "Barack Obama and Doris Kearns Goodwin: The Ultimate Exit Interview," *Vanity Fair*, Sept. 21, 2016, http://www.vanityfair.com/news/2016/09/barack-obama-doris-kearns -goodwin-interview; Barack Obama, "The Way Ahead," *Economist*, Oct. 8, 2016, https://www.economist.com/briefing/2016/10/08/the-way-ahead.

20. Mattathias Schwartz, "Obama Had a Secret Plan in Case Trump Rejected 2016 Election Results," *New York Magazine*, Oct. 10, 2018, http://nymag .com/intelligencer/2018/10/obama-had-a-secret-plan-in-case-trump-rejected -2016-results.html; Michael Wines, "All This Talk of Voter Fraud? Across U.S. Officials Found Next to None," *New York Times*, Dec. 18, 2016, https:// www.nytimes.com/2016/12/18/us/voter-fraud.html.

21. Alec Tyson and Shiva Maniam, "Behind Trump's Victory: Divisions by Race, Gender, Education," Pew Research Center, Nov. 9, 2016, https://www.pew research.org/fact-tank/2016/11/09/behind-trumps-victory-divisions-by-race -gender-education/; "Exit Polls," CNN, Nov. 23, 2016, https://edition.cnn .com/election/2016/results/exit-polls/national/president; Nate Cohn, "How the Obama Coalition Crumbled, Leaving an Opening for Trump," *New York Times*, Dec. 23, 2016, https://www.nytimes.com/2016/12/23/upshot /how-the-obama-coalition-crumbled-leaving-an-opening-for-trump.html; Alex Seitz-Wald, "Hillary Clinton's Loss Triggers Leadership Crisis for Democrats," NBC News, Nov. 9, 2016, http://www.nbcnews.com/storyline /2016-election-day/hillary-clinton-s-loss-triggers-leadership-crisis-democrats -n681266; Steven T. Dennis and Ben Brody, "Russian Operative Said 'We Made America Great' after Trump's Win," *Bloomberg*, Oct. 8, 2019, https://

www.bloomberg.com/news/articles/2019-10-08/senate-intelligence-panel
-warns-russian-meddling-continues; US Senate, *Report of the Select Committee on Intelligence*, vol. 2; Scott Shane and Sheera Frenkel, "Russian
2016 Influence Operation Targeted African-Americans on Social Media,"
New York Times, Dec. 17, 2018, https://www.nytimes.com/2018/12/17/us
/politics/russia-2016-influence-campaign.html.

22. Travis M. Andrews, " 'How Do I Explain This to My Children?': Van Jones
Gives Voice to the 'Nightmare' Some Are Feeling," *Washington Post*, Nov.
9, 2016, https://www.washingtonpost.com/news/morning-mix/wp/2016
/11/09/how-do-i-explain-this-to-my-children-van-jones-gives-voice-to-the
-nightmare-some-are-feeling/; Christopher Rosen, "SNL: Dave Chappelle
Monologue includes Message to Donald Trump," *Entertainment Weekly*,
Nov. 13, 2016 (updated Sept. 27, 2019), https://ew.com/article/2016/11/13
/snl-dave-chappelle-monologue-donald-trump/; David A. Love, "Trump's
Victory Reveals White People Lied to Us," TheGrio.com, Nov. 9, 2016,
https://thegrio.com/2016/11/09/white-people-lied-to-us/.

23. Kennedy interview; Fuller interview.

24. Sophia Tareen and Rachel Zoll, "Farrakhan Sees a New Opening for Black
Separatist Message," Associated Press, Dec. 18, 2016, https://www.apnews
.com/62ba650c823145b1a425e184294e81e6.

25. "NAACP Statement on Presidential Election," NAACP, Nov. 9, 2016,
https://www.naacp.org/latest/naacp-statement-presidential-election/; Aaron
Morrison, "Exclusive: Black Lives Matter Issues a Statement on Trump's
Election," mic.com, Nov. 15, 2016, https://www.mic.com/articles/159496
/exclusive-black-lives-matter-issues-a-statement-on-trump-s-election; Jay
Reeves, "Some Minorities Find 'President-Elect Trump' Scary Prospect,"
Associated Press, Nov. 9, 2016, https://www.apnews.com/69e53af8f0454de
388b1e11e5224ef76.

26. "President-Elect Trump Speaks to a Divided Country," *60 Minutes*, Nov. 13,
2016, https://www.cbsnews.com/news/60-minutes-donald-trump-family
-melania-ivanka-lesley-stahl/; "Thousands Join Anti-Trump Protests
around Country," Associated Press, Nov. 10, 2016, https://abc13.com/news
/thousands-join-anti-trump-protests-around-country/1599429/; Abigail
Hauslohner, Sandhya Somashekhar, and Susan Svrluga, "Vitriol Only Intensifies after Bitter Election," *Washington Post*, Nov. 11, 2016, https://www
.washingtonpost.com/national/vitriol-only-intensifies-after-bitter-election
/2016/11/11/3cc4ea42-a828-11e6-8042-f4d111c862d1_story.html; Holly Yan,
Kristina Sgueglia, and Kylie Walker, " 'Make America White Again': Hate
Speech and Crimes Post-Election," CNN, Dec. 22, 2016, https://www.cnn
.com/2016/11/10/us/post-election-hate-crimes-and-fears-trnd/index.html;
Nadia Dreid and Shannon Najmabadi, "Here's a Rundown of the Latest
Campus-Climate Incidents since Trump's Election," *Chronicle of Higher
Education*, Dec. 13, 2016, https://www.chronicle.com/blogs/ticker/heres-a
-rundown-of-the-latest-campus-climate-incidents-since-trumps-election
/115553; Hatewatch Staff, "Update: Incidents of Hateful Harassment since

Election Day Now Number 701," Southern Poverty Law Center, Nov. 18, 2016, https://www.splcenter.org/hatewatch/2016/11/18/update-incidents -hateful-harassment-election-day-now-number-701; Shiva Maniam, "Many Voters, Especially Blacks, Expect Race Relations to Worsen following Trump's Election," Pew Research Center, Nov. 21, 2016, https://www.pewresearch .org/fact-tank/2016/11/21/race-relations-following-trumps-election/.

27. David Remnick, "Obama Reckons with a Trump Presidency," *New Yorker*, Nov. 28, 2016, https://www.newyorker.com/magazine/2016/11/28/obama -reckons-with-a-trump-presidency; Rhodes, *World as It Is*, 401-402.

28. Remnick, "Obama Reckons with a Trump Presidency."

29. Jann S. Wenner, "The Day After: Obama on His Legacy, Trump's Win and the Path Forward," *Rolling Stone*, Nov. 29, 2016, https://www.rollingstone .com/politics/politics-features/the-day-after-obama-on-his-legacy-trumps -win-and-the-path-forward-113422/; Obama, *A Promised Land*, 206-207.

30. Remnick, "Obama Reckons with a Trump Presidency"; "Full Transcript: David Axelrod Interviews President Barack Obama for the Axe Files," CNN, Dec. 26, 2016, https://www.cnn.com/2016/12/26/politics/axe-files -obama-transcript/; Michael Kranish, "President Obama Says He Could Have Beaten Trump—Trump Says 'NO WAY!,'" *Washington Post*, Dec. 26, 2016, https://www.washingtonpost.com/news/post-politics/wp/2016/12/26 /president-obama-says-he-would-have-beaten-trump-if-i-had-run-again/. On New Year's Day 2017, President Obama's Twitter account posted a series of tweets that memorialized the achievements of his administration, including presiding over years of job growth, passage of the ACA, strengthening fuel efficiency standards, reducing troop deployments abroad, and standing behind marriage equality. President Obama, Twitter, Jan. 1, 2017, 11:49-11:59 a.m., https://twitter.com/POTUS44.

31. Melanie Garunay, "President Obama Speaks on the Results of the Election: 'We Are Americans First,'" White House, Nov. 9, 2016, https://obama whitehouse.archives.gov/blog/2016/11/09/president-obama-speaks-results -election; Mark Hensch, "Obama Invites Trump to White House on Thursday," TheHill.com, Nov. 9, 2016, https://thehill.com/blogs/ballot-box/presi dential-races/305155-obama-invites-trump-to-wh-thursday; Stephen Collinson and Eric Bradner, "Trump Calls Obama 'a Very Good Man' after Historic White House Meeting," CNN, Nov. 11, 2016, https://www.cnn.com /2016/11/10/politics/donald-trump-obama-paul-ryan-washington/index.html; Edward-Isaac Dovere, "Obama Meets His Nemesis," *Politico*, Nov. 10, 2016, https://www.politico.com/story/2016/11/obama-meets-trump-nemesis-231 200; Remnick, "Obama Reckons with a Trump Presidency"; Hauslohner, Somashekhar, and Svrluga, "Vitriol Only Intensifies after Bitter Election"; Eugene Scott, "Donald Trump Seeks Obama Advice on Appointments," CNN, Dec. 7, 2016, https://www.cnn.com/2016/12/07/politics/trump -obama-appointments/index.html.

32. "Trump Says He Had a 'Very Good Talk' with Obama on Wednesday," Reuters, Dec. 28, 2016, https://www.reuters.com/article/us-usa-trump

-obama-idUSKBN14I03N; Josh Gerstein et al., "Trump Breaks with Obama, Intel Agencies on Election Hacking," *Politico*, Dec. 9, 2016, https://www.politico.com/story/2016/12/obama-orders-full-review-of-election-relate-hacking-232419; Matthew Rosenberg, Adam Goldman, and Michael S. Schmidt, "Obama Administration Rushed to Preserve Intelligence of Russian Election Hacking," *New York Times*, Mar. 1, 2017, https://www.nytimes.com/2017/03/01/us/politics/obama-trump-russia-election-hacking.html; US Senate, *Report of the Select Committee on Intelligence*, vol. 5.

33. Kevin Liptak, "Exclusive: Read the Inauguration Day Letter Obama Left for Trump," CNN, Sept. 5, 2017, https://www.cnn.com/2017/09/03/politics/obama-trump-letter-inauguration-day/index.html; Juliet Eilperin and Krissah Thompson, "The Obamas Quietly Move On as Trump Moves In," *Washington Post*, Jan. 20, 2017, https://www.washingtonpost.com/politics/the-obamas-quietly-move-on-as-trump-moves-in/2017/01/20/584ab072-de8c-11e6-ad42-f3375f271c9c_story.html.

34. Barack Obama's last tweet as president read: "I'm still asking you to believe—not in my ability to bring about change, but in yours. I believe in change because I believe in you." President Obama, Twitter, Jan. 20, 2017, 9:13 a.m., https://twitter.com/POTUS44/status/822446982648201216. Also see Eilperin and Thompson, "Obamas Quietly Move On."

35. Karenna Meredith, "The Story of How Barack Obama Proposed to Michelle Is So Nerdy, It's Perfect" (embedded video of Michelle Obama interview on *The Late Show with Stephen Colbert*), PopSugar, Dec. 5, 2018, https://www.popsugar.com/celebrity/How-Did-Barack-Obama-Propose-Michelle-45548396; Remnick, "Obama Reckons with a Trump Presidency."

36. Eugene Scott, "Michelle Obama Goes Off on Donald Trump," CNN, Sept. 29, 2016, https://www.cnn.com/2016/09/28/politics/michelle-obama-hillary-clinton-donald-trump/index.html; Kevin Liptak, "Michelle Obama: The Clinton Surrogate That Could Finish Off Trump," CNN, Oct. 14, 2016, https://www.cnn.com/2016/10/13/politics/michelle-obama-donald-trump-criticism/index.html; "Full Tape with Lewd Donald Trump Remarks (Access Hollywood)," YouTube, accessed Oct. 18, 2019, https://www.youtube.com/watch?v=NcZcTnykYbw; Gregory Krieg, Eric Bradner, and Eugene Scott, "No One to Be Fired after Melania Trump Speech Plagiarism Episode," CNN, July 19, 2016, https://www.cnn.com/2016/07/19/politics/melania-trump-michelle-obama-speech/index.html; Meredith, "Story of How Barack Obama Proposed to Michelle."

37. Nancy Benac and Ben Nuckols, "Defiant Women to Trump: Your Agenda Won't Go Unchallenged," Associated Press, Jan. 22, 2017, https://www.apnews.com/aacac1eef359481bace23660199e230c; Michael D. Shear, "Trump Discards Obama Legacy, One Rule at a Time," *New York Times*, May 1, 2017, https://www.nytimes.com/2017/05/01/us/politics/trump-overturning-regulations.html; "Watch: Jeff Sessions Announces Guidelines for Stricter Sentencing," PBS NewsHour, May 12, 2017, https://www.pbs.org/news

hour/politics/watch-jeff-sessions-announces-guidelines-stricter-sentencing; Peter Baker, "Can Trump Destroy Obama's Legacy?," *New York Times*, June 23, 2017, https://www.nytimes.com/2017/06/23/sunday-review/donald -trump-barack-obama.html; Suzy Khimm, "Ben Carson Moves to Roll Back Obama-Era Fair Housing Rule," NBC News, Aug. 13, 2018, https:// www.nbcnews.com/politics/white-house/ben-carson-moves-roll-back -obama-era-fair-housing-rule-n900366; John Wagner, "Trump Signs Bipartisan Criminal Justice Bill amid Partisan Rancor over Stopgap Spending Measure," *Washington Post*, Dec. 21, 2018, https://www.washingtonpost .com/politics/trump-to-sign-bipartisan-criminal-justice-bill-amid-partisan -rancor-over-stopgap-spending-measure/2018/12/21/234f9ffc-0510-11e9-b5df -5d3874f1ac36_story.html; Mark Handler, "Trump Abandons Iran Nuclear Deal He Long Scorned," *New York Times*, May 8, 2018, https://www.ny times.com/2018/05/08/world/middleeast/trump-iran-nuclear-deal.html; Betsy Klein and Jennifer Hansler, "Trump Pardons Heavyweight Boxer Jack Johnson Posthumously," CNN, May 24, 2018, https://www.cnn.com /2018/05/24/politics/sylvester-stallone-jack-johnson-donald-trump/index .html; Anne Flaherty, "No Plans to Put Harriet Tubman on $20 Bill Next Year: Treasury Secretary Mnuchin," ABC News, May 22, 2019, https://abc news.go.com/Politics/treasury-secretary-mnuchin-plans-put-harriet-tub man-20/story?id=63206762; Nicholas Wu, Ledyard King, and Deborah Barfield Berry, "Should the Harriet Tubman $20 Bill Be Delayed? The Currency Process, Explained," *USA Today*, May 29, 2019, https://www .usatoday.com/story/news/politics/2019/05/28/steve-mnuchins-delay-20 -harriet-tubman-bill-design-explained/1227638001/.

38. "Acting Secretary Elaine Duke Announcement on Temporary Protected Status for Haiti," Department of Homeland Security, Nov. 20, 2017, https:// www.dhs.gov/news/2017/11/20/acting-secretary-elaine-duke-announcement -temporary-protected-status-haiti; Miriam Jordan, "Trump Administration Ends Temporary Protection for Haitians," *New York Times*, Nov. 20, 2017, https://www.nytimes.com/2017/11/20/us/haitians-temporary-status.html; Josh Delk, "NAACP President: We Know Trump Is Racist," TheHill.com, Jan. 13, 2018, https://thehill.com/blogs/blog-briefing-room/368926-naacp -president-we-know-trumps-racist; Eli Watkins and Abby Phillip, "Trump Decries Immigrants from 'Shithole Countries' Coming to US," CNN, Jan. 12, 2018, https://www.cnn.com/2018/01/11/politics/immigrants-shithole -countries-trump/index.html.

39. Jason Lange, "White and Male: Broader Bureaucracy Mirrors Trump Cabinet's Profile," Reuters, Oct. 20, 2017, https://www.reuters.com/article/us -trump-effect-diversity/white-and-male-broader-bureaucracy-mirrors -trump-cabinets-profile-idUSKBN1CP1D1; Catherine Lucey and Meghan Hoyer, "Trump Choosing White Men as Judges, Highest Rate in Decades," Associated Press, Nov. 13, 2017, https://apnews.com/a2c7a89828c747ed 9439f60e4a89193e; Emily Swanson and Russell Contreras, "AP-NORC Poll: Most Americans Say Trump Is Racist," Associated Press, Feb. 28, 2018, https://apnews.com/9961ee5b3c3b42d29aebdee837c17a11.

40. "In 1,372 Days, President Trump Has Made 26,548 False or Misleading Claims," *Washington Post*, Oct. 22, 2020, https://www.washingtonpost .com/graphics/politics/trump-claims-database/; "In 993 Days, President Trump Has Made 13,435 False or Misleading Claims," *Washington Post*, Oct. 9, 2019, https://www.washingtonpost.com/graphics/politics/trump -claims-database/; David Shepardson, "Trump Claims Obama Wiretapped Him during Campaign; Obama Refutes It," Reuters, Mar. 4, 2017, https:// www.reuters.com/article/us-usa-trump-obama-idUSKBN16B0CC; Max Greenwood, "Justice Dept.: No Evidence of Trump Tower Wiretapping," TheHill.com, Sept. 2, 2017, https://thehill.com/homenews/administration /348987-justice-dept-says-it-has-no-evidence-of-trump-tower-wiretapping.

41. Eric Lipton, "Trump's Choice to Bring G7 to His Own Resort Would Violate Conflict-of-Interest Law, if He Weren't President," *New York Times*, Oct. 18, 2019, https://www.nytimes.com/2019/10/18/us/politics/trump-g7-ethics .html; Office of the Special Counsel, Robert S. Mueller III, *Report on the Investigation into Russian Interference*; Jeremy Diamond, Kevin Liptak and Katelyn Polantz, "Mulvaney Brashly Admits Quid Pro Quo over Ukraine Aid as Key Details Emerge—and Then Denies Doing So," CNN, Oct. 17, 2019, https://www.cnn.com/2019/10/17/politics/mick-mulvaney-quid-pro -quo-donald-trump-ukraine-aid/index.html; Donald J. Trump (comparing investigations to lynching), Twitter, Oct. 22, 2019, 7:52 a.m., https://twitter .com/realDonaldTrump/status/1186611272231636992.

42. Committee of the Judiciary, US House of Representatives, *Impeachment of Donald J. Trump*; Jeremy Herb and Manu Raju, "House of Representatives Impeaches President Donald Trump," CNN, Dec. 19, 2019, https://www .cnn.com/2019/12/18/politics/house-impeachment-vote/index.html; Lisa Mascaro, Mary Clare Jalonick, and Eric Tucker, "Not Guilty: Senate Acquits Trump of Impeachment Charges," Associated Press, Feb. 6, 2020, https:// apnews.com/93c85dcfb0e6b2185391965e77ebea51.

EPILOGUE

1. Krissah Thompson, Kathy Orton, and Emily Heil, "The Obamas Just Bought Their Rental Home in Washington," *Washington Post*, May 31, 2017, https:// www.washingtonpost.com/news/reliable-source/wp/2017/05/31/the-obamas -are-buying-their-rental-home-in-washington/; Greg Jaffe and Juliet Eilperin, "Sasha Obama's High School Classes Will Keep First Family in Washington for a While," *Washington Post*, Mar. 3, 2016, https://www.washing tonpost.com/politics/sasha-obamas-high-school-classes-will-keep first-fam ily-in-washington-for-a-while/2016/03/03/39afd704-e181-11e5-9c36-e1902f6 b6571_story.html; Julie Hirschfeld Davis, "Obamas' Next Home: 9 Bedrooms in a Wealthy Washington Neighborhood," *New York Times*, May 25, 2016, https://www.nytimes.com/2016/05/26/us/politics/obama-kalorama -washington-house.html; Brittany Brolley, "Inside Barack and Michelle Obama's Gorgeous D.C. Home," *List*, Apr. 6, 2020, https://www.thelist.com /146336inside-barack-and-michelle-obamas-gorgeous-d-c-home/; Roxanne

Roberts, "How the Obamas Managed to Become Invisible in Washington," *Washington Post*, July 17, 2018, https://www.washingtonpost.com/lifestyle /style/how-the-obamas-managed-to-become-invisible-in-washington/2018 /07/16/c150863c-8606-11e8-8553-a3ce89036c78_story.html; Krissah Thompson and Juliet Eilperin, "Two Months out of Office, Barack Obama Is Having a Post-Presidency like No Other," *Washington Post*, Mar. 26, 2017, https://www.washingtonpost.com/lifestyle/two-months-out-of-office-bar ack-obama-is-having-a-post-presidency-like-no-other/2017/03/24/6b4d1c 05-f4a8-462b-ad7f-664ac35d0c06_story.html; Jeff Stein, "The Obamas Just Inked a Book Deal for More than $65 Million," *Vox*, Mar. 1, 2017, https:// www.vox.com/2017/3/1/14776542/obama-book-deal; Daniel Holloway, "Barack and Michelle Obama Sign Netflix Production Deal," *Variety*, May 21, 2018, https://variety.com/2018/digital/news/barack-michelle-obama-net flix-deal-1202817723/; Judy Kurtz, "Obama Becomes Presidential Taste-maker," TheHill.com, Sept. 4, 2019, https://thehill.com/blogs/in-the-know /in-the-know/459825-barack-obama-relishes-role-as-cultural-tastemaker. Ostensibly to deflect attention from the various controversies swirling around his own White House, Donald Trump called for an investigation of the Obamas' book deal. "Let's subpoena all of his records," the Republican president demanded in July 2019, as he also proceeded to criticize his predecessor for an allegedly errant air conditioning system in the West Wing. Kevin Fitzpatrick, "Trump: Obama's Book Deal Way Sketchier than Potential Obstruction of Justice," *Vanity Fair*, July 27, 2019, https://www .vanityfair.com/news/2019/07/trump-obama-book-deal-air-conditioning. Despite repeated attempts during the writing of this book, I was unable to obtain an interview with President Barack Obama. In an email response to one query, a member of the former president's press office stated, "President Obama is now a private citizen, and due to the large volume of requests that we receive, he unfortunately will not be able to participate." Press Office of Barack and Michelle Obama, Aug. 20, 2019, email.

2. Betsy Klein, "Obamas Donating $2 Million to South Side Summer Jobs Program," CNN, May 3, 2017, https://www.cnn.com/2017/05/03/politics /barack-michelle-obama-south-side/index.html; Edward-Isaac Dovere, "The Man Building Barack Obama's Future," *Politico*, Aug. 20, 2015, https://www .politico.eu/article/marty-nesbitt-building-barack-obama-future-us-legacy -chicago/; Krissah Thompson, "Barack Obama Is Building a Library—and Grappling Again with Chicago Politics," *Washington Post*, Nov. 7, 2017, https://www.washingtonpost.com/lifestyle/style/barack-obama-is-building -a-library—and-grappling-again-with-chicago-politics/2017/11/07/ee016 d36-c31f-11e7-84bc-5e285c7f4512_story.html; Gabriel Debenedetti, "Where Is Barack Obama?," *New York Magazine*, June 25, 2018, http://nymag.com /intelligencer/2018/06/where-is-barack-obama.html; Josh McGhee, "After Federal Assessment, What's Next for the Obama Presidential Center?," *Chicago Reporter*, Aug. 7, 2019, https://www.chicagoreporter.com/after-fed eral-assessment-whats-next-for-the-obama-presidential-center/; Alice Yin,

"One of the Multiple Long-Running Federal Reviews into Obama Center Concludes, Groundbreaking Tentatively Set for 2021," *Chicago Tribune*, Dec. 18, 2020, https://www.chicagotribune.com/politics/ct-obama-presi dential-center-section-106-memorandum-20201218-tzbwnjmz5bdj3l7nqnk 5unx7y4-story.html. To the consternation of some historians and others, in February 2019 the Barack Obama Foundation announced a decision not to house a physical collection of presidential papers in the planned Chicago center. Instead, the declassified records of the administration will be digitized and made available online through a partnership with the National Archives and Records Administration. See Memorandum of Understanding between the Barack Obama Foundation and National Archives and Records Administration regarding the Digitization of Obama Presidential Records, National Archives, Feb. 19, 2019, https://www.archives.gov/files/foia /obama-digitization-mou-executed-2-15-19.pdf; "Information about New Model for Obama Presidential Library," National Archives, accessed May 4, 2020, https://www.archives.gov/presidential-libraries/information-about -new-model-for-obama-presidential-library; "About the Library," Barack Obama Presidential Library, accessed May 4, 2020, https://www.obama library.gov/about-us; Jennifer Schuessler, "The Obama Presidential Library That Isn't," *New York Times*, Feb. 20, 2019, https://www.nytimes.com/2019 /02/20/arts/obama-presidential-center-library-national-archives-and-records -administration.html.

3. Madeline Conway, "Obama Slams Trump for Leaving Paris Climate Agreement," *Politico*, June 1, 2017, https://www.politico.com/story/2017/06/01 /barack-obama-slams-donald-trump-paris-climate-239032; Eli Watkins, "Obama: Leaving Iran Deal 'Misguided,'" CNN, May 8, 2018, https:// www.cnn.com/2018/05/08/politics/barack-obama-iran-deal-trump/index .html; William Cummings, "Obama Charlottesville Tweet Is Now the Most Liked Ever," *USA Today*, Aug. 15, 2017, https://www.usatoday.com /story/news/politics/onpolitics/2017/08/14/obama-charlottesville-tweet -likes/567196001/; Jane Coaston, "Trump's New Defense of His Charlottesville Comments Is Incredibly False," *Vox*, Apr. 26, 2019, https://www .vox.com/2019/4/26/18517980/trump-unite-the-right-racism-defense-char lottesville; Andrew Meldrum, "Obama Delivers Veiled Rebuke to Trump in Mandela Address," Associated Press, July 17, 2018, https://www.apnews .com/9c415f558c874ddba99ef23f2cd04of5.

4. Mikes Ives, "Obama Visits Kenya, Land of His Father, to Promote Local Charity," *New York Times*, July 16, 2018, https://www.nytimes.com/2018 /07/16/world/africa/obama-kcnya-visit-africa.html; Faith Karimi, "Obama Is in Kenya for His Sister's Project. Then He's Off to South Africa," CNN, July 15, 2018, https://www.cnn.com/2018/07/15/africa/obama-kenya-south -africa-visit/index.html; Hilary Weaver, "Barack Obama Has Another Dance Party in Kenya," *Vanity Fair*, July 18, 2018, https://www.vanityfair .com/style/2018/07/barack-obama-dances-in-kenya; "Barack Obama Makes First Post-Presidency Visit to Kenya," Associated Press, July 16, 2018,

https://www.nbcnews.com/politics/barack-obama/barack-obama-makes
-first-post-presidency-visit-kenya-n891671; NTV Kenya, Twitter, July 16,
2018, 5:14 a.m., https://twitter.com/ntvkenya/status/1018785890112397313.

5. Dan Merica and Jeff Zeleny, "Deval Patrick Announces Presidential Campaign," CNN, Nov. 14, 2019, https://www.cnn.com/2019/11/14/politics/deval
-patrick-president-2020-campaign/index.html; Nick Corasaniti, "Cory
Booker's Exit from 2020 Race Ends a Once-Promising Political Chapter,"
New York Times, Jan. 13, 2020, https://www.nytimes.com/2020/01/13/us
/politics/cory-booker-drops-out.html; Alexandra Jaffe, "Deval Patrick, Last
Black Candidate in 2020 Race, Drops Out," Associated Press, Feb. 12, 2020,
https://apnews.com/bb7101d62ffoa8918d3e25de65aa567a.

6. Astead W. Herndon and Susan Chira, "Can Kamala Harris Repeat Obama's
Success with Black Voters? It's Complicated," *New York Times*, Jan. 29, 2019,
https://www.nytimes.com/2019/01/29/us/politics/kamala-harris-black-voters
.html; Maeve Reston, "Kamala Harris Takes on Questions about Her 'Blackness,'" CNN, Mar. 6, 2019, https://www.cnn.com/2019/02/11/politics
/kamala-harris-prosecutor-breakfast-club/index.html; Jaweed Kaleem and
Melanie Mason, "Booker, Harris Redefine Black Presidential Candidates,"
Philadelphia Inquirer, Mar. 31, 2019, https://www.inquirer.com/news/nation
-world/booker-harris-redefine-black-presidential-candidates-20190331.html;
Christopher Cadelago, "'No Discipline. No Plan. No Strategy': Kamala
Harris Campaign in Meltdown," *Politico*, Nov. 15, 2019, https://www.poli
tico.com/news/2019/11/15/kamala-harris-campaign-2020-071105; Chelsea
Janes, "Harris Faces Uphill Climb amid Questions about Who She Is,"
Washington Post, Nov. 28, 2019, https://www.washingtonpost.com/politics
/harris-faces-uphill-climb-amid-questions-about-who-she-is/2019/11/28/7c
79d12a-0707-11ea-b17d-8b867891d39d_story.html; Janell Ross, "With Sen.
Kamala Harris' Exit, Democrats Can't Avoid a Tough Conversation about
Diversity," NBC News, Dec. 3, 2019, https://www.nbcnews.com/news/nbc
blk/sen-kamala-harris-exit-democrats-can-t-avoid-tough-conversation-n10
95196.

7. Edward-Isaac Dovere, "Inside Obama's Secret Meetings with 2020 Contenders," *Politico*, June 11, 2018, https://www.politico.com/story/2018/06/11
/obama-2020-elections-sanders-warren-635165; Ryan Lizza, "Waiting for
Obama," *Politico*, Nov. 26, 2019, https://www.politico.com/news/magazine
/2019/11/26/barack-obama-2020-democrats-candidates-biden-073025; "President Barack Obama Endorses Joe Biden for President," YouTube, accessed
May 23, 2020, https://www.youtube.com/watch?v=5-s3ANu4eMs; Amie
Parnes, "Obama, Trump Battle in New Wrinkle for 2020 Campaign,"
TheHill.com, Oct. 29, 2020, https://thehill.com/homenews/campaign/52
3259-obama-trump-battle-in-new-wrinkle-for-2020-campaign; Adam Edel-
man, Deepa Shivaram, and Kristen Welker, "Kamala Harris Named by Joe
Biden as His VP Pick," NBC News, Aug. 12, 2020, https://www.nbcnews
.com/politics/2020-election/joe-biden-selects-kamala-harris-his-running-
mate-n1235771; "COVID-19 Dashboard," Center for Systems Science and

Engineering, Johns Hopkins University, accessed Sept. 27, 2020, https://coronavirus.jhu.edu/map.html; Bureau of Labor Statistics, US Department of Labor, *The Employment Situation—April 2020*; Donald J. Trump (COVID-19 announcement), Twitter, Oct. 2, 2020, 12:54 a.m., https://twitter.com/realDonaldTrump/status/1311892190680014849; Tamara Keith, "Trump Says He Downplayed Coronavirus Threat in U.S. to Avert Panic," NPR, Sept. 11, 2020, https://www.npr.org/2020/09/11/911828384/trump-says-he-downplayed-coronavirus-threat-in-u-s-to-avert-panic; Eliza Barclay, "Trump and His Staff's Refusal to Wear a Face Mask Is a Catastrophe," *Vox*, Oct. 5, 2020, https://www.vox.com/2020/10/2/21498414/trump-tests-positive-coronavirus-mask-biden.

8. David Wasserman et al., "2020 National Popular Vote Tracker," *Cook Political Report*, accessed Dec. 21, 2020, https://cookpolitical.com/2020-national-popular-vote-tracker; "National Exit Poll: President" (2020), ABC News, accessed Dec. 21, 2020, https://abcnews.go.com/Elections/exit-polls-2020-us-presidential-election-results-analysis; "Exit Polls" (2020), CNN, accessed Dec. 21, 2020, https://www.cnn.com/election/2020/exit-polls/president/national-results; "Exit Polls" (2016), CNN, Nov. 23, 2016, https://www.cnn.com/election/2016/results/exit-polls/national/president.

9. In an audiotaped phone conversation with Georgia secretary of state Brad Raffensperger on January 2, 2021, Trump attempted to pressure the election supervisor into issuing a "recalculated" vote tally that would overturn Joe Biden's certified win of the state. "I just want to find 11,780 votes, which is one more than we have, because we won the state," Trump claimed. In response, Raffensperger, who apparently recorded the call and leaked it to the press, rejected the president's request and denied Trump's charges of election fraud and official misconduct. Amy Gardner, " 'I Just Want to Find 11,780 Votes': In Extraordinary Hour-Long Call, Trump Pressures Georgia Secretary of State to Recalculate the Vote in His Favor," *Washington Post*, Jan. 3, 2021, https://www.washingtonpost.com/politics/trump-raffensperger-call-georgia-vote/2021/01/03/d45acb92-4dc4-11eb-bda4-615aaefd0555_story.html; Brad Raffensperger, Twitter, Jan. 3, 2021, 10:27 a.m., https://twitter.com/GaSecofState/status/1345753643593687040; Amy Gardner, " 'Find the Fraud': Trump Pressured a Georgia Elections Investigator in a Separate Call Legal Experts Say Could Amount to Obstruction," *Washington Post*, Jan. 9, 2021, https://www.washingtonpost.com/politics/trump-call-georgia-investigator/2021/01/09/7a55c7fa-51cf-11eb-83e3-322644d82356_story.html; David Siders and Zach Montellaro, "Trump Confronts His 50 Percent Problem," *Politico*, Oct. 29, 2020, https://www.politico.com/news/2020/10/29/trump-suppress-vote-win-433460; Stephen Collinson, "Trump's Call to Halt Vote Counts Is His Most Brazen Swipe at Democracy Yet," CNN, Nov. 4, 2020, https://www.cnn.com/2020/11/04/politics/election-2020-donald-trump-joe-biden-voting-speech/index.html; "NBC News Fact Checks Trump's False Election Fraud Claims as Battleground Vote Counts Continue," YouTube, accessed Dec. 21, 2020, https://www.you

tube.com/watch?v=LZ-9R1ElhLo; "Trump Flips Out on Reporter: 'I'm the President of the United States!,' " YouTube, accessed Dec. 21, 2020, https://www.youtube.com/watch?v=vVR2_JyVzHE; Elise Viebeck, Emma Brown, and Rosalind S. Helderman, "Judges Turn Back Claims by Trump and His Allies in Six States as the President's Legal Effort Founders," *Washington Post*, Dec. 4, 2020, https://www.washingtonpost.com/politics/nevada-trump-lawsuit-dismissed/2020/12/04/844d420a-3682-11eb-a997-1f4c53d2a747_story.html; Jim Rutenberg, Nick Corasaniti, and Alan Feuer, "Trump's Fraud Claims Died in Court, but the Myth of Stolen Elections Lives On," *New York Times*, Dec. 26, 2020, https://www.nytimes.com/2020/12/26/us/politics/republicans-voter-fraud.html; Amy Gardner, Josh Dawsey, and Rachael Bade, "Trump Asks Pennsylvania House Speaker for Help Overturning Election Results, Personally Intervening in a Third State," *Washington Post*, Dec. 8, 2020, https://www.washingtonpost.com/politics/trump-pennsylvania-speaker-call/2020/12/07/d65fe8c4-38bf-11eb-98c4-25dc9f4987e8_story.html; Colleen Long and Ed White, "Trump Thought Courts Were Key to Winning: Judges Disagreed," Associated Press, Dec. 8, 2020, https://apnews.com/article/donald-trump-courts-election-results-e1297d874f45d2b14bc99c403abd0457; Anita Kumar and Gabby Orr, "Inside Trump's Pressure Campaign to Overturn the Election," *Politico*, Dec. 21, 2020, https://www.politico.com/news/2020/12/21/trump-pressure-campaign-overturn-election-449486.

10. In response to Trump's reported contemplation of using the military to subvert the outcome of the presidential election, ten former secretaries of defense published an editorial in the *Washington Post* that counseled, "Efforts to involve the U.S. armed forces in resolving election disputes would take us into dangerous, unlawful and unconstitutional territory." The bipartisan group explicitly reminded acting defense secretary Christopher C. Miller and his subordinates that they "are each bound by oath, law and precedent to facilitate the entry into office of the incoming administration, and to do so wholeheartedly." Ashton Carter et al., "All 10 Living Former Defense Secretaries: Involving the Military in Election Disputes Would Cross into Dangerous Territory," *Washington Post*, Jan. 3, 2021, https://www.washingtonpost.com/opinions/10-former-defense-secretaries-military-peaceful-transfer-of-power/2021/01/03/2a23d52e-4c4d-11eb-a9f4-0e668b9772ba_story.html; Maggie Haberman and Zolan Kanno-Youngs, "Trump Weighed Naming Election Conspiracy Theorist as Special Counsel," *New York Times*, Dec. 19, 2020, https://www.nytimes.com/2020/12/19/us/politics/trump-sidney-powell-voter-fraud.html; Philip Bump, "A Pillow Salesman Apparently Has Some Ideas about Declaring Martial Law," *Washington Post*, Jan. 15, 2021, https://www.washingtonpost.com/politics/2021/01/15/pillow-salesman-apparently-has-some-ideas-about-declaring-martial-law/.

11. By December 31, 2020, researchers at Johns Hopkins University had tallied 1.8 million known COVID-19-related deaths worldwide, with 345,736 (19 percent) in the United States. Coronavirus Resource Center, "Mortality

Analyses," Johns Hopkins University of Medicine, accessed Dec. 31, 2020, https://coronavirus.jhu.edu/map.html; Charlie Savage, Eric Schmitt, and Michael Schwirtz, "Russia Secretly Offered Afghan Militants Bounties to Kill U.S. Troops, Intelligence Says," *New York Times*, July 29, 2020, https://www.nytimes.com/2020/06/26/us/politics/russia-afghanistan-bounties.html; "Helsinki Summit: President Trump Backs Vladimir Putin on Election Interference," YouTube, accessed Jan. 16, 2021, https://www.youtube.com/watch?v=mBtsNNXjBPw; Ellen Nakashima and Craig Timberg, "DHS, State and NIH Join List of Federal Agencies—Now Five—Hacked in Major Russian Cyberespionage Campaign," *Washington Post*, Dec. 14, 2020, https://www.washingtonpost.com/national-security/dhs-is-third-federal-agency-hacked-in-major-russian-cyberespionage-campaign/2020/12/14/41f8fc98-3e3c-11eb-8bc0-ae155bee4aff_story.html; Kevin Johnson and Nathan Bomey, "US under Cyber Attack Believed to Be Tied to Russia: Private Sector, Infrastructure, All Levels of Government at Risk," *USA Today*, Dec. 17, 2020, https://www.usatoday.com/story/news/politics/2020/12/17/ongoing-cyber-attack-poses-grave-risk-government-private-sector/3946658001/; Veronica Stracqualursi, "Ex-DHS Adviser under Trump Calls for Urgent Action to Address Suspected Russian Cyberattack," CNN, Dec. 17, 2020, https://www.cnn.com/2020/12/17/politics/tom-bossert-trump-us-agencies-hack-russia/index.html; "My Interview with Secretary of State Mike Pompeo," *Mark Levin Show*, Dec. 18, 2020, https://www.marklevinshow.com/2020/12/18/my-interview-with-secretary-of-state-mike-pompeo/; Donald J. Trump (about Russian cyberespionage), Twitter, Dec. 19, 2020, 11:30 a.m., https://twitter.com/realDonaldTrump/status/1340333618691002368; Glenn Kessler, Salvador Rizzo, and Meg Kelly, "Trump Is Averaging More than 50 False or Misleading Claims a Day," *Washington Post*, Oct. 22, 2020, https://www.washingtonpost.com/politics/2020/10/22/president-trump-is-averaging-more-than-50-false-or-misleading-claims-day/.

12. Donald J. Trump, Twitter, Jan. 1, 2021, 2:53 p.m., https://twitter.com/realDonaldTrump/status/1345095714687377418; Donald J. Trump, Twitter, Dec. 27, 2020, 5:51 p.m., https://twitter.com/realDonaldTrump/status/1343328708963299338; Gardner, Dawsey, and Bade, "Trump Asks Pennsylvania House Speaker for Help"; William Saletan, "The GOP Is the Party of Civil War," *Slate*, Dec. 4, 2020, https://slate.com/news-and-politics/2020/12/georgia-senate-runoff-republicans-civil-war.html; Sarah Ferris et al., "Hill Chaos Turns Deadly after Rioters Storm Capitol," *Politico*, Jan. 6, 2021, https://www.politico.com/news/2021/01/06/electoral-college-certification-halted-amid-massive-pro-trump-demonstration-455495; Lisa Mascaro, Eric Tucker, and Mary Clare Jalonick, "Pro-Trump Mob Storms US Capitol in Bid to Overturn Election," Associated Press, Jan. 6, 2021, https://apnews.com/article/congress-confirm-joe-biden-78104aea082995bbd7412a6e6cd13818; Brian Stelter, "Now It's Sinking In: Wednesday's Capitol Hill Riot Was Even More Violent than It First Appeared," CNN, Jan. 9, 2021, https://www.cnn.com/2021/01/09/media/reliable-sources-january-8/index.html;

Rosalind S. Helderman, Spencer S. Hsu, and Rachel Weiner, " 'Trump Said to Do So': Accounts of Rioters Who Say the President Spurred Them to Rush the Capitol Could Be Pivotal Testimony," *Washington Post*, Jan. 16, 2021, https://www.washingtonpost.com/politics/trump-rioters-testimony /2021/01/16/01b3d5c6-575b-11eb-a931-5b162d0d033d_story.html; Ted Barrett, Manu Raju, and Peter Nickeas, "US Capitol Secured, Woman Dead after Rioters stormed the Halls of Congress to Block Biden's Win," CNN, Jan. 6, 2021, https://www.cnn.com/2021/01/06/politics/us-capitol-lockdown /index.html; "Watch: President Trump Speaks at 'Save America March,' " WSLS 10 News (Roanoke, VA), Jan. 6, 2021, https://www.wsls.com/news /2021/01/06/watch-president-trump-expected-to-speak-at-save-america -rally/; Jens Stoltenberg, Twitter, Jan. 6, 2021, 3:32 p.m., https://twitter.com /jensstoltenberg/status/1346917585535823872; "World Leaders Condemn Pro-Trump Riot at US Capitol," Voice of America, Jan. 6, 2021, https://www .voanews.com/usa/us-politics/world-leaders-condemn-pro-trump-riot-us -capitol.

13. According to news reports, Vice President Pence pushed for a more rapid deployment of the National Guard in the wake of the Capitol rioting than Trump had initially authorized. Helene Cooper et al., "Army Deploys D.C. National Guard to Capitol, and F.B.I. Mobilizes Agents," *New York Times*, Jan. 6, 2021, https://www.nytimes.com/2021/01/06/us/politics/national -guard-capitol-army.html; Kaitlin Collins et al., "Pence Took Lead as Trump Initially Resisted Sending National Guard to Capitol," CNN, Jan. 6, 2021, https://www.cnn.com/2021/01/06/politics/pence-national-guard/index .html; Lauren Giella, "Fact Check: Did Trump Call in the National Guard after Rioters Stormed the Capitol?," *Newsweek*, Jan. 8, 2021, https://www .newsweek.com/fact-check-did-trump-call-national-guard-after-rioters -stormed-capitol-1560186; Mike Pence, Twitter, Jan. 6, 2021, 3:35 p.m., https://twitter.com/Mike_Pence/status/1346918219991420928; "President Trump Video Statement on Capitol Protesters," C-SPAN, Jan. 6, 2021, https://www.c-span.org/video/?507774-1/president-trump-claims-election -stolen-tells-protesters-leave-capitol; "Mayor Bowser Orders Citywide Curfew Beginning at 6PM Today," Office of the Mayor (Washington, DC), Jan. 6, 2021, https://mayor.dc.gov/release/mayor-bowser-orders-citywide -curfew-beginning-6pm-today; Devlin Barrett and Missy Ryan, "Inspectors General of Several Federal Agencies Open Sweeping Review of Security, Intelligence Surrounding Capitol Attack," *Washington Post*, Jan. 15, 2021, https://www.washingtonpost.com/national-security/inspectors-general -capitol-riot/2021/01/15/c88474ba-573f-11eb-a817-e5e7f8a406d6_story.html; Luke Broadwater and Nicholas Fandos, "The Capitol Police Are Investigating whether Lawmakers Gave Pre-Riot Building Tours, as Pelosi Names Leader of Security Review," *New York Times*, Jan. 15, 2021, https://www.ny times.com/live/2021/01/15/us/impeachment-trump/the-capitol-police-are -investigating-whether-lawmakers-gave-pre-riot-building-tours-as-pelosi -names-leader-of-security-review; Carol D. Leonnig, "Capitol Police

Intelligence Report Warned Three Days before Attack That 'Congress Itself'
Could Be Targeted," *Washington Post*, Jan. 15, 2021, https://www.washington
post.com/politics/capitol-police-intelligence-warning/2021/01/15/c8b50744
-5742-11eb-a08b-f1381ef3d207_story.html; Nicole Gaouette, "Terrifying
Scope of Capitol Attack Becoming Clearer as Washington Locks Down for
Biden's Inauguration," CNN, Jan. 16, 2021, https://www.cnn.com/2021/01
/16/politics/insurrection-investigation-washington-lockdown/index.html;
Nomaan Merchant and Colleen Long, "Police Command Structure Crumbled Fast during Capitol Riot," Associated Press, Jan. 18, 2021, https://ap
news.com/article/capitol-siege-donald-trump-riots-only-on-ap-michael
-pence-a27921d08ca949c0b1e64c33628dd80e; Kate Riga, "Congressman
Recalls Rep. Boebert Giving Large Tour Days before January 6," *Talking
Points Memo*, Jan. 18, 2021, https://talkingpointsmemo.com/news/boebert
-tour-capitol-cohen-insurrection; Lauren Boebert, Twitter, Jan. 6, 2021,
2:18 p.m., https://twitter.com/laurenboebert/status/1346898958900199429.

14. In the wake of Congress's early morning affirmation of Joe Biden as
president-elect on January 7, Trump issued a commitment to move
ahead with the transition, though his statement was laced with caveats.
"Even though I totally disagree with the outcome of the election, and the
facts bear me out, nevertheless there will be an orderly transition on January 20th. I have always said we would continue our fight to ensure that
only legal votes were counted. While this represents the end of the greatest first term in presidential history, it's only the beginning of our fight to
Make America Great Again!" Trump had the statement posted through the
Twitter account of deputy chief of staff Dan Scavino; his own account had
been temporarily suspended the previous day due to the platform's (belated)
enforcement of its policies concerning the serial posting of disinformation and
inflammatory content. Dan Scavino (two tweets), Twitter, Jan. 7, 2021, 3:49
a.m., https://twitter.com/DanScavino/status/1347103015493361664, https://
twitter.com/DanScavino/status/1347103016311259136; Kevin Liptak, Veronica
Stracqualursi, and Allie Malloy, "Isolated Trump Reluctantly Pledges 'Orderly' Transition after Inciting Mob," CNN, Jan. 7, 2021, https://www.cnn
.com/2021/01/07/politics/trump-biden-us-capitol-electoral-college-insur
rection/index.html; Meg Wagner et al., "Congress Reconvenes to Certify
Biden's Win after Rioters Breach Capitol," CNN, Jan. 6, 2021, https://www
.cnn.com/politics/live-news/congress-electoral-college-vote-count-2021
/index.html; US Senate, "Roll Call Votes 117th Congress—1st Session" (Vote
No. 1), Jan. 6, 2021, https://www.senate.gov/legislative/LIS/roll_call_lists
/roll_call_vote_cfm.cfm?congress=117&session=1&vote=00001; US Senate,
"Roll Call Votes 117th Congress—1st Session" (Vote No. 2), Jan. 7, 2021,
https://www.senate.gov/legislative/LIS/roll_call_lists/roll_call_vote_cfm
.cfm?congress=117&session=1&vote=00002; US House of Representatives,
"Final Vote Results for Roll Call 10," Jan. 6, 2021, https://clerk.house.gov
/evs/2021/roll010.xml; US House of Representatives, "Final Vote Results
for Roll Call 11," Jan. 7, 2021, https://clerk.house.gov/evs/2021/roll011.xml;

Nicholas Fandos and Emily Cochrane, "After Pro-Trump Mob Storms Capitol, Congress Confirms Biden's Win," *New York Times*, Jan. 7, 2021, https://www.nytimes.com/2021/01/06/us/politics/congress-gop-subvert-election.html.

15. Zignal Labs, an analytics firm in San Francisco, found that online misinformation about election fraud declined 73 percent in the week following the banning of Donald Trump and several of his allies from Twitter and other social media platforms. Elizabeth Dwoskin and Craig Timberg, "Misinformation Dropped Dramatically the Week after Twitter Banned Trump," *Washington Post*, Jan. 16, 2021, https://www.washingtonpost.com/technology/2021/01/16/misinformation-trump-twitter/; "Permanent suspension of @realDonaldTrump," Twitter, Jan. 8, 2021, https://blog.twitter.com/en_us/topics/company/2020/suspension.html; Kaitlin Collins et al., "Second Cabinet Member Announces Resignation over Trump's Response to Riot," CNN, Jan. 8, 2021, https://www.cnn.com/2021/01/07/politics/elaine-chao-cabinet-resignation-trump/index.html; Michael Warren and Jamie Gangel, "Multiple Republicans Are Considering Supporting Impeachment, Sources Say," CNN, Jan. 8, 2021, https://www.cnn.com/2021/01/08/politics/capitol-hill-republicans-impeachment-removal-trump/index.html; James Brooks, "Alaska Sen. Lisa Murkowski Calls on President Trump to Resign, Questions Her Future as a Republican," *Anchorage Daily News* (AK), Jan. 8, 2021, https://www.adn.com/politics/2021/01/08/alaska-sen-lisa-murkowski-calls-on-president-trump-to-resign-questions-her-future-as-a-republican/; Julie Gerstein, "Trump Said to Have Told Pence 'I Don't Want to Be Your Friend' after the Vice President Refused to Block Biden's Election Certification," *Business Insider*, Jan. 8, 2021, https://www.businessinsider.com/trump-tells-pence-i-dont-want-to-be-your-friend-2021-1; Michael R. Pence to the Honorable Nancy Pelosi, Jan. 12, 2021, reprinted in "READ: Pence Letter to Pelosi Rejecting Calls to Invoke 25th Amendment," TheHill.com, Jan. 12, 2021, https://thehill.com/homenews/administration/533958-read-pence-letter-to-pelosi-rejecting-calls-to-invoke-25th-amendment.

16. Dan Lamothe, John Wagner, and Paul Sonne, "Pelosi Says She Spoke to Top General about Ensuring Trump Doesn't Launch Nuclear Attack," *Washington Post*, Jan. 8, 2021, https://www.washingtonpost.com/national-security/pelosi-trump-nuclear-codes/2021/01/08/032d95ac-51e0-11eb-bda4-615a aefd0555_story.html; "H. Res.24—Impeaching Donald John Trump, President of the United States, for High Crimes and Misdemeanors," Congress.gov, Jan. 11, 2021, https://www.congress.gov/bill/117th-congress/house-resolution/24/text; "Roll Call 17, Bill Number: H. Res. 24," US House of Representatives, Jan. 13, 2021, https://clerk.house.gov/Votes/202117; Mike DeBonis and Seung Min Kim, "House Impeaches Trump with 10 Republicans Joining, but Senate Plans Unclear," *Washington Post*, Jan. 13, 2021, https://www.washingtonpost.com/politics/house-impeachment-trump/2021/01/13/05fe731c-55c5-11eb-a931-5b162d0d033d_story.html; Seung Min Kim (Mitch McConnell memo on impeachment process), Twitter, Jan. 8, 2021,

8:52 p.m., https://twitter.com/seungminkim/status/1347722877521567747; Michael S. Schmidt and Maggie Haberman, "Trump Is Said to Have Discussed Pardoning Himself," *New York Times*, Jan. 7, 2021, https://www.nytimes.com/2021/01/07/us/politics/trump-self-pardon.html; Kristine Phillips and Kevin Johnson, "Capitol Police Officer's Death Investigated as Homicide: Trump's Legal Exposure Questioned," *USA Today*, Jan. 8, 2021, https://www.usatoday.com/story/news/politics/2021/01/08/capitol-riots-brian-sicknicks-death-being-investigated-homicide/6593630002/.

17. Trump's decision to skip the Biden inauguration placed him in the dubious company of Andrew Johnson, another impeached president, who had forgone attending his successor's inauguration more than 150 years earlier. Quint Forgey, "Biden: Trump Skipping Inauguration a 'Good Thing,'" *Politico*, Jan. 8, 2021, https://www.politico.com/news/2021/01/08/trump-wont-attend-biden-inauguration-456480; "The Inauguration of Joe Biden and Kamala Harris," YouTube, accessed Jan. 20, 2021, https://www.youtube.com/watch?v=C-qYgs_yOXA; Ken Thomas and Nancy A. Youssef, "Biden Team Says It Is Facing Transition 'Resistance' from Pentagon," *Wall Street Journal*, Dec. 18, 2020, https://www.wsj.com/articles/biden-team-says-it-is-facing-transition-resistance-from-pentagon-11608329195; Tyler Pager et al., "Biden Team Fears Rocky Transition May Have Revealed Only 'Tip of the Iceberg,'" *Politico*, Jan. 20, 2021, https://www.politico.com/news/2021/01/20/biden-staff-takeover-government-460600; Kate Sullivan and Eric Bradner, "Biden Says US Democracy under 'Unprecedented Assault' and Calls on Trump to 'Demand an End to This Siege,'" CNN, Jan. 6, 2021, https://www.cnn.com/2021/01/06/politics/joe-biden-riots-capitol-speech/index.html.

18. Amanda Sakuma, "Obama Leaves Behind a Mixed Legacy on Immigration," NBC News, Jan. 15, 2017, https://www.nbcnews.com/storyline/president-obama-the-legacy/obama-leaves-behind-mixed-legacy-immigration-n703656; Muzaffar Chishti, Sarah Pierce, and Jessica Bolter, "The Obama Record on Deportations: Deporter in Chief or Not?," Migration Policy Institute, Jan. 26, 2017, https://www.migrationpolicy.org/article/obama-record-deportations-deporter-chief-or-not; "Deporter-in-Chief Label Ups the Pressure for Action from Obama," NBC News, Mar. 6, 2014, https://www.nbcnews.com/news/latino/deporter-chief-label-ups-pressure-action-obama-n45346; Sarah R. Coleman, "A Promise Unfulfilled, an Imperfect Legacy: Obama and Immigration Policy," in Zelizer, *Presidency of Barack Obama*, 179–194; Obama, *A Promised Land*.

19. Obama, *A Promised Land*, 614–619.

SELECTED BIBLIOGRAPHY

BOOKS

Alexander, Michelle. *The New Jim Crow: Mass Incarceration in the Age of Color-blindness*. New York: New Press, 2010.

Alim, H. Samy, and Geneva Smitherman. *Articulate while Black: Barack Obama, Language, and Race in the U.S.* New York: Oxford University Press, 2012.

Alter, Jonathan. *The Center Holds: Obama and His Enemies*. New York: Simon and Schuster, 2013.

———. *The Promise: President Obama, Year One*. New York: Simon and Schuster, 2010.

Anderson, Carol. *One Person, No Vote: How Voter Suppression Is Destroying Our Democracy*. New York: Bloomsbury, 2018.

Asante, Molefi Kete, and Abu S. Abarry, eds. *African Intellectual Heritage: A Book of Sources*. Philadelphia, PA: Temple University Press, 1996.

Asch, Chris M., and George D. Musgrove. *Chocolate City: A History of Race and Democracy in the Nation's Capital*. Chapel Hill: University of North Carolina Press, 2017.

Axelrod, David. *Believer: My Forty Years in Politics*. New York: Penguin, 2015.

Balz, Dan. *Collision 2012: Obama vs. Romney and the Future of Elections in America*. New York: Viking, 2012.

Balz, Dan, and Haynes Johnson. *The Battle for America 2008: The Story of an Extraordinary Election*. New York: Viking, 2009.

Bangura, Abdul Karim, ed. *Assessing Barack Obama's Africa Policy: Suggestions for Him and African Leaders*. Lanham, MD: University Press of America, 2015.

Belafonte, Harry. *My Song: A Memoir of Art, Race, and Defiance*. New York: Vintage, 2012.

Belcher, Cornell. *A Black Man in the White House: Barack Obama and the Triggering of America's Racial Aversion Crisis*. Healdsburg, CA: Uptown Professional Press, 2016.

Berman, Ari. *Give Us the Ballot: The Modern Struggle for Voting Rights in America.* New York: Farrar, Straus and Giroux, 2015.

Biden, Joe. *Promises to Keep: On Life and Politics.* New York: Random House, 2007.

Brower, Kate Andersen. *The Residence: Inside the Private World of the White House.* New York: Harper, 2015.

———. *Team of Five: The Presidents Club in the Age of Trump.* New York: Harper-Collins, 2020.

Bush, George W. *Decision Points.* New York: Crown, 2010.

Cain, Herman. *This Is Herman Cain! My Journey to the White House.* New York: Threshold, 2011.

Carson, Ben (with Candy Carson). *America the Beautiful: Rediscovering What Made This Nation Great.* Grand Rapids, MI: Zondervan, 2012.

Carson, Ben (with Cecil Murphey). *Gifted Hands: The Ben Carson Story.* Grand Rapids, MI: Zondervan, 1990.

Chambers, Veronica, ed. *The Meaning of Michelle.* New York: St. Martin's, 2017.

Clinton, Hillary Rodham. *Hard Choices.* New York: Simon and Schuster, 2014.

Clyburn, James E. *Blessed Experiences: Genuinely Southern, Proudly Black.* Columbia: University of South Carolina Press, 2014.

Cobb, William Jelani. *The Substance of Hope: Barack Obama and the Paradox of Progress.* New York: Walker, 2010.

Corn, David. *Showdown: The Inside Story of How Obama Fought Back against Boehner, Cantor, and the Tea Party.* New York: William Morrow, 2012.

Daniel, C. Reginald, and Hettie V. Williams, eds. *Race and the Obama Phenomenon: The Vision of the More Perfect Multiracial Union.* Oxford: University Press of Mississippi, 2014.

Dionne, E. J., Jr., and Joy-Ann Reid, eds. *We Are the Change We Seek: The Speeches of Barack Obama.* New York: Bloomsbury, 2017.

Dyson, Michael E. *The Black Presidency: Barack Obama and the Politics of Race in America.* New York: Houghton Mifflin Harcourt, 2016.

Eisinger, Jesse. *The Chickenshit Club: Why the Justice Department Fails to Prosecute Executives.* New York: Simon and Schuster, 2017.

Farrington, Joshua. *Black Republicans and the Transformation of the GOP.* Philadelphia: University of Pennsylvania Press, 2016.

Feinman, Ronald L. *Assassinations, Threats, and the American Presidency: From Andrew Jackson to Barack Obama.* Lanham, MD: Rowman and Littlefield, 2015.

Felix, Antonia, and Christopher Measom. *Michelle Obama: A Photographic Journey.* New York: Sterling, 2017.

Fields, Corey D. *Black Elephants in the Room: The Unexpected Politics of African American Republicans.* Berkeley: University of California Press, 2016.

Firstbrook, Peter. *The Obamas: The Untold Story of an African Family.* New York: Crown, 2011.

Frey, William H. *Diversity Explosion: How New Racial Demographics Are Remaking America.* Washington, DC: Brookings Institution Press, 2015.

Garrow, David. *Rising Star: The Making of Barack Obama.* New York: William Morrow, 2017.

Gidlow, Liette, ed. *Obama, Clinton, Palin: Making History in Election 2008.* Urbana: University of Illinois Press, 2011.

Gillespie, Andra. *Race and the Obama Administration: Substance, Symbols, and Hope.* Manchester, England: Manchester University Press, 2019.

Glasrud, Bruce A., and Cary D. Wintz, eds. *African Americans and the Presidency.* New York: Routledge, 2010.

Glaude, Eddie S., Jr. *Democracy in Black: How Race Still Enslaves the American Soul.* New York: Crown, 2016.

Grove, Neil. *Inside the White House.* Washington, DC: National Geographic, 2013.

Grunwald, Michael. *The New New Deal: The Hidden Story of Change in the Obama Era.* New York: Simon and Schuster, 2012.

Halperin, Mark, and John Heilemann. *Double Down: Game Change 2012.* New York: Penguin, 2013.

———. *Game Change: Obama and the Clintons, McCain and Palin, and the Race of a Lifetime.* New York: Harper, 2010.

Harlan, Louis R. *Booker T. Washington: The Making of a Black Leader, 1856-1901.* New York: Oxford University Press, 1972.

Harris, Fredrick. *The Price of the Ticket: Barack Obama and the Rise and Decline of Black Politics.* New York: Oxford University Press, 2012.

Harris, Matthew L., and Newell G. Bringhurst, eds. *The Mormon Church and Blacks.* Urbana: University of Illinois Press, 2015.

Holloway, Pippa. *Living in Infamy: Felon Disfranchisement and the History of American Citizenship.* New York: Oxford University Press, 2013.

Holmes, David L. *The Faith of the Postwar Presidents: From Truman to Obama.* Athens: University of Georgia Press, 2012.

Indyk, Martin S., Kenneth G. Lieberthal, and Michael E. O'Hanlon. *Bending History: Barack Obama's Foreign Policy.* Washington, DC: Brookings Institution Press, 2012.

Jacobs, Sally H. *The Other Obama: The Bold and Reckless Life of President Obama's Father.* New York: Public Affairs, 2011.

Jarrett, Valerie. *Finding My Voice: My Journey to the West Wing and the Path Forward.* New York: Viking, 2019.

Johnson, Ollie A., III, and Karin L. Stanford, eds. *Black Political Organizations in the Post–Civil Rights Era.* New Brunswick, NJ: Rutgers University Press, 2002.

Joseph, Peniel E. *Dark Days, Bright Nights: From Black Power to Barack Obama.* New York: Basic, 2010.

Keckley, Elizabeth. *Behind the Scenes: Thirty Years a Slave, and Four Years in the White House.* New York: Oxford University Press, 1988.

Kennedy, Randall. *The Persistence of the Color Line: Racial Politics and the Obama Presidency.* New York: Pantheon, 2011.

Kessler, Ronald. *The First Family Detail: Secret Service Agents Reveal the Hidden Lives of the Presidents.* New York: Crown Forum, 2014.

Kinder, Donald, and Allison Dale-Riddle. *The End of Race? Obama, 2008, and Racial Politics in America*. New Haven, CT: Yale University Press, 2012.

King, Desmond S., and Rogers M. Smith. *Still a House Divided: Race and Politics in Obama's America*. Princeton, NJ: Princeton University Press, 2013.

Kirk, Elise K. *Music at the White House: A History of the American Spirit*. Urbana: University of Illinois Press, 1986.

Kloppenberg, James T. *Reading Obama: Dreams, Hope, and the American Political Tradition*. Princeton, NJ: Princeton University Press, 2011.

Kranish, Michael, and Marc Fisher. *Trump Revealed: An American Journey of Ambition, Ego, Money, and Power*. New York: Scribner, 2016.

Levingston, Steven. *Barack and Joe: The Making of an Extraordinary Partnership*. New York: Hachette, 2019.

Malveaux, Julianne. *Are We Better Off? Race, Obama and Public Policy*. Washington, DC: Malveaux Enterprises, 2016.

Mann, James. *The Obamians: The Struggle inside the White House to Redefine American Power*. New York: Viking, 2012.

Maraniss, David. *Barack Obama: The Story*. New York: Simon and Schuster, 2012.

Mayer, Jane. *Dark Money: The Hidden History of the Billionaires behind the Rise of the Radical Right*. New York: Anchor, 2017.

McClelland, Edward. *Young Mr. Obama: Chicago and the Making of a Black President*. New York: Bloomsbury, 2010.

McKenna, Elizabeth, and Hahrie Han. *Groundbreakers: How Obama's 2.2 Million Volunteers Transformed Campaigning in America*. New York: Oxford University Press, 2015.

Mendell, David. *Obama: From Promise to Power*. New York: Amistad, 2007.

Meriwether, James H. *Proudly We Can Be Africans: Black Americans and Africa, 1935-1961*. Chapel Hill: University of North Carolina Press, 2002.

Michelle Obama: A Portrait of the First Lady. New York: Life Books, 2013.

Milkis, Sidney M., and Michael Nelson. *The American Presidency. Origins and Development, 1776-2011*. 6th ed. Washington, DC: CQ Press, 2012.

Monkman, Betty C. *The White House: Its Historical Furnishings and First Families*. 2nd ed. Washington, DC: White House Historical Association, 2014.

Moore, Wes (with Erica L. Green). *Five Days: The Fiery Reckoning of an American City*. New York: One World, 2020.

Morial, Marc. *The Gumbo Coalition: Ten Leadership Lessons That Help You Inspire, Unite, and Achieve*. New York: HarperCollins Leadership, 2020.

Obama, Auma. *And Then Life Happens: A Memoir*. New York: St. Martin's, 2012.

Obama, Barack. *The Audacity of Hope: Thoughts on Reclaiming the American Dream*. New York: Three Rivers, 2006.

———. *Dreams from My Father: A Story of Race and Inheritance*. 1995; repr., New York: Crown, 2004.

———. *A Promised Land*. New York: Crown, 2020.

Obama, Michelle. *Becoming*. New York: Crown, 2018.

O'Brien, Cormac. *Secret Lives of the First Ladies*. Philadelphia, PA: Quirk Books, 2009.

Ogletree, Charles. *The Presumption of Guilt: The Arrest of Henry Louis Gates Jr. and Race, Class and Crime in America*. New York: St. Martin's, 2010.

O'Keefe, James. *American Pravda: My Fight for Truth in the Era of Fake News*. New York: St. Martin's, 2018.

Oliveira-Monte, Emanuelle. *Barack Obama Is Brazilian: (Re)Signifying Race Relations in Contemporary Brazil*. New York: Palgrave Macmillan, 2018.

Pfiffner, James P., and Roger H. Davidson, eds. *Understanding the Presidency*. 7th ed. Boston, MA: Pearson, 2013.

Plouffe, David. *The Audacity to Win: The Inside Story and Lessons of Barack Obama's Historic Victory*. New York: Viking, 2009.

Poniewozik, James. *Audience of One: Donald Trump, Television, and the Fracturing of America*. New York: Liveright, 2019.

President Obama: A Day in the Life of America's Leader. New York: Time for Kids Books, 2009.

Rabinowitz, Howard N., ed. *Southern Black Leaders of the Reconstruction Era*. Urbana: University of Illinois Press, 1982.

Ransby, Barbara. *Making All Black Lives Matter: Reimagining Freedom in the 21st Century*. Berkeley: University of California Press, 2018.

Reid, Joy-Ann. *Fracture: Barack Obama, the Clintons, and the Racial Divide*. New York: William Morrow, 2015.

Remnick, David. *The Bridge: The Life and Rise of Barack Obama*. New York: Knopf, 2010.

Rhodes, Ben. *The World as It Is: A Memoir of the Obama White House*. New York: Random House, 2018.

Rice, Susan. *Tough Love: My Story of the Things Worth Fighting For*. New York: Simon and Schuster, 2019.

Rigueur, Leah Wright. *The Loneliness of the Black Republican: Pragmatic Politics and the Pursuit of Power*. Princeton, NJ: Princeton University Press, 2015.

Romney, Mitt. *No Apology: The Case for American Greatness*. New York: St. Martin's, 2010.

Sahle, Eunice. *World Orders, Development and Transformation*. New York: Palgrave Macmillan, 2009.

Sarson, Steven. *Barack Obama: American Historian*. New York: Bloomsbury Academic, 2018.

Schmitt, Robert C. *Demographic Statistics of Hawaii, 1778-1965*. Honolulu: University of Hawaii Press, 1968.

Scott, Janny. *A Singular Woman: The Untold Story of Barack Obama's Mother*. New York: Riverhead, 2011.

Shachtman, Tom. *Airlift to America: How Barack Obama, Sr., John F. Kennedy, Tom Mboya, and 800 East African Students Changed Their World and Ours*. New York: St. Martin's, 2009.

Sharpton, Al (with Nick Chiles). *The Rejected Stone: Al Sharpton and the Path to American Leadership*. New York: Cash Money Content, 2013.

Sherman, Gabriel. *The Loudest Voice in the Room: How the Brilliant, Bombastic Roger Ailes Built Fox News—and Divided a Country*. New York: Random House, 2014.

Sherrod, Shirley. *The Courage to Hope: How I Stood Up to the Politics of Fear*. New York: Atria, 2012.

Skocpol, Theda. *Obama and America's Political Future*. Cambridge, MA: Harvard University Press, 2012.

Slevin, Peter. *Michelle Obama: A Life*. New York: Knopf, 2015.

Smith, Candis Watts. *Black Mosaic: The Politics of Black Pan-Ethnic Diversity*. New York: New York University Press, 2014.

Steele, Michael. *Right Now: A 12-Step Program for Defeating the Obama Agenda*. Washington, DC: Regnery, 2009.

Sugrue, Thomas J. *Not Even Past: Barack Obama and the Burden of Race*. Princeton, NJ: Princeton University Press, 2010.

Suskind, Ron. *Confidence Men: Wall Street, Washington, and the Education of a President*. New York: Harper, 2011.

Swarns, Rachel L. *American Tapestry: The Story of the Black, White, and Multiracial Ancestors of Michelle Obama*. New York: Amistad, 2012.

Taylor, Keeanga-Yamahtta. *From #BlackLivesMatter to Black Liberation*. Chicago, IL: Haymarket, 2016.

Tesler, Michael. *Post-Racial or Most-Racial? Race and Politics in the Obama Era*. Chicago, IL: University of Chicago Press, 2016.

Thurber, Timothy N. *Republicans and Race: The GOP's Frayed Relationship with African Americans, 1945-1974*. Lawrence: University Press of Kansas, 2013.

Todd, Chuck, and Sheldon Gawiser. *How Barack Obama Won*. New York: Vintage, 2009.

Toobin, Jeffrey. *The Oath: The Obama White House and the Supreme* Court. New York: Doubleday, 2012.

Trump, Donald J. *Crippled America: How to Make America Great Again*. New York: Threshold, 2015.

Trump, Mary L. *Too Much and Never Enough: How My Family Created the World's Most Dangerous Man*. New York: Simon and Schuster, 2020.

Walker, Clarence E., and Gregory D. Smithers. *The Preacher and the Politician: Jeremiah Wright, Barack Obama, and Race in America*. Charlottesville: University of Virginia Press, 2009.

Walton, Hanes, Jr., et al., eds. *Letters to President Obama: Americans Share Their Hopes and Dreams with the First African-American President*. New York: Skyhorse, 2009.

Watson, Robert P., et al., eds. *The Obama Presidency: A Preliminary Assessment*. Albany: State University of New York Press, 2012.

Weiss, Nancy J. *Whitney M. Young, Jr., and the Struggle for Civil Rights*. Princeton, NJ: Princeton University Press, 1989.

White House Historical Association. *The White House: An Historical Guide*. Washington, DC: National Geographic, 1982.

Wolffe, Richard. *Renegade: The Making of a President*. New York: Three Rivers, 2010.

Zelizer, Julian E., ed. *The Presidency of Barack Obama: A First Historical Assessment*. Princeton, NJ: Princeton University Press, 2018.

JOURNAL ARTICLES

Anwar, Shamena, Patrick Bayer, and Randi Hjalmarsson. "The Impact of Jury Race in Criminal Trials." *Quarterly Journal of Economics* 127.2 (May 2012): 1017-1055. https://academic.oup.com/qje/article-pdf/127/2/1017/5168118/qjs014.pdf.

Crouch, Jeffrey. "Barack Obama and the Clemency Power: Real Reform on the Way?" *Presidential Studies Quarterly* 45.4 (Dec. 2015): 778-795.

D'Elia, Justine, and Helmut Norpoth. "Winning with a Bad Economy." *Presidential Studies Quarterly* 44.3 (Sept. 2014): 467-483.

Gittinger, Ted, and Allen Fisher. "LBJ Champions the Civil Rights Act of 1964." *Prologue Magazine* 36.2 (Summer 2004). https://www.archives.gov/publications/prologue/2004/summer/civil-rights-act-1.html.

Knuckey, Jonathan, and Myunghee Kim. "Evaluations of Michelle Obama as First Lady: The Role of Racial Resentment." *Presidential Studies Quarterly* 46.2 (June 2016): 365-386.

Kolbe, Athena R. "Mortality, Crime and Access to Basic Needs before and after the Haiti Earthquake: A Random Survey of Port-au-Prince Households." *Medicine, Conflict and Survival* 26.4 (2010): 281-297.

Lee, Ronald, and Aysel Morin. "Using the 2008 Presidential Election to Think about 'Playing the Race Card.'" *Communication Studies* 60.4 (Sept.–Oct. 2009): 376-391.

Liu, Huchen, and Gary C. Jacobson. "Republican Candidates' Positions on Donald Trump in the 2016 Congressional Elections: Strategies and Consequences." *Presidential Studies Quarterly* 48.1 (Mar. 2018): 49-71.

Nordyke, Eleanor C. "Blacks in Hawai'i: A Demographic and Historical Perspective." *Hawaiian Journal of History* 22 (1988): 241-255.

Obama, Barack. "The President's Role in Advancing Criminal Justice Reform." *Harvard Law Review* 130.3 (Jan. 2017): 812-865.

Oberlander, Jonathan. "Long Time Coming: Why Health Reform Finally Passed." *Health Affairs* 29.6 (June 2010): 1112-1116. https://web.archive.org/web/20161205105530/http://content.healthaffairs.org/content/29/6/1112.

Rudalevige, Andrew. "The Contemporary Presidency: The Obama Administrative Presidency: Some Late-Term Patterns." *Presidential Studies Quarterly* 46.4 (Dec. 2016): 868-890.

Zeleza, Paul Tiyambe. "Obama's Africa Policy: The Limits of Symbolic Power." *African Studies Review* 56.2 (Sept. 2013): 165-178.

GOVERNMENT RECORDS

Bishaw, Alemayehu. *Poverty: 2000 to 2012*. US Census Bureau, Sept. 2013. https://www2.census.gov/library/publications/2013/acs/acsbr12-01.pdf.

Bronson, Jennifer, and E. Ann Carson. *Prisoners in 2017*. Bureau of Justice Statistics, US Department of Justice, Apr. 2019. https://www.bjs.gov/content/pub/pdf/p17.pdf.

Bureau of Labor Statistics, US Department of Labor. *The Employment Situation—April 2020*. USDL-20-0815, May 2020. https://www.bls.gov/news.release/archives/empsit_05082020.htm.

Carson, E. Ann. *Prisoners in 2018*. Bureau of Justice Statistics, US Department of Justice, Apr. 2020. https://www.bjs.gov/content/pub/pdf/p18.pdf.

Centers for Disease Control and Prevention. "HIV Surveillance—United States, 1981-2008." *Morbidity and Mortality Weekly Report*, June 3, 2011. https://www.cdc.gov/mmwr/preview/mmwrhtml/mm6021a2.htm.

Civil Rights Division, US Department of Justice. *Investigation of the Baltimore City Police Department*. Aug. 10, 2016. https://www.justice.gov/crt/file/883296.

Civil Rights Division, US Department of Justice, and US Attorney's Office, District of New Jersey. *Investigation of the Newark Police Department*. July 22, 2014. https://www.justice.gov/sites/default/files/crt/legacy/2014/07/22/newark_findings_7-22-14.pdf.

Committee of the Judiciary, US House of Representatives. *Impeachment of Donald J. Trump, President of the United States*. Report 116-346. 116th Cong. 1st sess., 2019. https://www.congress.gov/congressional-report/116th-congress/house-report/346/1.

Executive Office of the President of the United States. *Economic Perspectives on Incarceration and the Criminal Justice System*. Apr. 2016. https://obamawhitehouse.archives.gov/sites/whitehouse.gov/files/documents/CEA%2BCriminal%2BJustice%2BReport.pdf.

File, Thom. *The Diversifying Electorate—Voting Rates by Race and Hispanic Origin in 2012 (and Other Recent Elections)*. US Census Bureau, May 2013. https://www.census.gov/prod/2013pubs/p20-568.pdf.

Joint and Coalition Operational Analysis. *Operation United Assistance: The DOD Response to Ebola in West Africa*. Jan. 6, 2016. https://www.jcs.mil/Portals/36/Documents/Doctrine/ebola/OUA_report_jan2016.pdf.

Obama, Barack. "Presidential Documents: 2009-2014." In *Public Papers of the Presidents of the United States*. Washington, DC: US Government Publishing Office, 2011-2020.

Office of the Inspector General, US Department of Justice. *A Review of ATF's Operation Fast and Furious and Related Matters*. Redacted report, Nov. 2012. http://www.justice.gov/oig/reports/2012/s1209.pdf.

Office of Intelligence and Analysis, US Department of Homeland Security. *Rightwing Extremism: Current Economic and Political Climate Fueling Resurgence in Radicalization and Recruitment*. Apr. 7, 2009. https://fas.org/irp/eprint/rightwing.pdf.

Office of the Legislative Counsel, US House of Representatives. *Compilation of Patient Protection and Affordable Care Act*. 111th Cong., 2nd sess., May 2010. https://www.hhs.gov/sites/default/files/ppacacon.pdf.

Office of the Special Counsel, Robert S. Mueller III. *Report on the Investigation into Russian Interference in the 2016 Presidential Election.* Vols. 1-2. Washington, DC: US Department of Justice, 2019. https://www.justice.gov/storage/report.pdf.

Omnibus Appropriations Act, 2009. 111th Cong., 1st sess., Mar. 11, 2009. Public Law 111-8. https://www.congress.gov/111/plaws/publ8/PLAW-111publ8.pdf.

Presidential Commission on Election Administration. *The American Voting Experience: Report and Recommendations of the Presidential Commission on Election Administration.* Jan. 2014. https://www.eac.gov/sites/default/files/eac_assets/1/6/Amer-Voting-Exper-final-draft-01-09-14-508.pdf. *The President's Malaria Initiative.* USAID and Centers for Disease Control. Apr. 2014. https://www.pmi.gov/docs/default-source/default-document-library/pmi-reports/pmireport_final.pdf.

President's Task Force on 21st Century Policing. *Final Report of the President's Task Force on 21st Century Policing.* Washington, DC: Office of Community Oriented Policing Services, May 2015. https://cops.usdoj.gov/pdf/taskforce/taskforce_finalreport.pdf.

US Commission on Civil Rights. *Environmental Justice: Examining the Environmental Protection Agency's Compliance and Enforcement of Title VI and Executive Order 12,898.* Sept. 2016. https://www.usccr.gov/pubs/2016/Statutory_Enforcement_Report2016.pdf.

US Department of Health and Human Services. *Health Insurance Marketplace: Summary Enrollment Report for the Initial Annual Open Enrollment Period.* May 1, 2014. https://aspe.hhs.gov/system/files/pdf/76876/ib_2014Apr_enrollment.pdf.

US District Court, Eastern District of Missouri, Eastern Division. *United States of America v. the City of Ferguson: Consent Decree.* No. 4:16-cv-00180-CDP. Apr. 19, 2016. https://www.justice.gov/crt/file/883846/download.

US District Court, Northern District of Ohio, Eastern Division. *United States of America v. City of Cleveland: Settlement Agreement.* May 26, 2015. http://www.city.cleveland.oh.us/sites/default/files/forms_publications/SAD0c2016.pdf.

US District Court, Southern District of Ohio, Eastern Division. *Obama for America, et al., v. Jon Husted, et al.* No. 2:12-cv-636. Sept. 5, 2012. https://www.clearinghouse.net/chDocs/public/VR-OH-0079-0004.pdf.

US Government Accountability Office. *Elections: Issues Related to State Voter Identification Laws.* Sept. 2014. https://www.gao.gov/assets/670/665966.pdf.

———. *K-12 Education: Better Use of Information Could Help Agencies Identify Disparities and Address Racial Discrimination.* Apr. 2016. https://www.gao.gov/assets/680/676745.pdf.

US Senate. *Report of the Select Committee on Intelligence, United States Senate, on Russian Active Measures Campaigns and Interference in the 2016 U.S. Election.* Vol. 2: *Russia's Use of Social Media with Additional Views.* 116th Cong., 1st sess., 2019. https://bit.ly/2oe4OYV.

———. *Report of the Select Committee on Intelligence, United States Senate, on Russian Active Measures Campaigns and Interference in the 2016 U.S. Election.* Vol. 5: *Counterintelligence Threats and Vulnerabilities.* 116th Cong., 1st sess.,

2019. https://www.intelligence.senate.gov/sites/default/files/documents/re
port_volume5.pdf.

White House. *Promoting Responsible Fatherhood*. June 2012. https://obamawhite
house.archives.gov/sites/default/files/docs/fatherhood_report_6.13.12_final.pdf.

———. *U.S. Strategy toward Sub-Saharan Africa*. June 2012. https://obamawhite
house.archives.gov/sites/default/files/docs/africa_strategy_2.pdf.

White House Office of National AIDS Policy. *National HIV/AIDS Strategy: Federal Implementation Plan*. July 2010. https://obamawhitehouse.archives.gov
/files/documents/nhas-implementation.pdf.

———. *National HIV/AIDs Strategy for the United States*. July 2010. https://
obamawhitehouse.archives.gov/sites/default/files/uploads/NHAS.pdf.

White House Task Force on Childhood Obesity. *Solving the Problem of Childhood
Obesity within a Generation: Report to the President*. May 2010. https://letsmove
.obamawhitehouse.archives.gov/sites/letsmove.gov/files/TaskForce_on_Child
hood_Obesity_May2010_FullReport.pdf.

REPORTS AND STUDIES

Antonovics, Kate L., and Brian G. Knight. *A New Look at Racial Profiling: Evidence from the Boston Police Department*. Working Paper 10634. National Bureau of Economic Research, July 2004. https://www.nber.org/system/files
/working_papers/w10634/w10634.pdf.

Bositis, David A. *Blacks and the 2012 Democratic National Convention*. Washington, DC: Joint Center for Political and Economic Studies, 2012. https://joint
center.org/wp-content/uploads/2020/10/Blacks-and-the-2012-Democratic
-National-Convention.pdf.

———. *Blacks and the 2012 Republican National Convention*. Washington, DC:
Joint Center for Political and Economic Studies, 2012. https://coalchicago
.com/Images/2012/08/Blacks-and-the-2012-Republican-National-Conven
tion.pdf.

College Republican National Committee. *Grand Old Party for a Brand New Generation*. 2013. https://www.scribd.com/embeds/145467470/content.

Gaskins, Keesha, and Sundeep Iyer. *The Challenge of Obtaining Voter Identification*.
New York: Brennan Center for Justice, New York University School of Law,
2012.

Jones, Robert P., and Daniel Cox. *Religion, Values, and Experiences: Black and
Hispanic American Attitudes on Abortion and Reproductive Issues*. Washington,
DC: Public Religion Research Institute, 2012. https://www.prri.org
/research/african-american-and-hispanic-reproductive-issues-survey/.

National Coalition on Black Civic Participation. *Black Women in the United States,
2014: Progress and Challenges*. Mar. 2014. www.washingtonpost.com/r/2010
-2019/WashingtonPost/2014/03/27/National-Politics/Stories/2FinalBlack
WomenintheUS2014.pdf.

National Urban League. *Obama Administration Scorecard*. Jan. 2017. https://org2
.salsalabs.com/o/5666/images/2017-Obama-Scorecard-FINAL.pdf.

Police Accountability Task Force. *Recommendations for Reform: Restoring Trust between the Chicago Police and the Communities They Serve.* Apr. 2016. https://chi cagopatf.org/wp-content/uploads/2016/04/PATF_Final_Report_4_13_16-1.pdf.

Power Africa. *Annual Report 2019.* https://www.usaid.gov/sites/default/files/docu ments/1860/power_africa_annual_report_2019.pdf.

Republican National Committee. *Growth and Opportunity Project.* 2013. https:// assets.documentcloud.org/documents/623664/republican-national-commit tees-growth-and.pdf.

Smith, E. J., and S. R. Harper. *Disproportionate Impact of K-12 School Suspension and Expulsion on Black Students in Southern States.* Philadelphia: University of Pennsylvania, Center for the Study of Race and Equity in Education, 2015. https://web-app.usc.edu/web/rossier/publications/231/Smith%20and%20Har per%20(2015)-573.pdf.

Sobel, Richard. *The High Cost of "Free" Photo Voter Identification Cards.* Cambridge, MA: Charles Hamilton Houston Institute for Race and Justice, Harvard Law School, June 2014. https://today.law.harvard.edu/wp-content/uploads/2014 /06/FullReportVoterIDJune20141.pdf.

World Health Organization. "Liberia." *World Malaria Report 2018.* https://www .who.int/malaria/publications/country-profiles/profile_lbr_en.pdf.

CONVERSATIONS, INTERVIEWS, AND CORRESPONDENCE

Barnes, Melody C. Assistant to the president, director of the White House Domestic Policy Council (2009-2012). Interview with author via Zoom.com, July 22, 2020.

Brazile, Donna. Acting chair of the Democratic National Committee (2011, 2016-2017). Email correspondence with author, Sept. 8-9, 2020.

Brooks, Cornell William. President of the National Association for the Advancement of Colored People (2014-2017). Phone interview with author, July 9, 2020.

Clegg, Claude A., Jr. Conversations with author, Nov. 2008, Nov. 2016, Oct. 2020.

Clyburn, James E. US representative from South Carolina (Sixth District). Phone interview with author, Aug. 27, 2020.

Cook, Suzan Johnson. US ambassador-at-large for international religious freedom, Office of International Religious Freedom, US Department of State (2011-2013). Phone interview with author, Sept. 25, 2020.

Dyer, Deesha. White House social secretary (2015-2017). Email correspondence with author, June 29-30, 2020.

Edwards, Donna F. US representative from Maryland (Fourth District, 2008-2017). Email correspondence with author, July 16, 2020.

Fuller, Stanley. Pastor, Star of Bethlehem AME Church, Baltimore, MD. Phone interview with author, Sept. 18, 2020.

Harwell, Jerri A. Associate professor, Salt Lake Community College. Interview with author via webex.com, June 9, 2020.

Jealous, Benjamin. President of the National Association for the Advancement of Colored People (2008-2013). Email correspondence with author, May 31–June 1, 2020.

Kennedy, Randall. Michael R. Klein Professor of Law, Harvard University. Phone interview with author, Sept. 20, 2020.

Kirk, Ronald. US trade representative (2009-2013). Email correspondence with author, July 14 and Aug. 1, 2020.

Moore, Gwen. US representative from Wisconsin (Fourth District). Email correspondence with author, June 1, 2020.

Morial, Marc. President of the National Urban League. Phone interview with author, Sept. 20, 2020.

Nichols, Wil. Pastor, Victorious Praise Fellowship Church, Durham, NC. Phone interview with author, June 4, 2020.

Press Office of Barack and Michelle Obama. Email correspondence with author, Aug. 20-21, 2019.

Robinson, Laurie O. Cochair of President's Task Force on 21st Century Policing (2014-2015) and Clarence J. Robinson Professor of Criminology, Law and Society, George Mason University. Phone interview with author, June 4, 2020.

Rogers, Desirée. White House social secretary (2009-2010). Email interview with author, July 31, 2020.

Scott, Tim. US senator from South Carolina. Email correspondence with author, May 31, 2020.

Vance-Cooks, Davita. Public printer of the United States, first director of the Government Publishing Office (2013-2017). Email interview with author, Nov. 29, 2020.

Wilson, William Julius. Professor emeritus, Harvard University. Email correspondence with author, Aug. 24-25, 2020.

OTHER SOURCES

"Making Obama." Six-part podcast. WBEZ (Chicago), 2018. https://www.wbez.org/shows/making/71b8de57-b2be-4e03-8481-683258de3ec1.

Mitt. Directed by Greg Whiteley. Los Gatos, CA: Netflix, 2014.

PHOTO CREDITS

INDEX

Aaron, Henry, 259
Abe, Shinzo, 416
Acree, Angela, 272
Adams, Abigail, 266
Adams, Yolanda, 252
Adelson, Sheldon, 316
affirmative action: as applied during
the Obama presidency, 143–44;
Obama's changing positions on,
38–39; Supreme Court cases
relating to, 144–45
Affordable Care Act (ACA), 115, 129–
30, 132, 200, 490; benefits of, 137;
Republican opposition to, 354–56;
support for, 354; and uninsured
Americans, 354–55
Afghanistan: troop levels in, 430
African Americans. *See* Black
Americans
African American Students Foundation
(AASF), 5
African countries (1960): and quest
for independence from foreign
domination, 3–4. *See also names
of individual countries*
African countries, during Obama's
presidency, 276–84, 490–91;
achievements in, 305–7; China as
trading partner with, 283–84; complex dynamics involving, 282–83,

284, 289–90, 294–95, 306–7;
drone aircraft as used in, 290–95;
gay rights in, 298–99; humanitarian
aid to, 284–87; Michelle's impressions of, 307–8; Obama's approval
ratings in, 277–78; and Obama's
connections to Kenya, 4–5,
295–305; peacekeeping efforts in,
287–90; US policy toward, 280–82.
See also names of individual countries
African Growth and Opportunity Act,
281
Air Force One, 110–11
al-Bashir, Omar, 287, 306
Alim, H. Samy, 41
al-Qaeda, 281
al-Shabaab: US engagement with, 292,
293, 298, 299
American International Group, 81
American Jobs Act, 137, 162
American Recovery and Reinvestment
Act, 127–28
Americans for Prosperity, 201
AmeriCorps program, 129
Anderson, Marcia, 339
Anderson, Marian, 109
Angelou, Maya, 267
Anglin, Andrew, 457–58
Angola, 283
Anthony, Carmelo, 258

Nichols, Wil, 192
Niger, 283, 291
Nigeria, 3–4, 283, 291
1911 United, 316
Nixon, Jay, 398, 399
Nixon, Richard, 109
Norris, Michele, 126
Nyandega, Grace Kezia, 4

Obama, Auma, 11–12, 18, 303,
    480, 481
Obama, Barack Hussein, Jr.: *The
    Audacity of Hope*, 15–16, 32,
    36–37, 38, 43, 58, 70, 132, 278,
    416; birth of, 8; and Black politi-
    cians, 22–24; and campaign against
    Bobby Rush, 24–26; and campaign
    for the US Senate, 27–29; and Bill
    Clinton, 43–44; and Artur Davis,
    240; *Dreams from My Father*, 11,
    13–14, 20, 65, 178, 298, 304,
    416; early life of, 13–15; on father-
    hood, 69–71; in the Illinois Senate,
    20–24; in Indonesia, 8–9; Kenyan
    relatives of, 18–19, 300–305; and
    marital stress, 27; and marriage to
    Michelle, 19; on memories of his
    father, 11–12; and Michelle's trep-
    idation about a presidential run,
    32–33; on his mother, 9; political
    ambitions of, 19–34; presidential
    aspirations of, 32–34, 88; shifting
    racial identity of, 14–16, 211, 254–
    55, 537n19; at Sidley & Austin,
    17; as a smoker, 18, 40, 115; and
    speech at the Democratic National
    Convention (2004), 29–30; as US
    senator, 31–32; at the University of
    Chicago Law School, 20; and visit
    with his father, 10, 11
Obama, Barack Hussein, Jr. (presiden-
    tial primary campaign, 2007–2008):
    absentee fatherhood as issue dur-
    ing, 69–71; advisors to, 40; and

affirmative action, 38–39; announce-
    ment of, 35–36; and Black political
    figures, 65–68; and Bill Clinton's
    efforts on Hillary's behalf, 45–49;
    Hillary Clinton's support of, fol-
    lowing her defeat, 78–79; and
    Louis Farrakhan, 49–51, 120; hope
    and change as themes of, 35; and
    the Iowa caucuses, 44–45; issues
    important to, 36–38; and Jesse Jack-
    son Sr., 71–75; as part of the Joshua
    generation, 42; as perceived by Afri-
    can Americans, 62–75; Ted Ken-
    nedy as supporter of, 45–46; pri-
    mary opponents of, 43; race as issue
    in, 38–43, 54–61; in Selma, 42; on
    Super Tuesday, 49; as top vote–get-
    ter in various states, 44–45; as win-
    ner of the nomination, 78–80; and
    Jeremiah Wright, 51–61, 62, 119
Obama, Barack Hussein, Jr. (presiden-
    tial election campaign/inauguration,
    2008–2009): at the Democratic
    National Convention, 88–89;
    factors contributing to his victory,
    97–98; inauguration speech by,
    103; racist aspects of the Republican
    campaign against, 90–95; and the
    symbolic significance of a Black
    president, 88, 98–103; threats
    against, 93–95; vote totals received
    by, 96
Obama, Barack Hussein, Jr. (first term
    as president, 2009–2013): achieve-
    ments of, 136–38, 156–57; address
    to Congress (2009), 197–98; as
    basketball fan, 258; and the birther-
    ism conspiracy, 206–10; and the
    Black community, 136–38; and
    Black entertainers, 109, 245–55;
    Black leaders' criticism of, 180–83,
    185–87; in Brazil, 311–12; and
    Caribbean nations, 308–11; cere-
    monial responsibilities of, 255–56;